Spring 5 Recipes

A Problem-Solution Approach

Fourth Edition

Marten Deinum

Daniel Rubio

Josh Long

Spring 5 Recipes: A Problem-Solution Approach

Marten Deinum
Meppel, Drenthe, The Netherlands

Daniel Rubio
Ensenada, Baja California, Mexico

Josh Long
Canyon Country, California, USA

ISBN-13 (pbk): 978-1-4842-2789-3
DOI 10.1007/978-1-4842-2790-9

ISBN-13 (electronic): 978-1-4842-2790-9

Library of Congress Control Number: 2017954984

Cover image by Freepik (`www.freepik.com`)

Managing Director: Welmoed Spahr
Editorial Director: Todd Green
Acquisitions Editor: Steve Anglin
Development Editor: Matthew Moodie
Technical Reviewer: Massimo Nardone
Coordinating Editor: Mark Powers
Copy Editor: Kim Wimpsett

Distributed to the book trade worldwide by Springer Science+Business Media New York, 233 Spring Street, 6th Floor, New York, NY 10013. Phone 1-800-SPRINGER, fax (201) 348-4505, e-mail `orders-ny@springer-sbm.com`, or visit `www.springeronline.com`. Apress Media, LLC is a California LLC and the sole member (owner) is Springer Science + Business Media Finance Inc (SSBM Finance Inc). SSBM Finance Inc is a **Delaware** corporation.

For information on translations, please e-mail `rights@apress.com`, or visit `www.apress.com/rights-permissions`.

Apress titles may be purchased in bulk for academic, corporate, or promotional use. eBook versions and licenses are also available for most titles. For more information, reference our Print and eBook Bulk Sales web page at `www.apress.com/bulk-sales`.

Any source code or other supplementary material referenced by the author in this book is available to readers on GitHub via the book's product page, located at `www.apress.com/9781484227893`. For more detailed information, please visit `www.apress.com/source-code`.

Printed on acid-free paper

Contents at a Glance

Contents

About the Authors

Marten Deinum is a submitter on the open source Spring Framework project. He is also a Java/software consultant working for Conspect. He has developed and architected software, primarily in Java, for small and large companies. He is an enthusiastic open source user and longtime fan, user, and advocate of the Spring Framework. He has held a number of positions including software engineer, development lead, coach, and Java and Spring trainer.

Daniel Rubio has more than ten years of experience in enterprise and web-based software and is currently the founder and technical lead at MashupSoft.com. He has authored several books for Apress. Daniel's expertise lies in Java, Spring, Python, Django, JavaScript/CSS, and HTML.

Josh Long is the Spring developer advocate at Pivotal. Josh is a Java champion, the author of five books (including O'Reilly's upcoming *Cloud Native Java*) and three best-selling training videos (including *Building Microservices with Spring Boot* with Phil Webb), and an open source contributor (Spring Boot, Spring Integration, Spring Cloud, Activiti, and Vaadin).

About the Technical Reviewer

Massimo Nardone has more than 23 years of experience in security, web/mobile development, cloud computing, and IT architecture. His true IT passions are security and Android.

He currently works as the chief information security officer (CISO) for Cargotec Oyj and is a member of the ISACA Finland Chapter board. Over his long career, he has held these positions: project manager, software engineer, research engineer, chief security architect, information security manager, PCI/SCADA auditor, and senior lead IT security/cloud/SCADA architect. In addition, he has been a visiting lecturer and supervisor for exercises at the Networking Laboratory of the Helsinki University of Technology (Aalto University).

Massimo has a master of science degree in computing science from the University of Salerno in Italy, and he holds four international patents (PKI, SIP, SAML, and proxy areas).

Besides working on this book, Massimo has reviewed more than 40 IT books for different publishing companies and is the coauthor of *Pro Android Games* (Apress, 2015).

Acknowledgments

The acknowledgments are probably the hardest thing to write in a book. It is impossible to name everyone personally that I want to thank, and I will forget someone. For that, I want to apologize beforehand.

Although this is the third book I have written, I couldn't have done it without the great team at Apress. Special thanks to Mark Powers for keeping me focused and on schedule and to Amrita for keeping me on track with the final reviews.

I thank Massimo Nardone, without whose comments and suggestions this book would never have become what it is now.

Thanks to my family and friends for the times they had to miss me and to my dive buddies for all the dives and trips I missed.

Last but definitely not least, I thank my wife, Djoke Deinum, and daughters, Geeske and Sietske, for their endless support, love, and dedication, despite the long evenings and sacrificed weekends and holidays to finish the book. Without your support, I probably would have abandoned the endeavor long ago.

—Marten Deinum

Introduction

The Spring Framework is growing. It has always been about choice. Java EE focused on a few technologies, largely to the detriment of alternative, better solutions. When the Spring Framework debuted, few would have agreed that Java EE represented the best-in-breed architectures of the day. Spring debuted to great fanfare, because it sought to simplify Java EE. Each release since has marked the introduction of new features designed to both simplify and enable solutions.

With version 2.0 and newer, the Spring Framework started targeting multiple platforms. The framework provided services on top of existing platforms, as always, but was decoupled from the underlying platform wherever possible. Java EE is a still a major reference point, but it's not the only target. Additionally, the Spring Framework runs on different cloud environments. Frameworks built on top of Spring have emerged to support application integration, batch processing, messaging, and much more. Version 5 of the the Spring Framework is a major upgrade, the baseline was raised to Java 8, more support for annotation based configuration has been added and support for jUnit 5 was introduced. A newly added feature is the support for reactive programming in the form o Spring WebFlux.

This is the fourth edition of this superb recipe book, and it covers the updated framework, describing the new features and explaining the different configuration options.

It was impossible to describe every project in the Spring ecosystem, so we had to decide what to keep, what to add, and what to update. This was a hard decision, but we think we have included the most important content.

Who This Book Is For

This book is for Java developers who want to simplify their architecture and solve problems outside the scope of the Java EE platform. If you are already using Spring in your projects, the more advanced chapters discuss newer technologies that you might not know about already. If you are new to the framework, this book will get you started in no time.

This book assumes you have some familiarity with Java and an IDE of some sort. While it is possible, and indeed useful, to use Java exclusively with client applications, Java's largest community lives in the enterprise space, and that, too, is where you'll see these technologies deliver the most benefit. Thus, some familiarity with basic enterprise programming concepts such as the Servlet API is assumed.

How This Book Is Structured

Chapter 1, "Spring Development Tools," gives an overview of tools supporting the Spring Framework and how to use them.

Chapter 2, "Spring Core Tasks," gives a general overview of the Spring Framework, including how to set it up, what it is, and how it's used.

Chapter 3, "Spring MVC," covers web-based application development using the Spring Web MVC framework.

Chapter 4, "Spring REST," introduces Spring's support for RESTful web services.

Chapter 5, "Spring MVC: Async Processing," introduces async processing using Spring MVC.

Chapter 6, "Spring Social," introduces Spring Social, which lets you integrate easily with social networks.

Chapter 7, "Spring Security," provides an overview of the Spring Security project to help you better secure your application.

Chapter 8, "Spring Mobile," introduces Spring Mobile, which lets you integrate mobile device detection and usage in your application.

Chapter 9, "Data Access," discusses how to use Spring to talk to data stores using APIs such as JDBC, Hibernate, and JPA.

Chapter 10, "Spring Transaction Management," introduces the concepts behind Spring's robust transaction management facilities.

Chapter 11, "Spring Batch," introduces the Spring Batch framework, which provides a way to model solutions traditionally considered the domain of mainframes.

Chapter 12, "Spring with NoSQL," introduces multiple Spring Data portfolio projects, covering different NoSQL technologies and Big Data with Hadoop.

Chapter 13, "Spring Java Enterprise Services and Remoting Technologies," introduces you to JMX support, scheduling, e-mail support, and various facilities for RPC, including the Spring Web Services project.

Chapter 14, "Spring Messaging," discusses using Spring with message-oriented middleware through JMS and RabbitMQ and the simplifying Spring abstractions.

Chapter 15, "Spring Integration," discusses using the Spring Integration framework to integrate disparate services and data.

Chapter 16, "Spring Testing," discusses unit testing with the Spring Framework.

Chapter 17, "Grails," discusses the Grails framework, with which you can increase your productivity by using best-of-breed pieces and gluing them together with Groovy code.

Appendix A, "Deploying to the Cloud," shows how to deploy a Java (web) application to the cloud using the Pivotal's CloudFoundry solution.

Appendix B, "Caching," introduces the Spring Caching abstraction, including how to configure it and how to transparently add caching to your application.

Conventions

Sometimes when we want you to pay particular attention to a part within a code example, we will make the font **bold**. Please note that the bold doesn't necessarily reflect a code change from the previous version.

In cases when a code line is too long to fit the page's width, we will break it with a code continuation character. Please note that when you enter the code, you have to concatenate the line without any spaces.

Prerequisites

Because the Java programming language is platform independent, you are free to choose any supported operating system. However, some of the examples in this book use platform-specific paths. Translate them as necessary to your operating system's format before typing the examples.

To make the most of this book, install JDK version 1.8 or higher. You should have a Java IDE installed to make development easier. For this book, the sample code is Gradle-based. If you're running Eclipse and install the Gradle plug-in, you can open the same code in Eclipse and the CLASSPATH and dependencies will be filled in by the Gradle metadata.

If you're using Eclipse, you might prefer the SpringSource Tool Suite (STS), as it comes preloaded with the plug-ins you'll need to be productive with the Spring Framework in Eclipse. If you use IntelliJ IDEA, you need to enable the Gradle (and Groovy) plug-ins.

Downloading the Code

The source code for this book is available from the Apress web site (www.apress.com/9781484227893). The source code is organized by chapters, each of which includes one or more independent examples.

Contacting the Authors

We always welcome your questions and feedback regarding the contents of this book. You can contact Marten Deinum at marten@deinum.biz.

CHAPTER 1

Spring Development Tools

In this chapter, you'll learn how to set up and work with the most popular development tools to create Spring applications. Like many other software frameworks, Spring has a wide array of development tools to choose from, from bare-bones command-line tools to sophisticated graphical tools called *integrated development environments* (IDEs).

Whether you already use certain Java development tools or are a first-time developer, the following recipes will guide you through how to set up different toolboxes to do the exercises in the upcoming chapters, as well as develop any Spring application.

The following are the three toolboxes and the corresponding recipes you need to follow to get set up to start a Spring application:

- *Spring Tool Suite*: Recipe 1-1

- *IntelliJ IDE*: Recipe 1-2 (and recipes 1-3 and 1-4 for the Maven command-line interface; recipes 1-5 and 1-6 for the Gradle command-line interface)

- *Text editor*: Recipes 1-3 and 1-4 for the Maven command-line interface; recipes 1-5 and 1-6 for the Gradle command-line interface

Bear in mind you don't need to install all three toolboxes to work with Spring. It can be helpful to try them all out, but you can use the toolbox you feel most comfortable with.

1-1. Build a Spring Application with the Spring Tool Suite

Problem

You want to use the Spring Tool Suite (STS) to build a Spring application.

Solution

Install STS on your workstation. Open STS and click the Open Dashboard link. To create a new Spring application, click the "Spring project" link in the Dashboard window inside the Create table. To open a Spring application that uses Maven, from the top-level File menu select the Import option, click the Maven icon, and select "Existing Maven projects." Next, select the Spring application based on Maven from your workstation.

To install Gradle on STS, click the Extensions tab at the bottom of the Dashboard window. Click the Gradle Support check box. Proceed with the Gradle extension installation and restart STS once the installation is complete. To open a Spring application that uses Gradle, from the top-level File menu, select the Import option, click the Gradle icon, and select the Gradle project. Next, select the Spring application based on Gradle from your workstation. Click the Build Model button and finally click Finish to start working on the project.

© Marten Deinum, Daniel Rubio, and Josh Long 2017
M. Deinum et al., *Spring 5 Recipes*, DOI 10.1007/978-1-4842-2790-9_1

How It Works

STS is the IDE developed by SpringSource, which is a division of Pivotal, the creators of the Spring Framework. STS is specifically designed to develop Spring applications, making it one of the most complete tools for this purpose. STS is an Eclipse-powered tool, so it has the same look and feel as the open source Eclipse IDE.

STS can be downloaded for free from `http://spring.io/tools/sts`. STS is available for all major operating system (OS) versions: Windows (32 bit or 64 bit), macOS (Cocoa, 64 bit), and Linux (GTK, 32 bit and 64 bit). In addition, STS is versioned, so you have the option to download the latest stable release or a milestone/development version. Download the version suited to your OS.

Once you download STS, ensure you have a Java SDK installed on your system since this is an STS installation requirement. Proceed to install STS. Follow the installation wizard and you should have STS set up in five to ten minutes. Upon termination, a folder with the name `STS_<VERSION>` is created under the home folder of the user making the installation or where the user chooses to place the installation-based folder. If you inspect this folder, you'll see the STS executable that is used to start STS.

Start STS. At startup, STS asks you to define a workspace location. A *workspace* is where STS places all project information. You can keep the default directory that is under the main STS installation directory or define a different directory to your liking. After startup is complete, you'll see a screen like the one in Figure 1-1.

Figure 1-1. *STS startup screen*

On the STS Dashboard, in the center column inside the Get Started! box, there's a link called Create Spring Starter Project. You can click this link to create a new Spring application. You can go ahead and create an empty application if you like. You'll be asked for a name and to define a series of parameters, which you can leave with the default values.

A more common case than creating a Spring application from scratch is to continue development on an existing Spring application. Under such circumstances, the owner of an application generally distributes the application's source code with a build script to facilitate its ongoing development.

The build script of choice for most Java applications is a pom.xml file designed around the Maven build tool or, more recently, a build.gradle file designed around the Gradle build tool. The book's source code and its applications are provided with Gradle build files, in addition to a single application with a Maven build file.

In a Java application there can be dozens or hundreds of menial tasks required to put together an application (e.g., copying JARs or configuration files, setting up Java's classpath to perform compilation, downloading JAR dependencies, etc.). Java build tools can perform such tasks in Java applications.

Java build tools continue to have their place because applications distributed with build files ensure that all menial tasks intended by the creator of an application are replicated exactly by anyone else using the application. If an application is distributed with an Ant build.xml file, a Maven pom.xml file, an Ivy ivy.xml file, or a Gradle build.gradle file, each of these build files guarantees build consistency across users and different systems.

Some of the newer Java build tools are more powerful and enhance the way their earlier counterparts work, and each build file uses its own syntax to define actions, dependencies, and practically any other task required to build an application. However, you should never lose sight of the fact that a Java build tool is just a means to an end. It's a choice made by the creator of an application to streamline the build process. Don't panic if you see an application distributed with a build file from the oldest Ant version or the newest Gradle version; from an end user perspective, all you need to do is download and install the build tool to create the application as its creator intended.

Since many Spring applications continue to use Maven and some of the newer Spring applications use Gradle, we'll describe the import process into STS for both types of projects.

Importing and Building a Maven Project

Once you download the book's source and unpack it to a local directory, click the STS top-level File menu and select the Import option. A pop-up window appears. In the pop-up window, click the Maven icon and select the Existing Maven Projects option, as illustrated in Figure 1-2.

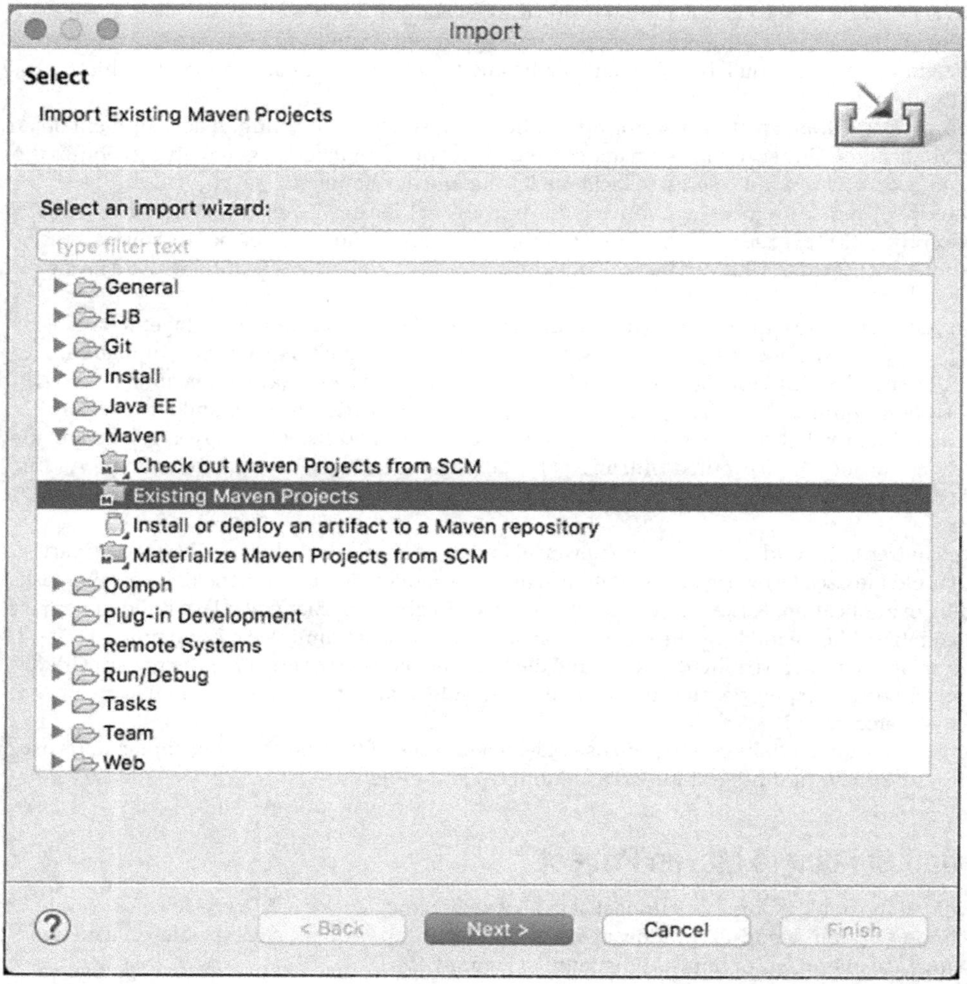

Figure 1-2. *Importing an existing Maven project*

Click the Next button. On the following screen, click the Browse button and select the directory of the book's source code in ch01 called springintro_mvn, as illustrated in Figure 1-3.

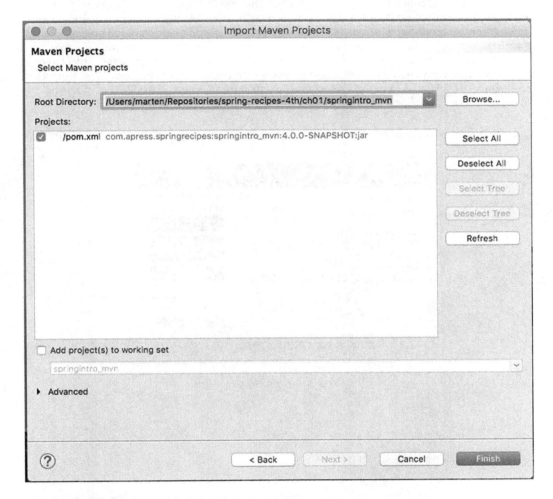

Figure 1-3. *Selecting a Maven project*

Notice in Figure 1-3 the Import Maven Projects window is updated to include the line pom.xml com. apress.springrecipes..., which reflects the Maven project to import. Select the project check box and click the Finish button to import the project. All projects in STS are accessible on the left side of the Package Explorer window. In this case, the project appears with the name springintro_mvn.

If you click the project icon in the Package Explorer, you'll be able to see the project structure (i.e., java classes, dependencies, configuration files, etc.). If you double-click any of the project files in the Package Explorer, the file is opened in a separate tab in the center window—alongside the Dashboard. Once a file is opened, you can inspect, edit, or delete its contents.

Select the project icon in the Package Explorer and right-click. A contextual menu appears with various project commands. Select the "Run as" option followed by the "Maven build" option. A pop-up window appears do you can edit and configure the project build. Just click the Run button in the bottom right. In the bottom center of STS you'll see the Console window appear. In this case, the Console window displays a series of build messages produced by Maven, as well as any possible errors in case the build process fails.

You've just built the application, congratulations! Now let's run it. Select the project icon from the Package Explorer once again and press the F5 key to refresh the project directory. Expand the project tree. Toward the bottom you'll see a new directory called `target`, which contains the built application. Expand the target directory by clicking its icon. Next, select the file `springintro_mvn-4.0.0-SNAPSHOT.jar`, as illustrated in Figure 1-4.

Figure 1-4. *Selecting the executable in STS*

With the file selected, right-click to open a contextual menu with various project commands. Select the "Run as" option followed by the "Run configurations" option. A pop-up window to edit and configure the run appears. Ensure the "Java application" option is selected on the left side. In the "Main class" box, enter **com.apress.springrecipes.hello.Main**. This is the main class for this project, as illustrated in Figure 1-5.

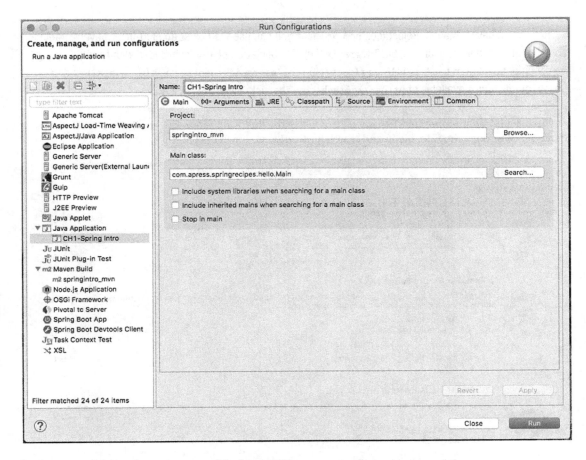

Figure 1-5. *Defining the main executable class in STS*

Click the Run button in the bottom right. In the bottom center of STS, you'll see the Console window. In this case, the Console window displays the application logging messages, as well as a greeting message defined by the application.

Even though you've built and run a Spring application with STS, you're still not done. The process you just completed with STS was mostly done behind the scenes by the Maven build tool. Next, it's time to import a Spring application that uses one of the newer build tools, called Gradle.

Importing and Building a Gradle Project

While Gradle is still a relatively new tool, there are signs that Gradle will supplant Maven in the future. For example, many large Java projects—such as the Spring Framework itself—now use Gradle instead of Maven because of its greater power. Given this tendency, it's worth describing how to use Gradle with STS.

■ **Tip** If you have a Maven project (i.e., `pom.xml` file), you can use the bootstrap plug-in or maven2gradle tool to create a Gradle project (i.e., `build.gradle` file). The bootstrap plug-in is included with Gradle (see the documentation at `http://gradle.org/docs/current/userguide/bootstrap_plugin.html`), and the maven2gradle tool is available at `https://github.com/jbaruch/maven2gradle.git`.

To install Gradle support in STS, you need to install the Buildship extension. For that, open the Eclipse Marketplace through the Help menu and search for *Gradle*, as shown in Figure 1-6.

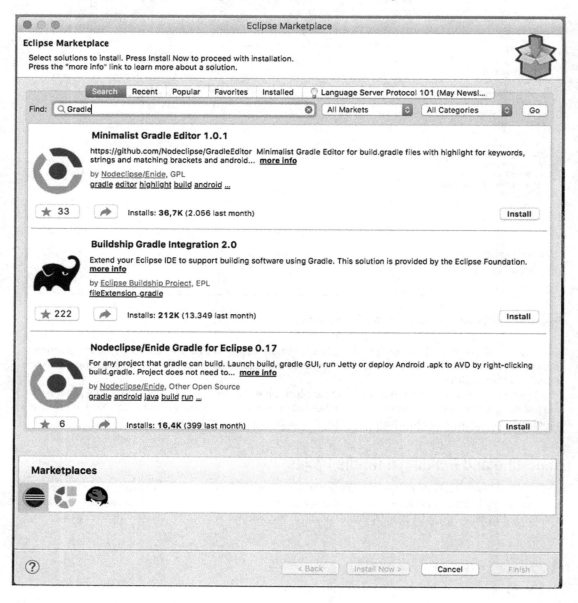

Figure 1-6. Buildship STS installation

Click the Install button at the bottom right of the BuildShip integration to proceed with the installation.

Click the pop-up window's Next button. Once you read the license and accept the terms, click the pop-up window's Finish button. The Gradle extension installation process starts. Once the installation process finishes, you'll be prompted to restart STS for the changes to take effect. Confirm the STS restart to finish the Gradle installation.

The book's source contains numerous Spring applications designed to be built with Gradle, so we'll describe how to import these Spring applications into STS. Once you download the book's source and unpack it to a local directory, in STS click the top-level File menu and select the Import option. A pop-up window appears. In the pop-up window, click the Gradle icon and select the Existing Gradle Project option, as illustrated in Figure 1-7.

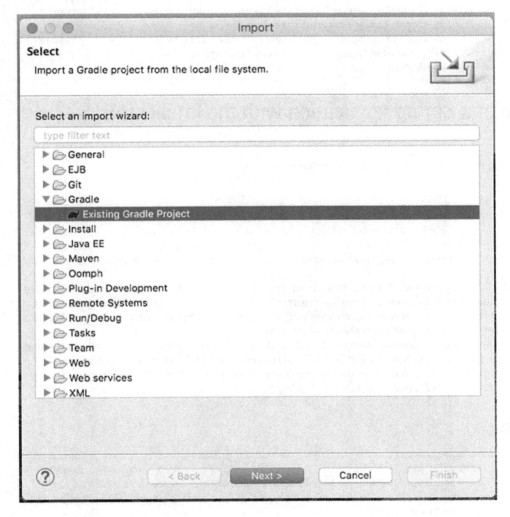

Figure 1-7. *Importing a Gradle project*

Click the Next button. On the following screen, click the Browse button and select the book's Ch01/ `springintro` directory. Click the Finish button to import the projects. If you look at the left side of STS in the Package Explorer, you'll see the project is loaded with the name `springintro`. If you click the project icon, you'll be able to see the project structure (i.e., Java classes, dependencies, configuration files, etc.).

In the right corner of the IDE there is a Gradle Tasks tab. Find the `springintro` project, open the Build menu, and select Build. Now right-click and select Run Gradle Tasks. You've just built the application. Now let's run it.

Select the project icon once again and press the F5 key to refresh the project directory. Expand the project tree. Toward the middle you'll see a new directory called `libs`, which contains the built application. Expand the `libs` directory by clicking the icon. Next, select the file `springintro.jar`.

With the file selected, from the top-level menu Run, select the "Run configurations" option. A pop-up window appears to edit and configure the run. Ensure the "Java application" option is selected on the left side. In the "Main class" box, enter **com.apress.springrecipes.hello.Main**. This is the main class for this project. Click the Run button in the bottom right. In the bottom center of STS, you'll see the Console window. In this case, the Console window displays the application logging messages, as well as a greeting message defined by the application.

1-2. Build a Spring Application with the IntelliJ IDE

Problem

You want to use the IntelliJ IDE to build Spring applications.

Solution

To start a new Spring application in the IntelliJ Quick Start window, click the Create New Project link. In the next window, assign a name to the project, select a runtime JDK, and select the Java Module option. In the next window, click the various Spring check boxes so IntelliJ downloads the necessary Spring dependencies for the project.

To open a Spring application that uses Maven, you first need to install Maven to work from a command-line interface (see recipe 1-4). From the IntelliJ top-level File menu, select the Import Project option. Next, select the Spring application based on Maven from your workstation. On the next screen, select the "Import project from external model" option and select a Maven type.

To open a Spring application that uses Gradle, you first need to install Gradle to work from a command-line interface (see recipe 1-5). From the IntelliJ top-level File menu, select the Import Project option. Next, select the Spring application based on Gradle from your workstation. In the next screen, select the "Import project from external model" option and select a Gradle type.

How It Works

IntelliJ is one of the most popular commercial IDEs in the market. Unlike other IDEs that are produced by a foundation, such as Eclipse, or are made to support the flagship software of a company, such as STS for the Spring Framework, IntelliJ is produced by a company called JetBrains whose sole business is to commercialize development tools. It's this focus that makes IntelliJ particularly popular for professional developers in corporate environments.

For this recipe, we'll assume you've already installed the IntelliJ Ultimate edition and just want to get up and running with Spring applications.

■ **Warning** IntelliJ is available in a free Community edition and an Ultimate edition with a 30-day free trial. Although the free Community edition provides good value for application development, the Community edition does not include support for Spring applications. The instructions that follow are based on the assumption that you're using the IntelliJ Ultimate edition.

Creating a Spring Application

To start a Spring application, in the IntelliJ Quick Start window click the Create New Project link. In the New Project window, select the Spring option and click the various Spring check boxes, as illustrated in Figure 1-8.

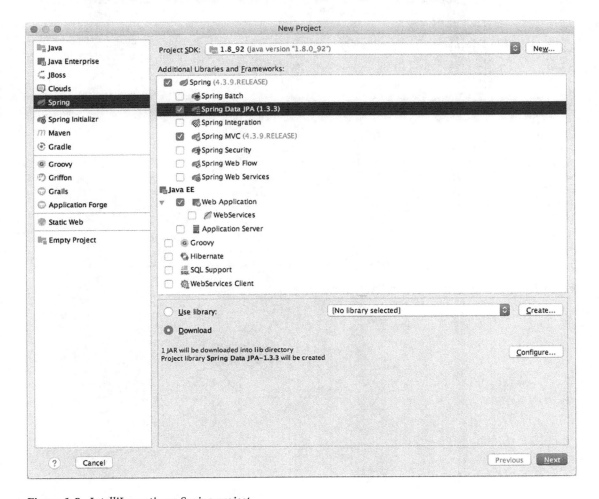

Figure 1-8. IntelliJ, creating a Spring project

Click the Next button. In the next window, assign a name to the project and click Finish.

Importing and Building a Maven Project

A more common case than creating a Spring application from scratch is to continue development of an existing Spring application. Under such circumstances, the owner of an application generally distributes the application's source code with a build script to facilitate its ongoing development.

The build script of choice for most Java application is a `pom.xml` file designed around the Maven build tool or, more recently, a `build.gradle` file designed around the Gradle build tool. The book's source code and its applications are provided with Gradle build files, in addition to a single application with a Maven build file.

Once you download the book's source and unpack it to a local directory, click the IntelliJ top-level File menu and select the Import Project option. A pop-up window appears, as illustrated in Figure 1-9.

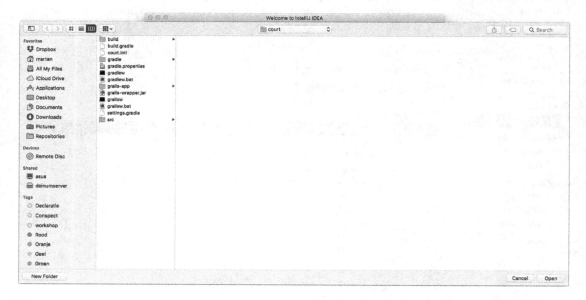

Figure 1-9. *IntelliJ, selecting a file or directory to import*

In this window, drill down in the directory tree until you get to the directory of the book's source code inside ch01 and then select springintro_mvn. Click the Open button. In the next screen, select the "Import project from external model" option and select a Maven type, as illustrated in Figure 1-10.

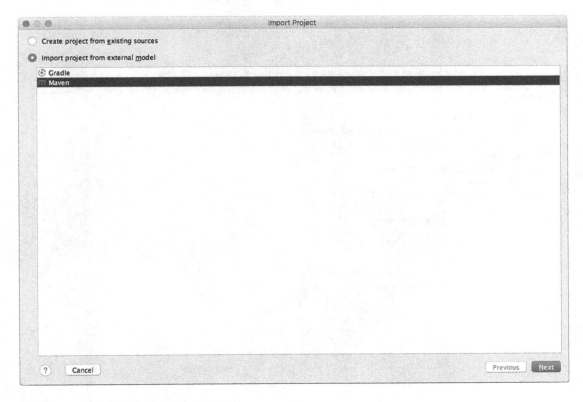

Figure 1-10. IntelliJ, selecting a project type

In the next window (see Figure 1-11), you can fine-tune some of the Maven project settings, such as automatically importing changes to pom.xml, downloading sources for dependencies, and so on. When satisfied with the settings, click Next.

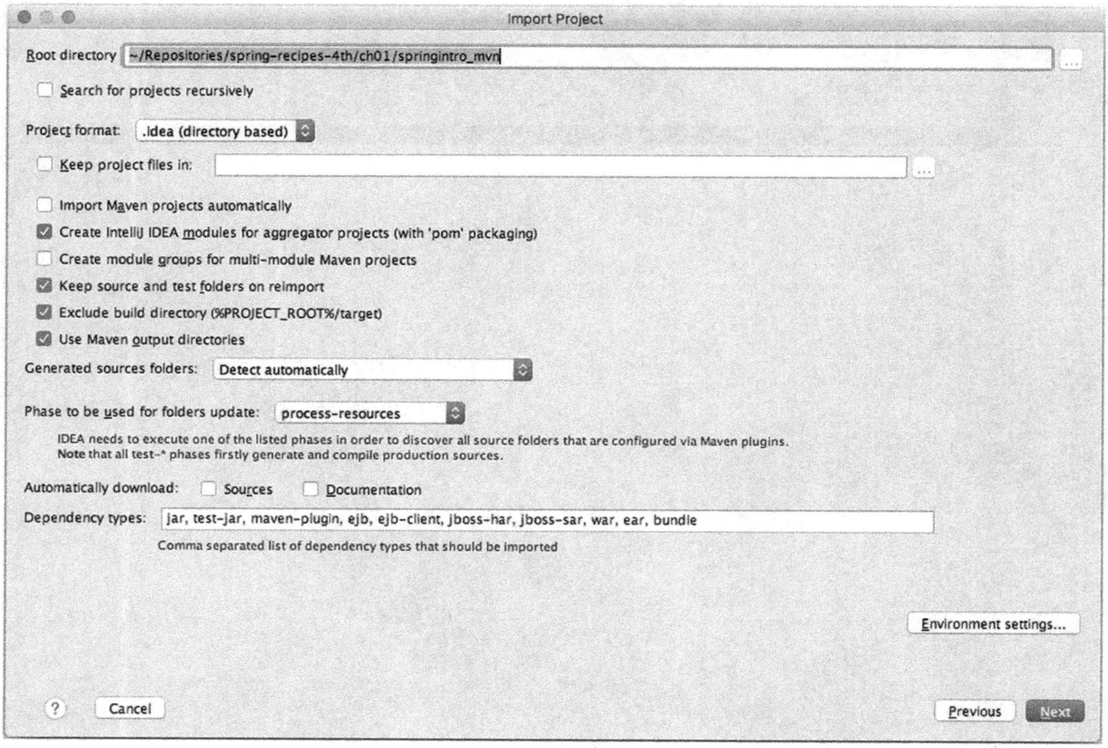

Figure 1-11. *IntelliJ, fine-tuning the Maven project settings*

Ensure the project check box is selected, as shown in Figure 1-12, and click the Next button to import the project.

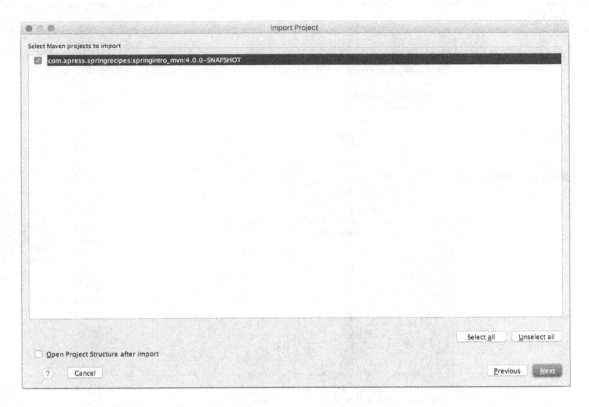

Figure 1-12. *IntelliJ, selecting the Maven project*

Next, choose the SDK version for the project. Confirm the project name and location and click the Finish button. All projects in IntelliJ are loaded on the left side of the Project window. In this case, the project appears with the name `springintro_mvn`.

If you click the project icon, you'll be able to see the project structure (i.e., Java classes, dependencies, configuration files, etc.). If you double-click any of the project files in the Project window, the file is opened in a separate tab in the center window. You can inspect the contents of the file, as well as edit or delete its contents.

Next, you need to set up Maven to work with IntelliJ. Follow the instructions in recipe 1-3 to install Maven to work from the command line. Once you do this, you can set up IntelliJ to work with Maven.

Click the IntelliJ top-level File menu and select the Settings option. A pop-up window appears to configure the IntelliJ settings. Click the Maven option and in the Maven home directory introduce the Maven installation directory based on your system, as illustrated in Figure 1-13. Click the Apply button, followed by the OK button.

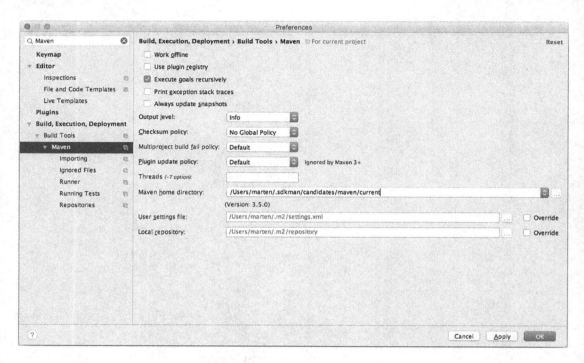

Figure 1-13. *IntelliJ, setting the Maven settings*

Next, on the right side of IntelliJ, click the vertical tab Maven Projects to show the Maven Projects pane, as illustrated in Figure 1-14.

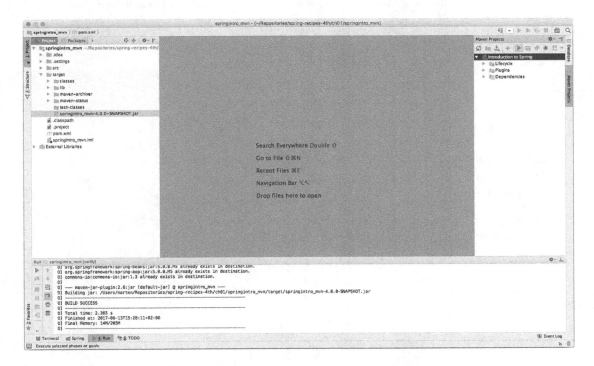

Figure 1-14. IntelliJ, Maven Projects pane

Select the project's Introduction to Spring line in the Maven Projects pane and right-click to open a contextual menu with various commands for the project. Select the Run Maven Build option. In the bottom center of IntelliJ, you'll see the Run window appear. In this case, the Run window displays a series of build messages produced by Maven, as well as any possible errors in case the build process fails.

■ **Warning** If you see the error message "No valid Maven installation found. Either set the home directory in the configuration dialog or set the M2_HOME environment variable on your system," it means Maven is not being found by IntelliJ. Verify the Maven installation and configuration process.

You've just built the application, congratulations! Now let's run it. If you don't see the target directory, press the Ctrl+Alt+Y key combination to synchronize the project. Expand the target directory by clicking its icon. Next, right-click the file springintro_mvn-4.0.0-SNAPSHOT.jar, as illustrated in Figure 1-15, and select the Run option.

Figure 1-15. *IntelliJ, running the application*

In the bottom center of IntelliJ in the Run window, you'll see the application logging messages, as well as a greeting message defined by the application.

Importing and Building a Gradle Project

Now let's build a Gradle application with IntelliJ. First you need to install Gradle. Follow the instructions in recipe 1-4 to install Gradle to work from the command line. Once you do this, you can set up IntelliJ to work with Gradle.

Click the IntelliJ top-level File menu and select the Import Project option. A pop-up window appears, as illustrated in Figure 1-9. Drill down in the directory tree in the pop-up window until you can select the file build.gradle in the ch01/springintro directory of the book's source code.

Click the Open button. On the next screen, select the "Import project from external model" option and select Gradle. On the next screen, enter the Gradle home directory in the "Gradle home" box, based on the Gradle installation of your system, as illustrated in Figure 1-16.

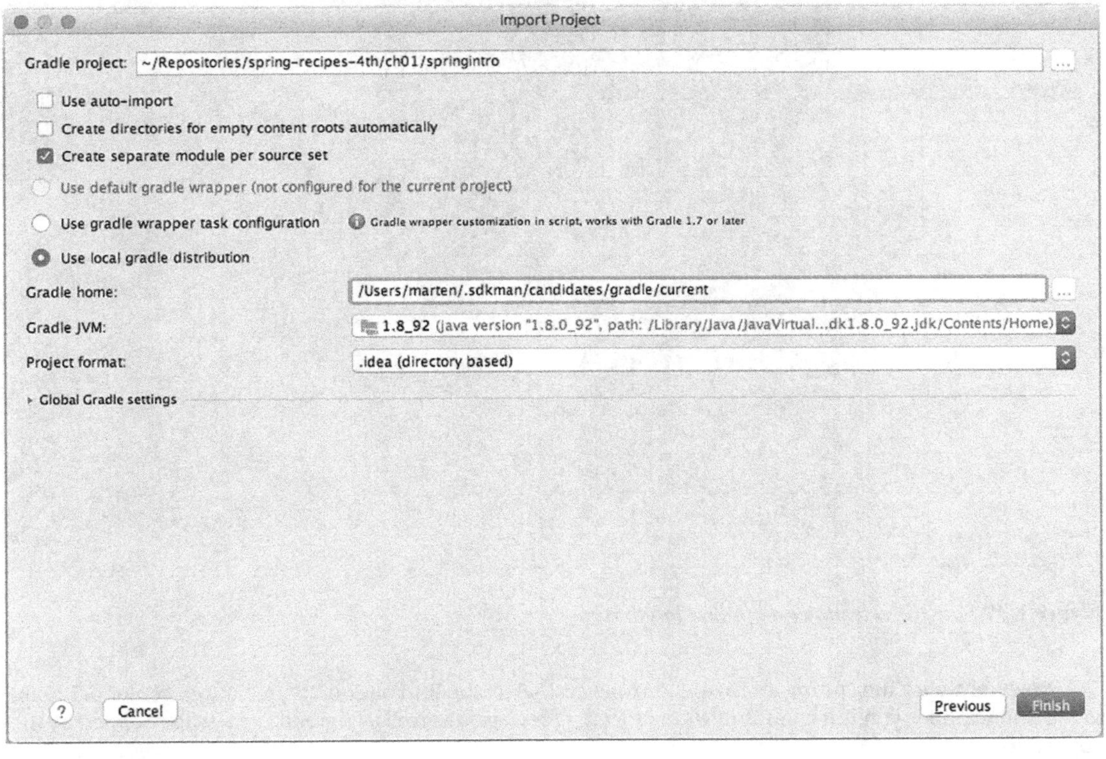

Figure 1-16. *Defining the Gradle home for IntelliJ*

Click the Finish button to confirm the import process and then click the Finish button to complete the import process. Next, in the Project window, right-click build.gradle and select Run Build.

You've just built the application. Now let's run it. In the Project window, expand the build directory and go into the libs directory. Find springintro-all.jar, as illustrated in Figure 1-17.

■ **Note**   The build.gradle file is configured to produce a shadow JAR, which means it contains all the classes and dependencies it needs to run.

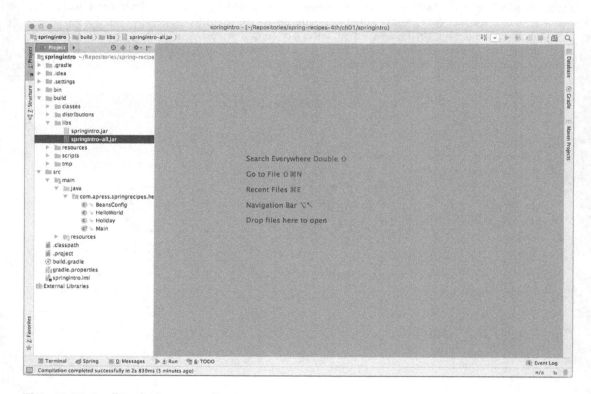

Figure 1-17. *IntelliJ, selecting an application to run*

Now right-click the springintro-all.jar file and select the Run option. In the bottom center of IntelliJ in the Run window, you'll see the application logging messages, as well as a greeting message defined by the application.

1-3. Build a Spring Application with the Maven Command-Line Interface

Problem

You want to build a Spring application with Maven from the command line.

Solution

Download Maven from `http://maven.apache.org/download.cgi`. Ensure the JAVA_HOME environment variable is set to Java's SDK main directory. Modify the PATH environment variable to include Maven's `bin` directory.

How It Works

Maven is available as a stand-alone command-line interface tool. This allows Maven to be leveraged from a wide variety of development environments. For example, if you prefer to use a text editor like emacs or vi to edit an application's code, it becomes essential to be able to access a build tool like Maven to automate the grunt work (e.g., copying files, one-step compiling) typically associated with the build process for Java applications.

Maven can be downloaded for free from `http://maven.apache.org/download.cgi`. Maven is available in both source code and binary versions. Since Java tools are cross-platform, we recommend you download the binary version to avoid the additional compilation step. At the time of this writing, the latest stable release of Maven is the 3.5.0 version.

Once you download Maven, ensure you have a Java SDK installed on your system because Maven requires it at runtime. Proceed to install Maven by unpacking it and defining the JAVA_HOME and PATH environment variables.

Run the following command to unpack it:

```
www@ubuntu:~$ tar -xzvf apache-maven-3.5.0-bin.tar.gz
```

Add the JAVA_HOME variable with the following command:

```
www@ubuntu:~$ export JAVA_HOME=/usr/lib/jvm/java-8-openjdk/
```

Add the Maven executable to the PATH variable with the following command:

```
www@ubuntu:~$ export PATH=$PATH:/home/www/apache-maven-3.5.0/bin/
```

■ **Tip** If you declare the variables JAVA_HOME and PATH as illustrated previously, you'll need to do this process every time you open a new shell session to use Maven. On Unix/Linux systems, you can open the `.bashrc` file inside a user's home directory and add the same export lines to avoid the need to declare the environment variables each session. On Windows systems, you can set environment variables permanently by selecting the My Computer icon, right-clicking, and then selecting the Properties option. In the pop-up window, select the Advanced tab and click the "Environment variables" button.

The Maven executable is available through the mvn command. If you set the environment variables correctly as described previously, typing mvn from any directory on your system invokes Maven. Describing any more details about Maven execution would go beyond the scope of this recipe. However, next we'll describe how to use Maven to build a Spring application from the book's source code.

Once you download the book's source code and unpack it to a local directory, go to the directory called ch01/springintro_mvn. Type mvn to invoke Maven and build the application under springintro_mvn. The output should look like Figure 1-18.

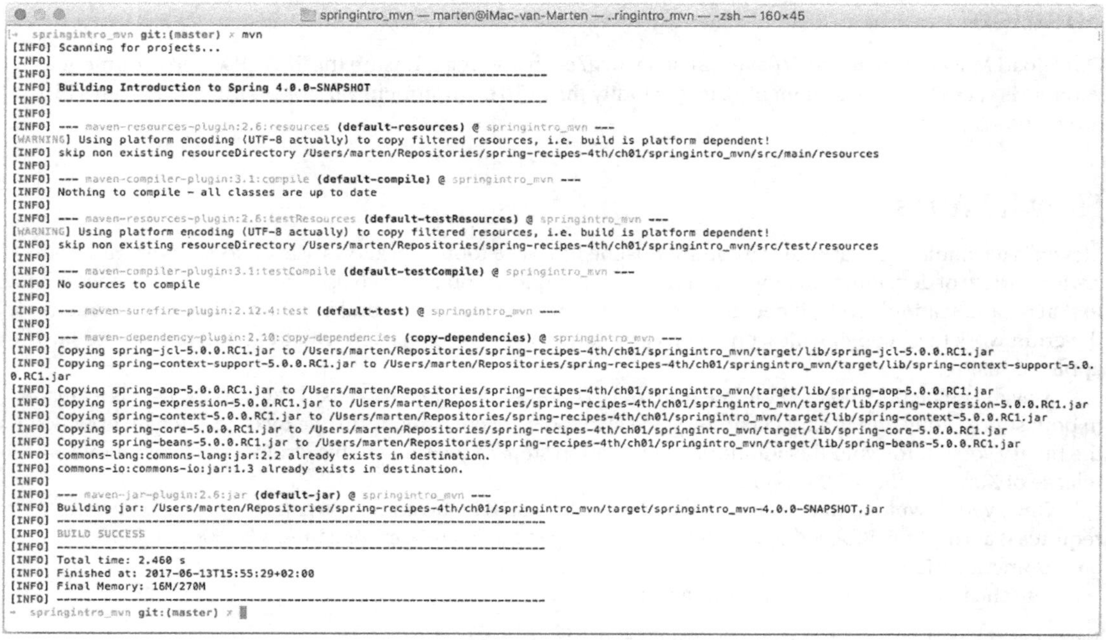

```
springintro_mvn — marten@iMac-van-Marten — ..ringintro_mvn — -zsh — 160×45
→ springintro_mvn git:(master) ✗ mvn
[INFO] Scanning for projects...
[INFO]
[INFO] ------------------------------------------------------------------------
[INFO] Building Introduction to Spring 4.0.0-SNAPSHOT
[INFO] ------------------------------------------------------------------------
[INFO]
[INFO] --- maven-resources-plugin:2.6:resources (default-resources) @ springintro_mvn ---
[WARNING] Using platform encoding (UTF-8 actually) to copy filtered resources, i.e. build is platform dependent!
[INFO] skip non existing resourceDirectory /Users/marten/Repositories/spring-recipes-4th/ch01/springintro_mvn/src/main/resources
[INFO]
[INFO] --- maven-compiler-plugin:3.1:compile (default-compile) @ springintro_mvn ---
[INFO] Nothing to compile - all classes are up to date
[INFO]
[INFO] --- maven-resources-plugin:2.6:testResources (default-testResources) @ springintro_mvn ---
[WARNING] Using platform encoding (UTF-8 actually) to copy filtered resources, i.e. build is platform dependent!
[INFO] skip non existing resourceDirectory /Users/marten/Repositories/spring-recipes-4th/ch01/springintro_mvn/src/test/resources
[INFO]
[INFO] --- maven-compiler-plugin:3.1:testCompile (default-testCompile) @ springintro_mvn ---
[INFO] No sources to compile
[INFO]
[INFO] --- maven-surefire-plugin:2.12.4:test (default-test) @ springintro_mvn ---
[INFO]
[INFO] --- maven-dependency-plugin:2.10:copy-dependencies (copy-dependencies) @ springintro_mvn ---
[INFO] Copying spring-jcl-5.0.0.RC1.jar to /Users/marten/Repositories/spring-recipes-4th/ch01/springintro_mvn/target/lib/spring-jcl-5.0.0.RC1.jar
[INFO] Copying spring-context-support-5.0.0.RC1.jar to /Users/marten/Repositories/spring-recipes-4th/ch01/springintro_mvn/target/lib/spring-context-support-5.0.
0.RC1.jar
[INFO] Copying spring-aop-5.0.0.RC1.jar to /Users/marten/Repositories/spring-recipes-4th/ch01/springintro_mvn/target/lib/spring-aop-5.0.0.RC1.jar
[INFO] Copying spring-expression-5.0.0.RC1.jar to /Users/marten/Repositories/spring-recipes-4th/ch01/springintro_mvn/target/lib/spring-expression-5.0.0.RC1.jar
[INFO] Copying spring-context-5.0.0.RC1.jar to /Users/marten/Repositories/spring-recipes-4th/ch01/springintro_mvn/target/lib/spring-context-5.0.0.RC1.jar
[INFO] Copying spring-core-5.0.0.RC1.jar to /Users/marten/Repositories/spring-recipes-4th/ch01/springintro_mvn/target/lib/spring-core-5.0.0.RC1.jar
[INFO] Copying spring-beans-5.0.0.RC1.jar to /Users/marten/Repositories/spring-recipes-4th/ch01/springintro_mvn/target/lib/spring-beans-5.0.0.RC1.jar
[INFO] commons-lang:commons-lang:jar:2.2 already exists in destination.
[INFO] commons-io:commons-io:jar:1.3 already exists in destination.
[INFO]
[INFO] --- maven-jar-plugin:2.6:jar (default-jar) @ springintro_mvn ---
[INFO] Building jar: /Users/marten/Repositories/spring-recipes-4th/ch01/springintro_mvn/target/springintro_mvn-4.0.0-SNAPSHOT.jar
[INFO] ------------------------------------------------------------------------
[INFO] BUILD SUCCESS
[INFO] ------------------------------------------------------------------------
[INFO] Total time: 2.460 s
[INFO] Finished at: 2017-06-13T15:55:29+02:00
[INFO] Final Memory: 16M/270M
[INFO] ------------------------------------------------------------------------
→ springintro_mvn git:(master) ✗
```

Figure 1-18. *Maven build output*

You've just built the application, congratulations! Now let's run it. Drill down into the directory called `target` created by Maven under the `ch01/springintro_mvn` directory. You'll see the file `springintro_mvn-4.0.0-SNAPSHOT.jar`, which is the built application. Execute the command `java -jar springintro_mvn-1-0.SNAPSHOT.jar` to run the application. You'll see application logging messages, as well as a greeting message defined by the application.

1-4. Build a Spring Application with the Gradle Wrapper

Problem

You want to build a Spring application utilizing the Maven wrapper from the command line.

Solution

Run the `mvnw` script from the command line.

How It Works

Although Maven (see recipe 1-3) is available as a stand-alone command-line tool, a lot of (open source) projects use the Maven wrapper to give you access to Maven. The advantage of this approach is that the application is completely self-providing. You as a developer don't need to have Maven installed, as the Maven wrapper will download a specific version of Maven to build the project.

Once you have a project that utilizes the Maven wrapper, you can simply type `./mvnw package` on the command line to have Maven automatically download and run the build. The only prerequisite is to have a Java SDK installed because Maven requires it at runtime and the Maven wrapper needs it to run.

Once you download the book's source code and unpack it to a local directory, go to the directory called `ch01/springintro_mvnw`. Type `./mvnw` to invoke the Maven wrapper and automatically build the application. The output will look something like Figure 1-19.

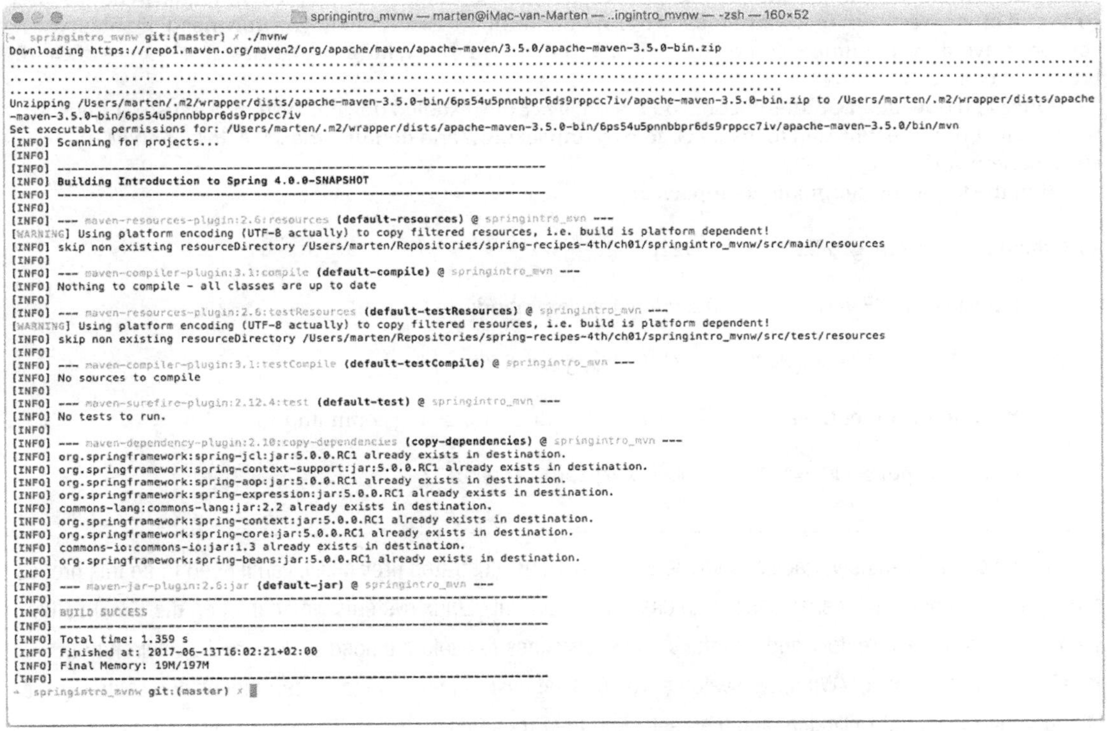

Figure 1-19. Maven wrapper build output

Notice that the first part of the output is downloading the actual Maven version used for this project.

1-5. Build a Spring Application with the Gradle Command-Line Interface

Problem

You want to build a Spring application with Gradle from the command line.

Solution

Download Gradle from `www.gradle.org/downloads`. Ensure the `JAVA_HOME` environment variable is set to Java's SDK main directory. Modify the `PATH` environment variable to include Gradle's `bin` directory.

How It Works

Gradle is available as a stand-alone command-line tool. This allows Gradle to be leveraged from a wide variety of development environments. For example, if you prefer to use a text editor like emacs or vi to edit an application's code, it becomes essential to be able to access a build tool like Gradle to automate the grunt work (e.g., copying files, one-step compiling) typically associated with the build process for Java applications.

Gradle can be downloaded for free from www.gradle.org/downloads. Gradle is available in both source code and binary versions. Since Java tools are cross-platform, we recommend you download the binary version to avoid the additional compilation step. At the time of this writing, the latest stable release of Gradle is the 3.5 version.

Once you download Gradle, ensure you have a Java SDK installed on your system because Gradle requires it at runtime. Proceed to install Gradle by unpacking it and defining the JAVA_HOME and PATH environment variables.

Run the following command to unpack it:

```
www@ubuntu:~$ unzip gradle-3.5-bin.zip
```

Add the JAVA_HOME variable with the following command:

```
www@ubuntu:~$ export JAVA_HOME=/usr/lib/jvm/java-8-openjdk/
```

Add the Gradle executable to the PATH variable with the following command:

```
www@ubuntu:~$ export PATH=$PATH:/home/www/gradle-3.5/bin/
```

■ **Tip** If you declare the variables JAVA_HOME and PATH as illustrated previously, you'll need to do this process every time you open a new shell session to use Gradle. On Unix/Linux systems, you can open the .bashrc file inside a user's home directory and add the same export lines to avoid the need to declare the environment variables each session. On Windows systems, you can set environment variables permanently by selecting the My Computer icon, right-clicking, and then selecting the Properties option. In the pop-up window, select the Advanced tab and click the "Environment variables" button.

The Gradle executable is available through the gradle command. If you set the environment variables correctly as described previously, typing gradle from any directory on your system invokes Gradle. Describing any more details about Gradle execution would go beyond the scope of this recipe. However, since the book's source code has numerous Spring applications that use Gradle, we'll describe how to use Gradle to build one of these Spring applications.

Once you download the book's source and unpack it to a local directory, go to the directory called ch01/springintro. Type gradle to invoke Gradle and build the application under springintro. The output should look like the output in Figure 1-20.

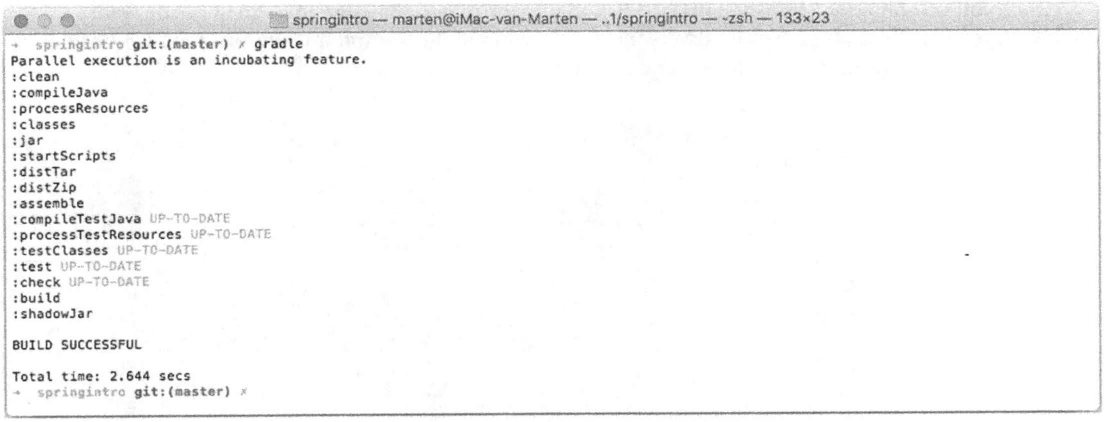

```
                    springintro — marten@iMac-van-Marten — ..1/springintro — -zsh — 133×23
→  springintro git:(master) ✗ gradle
Parallel execution is an incubating feature.
:clean
:compileJava
:processResources
:classes
:jar
:startScripts
:distTar
:distZip
:assemble
:compileTestJava UP-TO-DATE
:processTestResources UP-TO-DATE
:testClasses UP-TO-DATE
:test UP-TO-DATE
:check UP-TO-DATE
:build
:shadowJar

BUILD SUCCESSFUL

Total time: 2.644 secs
→  springintro git:(master) ✗
```

Figure 1-20. *Gradle build output*

You've just built the application, congratulations! Now let's run it. Drill down into the directory called `libs` created by Gradle under the `ch01/springintro` directory. You'll see the file `springintro-all.jar`, which is the built application. Execute the command `java -jar springintro-all.jar` to run the application. You'll see application logging messages, as well as a greeting message defined by the application.

1-6. Build a Spring Application with the Gradle Wrapper

Problem

You want to build a Spring application utilizing the Gradle wrapper from the command line.

Solution

Run the `gradlew` script from the command line.

How It Works

Although Gradle (see recipe 1-5) is available as a stand-alone command-line tool, a lot of (open source) projects use the Gradle wrapper to give you access to Gradle. The advantage of this approach is that the application is completely self-providing. You as a developer don't need to have Gradle installed because the Gradle wrapper will download a specific version of Gradle to build the project.

Once you have a project that utilizes the Gradle wrapper, you can simply type `./gradlew build` on the command line to have Gradle automatically download and run the build. The only prerequisite is to have a Java SDK installed because Gradle requires it at runtime and the Gradle wrapper needs it to run.

Once you download the book's source code and unpack it to a local directory, go to the directory called ch01/Recipe_1_6. Type ./gradlew to invoke the Gradle wrapper and automatically build the application under Recipe_1_6. The output will look something like Figure 1-21.

Figure 1-21. *Gradle build output*

■ **Tip** The source code from the book can be built with either plain Gradle or the Gradle wrapper. The latter is preferable as the code will be built using the same Gradle version while developing the samples.

Summary

In this chapter, you learned how to set up the most popular development tools to create Spring applications. You explored how to build and run the Spring application with four toolboxes. Two toolboxes consisted of using IDEs: the Spring Tool Suite distributed by the creators of the Spring Framework and the IntelliJ IDE distributed by JetBrains. The other two toolboxes consisted of using command-line tools: the Maven build tool and the newer Gradle build tool, which is gaining popularity over the Maven build tool.

CHAPTER 2

Spring Core Tasks

In this chapter, you'll learn about the core tasks associated with Spring. At the heart of the Spring Framework is the Spring Inversion of Control (Io0043) container. The IoC container is used to manage and configure Plain Old Java Objects (POJOs). Because one of the primary appeals of the Spring Framework is to build Java applications with POJOs, many of Spring's core tasks involve managing and configuring POJOs in the IoC container.

So, whether you plan to use the Spring Framework for web applications, enterprise integration, or some other type of project, working with POJOs and the IoC container is one of the first steps you need to take. The majority of the recipes in this chapter cover tasks that you'll use throughout the book and on a daily basis to develop Spring applications.

Note The term *bean* is used interchangeably with a POJO instance both in the book and in the Spring documentation. Both refer to an object instance created from a Java class. In addition, the term *component* is used interchangeably with a POJO class both in the book and in the Spring documentation. Both refer to the actual Java class from which object instances are created.

Tip The source code download is organized to use Gradle (through the Gradle wrapper) to build the recipe applications. Gradle takes care of loading all the necessary Java classes and dependencies and creating an executable JAR file. Chapter 1 describes how to set up the Gradle tool. Furthermore, if a recipe illustrates more than one approach, the source code is classified with various examples with roman letters (e.g., Recipe_2_1_i, Recipe_2_1_ii, Recipe_2_1_iii, etc.).

To build each application, go in the Recipe directory (e.g., Ch2/Recipe_2_1_i/) and execute the ./gradlew build command to compile the source code. Once the source code is compiled, a build/libs subdirectory is created with the application executable. You can then run the application JAR from the command line (e.g., java -jar Recipe_2_1_i-4.0.0.jar).

© Marten Deinum, Daniel Rubio, and Josh Long 2017
M. Deinum et al., *Spring 5 Recipes*, DOI 10.1007/978-1-4842-2790-9_2

2-1. Use a Java Config to Configure POJOs

Problem

You want to manage POJOs with annotations with Spring's IoC container.

Solution

Design a POJO class. Next, create a Java config class with @Configuration and @Bean annotations to configure POJO instance values or set up Java components with @Component, @Repository, @Service, or @Controller annotations to later create POJO instance values. Next, instantiate the Spring IoC container to scan for Java classes with annotations. The POJO instances or bean instances then become accessible to put together as part of an application.

How It Works

Suppose you're going to develop an application to generate sequence numbers and you are going to need many series of sequence numbers for different purposes. Each sequence will have its own prefix, suffix, and initial values. So, you have to create and maintain multiple generator instances for the application. Create a POJO class to create beans with a Java config.

In accordance with the requirements, you create a SequenceGenerator class that has three properties: prefix, suffix, and initial. You also create a private field counter to store the numeric value of each generator. Each time you call the getSequence() method on a generator instance, you get the last sequence number with the prefix and suffix joined.

```
package com.apress.springrecipes.sequence;

import java.util.concurrent.atomic.AtomicInteger;

public class SequenceGenerator {

    private String prefix;
    private String suffix;
    private int initial;
    private final AtomicInteger counter = new AtomicInteger();

    public SequenceGenerator() {
    }

    public void setPrefix(String prefix) {
        this.prefix = prefix;
    }

    public void setSuffix(String suffix) {
        this.suffix = suffix;
    }

    public void setInitial(int initial) {
        this.initial = initial;
    }
```

```
public String getSequence() {
    StringBuilder builder = new StringBuilder();
    builder.append(prefix)
           .append(initial)
           .append(counter.getAndIncrement())
           .append(suffix);
    return builder.toString();
}
}
```

Create a Java Config with @Configuration and @Bean to Create POJOs

To define instances of a POJO class in the Spring IoC container, you can create a Java config class with instantiation values. A Java config class with a POJO or bean definition looks like this:

```
package com.apress.springrecipes.sequence.config;

import org.springframework.context.annotation.Bean;
import org.springframework.context.annotation.Configuration;
import com.apress.springrecipes.sequence.SequenceGenerator;

@Configuration
public class SequenceGeneratorConfiguration {

    @Bean
    public SequenceGenerator sequenceGenerator() {
        SequenceGenerator seqgen = new SequenceGenerator();
        seqgen.setPrefix("30");
        seqgen.setSuffix("A");
        seqgen.setInitial("100000");
        return seqgen;
    }
}
```

Notice the SequenceGeneratorConfiguration class is decorated with the @Configuration annotation; this tells Spring it's a configuration class. When Spring encounters a class with the @Configuration annotation, it looks for bean instance definitions in the class, which are Java methods decorated with the @Bean annotation. The Java methods create and return a bean instance.

Any method definitions decorated with the @Bean annotation generates a bean name based on the method name. Alternatively, you can explicitly specify the bean name in the @Bean annotation with the name attribute. For example, @Bean(name="mys1") makes the bean available as mys1.

■ **Note** If you explicitly specify the bean name, the method name is ignored for the purposes of bean creation.

Instantiate the Spring IoC Container to Scan for Annotations

You have to instantiate the Spring IoC container to scan for Java classes that contain annotations. In doing so, Spring detects @Configuration and @Bean annotations so you can later get bean instances from the IoC container itself.

Spring provides two types of IoC container implementations. The basic one is called a *bean factory*. The more advanced one is called an *application context*, which is compatible with the bean factory. Note the configuration files for these two types of IoC containers are identical.

The application context provides more advanced features than the bean factory while keeping the basic features compatible. Therefore, we strongly recommend using the application context for every application unless the resources of an application are restricted (e.g., such as when running Spring for an applet or a mobile device). The interfaces for the bean factory and the application context are BeanFactory and ApplicationContext, respectively. The ApplicationContext interface is a subinterface of BeanFactory for maintaining compatibility.

Since ApplicationContext is an interface, you have to instantiate an implementation of it. Spring has several application context implementations; we recommend you use AnnotationConfigApplicationContext, which is the newest and most flexible implementation. With this class you can load the Java config file.

```
ApplicationContext context = new AnnotationConfigApplicationContext
    (SequenceGeneratorConfiguration.class);
```

Once the application context is instantiated, the object reference—in this case context—provides an entry point to access the POJO instances or beans.

Get POJO Instances or Beans from the IoC Container

To get a declared bean from a bean factory or an application context, you just make a call to the getBean() method and pass in the unique bean name. The return type of the getBean() method is java.lang.Object, so you have to cast it to its actual type before using it.

```
SequenceGenerator generator =
    (SequenceGenerator) context.getBean("sequenceGenerator");
```

The getBean() method also supports another variation where you can provide the bean class name to avoid making the cast.

```
SequenceGenerator generator = context.getBean("sequenceGenerator",SequenceGenerator.class);
```

If there is only a single bean, you can omit the bean name.

```
SequenceGenerator generator = context.getBean(SequenceGenerator.class);
```

Once you reach this step, you can use the POJO or bean just like any object created using a constructor outside of Spring.

A Main class to run the sequence generator application would look like the following:

```
package com.apress.springrecipes.sequence;

import com.apress.springrecipes.sequence.config.SequenceGeneratorConfiguration;
import org.springframework.context.ApplicationContext;
import org.springframework.context.annotation.AnnotationConfigApplicationContext;
```

```
public class Main {

    public static void main(String[] args) {
        ApplicationContext context =
            new AnnotationConfigApplicationContext(SequenceGeneratorConfiguration.class);

        SequenceGenerator generator = context.getBean(SequenceGenerator.class);

        System.out.println(generator.getSequence());
        System.out.println(generator.getSequence());
    }
}
```

If everything is available in the Java classpath (the SequenceGenerator POJO class and the Spring JAR dependencies), you should see the following output, along with some logging messages:

```
30100000A
30100001A
```

Create POJO Class with the @Component Annotation to Create Beans with DAO

Up to this point, the Spring bean instantiations have been done by hard-coding the values in a Java config class. This was the preferred approach to simplify the Spring examples.

However, the POJO instantiation process for most applications is done from either a database or user input. So, now it's time to move forward and use a more real-world scenario. For this section, we'll use a Domain class and a Data Access Object (DAO) class to create POJOs. You still won't need to set up a database—you'll actually hard-code values in the DAO class—but familiarizing yourself with this type of application structure is important since it's the basis for most real-world applications and future recipes.

Suppose you are asked to develop a sequence generator application like the one you did in the previous section. You'll need to modify the class structure slightly to accommodate a Domain class and DAO pattern. First, create a domain class called Sequence containing the id, prefix, and suffix properties.

```
package com.apress.springrecipes.sequence;

public class Sequence {

    private final String id;
    private final String prefix;
    private final String suffix;

    public Sequence(String id, String prefix, String suffix) {
        this.id = id;
        this.prefix = prefix;
        this.suffix = suffix;
    }

    public String getId() {
        return id;
    }
```

```
    public String getPrefix() {
        return prefix;
    }

    public String getSuffix() {
        return suffix;
    }

}
```

Then, you create an interface for the DAO, which is responsible for accessing data from the database. The getSequence() method loads a POJO or Sequence object from a database table by its ID, while the getNextValue() method retrieves the next value of a particular database sequence.

```
package com.apress.springrecipes.sequence;

public interface SequenceDao {

    public Sequence getSequence(String sequenceId);
    public int getNextValue(String sequenceId);
}
```

In a production application, you would implement this DAO interface to use a data-access technology. But to simplify this example, you'll implement a DAO with hard-coded values in a Map to store the sequence instances and values.

```
package com.apress.springrecipes.sequence;

import org.springframework.stereotype.Component;

import java.util.HashMap;
import java.util.Map;
import java.util.concurrent.atomic.AtomicInteger;

@Component("sequenceDao")
public class SequenceDaoImpl implements SequenceDao {

    private final Map<String, Sequence> sequences = new HashMap<>();
    private final Map<String, AtomicInteger> values = new HashMap<>();

    public SequenceDaoImpl() {
        sequences.put("IT", new Sequence("IT", "30", "A"));
        values.put("IT", new AtomicInteger(10000));
    }

    public Sequence getSequence(String sequenceId) {
        return sequences.get(sequenceId);
    }
```

```
    public int getNextValue(String sequenceId) {
        AtomicInteger value = values.get(sequenceId);
        return value.getAndIncrement();
    }
}
```

Observe how the SequenceDaoImpl class is decorated with the @Component("sequenceDao") annotation. This marks the class so Spring can create POJOs from it. The value inside the @Component annotation defines the bean instance ID, in this case sequenceDao. If no bean value name is provided in the @Component annotation, by default the bean name is assigned as the uncapitalized nonqualified class name. For example, for the SequenceDaoImpl class, the default bean name would be sequenceDaoImpl.

A call to the getSequence method returns the value of the given sequenceID. And a call to the getNextValue method creates a new value based on the value of the given sequenceID and returns the new value.

POJOs are classified in application layers. In Spring there are three layers: persistence, service, and presentation. @Component is a general-purpose annotation to decorate POJOs for Spring detection, whereas @Repository, @Service, and @Controller are specializations of @Component for more specific cases of POJOs associated with the persistence, service, and presentation layers.

If you're unsure about a POJO's purpose, you can decorate it with the @Component annotation. However, it's better to use the specialization annotations where possible because these provide extra facilities based on a POJO's purpose (e.g., @Repository causes exceptions to be wrapped up as DataAccessExceptions, which makes debugging easier).

Instantiate the Spring IoC Container with Filters to Scan for Annotations

By default, Spring detects all classes decorated with @Configuration, @Bean, @Component, @Repository, @Service, and @Controller annotations, among others. You can customize the scan process to include one or more include/exclude filters. This is helpful when a Java package has dozens or hundreds of classes. For certain Spring application contexts, it can be necessary to exclude or include POJOs with certain annotations.

■ **Warning**   Scanning every package can slow down the startup process unnecessarily.

Spring supports four types of filter expressions. The annotation and assignable types are to specify an annotation type and a class/interface for filtering. The regex and aspectj types allow you to specify a regular expression and an AspectJ pointcut expression for matching the classes. You can also disable the default filters with the use-default-filters attribute.

For example, the following component scan includes all classes in com.apress.springrecipes.sequence whose name contains the word Dao or Service and excludes the classes with the @Controller annotation:

```
@ComponentScan(
    includeFilters = {
        @ComponentScan.Filter(
            type = FilterType.REGEX,
            pattern = {"com.apress.springrecipes.sequence.*Dao",
                       "com.apress.springrecipes.sequence.*Service"})
    },
    excludeFilters = {
        @ComponentScan.Filter(
            type = FilterType.ANNOTATION,
            classes = {org.springframework.stereotype.Controller.class}) }
    )
```

When applying include filters to detect all classes whose name contains the word Dao or Service, even classes that don't have annotations are autodetected.

Get POJO Instances or Beans from the IoC Container

Then, you can test the preceding components with the following Main class:

```
package com.apress.springrecipes.sequence;

import org.springframework.context.ApplicationContext;
import org.springframework.context.annotation.AnnotationConfigApplicationContext;

public class Main {

    public static void main(String[] args) {

        ApplicationContext context =
            new AnnotationConfigApplicationContext("com.apress.springrecipes.sequence");

        SequenceDao sequenceDao = context.getBean(SequenceDao.class);

        System.out.println(sequenceDao.getNextValue("IT"));
        System.out.println(sequenceDao.getNextValue("IT"));
    }
}
```

2-2. Create POJOs by Invoking a Constructor

Problem

You want to create a POJO instance or bean in the Spring IoC container by invoking its constructor, which is the most common and direct way of creating beans. It is equivalent to using the new operator to create objects in Java.

Solution

Define a POJO class with a constructor or constructors. Next, create a Java config class to configure POJO instance values with constructors for the Spring IoC container. Next, instantiate the Spring IoC container to scan for Java classes with annotations. The POJO instances or bean instances become accessible to be put together as part of an application.

How It Works

Suppose you're going to develop a shop application to sell products online. First, you create the Product POJO class, which has several properties, such as the product name and price. As there are many types of products in your shop, you make the Product class abstract to extend it for different product subclasses.

```
package com.apress.springrecipes.shop;

public abstract class Product {

    private String name;
    private double price;

    public Product() {}

    public Product(String name, double price) {
        this.name = name;
        this.price = price;
    }

    // Getters and Setters
    ...

    public String toString() {
        return name + " " + price;
    }
}
```

Create the POJO Classes with Constructors

Then you create two product subclasses, Battery and Disc. Each of them has its own properties.

```
package com.apress.springrecipes.shop;

public class Battery extends Product {

    private boolean rechargeable;

    public Battery() {
        super();
    }

    public Battery(String name, double price) {
        super(name, price);
    }

    // Getters and Setters
    ...
}
```

```
package com.apress.springrecipes.shop;

public class Disc extends Product {

    private int capacity;
```

```java
    public Disc() {
        super();
    }

    public Disc(String name, double price) {
        super(name, price);
    }

    // Getters and Setters
    ...
}
```

Create a Java Config for Your POJO

To define instances of a POJO class in the Spring IoC container, you have to create a Java config class with instantiation values. A Java config class with a POJO or bean definition made by invoking constructors would look like this:

```java
package com.apress.springrecipes.shop.config;

import com.apress.springrecipes.shop.Battery;
import com.apress.springrecipes.shop.Disc;
import com.apress.springrecipes.shop.Product;
import org.springframework.context.annotation.Bean;
import org.springframework.context.annotation.Configuration;

@Configuration
public class ShopConfiguration {

    @Bean
    public Product aaa() {
        Battery p1 = new Battery("AAA", 2.5);
        p1.setRechargeable(true);
        return p1;
    }

    @Bean
    public Product cdrw() {
        Disc p2 = new Disc("CD-RW", 1.5);
        p2.setCapacity(700);
        return p2;
    }
}
```

Next, you can write the following Main class to test your products by retrieving them from the Spring IoC container:

```java
package com.apress.springrecipes.shop;

import com.apress.springrecipes.shop.config.ShopConfiguration;
import org.springframework.context.ApplicationContext;
import org.springframework.context.annotation.AnnotationConfigApplicationContext;
```

```java
public class Main {

    public static void main(String[] args) throws Exception {

        ApplicationContext context =
            new AnnotationConfigApplicationContext(ShopConfiguration.class);

        Product aaa = context.getBean("aaa", Product.class);
        Product cdrw = context.getBean("cdrw", Product.class);
        System.out.println(aaa);
        System.out.println(cdrw);
    }
}
```

2-3. Use POJO References and Autowiring to Interact with Other POJOs

Problem

The POJO instances or beans that make up an application often need to collaborate with each other to complete the application's functions. You want to use annotations to use POJO references and autowiring.

Solution

For POJO instances defined in a Java config class, you can use standard Java code to create references between beans. To autowire POJO references, you can mark a field, a setter method, a constructor, or even an arbitrary method with the @Autowired annotation.

How It Works

First we will introduce you to different methods of autowiring using constructors, fields and properties. Finally you will see how you could solve issues in autowiring.

Reference POJOs in a Java Config Class

When POJO instances are defined in a Java config class—as illustrated in recipe 2-1 and recipe 2-2—POJO references are straightforward to use because everything is Java code. In the following example, a bean property references another bean:

```java
package com.apress.springrecipes.sequence.config;

import com.apress.springrecipes.sequence.DatePrefixGenerator;
import com.apress.springrecipes.sequence.SequenceGenerator;
import org.springframework.context.annotation.Bean;
import org.springframework.context.annotation.Configuration;
```

```
@Configuration
public class SequenceConfiguration {

    @Bean
    public DatePrefixGenerator datePrefixGenerator() {
        DatePrefixGenerator dpg = new DatePrefixGenerator();
        dpg.setPattern("yyyyMMdd");
        return dpg;
    }

    @Bean
    public SequenceGenerator sequenceGenerator() {
        SequenceGenerator sequence = new SequenceGenerator();
        sequence.setInitial(100000);
        sequence.setSuffix("A");
        sequence.setPrefixGenerator(datePrefixGenerator());
        return sequence;
    }
}
```

The prefixGenerator property of the SequenceGenerator class is an instance of a DatePrefixGenerator bean.

The first bean declaration creates a DatePrefixGenerator POJO. By convention, the bean becomes accessible with the bean name datePrefixGenerator (i.e., the method name). But since the bean instantiation logic is also a standard Java method, the bean is also accessible by making a standard Java call. When the prefixGenerator property is set—in the second bean, via a setter—a standard Java call is made to the method datePrefixGenerator() to reference the bean.

Autowire POJO Fields with the @Autowired Annotation

Next, let's use autowiring on the SequenceDao field of the DAO SequenceDaoImpl class introduced in the second part of recipe 2-1. You'll add a service class to the application to illustrate autowiring with the DAO class.

A service class to generate service objects is another real-world application best practice, which acts as a façade to access DAOs—instead of accessing DAOs directly. Internally, the service object interacts with the DAO to handle the sequence generation requests.

```
package com.apress.springrecipes.sequence;
import org.springframework.beans.factory.annotation.Autowired;
import org.springframework.stereotype.Component;

@Component
public class SequenceService {

    @Autowired
    private SequenceDao sequenceDao;

    public void setSequenceDao(SequenceDao sequenceDao) {
        this.sequenceDao = sequenceDao;
    }
```

```
public String generate(String sequenceId) {
    Sequence sequence = sequenceDao.getSequence(sequenceId);
    int value = sequenceDao.getNextValue(sequenceId);
    return sequence.getPrefix() + value + sequence.getSuffix();
}
}
```

The SequenceService class is decorated with the @Component annotation. This allows Spring to detect the POJO. Because the @Component annotation has no name, the default bean name is sequenceService, which is based on the class name.

The sequenceDao property of the SequenceService class is decorated with the @Autowired annotation. This allows Spring to autowire the property with the sequenceDao bean (i.e., the SequenceDaoImpl class).

The @Autowired annotation can also be applied to a property of an array type to have Spring autowire all the matching beans. For example, you can annotate a PrefixGenerator[] property with @Autowired. Then, Spring will autowire all the beans whose type is compatible with PrefixGenerator at one time.

```
package com.apress.springrecipes.sequence;

import org.springframework.beans.factory.annotation.Autowired;

public class SequenceGenerator {

    @Autowired
    private PrefixGenerator[] prefixGenerators;
    ...
}
```

If you have multiple beans whose type is compatible with the PrefixGenerator defined in the IoC container, they will be added to the prefixGenerators array automatically.

In a similar way, you can apply the @Autowired annotation to a type-safe collection. Spring can read the type information of this collection and autowire all the beans whose type is compatible.

```
package com.apress.springrecipes.sequence;

import org.springframework.beans.factory.annotation.Autowired;

public class SequenceGenerator {

    @Autowired
    private List<PrefixGenerator> prefixGenerators;
    ...
}
```

If Spring notices that the @Autowired annotation is applied to a type-safe java.util.Map with strings as the keys, it will add all the beans of the compatible type, with the bean names as the keys, to this map.

```
package com.apress.springrecipes.sequence;

import org.springframework.beans.factory.annotation.Autowired;

public class SequenceGenerator {

    @Autowired
    private Map<String, PrefixGenerator> prefixGenerators;
    ...
}
```

Autowire POJO Methods and Constructors with the @Autowired Annotation and Make Autowiring Optional

The @Autowired annotation can also be applied directly to the setter method of a POJO. As an example, you can annotate the setter method of the prefixGenerator property with @Autowired. Then, Spring attempts to wire a bean whose type is compatible with prefixGenerator.

```
package com.apress.springrecipes.sequence;

import org.springframework.beans.factory.annotation.Autowired;

public class SequenceGenerator {
    ...
    @Autowired
    public void setPrefixGenerator(PrefixGenerator prefixGenerator) {
        this.prefixGenerator = prefixGenerator;
    }
}
```

By default, all the properties with @Autowired are required. When Spring can't find a matching bean to wire, it will throw an exception. If you want a certain property to be optional, set the required attribute of @Autowired to false. Then, when Spring can't find a matching bean, it will leave this property unset.

```
package com.apress.springrecipes.sequence;

import org.springframework.beans.factory.annotation.Autowired;

public class SequenceGenerator {
    ...
    @Autowired(required=false)
    public void setPrefixGenerator(PrefixGenerator prefixGenerator) {
        this.prefixGenerator = prefixGenerator;
    }
}
```

You may also apply the @Autowired annotation to a method with an arbitrary name and an arbitrary number of arguments; in that case, Spring attempts to wire a bean with the compatible type for each of the method arguments.

```
package com.apress.springrecipes.sequence;

import org.springframework.beans.factory.annotation.Autowired;

public class SequenceGenerator {
    ...
    @Autowired
    public void myOwnCustomInjectionName(PrefixGenerator prefixGenerator) {
        this.prefixGenerator = prefixGenerator;
    }
}
```

Finally, you may also apply the @Autowired annotation to a constructor that you want to be used for autowiring. The constructor can have any number of arguments, and Spring will attempt to wire a bean with the compatible type for each of the constructor arguments.

```
@Service
public class SequenceService {

    private final SequenceDao sequenceDao;

    @Autowired
    public SequenceService(SequenceDao sequenceDao) {
        this.sequenceDao=sequenceDao;
    }

    public String generate(String sequenceId) {
        Sequence sequence = sequenceDao.getSequence(sequenceId);
        int value = sequenceDao.getNextValue(sequenceId);
        return sequence.getPrefix() + value + sequence.getSuffix();
    }
}
```

■ **Tip**   As of Spring Framework 4.3, if you have only a single constructor, Spring will automatically use that constructor for autowiring. In that case, you can omit the @Autowired annotation.

Resolve Autowire Ambiguity with Annotations

By default, autowiring by type will not work when there is more than one bean with the compatible type in the IoC container and the property isn't a group type (e.g., array, list, map), as illustrated previously. However, there are two workarounds to autowiring by type if there's more than one bean of the same type: the @Primary annotation and the @Qualifier annotation.

Resolve Autowire Ambiguity with the @Primary Annotation

Spring allows you to specify a candidate bean by type by decorating the candidate with the @Primary annotation. The @Primary annotation gives preference to a bean when multiple candidates are qualified to autowire a single-valued dependency.

```
package com.apress.springrecipes.sequence;
...
import org.springframework.stereotype.Component;
import org.springframework.context.annotation.Primary;

@Component
@Primary
public class DatePrefixGenerator implements PrefixGenerator {

    public String getPrefix() {
        DateFormat formatter = new SimpleDateFormat("yyyyMMdd");
        return formatter.format(new Date());
    }
}
```

Notice that the previous POJO implements the PrefixGenerator interface and is decorated with the @Primary annotation. If you attempted to autowire a bean with a PrefixGenerator type, even if Spring had more than one bean instance with the same PrefixGenerator type, Spring would autowire the DatePrefixGenerator because it's marked with the @Primary annotation.

Resolve Autowire Ambiguity with the @Qualifier Annotation

Spring also allows you to specify a candidate bean by type by providing its name in the @Qualifier annotation.

```
package com.apress.springrecipes.sequence;

import org.springframework.beans.factory.annotation.Autowired;
import org.springframework.beans.factory.annotation.Qualifier;

public class SequenceGenerator {

    @Autowired
    @Qualifier("datePrefixGenerator")
    private PrefixGenerator prefixGenerator;
    ...
}
```

Once you've done this, Spring attempts to find a bean with that name in the IoC container and wire it into the property.

The @Qualifier annotation can also be applied to a method argument for autowiring.

```
package com.apress.springrecipes.sequence;

import org.springframework.beans.factory.annotation.Autowired;
import org.springframework.beans.factory.annotation.Qualifier;
```

```
public class SequenceGenerator {
    ...
    @Autowired
    public void myOwnCustomInjectionName(
        @Qualifier("datePrefixGenerator") PrefixGenerator prefixGenerator) {
        this.prefixGenerator = prefixGenerator;
    }
}
```

If you want to autowire bean properties by name, you can annotate a setter method, a constructor, or a field with the JSR-250 @Resource annotation described in the next recipe.

Resolve POJO References from Multiple Locations

As an application grows, it can become difficult to manage every POJO in a single Java configuration class. A common practice is to separate POJOs into multiple Java configuration classes according to their functionalities. When you create multiple Java configuration classes, obtaining references and autowiring POJOs that are defined in different classes isn't as straightforward as when everything is in a single Java configuration class.

One approach is to initialize the application context with the location of each Java configuration class. In this manner, the POJOs for each Java configuration class are loaded into the context and references, and autowiring between POJOs is possible.

```
AnnotationConfigApplicationContext context = new AnnotationConfigApplicationContext
    (PrefixConfiguration.class, SequenceGeneratorConfiguration.class);
```

Another alternative is to use the @Import annotation so Spring makes the POJOs from one configuration file available in another.

```
package com.apress.springrecipes.sequence.config;

import org.springframework.context.annotation.Bean;
import org.springframework.context.annotation.Import;
import org.springframework.beans.factory.annotation.Value;
import org.springframework.context.annotation.Configuration;
import com.apress.springrecipes.sequence.SequenceGenerator;
import com.apress.springrecipes.sequence.PrefixGenerator;

@Configuration
@Import(PrefixConfiguration.class)
public class SequenceConfiguration {
    @Value("#{datePrefixGenerator}")
    private PrefixGenerator prefixGenerator;

    @Bean
    public SequenceGenerator sequenceGenerator() {
        SequenceGenerator sequence= new SequenceGenerator();
        sequence.setInitial(100000);
        sequence.setSuffix("A");
        sequence.setPrefixGenerator(prefixGenerator);
        return sequence;
    }
}
```

The sequenceGenerator bean requires you to set a prefixGenerator bean. But notice no prefixGenerator bean is defined in the Java configuration class. The prefixGenerator bean is defined in a separate Java configuration class called PrefixConfiguration. With the @Import(PrefixConfiguration. class) annotation, Spring brings all the POJOs in the Java configuration class into the scope of the present configuration class. With the POJOs from PrefixConfiguration in scope, you use the @Value annotation and SpEL to inject the bean named datePrefixGenerator into the prefixGenerator field. Once the bean is injected, it can be used to set a prefixGenerator bean for the sequenceGenerator bean.

2-4. Autowire POJOs with the @Resource and @Inject Annotations

Problem

You want to use the Java standard @Resource and @Inject annotations to reference POJOs via autowiring, instead of using the Spring-specific @Autowired annotation.

Solution

JSR-250, or Common Annotations for the Java Platform, defines the @Resource annotation to autowire POJO references by name. JSR-330, or Standard Annotations for Injection, defines the @Inject annotations to autowire POJO references by type.

How It Works

The @Autowired annotation described in the previous recipe belongs to the Spring Framework, specifically to the org.springframework.beans.factory.annotation package. This means it can be used only in the context of the Spring Framework.

Soon after Spring added support for the @Autowired annotation, the Java language standardized various annotations to fulfill the same purpose of the @Autowired annotation. These annotations are @Resource, which belongs to the javax.annotation package, and @Inject, which belongs to the javax.inject package.

Autowire POJOs with the @Resource Annotation

By default, the @Resource annotation works like Spring's @Autowired annotation and attempts to autowire by type. For example, the following POJO attribute is decorated with the @Resource annotation, so Spring attempts to locate a POJO that matches the PrefixGenerator type.

```
package com.apress.springrecipes.sequence;

import javax.annotation.Resource;

public class SequenceGenerator {

    @Resource
    private PrefixGenerator prefixGenerator;
    ...
}
```

However, unlike the @Autowired annotation, which requires the @Qualifier annotation to autowire a POJO by name, the @Resource ambiguity is eliminated if more than one POJO type of the same kind exists. Essentially, the @Resource annotation provides the same functionality as putting together the @Autowired annotation and the @Qualifier annotation.

Autowire POJOs with the @Inject Annotation

Also, the @Inject annotation attempts to autowire by type, like the @Resource and @Autowired annotations. For example, the following POJO attribute is decorated with the @Inject annotation, so Spring attempts to locate a POJO that matches the PrefixGenerator type:

```
package com.apress.springrecipes.sequence;

import javax.inject.Inject;

public class SequenceGenerator {

    @Inject
    private PrefixGenerator prefixGenerator;
    ...
}
```

But just like the @Resource and @Autowired annotations, a different approach has to be used to match POJOs by name or avoid ambiguity if more than one POJO type of the same kind exists. The first step to do autowiring by name with the @Inject annotation is to create a custom annotation to identify both the POJO injection class and the POJO injection point.

```
package com.apress.springrecipes.sequence;

import java.lang.annotation.Documented;
import java.lang.annotation.ElementType;
import java.lang.annotation.Retention;
import java.lang.annotation.RetentionPolicy;
import java.lang.annotation.Target;

import javax.inject.Qualifier;

@Qualifier
@Target({ElementType.TYPE, ElementType.FIELD, ElementType.PARAMETER})
@Documented
@Retention(RetentionPolicy.RUNTIME)
public @interface DatePrefixAnnotation {
}
```

Notice the custom annotation makes use of the @Qualifier annotation. This annotation is different from the one used with Spring's @Qualifier annotation, as this last class belongs to the same Java package as the @Inject annotation (i.e., javax.inject).

Once the custom annotation is done, it's necessary to decorate the POJO injection class that generates the bean instance, which in this case is the DatePrefixGenerator class.

```
package com.apress.springrecipes.sequence;
...
@DatePrefixAnnotation
public class DatePrefixGenerator implements PrefixGenerator {
...
}
```

Finally, the POJO attribute or injection point is decorated with the same custom annotation to qualify the POJO and eliminate any ambiguity.

```
package com.apress.springrecipes.sequence;

import javax.inject.Inject;

public class SequenceGenerator {

    @Inject @DataPrefixAnnotation
    private PrefixGenerator prefixGenerator;
    ...
}
```

As you've seen in recipes 2-3 and 2-4, the three annotations @Autowired, @Resource, and @Inject can achieve the same result. The @Autowired annotation is a Spring-based solution, whereas the @Resource and @Inject annotations are Java standard (i.e., JSR) solutions. If you're going to do name-based autowiring, the @Resource annotation offers the simplest syntax. For autowiring by class type, all three annotations are straightforward to use because all three require a single annotation.

2-5. Set a POJO's Scope with the @Scope Annotation

Problem

When you declare a POJO instance with an annotation like @Component, you are actually defining a template for bean creation, not an actual bean instance. When a bean is requested by the getBean() method or referenced from other beans, Spring decides which bean instance should be returned according to the bean scope. Sometimes you have to set an appropriate scope for a bean other than the default scope.

Solution

A bean's scope is set with the @Scope annotation. By default, Spring creates exactly one instance for each bean declared in the IoC container, and this instance is shared in the scope of the entire IoC container. This unique bean instance is returned for all subsequent getBean() calls and bean references. This scope is called singleton, which is the default scope of all beans. Table 2-1 lists all valid bean scopes in Spring.

Table 2-1. *Valid Bean Scopes in Spring*

Scope	Description
singleton	Creates a single bean instance per Spring IoC container
prototype	Creates a new bean instance each time when requested
request	Creates a single bean instance per HTTP request; valid only in the context of a web application
session	Creates a single bean instance per HTTP session; valid only in the context of a web application
globalSession	Creates a single bean instance per global HTTP session; valid only in the context of a portal application

How It Works

To demonstrate the concept of bean scope, let's consider a shopping cart example in a shopping application. First, you create the ShoppingCart class as follows:

```
package com.apress.springrecipes.shop;
...
@Component
public class ShoppingCart {

    private List<Product> items = new ArrayList<>();

    public void addItem(Product item) {
        items.add(item);
    }

    public List<Product> getItems() {
        return items;
    }
}
```

Then, you declare some product beans in a Java config file so they can later be added to the shopping cart.

```
package com.apress.springrecipes.shop.config;

import com.apress.springrecipes.shop.Battery;
import com.apress.springrecipes.shop.Disc;
import com.apress.springrecipes.shop.Product;
import org.springframework.context.annotation.Bean;
import org.springframework.context.annotation.ComponentScan;
import org.springframework.context.annotation.Configuration;

@Configuration
@ComponentScan("com.apress.springrecipes.shop")
public class ShopConfiguration {
```

```java
@Bean
public Product aaa() {
    Battery p1 = new Battery();
    p1.setName("AAA");
    p1.setPrice(2.5);
    p1.setRechargeable(true);
    return p1;
}

@Bean
public Product cdrw() {
    Disc p2 = new Disc("CD-RW", 1.5);
    p2.setCapacity(700);
    return p2;
}

@Bean
public Product dvdrw() {
    Disc p2 = new Disc("DVD-RW", 3.0);
    p2.setCapacity(700);
    return p2;
}
}
```

Once you do this, you can define a Main class to test the shopping cart by adding some products to it. Suppose there are two customers navigating in your shop at the same time. The first one gets a shopping cart by the getBean() method and adds two products to it. Then, the second customer also gets a shopping cart by the getBean() method and adds another product to it.

```java
package com.apress.springrecipes.shop;

import com.apress.springrecipes.shop.config.ShopConfiguration;
import org.springframework.context.ApplicationContext;
import org.springframework.context.annotation.AnnotationConfigApplicationContext;

public class Main {

    public static void main(String[] args) throws Exception {
        ApplicationContext context =
            new AnnotationConfigApplicationContext(ShopConfiguration.class);

        Product aaa = context.getBean("aaa", Product.class);
        Product cdrw = context.getBean("cdrw", Product.class);
        Product dvdrw = context.getBean("dvdrw", Product.class);

        ShoppingCart cart1 = context.getBean("shoppingCart", ShoppingCart.class);
        cart1.addItem(aaa);
        cart1.addItem(cdrw);
        System.out.println("Shopping cart 1 contains " + cart1.getItems());
```

```
ShoppingCart cart2 = context.getBean("shoppingCart", ShoppingCart.class);
cart2.addItem(dvdrw);
System.out.println("Shopping cart 2 contains " + cart2.getItems());

    }
}
```

As a result of the preceding bean declaration, you can see that the two customers get the same shopping cart instance.

```
Shopping cart 1 contains [AAA 2.5, CD-RW 1.5]
Shopping cart 2 contains [AAA 2.5, CD-RW 1.5, DVD-RW 3.0]
```

This is because Spring's default bean scope is singleton, which means Spring creates exactly one shopping cart instance per IoC container.

In your shop application, you expect each customer to get a different shopping cart instance when the getBean() method is called. To ensure this behavior, the scope of the shoppingCart bean needs to be set to prototype. Then Spring creates a new bean instance for each getBean() method call.

```
package com.apress.springrecipes.shop;
...
import org.springframework.stereotype.Component;
import org.springframework.context.annotation.Scope;

@Component
@Scope("prototype")
public class ShoppingCart { ... }
```

Now if you run the Main class again, you can see the two customers get a different shopping cart instance.

```
Shopping cart 1 contains [AAA 2.5, CD-RW 1.5]
Shopping cart 2 contains [DVD-RW 3.0]
```

2-6. Use Data from External Resources (Text Files, XML Files, Properties Files, or Image Files)

Problem

Sometimes applications need to read external resources (e.g., text files, XML files, properties file, or image files) from different locations (e.g., a file system, classpath, or URL). Usually, you have to deal with different APIs for loading resources from different locations.

Solution

Spring offers the @PropertySource annotation as a facility to load the contents of a .properties file (i.e., key-value pairs) to set up bean properties.

Spring also has a resource loader mechanism that provides a unified Resource interface to retrieve any type of external resource by a resource path. You can specify different prefixes for this path to load resources from different locations with the @Value annotation. To load a resource from a file system, you use the file prefix. To load a resource from the classpath, you use the classpath prefix. You can also specify a URL in the resource path.

How It Works

To read the contents of a properties file (i.e., key-value pairs) to set up bean properties, you can use Spring's @PropertySource annotation with PropertySourcesPlaceholderConfigurer. If you want to read the contents of any file, you can use Spring's Resource mechanism decorated with the @Value annotation.

Use Properties File Data to Set Up POJO Instantiation Values

Let's assume you have a series of values in a properties file you want to access to set up bean properties. Typically this can be the configuration properties of a database or some other application values composed of key values. For example, take the following key values stored in a file called discounts.properties:

```
specialcustomer.discount=0.1
summer.discount=0.15
endofyear.discount=0.2
```

■ **Note**   To read properties files for the purpose of internationalization (i18n), see the next recipe.

To make the contents of the discounts.properties file accessible to set up other beans, you can use the @PropertySource annotation to convert the key values into a bean inside a Java config class.

```java
package com.apress.springrecipes.shop.config;

import com.apress.springrecipes.shop.Battery;
import com.apress.springrecipes.shop.Disc;
import com.apress.springrecipes.shop.Product;
import org.springframework.beans.factory.annotation.Value;
import org.springframework.context.annotation.Bean;
import org.springframework.context.annotation.ComponentScan;
import org.springframework.context.annotation.Configuration;
import org.springframework.context.annotation.PropertySource;
import org.springframework.context.support.PropertySourcesPlaceholderConfigurer;

@Configuration
@PropertySource("classpath:discounts.properties")
@ComponentScan("com.apress.springrecipes.shop")
public class ShopConfiguration {

    @Value("${endofyear.discount:0}")
    private double specialEndofyearDiscountField;
```

```
@Bean
public static PropertySourcesPlaceholderConfigurer
    propertySourcesPlaceholderConfigurer() {
    return new PropertySourcesPlaceholderConfigurer();
}

@Bean
public Product dvdrw() {
    Disc p2 = new Disc("DVD-RW", 3.0, specialEndofyearDiscountField);
    p2.setCapacity(700);
    return p2;
}
}
```

You define a @PropertySource annotation with a value of classpath:discounts.properties to decorate the Java config class. The classpath: prefix tells Spring to look for the discounts.properties file in the Java classpath.

Once you define the @PropertySource annotation to load the properties file, you also need to define a PropertySourcePlaceholderConfigurer bean with the @Bean annotation. Spring automatically wires the @PropertySource discounts.properties file so its properties become accessible as bean properties.

Next, you need to define Java variables to take values from the discount discounts.properties file. To define the Java variable values with these values, you make use of the @Value annotation with a placeholder expression.

The syntax is @Value("${key:default_value}"). A search is done for the key value in all the loaded application properties. If a matching key=value is found in the properties file, the corresponding value is assigned to the bean property. If no matching key=value is found in the loaded application properties, default_value (i.e., after ${key:) is assigned to the bean property.

Once a Java variable is set with a discount value, you can use it to set up bean instances for a bean's discount property.

If you want to use properties file data for a different purpose than setting up bean properties, you should use Spring's Resource mechanism, which is described next.

Use Data from Any External Resource File for Use in a POJO

Suppose you want to display a banner on application startup. The banner consists of the following characters and stored in a text file called banner.txt. This file can be put in the classpath of your application.

```
*************************
*  Welcome to My Shop!  *
*************************
```

Next, let's write a BannerLoader POJO class to load the banner and output it to the console.

```
package com.apress.springrecipes.shop;
import org.springframework.core.io.Resource;
...
import javax.annotation.PostConstruct;
public class BannerLoader {

    private Resource banner;
```

```
    public void setBanner(Resource banner) {
        this.banner = banner;
    }


    @PostConstruct
    public void showBanner() throws IOException {
        InputStream in = banner.getInputStream();

        BufferedReader reader = new BufferedReader(new InputStreamReader(in));
        while (true) {
            String line = reader.readLine();
            if (line == null)
                break;
            System.out.println(line);
        }
        reader.close();
    }
}
```

Notice the POJO banner field is a Spring Resource type. The field value will be populated through setter injection when the bean instance is created—to be explained shortly. The showBanner() method makes a call to the getInputStream() method to retrieve the input stream from the Resource field. Once you have an InputStream, you're able to use a standard Java file manipulation class. In this case, the file contents are read line by line with BufferedReader and output to the console.

Also notice the showBanner() method is decorated with the @PostConstruct annotation. Because you want to show the banner at startup, you use this annotation to tell Spring to invoke the method automatically after creation. This guarantees the showBanner() method is one of the first methods to be run by the application and therefore ensures the banner appears at the outset.

Next, the POJO BannerLoader needs to be initialized as an instance. In addition, the banner field of the BannerLoader also needs to be injected. So, let's create a Java config class for these tasks.

```
@Configuration
@PropertySource("classpath:discounts.properties")
@ComponentScan("com.apress.springrecipes.shop")
public class ShopConfiguration {

    @Value("classpath:banner.txt")
    private Resource banner;

    @Bean
    public static PropertySourcesPlaceholderConfigurer propertySourcesPlaceholderConfigurer() {
        return new PropertySourcesPlaceholderConfigurer();
    }

    @Bean
    public BannerLoader bannerLoader() {
        BannerLoader bl = new BannerLoader();
        bl.setBanner(banner);
        return bl;
    }
}
```

See how the `banner` property is decorated with the `@Value("classpath:banner.txt")` annotation. This tells Spring to search for the `banner.txt` file in the classpath and inject it. Spring uses the preregistered property editor `ResourceEditor` to convert the file definition into a `Resource` object before injecting it into the bean.

Once the `banner` property is injected, it's assigned to the `BannerLoader` bean instance via setter injection.

Because the banner file is located in the Java classpath, the resource path starts with the `classpath:` prefix. The previous resource path specifies a resource in the relative path of the file system. You can specify an absolute path as well.

```
file:c:/shop/banner.txt
```

When a resource is located in Java's classpath, you have to use the classpath prefix. If there's no path information presented, it will be loaded from the root of the classpath.

```
classpath:banner.txt
```

If the resource is located in a particular package, you can specify the absolute path from the classpath root.

```
classpath:com/apress/springrecipes/shop/banner.txt
```

Besides support to load from a file system path or the classpath, a resource can also be loaded by specifying a URL.

```
http://springrecipes.apress.com/shop/banner.txt
```

Since the bean class uses the `@PostConstruct` annotation on the `showBanner()` method, the banner is sent to output when the IoC container is set up. Because of this, there's no need to tinker with an application's context or explicitly call the bean to output the banner. However, sometimes it can be necessary to access an external resource to interact with an application's context. Now suppose you want to display a legend at the end of an application. The legend consists of the discounts previously described in the `discounts.properties` file. To access the contents of the properties file, you can also leverage Spring's Resource mechanism.

Next, let's use Spring's Resource mechanism, but this time directly inside an application's `Main` class to output a legend when the application finishes.

```java
import org.springframework.core.io.ClassPathResource;
import org.springframework.core.io.support.PropertiesLoaderUtils;
...
...
public class Main {

    public static void main(String[] args) throws Exception {
        ...
        Resource resource = new ClassPathResource("discounts.properties");
        Properties props = PropertiesLoaderUtils.loadProperties(resource);
        System.out.println("And don't forget our discounts!");
        System.out.println(props);

    }
}
```

Spring's ClassPathResource class is used to access the discounts.properties file, which casts the file's contents into a Resource object. Next, the Resource object is processed into a Properties object with Spring's PropertiesLoaderUtils class. Finally, the contents of the Properties object are sent to the console as the final output of the application.

Because the legend file (i.e., discounts.properties) is located in the Java classpath, the resource is accessed with Spring's ClassPathResource class. If the external resource were in a file system path, the resource would be loaded with Spring's FileSystemResource.

```
Resource resource = new FileSystemResource("c:/shop/banner.txt")
```

If the external resource were at a URL, the resource would be loaded with Spring's UrlResource.

```
Resource resource = new UrlResource("http://www.apress.com/")
```

2-7. Resolve I18N Text Messages for Different Locales in Properties Files

Problem

You want an application to support internationalization via annotations.

Solution

MessageSource is an interface that defines several methods for resolving messages in resource bundles. ResourceBundleMessageSource is the most common MessageSource implementation that resolves messages from resource bundles for different locales. After you implement a ResourceBundleMessageSource POJO, you can use the @Bean annotation in a Java config file to make the i18n data available in an application.

How It Works

As an example, create a resource bundle called messages_en_US.properties for the English language in the United States. Resource bundles are loaded from the root of the classpath, so ensure it's available on the Java classpath. Place the following key-value in the file:

```
alert.checkout=A shopping cart has been checked out.
alert.inventory.checkout=A shopping cart with {0} has been checked out at {1}.
```

To resolve messages from resource bundles, let's create a Java config file with an instance of a ReloadableResourceBundleMessageSource bean.

```
package com.apress.springrecipes.shop.config;

import org.springframework.context.annotation.Bean;
import org.springframework.context.annotation.Configuration;
import org.springframework.context.support.ReloadableResourceBundleMessageSource;
```

```
@Configuration
public class ShopConfiguration {

    @Bean
    public ReloadableResourceBundleMessageSource messageSource() {
        ReloadableResourceBundleMessageSource messageSource =
            new ReloadableResourceBundleMessageSource();
        messageSource.setBasenames("classpath:messages");
        messageSource.setCacheSeconds(1);
        return messageSource;
    }
}
```

The bean instance must have the name messageSource for the application context to detect it.

Inside the bean definition you declare a String list via the setBasenames method to locate bundles for the ResourceBundleMessageSource. In this case, you just specify the default convention to look up files located in the Java classpath that start with messages. In addition, the setCacheSeconds methods sets the caching to 1 second to avoid reading stale messages. Note that a refresh attempt first checks the last-modified timestamp of the properties file before actually reloading it, so if files don't change, the setCacheSeconds interval can be set rather low, as refresh attempts aren't actually reloaded.

For this MessageSource definition, if you look up a text message for the United States locale, whose preferred language is English, the resource bundle messages_en_US.properties is considered first. If there's no such resource bundle or the message can't be found, then a messages_en.properties file that matches the language is considered. If a resource bundle still can't be found, the default messages.properties for all locales is chosen. For more information on resource bundle loading, you can refer to the Javadoc of the java.util.ResourceBundle class.

Next, you can configure the application context to resolve messages with the getMessage() method. The first argument is the key corresponding to the message, and the third is the target locale.

```
package com.apress.springrecipes.shop;

import com.apress.springrecipes.shop.config.ShopConfiguration;
import org.springframework.context.ApplicationContext;
import org.springframework.context.annotation.AnnotationConfigApplicationContext;

import java.util.Date;
import java.util.Locale;

public class Main {

    public static void main(String[] args) throws Exception {

        ApplicationContext context =
            new AnnotationConfigApplicationContext(ShopConfiguration.class);

        String alert = context.getMessage("alert.checkout", null, Locale.US);
        String alert_inventory = context.getMessage("alert.inventory.checkout", new Object[]
        {"[DVD-RW 3.0]", new Date()}, Locale.US);
```

```
        System.out.println("The I18N message for alert.checkout is: " + alert);
        System.out.println("The I18N message for alert.inventory.checkout is: " +
        alert_inventory);
    }
}
```

The second argument of the getMessage() method is an array of message parameters. In the first String statement the value is null, and in the second String statement an object array to fill in the message parameters is used.

In the Main class, you can resolve text messages because you can access the application context directly. But for a bean to resolve text messages, you have to inject a MessageSource implementation into the bean that needs to resolve text messages. Let's implement a Cashier class for the shopping application that illustrates how to resolve messages.

```
package com.apress.springrecipes.shop;
...
@Component
public class Cashier {

    @Autowired
    private MessageSource messageSource;

    public void setMessageSource(MessageSource messageSource) {
        this.messageSource = messageSource;
    }

    public void checkout(ShoppingCart cart) throws IOException {
        String alert = messageSource.getMessage("alert.inventory.checkout",
                                        new Object[] { cart.getItems(), new Date() },
                                        Locale.US);
        System.out.println(alert);
    }
}
```

Notice the POJO messageSource field is a Spring MessageSource type. The field value is decorated with the @Autowired annotation, so it's populated through injection when the bean instance is created. Then the checkout method can access the messageSource field, which gives the bean access to the getMessage method to gain access to text messages based on i18n criteria.

2-8. Customize POJO Initialization and Destruction with Annotations

Problem

Some POJOs have to perform certain types of initialization tasks before they're used. These tasks can include opening a file, opening a network/database connection, allocating memory, and so on. In addition, these same POJOs have to perform the corresponding destruction tasks at the end of their life cycle. Therefore, sometimes it's necessary to customize bean initialization and destruction in the Spring IoC container.

Solution

Spring can recognize initialization and destruction callback methods by setting the `initMethod` and `destroyMethod` attributes of the @Bean definition in a Java config class. Or Spring can also recognize initialization and destruction callback methods if POJO methods are decorated with the @PostConstruct and @PreDestroy annotations, respectively. Spring can also delay the creation of a bean up until the point it's required—a process called *lazy initialization*—with the @Lazy annotation. Spring can also ensure the initialization of certain beans before others with the @DependsOn annotation.

How It Works

Define methods to run before POJO initialization and destruction with @Bean. Let's take the case of the shopping application and consider an example involving a checkout function. Let's modify the `Cashier` class to record a shopping cart's products and the checkout time to a text file.

```java
package com.apress.springrecipes.shop;

import java.io.*;
import java.util.Date;

public class Cashier {

    private String fileName;
    private String path;
    private BufferedWriter writer;

    public void setFileName(String fileName) {
        this.fileName = fileName;
    }

    public void setPath(String path) {
        this.path = path;
    }

    public void openFile() throws IOException {

        File targetDir = new File(path);
        if (!targetDir.exists()) {
            targetDir.mkdir();
        }

        File checkoutFile = new File(path, fileName + ".txt");
        if (!checkoutFile.exists()) {
            checkoutFile.createNewFile();
        }

        writer = new BufferedWriter(new OutputStreamWriter(
                new FileOutputStream(checkoutFile, true)));
    }
```

```
    public void checkout(ShoppingCart cart) throws IOException {
        writer.write(new Date() + "\t" + cart.getItems() + "\r\n");
        writer.flush();
    }

    public void closeFile() throws IOException {
        writer.close();
    }

}
```

In the Cashier class, the openFile() method first verifies whether the target directory and the file to write the data exists. It then opens the text file in the specified system path and assigns it to the writer field. Then each time the checkout() method is called, the date and cart items are appended to the text file. Finally, the closeFile() method closes the file to release its system resources.

Next, let's explore how this bean definition has to be set up in a Java config class to execute the openFile() method just before the bean is created and the closeFile() method just before it's destroyed.

```
@Configuration
public class ShopConfiguration {

    @Bean(initMethod = "openFile", destroyMethod = "closeFile")
    public Cashier cashier() {

        String path = System.getProperty("java.io.tmpdir") + "/cashier";
        Cashier c1 = new Cashier();
        c1.setFileName("checkout");
        c1.setPath(path);
        return c1;
    }
}
```

Notice the POJO's initialization and destruction tasks are defined with the initMethod and destroyMethod attributes of an @Bean annotation. With these two attributes set in the bean declaration, when the Cashier class is created, it first triggers the openFile() method, verifying whether the target directory and the file to write the data exist, as well as opening the file to append records. When the bean is destroyed, it triggers the closeFile() method, ensuring the file reference is closed to release system resources.

Define Methods to Run Before POJO Initialization and Destruction with @PostConstruct and @PreDestroy

Another alterative if you're defining POJO instances outside a Java config class (e.g., with the @Component annotation) is to use the @PostConstruct and @PreDestroy annotations directly in the POJO class.

```
@Component
public class Cashier {

    @Value("checkout")
    private String fileName;
    @Value("c:/Windows/Temp/cashier")
```

```java
private String path;
private BufferedWriter writer;

public void setFileName(String fileName) {
    this.fileName = fileName;
}

public void setPath(String path) {
    this.path = path;
}

@PostConstruct
public void openFile() throws IOException {
    File targetDir = new File(path);
    if (!targetDir.exists()) {
        targetDir.mkdir();
    }
    File checkoutFile = new File(path, fileName + ".txt");
    if(!checkoutFile.exists()) {
        checkoutFile.createNewFile();
    }
    writer = new BufferedWriter(new OutputStreamWriter(
            new FileOutputStream(checkoutFile, true)));
}

public void checkout(ShoppingCart cart) throws IOException {
    writer.write(new Date() + "\t" +cart.getItems() + "\r\n");
    writer.flush();
}

@PreDestroy
public void closeFile() throws IOException {
    writer.close();
}
}
```

The @Component annotation tells Spring to manage the POJO, just like it's been used in previous recipes. Two of the POJO fields' values are set with the @Value annotation, a concept that was also explored in a previous recipe. The openFile() method is decorated with the @PostConstruct annotation, which tells Spring to execute the method right after a bean is constructed. The closeFile() method is decorated with the @PreDestroy annotation, which tells Spring to execute the method right before a bean is destroyed.

Define Lazy Initialization for POJOs with @Lazy

By default, Spring performs eager initialization on all POJOs. This means POJOs are initialized at startup. In certain circumstances, though, it can be convenient to delay the POJO initialization process until a bean is required. Delaying the initialization is called *lazy initialization*.

Lazy initialization helps limit resource consumption peaks at startup and save overall system resources. Lazy initialization can be particularly relevant for POJOs that perform heavyweight operations (e.g., network connections, file operations). To mark a bean with lazy initialization, you decorate a bean with the @Lazy annotation.

```
package com.apress.springrecipes.shop;
...
import org.springframework.stereotype.Component;
import org.springframework.context.annotation.Scope;
import org.springframework.context.annotation.Lazy;

@Component
@Scope("prototype")
@Lazy
public class ShoppingCart {

    private List<Product> items = new ArrayList<>();

    public void addItem(Product item) {
        items.add(item);
    }

    public List<Product> getItems() {
        return items;
    }
}
```

In the previous declaration, because the POJO is decorated with the @Lazy annotation, if the POJO is never required by the application or referenced by another POJO, it's never instantiated.

Define Initialization of POJOs Before Other POJOs with @DependsOn

As an application's POJOs grow, so does the number of POJO initializations. This can create race conditions if POJOs reference one another and are spread out in different Java configuration classes. What happens if bean *C* requires the logic in bean *B* and bean *F*? If bean *C* is detected first and Spring hasn't initialized bean *B* and bean *F*, you'll get an error that can be hard to detect. To ensure that certain POJOs are initialized before other POJOs and to get a more descriptive error in case of a failed initialization process, Spring offers the @DependsOn annotation. The @DependsOn annotation ensures a given bean is initialized before another bean.

```
package com.apress.springrecipes.sequence.config;

import org.springframework.context.annotation.Bean;
import org.springframework.context.annotation.DependsOn;
import org.springframework.context.annotation.Configuration;
import com.apress.springrecipes.sequence.DatePrefixGenerator;
import com.apress.springrecipes.sequence.NumberPrefixGenerator;
import com.apress.springrecipes.sequence.SequenceGenerator;

@Configuration
public class SequenceConfiguration {
    @Bean
    @DependsOn("datePrefixGenerator")
    public SequenceGenerator sequenceGenerator() {
        SequenceGenerator sequence= new SequenceGenerator();
        sequence.setInitial(100000);
```

```
        sequence.setSuffix("A");
        return sequence;
    }
}
```

In the previous snippet, the declaration @DependsOn("datePrefixGenerator") ensures the datePrefixGenerator bean is created before the sequenceGenerator bean. The @DependsOn attribute also supports defining multiple dependency beans with a CSV list surrounded by {} (e.g., @DependsOn({"datePrefixGenerator,numberPrefixGenerator,randomPrefixGenerator"})

2-9. Create Post-Processors to Validate and Modify POJOs

Problem

You want to apply tasks to all bean instances or specific types of instances during construction to validate or modify bean properties according to particular criteria.

Solution

A bean post-processor allows bean processing before and after the initialization callback method (i.e., the one assigned to the initMethod attribute of the @Bean annotation or the method decorated with the @PostConstruct annotation). The main characteristic of a bean post-processor is that it processes all the bean instances in the IoC container, not just a single bean instance. Typically, bean post-processors are used to check the validity of bean properties, alter bean properties according to particular criteria, or apply certain tasks to all bean instances.

Spring also supports the @Required annotation, which is backed by the built-in Spring post-processor RequiredAnnotationBeanPostProcessor. The RequiredAnnotationBeanPostProcessor bean post-processor checks whether all the bean properties with the @Required annotation have been set.

How It Works

Suppose you want to audit the creation of every bean. You may want to do this to debug an application, to verify the properties of every bean, or in some other scenario. A bean post-processor is an ideal choice to implement this feature because you don't have to modify any preexisting POJO code.

Create POJO to Process Every Bean Instance

To write a bean post-processor, a class has to implement BeanPostProcessor. When Spring detects a bean that implements this class, it applies the postProcessBeforeInitialization() and postProcessAfterInitialization() methods to all bean instances managed by Spring. You can implement any logic you want in these methods to either inspect, modify, or verify the status of a bean.

```
package com.apress.springrecipes.shop;

import org.springframework.beans.BeansException;
import org.springframework.beans.factory.config.BeanPostProcessor;

import org.springframework.stereotype.Component;
```

```
@Component
public class AuditCheckBeanPostProcessor implements BeanPostProcessor {

    public Object postProcessBeforeInitialization(Object bean, String beanName)
        throws BeansException {
            System.out.println("In AuditCheckBeanPostProcessor.
            postProcessBeforeInitialization, processing bean type: " + bean.getClass());
        return bean;
    }

    public Object postProcessAfterInitialization(Object bean, String beanName)
        throws BeansException {
        return bean;
    }
}
```

Notice the postProcessBeforeInitialization() and postProcessAfterInitialization() methods must return the original bean instance even if you don't do anything in the method.

To register a bean post-processor in an application context, just annotate the class with the @Component annotation. The application context is able to detect which bean implements the BeanPostProcessor interface and register it to process all other bean instances in the container.

Create a POJO to Process Selected Bean Instances

During bean construction, the Spring IoC container passes all the bean instances to the bean post-processor one by one. This means if you want to apply a bean post-processor to only certain types of beans, you must filter the beans by checking their instance type. This allows you to apply logic more selectively across beans.

Suppose you now want to apply a bean post-processor but just to Product bean instances. The following example is another bean post-processor that does this:

```
package com.apress.springrecipes.shop;

import org.springframework.beans.BeansException;
import org.springframework.beans.factory.config.BeanPostProcessor;

import org.springframework.stereotype.Component;

@Component
public class ProductCheckBeanPostProcessor implements BeanPostProcessor {

    public Object postProcessBeforeInitialization(Object bean, String beanName)
        throws BeansException {
        if (bean instanceof Product) {
            String productName = ((Product) bean).getName();
                System.out.println("In ProductCheckBeanPostProcessor.
                postProcessBeforeInitialization, processing Product: " + productName);
        }
        return bean;
    }
```

```
public Object postProcessAfterInitialization(Object bean, String beanName)
    throws BeansException {
    if (bean instanceof Product) {
        String productName = ((Product) bean).getName();
            System.out.println("In ProductCheckBeanPostProcessor.
            postProcessAfterInitialization, processing Product: " + productName);
    }
    return bean;
}
}
```

Both the postProcessBeforeInitialization() and postProcessAfterInitialization() methods
must return an instance of the bean being processed. However, this also means you can even replace the
original bean instance with a new instance in your bean post-processor.

Verify POJO Properties with the @Required Annotation

In certain cases, it may be necessary to check whether particular properties have been set. Instead
of creating of custom post-constructor to verify the particular properties of a bean, it's possible to
decorate a property with the @Required annotation. The @Required annotation provides access to the
RequiredAnnotationBeanPostProcessor class—a Spring bean post-processor that can check whether
certain bean properties have been set. Note that this processor can check only whether the properties have
been set but can't check whether their value is null or something else.

Suppose that both the prefixGenerator and suffix properties are required for a sequence generator.
You can annotate their setter methods with @Required.

```
package com.apress.springrecipes.sequence;

import org.springframework.beans.factory.annotation.Required;

public class SequenceGenerator {

    private PrefixGenerator prefixGenerator;
    private String suffix;
    ...
    @Required
    public void setPrefixGenerator(PrefixGenerator prefixGenerator) {
        this.prefixGenerator = prefixGenerator;
    }

    @Required
    public void setSuffix(String suffix) {
        this.suffix = suffix;
    }
    ...
}
```

To ask Spring to check whether these properties have been set, you just need to enable scanning so
Spring can detect and enforce the @Required annotation. If any properties with @Required have not been set,
a BeanInitializationException error is thrown.

2-10. Create POJOs with a Factory (Static Method, Instance Method, Spring's FactoryBean)

Problem

You want to create a POJO instance in the Spring IoC container by invoking a static factory method or instance factory method. The purpose of this approach is to encapsulate the object-creation process either in a static method or in a method of another object instance, respectively. The client who requests an object can simply make a call to this method without knowing about the creation details. You want to create a POJO instance in the Spring IoC container using Spring's factory bean. A factory bean is a bean that serves as a factory for creating other beans within the IoC container. Conceptually, a factory bean is similar to a factory method, but it's a Spring-specific bean that can be identified by the Spring IoC container during bean construction.

Solution

To create a POJO by invoking a static factory inside an @Bean definition of a Java configuration class, you use standard Java syntax to call the static factory method. To create a POJO by invoking an instance factory method inside an @Bean definition of a Java configuration class, you create a POJO to instantiate the factory values and another POJO to act as a façade to access the factory.

As a convenience, Spring provides an abstract template class called AbstractFactoryBean to extend Spring's FactoryBean interface.

How It Works

You will explore the different ways of defining and using factory methods with Spring. First you will learn how to use a static factory method, next an instance based factory method and finally you will look at the Spring FactoryBean.

Create POJOs by Invoking a Static Factory Method

For example, you can write the following createProduct static factory method to create a product from a predefined product ID. According to the product ID, this method decides which concrete product class to instantiate. If there is no product matching this ID, it throws an IllegalArgumentException.

```java
package com.apress.springrecipes.shop;

public class ProductCreator {

    public static Product createProduct(String productId) {
        if ("aaa".equals(productId)) {
            return new Battery("AAA", 2.5);
        } else if ("cdrw".equals(productId)) {
            return new Disc("CD-RW", 1.5);
        } else if ("dvdrw".equals(productId)) {
            return new Disc("DVD-RW", 3.0);
        }
        throw new IllegalArgumentException("Unknown product");
    }
}
```

To create a POJO with a static factory method inside an @Bean definition of a Java configuration class, you use regular Java syntax to call the factory method.

```
package com.apress.springrecipes.shop.config;

import com.apress.springrecipes.shop.Product;
import com.apress.springrecipes.shop.ProductCreator;
import org.springframework.context.annotation.Bean;
import org.springframework.context.annotation.Configuration;

@Configuration
public class ShopConfiguration {
    @Bean
    public Product aaa() {
        return ProductCreator.createProduct("aaa");
    }

    @Bean
    public Product cdrw() {
        return ProductCreator.createProduct("cdrw");
    }

    @Bean
    public Product dvdrw() {
        return ProductCreator.createProduct("dvdrw");
    }
}
```

Create POJOs by Invoking an Instance Factory Method

For example, you can write the following ProductCreator class by using a configurable map to store predefined products. The createProduct() instance factory method finds a product by looking up the supplied productId value in the map. If there is no product matching this ID, it will throw an IllegalArgumentException.

```
package com.apress.springrecipes.shop;
...
public class ProductCreator {

    private Map<String, Product> products;

    public void setProducts(Map<String, Product> products) {
        this.products = products;
    }
```

```
    public Product createProduct(String productId) {
        Product product = products.get(productId);
        if (product != null) {
            return product;
        }
        throw new IllegalArgumentException("Unknown product");
    }
}
```

To create products from this ProductCreator, you first declare an @Bean to instantiate the factory values. Next, you declare a second bean to act as a façade to access the factory. Finally, you can call the factory and execute the createProduct() method to instantiate other beans.

```
package com.apress.springrecipes.shop.config;

import com.apress.springrecipes.shop.Battery;
import com.apress.springrecipes.shop.Disc;
import com.apress.springrecipes.shop.Product;
import com.apress.springrecipes.shop.ProductCreator;
import org.springframework.context.annotation.Bean;
import org.springframework.context.annotation.Configuration;

import java.util.HashMap;
import java.util.Map;

@Configuration
public class ShopConfiguration {

    @Bean
    public ProductCreator productCreatorFactory() {

        ProductCreator factory = new ProductCreator();
        Map<String, Product> products = new HashMap<>();
        products.put("aaa", new Battery("AAA", 2.5));
        products.put("cdrw", new Disc("CD-RW", 1.5));
        products.put("dvdrw", new Disc("DVD-RW", 3.0));
        factory.setProducts(products);
        return factory;
    }
    @Bean
    public Product aaa() {
        return productCreatorFactory().createProduct("aaa");
    }

    @Bean
    public Product cdrw() {
        return productCreatorFactory().createProduct("cdrw");
    }
```

```
    @Bean
    public Product dvdrw() {
        return productCreatorFactory().createProduct("dvdrw");
    }

}
```

Create POJOs Using Spring's Factory Bean

Although you'll seldom have to write custom factory beans, you may find it helpful to understand their internal mechanisms through an example. For example, you can write a factory bean for creating a product with a discount applied to the price. It accepts a `product` property and a `discount` property to apply the discount to the product and return it as a new bean.

```
package com.apress.springrecipes.shop;

import org.springframework.beans.factory.config.AbstractFactoryBean;

public class DiscountFactoryBean extends AbstractFactoryBean<Product> {

    private Product product;
    private double discount;

    public void setProduct(Product product) {
        this.product = product;
    }

    public void setDiscount(double discount) {
        this.discount = discount;
    }

    public Class<?> getObjectType() {
        return product.getClass();
    }

    protected Product createInstance() throws Exception {
        product.setPrice(product.getPrice() * (1 - discount));
        return product;
    }
}
```

By extending the `AbstractFactoryBean` class, the factory bean can simply override the `createInstance()` method to create the target bean instance. In addition, you have to return the target bean's type in the `getObjectType()` method for the autowiring feature to work properly.

Next, you can declare product instances using a regular @Bean annotation to apply `DiscountFactoryBean`.

```
package com.apress.springrecipes.shop.config;

import com.apress.springrecipes.shop.Battery;
import com.apress.springrecipes.shop.Disc;
import com.apress.springrecipes.shop.DiscountFactoryBean;
```

```java
import org.springframework.context.annotation.Bean;
import org.springframework.context.annotation.ComponentScan;
import org.springframework.context.annotation.Configuration;

@Configuration
@ComponentScan("com.apress.springrecipes.shop")
public class ShopConfiguration {
    @Bean
    public Battery aaa() {
        Battery aaa = new Battery("AAA", 2.5);
        return aaa;
    }

    @Bean
    public Disc cdrw() {
        Disc aaa = new Disc("CD-RW", 1.5);
        return aaa;
    }

    @Bean
    public Disc dvdrw() {
        Disc aaa = new Disc("DVD-RW", 3.0);
        return aaa;
    }

    @Bean
    public DiscountFactoryBean discountFactoryBeanAAA() {
        DiscountFactoryBean factory = new DiscountFactoryBean();
        factory.setProduct(aaa());
        factory.setDiscount(0.2);
        return factory;
    }

    @Bean
    public DiscountFactoryBean discountFactoryBeanCDRW() {
        DiscountFactoryBean factory = new DiscountFactoryBean();
        factory.setProduct(cdrw());
        factory.setDiscount(0.1);
        return factory;
    }

    @Bean
    public DiscountFactoryBean discountFactoryBeanDVDRW() {
        DiscountFactoryBean factory = new DiscountFactoryBean();
        factory.setProduct(dvdrw());
        factory.setDiscount(0.1);
        return factory;
    }
}
```

2-11. Use Spring Environments and Profiles to Load Different Sets of POJOs

Problem

You want to use the same set of POJO instances or beans but with different instantiation values for different application scenarios (e.g., production and development and testing).

Solution

Create multiple Java configuration classes and group POJOs instances or beans into each of these classes. Assign a profile name to the Java configuration class with the @Profile annotation based on the purpose of the group. Get the environment for an application's context and set the profile to load a specific group of POJOs.

How It Works

POJO instantiation values can vary depending on different application scenarios. For example, a common scenario can occur when an application goes from development to testing and on to production. In each of these scenarios, the properties for certain beans can vary slightly to accommodate environment changes (e.g., database username/password, file paths, etc.).

You can create multiple Java configuration classes each with different POJOs (e.g., ShopConfigurationGlobal, ShopConfigurationStr, and ShopConfigurationSumWin) and, in the application context, only load a given configuration class file based on the scenario.

Create a Java Configuration Class with the @Profile Annotation

Let's create a multiple Java configuration class with an @Profile annotation for the shopping application presented in previous recipes.

```
package com.apress.springrecipes.shop.config;

import com.apress.springrecipes.shop.Cashier;
import org.springframework.context.annotation.Bean;
import org.springframework.context.annotation.ComponentScan;
import org.springframework.context.annotation.Configuration;
import org.springframework.context.annotation.Profile;

@Configuration
@Profile("global")
@ComponentScan("com.apress.springrecipes.shop")
public class ShopConfigurationGlobal {

    @Bean(initMethod = "openFile", destroyMethod = "closeFile")
    public Cashier cashier() {
        final String path = System.getProperty("java.io.tmpdir") + "cashier";
        Cashier c1 = new Cashier();
        c1.setFileName("checkout");
```

```
            c1.setPath(path);
            return c1;
        }
}
package com.apress.springrecipes.shop.config;

import com.apress.springrecipes.shop.Battery;
import com.apress.springrecipes.shop.Disc;
import com.apress.springrecipes.shop.Product;
import org.springframework.context.annotation.Bean;
import org.springframework.context.annotation.Configuration;
import org.springframework.context.annotation.Profile;

@Configuration
@Profile({"summer", "winter"})
public class ShopConfigurationSumWin {
    @Bean
    public Product aaa() {
        Battery p1 = new Battery();
        p1.setName("AAA");
        p1.setPrice(2.0);
        p1.setRechargeable(true);
        return p1;
    }

    @Bean
    public Product cdrw() {
        Disc p2 = new Disc("CD-RW", 1.0);
        p2.setCapacity(700);
        return p2;
    }

    @Bean
    public Product dvdrw() {
        Disc p2 = new Disc("DVD-RW", 2.5);
        p2.setCapacity(700);
        return p2;
    }
}
```

The @Profile annotation decorates the entire Java configuration class, so all the @Bean instances belong to the same profile. To assign an @Profile name, you just place the name inside "". Notice it's also possible to assign multiple @Profile names using a comma-separated value (CSV) syntax surrounded by {} (e.g., {"summer","winter"}).

Load the Profile into Environment

To load the beans from a certain profile into an application, you need to activate a profile. You can load multiple profiles at a time, and it's also possible to load profiles programmatically, through a Java runtime flag or even as an initialization parameter of a WAR file.

To load profiles programmatically (i.e., via the application context), you get the context environment from where you can load profiles via the setActiveProfiles() method.

```
AnnotationConfigApplicationContext context = new AnnotationConfigApplicationContext();
context.getEnvironment().setActiveProfiles("global", "winter");
context.scan("com.apress.springrecipes.shop");
context.refresh();
```

It's also possible to indicate which Spring profile to load via a Java runtime flag. In this manner, you can pass the following runtime flag to load all beans that belong to the global and winter profiles:

```
-Dspring.profiles.active=global,winter
```

Set a Default Profile

To avoid the possibility of errors because no profiles are loaded into an application, you can define default profiles. Default profiles are used only when Spring can't detect any active profiles, which are defined programmatically, via a Java runtime flag, or with a web application initialization parameter.

To set up default profiles, you can also use any of the three methods to set up active profiles. Programmatically you use the method setDefaultProfiles() instead of setActiveProfiles(), and via a Java runtime flag or web application initialization parameter, you can use the spring.profiles.default parameter instead of spring.profiles.active.

2-12. Make POJOs Aware of Spring's IoC Container Resources

Problem

Even though a well-designed component should not have direct dependencies on Spring's IoC container, sometimes it's necessary for beans to be aware of the container's resources.

Solution

Your beans can be aware of the Spring IoC container's resources by implementing certain "aware" interfaces. Table 2-2 lists the most common ones. Spring injects the corresponding resources to beans that implement these interfaces via the setter methods defined in these interfaces.

Table 2-2. *Common Aware Interfaces in Spring*

Aware Interface	Target Resource Type
BeanNameAware	The bean name of its instances configured in the IoC container.
BeanFactoryAware	The current bean factory, through which you can invoke the container's services
ApplicationContextAware	The current application context, through which you can invoke the container's services
MessageSourceAware	A message source, through which you can resolve text messages
ApplicationEventPublisherAware	An application event publisher, through which you can publish application events
ResourceLoaderAware	A resource loader, through which you can load external resources
EnvironmentAware	The org.springframework.core.env.Environment instance associated with the ApplicationContext interface

■ **Note** The ApplicationContext interface in fact extends the MessageSource, ApplicationEventPublisher, and ResourceLoader interfaces, so you only need to be aware of the application context to access all these services. However, the best practice is to choose an aware interface with minimum scope that can satisfy your requirement.

The setter methods in the aware interfaces are called by Spring after the bean properties have been set but before the initialization callback methods are called, as illustrated in the following list:

1. Create the bean instance either by a constructor or by a factory method.

2. Set the values and bean references to the bean properties.

3. Call the setter methods defined in the aware interfaces.

4. Pass the bean instance to the postProcessBeforeInitialization() method of each bean post-processor. Call the initialization callback methods.

5. Pass the bean instance to the postProcessAfterInitialization() method of each bean post-processor. The bean is ready to be used.

6. When the container is shut down, call the destruction callback methods.

Keep in mind that once a class implements an aware interface, they are bound to Spring and won't work properly outside the Spring IoC container. So, consider carefully whether it's necessary to implement such proprietary interfaces.

■ **Note** With the newer versions of Spring, it is not strictly necessary to implement the aware interfaces. You could also use @Autowired to get, for instance, access to the ApplicationContext. However, if you are writing a framework/library, it might be better to implement the interfaces.

How It Works

For example, you can make the shopping application's POJO instances of the Cashier class aware of their corresponding bean names by implementing the BeanNameAware interface. By implementing the interface, Spring automatically injects the bean name into the POJO instance. In addition to implementing the interface, you also need to add the necessary setter method to handle the bean name.

```
package com.apress.springrecipes.shop;
...
import org.springframework.beans.factory.BeanNameAware;

public class Cashier implements BeanNameAware {
    ...
    private String fileName;

    public void setBeanName(String beanName) {
        this.fileName = beanName;
    }
}
```

When a bean name is injected, you can use the value to do a related POJO task that requires the bean name. For example, you could use the value to set the file name to record a cashier's checkout data. In this way, you can erase the configuration of the fileName property and setFileName() method.

```
@Bean(initMethod = "openFile", destroyMethod = "closeFile")
public Cashier cashier() {
    final String path = System.getProperty("java.io.tmpdir") + "cashier";
    Cashier cashier = new Cashier();
    cashier.setPath(path);
    return c1;
}
```

2-13. Use Aspect-Oriented Programming with Annotations

Problem

You want to use aspect-oriented programming with Spring and annotations.

Solution

You define an aspect by decorating a Java class with the @Aspect annotation. Each of the methods in a class can become an advice with another annotation. You can use five types of advice annotations: @Before, @After, @AfterReturning, @AfterThrowing, and @Around.

To enable annotation support in the Spring IoC container, you have to add @EnableAspectJAutoProxy to one of your configuration classes. To apply AOP, Spring creates proxies, and by default it creates JDK dynamic proxies, which are interface-based. For cases in which interfaces are not available or not used in an application's design, it's possible to create proxies by relying on CGLIB. To enable CGLIB, you need to set the attribute proxyTargetClass=true on the @EnableAspectJAutoProxy annotation.

How It Works

To support aspect-oriented programming with annotations, Spring uses the same annotations as AspectJ, using a library supplied by AspectJ for pointcut parsing and matching. However, the AOP runtime is still pure Spring AOP, and there is no dependency on the AspectJ compiler or weaver.

To illustrate the enablement of aspect-oriented programming with annotations, you'll use the following calculator interfaces to define a set of sample POJOs:

```
package com.apress.springrecipes.calculator;

public interface ArithmeticCalculator {

    public double add(double a, double b);
    public double sub(double a, double b);
    public double mul(double a, double b);
    public double div(double a, double b);
}
package com.apress.springrecipes.calculator;

public interface UnitCalculator {

    public double kilogramToPound(double kilogram);
    public double kilometerToMile(double kilometer);
}
```

Next, let's create POJO classes for each interface with println statements to know when each method is executed:

```
package com.apress.springrecipes.calculator;

import org.springframework.stereotype.Component;

@Component("arithmeticCalculator")
public class ArithmeticCalculatorImpl implements ArithmeticCalculator {

    public double add(double a, double b) {
        double result = a + b;
        System.out.println(a + " + " + b + " = " + result);
        return result;
    }

    public double sub(double a, double b) {
        double result = a - b;
        System.out.println(a + " - " + b + " = " + result);
        return result;
    }
    public double mul(double a, double b) {
        double result = a * b;
        System.out.println(a + " * " + b + " = " + result);
        return result;
    }
```

```java
    public double div(double a, double b) {
        if (b == 0) {
            throw new IllegalArgumentException("Division by zero");
        }
        double result = a / b;
        System.out.println(a + " / " + b + " = " + result);
        return result;
    }
}

package com.apress.springrecipes.calculator;

import org.springframework.stereotype.Component;

@Component("unitCalculator")
public class UnitCalculatorImpl implements UnitCalculator {

    public double kilogramToPound(double kilogram) {
        double pound = kilogram * 2.2;
        System.out.println(kilogram + " kilogram = " + pound + " pound");
        return pound;
    }

    public double kilometerToMile(double kilometer) {
        double mile = kilometer * 0.62;
        System.out.println(kilometer + " kilometer = " + mile + " mile");
        return mile;
    }
}
```

Note that each POJO implementation is decorated with the @Component annotation to create bean instances.

Declare Aspects, Advices, and Pointcuts

An aspect is a Java class that modularizes a set of concerns (e.g., logging or transaction management) that cuts across multiple types and objects. Java classes that modularize such concerns are decorated with the @Aspect annotation. In AOP terminology, aspects are also complemented by advices, which in themselves have pointcuts. An advice is a simple Java method with one of the advice annotations. AspectJ supports five types of advice annotations: @Before, @After, @AfterReturning, @AfterThrowing, and @Around. A pointcut is an expression that looks for types and objects on which to apply the aspect's advices.

Aspect with @Before Advice

To create a before advice to handle crosscutting concerns before particular program execution points, you use the @Before annotation and include the pointcut expression as the annotation value.

```java
package com.apress.springrecipes.calculator;

import org.apache.commons.logging.Log;
import org.apache.commons.logging.LogFactory;
import org.aspectj.lang.annotation.Aspect;
import org.aspectj.lang.annotation.Before;
import org.springframework.stereotype.Component;
```

```
@Aspect
@Component
public class CalculatorLoggingAspect {

    private Log log = LogFactory.getLog(this.getClass());

    @Before("execution(* ArithmeticCalculator.add(..))")
    public void logBefore() {
        log.info("The method add() begins");
    }
}
```

This pointcut expression matches the add() method execution of the ArithmeticCalculator interface. The preceding wildcard in this expression matches any modifier (public, protected, and private) and any return type. The two dots in the argument list match any number of arguments.

For the previous aspect to work (i.e., output its message), you need to set up logging. Specifically, create a logback.xml file with configuration properties like the following.

```
<?xml version="1.0" encoding="UTF-8"?>
<configuration>

    <appender name="STDOUT" class="ch.qos.logback.core.ConsoleAppender">
        <layout class="ch.qos.logback.classic.PatternLayout">
            <Pattern>%d [%15.15t] %-5p %30.30c - %m%n</Pattern>
        </layout>
    </appender>

    <root level="INFO">
        <appender-ref ref="STDOUT" />
    </root>

</configuration>
```

■ **Note** The @Aspect annotation is not sufficient for autodetection in the classpath. Therefore, you need to add a separate @Component annotation for the POJO to be detected.

Next, you create a Spring configuration to scan all POJOs, including the POJO calculator implementation and aspect and including the @EnableAspectJAutoProxy annotation.

```
@Configuration
@EnableAspectJAutoProxy
@ComponentScan
public class CalculatorConfiguration {
}
```

As the last step, you can test the aspect with the following `Main` class:

```
package com.apress.springrecipes.calculator;

import org.springframework.context.ApplicationContext;
import org.springframework.context.annotation.AnnotationConfigApplicationContext;

public class Main {

    public static void main(String[] args) {

        ApplicationContext context =
            new AnnotationConfigApplicationContext(CalculatorConfiguration.class);

        ArithmeticCalculator arithmeticCalculator =
            context.getBean("arithmeticCalculator", ArithmeticCalculator.class);
        arithmeticCalculator.add(1, 2);
        arithmeticCalculator.sub(4, 3);
        arithmeticCalculator.mul(2, 3);
        arithmeticCalculator.div(4, 2);

        UnitCalculator unitCalculator = context.getBean("unitCalculator", UnitCalculator.class);
        unitCalculator.kilogramToPound(10);
        unitCalculator.kilometerToMile(5);
    }
}
```

The execution points matched by a pointcut are called *join points*. In this term, a pointcut is an expression to match a set of join points, while an advice is the action to take at a particular join point.

For your advice to access the detail of the current join point, you can declare an argument of type `JoinPoint` in your advice method. Then, you can get access to join point details such as the method name and argument values. Now, you can expand your pointcut to match all methods by changing the class name and method name to wildcards.

```
package com.apress.springrecipes.calculator;
...
import java.util.Arrays;

import org.aspectj.lang.JoinPoint;
import org.aspectj.lang.annotation.Aspect;
import org.aspectj.lang.annotation.Before;

@Aspect
@Component
public class CalculatorLoggingAspect {
    ...
    @Before("execution(* *.*(..))")
    public void logBefore(JoinPoint joinPoint) {
        log.info("The method " + joinPoint.getSignature().getName()
            + "() begins with " + Arrays.toString(joinPoint.getArgs()));
    }
}
```

Use an Aspect with @After Advice

An after advice is executed after a join point finishes and is represented by a method annotated with @After, whenever it returns a result or throws an exception. The following after advice logs the calculator method ending:

```
package com.apress.springrecipes.calculator;
...
import org.aspectj.lang.JoinPoint;
import org.aspectj.lang.annotation.After;
import org.aspectj.lang.annotation.Aspect;

@Aspect
public class CalculatorLoggingAspect {
    ...
    @After("execution(* *.*(..))")
    public void logAfter(JoinPoint joinPoint) {
        log.info("The method " + joinPoint.getSignature().getName()
            + "() ends");
    }
}
```

Use an Aspect with @AfterReturning Advice

An after advice is executed regardless of whether a join point returns normally or throws an exception. If you would like to perform logging only when a join point returns, you should replace the after advice with an after returning advice.

```
package com.apress.springrecipes.calculator;
...
import org.aspectj.lang.JoinPoint;
import org.aspectj.lang.annotation.AfterReturning;
import org.aspectj.lang.annotation.Aspect;

@Aspect
public class CalculatorLoggingAspect {
    ...
    @AfterReturning("execution(* *.*(..))")
    public void logAfterReturning(JoinPoint joinPoint) {
        log.info("The method {}() ends with {}", joinPoint.getSignature().getName(), result);
    }
}
```

In an after returning advice, you can get access to the return value of a join point by adding a returning attribute to the @AfterReturning annotation. The value of this attribute should be the argument name of this advice method for the return value to pass in. Then, you have to add an argument to the advice method signature with this name. At runtime, Spring AOP will pass in the return value through this argument. Also note that the original pointcut expression needs to be presented in the pointcut attribute instead.

```
package com.apress.springrecipes.calculator;
...
import org.aspectj.lang.JoinPoint;
import org.aspectj.lang.annotation.AfterReturning;
import org.aspectj.lang.annotation.Aspect;

@Aspect
public class CalculatorLoggingAspect {
    ...
    @AfterReturning(
        pointcut = "execution(* *.*(..))",
        returning = "result")
    public void logAfterReturning(JoinPoint joinPoint, Object result) {
        log.info("The method " + joinPoint.getSignature().getName()
            + "() ends with " + result);
    }
}
```

Use an Aspect with @AfterThrowing Advice

An after throwing advice is executed only when an exception is thrown by a join point.

```
package com.apress.springrecipes.calculator;
...
import org.aspectj.lang.JoinPoint;
import org.aspectj.lang.annotation.AfterThrowing;
import org.aspectj.lang.annotation.Aspect;

@Aspect
public class CalculatorLoggingAspect {
    ...
    @AfterThrowing("execution(* *.*(..))")
    public void logAfterThrowing(JoinPoint joinPoint) {
        log.error("An exception has been thrown in {}()", joinPoint.getSignature().getName());
    }
}
```

Similarly, the exception thrown by the join point can be accessed by adding a throwing attribute to the @AfterThrowing annotation. The type Throwable is the superclass of all errors and exceptions in the Java language. So, the following advice will catch any of the errors and exceptions thrown by the join points:

```
package com.apress.springrecipes.calculator;
...
import org.aspectj.lang.JoinPoint;
import org.aspectj.lang.annotation.AfterThrowing;
import org.aspectj.lang.annotation.Aspect;
```

```
@Aspect
public class CalculatorLoggingAspect {
    ...
    @AfterThrowing(
        pointcut = "execution(* *.*(..))",
        throwing = "e")
    public void logAfterThrowing(JoinPoint joinPoint, Throwable e) {
        log.error("An exception {} has been thrown in {}()", e, joinPoint.getSignature().
        getName());
    }
}
```

However, if you are interested in one particular type of exception only, you can declare it as the argument type of the exception. Then your advice will be executed only when exceptions of compatible types (i.e., this type and its subtypes) are thrown.

```
package com.apress.springrecipes.calculator;
...
import java.util.Arrays;

import org.aspectj.lang.JoinPoint;
import org.aspectj.lang.annotation.AfterThrowing;
import org.aspectj.lang.annotation.Aspect;

@Aspect
public class CalculatorLoggingAspect {
    ...
    @AfterThrowing(
        pointcut = "execution(* *.*(..))",
        throwing = "e")
    public void logAfterThrowing(JoinPoint joinPoint, IllegalArgumentException e) {
        log.error("Illegal argument {} in {}()", Arrays.toString(joinPoint.getArgs()),
        joinPoint.getSignature().getName());
    }
}
```

Use an Aspect with @Around Advice

The last type of advice is an around advice. It is the most powerful of all the advice types. It gains full control of a join point, so you can combine all the actions of the preceding advices into one single advice. You can even control when, and whether, to proceed with the original join point execution.

The following around advice is the combination of the before, after returning, and after throwing advices you created earlier. Note that for an around advice, the argument type of the join point must be ProceedingJoinPoint. It's a subinterface of JoinPoint that allows you to control when to proceed with the original join point.

```
package com.apress.springrecipes.calculator;

import org.aspectj.lang.ProceedingJoinPoint;
import org.aspectj.lang.annotation.Around;
import org.aspectj.lang.annotation.Aspect;
```

```
import org.slf4j.Logger;
import org.slf4j.LoggerFactory;
import org.springframework.stereotype.Component;

import java.util.Arrays;

@Aspect
@Component
public class CalculatorLoggingAspect {

    private Logger log = LoggerFactory.getLogger(this.getClass());

    @Around("execution(* *.*(..))")
    public Object logAround(ProceedingJoinPoint joinPoint) throws Throwable {

        log.info("The method {}() begins with {}", joinPoint.getSignature().getName(),
        Arrays.toString(joinPoint.getArgs()));
        try {
            Object result = joinPoint.proceed();
            log.info("The method {}() ends with ", joinPoint.getSignature().getName(),
            result);
            return result;
        } catch (IllegalArgumentException e) {
            log.error("Illegal argument {} in {}()", Arrays.toString(joinPoint.getArgs()) ,
            joinPoint.getSignature().getName());
            throw e;
        }
    }
}
```

The around advice type is powerful and flexible in that you can even alter the original argument values and change the final return value. You must use this type of advice with great care, as the call to proceed with the original join point may easily be forgotten.

■ **Tip**   A common rule for choosing an advice type is to use the least powerful one that can satisfy your requirements.

2-14. Access the Join Point Information

Problem

In AOP, an advice is applied to different program execution points that are called *join points*. For an advice to take the correct action, it often requires detailed information about join points.

Solution

An advice can access the current join point information by declaring an argument of type org.aspectj. lang.JoinPoint in the advice method signature.

How It Works

For example, you can access the join point information through the following advice. The information includes the join point kind (only method execution in Spring AOP), the method signature (declaring type and method name), and the argument values, as well as the target object and proxy object.

```
package com.apress.springrecipes.calculator;

import org.aspectj.lang.JoinPoint;
import org.aspectj.lang.annotation.Aspect;
import org.aspectj.lang.annotation.Before;
import org.slf4j.Logger;
import org.slf4j.LoggerFactory;
import org.springframework.stereotype.Component;

import java.util.Arrays;

@Aspect
@Component
public class CalculatorLoggingAspect {

    private Logger log = LoggerFactory.getLogger(this.getClass());

    @Before("execution(* *.*(..))")
    public void logJoinPoint(JoinPoint joinPoint) {

        log.info("Join point kind : {}", joinPoint.getKind());
        log.info("Signature declaring type : {}", joinPoint.getSignature().
        getDeclaringTypeName());
        log.info("Signature name : {}", joinPoint.getSignature().getName());
        log.info("Arguments : {}", Arrays.toString(joinPoint.getArgs()));
        log.info("Target class : {}", joinPoint.getTarget().getClass().getName());
        log.info("This class : {}", joinPoint.getThis().getClass().getName());
    }
}
```

The original bean that was wrapped by a proxy is called the *target object*, while the proxy object is the this object. They can be accessed by the join point's getTarget() and getThis() methods. From the following outputs, you can see that the classes of these two objects are not the same:

```
Join point kind : method-execution
Signature declaring type : com.apress.springrecipes.calculator.ArithmeticCalculator
Signature name : add
Arguments : [1.0, 2.0]
Target class : com.apress.springrecipes.calculator.ArithmeticCalculatorImpl
This class : com.sun.proxy.$Proxy6
```

2-15. Specify Aspect Precedence with the @Order Annotation

Problem

When there's more than one aspect applied to the same join point, the precedence of the aspects is undefined unless you have explicitly specified it.

Solution

The precedence of aspects can be specified either by implementing the Ordered interface or by using the @Order annotation.

How It Works

Suppose you have written another aspect to validate the calculator arguments. There's only one before advice in this aspect.

```
package com.apress.springrecipes.calculator;

import org.aspectj.lang.JoinPoint;
import org.aspectj.lang.annotation.Aspect;
import org.aspectj.lang.annotation.Before;

import org.springframework.stereotype.Component;

@Aspect
@Component
public class CalculatorValidationAspect {

    @Before("execution(* *.*(double, double))")
    public void validateBefore(JoinPoint joinPoint) {
        for (Object arg : joinPoint.getArgs()) {
            validate((Double) arg);
        }
    }

    private void validate(double a) {
        if (a < 0) {
            throw new IllegalArgumentException("Positive numbers only");
        }
    }
}
```

If you apply this aspect and the previous, you can't guarantee which one is applied first. To guarantee that one aspect is applied before another, you need to specify precedence. To specify precedence, you have to make both aspects implement the Ordered interface or use the @Order annotation.

If you decide to implement the Ordered interface, the lower value returned by the getOrder method represents higher priority. So, if you prefer the validation aspect to be applied first, it should return a value lower than the logging aspect.

```
package com.apress.springrecipes.calculator;
...
import org.springframework.core.Ordered;

@Aspect
@Component
public class CalculatorValidationAspect implements Ordered {
    ...
    public int getOrder() {
        return 0;
    }
}
package com.apress.springrecipes.calculator;
...
import org.springframework.core.Ordered;

@Aspect
@Component
public class CalculatorLoggingAspect implements Ordered {
    ...
    public int getOrder() {
        return 1;
    }
}
```

Another way to specify precedence is through the @Order annotation. The order number should be presented in the annotation value.

```
package com.apress.springrecipes.calculator;
...
import org.springframework.core.annotation.Order;

@Aspect
@Component
@Order(0)
public class CalculatorValidationAspect { ... }
package com.apress.springrecipes.calculator;
...
import org.springframework.core.annotation.Order;

@Aspect
@Component
@Order(1)
public class CalculatorLoggingAspect { ... }
```

2-16. Reuse Aspect Pointcut Definitions

Problem

When writing aspects, you can directly embed a pointcut expression in an advice annotation. You want to use the same pointcut expression in multiple advices without embedding it multiple times.

Solution

You can use the @Pointcut annotation to define a pointcut independently to be reused in multiple advices.

How It Works

In an aspect, a pointcut can be declared as a simple method with the @Pointcut annotation. The method body of a pointcut is usually empty because it is unreasonable to mix a pointcut definition with application logic. The access modifier of a pointcut method controls the visibility of this pointcut as well. Other advices can refer to this pointcut by the method name.

```
package com.apress.springrecipes.calculator;
...
import org.aspectj.lang.annotation.Pointcut;

@Aspect
@Component
public class CalculatorLoggingAspect {
    ...
    @Pointcut("execution(* *.*(..))")
    private void loggingOperation() {}

    @Before("loggingOperation()")
    public void logBefore(JoinPoint joinPoint) {
        ...
    }

    @AfterReturning(
        pointcut = "loggingOperation()",
        returning = "result")
    public void logAfterReturning(JoinPoint joinPoint, Object result) {
        ...
    }

    @AfterThrowing(
        pointcut = "loggingOperation()",
        throwing = "e")
    public void logAfterThrowing(JoinPoint joinPoint, IllegalArgumentException e) {
        ...
    }
```

```java
    @Around("loggingOperation()")
    public Object logAround(ProceedingJoinPoint joinPoint) throws Throwable {
        ...
    }
}
```

Usually, if your pointcuts are shared between multiple aspects, it is better to centralize them in a common class. In this case, they must be declared as public.

```java
package com.apress.springrecipes.calculator;

import org.aspectj.lang.annotation.Aspect;
import org.aspectj.lang.annotation.Pointcut;

@Aspect
public class CalculatorPointcuts {

    @Pointcut("execution(* *.*(..))")
    public void loggingOperation() {}
}
```

When you refer to this pointcut, you have to include the class name as well. If the class is not located in the same package as the aspect, you have to include the package name also.

```java
package com.apress.springrecipes.calculator;
...
@Aspect
public class CalculatorLoggingAspect {
    ...
    @Before("CalculatorPointcuts.loggingOperation()")
    public void logBefore(JoinPoint joinPoint) {
        ...
    }

    @AfterReturning(
        pointcut = "CalculatorPointcuts.loggingOperation()",
        returning = "result")
    public void logAfterReturning(JoinPoint joinPoint, Object result) {
        ...
    }

    @AfterThrowing(
        pointcut = "CalculatorPointcuts.loggingOperation()",
        throwing = "e")
    public void logAfterThrowing(JoinPoint joinPoint, IllegalArgumentException e) {
        ...
    }

    @Around("CalculatorPointcuts.loggingOperation()")
    public Object logAround(ProceedingJoinPoint joinPoint) throws Throwable {
        ...
    }
}
```

2-17. Write AspectJ Pointcut Expressions

Problem

Crosscutting concerns can happen at different program execution points called *join points*. Because of the variety of join points, you need a powerful expression language to help match them.

Solution

The AspectJ pointcut language is a powerful expression language that can match various kinds of join points. However, Spring AOP only supports method execution join points for beans declared in its IoC container. For this reason, only those pointcut expressions supported by Spring AOP are presented in this recipe. For a full description of the AspectJ pointcut language, please refer to the AspectJ programming guide available on AspectJ's web site (`www.eclipse.org/aspectj/`). Spring AOP makes use of the AspectJ pointcut language for its pointcut definition and interprets the pointcut expressions at runtime by using a library provided by AspectJ. When writing AspectJ pointcut expressions for Spring AOP, you must keep in mind that Spring AOP only supports method execution join points for the beans in its IoC container. If you use a pointcut expression out of this scope, an `IllegalArgumentException` is thrown.

How It Works

Lets explore the, by Spring, supported patterns for writing pointcut expression. First you will see how to write pointcuts based on message signatures, type patterns and how to use (and access) method arguments.

Use Method Signature Patterns

The most typical pointcut expressions are used to match a number of methods by their signatures. For example, the following pointcut expression matches all of the methods declared in the `ArithmeticCalculator` interface. The initial wildcard matches methods with any modifier (`public`, `protected`, and `private`) and any return type. The two dots in the argument list match any number of arguments.

```
execution(* com.apress.springrecipes.calculator.ArithmeticCalculator.*(..))
```

You can omit the package name if the target class or interface is located in the same package as the aspect.

```
execution(* ArithmeticCalculator.*(..))
```

The following pointcut expression matches all the `public` methods declared in the `ArithmeticCalculator` interface:

```
execution(public * ArithmeticCalculator.*(..))
```

You can also restrict the method return type. For example, the following pointcut matches the methods that return a double number:

```
execution(public double ArithmeticCalculator.*(..))
```

The argument list of the methods can also be restricted. For example, the following pointcut matches the methods whose first argument is of primitive double type. The two dots then match any number of followed arguments.

```
execution(public double ArithmeticCalculator.*(double, ..))
```

Or, you can specify all the argument types in the method signature for the pointcut to match.

```
execution(public double ArithmeticCalculator.*(double, double))
```

Although the AspectJ pointcut language is powerful in matching various join points, sometimes you may not be able to find any common characteristics (e.g., modifiers, return types, method name patterns, or arguments) for the methods you want to match. In such cases, you can consider providing a custom annotation for them. For instance, you can define the following marker annotation. This annotation can be applied to both method level and type level.

```
package com.apress.springrecipes.calculator;

import java.lang.annotation.Documented;
import java.lang.annotation.ElementType;
import java.lang.annotation.Retention;
import java.lang.annotation.RetentionPolicy;
import java.lang.annotation.Target;

@Target( { ElementType.METHOD, ElementType.TYPE })
@Retention(RetentionPolicy.RUNTIME)
@Documented
public @interface LoggingRequired {
}
```

Next, you can annotate all methods that require logging with this annotation or the class itself to apply the behavior to all methods. Note that the annotations must be added to the implementation class but not the interface, as they will not be inherited.

```
package com.apress.springrecipes.calculator;

@LoggingRequired
public class ArithmeticCalculatorImpl implements ArithmeticCalculator {

    public double add(double a, double b) {
        ...
    }

    public double sub(double a, double b) {
        ...
    }

    ...
}
```

Then you can write a pointcut expression to match a class or methods with the `@LoggingRequired` annotation using the annotation keyword on the `@Pointcut` annotation.

```
package com.apress.springrecipes.calculator;

import org.aspectj.lang.annotation.Aspect;
import org.aspectj.lang.annotation.Pointcut;

@Aspect
public class CalculatorPointcuts {

    @Pointcut("annotation(com.apress.springrecipes.calculator.LoggingRequired)")
    public void loggingOperation() {}

}
```

Use Type Signature Patterns

Another kind of pointcut expression matches all join points within certain types. When applied to Spring AOP, the scope of these pointcuts will be narrowed to matching all method executions within the types. For example, the following pointcut matches all the method execution join points within the `com.apress.springrecipes.calculator` package:

```
within(com.apress.springrecipes.calculator.*)
```

To match the join points within a package and its subpackage, you have to add one more dot before the wildcard.

```
within(com.apress.springrecipes.calculator..*)
```

The following pointcut expression matches the method execution join points within a particular class:

```
within(com.apress.springrecipes.calculator.ArithmeticCalculatorImpl)
```

Again, if the target class is located in the same package as this aspect, the package name can be omitted.

```
within(ArithmeticCalculatorImpl)
```

You can match the method execution join points within all classes that implement the `ArithmeticCalculator` interface by adding a plus symbol.

```
within(ArithmeticCalculator+)
```

The custom annotation `@LoggingRequired` can be applied to the class or method level, as illustrated previously.

```
package com.apress.springrecipes.calculator;

@LoggingRequired
public class ArithmeticCalculatorImpl implements ArithmeticCalculator {
    ...
}
```

Then you can match the join points within the classes or methods that have been annotated with @ LoggingRequired using the within keyword on the @Pointcut annotation.

```
@Pointcut("within(com.apress.springrecipes.calculator.LoggingRequired)")
public void loggingOperation() {}
```

Combine Pointcut Expressions

In AspectJ, pointcut expressions can be combined with the operators && (and), || (or), and ! (not). For example, the following pointcut matches the join points within classes that implement either the ArithmeticCalculator or UnitCalculator interface:

```
within(ArithmeticCalculator+) || within(UnitCalculator+)
```

The operands of these operators can be any pointcut expressions or references to other pointcuts.

```
package com.apress.springrecipes.calculator;

import org.aspectj.lang.annotation.Aspect;
import org.aspectj.lang.annotation.Pointcut;

@Aspect
public class CalculatorPointcuts {

    @Pointcut("within(ArithmeticCalculator+)")
    public void arithmeticOperation() {}

    @Pointcut("within(UnitCalculator+)")
    public void unitOperation() {}

    @Pointcut("arithmeticOperation() || unitOperation()")
    public void loggingOperation() {}
}
```

Declare Pointcut Parameters

One way to access join point information is by reflection (i.e., via an argument of type org.aspectj.lang. JoinPoint in the advice method). Besides, you can access join point information in a declarative way by using some kinds of special pointcut expressions. For example, the expressions target() and args() capture the target object and argument values of the current join point and expose them as pointcut parameters. These parameters are passed to your advice method via arguments of the same name.

```
package com.apress.springrecipes.calculator;
...
import org.aspectj.lang.annotation.Aspect;
import org.aspectj.lang.annotation.Before;

@Aspect
public class CalculatorLoggingAspect {
    ...
    @Before("execution(* *.*(..)) && target(target) && args(a,b)")
    public void logParameter(Object target, double a, double b) {
        log.info("Target class : {}", target.getClass().getName());
        log.info("Arguments : {}, {}", a,b);
    }
}
```

When declaring an independent pointcut that exposes parameters, you have to include them in the argument list of the pointcut method as well.

```
package com.apress.springrecipes.calculator;

import org.aspectj.lang.annotation.Aspect;
import org.aspectj.lang.annotation.Pointcut;

@Aspect
public class CalculatorPointcuts {
    ...
    @Pointcut("execution(* *.*(..)) && target(target) && args(a,b)")
    public void parameterPointcut(Object target, double a, double b) {}
}
```

Any advice that refers to this parameterized pointcut can access the pointcut parameters via method arguments of the same name.

```
package com.apress.springrecipes.calculator;
...
import org.aspectj.lang.annotation.Aspect;
import org.aspectj.lang.annotation.Before;

@Aspect
public class CalculatorLoggingAspect {
    ...
    @Before("CalculatorPointcuts.parameterPointcut(target, a, b)")
    public void logParameter(Object target, double a, double b) {
        log.info("Target class : {}", target.getClass().getName());
        log.info("Arguments : {}, {}"a,b);
    }
}
```

2-18. Use AOP for introductions for POJOs

Problem

Sometimes you may have a group of classes that share a common behavior. In OOP, they must extend the same base class or implement the same interface. This issue is actually a crosscutting concern that can be modularized with AOP. In addition, the single inheritance mechanism of Java only allows a class to extend one base class at most. So, you cannot inherit behaviors from multiple implementation classes at the same time.

Solution

An introduction is a special type of advice in AOP. It allows objects to implement an interface dynamically by providing an implementation class for that interface. It seems as if objects extend an implementation class at runtime. Moreover, you are able to introduce multiple interfaces with multiple implementation classes to your objects at the same time. This can achieve the same effect as multiple inheritance.

How It Works

Suppose you have two interfaces, `MaxCalculator` and `MinCalculator`, to define the `max()` and `min()` operations.

```
package com.apress.springrecipes.calculator;

public interface MaxCalculator {

    public double max(double a, double b);
}
```
```
package com.apress.springrecipes.calculator;

public interface MinCalculator {

    public double min(double a, double b);
}
```

Then you have an implementation for each interface with `println` statements to let you know when the methods are executed.

```
package com.apress.springrecipes.calculator;

public class MaxCalculatorImpl implements MaxCalculator {

    public double max(double a, double b) {
        double result = (a >= b) ? a : b;
        System.out.println("max(" + a + ", " + b + ") = " + result);
        return result;
    }
}
```
```
package com.apress.springrecipes.calculator;
```

```java
public class MinCalculatorImpl implements MinCalculator {

    public double min(double a, double b) {
        double result = (a <= b) ? a : b;
        System.out.println("min(" + a + ", " + b + ") = " + result);
        return result;
    }
}
```

Now, suppose you want `ArithmeticCalculatorImpl` to perform the `max()` and `min()` calculation also. As the Java language supports single inheritance only, it is not possible for the `ArithmeticCalculatorImpl` class to extend both the `MaxCalculatorImpl` and `MinCalculatorImpl` classes at the same time. The only possible way is to extend either class (e.g., `MaxCalculatorImpl`) and implement another interface (e.g., `MinCalculator`), either by copying the implementation code or by delegating the handling to the actual implementation class. In either case, you have to repeat the method declarations.

With an introduction, you can make `ArithmeticCalculatorImpl` dynamically implement both the `MaxCalculator` and `MinCalculator` interfaces by using the implementation classes `MaxCalculatorImpl` and `MinCalculatorImpl`. It has the same effect as multiple inheritance from `MaxCalculatorImpl` and `MinCalculatorImpl`. The idea behind an introduction is that you needn't modify the `ArithmeticCalculatorImpl` class to introduce new methods. That means you can introduce methods to your existing classes even without source code available.

■ **Tip** You may wonder how an introduction can do that in Spring AOP. The answer is a dynamic proxy. As you may recall, you can specify a group of interfaces for a dynamic proxy to implement. Introduction works by adding an interface (e.g., `MaxCalculator`) to the dynamic proxy. When the methods declared in this interface are called on the proxy object, the proxy will delegate the calls to the back-end implementation class (e.g., `MaxCalculatorImpl`).

Introductions, like advices, must be declared within an aspect. You may create a new aspect or reuse an existing aspect for this purpose. In this aspect, you can declare an introduction by annotating an arbitrary field with the `@DeclareParents` annotation.

```java
package com.apress.springrecipes.calculator;

import org.aspectj.lang.annotation.Aspect;
import org.aspectj.lang.annotation.DeclareParents;

import org.springframework.stereotype.Component;

@Aspect
@Component
public class CalculatorIntroduction {

    @DeclareParents(
        value = "com.apress.springrecipes.calculator.ArithmeticCalculatorImpl",
        defaultImpl = MaxCalculatorImpl.class)
    public MaxCalculator maxCalculator;
```

```
@DeclareParents(
    value = "com.apress.springrecipes.calculator.ArithmeticCalculatorImpl",
    defaultImpl = MinCalculatorImpl.class)
public MinCalculator minCalculator;
}
```

The value attribute of the @DeclareParents annotation type indicates which classes are the targets for this introduction. The interface to introduce is determined by the type of the annotated field. Finally, the implementation class used for this new interface is specified in the defaultImpl attribute.

Through these two introductions, you can dynamically introduce a couple of interfaces to the ArithmeticCalculatorImpl class. Actually, you can specify an AspectJ type-matching expression in the value attribute of the @DeclareParents annotation to introduce an interface to multiple classes.

As you have introduced both the MaxCalculator and MinCalculator interfaces to your arithmetic calculator, you can cast it to the corresponding interface to perform the max() and min() calculations.

```
package com.apress.springrecipes.calculator;

public class Main {

    public static void main(String[] args) {
        ...
        ArithmeticCalculator arithmeticCalculator =
            (ArithmeticCalculator) context.getBean("arithmeticCalculator");
        ...
        MaxCalculator maxCalculator = (MaxCalculator) arithmeticCalculator;
        maxCalculator.max(1, 2);

        MinCalculator minCalculator = (MinCalculator) arithmeticCalculator;
        minCalculator.min(1, 2);
    }
}
```

2-19. Introduce States to Your POJOs with AOP

Problem

Sometimes you may want to add new states to a group of existing objects to keep track of their usage, such as the calling count, the last modified date, and so on. It should not be a solution if all the objects have the same base class. However, it's difficult to add such states to different classes if they are not in the same class hierarchy.

Solution

You can introduce a new interface to your objects with an implementation class that holds the state field. Then, you can write another advice to change the state according to a particular condition.

How It Works

Suppose you want to keep track of the calling count of each calculator object. Since there is no field for storing the counter value in the original calculator classes, you need to introduce one with Spring AOP. First, let's create an interface for the operations of a counter.

```
package com.apress.springrecipes.calculator;

public interface Counter {

    public void increase();
    public int getCount();
}
```

Next, just write a simple implementation class for this interface. This class has a count field for storing the counter value.

```
package com.apress.springrecipes.calculator;

public class CounterImpl implements Counter {

    private int count;

    public void increase() {
        count++;
    }

    public int getCount() {
        return count;
    }
}
```

To introduce the Counter interface to all your calculator objects with CounterImpl as the implementation, you can write the following introduction with a type-matching expression that matches all the calculator implementations:

```
package com.apress.springrecipes.calculator;
...
import org.aspectj.lang.annotation.Aspect;
import org.aspectj.lang.annotation.DeclareParents;

@Aspect
@Component
public class CalculatorIntroduction {
    ...
    @DeclareParents(
        value = "com.apress.springrecipes.calculator.*CalculatorImpl",
        defaultImpl = CounterImpl.class)
    public Counter counter;
}
```

This introduction introduces CounterImpl to each of your calculator objects. However, it's still not enough to keep track of the calling count. You have to increase the counter value each time a calculator method is called. You can write an after advice for this purpose. Note that you must get this object but not the target object, as only the proxy object implements the Counter interface.

```
package com.apress.springrecipes.calculator;
...
import org.aspectj.lang.annotation.After;
import org.aspectj.lang.annotation.Aspect;

@Aspect
@Component
public class CalculatorIntroduction {
    ...
    @After("execution(* com.apress.springrecipes.calculator.*Calculator.*(..))"
        + " && this(counter)")
    public void increaseCount(Counter counter) {
        counter.increase();
    }
}
```

In the Main class, you can output the counter value for each of the calculator objects by casting them into the Counter type.

```
package com.apress.springrecipes.calculator;

public class Main {

    public static void main(String[] args) {
        ...
        ArithmeticCalculator arithmeticCalculator =
            (ArithmeticCalculator) context.getBean("arithmeticCalculator");
        ...

        UnitCalculator unitCalculator =
            (UnitCalculator) context.getBean("unitCalculator");
        ...

        Counter arithmeticCounter = (Counter) arithmeticCalculator;
        System.out.println(arithmeticCounter.getCount());

        Counter unitCounter = (Counter) unitCalculator;
        System.out.println(unitCounter.getCount());
    }
}
```

2-20. Use Load-Time Weaving AspectJ Aspects in Spring

Problem

The Spring AOP framework supports only limited types of AspectJ pointcuts and allows aspects to apply to beans declared in the IoC container. If you want to use additional pointcut types or apply your aspects to objects created outside the Spring IoC container, you have to use the AspectJ framework in your Spring application.

Solution

Weaving is the process of applying aspects to your target objects. With Spring AOP, weaving happens at runtime through dynamic proxies. In contrast, the AspectJ framework supports both compile-time and load-time weaving.

AspectJ *compile-time weaving* is done through a special AspectJ compiler called *ajc*. It can weave aspects into your Java source files and output woven binary class files. It can also weave aspects into your compiled class files or JAR files. This process is known as *post-compile-time weaving*. You can perform compile-time and post-compile-time weaving for your classes before declaring them in the Spring IoC container. Spring is not involved in the weaving process at all. For more information on compile-time and post-compile-time weaving, please refer to the AspectJ documentation.

AspectJ load-time weaving (also known as LTW) happens when the target classes are loaded into JVM by a class loader. For a class to be woven, a special class loader is required to enhance the bytecode of the target class. Both AspectJ and Spring provide load-time weavers to add load-time weaving capability to the class loader. You need only simple configurations to enable these load-time weavers.

How It Works

To understand the AspectJ load-time weaving process in a Spring application, let's consider a calculator for complex numbers. First, you create the `Complex` class to represent complex numbers. You define the `toString()` method for this class to convert a complex number into the string representation (a + bi).

```
package com.apress.springrecipes.calculator;

public class Complex {

    private int real;
    private int imaginary;

    public Complex(int real, int imaginary) {
        this.real = real;
        this.imaginary = imaginary;
    }

    // Getters and Setters
    ...

    public String toString() {
        return "(" + real + " + " + imaginary + "i)";
    }
}
```

Next, you define an interface for the operations on complex numbers. For simplicity's sake, only add() and sub() are supported.

```
package com.apress.springrecipes.calculator;

public interface ComplexCalculator {

    public Complex add(Complex a, Complex b);
    public Complex sub(Complex a, Complex b);
}
```

The implementation code for this interface is as follows. Each time, you return a new complex object as the result.

```
package com.apress.springrecipes.calculator;

import org.springframework.stereotype.Component;

@Component("complexCalculator")
public class ComplexCalculatorImpl implements ComplexCalculator {

    public Complex add(Complex a, Complex b) {
        Complex result = new Complex(a.getReal() + b.getReal(),
            a.getImaginary() + b.getImaginary());
        System.out.println(a + " + " + b + " = " + result);
        return result;
    }

    public Complex sub(Complex a, Complex b) {
        Complex result = new Complex(a.getReal() - b.getReal(),
            a.getImaginary() - b.getImaginary());
        System.out.println(a + " - " + b + " = " + result);
        return result;
    }
}
```

Now, you can test this complex number calculator with the following code in the Main class:

```
package com.apress.springrecipes.calculator;

import org.springframework.context.ApplicationContext;
import org.springframework.context.annotation.AnnotationConfigApplicationContext;

public class Main {

    public static void main(String[] args) {
```

```
    ApplicationContext context =
        new AnnotationConfigApplicationContext(CalculatorConfiguration.class);

    ComplexCalculator complexCalculator =
        context.getBean("complexCalculator", ComplexCalculator.class);

    complexCalculator.add(new Complex(1, 2), new Complex(2, 3));
    complexCalculator.sub(new Complex(5, 8), new Complex(2, 3));
    }
}
```

So far, the complex calculator is working fine. However, you may want to improve the performance of the calculator by caching complex number objects. As caching is a well-known crosscutting concern, you can modularize it with an aspect.

```
package com.apress.springrecipes.calculator;

import java.util.Collections;
import java.util.HashMap;
import java.util.Map;

import org.aspectj.lang.ProceedingJoinPoint;
import org.aspectj.lang.annotation.Around;
import org.aspectj.lang.annotation.Aspect;

@Aspect
public class ComplexCachingAspect {

    private final Map<String, Complex> cache = new ConcurrentHashMap<>();

    @Around("call(public Complex.new(int, int)) && args(a,b)")
    public Object cacheAround(ProceedingJoinPoint joinPoint, int a, int b)
        throws Throwable {
        String key = a + "," + b;
        Complex complex = cache.get(key);
        if (complex == null) {
            System.out.println("Cache MISS for (" + key + ")");
            complex = (Complex) joinPoint.proceed();
            cache.put(key, complex);
        }
        else {
            System.out.println("Cache HIT for (" + key + ")");
        }
        return complex;
    }
}
```

In this aspect, you cache the complex objects in a map with their real and imaginary values as keys. Then, the most suitable time to look up the cache is when a complex object is created by invoking the constructor. You use the AspectJ pointcut expression `call` to capture the join points of calling the `Complex(int,int)` constructor.

Next, you need an around advice to alter the return value. If a complex object of the same value is found in the cache, you return it to the caller directly. Otherwise, you proceed with the original constructor invocation to create a new complex object. Before you return it to the caller, you cache it in the map for subsequent usages.

The call pointcut is not supported by Spring AOP, so if you attempt to let Spring scan the pointcut annotation, you'll get the error "unsupported pointcut primitive call."

Because this type of pointcut is not supported by Spring AOP, you have to use the AspectJ framework to apply this aspect. The configuration of the AspectJ framework is done through a file named aop.xml in the META-INF directory of the classpath root.

```
<!DOCTYPE aspectj PUBLIC "-//AspectJ//DTD//EN"
    "http://www.eclipse.org/aspectj/dtd/aspectj.dtd">

<aspectj>
    <weaver>
        <include within="com.apress.springrecipes.calculator.*" />
    </weaver>

    <aspects>
        <aspect
            name="com.apress.springrecipes.calculator.ComplexCachingAspect" />
    </aspects>
</aspectj>
```

In this AspectJ configuration file, you have to specify the aspects and which classes you want your aspects to weave in. Here, you specify weaving `ComplexCachingAspect` into all the classes in the `com.apress.springrecipes.calculator` package.

Finally, to make this load-time weaving, you need to run the application in one of two ways, as described in the next sections.

Implement Load-Time Weaving with the AspectJ Weaver

AspectJ provides a load-time weaving agent to enable load-time weaving. You need only to add a VM argument to the command that runs your application. Then your classes will get woven when they are loaded into the JVM.

```
java -javaagent:lib/aspectjweaver-1.9.0.jar -jar Recipe_2_19_ii-4.0.0.jar
```

If you run your application with the preceding argument, you will get the following output and cache status. The AspectJ agent advises all calls to the `Complex(int,int)` constructor.

```
Cache MISS for (1,2)
Cache MISS for (2,3)
Cache MISS for (3,5)
(1 + 2i) + (2 + 3i) = (3 + 5i)
Cache MISS for (5,8)
Cache HIT for (2,3)
Cache HIT for (3,5)
(5 + 8i) - (2 + 3i) = (3 + 5i)
```

Implement Load-Time Weaving with Spring Load-Time Weaver

Spring has several load-time weavers for different runtime environments. To turn on a suitable load-time weaver for your Spring application, you need only to add @EnableLoadTimeWeaving to your configuration class.

Spring will be able to detect the most suitable load-time weaver for your runtime environment. Some Java EE application servers have class loaders that support the Spring load-time weaver mechanism, so there's no need to specify a Java agent in their startup commands.

However, for a simple Java application, you still require a weaving agent provided by Spring to enable load-time weaving. You have to specify the Spring agent in the VM argument of the startup command.

```
java -javaagent:lib/spring-instrument-5.0.0.jar -jar Recipe_2_19_iii-4.0.0.jar
```

However, if you run your application, you will get the following output and cache status:

```
Cache MISS for (3,5)
(1 + 2i) + (2 + 3i) = (3 + 5i)
Cache HIT for (3,5)
(5 + 8i) - (2 + 3i) = (3 + 5i)
```

This is because the Spring agent advises only the Complex(int,int) constructor calls made by beans declared in the Spring IoC container. As the complex operands are created in the Main class, the Spring agent will not advise their constructor calls.

2-21. Configure AspectJ Aspects in Spring

Problem

Aspects used in the AspectJ framework are instantiated by the AspectJ framework itself. Therefore, you have to retrieve the aspect instances from the AspectJ framework to configure them.

Solution

Each AspectJ aspect provides a factory class called Aspects that has a static factory method called aspectOf(), which allows you to access the current aspect instance. In the Spring IoC container, you can declare a bean created by this factory method by calling Aspects.aspectOf(ComplexCachingAspect.class).

How It Works

For instance, you can allow the cache map of `ComplexCachingAspect` to be preconfigured via a setter method.

```
package com.apress.springrecipes.calculator;

import org.aspectj.lang.ProceedingJoinPoint;
import org.aspectj.lang.annotation.Around;
import org.aspectj.lang.annotation.Aspect;

import java.util.Map;
import java.util.concurrent.ConcurrentHashMap;

@Aspect
public class ComplexCachingAspect {

    private Map<String, Complex> cache = new ConcurrentHashMap<>();

    public void setCache(Map<String, Complex> cache) {
        this.cache.clear();
        this.cache.putAll(cache);
    }

    @Around("call(public Complex.new(int, int)) && args(a,b)")
    public Object cacheAround(ProceedingJoinPoint joinPoint, int a, int b) throws Throwable {
        String key = a + "," + b;
        Complex complex = cache.get(key);
        if (complex == null) {
            System.out.println("Cache MISS for (" + key + ")");
            complex = (Complex) joinPoint.proceed();
            cache.put(key, complex);
        } else {
            System.out.println("Cache HIT for (" + key + ")");
        }
        return complex;
    }

}
```

To configure the aspect, create an @Bean annotated method that calls the aforementioned factory method `Aspects.aspectOf`; this will give you the instance of the aspect. This instance can in turn be configured.

```
package com.apress.springrecipes.calculator;

import org.aspectj.lang.Aspects;
import org.springframework.context.annotation.Bean;
import org.springframework.context.annotation.ComponentScan;
import org.springframework.context.annotation.Configuration;
```

```
import java.util.HashMap;
import java.util.Map;

@Configuration
@ComponentScan
public class CalculatorConfiguration {

    @Bean
    public ComplexCachingAspect complexCachingAspect() {

        Map<String, Complex> cache = new HashMap<>();
        cache.put("2,3", new Complex(2,3));
        cache.put("3,5", new Complex(3,5));

        ComplexCachingAspect complexCachingAspect =
            Aspects.aspectOf(ComplexCachingAspect.class);
        complexCachingAspect.setCache(cache);
        return complexCachingAspect;
    }
}
```

To run the application, you use AspectJ's weaver.

```
java -javaagent:lib/aspectjweaver-1.9.0.jar -jar Recipe_2_20-4.0.0.jar
```

2-22. Inject POJOs into Domain Objects with AOP

Problem

Beans declared in the Spring IoC container can wire themselves to one another through Spring's dependency injection capability. However, objects created outside the Spring IoC container cannot wire themselves to Spring beans via configuration. You have to perform the wiring manually with programming code.

Solution

Objects created outside the Spring IoC container are usually domain objects. They are often created using the new operator or from the results of database queries. To inject a Spring bean into domain objects created outside Spring, you need the help of AOP. Actually, the injection of Spring beans is also a kind of crosscutting concern. As the domain objects are not created by Spring, you cannot use Spring AOP for injection. Spring supplies an AspectJ aspect specialized for this purpose. You can enable this aspect in the AspectJ framework.

How It Works

Suppose you have a global formatter to format complex numbers. This formatter accepts a pattern for formatting and uses the standard @Component and @Value annotations to instantiate a POJO.

```
package com.apress.springrecipes.calculator;

@Component
public class ComplexFormatter {

    @Value("(a + bi)")
    private String pattern;

    public void setPattern(String pattern) {
        this.pattern = pattern;
    }

    public String format(Complex complex) {
        return pattern.replaceAll("a", Integer.toString(complex.getReal()))
                .replaceAll("b", Integer.toString(complex.getImaginary()));
    }
}
```

In the Complex class, you want to use this formatter in the toString() method to convert a complex number into a string. It exposes a setter method for ComplexFormatter.

```
package com.apress.springrecipes.calculator;

public class Complex {

    private int real;
    private int imaginary;
    ...
    private ComplexFormatter formatter;

    public void setFormatter(ComplexFormatter formatter) {
        this.formatter = formatter;
    }

    public String toString() {
        return formatter.format(this);
    }
}
```

However, because Complex objects are not instantiated by the Spring IoC container, they cannot be configured for dependency injection in the regular manner. Spring includes AnnotationBeanConfigurerAspect in its aspect library to configure the dependencies of any objects, even if they were not created by the Spring IoC container.

First, you have to annotate your object type with the @Configurable annotation to declare that this type of object is configurable.

```
package com.apress.springrecipes.calculator;

import org.springframework.beans.factory.annotation.Configurable;
import org.springframework.beans.factory.annotation.Configurable;
import org.springframework.context.annotation.Scope;

@Configurable
@Component
@Scope("prototype")
public class Complex {
    ...
    @Autowired
    public void setFormatter(ComplexFormatter formatter) {
        this.formatter = formatter;
    }

}
```

In addition to the @Configurable annotation, you decorate the POJO with the standard @Component, @Scope, and @Autowired annotations so the bean gets its standard Spring behaviors. However, the @Configurable annotation is the most important configuration piece, and for this Spring defines a convenient annotation, @EnableSpringConfigured, for you to enable the mentioned aspect.

```
@Configuration
@EnableSpringConfigured
@ComponentScan
public class CalculatorConfiguration {}
```

When a class with the @Configurable annotation is instantiated, the aspect will look for a prototype-scoped bean definition whose type is the same as this class. Then, it will configure the new instances according to this bean definition. If there are properties declared in the bean definition, the new instances will also have the same properties set by the aspect.

Finally, to run the application, you weave the aspect into your classes at load time with the AspectJ agent.

```
java -javaagent:lib/aspectjweaver-1.9.0.jar -jar Recipe_2_21-4.0.0.jar
```

2-23. Applying Concurrency with Spring and TaskExecutors

Problem

You want to build a threaded, concurrent program with Spring but don't know what approach to use since there's no standard approach.

Solution

Use Spring's TaskExecutor abstraction. This abstraction provides numerous implementations for many environments, including basic Java SE Executor implementations, CommonJ WorkManager implementations, and custom implementations.

In Spring all the implementations are unified and can be cast to Java SE's Executor interface, too.

How It Works

Threading is a difficult issue that can be particularly tedious to implement using standard threading in the Java SE environment. Concurrency is another important aspect of server-side components but has little to no standardization in the enterprise Java space. In fact, some parts of the Java Enterprise Edition specifications forbid the explicit creation and manipulation of threads.

In the Java SE landscape, many options have been introduced over the years to deal with threading and concurrency. First, there was the standard java.lang.Thread support present since Java Development Kit (JDK) 1.0. Java 1.3 saw the introduction of java.util.TimerTask to support doing some sort of work periodically. Java 5 debuted the java.util.concurrent package, as well as a reworked hierarchy for building thread pools, oriented around java.util.concurrent.Executor.

The application programming interface (API) for Executor is simple.

```
package java.util.concurrent;
public interface Executor {
    void execute(Runnable command);
}
```

ExecutorService, a subinterface, provides more functionality for managing threads and provides support to raise events to threads, such as shutdown(). There are several implementations that have shipped with the JDK since Java SE 5.0. Many of them are available via static factory methods in the java.util.concurrent package. What follows are several examples using Java SE classes.

The ExecutorService class provides a submit() method, which returns a Future<T> object. An instance of Future<T> can be used to track the progress of a thread that's usually executing asynchronously. You can call Future.isDone() or Future.isCancelled() to determine whether the job is finished or cancelled, respectively. When you use ExecutorService and submit() inside a Runnable instance whose run method has no return type, calling get() on the returned Future returns null, or the value specified on submission.

```
Runnable task = new Runnable(){
    public void run(){
        try{
            Thread.sleep( 1000 * 60 ) ;
            System.out.println("Done sleeping for a minute, returning! " );
        } catch (Exception ex) { /* ... */ }
    }
};

ExecutorService executorService  = Executors.newCachedThreadPool() ;

if(executorService.submit(task, Boolean.TRUE).get().equals( Boolean.TRUE ))
    System.out.println( "Job has finished!");
```

With this background information, you can explore some of the characteristics of the various implementations. For example, the following is a class designed to mark the passage of time using Runnable:

```
package com.apress.springrecipes.spring3.executors;

import java.util.Date;

public class DemonstrationRunnable implements Runnable {
    public void run() {
        try {
```

```
            Thread.sleep(1000);
        } catch (InterruptedException e) {
            e.printStackTrace();
        }
        System.out.println(Thread.currentThread().getName());
        System.out.printf("Hello at %s \n", new Date());
    }
}
```

You'll use the same instance when you explore Java SE Executors and Spring's TaskExecutor support.

```java
package com.apress.springrecipes.spring3.executors;
import java.util.Date;
import java.util.concurrent.ExecutorService;
import java.util.concurrent.Executors;
import java.util.concurrent.ScheduledExecutorService;
import java.util.concurrent.TimeUnit;

public class ExecutorsDemo {

    public static void main(String[] args) throws Throwable {
        Runnable task = new DemonstrationRunnable();

        ExecutorService cachedThreadPoolExecutorService =
            Executors.newCachedThreadPool();
        if (cachedThreadPoolExecutorService.submit(task).get() == null)
            System.out.printf("The cachedThreadPoolExecutorService "
                + "has succeeded at %s \n", new Date());

        ExecutorService fixedThreadPool = Executors.newFixedThreadPool(100);
        if (fixedThreadPool.submit(task).get() == null)
            System.out.printf("The fixedThreadPool has " +
                "succeeded at %s \n",
                new Date());

        ExecutorService singleThreadExecutorService =
            Executors.newSingleThreadExecutor();
        if (singleThreadExecutorService.submit(task).get() == null)
            System.out.printf("The singleThreadExecutorService "
                + "has succeeded at %s \n", new Date());

        ExecutorService es = Executors.newCachedThreadPool();
        if (es.submit(task, Boolean.TRUE).get().equals(Boolean.TRUE))
            System.out.println("Job has finished!");
```

```
        ScheduledExecutorService scheduledThreadExecutorService =
            Executors.newScheduledThreadPool(10);
        if (scheduledThreadExecutorService.schedule(
            task, 30, TimeUnit.SECONDS).get() == null)
            System.out.printf("The scheduledThreadExecutorService "
                + "has succeeded at %s \n", new Date());

        scheduledThreadExecutorService.scheduleAtFixedRate(task, 0, 5,
            TimeUnit.SECONDS);

    }
}
```

If you use the submit() method version of the ExecutorService subinterface that accepts Callable<T>, then submit() returns whatever was returned from the main call() method in Callable. The following is the interface for Callable:

```
package java.util.concurrent;

public interface Callable<V> {
    V call() throws Exception;
}
```

In the Java EE landscape, different approaches for solving these sorts of problems have been created, since Java EE by design restricts the handling of threads.

Quartz (a job scheduling framework) was among the first solutions to fill this thread feature gap with a solution that provided scheduling and concurrency. JCA 1.5 (or the J2EE Connector Architecture) is another specification that provides a primitive type of gateway for integration functionality and supports ad hoc concurrency. With JCA, components are notified about incoming messages and respond concurrently. JCA 1.5 provides a primitive, limited enterprise service bus—similar to integration features without nearly as much of the finesse of something like SpringSource's Spring Integration framework.

The requirement for concurrency wasn't lost on application server vendors, though. Many other initiatives came to the forefront. For example, in 2003, IBM and BEA jointly created the Timer and WorkManager APIs, which eventually became JSR-237 and was then merged with JSR-236 to focus on how to implement concurrency in a managed environment. The Service Data Object (SDO) specification, JSR-235, had a similar solution. In addition, open source implementations of the CommonJ API have sprung up in recent years to achieve the same solution.

The issue is that there's no portable, standard, simple way of controlling threads and providing concurrency for components in a managed environment, similar to the case of Java SE solutions.

Spring provides a unified solution via the org.springframeworks.core.task.TaskExecutor interface. The TaskExecutor abstraction extends java.util.concurrent.Executor, which is part of Java 1.5.

In fact, the TaskExecutor interface is used quite a bit internally in the Spring Framework. For example, for Spring Quartz integration (which supports threading) and the message-driven POJO container support, there's wide use of TaskExecutor.

```
package org.springframework.core.task;

import java.util.concurrent.Executor;

public interface TaskExecutor extends Executor {
    void execute(Runnable task);
}
```

In some places, the various solutions mirror the functionality provided by the core JDK options. In others, they're quite unique and provide integrations with other frameworks such as with CommonJ WorkManager. These integrations usually take the form of a class that can exist in the target framework but that you can manipulate just like any other TaskExecutor abstraction.

Although there's support for adapting an existing Java SE Executor or ExecutorService as a TaskExecutor, this isn't so important in Spring because the base class for TaskExecutor is an Executor anyway. In this way, the TaskExecutor in Spring bridges the gap between various solutions on Java EE and Java SE.

Next, let's see a simple example of the TaskExecutor, using the same Runnable defined previously. The client for the code is a simple Spring POJO, into which you've injected various instances of TaskExecutor with the sole aim of submitting Runnable.

```java
package com.apress.springrecipes.executors;

import org.springframework.beans.factory.annotation.Autowired;
import org.springframework.context.ApplicationContext;
import org.springframework.context.annotation.AnnotationConfigApplicationContext;
import org.springframework.core.task.SimpleAsyncTaskExecutor;
import org.springframework.core.task.SyncTaskExecutor;
import org.springframework.core.task.support.TaskExecutorAdapter;
import org.springframework.scheduling.concurrent.ThreadPoolTaskExecutor;
import org.springframework.stereotype.Component;

import javax.annotation.PostConstruct;

@Component
public class SpringExecutorsDemo {

    @Autowired
    private SimpleAsyncTaskExecutor asyncTaskExecutor;
    @Autowired
    private SyncTaskExecutor syncTaskExecutor;
    @Autowired
    private TaskExecutorAdapter taskExecutorAdapter;
    @Autowired
    private ThreadPoolTaskExecutor threadPoolTaskExecutor;
    @Autowired
    private DemonstrationRunnable task;

    @PostConstruct
    public void submitJobs() {
        syncTaskExecutor.execute(task);
        taskExecutorAdapter.submit(task);
        asyncTaskExecutor.submit(task);

        for (int i = 0; i < 500; i++)
            threadPoolTaskExecutor.submit(task);
    }
}
```

```
    public static void main(String[] args) {

        new AnnotationConfigApplicationContext(ExecutorsConfiguration.class)
            .registerShutdownHook();
    }
}
```

The application context demonstrates the creation of these various TaskExecutor implementations. Most are so simple that you could create them manually. Only in one case do you delegate to a factory bean to automatically trigger the execution, shown here:

```
package com.apress.springrecipes.executors;

import org.springframework.context.annotation.Bean;
import org.springframework.context.annotation.ComponentScan;
import org.springframework.context.annotation.Configuration;
import org.springframework.core.task.SimpleAsyncTaskExecutor;
import org.springframework.core.task.SyncTaskExecutor;
import org.springframework.core.task.support.TaskExecutorAdapter;
import org.springframework.scheduling.concurrent.ScheduledExecutorFactoryBean;
import org.springframework.scheduling.concurrent.ScheduledExecutorTask;
import org.springframework.scheduling.concurrent.ThreadPoolTaskExecutor;

import java.util.concurrent.Executors;

@Configuration
@ComponentScan
public class ExecutorsConfiguration {

    @Bean
    public TaskExecutorAdapter taskExecutorAdapter() {
        return new TaskExecutorAdapter(Executors.newCachedThreadPool());
    }

    @Bean
    public SimpleAsyncTaskExecutor simpleAsyncTaskExecutor() {
        return new SimpleAsyncTaskExecutor();
    }

    @Bean
    public SyncTaskExecutor syncTaskExecutor() {
        return new SyncTaskExecutor();
    }
    @Bean
    public ScheduledExecutorFactoryBean scheduledExecutorFactoryBean(ScheduledExecutorTask
    scheduledExecutorTask) {
        ScheduledExecutorFactoryBean scheduledExecutorFactoryBean =
        new ScheduledExecutorFactoryBean();
        scheduledExecutorFactoryBean.setScheduledExecutorTasks(scheduledExecutorTask);
        return scheduledExecutorFactoryBean;
    }
```

```
@Bean
public ScheduledExecutorTask scheduledExecutorTask(Runnable runnable) {
    ScheduledExecutorTask scheduledExecutorTask = new ScheduledExecutorTask();
    scheduledExecutorTask.setPeriod(1000);
    scheduledExecutorTask.setRunnable(runnable);
    return scheduledExecutorTask;
}

@Bean
public ThreadPoolTaskExecutor threadPoolTaskExecutor() {
    ThreadPoolTaskExecutor taskExecutor = new ThreadPoolTaskExecutor();
    taskExecutor.setCorePoolSize(50);
    taskExecutor.setMaxPoolSize(100);
    taskExecutor.setAllowCoreThreadTimeOut(true);
    taskExecutor.setWaitForTasksToCompleteOnShutdown(true);
    return taskExecutor;
}
}
```

The previous code shows different implementations of the TaskExecutor interface. The first bean, the TaskExecutorAdapter instance, is a simple wrapper around a java.util.concurrence.Executors instance so you can deal with it in terms of the Spring TaskExecutor interface. You use Spring here to configure an instance of an Executor and pass it in as the constructor argument.

SimpleAsyncTaskExecutor provides a new Thread for each submitted job. It does no thread pooling or reuse. Each job submitted runs asynchronously in a thread.

SyncTaskExecutor is the simplest of the implementations of TaskExecutor. Submission of a job is synchronous and tantamount to launching a Thread, running it, and then using join() to connect it immediately. It's effectively the same as manually invoking the run() method in the calling thread, skipping threading altogether.

ScheduledExecutorFactoryBean automatically triggers jobs defined as ScheduledExecutorTask beans. You can specify a list of ScheduledExecutorTask instances to trigger multiple jobs simultaneously. A ScheduledExecutorTask instance can accept a period to space out the execution of tasks.

The last example is ThreadPoolTaskExecutor, which is a full-on thread pool implementation built on java.util.concurrent.ThreadPoolExecutor.

If you want to build applications using the CommonJ WorkManager/TimerManager support available in application servers like IBM WebSphere, you can use org.springframework.scheduling.commonj.Work ManagerTaskExecutor. This class delegates to a reference to the CommonJ Work Manager available inside of WebSphere. Usually, you'll provide it with a JNDI reference to the appropriate resource.

In JEE 7, the javax.enterprise.concurrent package and specifically the ManagedExecutorService, was added. An instance of this ManagedExecutorService must be provided by JEE 7-compliant servers. If you want to use this mechanism with Spring TaskExecutor support, you can configure a DefaultManagedTaskExecutor, which will try to detect the default ManagedExecutorService (as mentioned by the specification), or you can explictly configure it.

The TaskExecutor support provides a powerful way to access scheduling services on an application server via a unified interface. If you're looking for more robust (albeit much more heavyweight) support that can be deployed on any app server (e.g., Tomcat and Jetty), you might consider Spring's Quartz support.

2-24. Communicate Application Events Between POJOs

Problem

In a typical communication between POJOs, the sender has to locate the receiver to call a method on it. In this case, the sender POJO must be aware of the receiver component. This kind of communication is direct and simple, but the sender and receiver POJOs are tightly coupled.

When using an IoC container, POJOs can communicate by interface rather than by implementation. This communication model helps reduce coupling. However, it is efficient only when a sender component has to communicate with one receiver. When a sender needs to communicate with multiple receivers, it has to call the receivers one by one.

Solution

Spring's application context supports event-based communication between its beans. In the event-based communication model, the sender POJO just publishes an event without knowing who the receiver is since there can actually be more than one receiver. Also, the receiver doesn't necessarily know who is publishing the event. It can listen to multiple events from different senders at the same time. In this way, the sender and receiver components are loosely coupled.

Traditionally to listen for events, a bean has to implement the `ApplicationListener` interface and specify the type of events they want to be notified about by specifying the type parameter, i.e., `ApplicationListener<CheckoutEvent>`. Listeners of this kind can only listen to events that extend from `ApplicationEvent` as that is the type signature of the `ApplicationListener` interface.

To publish an event, a bean needs access to the `ApplicationEventPublisher`, and for sending, an event needs to call the `publishEvent` method. To get access to the `ApplicationEventPublisher`, a class can either implement `ApplicationEventPublisherAware` or use `@Autowired` on a field of type `ApplicationEventPublisher`.

How It Works

First you will write a custom ApplicationEvent then publish it and finally write a component to receive those events and act upon it.

Define Events Using ApplicationEvent

The first step of enabling event-based communication is to define the event. Suppose you want a cashier bean to publish a `CheckoutEvent` after the shopping cart is checked out. This event includes a checkout time property.

```
package com.apress.springrecipes.shop;

import org.springframework.context.ApplicationEvent;

import java.util.Date;

public class CheckoutEvent extends ApplicationEvent {

    private final ShoppingCart cart;
    private final Date time;
```

```
    public CheckoutEvent(ShoppingCart cart, Date time) {
        super(cart);
        this.cart=cart;
        this.time = time;
    }

    public ShoppingCart getCart() {
        return cart;
    }

    public Date getTime() {
        return this.time;
    }
}
```

Publish Events

To publish an event, you just create an event instance and make a call to the publishEvent()
method of an application event publisher, which becomes accessible by implementing the
ApplicationEventPublisherAware interface.

```
package com.apress.springrecipes.shop;
...
import org.springframework.context.ApplicationEventPublisher;
import org.springframework.context.ApplicationEventPublisherAware;

public class Cashier implements ApplicationEventPublisherAware {
    ...
    private ApplicationEventPublisher applicationEventPublisher;

    public void setApplicationEventPublisher(
        ApplicationEventPublisher applicationEventPublisher) {
        this.applicationEventPublisher = applicationEventPublisher;
    }

    public void checkout(ShoppingCart cart) throws IOException {
        ...
        CheckoutEvent event = new CheckoutEvent(this, new Date());
        applicationEventPublisher.publishEvent(event);
    }
}
```

Or you could simply autowire it on a field property.

```
package com.apress.springrecipes.shop;
...
import org.springframework.context.ApplicationEventPublisher;

public class Cashier {
    ...
    @Autowired
    private ApplicationEventPublisher applicationEventPublisher;

    public void checkout(ShoppingCart cart) throws IOException {
        ...
        CheckoutEvent event = new CheckoutEvent(cart, new Date());
        applicationEventPublisher.publishEvent(event);
    }
}
```

Listen to Events

Any bean defined in the application context that implements the ApplicationListener interface is notified of all type of events that match the type parameter (this way you can listen for a certain group of events such as ApplicationContextEvent).

```
package com.apress.springrecipes.shop;
...
import org.springframework.context.ApplicationListener;

@Component
public class CheckoutListener implements ApplicationListener<CheckoutEvent> {

    public void onApplicationEvent(CheckoutEvent event) {
        // Do anything you like with the checkout amount and time
        System.out.println("Checkout event [" + event.getTime() + "]");
    }
}
```

Newer versions of Spring also allow you to create event listeners using the @EventListener annotation instead of implementing the ApplicationListener interface.

```
package com.apress.springrecipes.shop;

...

@Component
public class CheckoutListener {

    @EventListener
    public void onApplicationEvent(CheckoutEvent event) {
        // Do anything you like with the checkout amount and time
        System.out.println("Checkout event [" + event.getTime() + "]");
    }
}
```

Next, you have to register the listener in the application context to listen for all events. The registration is as simple as declaring a bean instance of this listener or letting component scanning detect it. The application context recognizes beans that implement the ApplicationListener interface and beans that have methods annotated with @EventListener and notify them of each event they are interested in.

Using @EventListener has another nice feature, which is that the events don't have to extend ApplicationEvent anymore. This way, your events don't rely on Spring Framework classes but are plain POJOs again.

```
package com.apress.springrecipes.shop;

import java.util.Date;

public class CheckoutEvent {

    private final ShoppingCart cart;
    private final Date time;

    public CheckoutEvent(ShoppingCart cart, Date time) {
        this.cart=cart;
        this.time = time;
    }

    public ShoppingCart getCart() {
        return cart;
    }

    public Date getTime() {
        return this.time;
    }
}
```

■ **Note**   Finally, remember the application context itself also publishes container events such as ContextClosedEvent, ContextRefreshedEvent, and RequestHandledEvent. If any beans want to be notified of these events, they can implement the ApplicationListener interface.

Summary

In this chapter, you learned about Spring's core tasks. You learned how Spring supports the @Configuration and @Bean annotations to instantiate POJO via a Java config class. You also learned how to use the @Component annotation to administer POJOs with Spring. In addition, you learned about the @Repository, @Service, and @Controller annotations, which provide more specific behavior than the @Component annotation.

You also learned how to reference POJOs from other POJOs, as well as how to use the @Autowired annotation, which can automatically associate POJOs by either type or name. In addition, you explored how the standard @Resource and @Inject annotations work to reference POJOs via autowiring, instead of using the Spring-specific @Autowired annotation.

You then learned how to set a Spring POJOs scope with the `@Scope` annotation. You also learned how Spring can read external resources and use this data in the context of POJO configuration and creation using the `@PropertySource` and `@Value` annotations. In addition, you learned how Spring supports different languages in POJOs through the use of i18n resource bundles.

Next, you learned how to customize the initialization and destruction of POJOs with the `initmethod` and `destroyMethod` attributes of an `@Bean` annotation, as well as the `@PostConstruct` and `@PreDestroy` annotations. In addition, you learned how to do lazy initialization with the `@PreDestroy` annotation and define initialization dependencies with the `@DependsOn` annotation.

You then learned about Spring post-processors to validate and modify POJO values, including how to use the `@Required` annotation. Next, you explored how to work with Spring environments and profiles to load different sets of POJOs, including how to use the `@Profile` annotation.

Next, you explored aspect-oriented programming in the context of Spring and learned how to create aspects, pointcuts, and advices. This included the use of the `@Aspect` annotation, as well as the `@Before`, `@After`, `@AfterReturning`, `@AfterThrowing`, and `@Around` annotations.

Next, you learned how to access AOP join point information and apply it to different program execution points. And then you learned how specify aspect precedence with the `@Order` annotations, followed by how to reuse aspect pointcut definition.

In this chapter, you also learned how to write AspectJ pointcut expressions, as well as how to apply the concept of AOP introductions so a POJO can inherit behaviors from multiple implementation classes at the same time. You also learned how to introduce states to POJOs with AOP, as well as how to apply the technique of load-time weaving.

Finally, you learned how to configure AspectJ aspects in Spring, how to inject POJOs into domain objects, how to deal with concurrency with Spring and `TaskExecutors`, and, last but not least, how to create, publish, and listen to events in Spring.

CHAPTER 3

Spring MVC

MVC is one of the most important modules of the Spring Framework. It builds on the powerful Spring IoC container and makes extensive use of the container features to simplify its configuration.

Model-View-Controller (MVC) is a common design pattern in UI design. It decouples business logic from UIs by separating the roles of model, view, and controller in an application. *Models* are responsible for encapsulating application data for views to present. *Views* should only present this data, without including any business logic. *Controllers* are responsible for receiving requests from users and invoking back-end services for business processing. After processing, back-end services may return some data for views to present. Controllers collect this data and prepare models for views to present. The core idea of the MVC pattern is to separate business logic from UIs to allow them to change independently without affecting each other.

In a Spring MVC application, models usually consist of domain objects that are processed by the service layer and persisted by the persistence layer. Views are usually JSP templates written with the Java Standard Tag Library (JSTL). However, it's also possible to define views as PDF files, Excel files, RESTful web services, or even Flex interfaces, the last of which are often dubbed rich Internet applications (RIAs).

Upon finishing this chapter, you will be able to develop Java web applications using Spring MVC. You will also understand Spring MVC's common controller and view types, including what has become the de facto use of annotations for creating controllers since the release of Spring 3.0. Moreover, you will understand the basic principles of Spring MVC, which will serve as the foundation for more advanced topics covered in the upcoming chapters.

3-1. Develop a Simple Web Application with Spring MVC

Problem

You want to develop a simple web application with Spring MVC to learn the basic concepts and configurations of this framework.

Solution

The central component of Spring MVC is a front controller. In the simplest Spring MVC application, this controller is the only servlet you need to configure in a Java web deployment descriptor (i.e., the web.xml file or a ServletContainerInitializer). A Spring MVC controller—often referred to as a *dispatcher servlet*—implements one of Sun's core Java EE design patterns called Front Controller. It acts as the front controller of the Spring MVC framework, and every web request must go through it so that it can manage the entire request-handling process.

When a web request is sent to a Spring MVC application, a controller first receives the request. Then it organizes the different components configured in Spring's web application context or annotations present in the controller itself, all needed to handle the request. Figure 3-1 shows the primary flow of request handling in Spring MVC.

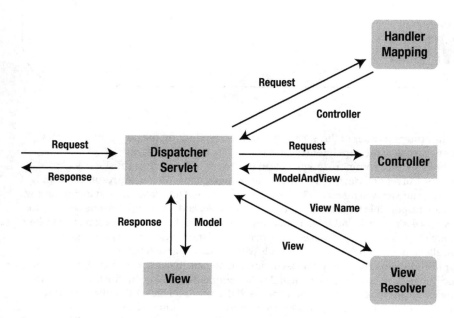

Figure 3-1. *Primary flow of request handling in Spring MVC*

To define a controller class in Spring, a class has to be marked with the @Controller or @RestController annotation.

When an @Controller annotated class (i.e., a controller class) receives a request, it looks for an appropriate handler method to handle the request. This requires that a controller class map each request to a handler method by one or more handler mappings. To do so, a controller class's methods are decorated with the @RequestMapping annotation, making them handler methods.

The signature for these handler methods—as you can expect from any standard class—is open ended. You can specify an arbitrary name for a handler method and define a variety of method arguments. Equally, a handler method can return any of a series of values (e.g., String or void), depending on the application logic it fulfills. As the book progresses, you will encounter the various method arguments that can be used in handler methods using the @RequestMapping annotation. The following is only a partial list of valid argument types, just to give you an idea.

- HttpServletRequest or HttpServleResponse

- Request parameters of arbitrary type, annotated with @RequestParam

- Model attributes of arbitrary type, annotated with @ModelAttribute

- Cookie values included in an incoming request, annotated with @CookieValue

- Map or ModelMap, for the handler method to add attributes to the model

- `Errors` or `BindingResult`, for the handler method to access the binding and validation result for the command object

- `SessionStatus`, for the handler method to notify its completion of session processing

Once the controller class has picked an appropriate handler method, it invokes the handler method's logic with the request. Usually, a controller's logic invokes back-end services to handle the request. In addition, a handler method's logic is likely to add or remove information from the numerous input arguments (e.g., `HttpServletRequest`, `Map`, `Errors`, or `SessionStatus`) that will form part of the ongoing Spring MVC flow.

After a handler method has finished processing the request, it delegates control to a view, which is represented as the handler method's return value. To provide a flexible approach, a handler method's return value doesn't represent a view's implementation (e.g., `user.jsp` or `report.pdf`) but rather a logical view (e.g., `user` or `report`)—note the lack of file extension.

A handler method's return value can be either a `String`, representing a logical view name, or `void`, in which case a default logical view name is determined on the basis of a handler method's or controller's name.

To pass information from a controller to a view, it's irrelevant that a handler's method returns a logical view name—`String` or a `void`—since the handler method input arguments will be available to a view. For example, if a handler method takes a `Map` and `SessionStatus` objects as input parameters—modifying their contents inside the handler method's logic—these same objects will be accessible to the view returned by the handler method.

When the controller class receives a view, it resolves the logical view name into a specific view implementation (e.g., `user.jsp` or `report.pdf`) by means of a view resolver. A *view resolver* is a bean configured in the web application context that implements the `ViewResolver` interface. Its responsibility is to return a specific view implementation (HTML, JSP, PDF, or other) for a logical view name.

Once the controller class has resolved a view name into a view implementation, per the view implementation's design, it renders the objects (e.g., `HttpServletRequest`, `Map`, `Errors`, or `SessionStatus`) passed by the controller's handler method. The view's responsibility is to display the objects added in the handler method's logic to the user.

How It Works

Suppose you are going to develop a court reservation system for a sports center. The UIs of this application are web-based so that users can make online reservations through the Internet. You want to develop this application using Spring MVC. First, you create the following domain classes in the `domain` subpackage:

```
package com.apress.springrecipes.court.domain;

public class Reservation {

    private String courtName;
    private Date date;
    private int hour;
    private Player player;
    private SportType sportType;

    // Constructors, Getters and Setters
    ...
}
package com.apress.springrecipes.court.domain;
```

```
public class Player {

    private String name;
    private String phone;

    // Constructors, Getters and Setters
    ...
}
package com.apress.springrecipes.court.domain;

public class SportType {

    private int id;
    private String name;

    // Constructors, Getters and Setters
    ...
}
```

Then, you define the following service interface in the service subpackage to provide reservation services to the presentation layer:

```
package com.apress.springrecipes.court.service;

import com.apress.springrecipes.court.domain.Reservation;

import java.util.List;

public interface ReservationService {

    public List<Reservation> query(String courtName);
}
```

In a production application, you should implement this interface with database persistence. But for simplicity's sake, you can store the reservation records in a list and hard-code several reservations for testing purposes.

```
package com.apress.springrecipes.court.service;

import com.apress.springrecipes.court.domain.Player;
import com.apress.springrecipes.court.domain.Reservation;
import com.apress.springrecipes.court.domain.SportType;
import org.springframework.stereotype.Service;

import java.time.LocalDate;
import java.util.ArrayList;
import java.util.List;
import java.util.Objects;
import java.util.stream.Collectors;
```

```
@Service
public class ReservationServiceImpl implements ReservationService {

    public static final SportType TENNIS = new SportType(1, "Tennis");
    public static final SportType SOCCER = new SportType(2, "Soccer");

    private final List<Reservation> reservations = new ArrayList<>();

    public ReservationServiceImpl() {

        reservations.add(new Reservation("Tennis #1", LocalDate.of(2008, 1, 14), 16,
            new Player("Roger", "N/A"), TENNIS));
        reservations.add(new Reservation("Tennis #2", LocalDate.of(2008, 1, 14), 20,
            new Player("James", "N/A"), TENNIS));
    }

    @Override
    public List<Reservation> query(String courtName) {

        return this.reservations.stream()
            .filter(reservation -> Objects.equals(reservation.getCourtName(), courtName))
            .collect(Collectors.toList());
    }
}
```

Set Up a Spring MVC Application

Next, you need to create a Spring MVC application layout. In general, a web application developed with Spring MVC is set up in the same way as a standard Java web application, except that you have to add a couple of configuration files and required libraries specific to Spring MVC.

The Java EE specification defines the valid directory structure of a Java web application made up of a web archive (WAR file). For example, you have to provide a web deployment descriptor (i.e., web.xml) in the WEB-INF root or one or more classes implementing ServletContainerInitializer. The class files and JAR files for this web application should be put in the WEB-INF/classes and WEB-INF/lib directories, respectively.

For your court reservation system, you create the following directory structure. Note that the highlighted files are Spring-specific configuration files.

■ **Note**   To develop a web application with Spring MVC, you have to add all the normal Spring dependencies (see Chapter 1 for more information) as well as the Spring Web and Spring MVC dependencies to your CLASSPATH. If you are using Maven, add the following dependencies to your Maven project:

```
<dependency>
    <groupId>org.springframework</groupId>
    <artifactId>spring-webmvc</artifactId>
    <version>${spring.version}</version>
</dependency>
```

If you are using Gradle, add the following:

```
dependencies {
    compile "org.springframework:spring-webmvc:$springVersion"

}
```

The files outside the WEB-INF directory are directly accessible to users via URLs, so the CSS files and image files must be put there. When using Spring MVC, the JSP files act as templates. They are read by the framework for generating dynamic content, so the JSP files should be put inside the WEB-INF directory to prevent direct access to them. However, some application servers don't allow the files inside WEB-INF to be read by a web application internally. In that case, you can only put them outside the WEB-INF directory.

Create the Configuration Files

The web deployment descriptor (web.xml or ServletContainerInitializer is the essential configuration file for a Java web application). In this file, you define the servlets for your application and how web requests are mapped to them. For a Spring MVC application, you have to define only a single DispatcherServlet instance that acts as the front controller for Spring MVC, although you are allowed to define more than one if required.

In large applications, it can be convenient to use multiple DispatcherServlet instances. This allows DispatcherServlet instances to be designated to specific URLs, making code management easier and letting individual team members work on an application's logic without getting in each other's way.

```
package com.apress.springrecipes.court.web;

import com.apress.springrecipes.court.config.CourtConfiguration;
import org.springframework.web.context.support.AnnotationConfigWebApplicationContext;
import org.springframework.web.servlet.DispatcherServlet;

import javax.servlet.ServletContainerInitializer;
import javax.servlet.ServletContext;
import javax.servlet.ServletException;
import javax.servlet.ServletRegistration;
import java.util.Set;

public class CourtServletContainerInitializer implements ServletContainerInitializer {

    @Override
    public void onStartup(Set<Class<?>> c, ServletContext ctx) throws ServletException {

        AnnotationConfigWebApplicationContext applicationContext =
            new AnnotationConfigWebApplicationContext();
        applicationContext.register(CourtConfiguration.class);

        DispatcherServlet dispatcherServlet = new DispatcherServlet(applicationContext);

        ServletRegistration.Dynamic courtRegistration =
            ctx.addServlet("court", dispatcherServlet);
        courtRegistration.setLoadOnStartup(1);
        courtRegistration.addMapping("/");
    }
}
```

In this `CourtServletContainerInitializer`, you define a servlet of type `DispatcherServlet`. This is the core servlet class in Spring MVC that receives web requests and dispatches them to appropriate handlers. You set this servlet's name to court and map all URLs using a slash (/), with the slash representing the root directory. Note that the URL pattern can be set to more granular patterns. In larger applications, it can make more sense to delegate patterns among various servlets, but for simplicity, all URLs in the application are delegated to the single court servlet.

To have the `CourtServletContainerInitializer` detected, you also have to add a file named `javax.servlet.ServletContainerInitializer` into the `META-INF/services` directory. The content of the file should be the full name of the `CourtServletContainerInitializer`. This file is loaded by the servlet container and used to bootstrap the application.

`com.apress.springrecipes.court.web.CourtServletContainerInitializer`

Finally, add the `CourtConfiguration` class, which is a simple `@Configuration` class.

```
package com.apress.springrecipes.court.config;

import org.springframework.context.annotation.ComponentScan;
import org.springframework.context.annotation.Configuration;

@Configuration
@ComponentScan("com.apress.springrecipes.court")
public class CourtConfiguration {}
```

This defines an `@ComponentScan` annotation, which will scan the `com.apress.springrecipes.court` package (and subpackages) and register all the detected beans (in this case, the `ReservationServiceImpl` and the yet to be created `@Controller` annotated classes).

Create Spring MVC Controllers

An annotation-based controller class can be an arbitrary class that doesn't implement a particular interface or extend a particular base class. You can annotate it with the `@Controller` annotation. There can be one or more handler methods defined in a controller to handle single or multiple actions. The signature of the handler methods is flexible enough to accept a range of arguments.

The `@RequestMapping` annotation can be applied to the class level or the method level. The first mapping strategy is to map a particular URL pattern to a controller class and then a particular HTTP method to each handler method.

```
package com.apress.springrecipes.court.web;

import org.springframework.stereotype.Controller;
import org.springframework.ui.Model;
import org.springframework.web.bind.annotation.RequestMapping;
import org.springframework.web.bind.annotation.RequestMethod;

import java.util.Date;

@Controller
@RequestMapping("/welcome")
public class WelcomeController {
```

```
@RequestMapping(method = RequestMethod.GET)
public String welcome(Model model) {

    Date today = new Date();
    model.addAttribute("today", today);
    return "welcome";
}
}
```

This controller creates a `java.util.Date` object to retrieve the current date and then adds it to the input Model object as an attribute so the target view can display it.

Since you've already activated annotation scanning on the `com.apress.springrecipes.court` package, the annotations for the controller class are detected upon deployment.

The `@Controller` annotation defines the class as a Spring MVC controller. The `@RequestMapping` annotation is more interesting since it contains properties and can be declared at the class or handler method level. The first value used in this class— `("/welcome")`—is used to specify the URL on which the controller is actionable, meaning any request received on the `/welcome` URL is attended by the `WelcomeController` class.

Once a request is attended by the controller class, it delegates the call to the default HTTP GET handler method declared in the controller. The reason for this behavior is that every initial request made on a URL is of the HTTP GET kind. So, when the controller attends a request on the `/welcome` URL, it subsequently delegates to the default HTTP GET handler method for processing.

The annotation `@RequestMapping(method = RequestMethod.GET)` is used to decorate the welcome method as the controller's default HTTP GET handler method. It's worth mentioning that if no default HTTP GET handler method is declared, a `ServletException` is thrown. Hence, it's important for a Spring MVC controller to have at a minimum a URL route and default HTTP GET handler method.

Another variation to this approach can be declaring both values—URL route and default HTTP GET handler method—in the `@RequestMapping` annotation used at the method level. This declaration is illustrated next:

```
@Controller
public class WelcomeController {

    @RequestMapping(value = "/welcome", method=RequestMethod.GET)
    public String welcome(Model model) { ... }

}
```

This declaration is equivalent to the earlier one. The `value` attribute indicates the URL to which the handler method is mapped, and the `method` attribute defines the handler method as the controller's default HTTP GET method. Finally, there are also some convenient annotations such as `@GetMapping`, `@PostMapping`, and so on, to minimize the configuration. The following mapping will do the same as the earlier mentioned declarations:

```
@Controller
public class WelcomeController {

    @GetMapping("/welcome")
    public String welcome(Model model) { ... }

}
```

The @GetMapping annotation makes the class a bit shorter and maybe easier to read.

This last controller illustrates the basic principles of Spring MVC. However, a typical controller may invoke back-end services for business processing. For example, you can create a controller for querying reservations of a particular court as follows:

```
package com.apress.springrecipes.court.web;

import com.apress.springrecipes.court.domain.Reservation;
import com.apress.springrecipes.court.service.ReservationService;
import org.springframework.beans.factory.annotation.Autowired;
import org.springframework.stereotype.Controller;
import org.springframework.ui.Model;
import org.springframework.web.bind.annotation.RequestMapping;
import org.springframework.web.bind.annotation.RequestMethod;
import org.springframework.web.bind.annotation.RequestParam;

import java.util.List;

@Controller
@RequestMapping("/reservationQuery")
public class ReservationQueryController {

    private final ReservationService reservationService;

    public ReservationQueryController(ReservationService reservationService) {
        this.reservationService = reservationService;
    }

    @GetMapping
    public void setupForm() {}

    @PostMapping
    public String sumbitForm(@RequestParam("courtName") String courtName, Model model) {

        List<Reservation> reservations = java.util.Collections.emptyList();
        if (courtName != null) {
            reservations = reservationService.query(courtName);
        }
            model.addAttribute("reservations", reservations);
        return "reservationQuery";
    }
}
```

As outlined earlier, the controller then looks for a default HTTP GET handler method. Since the public void setupForm() method is assigned the necessary @RequestMapping annotation for this purpose, it's called next.

Unlike the previous default HTTP GET handler method, notice that this method has no input parameters, has no logic, and has a void return value. This means two things. By having no input parameters and no logic, a view only displays data hard-coded in the implementation template (e.g., JSP) since no data is being added by the controller. By having a void return value, a default view name based on the request URL is used; therefore, since the requesting URL is /reservationQuery, a return view named reservationQuery is assumed.

The remaining handler method is decorated with the @PostMapping annotation. At first sight, having two handler methods with only the class-level /reservationQuery URL statement can be confusing, but it's really simple. One method is invoked when HTTP GET requests are made on the /reservationQuery URL; the other is invoked when HTTP POST requests are made on the same URL.

The majority of requests in web applications are of the HTTP GET kind, whereas requests of the HTTP POST kind are generally made when a user submits an HTML form. So, revealing more of the application's view (which we will describe shortly), one method is called when the HTML form is initially loaded (i.e., HTTP GET), whereas the other is called when the HTML form is submitted (i.e., HTTP POST).

Looking closer at the HTTP POST default handler method, notice the two input parameters. First notice the @RequestParam("courtName") String courtName declaration, used to extract a request parameter named courtName. In this case, the HTTP POST request comes in the form /reservationQuery?courtName=<value>; this declaration makes said value available in the method under the variable named courtName. Second, notice the Model declaration, which is used to define an object in which to pass data onto the returning view.

The logic executed by the handler method consists of using the controller's reservationService to perform a query using the courtName variable. The results obtained from this query are assigned to the Model object, which will later become available to the returning view for display.

Finally, note that the method returns a view named reservationQuery. This method could have also returned void, just like the default HTTP GET, and have been assigned to the same reservationQuery default view on account of the requesting URL. Both approaches are identical.

Now that you are aware of how Spring MVC controllers are constituted, it's time to explore the views to which a controller's handler methods delegate their results.

Create JSP Views

Spring MVC supports many types of views for different presentation technologies. These include JSPs, HTML, PDF, Excel worksheets (XLS), XML, JSON, Atom and RSS feeds, JasperReports, and other third-party view implementations.

In a Spring MVC application, views are most commonly JSP templates written with JSTL. When the DispatcherServlet—defined in an application's web.xml file—receives a view name returned from a handler, it resolves the logical view name into a view implementation for rendering. For example, you can configure the InternalResourceViewResolver bean, in this case in the CourtConfiguration, of a web application's context to resolve view names into JSP files in the /WEB-INF/jsp/ directory.

```
@Bean
public InternalResourceViewResolver internalResourceViewResolver() {

    InternalResourceViewResolver viewResolver = new InternalResourceViewResolver();
    viewResolver.setPrefix("/WEB-INF/jsp/");
    viewResolver.setSuffix(".jsp");
    return viewResolver;
}
```

By using this last configuration, a logical view named reservationQuery is delegated to a view implementation located at /WEB-INF/jsp/reservationQuery.jsp. Knowing this, you can create the following JSP template for the welcome controller, naming it welcome.jsp and putting it in the /WEB-INF/jsp/ directory:

```
<%@ taglib prefix="fmt" uri="http://java.sun.com/jsp/jstl/fmt" %>

<html>
<head>
    <title>Welcome</title>
</head>

<body>
<h2>Welcome to Court Reservation System</h2>
Today is <fmt:formatDate value="${today}" pattern="yyyy-MM-dd" />.
</body>
</html>
```

In this JSP template, you make use of the fmt tag library in JSTL to format the today model attribute into the pattern yyyy-MM-dd. Don't forget to include the fmt tag library definition at the top of this JSP template.

Next, you can create another JSP template for the reservation query controller and name it reservationQuery.jsp to match the view name.

```
<%@ taglib prefix="c" uri="http://java.sun.com/jsp/jstl/core" %>
<%@ taglib prefix="fmt" uri="http://java.sun.com/jsp/jstl/fmt" %>

<html>
<head>
<title>Reservation Query</title>
</head>

<body>
<form method="post">
Court Name
<input type="text" name="courtName" value="${courtName}" />
<input type="submit" value="Query" />
</form>

<table border="1">
    <tr>
        <th>Court Name</th>
        <th>Date</th>
        <th>Hour</th>
        <th>Player</th>
    </tr>
    <c:forEach items="${reservations}" var="reservation">
    <tr>
        <td>${reservation.courtName}</td>
        <td><fmt:formatDate value="${reservation.date}" pattern="yyyy-MM-dd" /></td>
        <td>${reservation.hour}</td>
        <td>${reservation.player.name}</td>
    </tr>
    </c:forEach>
</table>
</body>
</html>
```

In this JSP template, you include a form for users to input the court name they want to query and then use the <c:forEach> tag to loop the reservation's model attribute to generate the result table.

127

Deploy the Web Application

In a web application's development process, we strongly recommend installing a local Java EE application server that comes with a web container for testing and debugging purposes. For the sake of easy configuration and deployment, we have chosen Apache Tomcat 8.5.x as the web container.

The deployment directory for this web container is located in the webapps directory. By default, Tomcat listens on port 8080 and deploys applications onto a context by the same name of an application WAR. Therefore, if you package the application in a WAR named court.war, the welcome controller and the reservation query controller can be accessed through the following URLs:

```
http://localhost:8080/court/welcome
http://localhost:8080/court/reservationQuery
```

■ **Tip** The project can also create a Docker container with the app. Run `../gradlew buildDocker` to get a container with Tomcat and the application. You can then start a Docker container to test the application (`docker run -p 8080:8080 spring-recipes-4th/court-web`).

Bootstrap the Application Using a WebApplicationInitializer

In the previous section, you created a CourtServletContainerInitializer together with a file in META-INF/ services to bootstrap the application.

Instead of implementing your own, you are now going to leverage the convenient Spring implementation the SpringServletContainerInitializer. This class is an implementation of the ServletContainerInitializer interface and scans the classpath for implementations of a WebApplicationInitializer interface. Luckily, Spring provides some convenience implementations of this interface, which you can leverage for the application; one of them is the AbstractAnnotationConfigDispatcherServletInitializer.

```
package com.apress.springrecipes.court.web;

import com.apress.springrecipes.court.config.CourtConfiguration;
import org.springframework.web.servlet.support.
AbstractAnnotationConfigDispatcherServletInitializer;

public class CourtWebApplicationInitializer extends
AbstractAnnotationConfigDispatcherServletInitializer {

    @Override
    protected Class<?>[] getRootConfigClasses() {
        return null;
    }

    @Override
    protected Class<?>[] getServletConfigClasses() {
        return new Class[] {CourtConfiguration.class};
    }
```

```
    @Override
    protected String[] getServletMappings() {
        return new String[] { "/"};
    }
}
```

The newly introduced CourtWebApplicationInitializer already creates a DispatcherServlet, so the only thing you need to do is to configure the mappings in the getServletMappings method and the configuration classes you want to load in the getServletConfigClasses. Next to the servlet there is also another component being created, optionally, which is the ContextLoaderListener. This is a ServletContextListener, which also creates an ApplicationContext, which will be used as a parent ApplicationContext for the DispatcherServlet. This is convenient if you have multiple servlets needing access to the same beans (services, data sources, etc.).

3-2. Map Requests with @RequestMapping

Problem

When DispatcherServlet receives a web request, it attempts to dispatch requests to the various controller classes that have been declared with the @Controller annotation. The dispatching process depends on the various @RequestMapping annotations declared in a controller class and its handler methods. You want to define a strategy for mapping requests using the @RequestMapping annotation.

Solution

In a Spring MVC application, web requests are mapped to handlers by one or more @RequestMapping annotations declared in controller classes.

Handler mappings match URLs according to their paths relative to the context path (i.e., the web application context's deployed path) and the servlet path (i.e., the path mapped to DispatcherServlet). So, for example, in the URL http://localhost:8080/court/welcome, the path to match is /welcome, as the context path is /court and there's no servlet path—recall the servlet path declared as / in the CourtWebApplicationInitializer.

How It Works

First you will see the request mapping applied at the method level, next you will explore the request mapping on the class level and combined together with method level request mapping. Finally you will see how you can use the HTTP method for request mapping methods as well.

Map Requests by Method

The simplest strategy for using @RequestMapping annotations is to decorate the handler methods directly. For this strategy to work, you have to declare each handler method with the @RequestMapping annotation containing a URL pattern. If a handler's @RequestMapping annotation matches a request's URL, DispatcherServlet dispatches the request to this handler for it to handle the request.

```
package com.apress.springrecipes.court.web;

import com.apress.springrecipes.court.domain.Member;
import com.apress.springrecipes.court.service.MemberService;
```

```
import org.springframework.stereotype.Controller;
import org.springframework.ui.Model;
import org.springframework.web.bind.annotation.RequestMapping;
import org.springframework.web.bind.annotation.RequestMethod;
import org.springframework.web.bind.annotation.RequestParam;

@Controller
public class MemberController {

    private MemberService memberService;

    public MemberController(MemberService memberService) {
        this.memberService = memberService;
    }

    @RequestMapping("/member/add")
    public String addMember(Model model) {

        model.addAttribute("member", new Member());
        model.addAttribute("guests", memberService.list());
        return "memberList";
    }

    @RequestMapping(value = {"/member/remove", "/member/delete"}, method = RequestMethod.GET)
    public String removeMember(@RequestParam("memberName")String memberName) {
        memberService.remove(memberName);
        return "redirect:";
    }
}
```

This code illustrates how each handler method is mapped to a particular URL using the @RequestMapping annotation. The second handler method illustrates the assignment of multiple URLs, so both /member/remove and /member/delete trigger the execution of the handler method. By default, it's assumed all incoming requests to URLs are of the HTTP GET kind.

Map Requests by Class

The @RequestMapping annotation can also be used to decorate a controller class. This allows handler methods to either forgo the use of @RequestMapping annotations, as illustrated in the ReservationQueryController controller in recipe 4-1, or use finer-grained URLs with their own @RequestMapping annotation. For broader URL matching, the @RequestMapping annotation also supports the use of wildcards (i.e., *).

The following code illustrates the use of URL wildcards in an @RequestMapping annotation, as well as finer-grained URL matching on @RequestMapping annotations for handler methods:

```
package com.apress.springrecipes.court.web;

import com.apress.springrecipes.court.domain.Member;
import com.apress.springrecipes.court.service.MemberService;
import org.springframework.stereotype.Controller;
```

```
import org.springframework.ui.Model;
import org.springframework.web.bind.annotation.PathVariable;
import org.springframework.web.bind.annotation.RequestMapping;
import org.springframework.web.bind.annotation.RequestMethod;
import org.springframework.web.bind.annotation.RequestParam;

@Controller
@RequestMapping("/member/*")
public class MemberController {

    private final MemberService memberService;

    public MemberController(MemberService memberService) {
        this.memberService = memberService;
    }

    @RequestMapping("add")
    public String addMember(Model model) {

        model.addAttribute("member", new Member());
        model.addAttribute("guests", memberService.list());
        return "memberList";
    }

    @RequestMapping(value={"remove","delete"}, method=RequestMethod.GET)
    public String removeMember(@RequestParam("memberName") String memberName) {
        memberService.remove(memberName);
        return "redirect:";
    }

    @RequestMapping("display/{member}")
    public String displayMember(@PathVariable("member") String member, Model model) {
        model.addAttribute("member", memberService.find(member).orElse(null));
        return "member";
    }

    @RequestMapping
    public void memberList() {}

    public void memberLogic(String memberName) {}

}
```

Note the class-level @RequestMapping annotation uses a URL wildcard: /member/* . This in turn delegates all requests under the /member/ URL to the controller's handler methods.

The first two handler methods make use of the @RequestMapping annotation. The addMember() method is invoked when an HTTP GET request is made on the /member/add URL, whereas the removeMember() method is invoked when an HTTP GET request is made on either the /member/remove or /member/delete URL.

The third handler method uses the special notation {path_variable} to specify its @RequestMapping value. By doing so, a value present in the URL can be passed as input to the handler method. Notice the handler method declares @PathVariable("user") String user. In this manner, if a request is received in the form member/display/jdoe, the handler method has access to the member variable with a jdoe value. This is mainly a facility that allows you to avoid tinkering with a handler's request object and an approach that is especially helpful when you design RESTful web services.

The fourth handler method also uses the @RequestMapping annotation, but in this case it lacks a URL value. Since the class level uses the /member/* URL wildcard, this handler method is executed as a catchall. So, any URL request (e.g., /member/abcdefg or /member/randomroute) triggers this method. Note the void return value, which in turn makes the handler method default to a view by its name (i.e., memberList).

The last method—memberLogic—lacks any @RequestMapping annotations, which means the method is a utility for the class and has no influence on Spring MVC.

Map Requests by HTTP Request Type

By default, @RequestMapping annotations handle all types of incoming requests. However, in most cases, you do not want the same method to be executed for both a GET request and a POST request. To differentiate on HTTP requests, it's necessary to specify the type explicitly in the @RequestMapping annotation as follows:

```
@RequestMapping(value= "processUser", method =  RequestMethod.POST)
public String submitForm(@ModelAttribute("member") Member member,
                         BindingResult result, Model model) {

}
```

The extent to which you require specifying a handler method's HTTP type depends on how and what is interacting with a controller. For the most part, web browsers perform the bulk of their operations using HTTP GET and HTTP POST requests. However, other devices or applications (e.g., RESTful web services) may require support for other HTTP request types. In all, there are nine different HTTP request types: HEAD, GET, POST, PUT, DELETE, PATCH, TRACE, OPTIONS, and CONNECT. However, support for handling all these request types goes beyond the scope of an MVC controller, since a web server, as well as the requesting party, needs to support such HTTP request types. Considering the majority of HTTP requests are of the GET or POST kind, you will rarely if ever need to implement support for these additional HTTP request types.

For the most commonly used request methods, Spring MVC provides specialized annotations, as shown in Table 3-1.

Table 3-1. *Request Method to Annotation Mapping*

Request Method	Annotation
POST	@PostMapping
GET	@GetMapping
DELETE	@DeleteMapping
PUT	@PutMapping

These convenience annotations are all specialized @RequestMapping annotations and make writing request-handling methods a bit more compact.

```
@PostMapping("processUser")
public String submitForm(@ModelAttribute("member") Member member,
                         BindingResult result, Model model) {

}
```

You might have noticed that in all the URLs specified in @RequestMapping annotations, there was no trace of a file extension like .html or .jsp. This is good practice in accordance with MVC design, even though it's not widely adopted.

A controller should not be tied to any type of extension that is indicative of a view technology, such as HTML or JSP. This is why controllers return logical views and also why matching URLs should be declared without extensions.

In an age where it's common to have applications serve the same content in different formats, such as XML, JSON, PDF, or XLS (Excel), it should be left to a view resolver to inspect the extension provided in a request—if any—and determine which view technology to use.

In this short introduction, you've seen how a resolver is configured in an MVC's configuration class to map logical views to JSP files, all without every using a URL file extension like .jsp.

In later recipes, you will learn how Spring MVC uses this same nonextension URL approach to serve content using different view technologies.

3-3. Intercept Requests with Handler Interceptors

Problem

Servlet filters defined by the Servlet API can pre-handle and post-handle every web request before and after it's handled by a servlet. You want to configure something with similar functions as filters in Spring's web application context to take advantage of the container features.

Moreover, sometimes you may want to pre-handle and post-handle web requests that are handled by Spring MVC handlers and manipulate the model attributes returned by these handlers before they are passed to the views.

Solution

Spring MVC allows you to intercept web requests for pre-handling and post-handling through handler interceptors. Handler interceptors are configured in Spring's web application context, so they can make use of any container features and refer to any beans declared in the container. A handler interceptor can be registered for particular URL mappings, so it only intercepts requests mapped to certain URLs.

Each handler interceptor must implement the HandlerInterceptor interface, which contains three callback methods for you to implement: preHandle(), postHandle(), and afterCompletion(). The first and second methods are called before and after a request is handled by a handler. The second method also allows you to get access to the returned ModelAndView object, so you can manipulate the model attributes in it. The last method is called after the completion of all request processing (i.e., after the view has been rendered).

How It Works

Suppose you are going to measure each web request's handling time by each request handler and allow the views to show this time to the user. You can create a custom handler interceptor for this purpose.

```java
package com.apress.springrecipes.court.web;
...
import org.springframework.web.servlet.HandlerInterceptor;
import org.springframework.web.servlet.ModelAndView;

public class MeasurementInterceptor implements HandlerInterceptor {

    public boolean preHandle(HttpServletRequest request,
        HttpServletResponse response, Object handler) throws Exception {
        long startTime = System.currentTimeMillis();
        request.setAttribute("startTime", startTime);
        return true;
    }

    public void postHandle(HttpServletRequest request,
        HttpServletResponse response, Object handler,
        ModelAndView modelAndView) throws Exception {
        long startTime = (Long) request.getAttribute("startTime");
        request.removeAttribute("startTime");

        long endTime = System.currentTimeMillis();
        modelAndView.addObject("handlingTime", endTime - startTime);
    }

    public void afterCompletion(HttpServletRequest request,
        HttpServletResponse response, Object handler, Exception ex)
        throws Exception {
    }
}
```

In the preHandle() method of this interceptor, you record the start time and save it to a request attribute. This method should return true, allowing DispatcherServlet to proceed with request handling. Otherwise, DispatcherServlet assumes that this method has already handled the request, so DispatcherServlet returns the response to the user directly. Then, in the postHandle() method, you load the start time from the request attribute and compare it with the current time. You can calculate the total duration and then add this time to the model for passing to the view. Finally, as there is nothing for the afterCompletion() method to do, you can leave its body empty.

When implementing an interface, you must implement all the methods even though you may not have a need for all of them. A better way is to extend the interceptor adapter class instead. This class implements all the interceptor methods by default. You can override only the methods that you need.

```java
package com.apress.springrecipes.court.web;
...
import org.springframework.web.servlet.ModelAndView;
import org.springframework.web.servlet.handler.HandlerInterceptorAdapter;

public class MeasurementInterceptor extends HandlerInterceptorAdapter {
```

```
    public boolean preHandle(HttpServletRequest request,
        HttpServletResponse response, Object handler) throws Exception {
        ...
    }

    public void postHandle(HttpServletRequest request,
        HttpServletResponse response, Object handler,
        ModelAndView modelAndView) throws Exception {
        ...
    }
}
```

To register an interceptor, you need to modify the CourtConfiguration that was created in the first recipe. You need to have it implement WebMvcConfigurer and override the addInterceptors method. The method gives you access to the InterceptorRegistry, which you can use to add interceptors. The modified class looks like the following:

```
@Configuration
public class InterceptorConfiguration implements WebMvcConfigurer {

    @Override
    public void addInterceptors(InterceptorRegistry registry) {
        registry.addInterceptor(measurementInterceptor());
    }

    @Bean
    public MeasurementInterceptor measurementInterceptor() {
        return new MeasurementInterceptor();
    }

    ...
}
```

Now you can show this time in welcome.jsp to verify this interceptor's functionality. As WelcomeController doesn't have much to do, you may likely see that the handling time is 0 milliseconds. If this is the case, you can add a sleep statement to this class to see a longer handling time.

```
<%@ taglib prefix="fmt" uri="http://java.sun.com/jsp/jstl/fmt" %>

<html>
<head>
<title>Welcome</title>
</head>

<body>
...
<hr />
Handling time : ${handlingTime} ms
</body>
</html>
```

By default HandlerInterceptors apply to all @Controllers; however, sometimes you want to discriminate on which controllers interceptors are applied. The namespace and the Java-based configuration allow for interceptors to be mapped to particular URLs. It is only a matter of configuration. The following is the Java configuration of this:

```
package com.apress.springrecipes.court.config;

import com.apress.springrecipes.court.web.ExtensionInterceptor;
import com.apress.springrecipes.court.web.MeasurementInterceptor;
import org.springframework.context.annotation.Bean;
import org.springframework.context.annotation.Configuration;
import org.springframework.web.servlet.config.annotation.InterceptorRegistry;
import org.springframework.web.servlet.config.annotation.WebMvcConfigurer;

@Configuration
public class InterceptorConfiguration implements WebMvcConfigurer {

    @Override
    public void addInterceptors(InterceptorRegistry registry) {

        registry.addInterceptor(measurementInterceptor());
        registry.addInterceptor(summaryReportInterceptor())
                .addPathPatterns("/reservationSummary*");
    }

    @Bean
    public MeasurementInterceptor measurementInterceptor() {
        return new MeasurementInterceptor();
    }

    @Bean
    public ExtensionInterceptor summaryReportInterceptor() {
        return new ExtensionInterceptor();
    }
}
```

First there is the addition of the interceptor bean summaryReportInterceptor. The structure of the backing class for this bean is identical to that of the measurementInterceptor (i.e., it implements the HandlerInterceptor interface). However, this interceptor performs logic that should be restricted to a particular controller, which is mapped to the /reservationSummary URI. When registering an interceptor, you can specify which URLs it maps to; by default this takes an Ant-style expression. You pass this pattern into the addPathPatterns method; there is also an excludePathPatterns method that you can use to exclude the interceptor for certain URLs.

3-4. Resolve User Locales

Problem

For your web application to support internationalization, you have to identify each user's preferred locale and display contents according to this locale.

Solution

In a Spring MVC application, a user's locale is identified by a locale resolver, which has to implement the LocaleResolver interface. Spring MVC comes with several LocaleResolver implementations for you to resolve locales by different criteria. Alternatively, you may create your own custom locale resolver by implementing this interface.

You can define a locale resolver by registering a bean of type LocaleResolver in the web application context. You must set the bean name of the locale resolver to localeResolver for DispatcherServlet to autodetect. Note that you can register only one locale resolver per DispatcherServlet.

How It Works

You will explore the different available LocaleResolvers avaiable in Spring MVC and how you can change the users locale using an interceptor.

Resolve Locales by an HTTP Request Header

The default locale resolver used by Spring is AcceptHeaderLocaleResolver. It resolves locales by inspecting the accept-language header of an HTTP request. This header is set by a user's web browser according to the locale setting of the underlying operating system. Note that this locale resolver cannot change a user's locale because it is unable to modify the locale setting of the user's operating system.

Resolve Locales by a Session Attribute

Another option of resolving locales is by SessionLocaleResolver. It resolves locales by inspecting a predefined attribute in a user's session. If the session attribute doesn't exist, this locale resolver determines the default locale from the accept-language HTTP header.

```
@Bean
public LocaleResolver localeResolver () {
    SessionLocaleResolver localeResolver = new SessionLocaleResolver();
    localeResolver.setDefaultLocale(new Locale("en"));
    return localeResolver;
}
```

You can set the defaultLocale property for this resolver in case the session attribute doesn't exist. Note that this locale resolver is able to change a user's locale by altering the session attribute that stores the locale.

Resolve Locales by a Cookie

You can also use CookieLocaleResolver to resolve locales by inspecting a cookie in a user's browser. If the cookie doesn't exist, this locale resolver determines the default locale from the accept-language HTTP header.

```
@Bean
public LocaleResolver localeResolver() {
    return new CookieLocaleResolver();
}
```

The cookie used by this locale resolver can be customized by setting the `cookieName` and `cookieMaxAge` properties. The `cookieMaxAge` property indicates how many seconds this cookie should be persisted. The value -1 indicates that this cookie will be invalid after the browser is closed.

```
@Bean
public LocaleResolver localeResolver() {
    CookieLocaleResolver cookieLocaleResolver = new CookieLocaleResolver();
    cookieLocaleResolver.setCookieName("language");
    cookieLocaleResolver.setCookieMaxAge(3600);
    cookieLocaleResolver.setDefaultLocale(new Locale("en"));
    return cookieLocaleResolver;
}
```

You can also set the `defaultLocale` property for this resolver in case the cookie doesn't exist in a user's browser. This locale resolver is able to change a user's locale by altering the cookie that stores the locale.

Changing a User's Locale

In addition to changing a user's locale by calling `LocaleResolver.setLocale()` explicitly, you can also apply `LocaleChangeInterceptor` to your handler mappings. This interceptor detects whether a special parameter is present in the current HTTP request. The parameter name can be customized with the `paramName` property of this interceptor. If such a parameter is present in the current request, this interceptor changes the user's locale according to the parameter value.

```
package com.apress.springrecipes.court.web.config;

import org.springframework.web.servlet.i18n.CookieLocaleResolver;
import org.springframework.web.servlet.i18n.LocaleChangeInterceptor;
import org.springframework.web.servlet.view.InternalResourceViewResolver;

import java.util.Locale;

// Other imports omitted

@Configuration
public class I18NConfiguration implements WebMvcConfigurer {

    @Override
    public void addInterceptors(InterceptorRegistry registry) {
        registry.addInterceptor(measurementInterceptor());
        registry.addInterceptor(localeChangeInterceptor());
        registry.addInterceptor(summaryReportInterceptor())
                .addPathPatterns("/reservationSummary*");
    }

    @Bean
    public LocaleChangeInterceptor localeChangeInterceptor() {
        LocaleChangeInterceptor localeChangeInterceptor = new LocaleChangeInterceptor();
        localeChangeInterceptor.setParamName("language");
        return localeChangeInterceptor;
    }
```

```
@Bean
public CookieLocaleResolver localeResolver() {
    CookieLocaleResolver cookieLocaleResolver = new CookieLocaleResolver();
    cookieLocaleResolver.setCookieName("language");
    cookieLocaleResolver.setCookieMaxAge(3600);
    cookieLocaleResolver.setDefaultLocale(new Locale("en"));
    return cookieLocaleResolver;
}
...
}
```

Now a user's locale can be changed by any URLs with the language parameter. For example, the following two URLs change the user's locale to English for the United States, and to German, respectively:

```
http://localhost:8080/court/welcome?language=en_US
http://localhost:8080/court/welcome?language=de
```

Then you can show the HTTP response object's locale in welcome.jsp to verify the locale interceptor's configuration.

```
<%@ taglib prefix="fmt" uri="http://java.sun.com/jsp/jstl/fmt" %>

<html>
<head>
<title>Welcome</title>
</head>

<body>
...
<br />
Locale : ${pageContext.response.locale}
</body>
</html>
```

3-5. Externalize Locale-Sensitive Text Messages

Problem

When developing an internationalized web application, you have to display your web pages in a user's preferred locale. You don't want to create different versions of the same page for different locales.

Solution

To avoid creating different versions of a page for different locales, you should make your web page independent of the locale by externalizing locale-sensitive text messages. Spring is able to resolve text messages for you by using a message source, which has to implement the MessageSource interface. Then your JSP files can use the <spring:message> tag, defined in Spring's tag library, to resolve a message given the code.

How It Works

You can define a message source by registering a bean of type MessageSource in the web application context. You must set the bean name of the message source to messageSource for DispatcherServlet to autodetect. Note that you can register only one message source per DispatcherServlet. The ResourceBundleMessageSource implementation resolves messages from different resource bundles for different locales. For example, you can register it in WebConfiguration to load resource bundles whose base name is messages.

```
@Bean
public MessageSource messageSource() {
    ResourceBundleMessageSource messageSource = new ResourceBundleMessageSource();
    messageSource.setBasename("messages");
    return messageSource;
}
```

Then you create two resource bundles, messages.properties and messages_de.properties, to store messages for the default and German locales. These resource bundles should be put in the root of the classpath.

```
welcome.title=Welcome
welcome.message=Welcome to Court Reservation System

welcome.title=Willkommen
welcome.message=Willkommen zum Spielplatz-Reservierungssystem
```

Now, in a JSP file such as welcome.jsp, you can use the <spring:message> tag to resolve a message given the code. This tag automatically resolves the message according to a user's current locale. Note that this tag is defined in Spring's tag library, so you have to declare it at the top of your JSP file.

```
<%@ taglib prefix="spring" uri="http://www.springframework.org/tags" %>

<html>
<head>
<title><spring:message code="welcome.title" text="Welcome" /></title>
</head>

<body>
<h2><spring:message code="welcome.message"
    text="Welcome to Court Reservation System" /></h2>
...
</body>
</html>
```

In <spring:message>, you can specify the default text to output when a message for the given code cannot be resolved.

3-6. Resolve Views by Name

Problem

After a handler has finished handling a request, it returns a logical view name, in which case DispatcherServlet has to delegate control to a view template so the information is rendered. You want to define a strategy for DispatcherServlet to resolve views by their logical names.

Solution

In a Spring MVC application, views are resolved by one or more view resolver beans declared in the web application context. These beans have to implement the ViewResolver interface for DispatcherServlet to autodetect them. Spring MVC comes with several ViewResolver implementations for you to resolve views using different strategies.

How It Works

You will explore different view resolving strategies, starting with a naming template using a prefix and suffix to generate the actual name to resolving views based on the name from either an XML file or ResourceBundle. Finally you will learn how to use multiple ViewResolvers together.

Resolve Views Based on a Template's Name and Location

The basic strategy of resolving views is to map them to a template's name and location directly. The view resolver InternalResourceViewResolver maps each view name to an application's directory by means of a prefix and a suffix declaration. To register InternalResourceViewResolver, you can declare a bean of this type in the web application context.

```
@Bean
public InternalResourceViewResolver viewResolver() {
    InternalResourceViewResolver viewResolver = new InternalResourceViewResolver();
    viewResolver.setPrefix("/WEB-INF/jsp/");
    viewResolver.setSuffix(".jsp");
    return viewResolver;
}
```

For example, InternalResourceViewResolver resolves the view names welcome and reservationQuery in the following way:

```
welcome --> /WEB-INF/jsp/welcome.jsp
reservationQuery --> /WEB-INF/jsp/reservationQuery.jsp
```

The type of the resolved views can be specified by the viewClass property. By default, InternalResourceViewResolver resolves view names into view objects of type JstlView if the JSTL library (i.e., jstl.jar) is present in the classpath. So, you can omit the viewClass property if your views are JSP templates with JSTL tags.

InternalResourceViewResolver is simple, but it can only resolve internal resource views that can be forwarded by the Servlet API's RequestDispatcher (e.g., an internal JSP file or a servlet). As for other view types supported by Spring MVC, you have to resolve them using other strategies.

Resolve Views from an XML Configuration File

Another strategy for resolving views is to declare them as Spring beans and resolve them by their bean names. You can declare the view beans in the same configuration file as the web application context, but it's better to isolate them in a separate configuration file. By default, XmlViewResolver loads view beans from /WEB-INF/views.xml, but this location can be overridden through the location property.

Configuration
```java
public class ViewResolverConfiguration implements WebMvcConfigurer, ResourceLoaderAware {

    private ResourceLoader resourceLoader;

    @Bean
    public ViewResolver viewResolver() {
        XmlViewResolver viewResolver = new XmlViewResolver();
        viewResolver.setLocation(resourceLoader.getResource("/WEB-INF/court-views.nl"));
        return viewResolver;
    }

    @Override
    public void setResourceLoader(ResourceLoader resourceLoader) {
        this.resourceLoader=resourceLoader;
    }
}
```

Note in the implementation of the ResourceLoaderAware interface, you need to load resources as the location property takes an argument of the type Resource. In a Spring XML file, the conversion from String to Resource is handled for you; however, when using a Java-based configuration, you have to do some additional work. In the court-views.xml configuration file, you can declare each view as a normal Spring bean by setting the class name and properties. In this way, you can declare any types of views (e.g., RedirectView and even custom view types).

```xml
<beans xmlns="http://www.springframework.org/schema/beans"
    xmlns:xsi="http://www.w3.org/2001/XMLSchema-instance"
    xsi:schemaLocation="http://www.springframework.org/schema/beans
        http://www.springframework.org/schema/beans/spring-beans.xsd">

    <bean id="welcome"
        class="org.springframework.web.servlet.view.JstlView">
        <property name="url" value="/WEB-INF/jsp/welcome.jsp" />
    </bean>

    <bean id="reservationQuery"
        class="org.springframework.web.servlet.view.JstlView">
        <property name="url" value="/WEB-INF/jsp/reservationQuery.jsp" />
    </bean>

    <bean id="welcomeRedirect"
        class="org.springframework.web.servlet.view.RedirectView">
        <property name="url" value="welcome" />
    </bean>
</beans>
```

Resolve Views from a Resource Bundle

In addition to an XML configuration file, you can declare view beans in a resource bundle. ResourceBundleViewResolver loads view beans from a resource bundle in the classpath root. Note that ResourceBundleViewResolver can also take advantage of the resource bundle capability to load view beans from different resource bundles for different locales.

```
@Bean
public ResourceBundleViewResolver viewResolver() {
    ResourceBundleViewResolver viewResolver = new ResourceBundleViewResolver();
    viewResolver.setBasename("court-views");
    return viewResolver;
}
```

As you specify court-views as the base name of ResourceBundleViewResolver, the resource bundle is court-views.properties. In this resource bundle, you can declare view beans in the format of properties. This type of declaration is equivalent to the XML bean declaration.

```
welcome.(class)=org.springframework.web.servlet.view.JstlView
welcome.url=/WEB-INF/jsp/welcome.jsp
reservationQuery.(class)=org.springframework.web.servlet.view.JstlView
reservationQuery.url=/WEB-INF/jsp/reservationQuery.jsp
welcomeRedirect.(class)=org.springframework.web.servlet.view.RedirectView
welcomeRedirect.url=welcome
```

Resolve Views with Multiple Resolvers

If you have a lot of views in your web application, it is often insufficient to choose only one view-resolving strategy. Typically, InternalResourceViewResolver can resolve most of the internal JSP views, but there are usually other types of views that have to be resolved by ResourceBundleViewResolver. In this case, you have to combine both strategies for view resolution.

```
@Bean
public ResourceBundleViewResolver viewResolver() {
    ResourceBundleViewResolver viewResolver = new ResourceBundleViewResolver();
    viewResolver.setOrder(0);
    viewResolver.setBasename("court-views");
    return viewResolver;
}

@Bean
public InternalResourceViewResolver internalResourceViewResolver() {
    InternalResourceViewResolver viewResolver = new InternalResourceViewResolver();
    viewResolver.setOrder(1);
    viewResolver.setPrefix("/WEB-INF/jsp/");
    viewResolver.setSuffix(".jsp");
    return viewResolver;
}
```

When choosing more than one strategy at the same time, it's important to specify the resolving priority. You can set the order properties of the view resolver beans for this purpose. The lower-order value represents the higher priority. Note that you should assign the lowest priority to InternalResourceViewResolver because it always resolves a view no matter whether it exists. So, other resolvers will have no chance to resolve a view if they have lower priorities. Now the resource bundle court-views.properties should only contain the views that can't be resolved by InternalResourceViewResolver (e.g., the redirect views).

```
welcomeRedirect.(class)=org.springframework.web.servlet.view.RedirectView
welcomeRedirect.url=welcome
```

Use the Redirect Prefix

If you have InternalResourceViewResolver configured in your web application context, it can resolve redirect views by using the redirect: prefix in the view name. Then the rest of the view name is treated as the redirect URL. For example, the view name redirect:welcome triggers a redirect to the relative URL welcome. You can also specify an absolute URL in the view name.

3-7. Use Views and Content Negotiation

Problem

You are relying on extension-less URLs in your controllers—welcome and not welcome.html or welcome.pdf. You want to devise a strategy so the correct content and type are returned for all requests.

Solution

When a request is received for a web application, it contains a series of properties that allow the processing framework, in this case Spring MVC, to determine the correct content and type to return to the requesting party. The main two properties include the URL extension provided in a request and the HTTP Accept header. For example, if a request is made to a URL in the form /reservationSummary.xml, a controller is capable of inspecting the extension and delegating it to a logical view representing an XML view. However, the possibility can arise for a request to be made to a URL in the form /reservationSummary. Should this request be delegated to an XML view or an HTML view? Or perhaps some other type of view? It's impossible to tell through the URL. But instead of deciding on a default view for such requests, a request can be inspected for its HTTP Accept header to decide what type of view is more appropriate.

Inspecting HTTP Accept headers in a controller can be a messy process. So, Spring MVC supports the inspection of headers through ContentNegotiatingViewResolver, allowing view delegation to be made based on either a URL file extension or an HTTP Accept header value.

How It Works

The first thing you need to realize about Spring MVC content negotiation is that it's configured as a resolver, just like those illustrated in recipe 3-6. The Spring MVC content negotiating resolver is based on the ContentNegotiatingViewResolver class. But before we describe how it works, we will illustrate how to configure and integrate it with other resolvers.

```
@Configuration
ublic class ViewResolverConfiguration implements WebMvcConfigurer {

    @Autowired
    private ContentNegotiationManager contentNegotiationManager;

    @Override
    public void configureContentNegotiation(ContentNegotiationConfigurer configurer) {
        Map<String, MediaType> mediatypes = new HashMap<>();
        mediatypes.put("html", MediaType.TEXT_HTML);
        mediatypes.put("pdf", MediaType.valueOf("application/pdf"));
        mediatypes.put("xls", MediaType.valueOf("application/vnd.ms-excel"));
        mediatypes.put("xml", MediaType.APPLICATION_XML);
        mediatypes.put("json", MediaType.APPLICATION_JSON);
        configurer.mediaTypes(mediatypes);
    }

    @Bean
    public ContentNegotiatingViewResolver contentNegotiatingViewResolver() {
        ContentNegotiatingViewResolver viewResolver = new ContentNegotiatingViewResolver();
        viewResolver.setContentNegotiationManager(contentNegotiationManager);
        return viewResolver;
    }
}
```

First you need to configure content negotiation. The default configuration adds a ContentNegotiationManager, which can be configured by implementing the configureContentNegotiation method. To get access to the configured ContentNegotiationManager, you can simply autowire it in your configuration class.

Turn your attention back to the ContentNegotiatingViewResolver resolver. This configuration sets up the resolver to have the highest priority among all resolvers, which is necessary to make the content negotiating resolver work. The reason for this resolver having the highest priority is that it does not resolve views themselves but rather delegates them to other view resolvers (which it automatically detects). Since a resolver that does not resolve views can be confusing, we will elaborate with an example.

Let's assume a controller receives a request for /reservationSummary.xml. Once the handler method finishes, it sends control to a logical view named reservation. At this point, Spring MVC resolvers come into play, the first of which is the ContentNegotiatingViewResolver resolver, since it has the highest priority.

The ContentNegotiatingViewResolver resolver first determines the media type for a request based on the following criteria: it checks a request path extension (e.g., .html, .xml, or .pdf) against the default media types (e.g., text/html) specified by the mediaTypes map in the configuration of the ContentNegotiatingManager bean. If a request path has an extension but no match can be found in the default mediaTypes section, an attempt is made to determine an extension's media type using FileTypeMap belonging to Java Activation Framework. If no extension is present in a request path, the HTTP Accept header of the request is used. For the case of a request made on /reservationSummary.xml, the media type is determined in step 1 to be application/xml. However, for a request made on a URL like /reservationSummary, the media type is not determined until step 3.

The HTTP Accept header contains values such as Accept: text/html or Accept: application/pdf. These values help the resolver determine the media type a requester is expecting, given that no extension is present in the requesting URL.

145

At this juncture, the ContentNegotiatingViewResolver resolver has a media type and logical view named reservation. Based on this information, an iteration is performed over the remaining resolvers—based on their order—to determine what view best matches the logical name based on the detected media type.

This process allows you to have multiple logical views with the same name, each supporting a different media type (e.g., HTML, PDF, or XLS), with ContentNegotiatingViewResolver resolving which is the best match. In such cases, a controller's design is further simplified, since it won't be necessary to hard-code the logical view necessary to create a certain media type (e.g., pdfReservation, xlsReservation, or htmlReservation) but instead a single view (e.g., reservation), letting the ContentNegotiatingViewResolver resolver determine the best match.

A series of outcomes for this process can be the following:

- The media type is determined to be application/pdf. If the resolver with the highest priority (lower order) contains a mapping to a logical view named reservation but such a view does not support the application/pdf type, no match occurs—the lookup process continues onto the remaining resolvers.

- The media type is determined to be application/pdf. The resolver with the highest priority (lower order) containing a mapping to a logical view named reservation and having support for application/pdf is matched.

- The media type is determined to be text/html. There are four resolvers with a logical view named reservation, but the views mapped to the two resolvers with highest priority do not support text/html. It's the remaining resolver containing a mapping for a view named reservation that supports text/html that is matched.

This search process for views automatically takes place on all the resolvers configured in an application. It's also possible to configure—within the ContentNegotiatingViewResolver bean— default views and resolvers, in case you don't want to fall back on configurations made outside the ContentNegotiatingViewResolver resolver.

Recipe 3-11 will illustrate a controller that relies on the ContentNegotiatingViewResolver resolver to determine an application's views.

3-8. Map Exceptions to Views

Problem

When an unknown exception occurs, your application server usually displays the evil exception stack trace to the user. Your users have nothing to do with this stack trace and complain that your application is not user friendly. Moreover, it's also a potential security risk, as you may expose the internal method call hierarchy to users. However, a web application's web.xml can be configured to display friendly JSP pages in case an HTTP error or class exception occur. Spring MVC supports a more robust approach to managing views for class exceptions.

Solution

In a Spring MVC application, you can register one or more exception resolver beans in the web application context to resolve uncaught exceptions. These beans have to implement the HandlerExceptionResolver interface for DispatcherServlet to autodetect them. Spring MVC comes with a simple exception resolver for you to map each category of exceptions to a view.

How It Works

Suppose your reservation service throws the following exception because of a reservation not being available:

```
package com.apress.springrecipes.court.service;
...
public class ReservationNotAvailableException extends RuntimeException {

    private String courtName;
    private Date date;
    private int hour;

    // Constructors and Getters
    ...
}
```

To resolve uncaught exceptions, you can write your custom exception resolver by implementing the HandlerExceptionResolver interface. Usually, you'll want to map different categories of exceptions into different error pages. Spring MVC comes with the exception resolver SimpleMappingExceptionResolver for you to configure the exception mappings in the web application context. For example, you can register the following exception resolver in your configuration:

```
@Override
public void configureHandlerExceptionResolvers(List<HandlerExceptionResolver>
    exceptionResolvers) {
    exceptionResolvers.add(handlerExceptionResolver());
}

@Bean
public HandlerExceptionResolver handlerExceptionResolver() {
    Properties exceptionMapping = new Properties();
    exceptionMapping.setProperty(
    ReservationNotAvailableException.class.getName(), "reservationNotAvailable");

    SimpleMappingExceptionResolver exceptionResolver = new SimpleMappingExceptionResolver();
    exceptionResolver.setExceptionMappings(exceptionMapping);
    exceptionResolver.setDefaultErrorView("error");
    return exceptionResolver;
}
```

In this exception resolver, you define the logical view name reservationNotAvailable for ReservationNotAvailableException. You can add any number of exception classes using the exceptionMappings property, all the way down to the more general exception class java.lang.Exception. In this manner, depending on the type of class exception, a user is served a view in accordance with the exception.

The property defaultErrorView is used to define a default view named error, used if an exception class not mapped in the exceptionMapping element is raised.

Addressing the corresponding views, if the `InternalResourceViewResolver` is configured in your web application context, the following `reservationNotAvailable.jsp` page is shown if a reservation is not available:

```
<%@ taglib prefix="fmt" uri="http://java.sun.com/jsp/jstl/fmt" %>
<html>
<head>
<title>Reservation Not Available</title>
</head>
<body>
Your reservation for ${exception.courtName} is not available on <fmt:formatDate
value="${exception.date}" pattern="yyyy-MM-dd" /> at ${exception.hour}:00.
</body>
```

In an error page, the exception instance can be accessed by the variable ${exception}, so you can show the user more details on this exception.

It's a good practice to define a default error page for any unknown exceptions. You can use the property `defaultErrorView` to define a default view or map a page to the key `java.lang.Exception` as the last entry of the mapping, so it will be shown if no other entry has been matched before. Then you can create this view's JSP— `error.jsp`—as follows:

```
<html>
<head>
<title>Error</title>
</head>
<body>
An error has occurred. Please contact our administrator for details.
</body>
</html>
```

Map Exceptions Using @ExceptionHandler

Instead of configuring a `HandlerExceptionResolver`, you can annotate a method with `@ExceptionHandler`. It works in a similar way as the `@RequestMapping` annotation.

```
@Controller
@RequestMapping("/reservationForm")
@SessionAttributes("reservation")
public class ReservationFormController {

    @ExceptionHandler(ReservationNotAvailableException.class)
    public String handle(ReservationNotAvailableException ex) {
        return "reservationNotAvailable";
    }

    @ExceptionHandler
    public String handleDefault(Exception e) {
        return "error";
    }
    ...
}
```

You have here two methods annotated as @ExceptionHandler. The first is for handling the specific ReservationNotAvailableException; the second is the general (catchall) exception-handling method. You also don't have to specify a HandlerExceptionResolver in the WebConfiguration anymore.

Methods annotated with @ExceptionHandler can have a variety of return types (like the @RequestMapping methods); here you just return the name of the view that needs to be rendered, but you could also have returned a ModelAndView, a View, and so on.

Although using @ExceptionHandler annotated methods is very powerful and flexible, there is a drawback when you put them in controllers. Those methods will work only for the controller they are defined in, so if you have an exception occurring in another controller (for instance, the WelcomeController), these methods won't be called. Generic exception-handling methods have to be moved to a separate class, and that class has to be annotated with @ControllerAdvice.

```
@ControllerAdvice
public class ExceptionHandlingAdvice {

    @ExceptionHandler(ReservationNotAvailableException.class)
    public String handle(ReservationNotAvailableException ex) {
        return "reservationNotAvailable";
    }

    @ExceptionHandler
    public String handleDefault(Exception e) {
        return "error";
    }
}
```

This class will apply to all controllers in the application context, which is why it's called @ControllerAdvice.

3-9. Handle Forms with Controllers

Problem

In a web application, you often have to deal with forms. A form controller has to show a form to a user and also handle the form submission. Form handling can be a complex and variable task.

Solution

When a user interacts with a form, it requires support for two operations from a controller. First, when a form is initially requested, it asks the controller to show a form by an HTTP GET request, which renders the form view to the user. Then when the form is submitted, an HTTP POST request is made to handle things such as validation and business processing for the data present in the form. If the form is handled successfully, it renders the success view to the user. Otherwise, it renders the form view again with errors.

How It Works

Suppose you want to allow a user to make a court reservation by filling out a form. To give you a better idea of the data handled by a controller, we will introduce the controller's view (i.e., the form) first.

Create a Form's Views

Let's create the form view `reservationForm.jsp`. The form relies on Spring's form tag library, as this simplifies a form's data binding, display of error messages, and the redisplay of original values entered by the user in case of errors.

```
<%@ taglib prefix="form" uri="http://www.springframework.org/tags/form"%>

<html>
<head>
<title>Reservation Form</title>
<style>
.error {
    color: #ff0000;
    font-weight: bold;
}
</style>
</head>

<body>
<form:form method="post" modelAttribute="reservation">
<form:errors path="*" cssClass="error" />
<table>
    <tr>
        <td>Court Name</td>
        <td><form:input path="courtName" /></td>
        <td><form:errors path="courtName" cssClass="error" /></td>
    </tr>
    <tr>
        <td>Date</td>
        <td><form:input path="date" /></td>
        <td><form:errors path="date" cssClass="error" /></td>
    </tr>
    <tr>
        <td>Hour</td>
        <td><form:input path="hour" /></td>
        <td><form:errors path="hour" cssClass="error" /></td>
    </tr>
    <tr>
        <td colspan="3"><input type="submit" /></td>
    </tr>
</table>
</form:form>
</body>
</html>
```

The Spring `<form:form>` declares two attributes. The `method="post"` attribute indicates that a form performs an HTTP POST request upon submission. The `modelAttribute="reservation"` attribute indicates that the form data is bound to a model named `reservation`. The first attribute should be familiar to you since it's used on most HTML forms. The second attribute will become clearer once we describe the controller that handles the form.

Bear in mind the `<form:form>` tag is rendered into standard HTML before it's sent to a user, so it's not that `modelAttribute="reservation"` is of use to a browser; the attribute is used as a facility to generate the actual HTML form.

Next, you can find the `<form:errors>` tag, used to define a location in which to place errors in case a form does not meet the rules set forth by a controller. The attribute `path="*"` is used to indicate the display of all errors—given the wildcard *—whereas the attribute `cssClass="error"` is used to indicate a CSS formatting class to display the errors.

Next, you can find the form's various `<form:input>` tags accompanied by another set of corresponding `<form:errors>` tags. These tags make use of the attribute path to indicate the form's fields, which in this case are courtName, date, and hour.

The `<form:input>` tags are bound to properties corresponding to `modelAttribute` by using the `path` attribute. They show the user the original value of the field, which will be either the bound property value or the value rejected because of a binding error. They must be used inside the `<form:form>` tag, which defines a form that binds to `modelAttribute` by its name.

Finally, you can find the standard HTML tag `<input type="submit" />` that generates a Submit button and trigger the sending of data to the server, followed by the `</form:form>` tag that closes out the form. If the form and its data are processed correctly, you need to create a success view to notify the user of a successful reservation. The `reservationSuccess.jsp` illustrated next serves this purpose:

```
<html>
<head>
<title>Reservation Success</title>
</head>

<body>
Your reservation has been made successfully.
</body>
</html>
```

It's also possible for errors to occur because of invalid values being submitted in a form. For example, if the date is not in a valid format or an alphabetic character is presented for hour, the controller is designed to reject such field values. The controller will then generate a list of selective error codes for each error to be returned to the form view, and the values are placed inside the `<form:errors>` tag.

For example, for an invalid value input in the date field, the following error codes are generated by a controller:

```
typeMismatch.command.date
typeMismatch.date
typeMismatch.java.time.LocalDate
typeMismatch
```

If you have a `ResourceBundleMessageSource` defined, you can include the following error messages in your resource bundle for the appropriate locale (e.g., `messages.properties` for the default locale):

```
typeMismatch.date=Invalid date format
typeMismatch.hour=Invalid hour format
```

The corresponding error codes and their values are returned to a user if a failure occurs when processing form data.

Now that you know the structure of the views involved with a form, as well as the data handled by it, let's take a look at the logic that handles the submitted data (i.e., the reservation) in a form.

Create a Form's Service Processing

This is not the controller but rather the service used by the controller to process the form's data reservation. First define a make() method in the ReservationService interface.

```
package com.apress.springrecipes.court.service;
...
public interface ReservationService {
    ...
    void make(Reservation reservation)
        throws ReservationNotAvailableException;
}
```

Then you implement this make() method by adding a Reservation item to the list that stores the reservations. You throw a ReservationNotAvailableException in case of a duplicate reservation.

```
package com.apress.springrecipes.court.service;
...
public class ReservationServiceImpl implements ReservationService {
    ...
    @Override
    public void make(Reservation reservation) throws ReservationNotAvailableException {
        long cnt = reservations.stream()
            .filter(made -> Objects.equals(made.getCourtName(), reservation.getCourtName()))
            .filter(made -> Objects.equals(made.getDate(), reservation.getDate()))
            .filter(made -> made.getHour() == reservation.getHour())
            .count();

        if (cnt > 0) {
            throw new ReservationNotAvailableException(reservation
                .getCourtName(), reservation.getDate(), reservation
                .getHour());
        } else {
            reservations.add(reservation);
        }
    }
}
```

Now that you have a better understanding of the two elements that interact with a controller—a form's views and the reservation service class—let's create a controller to handle the court reservation form.

Create a Form's Controller

A controller used to handle forms makes use of practically the same annotations you've already used in the previous recipes. So let's get right to the code.

```
package com.apress.springrecipes.court.web;
...

@Controller
@RequestMapping("/reservationForm")
```

```java
@SessionAttributes("reservation")
public class ReservationFormController {

    private final ReservationService reservationService;

    @Autowired
    public ReservationFormController(ReservationService reservationService) {
        this.reservationService = reservationService;
    }

    @RequestMapping(method = RequestMethod.GET)
    public String setupForm(Model model) {
        Reservation reservation = new Reservation();
        model.addAttribute("reservation", reservation);
        return "reservationForm";
    }

    @RequestMapping(method = RequestMethod.POST)
    public String submitForm(
        @ModelAttribute("reservation") Reservation reservation,
        BindingResult result, SessionStatus status) {
            reservationService.make(reservation);
            return "redirect:reservationSuccess";
    }
}
```

The controller starts by using the standard @Controller annotation, as well as the @RequestMapping annotation that allows access to the controller through the following URL:

```
http://localhost:8080/court/reservationForm
```

When you enter this URL in your browser, it will send an HTTP GET request to your web application. This in turn triggers the execution of the setupForm method, which is designated to handle this type of request based on its @RequestMapping annotation.

The setupForm method defines a Model object as an input parameter, which serves to send model data to the view (i.e., the form). Inside the handler method, an empty Reservation object is created that is added as an attribute to the controller's Model object. Then the controller returns the execution flow to the reservationForm view, which in this case is resolved to reservationForm.jsp (i.e., the form).

The most important aspect of this last method is the addition of an empty Reservation object. If you analyze the form reservationForm.jsp, you will notice the <form:form> tag declares the attribute modelAttribute="reservation". This means that upon rendering the view, the form expects an object named reservation to be available, which is achieved by placing it inside the handler method's Model. In fact, further inspection reveals that the path values for each <form:input> tag correspond to the field names belonging to the Reservation object. Since the form is being loaded for the first time, it should be evident that an empty Reservation object is expected.

Another aspect that is vital to describe prior to analyzing the other controller handler method is the @SessionAttributes("reservation") annotation—declared at the top of the controller class. Since it's possible for a form to contain errors, it can be an inconvenience to lose whatever valid data was already provided by a user on every subsequent submission. To solve this problem, the @SessionAttributes annotation is used to save a reservation field to a user's session so that any future reference to the reservation field is in fact made on the same reference, whether a form is submitted twice or more times. This is also the reason why only a single `Reservation` object is created and assigned to the reservation field in the entire controller. Once the empty `Reservation` object is created—inside the HTTP GET handler method—all actions are made on the same object, since it's assigned to a user's session.

Now let's turn our attention to submitting the form for the first time. After you have filled in the form fields, submitting the form triggers an HTTP POST request, which in turn invokes the `submitForm` method—on account of this method's `@RequestMapping` value. The input fields declared for the `submitForm` method are three. The `@ModelAttribute("reservation") Reservation reservation` is used to reference the reservation object. The `BindingResult` object contains newly submitted data by the user. The `SessionStatus` object is used so that it is possible to mark the processing as completed, after which the `Reservation` object will be removed from the `HttpSession`.

At this juncture, the handler method doesn't incorporate validation or perform access to a user's session, which is the purpose of the `BindingResult` object and `SessionStatus` object—we will describe and incorporate them shortly.

The only operation performed by the handler method is `reservationService.make(reservation);`. This operation invokes the reservation service using the current state of the reservation object. Generally, controller objects are first validated prior to performing this type of operation on them. Finally, note the handler method returns a view named `redirect:reservationSuccess`. The actual name of the view in this case is `reservationSuccess`, which is resolved to the `reservationSuccess.jsp` page you created earlier.

The `redirect:` prefix in the view name is used to avoid a problem known as *duplicate form submission*.

When you refresh the web page in the form success view, the form you just submitted is resubmitted. To avoid this problem, you can apply the post/redirect/get design pattern, which recommends redirecting to another URL after a form submission is handled successfully, instead of returning an HTML page directly. This is the purpose of prefixing a view name with `redirect:`.

Initialize a Model Attribute Object and Prepopulate a Form with Values

The form is designed to let users make reservations. However, if you analyze the `Reservation` domain class, you will note the form is still missing two fields to create a complete reservation object. One of these fields is the `player` field, which corresponds to a `Player` object. Per the `Player` class definition, a `Player` object has both a name field and a phone field.

So, can the player field be incorporated into a form view and controller? Let's analyze the form view first.

```
<html>
<head>
<title>Reservation Form</title>
</head>
<body>
<form method="post" modelAttribute="reservation">
<table>

    ...
    <tr>
        <td>Player Name</td>
        <td><form:input path="player.name" /></td>
        <td><form:errors path="player.name" cssClass="error" /></td>
    </tr>
    <tr>
        <td>Player Phone</td>
        <td><form:input path="player.phone" /></td>
        <td><form:errors path="player.phone" cssClass="error" /></td>
    </tr>
```

```
  <tr>
      <td colspan="3"><input type="submit" /></td>
  </tr>
</table>
</form>
</body>
</html>
```

Using a straightforward approach, you add two additional `<form:input>` tags to represent the Player object's fields. Though these form declarations are simple, you also need to perform modifications to the controller. Recall that by using `<form:input>` tags, a view expects to have access to model objects passed by the controller that match the path value for `<form:input>` tags.

Though the controller's HTTP GET handler method returns an empty reservation named Reservation to this last view, the player property is null, so it causes an exception when rendering the form. To solve this problem, you have to initialize an empty Player object and assign it to the Reservation object returned to the view.

```
@RequestMapping(method = RequestMethod.GET)
public String setupForm(
@RequestParam(required = false, value = "username") String username, Model model) {
    Reservation reservation = new Reservation();
    reservation.setPlayer(new Player(username, null));
    model.addAttribute("reservation", reservation);
    return "reservationForm";
}
```

In this case, after creating the empty Reservation object, the setPlayer method is used to assign it an empty Player object. Further note that the creation of the Person object relies on the username value. This particular value is obtained from the @RequestParam input value, which was also added to the handler method. By doing so, the Player object can be created with a specific username value passed in as a request parameter, resulting in the username form field being prepopulated with this value.

So, for example, if a request to the form is made in the following manner:

```
http://localhost:8080/court/reservationForm?username=Roger
```

this allows the handler method to extract the username parameter to create the Player object, in turn prepopulating the form's username form field with a Roger value. It's worth noting that the @RequestParam annotation for the username parameter uses the property required=false; this allows a form request to be processed even if such a request parameter is not present.

Provide Form Reference Data

When a form controller is requested to render the form view, it may have some types of reference data to provide to the form (e.g., the items to display in an HTML selection). Now suppose you want to allow a user to select the sport type when reserving a court—which is the final unaccounted field for the Reservation class.

```
<html>
<head>
<title>Reservation Form</title>
</head>
<body>
<form method="post" modelAttribute="reservation">
```

```
<table>
    ...
    <tr>
        <td>Sport Type</td>
        <td><form:select path="sportType" items="${sportTypes}"
            itemValue="id" itemLabel="name" /></td>
        <td><form:errors path="sportType" cssClass="error" /></td>
    </tr>
    <tr>
        <td colspan="3"><input type="submit" /></td>
    </tr>
</table>
</form>
</body>
</html>
```

The `<form:select>` tag provides a way to generate a drop-down list of values passed to the view by the controller. Thus, the form represents the `sportType` field as a set of HTML `<select>` elements, instead of the previous open-ended fields—`<input>`—that require a user to introduce text values.

Next, let's take a look at how the controller assigns the `sportType` field as a model attribute; the process is a little different from the previous fields.

First let's define the `getAllSportTypes()` method in the `ReservationService` interface for retrieving all available sport types.

```
package com.apress.springrecipes.court.service;
...
public interface ReservationService {
    ...
    public List<SportType> getAllSportTypes();
}
```

Then you can implement this method by returning a hard-coded list.

```
package com.apress.springrecipes.court.service;
...
public class ReservationServiceImpl implements ReservationService {
    ...
    public static final SportType TENNIS = new SportType(1, "Tennis");
    public static final SportType SOCCER = new SportType(2, "Soccer");

    public List<SportType> getAllSportTypes() {
        return Arrays.asList(TENNIS, SOCCER);
    }
}
```

Now that you have an implementation that returns a hard-coded list of SportType objects, let's take a look at how the controller associates this list for it to be returned to the form view.

```
package com.apress.springrecipes.court.service;
.....
    @ModelAttribute("sportTypes")
    public List<SportType> populateSportTypes() {
```

```
    return reservationService.getAllSportTypes();
}

@RequestMapping(method = RequestMethod.GET)
public String setupForm(
@RequestParam(required = false, value = "username") String username, Model model) {
    Reservation reservation = new Reservation();
    reservation.setPlayer(new Player(username, null));
    model.addAttribute("reservation", reservation);
    return "reservationForm";
}
```

Notice that the setupForm handler method charged with returning the empty Reservation object to the form view remains unchanged.

The new addition and what is responsible for passing a SportType list as a model attribute to the form view is the method decorated with the @ModelAttribute("sportTypes") annotation. The @ModelAttribute annotation is used to define global model attributes, available to any returning view used in handler methods. In the same way, a handler method declares a Model object as an input parameter and assigns attributes that can be accessed in the returning view.

Since the method decorated with the @ModelAttribute("sportTypes") annotation has a return type of List<SportType> and makes a call to reservationService.getAllSportTypes(), the hard-coded TENNIS and SOCCER SportType objects are assigned to the model attribute named sportTypes. This last model attribute is used in the form view to populate a drop-down list (i.e., <form:select> tag).

Bind Properties of Custom Types

When a form is submitted, a controller binds the form field values to the model object's properties of the same name, in this case a Reservation object. However, for properties of custom types, a controller is not able to convert them unless you specify the corresponding property editors for them.

For example, the sport type selection field only submits the selected sport type ID—as this is the way HTML <select> fields operate. Therefore, you have to convert this ID into a SportType object with a property editor. First, you require the getSportType() method in ReservationService to retrieve a SportType object by its ID.

```
package com.apress.springrecipes.court.service;
...
public interface ReservationService {
    ...
    public SportType getSportType(int sportTypeId);
}
```

For testing purposes, you can implement this method with a switch/case statement.

```
package com.apress.springrecipes.court.service;
...
public class ReservationServiceImpl implements ReservationService {
    ...
    public SportType getSportType(int sportTypeId) {
        switch (sportTypeId) {
        case 1:
            return TENNIS;
```

```
        case 2:
            return SOCCER;
        default:
            return null;
        }
    }
}
```

Then you create the SportTypeConverter class to convert a sport type ID into a SportType object. This converter requires ReservationService to perform the lookup.

```
package com.apress.springrecipes.court.domain;

import com.apress.springrecipes.court.service.ReservationService;
import org.springframework.core.convert.converter.Converter;

public class SportTypeConverter implements Converter<String, SportType> {

    private ReservationService reservationService;

    public SportTypeConverter(ReservationService reservationService) {
        this.reservationService = reservationService;
    }

    @Override
    public SportType convert(String source) {
        int sportTypeId = Integer.parseInt(source);
        SportType sportType = reservationService.getSportType(sportTypeId);
        return sportType;
    }
}
```

Now that you have the supporting SportTypeConverter class required to bind form properties to a custom class like SportType, you need to associate it with the controller. For this purpose, you can use the addFormatters method from the WebMvcConfigurer.

By overriding this method in your configuration class, custom types can be associated with a controller. This includes the SportTypeConverter class and other custom types like Date. Though we didn't mention the date field earlier, it suffers from the same problem as the sport type selection field. A user introduces date fields as text values. For the controller to assign these text values to the Reservation object's date field, this requires the date fields to be associated with a Date object. Given that the Date class is part of the Java language, it won't be necessary to create a special class like SportTypeConverter. For this purpose, the Spring Framework already includes a custom class.

Knowing you need to bind both the SportTypeConverter class and a Date class to the underlying controller, the following code illustrates the modifications to the configuration class:

```
package com.apress.springrecipes.court.web.config;
...
import com.apress.springrecipes.court.domain.SportTypeConverter;
import com.apress.springrecipes.court.service.ReservationService;
import org.springframework.beans.factory.annotation.Autowired;
import org.springframework.format.FormatterRegistry;
import org.springframework.format.datetime.DateFormatter;
```

```
@Configuration
@EnableWebMvc
@ComponentScan("com.apress.springrecipes.court.web")
public class WebConfiguration implements WebMvcConfigurer {

    @Autowired
    private ReservationService reservationService;

    @Override
    public void addFormatters(FormatterRegistry registry) {
        registry.addConverter(new SportTypeConverter(reservationService));
    }
}
```

The only field for this last class corresponds to reservationService, used to access the application's ReservationService bean. Note the use of the @Autowired annotation that enables the injection of the bean. Next, you can find the addFormatters method used to bind the Date and SportTypeConverter classes. You can then find two calls to register the converter and formatter. These methods belong to the FormatterRegistry object, which is passed as an input parameter to the addFormatters method.

The first call is used to bind a Date class to the DateFormatter class. The DateFormatter class is provided by the Spring Framework and offers functionality to parse and print Date objects.

The second call is used to register the SportTypeConverter class. Since you created the SportTypeConverter class, you should know that its only input parameter is a ReservationService bean. By using this approach, every annotation-based controller (i.e., classes using the @Controller annotation) can have access to the same custom converters and formatters in their handler methods.

Validate Form Data

When a form is submitted, it's standard practice to validate the data provided by a user before a submission is successful. Spring MVC supports validation by means of a validator object that implements the Validator interface. You can write the following validator to check whether the required form fields are filled and whether the reservation hour is valid on holidays and weekdays:

```
package com.apress.springrecipes.court.domain;

import org.springframework.stereotype.Component;
import org.springframework.validation.Errors;
import org.springframework.validation.ValidationUtils;
import org.springframework.validation.Validator;

import java.time.DayOfWeek;
import java.time.LocalDate;

@Component
public class ReservationValidator implements Validator {

    public boolean supports(Class<?> clazz) {
        return Reservation.class.isAssignableFrom(clazz);
    }

    public void validate(Object target, Errors errors) {
        ValidationUtils.rejectIfEmptyOrWhitespace(errors, "courtName",
            "required.courtName", "Court name is required.");
```

```
        ValidationUtils.rejectIfEmpty(errors, "date",
            "required.date", "Date is required.");
        ValidationUtils.rejectIfEmpty(errors, "hour",
            "required.hour", "Hour is required.");
        ValidationUtils.rejectIfEmptyOrWhitespace(errors, "player.name",
            "required.playerName", "Player name is required.");
        ValidationUtils.rejectIfEmpty(errors, "sportType",
            "required.sportType", "Sport type is required.");

        Reservation reservation = (Reservation) target;
        LocalDate date = reservation.getDate();
        int hour = reservation.getHour();
        if (date != null) {
            if (date.getDayOfWeek() == DayOfWeek.SUNDAY) {
                if (hour < 8 || hour > 22) {
                    errors.reject("invalid.holidayHour", "Invalid holiday hour.");
                }
            } else {
                if (hour < 9 || hour > 21) {
                    errors.reject("invalid.weekdayHour", "Invalid weekday hour.");
                }
            }
        }
    }
}
```

In this validator, you use utility methods such as rejectIfEmptyOrWhitespace() and rejectIfEmpty() in the ValidationUtils class to validate the required form fields. If any of these form fields are empty, these methods will create a field error and bind it to the field. The second argument of these methods is the property name, while the third and fourth are the error code and default error message.

You also check whether the reservation hour is valid on holidays and weekdays. In case of invalidity, you should use the reject() method to create an object error to be bound to the reservation object, not to a field.

Since the validator class is annotated with the @Component annotation, Spring attempts to instantiate the class as a bean in accordance with the class name, in this case reservationValidator.

Since validators may create errors during validation, you should define messages for the error codes for displaying to the user. If you have ResourceBundleMessageSource defined, you can include the following error messages in your resource bundle for the appropriate locale (e.g., messages.properties for the default locale):

```
required.courtName=Court name is required
required.date=Date is required
required.hour=Hour is required
required.playerName=Player name is required
required.sportType=Sport type is required
invalid.holidayHour=Invalid holiday hour
invalid.weekdayHour=Invalid weekday hour
```

To apply this validator, you need to perform the following modification to your controller:

```
package com.apress.springrecipes.court.service;
.....
    private ReservationService reservationService;
    private ReservationValidator reservationValidator;
```

```java
public ReservationFormController(ReservationService reservationService,
    ReservationValidator reservationValidator) {
    this.reservationService = reservationService;
    this.reservationValidator = reservationValidator;
}

@RequestMapping(method = RequestMethod.POST)
public String submitForm(
    @ModelAttribute("reservation") @Validated Reservation reservation,
    BindingResult result, SessionStatus status) {
    if (result.hasErrors()) {
        return "reservationForm";
    } else {
        reservationService.make(reservation);
        return "redirect:reservationSuccess";
    }
}

@InitBinder
public void initBinder(WebDataBinder binder) {
    binder.setValidator(reservationValidator);
}
```

The first addition to the controller is the ReservationValidator field, which gives the controller access to an instance of the validator bean.

The next modification takes place in the HTTP POST handler method, which is always called when a user submits a form. Next to the @ModelAttribute annotation there is now an @Validated annotation, which triggers validation of the object. After the validation, the result parameter—the BindingResult object—contains the results for the validation process. Next, a conditional based on the value of result. hasErrors() is made. If the validation class detects errors, this value is true.

If errors are detected in the validation process, the method handler returns the view reservationForm, which corresponds to the same form so a user can resubmit information. If no errors are detected in the validation process, a call is made to perform the reservation— reservationService. make(reservation);—followed by a redirection to the success view reservationSuccess.

The registration of the validator is done in the @InitBinder annotated method, and the validator is set on the WebDataBinder so that it can be used after binding. To register the validator, you need to use the setValidator method. You can also register multiple validators using the addValidators method, which takes a varargs argument for one or more Validator instances.

■ **Note**   The WebDataBinder can also be used to register additional ProperyEditor, Converter, and Formatter instances for type conversion. This can be used instead of registering global PropertyEditors, Converters, or Formatters.

Expire a Controller's Session Data

To support the possibility of a form being submitted multiple times and not losing data provided by a user between submissions, the controller relies on the use of the @SessionAttributes annotation. By doing so, a reference to the reservation field represented as a Reservation object is saved between requests.

However, once a form is submitted successfully and a reservation is made, there is no point in keeping the Reservation object in a user's session. In fact, if a user revisits the form within a short period of time, there is a possibility that remnants of this old Reservation object emerge if not removed.

Values assigned using the @SessionAttributes annotation can be removed using the SessionStatus object, which is an object that can be passed as an input parameter to handler methods. The following code illustrates how to expire the controller's session data:

```
package com.apress.springrecipes.court.web;

@Controller
@RequestMapping("/reservationForm")
@SessionAttributes("reservation")
public class ReservationFormController {

    @RequestMapping(method = RequestMethod.POST)
    public String submitForm(
        @ModelAttribute("reservation") Reservation reservation,
        BindingResult result, SessionStatus status) {

        if (result.hasErrors()) {
            return "reservationForm";
        } else {
            reservationService.make(reservation);
            status.setComplete();
            return "redirect:reservationSuccess";
        }
    }
}
```

Once the handler method performs the reservation by calling reservationService.make(reservation); and right before a user is redirected to a success page, it becomes an ideal time in which expire a controller's session data. This is done by calling the setComplete() method on the SessionStatus object. It's that simple.

3-10. Handle Multipage Forms with Wizard Form Controllers

Problem

In a web application, you sometimes have to deal with complex forms that span multiple pages. Forms like this are usually called *wizard forms* because users have to fill them page by page—just like using a software wizard. Undoubtedly, you can create one or more form controllers to handle a wizard form.

Solution

As there are multiple form pages for a wizard form, you have to define multiple page views for a wizard form controller. A controller then manages the form status across all these form pages. In a wizard form, there can also be a single controller handler method for form submissions, just like an individual form. However, to distinguish between a user's action, a special request parameter needs to be embedded in each form, usually specified as the name of a submit button.

`_finish`: Finish the wizard form.
`_cancel`: Cancel the wizard form.
`_targetx`: Step to the target page, where x is the zero-based page index.

Using these parameters, a controller's handler method can determine what steps to take based on the form and user's action.

How It Works

Suppose you want to provide a function that allows a user to reserve a court at fixed hours periodically. You first define the PeriodicReservation class in the domain subpackage.

```
package com.apress.springrecipes.court.domain;
...
public class PeriodicReservation {

    private String courtName;
    private Date fromDate;
    private Date toDate;
    private int period;
    private int hour;
    private Player player;

    // Getters and Setters
    ...
}
```

Then you add a makePeriodic() method to the ReservationService interface for making a periodic reservation.

```
package com.apress.springrecipes.court.service;
...
public interface ReservationService {
    ...
    public void makePeriodic(PeriodicReservation periodicReservation)
        throws ReservationNotAvailableException;
}
```

The implementation of this method involves generating a series of Reservation objects from PeriodicReservation and passing each reservation to the make() method. Obviously in this simple application, there's no transaction management support.

```
package com.apress.springrecipes.court.service;
...
public class ReservationServiceImpl implements ReservationService {
    ...
    @Override
    public void makePeriodic(PeriodicReservation periodicReservation)
        throws ReservationNotAvailableException {

        LocalDate fromDate = periodicReservation.getFromDate();
```

```
        while (fromDate.isBefore(periodicReservation.getToDate())) {
            Reservation reservation = new Reservation();
            reservation.setCourtName(periodicReservation.getCourtName());
            reservation.setDate(fromDate);
            reservation.setHour(periodicReservation.getHour());
            reservation.setPlayer(periodicReservation.getPlayer());
            make(reservation);

            fromDate = fromDate.plusDays(periodicReservation.getPeriod());

        }
    }
}
```

Create Wizard Form Pages

Suppose you want to show users the periodic reservation form split across three different pages. Each page has a portion of the form fields. The first page is reservationCourtForm.jsp, which contains only the court name field for the periodic reservation.

```
<%@ taglib prefix="form" uri="http://www.springframework.org/tags/form"%>

<html>
<head>
<title>Reservation Court Form</title>
<style>
.error {
    color: #ff0000;
    font-weight: bold;
}
</style>
</head>

<body>
<form:form method="post" modelAttribute="reservation">
<table>
    <tr>
        <td>Court Name</td>
        <td><form:input path="courtName" /></td>
        <td><form:errors path="courtName" cssClass="error" /></td>
    </tr>
    <tr>
        <td colspan="3">
            <input type="hidden" value="0" name="_page" />
            <input type="submit" value="Next" name="_target1" />
            <input type="submit" value="Cancel" name="_cancel" />
        </td>
    </tr>
</table>
</form:form>
</body>
</html>
```

The form and input fields in this page are defined with Spring's `<form:form>` and `<form:input>` tags. They are bound to the model attribute `reservation` and its properties. There's also an error tag for displaying the field error message to the user. Note that there are two submit buttons in this page. The Next button's name must be `_target1`. It asks the wizard form controller to step forward to the second page, whose page index is 1 (zero-based). The Cancel button's name must be `_cancel`. It asks the controller to cancel this form. In addition, there is also a hidden form field to keep track of the page a user is on; in this case, it corresponds to 0.

The second page is `reservationTimeForm.jsp`. It contains the date and time fields for a periodic reservation.

```jsp
<%@ taglib prefix="form" uri="http://www.springframework.org/tags/form"%>

<html>
<head>
<title>Reservation Time Form</title>
<style>
.error {
    color: #ff0000;
    font-weight: bold;
}
</style>
</head>

<body>
<form:form method="post" modelAttribute="reservation">
<table>
    <tr>
        <td>From Date</td>
        <td><form:input path="fromDate" /></td>
        <td><form:errors path="fromDate" cssClass="error" /></td>
    </tr>
    <tr>
        <td>To Date</td>
        <td><form:input path="toDate" /></td>
        <td><form:errors path="toDate" cssClass="error" /></td>
    </tr>
    <tr>
        <td>Period</td>
        <td><form:select path="period" items="${periods}" /></td>
        <td><form:errors path="period" cssClass="error" /></td>
    </tr>
    <tr>
        <td>Hour</td>
        <td><form:input path="hour" /></td>
        <td><form:errors path="hour" cssClass="error" /></td>
    </tr>
    <tr>
        <td colspan="3">
            <input type="hidden" value="1" name="_page"/>
            <input type="submit" value="Previous" name="_target0" />
            <input type="submit" value="Next" name="_target2" />
```

```
                <input type="submit" value="Cancel" name="_cancel" />
        </td>
    </tr>
</table>
</form:form>
</body>
</html>
```

There are three submit buttons in this form. The names of the Previous and Next buttons must be _target0 and _target2, respectively. They ask the wizard form controller to step to the first page and the third page. The Cancel button asks the controller to cancel this form. In addition, there is a hidden form field to keep track of the page a user is on; in this case, it corresponds to 1.

The third page is reservationPlayerForm.jsp. It contains the player information fields for a periodic reservation.

```
<%@ taglib prefix="form" uri="http://www.springframework.org/tags/form"%>

<html>
<head>
<title>Reservation Player Form</title>
<style>
.error {
    color: #ff0000;
    font-weight: bold;
}
</style>
</head>

<body>
<form:form method="POST" commandName="reservation">
<table>
    <tr>
        <td>Player Name</td>
        <td><form:input path="player.name" /></td>
        <td><form:errors path="player.name" cssClass="error" /></td>
    </tr>
    <tr>
        <td>Player Phone</td>
        <td><form:input path="player.phone" /></td>
        <td><form:errors path="player.phone" cssClass="error" /></td>
    </tr>
    <tr>
        <td colspan="3">
            <input type="hidden" value="2" name="_page"/>
            <input type="submit" value="Previous" name="_target1" />
            <input type="submit" value="Finish" name="_finish" />
            <input type="submit" value="Cancel" name="_cancel" />
        </td>
    </tr>
</table>
</form:form>
</body>
</html>
```

There are three submit buttons in this form. The Previous button asks the wizard form controller to step back to the second page. The Finish button's name must be _finish. It asks the controller to finish this form. The Cancel button asks the controller to cancel this form. In addition, there is a hidden form field to keep track of the page a user is on; in this case, it corresponds to 2.

Create a Wizard Form Controller

Now let's create a wizard form controller to handle this periodic reservation form. Like the previous Spring MVC controllers, this controller has four main handler methods—one for HTTP GET requests and others for HTTP POST requests—as well as makes use of the same controller elements (e.g., annotations, validation, or sessions) used in prior controllers. For a wizard form controller, all the form fields in different pages are bound to a single model attribute's Reservation object, which is stored in a user's session across multiple requests.

```java
package com.apress.springrecipes.court.web;

import com.apress.springrecipes.court.domain.PeriodicReservation;
import com.apress.springrecipes.court.domain.Player;
import com.apress.springrecipes.court.service.ReservationService;
import org.springframework.stereotype.Controller;
import org.springframework.ui.Model;
import org.springframework.validation.BindingResult;
import org.springframework.validation.annotation.Validated;
import org.springframework.web.bind.annotation.*;
import org.springframework.web.bind.support.SessionStatus;
import org.springframework.web.util.WebUtils;

import javax.annotation.PostConstruct;
import javax.servlet.http.HttpServletRequest;
import java.util.Enumeration;
import java.util.HashMap;
import java.util.Map;

@Controller
@RequestMapping("/periodicReservationForm")
@SessionAttributes("reservation")
public class PeriodicReservationController {

    private final Map<Integer, String> pageForms = new HashMap<>(3);
    private final ReservationService reservationService;

    public PeriodicReservationController(ReservationService reservationService) {
        this.reservationService = reservationService;
    }

    @PostConstruct
    public void initialize() {
        pageForms.put(0, "reservationCourtForm");
        pageForms.put(1, "reservationTimeForm");
        pageForms.put(2, "reservationPlayerForm");
    }
```

```java
@GetMapping
public String setupForm(Model model) {
    PeriodicReservation reservation = new PeriodicReservation();
    reservation.setPlayer(new Player());
    model.addAttribute("reservation", reservation);
    return "reservationCourtForm";
}

@PostMapping(params = {"_cancel"})
public String cancelForm(@RequestParam("_page") int currentPage) {

    return pageForms.get(currentPage);
}

@PostMapping(params = {"_finish"})
public String completeForm(
    @ModelAttribute("reservation") PeriodicReservation reservation,
    BindingResult result, SessionStatus status,
    @RequestParam("_page") int currentPage) {

    if (!result.hasErrors()) {
        reservationService.makePeriodic(reservation);
        status.setComplete();
        return "redirect:reservationSuccess";
    } else {
        return pageForms.get(currentPage);
    }
}

@PostMapping
public String submitForm(
    HttpServletRequest request,
    @ModelAttribute("reservation") PeriodicReservation reservation,
    BindingResult result, @RequestParam("_page") int currentPage) {

    int targetPage = getTargetPage(request, "_target", currentPage);
    if (targetPage < currentPage) {
        return pageForms.get(targetPage);
    }

    if (!result.hasErrors()) {
        return pageForms.get(targetPage);
    } else {
        return pageForms.get(currentPage);
    }
}

@ModelAttribute("periods")
public Map<Integer, String> periods() {
```

```
        Map<Integer, String> periods = new HashMap<Integer, String>();
        periods.put(1, "Daily");
        periods.put(7, "Weekly");
        return periods;
    }

    private int getTargetPage(HttpServletRequest request, String paramPrefix, int currentPage) {

        Enumeration<String> paramNames = request.getParameterNames();
        while (paramNames.hasMoreElements()) {
            String paramName = paramNames.nextElement();
            if (paramName.startsWith(paramPrefix)) {
                for (int i = 0; i < WebUtils.SUBMIT_IMAGE_SUFFIXES.length; i++) {
                    String suffix = WebUtils.SUBMIT_IMAGE_SUFFIXES[i];
                    if (paramName.endsWith(suffix)) {
                        paramName = paramName.substring(0, paramName.length() -
                        suffix.length());
                    }
                }
                return Integer.parseInt(paramName.substring(paramPrefix.length()));
            }
        }
        return currentPage;
    }
}
```

This controller uses some of the same elements used in the previous ReservationFormController controller, so we won't go into specifics about what's already been explained. But to recap, it uses the @SessionAttributes annotation to place the reservation object in a user's session. It has the same HTTP GET method used to assign empty Reservation and Player objects upon loading the first form view.

Next, the controller defines a HashMap in which it associates page numbers to view names. This HashMap is used various times in the controller since the controller needs to determine target views for a variety of scenarios (e.g., validation or a user clicking Cancel or Next).

You can also find the method decorated with the @ModelAttribute("periods") annotation. As it was illustrated in previous controllers, this declaration allows a list of values to be made available to any returning view placed in the controller. If you look at the previous form reservationTimeForm.jsp, you can see that it expects to have access to a model attribute named periods.

Then you can find that the first @PostMapping will be called if the incoming request has the _cancel parameter in the URL. It also tries to extract the currentPage value by extracting the page attribute from the request using @RequestParam("page"). When this method is called, it returns control to the view corresponding to the currentPage value. The result is that the input is reset to the input prior to changing the content of the input fields.

The next @PostMapping(params={"_finish"}) will be called if the incoming request has the _finish parameter in the URL, which is the case if the user clicked the Finish button. As this is the final step in the process, you want to validate the Reservation object, and for that you annotate the attribute with @Validated. When there are no errors, the handler method makes the reservation by calling reservationService. makePeriodic(reservation); and redirects the user to the reservationSuccess view.

The final handler method with @PostMapping handles the remaining cases and declares an input parameter for the HttpServletRequest, allowing the handler method to access this object's contents. Previous handler methods used parameters such as @RequestParam to input data typically located in these standard objects, as a shortcut mechanism. It demonstrates that full access to the standard HttpServletRequest and HttpServletResponse objects inside a handler method is possible. The names and notation for the remaining input parameters should be familiar to you from earlier controllers. If this handler method is called, it means the user clicked either the Next or Previous button on either of the forms. As a consequence, this means that inside the HttpServletRequest object there is a parameter named _target. This is because each of the form's Next and Previous buttons is assigned this parameter.

Using the getTargetPage method, the value for the _target parameter is extracted, which corresponds to either target0, target1, or target2 and is trimmed to 0, 1, or 2 representing the target page.

Once you have the target page number and the current page number, you can determine whether the user clicked the Next or Previous button. If the target page is lower than the current page, this means the user clicked the Previous button. If the target page number is greater than the current page number, this means the user clicked the Next button.

At this juncture, it isn't clear why you need to determine whether a user clicked the Next or Previous button, especially since a view corresponding to the target page is always returned. But the reason behind this logic is the following: if a user clicked the Next button, you will want to validate the data, whereas if a user clicked the Previous button, there is no need to validate anything. This will become obvious in the next section when validation is incorporated into the controller.

As you have the PeriodicReservationController class decorated with the @RequestMapping ("/periodicReservationForm") annotation, you can access this controller through the following URL:

```
http://localhost:8080/court/periodicReservation
```

Validate Wizard Form Data

In a simple form controller, you validate the entire model attribute object in one shot when the form is submitted. However, as there are multiple form pages for a wizard form controller, you have to validate each page when it's submitted. For this reason, you create the following validator, which splits the validate() method into several fine-grained validate methods, each of which validates fields in a particular page:

```java
package com.apress.springrecipes.court.domain;

import org.springframework.validation.Errors;
import org.springframework.validation.ValidationUtils;
import org.springframework.validation.Validator;

public class PeriodicReservationValidator implements Validator {

    public boolean supports(Class clazz) {
        return PeriodicReservation.class.isAssignableFrom(clazz);
    }

    public void validate(Object target, Errors errors) {
        validateCourt(target, errors);
        validateTime(target, errors);
        validatePlayer(target, errors);
    }
```

```
    public void validateCourt(Object target, Errors errors) {
        ValidationUtils.rejectIfEmptyOrWhitespace(errors, "courtName",
            "required.courtName", "Court name is required.");
    }

    public void validateTime(Object target, Errors errors) {
        ValidationUtils.rejectIfEmpty(errors, "fromDate",
            "required.fromDate", "From date is required.");
        ValidationUtils.rejectIfEmpty(errors, "toDate", "required.toDate",
            "To date is required.");
        ValidationUtils.rejectIfEmpty(errors, "period",
            "required.period", "Period is required.");
        ValidationUtils.rejectIfEmpty(errors, "hour", "required.hour",
            "Hour is required.");
    }

    public void validatePlayer(Object target, Errors errors) {
        ValidationUtils.rejectIfEmptyOrWhitespace(errors, "player.name",
            "required.playerName", "Player name is required.");
    }
}
```

Similar to the earlier validator example, notice that this validator also relies on the @Component annotation to automatically register the validator class as a bean. Once the validator bean is registered, the only thing left to do is incorporate the validator into the controller.

```
package com.apress.springrecipes.court.web;

import com.apress.springrecipes.court.domain.PeriodicReservation;
import com.apress.springrecipes.court.domain.PeriodicReservationValidator;
import com.apress.springrecipes.court.domain.Player;
import com.apress.springrecipes.court.service.ReservationService;
import org.springframework.stereotype.Controller;
import org.springframework.ui.Model;
import org.springframework.validation.BindingResult;
import org.springframework.validation.annotation.Validated;
import org.springframework.web.bind.WebDataBinder;
import org.springframework.web.bind.annotation.*;
import org.springframework.web.bind.support.SessionStatus;
import org.springframework.web.util.WebUtils;

import javax.annotation.PostConstruct;
import javax.servlet.http.HttpServletRequest;
import java.util.Enumeration;
import java.util.HashMap;
import java.util.Map;
```

```java
@Controller
@RequestMapping("/periodicReservationForm")
@SessionAttributes("reservation")
public class PeriodicReservationController {

    private final Map<Integer, String> pageForms = new HashMap<>(3);
    private final ReservationService reservationService;
    private final PeriodicReservationValidator validator;

    public PeriodicReservationController(ReservationService reservationService,
                                         PeriodicReservationValidator
                                         periodicReservationValidator) {
        this.reservationService = reservationService;
        this.validator = periodicReservationValidator;
    }

    @InitBinder
    public void initBinder(WebDataBinder binder) {
        binder.setValidator(this.validator);
    }

    @PostMapping(params = {"_finish"})
    public String completeForm(
        @Validated @ModelAttribute("reservation") PeriodicReservation reservation,
        BindingResult result, SessionStatus status,
        @RequestParam("_page") int currentPage) {
        if (!result.hasErrors()) {
            reservationService.makePeriodic(reservation);
            status.setComplete();
            return "redirect:reservationSuccess";
        } else {
            return pageForms.get(currentPage);
        }
    }

    @PostMapping
    public String submitForm(
        HttpServletRequest request,
        @ModelAttribute("reservation") PeriodicReservation reservation,
        BindingResult result, @RequestParam("_page") int currentPage) {
        int targetPage = getTargetPage(request, "_target", currentPage);
        if (targetPage < currentPage) {
            return pageForms.get(targetPage);
        }
        validateCurrentPage(reservation, result, currentPage);
        if (!result.hasErrors()) {
            return pageForms.get(targetPage);
        } else {
            return pageForms.get(currentPage);
        }
    }
}
```

```java
    private void validateCurrentPage(PeriodicReservation reservation,
        BindingResult result, int currentPage) {
        switch (currentPage) {
            case 0:
                validator.validateCourt(reservation, result);
                break;
            case 1:
                validator.validateTime(reservation, result);
                break;
            case 2:
                validator.validatePlayer(reservation, result);
                break;
        }
    }

    ...
}
```

The first addition to the controller is the validator field that is assigned an instance of the
PeriodicReservationValidator validator bean via the class's constructor. You can then find two references
to the validator in the controller.

The first one is when a user finishes submitting a form. To call the validator, you need to add the
@Validated annotation to the method's Reservation argument. To make that actually do something, you
also need to add an @InitBinder annotated method, which registers the PeriodicReservationValidator
with the data binder. If the validator returns no errors, the reservation is committed, a user's session is
reset, and the user is redirected to the reservationSuccess view. If the validator returns errors, a user is sent
to the current view form to correct the errors. (See also recipe 3-9.)

The second occasion the validator is used in the controller is when a user clicks the Next button on
a form. Since a user is attempting to advance to the next form, it's necessary to validate whatever data a
user provided. Given there are three possible form views to validate, a case statement is used to determine
what validator method to invoke. Once the execution of a validator method returns, if errors are detected, a
user is sent to the currentPage view to can correct the errors; if no errors are detected, a user is sent to the
targetPage view; note that these target pages numbers are mapped to a Map in the controller.

3-11. Use Bean Validation with Annotations (JSR-303)

Problem

You want to validate Java beans in a web application using annotations based on the JSR-303 standard.

Solution

JSR-303, or Bean Validation, is a specification whose objective is to standardize the validation of Java beans
through annotations.

In the previous examples, you saw how the Spring Framework supports an ad hoc technique for
validating beans. This requires you to extend one of the Spring Framework's classes to create a validator
class for a particular type of Java bean.

The objective of the JSR-303 standard is to use annotations directly in a Java bean class. This allows
validation rules to be specified directly in the code they are intended to validate, instead of creating
validation rules in separate classes—just like you did earlier using the Spring Validator class.

How It Works

The first thing you need to do is decorate a Java bean with the necessary JSR-303 annotations. The following code illustrates the Reservation domain class used in the court application decorated with JSR-303 annotations:

```
public class Reservation {

    @NotNull
    @Size(min = 4)
    private String courtName;

    @NotNull
    private Date date;

    @Min(9)
    @Max(21)
    private int hour;

    @Valid
    private Player player;

    @NotNull
    private SportType sportType;

    // Getter/Setter methods omitted for brevity
}
```

The courtName field is assigned two annotations: the @NotNull annotation, which indicates that a field cannot be null, and the @Size annotation, which is used to indicate a field has to have a minimum of four characters.

The date and sportType fields are annotated with @NotNull because those are required.

The hour field is annotated with @Min and @Max because those are the lower and upper limits of the hour field.

The player fields is annotated with @Valid to trigger validation of the nested Player object, both fields in the Player domain class are annotated with @NotNull.

Now that you know how a Java bean class is decorated with annotations belonging to the JSR-303 standard. Let's take a look at how these validator annotations are enforced in a controller.

```
package com.apress.springrecipes.court.service;
.....
    private final ReservationService reservationService;

    public ReservationFormController(ReservationService reservationService) {
        this.reservationService = reservationService;
    }

    @RequestMapping(method = RequestMethod.POST)
    public String submitForm(
        @ModelAttribute("reservation") @Valid Reservation reservation,
        BindingResult result, SessionStatus status) {
```

```
    if (result.hasErrors()) {
        return "reservationForm";
    } else {
        reservationService.make(reservation);
        return "redirect:reservationSuccess";
    }
}
```

The controller is almost similar to the one from recipe 3-9. The only difference is the absence of the @InitBinder annotated method. Spring MVC detects a javax.validation.Validator if that is on the classpath. We added hibernate-validator to the classpath, and that is a validation implementation.

Next, you find the controller's HTTP POST handler method, which is used to handle the submission of user data. Since the handler method is expecting an instance of the Reservation object, which you decorated with JSR-303 annotations, you can validate its data.

The remainder of the submitForm method is the same as from recipe 3-9.

■ **Note**   To use JSR-303 bean validation in a web application, you must add a dependency to an implementation to your CLASSPATH. If you are using Maven, add the following dependencies to your Maven project:

```
<dependency>
    <groupId>org.hibernate</groupId>
    <artifactId>hibernate-validator</artifactId>
    <version>5.4.0.Final</version>
</dependency>
```

Add the following for Gradle:

```
compile 'org.hibernate:hibernate-validator:5.4.0.Final'
```

3-12. Create Excel and PDF Views

Problem

Although HTML is the most common method of displaying web contents, sometimes your users may want to export contents from your web application in Excel or PDF format. In Java, several libraries can help generate Excel and PDF files. However, to use these libraries directly in a web application, you have to generate the files behind the scenes and return them to users as binary attachments. You have to deal with HTTP response headers and output streams for this purpose.

Solution

Spring integrates the generation of Excel and PDF files into its MVC framework. You can consider Excel and PDF files as special kinds of views so that you can consistently handle a web request in a controller and add data to a model for passing to Excel and PDF views. In this way, you have no need to deal with HTTP response headers and output streams. Spring MVC supports generating Excel files using the Apache POI library (http://poi.apache.org/). The corresponding view classes are AbstractExcelView, AbstractXlsxView and AbstractXlsxStreamingView. PDF files are generated by the iText library (www.lowagie.com/iText/), and the corresponding view class is AbstractPdfView.

How It Works

Suppose your users want to generate a report of the reservation summary for a particular day. They want this report to be generated in either Excel, PDF, or the basic HTML format. For this report generation function, you need to declare a method in the service layer that returns all the reservations of a specified day.

```
package com.apress.springrecipes.court.service;
...
public interface ReservationService {
    ...
    public List<Reservation> findByDate(LocalDate date);
}
```

Then you provide a simple implementation for this method by iterating over all the made reservations.

```
package com.apress.springrecipes.court.service;
...
public class ReservationServiceImpl implements ReservationService {
    ...
    public List<Reservation> findByDate(LocalDate date) {
        return reservations.stream()
            .filter(r -> Objects.equals(r.getDate(), date))
            .collect(Collectors.toList());
    }
}
```

Now you can write a simple controller to get the date parameters from the URL. The date parameter is formatted into a date object and passed to the service layer for querying reservations. The controller relies on the content negotiation resolver described in recipe 3-7. Therefore, the controller returns a single logic view and lets the resolver determine whether a report should be generated in Excel, PDF, or a default HTML web page.

```
package com.apress.springrecipes.court.web;
...
@Controller
@RequestMapping("/reservationSummary*")
public class ReservationSummaryController {
    private ReservationService reservationService;

    @Autowired
    public ReservationSummaryController(ReservationService reservationService) {
        this.reservationService = reservationService;
    }

    @RequestMapping(method = RequestMethod.GET)
    public String generateSummary(
        @RequestParam(required = true, value = "date")
        String selectedDate,
        Model model) {
        List<Reservation> reservations = java.util.Collections.emptyList();
```

```
try {
    Date summaryDate = new SimpleDateFormat("yyyy-MM-dd").parse(selectedDate);
    reservations = reservationService.findByDate(summaryDate);
} catch (java.text.ParseException ex) {
    StringWriter sw = new StringWriter();
    PrintWriter pw = new PrintWriter(sw);
    ex.printStackTrace(pw);
    throw new ReservationWebException("Invalid date format for reservation
    summary",new Date(),sw.toString());
}
model.addAttribute("reservations",reservations);
return "reservationSummary";
    }
}
```

This controller only contains a default HTTP GET handler method. The first action performed by this method is creating an empty Reservation list to place the results obtained from the reservation service. Next, you can find a try/catch block that attempts to create a Date object from the selectedDate @RequestParam, as well as invoke the reservation service with the created Date object. If creating a Date object fails, a custom Spring exception named ReservationWebException is thrown.

If no errors are raised in the try/catch block, the Reservation list is placed into the controller's Model object. Once this is done, the method returns control to the reservationSummary view.

Note that the controller returns a single view, even though it supports PDF, XLS, and HTML views. This is possible because of the ContentNegotiatingViewResolver resolver, which determines on the basis of this single view name which of these multiple views to use. See recipe 3-7 for more information on this resolver.

Create Excel Views

An Excel view can be created by extending the AbstractXlsView or AbstractXlsxView class (for Apache POI). Here, AbstractXlsxView is used as an example. In the buildExcelDocument() method, you can access the model passed from the controller and also a precreated Excel workbook. Your task is to populate the workbook with the data in the model.

■ **Note**   To generate Excel files with Apache POI in a web application, you must have the Apache POI dependencies on your CLASSPATH. If you are using Apache Maven, add the following dependencies to your Maven project:

```
<dependency>
    <groupId>org.apache.poi</groupId>
    <artifactId>poi</artifactId>
    <version>3.10-FINAL</version>
</dependency>
```

```
package com.apress.springrecipes.court.web.view;

import com.apress.springrecipes.court.domain.Reservation;
import org.apache.poi.ss.usermodel.Row;
import org.apache.poi.ss.usermodel.Sheet;
import org.apache.poi.ss.usermodel.Workbook;
import org.springframework.web.servlet.view.document.AbstractXlsxView;
```

```java
import javax.servlet.http.HttpServletRequest;
import javax.servlet.http.HttpServletResponse;
import java.text.DateFormat;
import java.text.SimpleDateFormat;
import java.util.List;
import java.util.Map;

public class ExcelReservationSummary extends AbstractXlsxView {

    @Override
    protected void buildExcelDocument(Map<String, Object> model, Workbook workbook,
                                      HttpServletRequest request, HttpServletResponse
                                      response) throws Exception {
        @SuppressWarnings({"unchecked"})
        final List<Reservation> reservations =
            (List<Reservation>) model.get("reservations");
        final DateFormat dateFormat = new SimpleDateFormat("yyyy-MM-dd");
        final Sheet sheet = workbook.createSheet();

        addHeaderRow(sheet);

        reservations.forEach(reservation -> createRow(dateFormat, sheet, reservation));
    }

    private void addHeaderRow(Sheet sheet) {
        Row header = sheet.createRow(0);
        header.createCell((short) 0).setCellValue("Court Name");
        header.createCell((short) 1).setCellValue("Date");
        header.createCell((short) 2).setCellValue("Hour");
        header.createCell((short) 3).setCellValue("Player Name");
        header.createCell((short) 4).setCellValue("Player Phone");
    }

    private void createRow(DateFormat dateFormat, Sheet sheet, Reservation reservation) {
        Row row = sheet.createRow(sheet.getLastRowNum() + 1);
        row.createCell((short) 0).setCellValue(reservation.getCourtName());
        row.createCell((short) 1).setCellValue(dateFormat.format(reservation.getDate()));
        row.createCell((short) 2).setCellValue(reservation.getHour());
        row.createCell((short) 3).setCellValue(reservation.getPlayer().getName());
        row.createCell((short) 4).setCellValue(reservation.getPlayer().getPhone());
    }
}
```

In the preceding Excel view, you first create a sheet in the workbook. In this sheet, you show the headers of this report in the first row. Then you iterate over the reservation list to create a row for each reservation.

As you have @RequestMapping("/reservationSummary*") configured in your controller and the handler method requires a date as a request parameter, you can access this Excel view through the following URL:

```
http://localhost:8080/court/reservationSummary.xls?date=2009-01-14
```

Create PDF Views

A PDF view is created by extending the AbstractPdfView class. In the buildPdfDocument() method, you can access the model passed from the controller and also a precreated PDF document. Your task is to populate the document with the data in the model.

■ **Note** To generate PDF files with iText in a web application, you must have the iText library on your CLASSPATH. If you are using Apache Maven, add the following dependency to your Maven project:

```
<dependency>
    <groupId>com.lowagie</groupId>
    <artifactId>itext</artifactId>
    <version>4.2.1</version>
</dependency>
```

```
package com.apress.springrecipes.court.web.view;
...
import org.springframework.web.servlet.view.document.AbstractPdfView;

import com.lowagie.text.Document;
import com.lowagie.text.Table;
import com.lowagie.text.pdf.PdfWriter;

public class PdfReservationSummary extends AbstractPdfView {

    protected void buildPdfDocument(Map model, Document document,
        PdfWriter writer, HttpServletRequest request,
        HttpServletResponse response) throws Exception {
        List<Reservation> reservations = (List) model.get("reservations");
        DateFormat dateFormat = new SimpleDateFormat("yyyy-MM-dd");
        Table table = new Table(5);

        table.addCell("Court Name");
        table.addCell("Date");
        table.addCell("Hour");
        table.addCell("Player Name");
        table.addCell("Player Phone");

        for (Reservation reservation : reservations) {
            table.addCell(reservation.getCourtName());
            table.addCell(dateFormat.format(reservation.getDate()));
            table.addCell(Integer.toString(reservation.getHour()));
            table.addCell(reservation.getPlayer().getName());
            table.addCell(reservation.getPlayer().getPhone());
        }

        document.add(table);
    }
}
```

As you have @RequestMapping("/reservationSummary*") configured in your controller and the handler method requires a date as a request parameter, you can access this PDF view through the following URL:

```
http://localhost:8080/court/reservationSummary.pdf?date=2009-01-14
```

Create Resolvers for Excel and PDF Views

In recipe 3-6, you learned different strategies for resolving logical view names to specific view implementations. One of these strategies was resolving views from a resource bundle; this is the better-suited strategy for mapping logical view names to view implementations consisting of PDF or XLS classes.

Ensuring you have the ResourceBundleViewResolver bean configured in your web application context as a view resolver, you can then define views in the views.properties file included in a web application's classpath root.

You can add the following entry to views.properties to map the XLS view class to a logical view name:

```
reservationSummary.(class)=com.apress.springrecipes.court.web.view.ExcelReservationSummary
```

Since the application relies on the process of content negotiation, this implies that the same view name is mapped to multiple view technologies. In addition, since it's not possible to have duplicate names in the same views.properties file, you need to create a separate file named secondaryviews.properties to map the PDF view class to a logical view name, as illustrated next:

```
reservationSummary.(class)=com.apress.springrecipes.court.web.view.PdfReservationSummary
```

Take note that this file—secondaryviews.properties—needs to be configured in its own ResourceBundleViewResolver resolver. The property name—reservationSummary—corresponds to the view's name returned by the controller. It's the task of the ContentNegotiatingViewResolver resolver to determine which of these classes to use based on a user's request. Once this is determined, the execution of the corresponding class generates either a PDF or XLS file.

Create Date-Based PDF and XLS File Names

When a user makes a request for a PDF or XLS file using any of the following URLs:

```
http://localhost:8080/court/reservationSummary.pdf?date=2008-01-14
http://localhost:8080/court/reservationSummary.xls?date=2008-02-24
```

the browser prompts a user with a question like "Save as reservationSummary.pdf ?" or "Save as reservationSummary.xls?" This convention is based on the URL a user is requesting a resource from. However, given that a user is also providing a date in the URL, a nice feature can be an automatic prompt in the form "Save as ReservationSummary_2009_01_24.xls?" or "Save as ReservationSummary_2009_02_24.xls?" This can be done by applying an interceptor to rewrite the returning URL. The following code illustrates this interceptor:

```
package com.apress.springrecipes.court.web
...

public class ExtensionInterceptor extends HandlerInterceptorAdapter {
```

```
public void postHandle(HttpServletRequest request,
    HttpServletResponse response, Object handler,
        ModelAndView modelAndView) throws Exception {
    // Report date is present in request
    String reportName = null;
    String reportDate = request.getQueryString().replace("date=","").replace("-","_");
    if(request.getServletPath().endsWith(".pdf")) {
        reportName= "ReservationSummary_" + reportDate + ".pdf";
    }
    if(request.getServletPath().endsWith(".xls")) {
        reportName= "ReservationSummary_" + reportDate + ".xls";
    }
    if (reportName != null) {
        response.setHeader("Content-Disposition","attachment; filename="+reportName);
    }
}
}
```

The interceptor extracts the entire URL if it contains a .pdf or .xls extension. If it detects such an extension, it creates a value for the return file name in the form ReservationSummary_<report_date>.<.pdf|.xls>. To ensure a user receives a download prompt in this form, the HTTP header Content-Disposition is set with this file name format.

To deploy this interceptor and that it only be applied to the URL corresponding to the controller charged with generating PDF and XLS files, we advise you to look over recipe 3-3, which contains this particular configuration and more details about interceptor classes.

CONTENT NEGOTIATION AND SETTING HTTP HEADERS IN AN INTERCEPTOR

Though this application uses the ContentNegotiatingViewResolver resolver to select an appropriate view, the process of modifying a return URL is outside the scope of view resolvers. Therefore, it's necessary to use an interceptor to manually inspect a request extension, as well as set the necessary HTTP headers to modify the outgoing URL.

Summary

In this chapter, you learned how to develop a Java web application using the Spring MVC framework. The central component of Spring MVC is DispatcherServlet, which acts as a front controller that dispatches requests to appropriate handlers for them to handle requests. In Spring MVC, controllers are standard Java classes that are decorated with the @Controller annotation. Throughout the various recipes, you learned how to leverage other annotations used in Spring MVC controllers, which included @RequestMapping to indicate access URLs, @Autowired to automatically inject bean references, and @SessionAttributes to maintain objects in a user's session, among many others. You also learned how to incorporate interceptors into an application; this allows you to alter request and response objects in a controller. In addition, you explored how Spring MVC supports form processing, including data validation using both Spring validators and the JSR-303 bean validation standard. You also explored how Spring MVC incorporates SpEL to facilitate certain configuration tasks and how Spring MVC supports different types of views for different presentation technologies. Finally, you also learned how Spring supports content negotiation to determine a view based on a request's extensions.

CHAPTER 4

■ ■ ■

Spring REST

In this chapter, you will learn how Spring addresses Representational State Transfer, usually referred to by its acronym REST. REST has had an important impact on web applications since the term was coined by Roy Fielding (http://en.wikipedia.org/wiki/Roy_Fielding) in 2000.

Based on the foundations of the Web's Hypertext Transfer Protocol (HTTP), the architecture set forth by REST has become increasingly popular in the implementation of web services. Web services in and of themselves have become the cornerstone for much machine-to-machine communication taking place on the Web. It's the fragmented technology choices (e.g., Java, Python, Ruby, .NET) made by many organizations that have necessitated a solution capable of bridging the gaps between these disparate environments. For example, how is information in an application backed by Java accessed by one written in Python? How can a Java application obtain information from an application written in .NET? Web services fill this void.

There are various approaches to implementing web services, but RESTful web services have become the most common choice in web applications. They are used by some of the largest Internet sites (e.g., Google and Yahoo) to provide access to their information, to back access to Ajax calls made by browsers, and to provide the foundations for the distribution of information such as news feeds (e.g., RSS).

In this chapter, you will learn how Spring applications can use REST so that you can both access and provide information using this popular approach.

4-1. Publish XML with REST Services

Problem

You want to publish an XML-based REST service with Spring.

Solution

There are two possibilities when designing REST services in Spring. One involves publishing an application's data as a REST service; the other involves accessing data from third-party REST services to be used in an application. This recipe describes how to publish an application's data as a REST service. Recipe 4-2 describes how to access data from third-party REST services. Publishing an application's data as a REST service revolves around the use of the Spring MVC annotations @RequestMapping and @PathVariable. By using these annotations to decorate a Spring MVC handler method, a Spring application is capable of publishing an application's data as a REST service.

In addition, Spring supports a series of mechanisms to generate a REST service's payload. This recipe will explore the simplest mechanism, which involves the use of Spring's MarshallingView class. As the recipes in this chapter progress, you will learn about more advanced mechanisms supported by Spring to generate REST service payloads.

© Marten Deinum, Daniel Rubio, and Josh Long 2017
M. Deinum et al., *Spring 5 Recipes*, DOI 10.1007/978-1-4842-2790-9_4

How It Works

Publishing a web application's data as a REST service (or as it's more technically known in web services parlance, "creating an endpoint") is strongly tied to Spring MVC, which you explored in Chapter 3. Since Spring MVC relies on the annotation @RequestMapping to decorate handler methods and define access points (i.e., URLs), it's the preferred way in which to define a REST service's endpoint.

Use MarshallingView to Produce XML

The following code illustrates a Spring MVC controller class with a handler method that defines a REST service endpoint:

```
package com.apress.springrecipes.court.web;

import com.apress.springrecipes.court.domain.Members;
import com.apress.springrecipes.court.service.MemberService;
import org.springframework.beans.factory.annotation.Autowired;
import org.springframework.stereotype.Controller;
import org.springframework.ui.Model;
import org.springframework.web.bind.annotation.RequestMapping;

@Controller
public class RestMemberController {

    private final MemberService memberService;

    @Autowired
    public RestMemberController(MemberService memberService) {
        super();
        this.memberService=memberService;
    }

    @RequestMapping("/members")
    public String getRestMembers(Model model) {
        Members members = new Members();
        members.addMembers(memberService.findAll());
        model.addAttribute("members", members);
        return "membertemplate";
    }
}
```

By using @RequestMapping("/members") to decorate a controller's handler method, a REST service endpoint is made accessible at host_name/[app-name]/members. You can observe that control is relinquished to a logical view named membertemplate. The following code illustrates the declaration used to define the logical view named membertemplate:

```
@Configuration
@EnableWebMvc
@ComponentScan(basePackages = "com.apress.springrecipes.court")
public class CourtRestConfiguration {
```

```
@Bean
public View membertemplate() {
    return new MarshallingView(jaxb2Marshaller());
}

@Bean
public Marshaller jaxb2Marshaller() {
    Jaxb2Marshaller marshaller = new Jaxb2Marshaller();
    marshaller.setClassesToBeBound(Members.class, Member.class);
    return marshaller;
}

@Bean
public ViewResolver viewResolver() {
    return new BeanNameViewResolver();
}
}
```

The membertemplate view is defined as a MarshallingView type, which is a general-purpose class that allows a response to be rendered using a marshaller. *Marshalling* is the process of transforming an in-memory representation of an object into a data format. Therefore, for this particular case, a marshaller is charged with transforming Members and Member objects into an XML data format. The marshaller used by MarshallingView belongs to one of a series of XML marshallers provided by Spring—Jaxb2Marshaller. Other marshallers provided by Spring include CastorMarshaller, JibxMarshaller, XmlBeansMarshaller, and XStreamMarshaller.

Marshallers themselves also require configuration. We opted to use the Jaxb2Marshaller marshaller because of its simplicity and Java Architecture for XML Binding (JAXB) foundations. However, if you're more comfortable using the Castor XML framework, you might find it easier to use CastorMarshaller; if you're more at ease using XStream, you would likely find it easier to use XStreamMarshaller; and it's similar for the rest of the available marshallers.

The Jaxb2Marshaller marshaller needs to be configured with either a property named classesToBeBound or a property named contextPath. In the case of classesToBeBound, the classes assigned to this property indicate the class (i.e., object) structure that is to be transformed into XML. The following code illustrates the Members and Member classes assigned to the Jaxb2Marshaller marshaller:

```
package com.apress.springrecipes.court.domain;

import javax.xml.bind.annotation.XmlRootElement;

@XmlRootElement
public class Member {
    private String name;
    private String phone;
    private String email;

    public String getEmail() {
        return email;
    }
```

```java
    public String getName() {
        return name;
    }

    public String getPhone() {
        return phone;
    }

    public void setEmail(String email) {
        this.email = email;
    }

    public void setName(String name) {
        this.name = name;
    }

    public void setPhone(String phone) {
        this.phone = phone;
    }
}
```

Here's the Members class:

```java
package com.apress.springrecipes.court.domain;

import javax.xml.bind.annotation.XmlAccessType;
import javax.xml.bind.annotation.XmlAccessorType;
import javax.xml.bind.annotation.XmlElement;
import javax.xml.bind.annotation.XmlRootElement;
import java.util.ArrayList;
import java.util.Collection;
import java.util.List;

@XmlRootElement
@XmlAccessorType(XmlAccessType.FIELD)
public class Members {

    @XmlElement(name="member")
    private List<Member> members = new ArrayList<>();

    public List<Member> getMembers() {
        return members;
    }

    public void setMembers(List<Member> members) {
        this.members = members;
    }

    public void addMembers(Collection<Member> members) {
        this.members.addAll(members);
    }
}
```

Note the Member class is a POJO decorated with the @XmlRootElement annotation. This annotation allows the Jaxb2Marshaller marshaller to detect a class's (i.e., object's) fields and transform them into XML data (e.g., name=John into <name>john</name>, email=john@doe.com into <email>john@doe.com</email>).

To recap what's been described, this means that when a request is made to a URL in the form http://[host_name]//app-name]/members.xml, the corresponding handler is charged with creating a Members object, which is then passed to a logical view named membertemplate. Based on this last view's definition, a marshaller is used to convert a Members object into an XML payload that is returned to the REST service's requesting party. The XML payload returned by the REST service is illustrated in the following code:

```
<?xml version="1.0" encoding="UTF-8" standalone="yes"?>
<members>
    <member>
        <email>marten@deinum.biz</email>
        <name>Marten Deinum</name>
        <phone>00-31-1234567890</phone>
    </member>
    <member>
        <email>john@doe.com</email>
        <name>John Doe</name>
        <phone>1-800-800-800</phone>
    </member>
    <member>
        <email>jane@doe.com</email>
        <name>Jane Doe</name>
        <phone>1-801-802-803</phone>
    </member>
</members>
```

This XML payload represents a simple approach to generating a REST service's response. As the recipes in this chapter progress, you will learn more sophisticated approaches, such as the ability to create widely used REST service payloads such as RSS, Atom, and JSON.

If you look closely at the REST service endpoint or URL described in the previous paragraph, you'll note that it has an .xml extension. If you try another extension—or even omit the extension—this particular REST service may not be triggered. This last behavior is directly tied to Spring MVC and how it handles view resolution. It has nothing do with REST services per se.

By default, since the view associated with this particular REST service handler method returns XML, it's triggered by an .xml extension. This allows the same handler method to support multiple views. For example, it can be convenient for a request like http://[host_name]/[app-name]/members.pdf to return the same information in a PDF document, as well as a request like http://[host_name]/[app-name]/members.html to return content in HTML or a request like http://[host_name]/[app-name]/members.xml to return XML for a REST request.

So, what happens to a request with no URL extension, like http://[host_name]/[app-name]/members? This also depends heavily on Spring MVC view resolution. For this purpose, Spring MVC supports a process called *content negotiation*, by which a view is determined based on a request's extension or HTTP headers.

Since REST service requests typically have HTTP headers in the form Accept: application/xml, Spring MVC configured to use content negotiation can determine to serve XML (REST) payloads to such requests even if requests are made extensionless. This also allows extensionless requests to be made in formats such as HTML, PDF, and XLS, all simply based on HTTP headers. Recipe 3-7 in Chapter 3 discusses content negotiation.

Use @ResponseBody to Produce XML

Using `MarshallingView` to produce XML is one way of producing results; however, when you want to have multiple representations (JSON, for instance) of the same data (a list of `Member` objects), adding another view can be a cumbersome task. Instead, you can rely on the Spring MVC `HttpMessageConverters` to convert an object to the representation requested by the user. The following code shows the changes made to `RestMemberController`:

```
@Controller
public class RestMemberController {
...
    @RequestMapping("/members")
    @ResponseBody
    public Members getRestMembers() {
        Members members = new Members();
        members.addMembers(memberService.findAll());
        return members;
    }
}
```

The first change is that you have now, additionally, annotated the controller method with `@ResponseBody`. This annotation tells Spring MVC that the result of the method should be used as the body of the response. Because you want XML, this marshalling is done by the `Jaxb2RootElementHttpMessageConverter` class provided by Spring. The second change is that because of the `@ResponseBody` annotation, you don't need the view name anymore but can simply return the `Members` object.

■ **Tip** When using Spring 4 or higher instead of annotating the method with `@ResponseBody`, you can also annotate your controller with `@RestController` instead of `@Controller`, which would give the same result. This is especially convenient if you have a single controller with multiple methods.

These changes also allow you to clean up your configuration, as you don't need `MarshallingView` and `Jaxb2Marshaller` anymore.

```
package com.apress.springrecipes.court.web.config;

import org.springframework.context.annotation.Bean;
import org.springframework.context.annotation.ComponentScan;
import org.springframework.context.annotation.Configuration;
import org.springframework.web.servlet.config.annotation.EnableWebMvc;

@Configuration
@EnableWebMvc
@ComponentScan(basePackages = "com.apress.springrecipes.court")
public class CourtRestConfiguration {}
```

When the application is deployed and you do request the members from `http://localhost:8080/court/members.xml`, it will yield the same results as before.

```xml
<?xml version="1.0" encoding="UTF-8" standalone="yes"?>
<members>
    <member>
        <email>marten@deinum.biz</email>
        <name>Marten Deinum</name>
        <phone>00-31-1234567890</phone>
    </member>
    <member>
        <email>john@doe.com</email>
        <name>John Doe</name>
        <phone>1-800-800-800</phone>
    </member>
    <member>
        <email>jane@doe.com</email>
        <name>Jane Doe</name>
        <phone>1-801-802-803</phone>
    </member>
</members>
```

Use @PathVariable to Limit the Results

It's common for REST service requests to have parameters. This is done to limit or filter a service's payload. For example, a request in the form http://[host_name]/[app-name]/member/353/ can be used to retrieve information exclusively on member 353. Another variation can be a request like http://[host_name]/[app-name]/reservations/07-07-2010/ to retrieve reservations made on the date July 7, 2010.

To use parameters for constructing a REST service in Spring, you use the @PathVariable annotation. The @PathVariable annotation is added as an input parameter to the handler method, per Spring's MVC conventions, for it to be used inside the handler method body. The following snippet illustrates a handler method for a REST service using the @PathVariable annotation:

```java
import org.springframework.web.bind.annotation.PathVariable;

@Controller
public class RestMemberController {
...
    @RequestMapping("/member/{memberid}")
    @ResponseBody
    public Member getMember(@PathVariable("memberid") long memberID) {
        return memberService.find(memberID);
    }
}
```

Notice the @RequestMapping value contains {memberid}. Values surrounded by { } are used to indicate that URL parameters are variables. Further note that the handler method is defined with the input parameter @PathVariable("memberid") long memberID. This last declaration associates whatever memberid value forms part of the URL and assigns it to a variable named memberID that can be accessible inside the handler method. Therefore, REST endpoints in the form /member/353/ and /member/777/ will be processed by this last handler method, with the memberID variable being assigned values of 353 and 777, respectively. Inside the handler method, the appropriate queries can be made for members 353 and 777—via the memberID variable—and returned as the REST service's payload.

189

A request to `http://localhost:8080/court/member/2` will result in an XML representation of the member with an ID of 2.

```xml
<?xml version="1.0" encoding="UTF-8" standalone="yes"?>
<member>
    <email>john@doe.com</email>
    <name>John Doe</name>
    <phone>1-800-800-800</phone>
</member>
```

In addition to the supporting { } notation, it's also possible to use a wildcard (*) notation for defining REST endpoints. This is often the case when a design team has opted to use expressive URLs (often called *pretty URLs*) or opts to use search engine optimization (SEO) techniques to make a REST URL search engine friendly. The following snippet illustrates a declaration for a REST service using the wildcard notation:

```java
@RequestMapping("/member/*/{memberid}")
@ResponseBody
public Member getMember(@PathVariable("memberid") long memberID) { ... }
```

In this case, the addition of a wildcard doesn't have any influence over the logic performed by the REST service. But it will match endpoint requests in the form of /member/John+Smith/353/ and /member/Mary+Jones/353/, which can have an important impact on end user readability and SEO.

It's also worth mentioning that data binding can be used in the definition of handler methods for REST endpoints. The following snippet illustrates a declaration for a REST service using data binding:

```java
@InitBinder
public void initBinder(WebDataBinder binder) {
    SimpleDateFormat dateFormat = new SimpleDateFormat("yyyy-MM-dd");
    binder.registerCustomEditor(Date.class, new CustomDateEditor(dateFormat, false));
}

@RequestMapping("/reservations/{date}")
public void getReservation(@PathVariable("date") Date resDate) { ... }
```

In this case, a request in the form http://[host_name]/[app-name]/reservations/07-07-2010/ is matched by this last handler method, with the value 07-07-2010 passed into the handler method—as the variable resDate—where it can be used to filter the REST web service payload.

Use ResponseEntity to Inform the Client

The endpoint for retrieving a single Member instance returns either a valid member or nothing at all. Both lead to a request that will send the HTTP response code 200, which means OK, back to the client. However, this is probably not what your users will expect. When working with resources, you should inform them of the fact that a resource cannot be found. Ideally, you would want to return the HTTP response code 404, which indicates "not found." The following code snippet shows the modified getMember method:

```java
package com.apress.springrecipes.court.web;

import org.springframework.http.HttpStatus;
import org.springframework.http.ResponseEntity;
...
```

```
@Controller
public class RestMemberController {
...
    @RequestMapping("/member/{memberid}")
    @ResponseBody
    public ResponseEntity<Member> getMember(@PathVariable("memberid") long memberID) {
        Member member = memberService.find(memberID);
        if (member != null) {
            return new ResponseEntity<Member>(member, HttpStatus.OK);
        }
        return new ResponseEntity(HttpStatus.NOT_FOUND);
    }
}
```

The return value of the method has been changed to ResponseEntity<Member>. The ResponseEntity class in Spring MVC acts as a wrapper for an object to be used as the body of the result together with an HTTP status code. When you find a Member, it is returned with HttpStatus.OK, which corresponds to an HTTP status code of 200. When there is no result, you return HttpStatus.NOT_FOUND, corresponding to the HTTP status code 404, which means "not found."

4-2. Publish JSON with REST Services

Problem

You want to publish a JavaScript Object Notation (JSON)–based REST service with Spring.

Solution

JSON has blossomed into a favorite payload format for REST services. However, unlike most REST service payloads, which rely on XML markup, JSON is different in the sense that its content is a special notation based on the JavaScript language. For this recipe, in addition to relying on Spring's REST support, you will also use the MappingJackson2JsonView class that forms part of Spring to facilitate the publication of JSON content.

Note The MappingJackson2JsonView class depends on the presence of the Jackson JSON processor library, version 2, which can be downloaded at http://wiki.fasterxml.com/JacksonDownload. If you are using Maven or Gradle you can simply add the Jackson library as a dependency in your projects build file.

If your Spring applications incorporate Ajax designs, it's likely that you'll find yourself designing REST services that publish JSON as their payload. This is mainly because of the limited processing capabilities in browsers. Although browsers can process and extract information from REST services that publish XML payloads, it's not very efficient. By instead delivering payloads in JSON, which is based on a language for which browsers have a native interpreter—JavaScript—the processing and extraction of data becomes more efficient. Unlike RSS and Atom feeds, which are standards, JSON has no specific structure it needs to follow—except its syntax, which you'll explore shortly. Therefore, a JSON element's payload structure is likely to be determined in coordination with the team members charged with an application's Ajax design.

How It Works

The first thing you need to do is determine the information you want to publish as a JSON payload. This information can be located in an RDBMS or text file, be accessed through JDBC or ORM, or inclusively be part of a Spring bean or some other type of construct. Describing how to obtain this information would go beyond the scope of this recipe, so we will assume you'll use whatever means you deem appropriate to access it. In case you're unfamiliar with JSON, the following snippet illustrates a fragment of this format:

```
{
    "glossary": {
        "title": "example glossary",
        "GlossDiv": {
            "title": "S",
            "GlossList": {
                "GlossEntry": {
                    "ID": "SGML",
                    "SortAs": "SGML",
                    "GlossTerm": "Standard Generalized Markup Language",
                    "Acronym": "SGML",
                    "Abbrev": "ISO 8879:1986",
                    "GlossDef": {
                        "para": "A meta-markup language, used to create markup
                        languages such as DocBook.",
                        "GlossSeeAlso": ["GML", "XML"]
                    },
                    "GlossSee": "markup"
                }
            }
        }
    }
}
```

As you can observe, a JSON payload consists of text and separators such as { , } ,[,] , :, and ". We won't go into details about using one separator over another, but it suffices to say this type of syntax makes it easier for a JavaScript engine to access and manipulate data than if it was to process it in an XML-type format.

Use MappingJackson2JsonView to Produce XML

Since you've already explored how to publish data using a REST service in recipes 4-1 and 4-3, we'll cut to the chase and show you the actual handler method needed in a Spring MVC controller to achieve this process.

```
@RequestMapping("/members")
public String getRestMembers(Model model) {

    Members members = new Members();
    members.addMembers(memberService.findAll());
    model.addAttribute("members", members);
    return "jsonmembertemplate";
}
```

You probably notice that it is quite similar to the controller method mentioned in recipe 4-1. The only difference is that you return a different name for the view. The name of the view you are returning here, jsonmembertemplate, is different and maps to a MappingJackson2JsonView view. You need to configure this view in your configuration class.

```
@Configuration
@EnableWebMvc
@ComponentScan(basePackages = "com.apress.springrecipes.court")
public class CourtRestConfiguration {
    ...
    @Bean
    public View jsonmembertemplate() {
        MappingJackson2JsonView view = new MappingJackson2JsonView();
        view.setPrettyPrint(true);
        return view;
    }
}
```

The MappingJackson2JsonView view uses the Jackson2 library to convert objects to and from JSON. It uses a Jackson2 ObjectMapper instance for the conversion. When a request is made to http://localhost:8080/court/members.json, the controller method will be invoked, and a JSON representation will be returned.

```
{
    "members" : {
        "members" : [ {
            "name" : "Marten Deinum",
            "phone" : "00-31-1234567890",
            "email" : "marten@deinum.biz"
        }, {
            "name" : "John Doe",
            "phone" : "1-800-800-800",
            "email" : "john@doe.com"
        }, {
            "name" : "Jane Doe",
            "phone" : "1-801-802-803",
            "email" : "jane@doe.com"
        } ]
    }
}
```

Actually, this JSON will be produced by each call to /members or /members.* (for instance, /members.xml will also produce JSON). Let's add the method and view from recipe 4-1 to the controller.

```
@Controller
public class RestMemberController {
...
    @RequestMapping(value="/members", produces=MediaType.APPLICATION_XML_VALUE)
    public String getRestMembersXml(Model model) {
        Members members = new Members();
        members.addMembers(memberService.findAll());
        model.addAttribute("members", members);
        return "xmlmembertemplate";
    }
```

193

```
@RequestMapping(value="/members", produces= MediaType.APPLICATION_JSON_VALUE)
public String getRestMembersJson(Model model) {
    Members members = new Members();
    members.addMembers(memberService.findAll());
    model.addAttribute("members", members);
    return "jsonmembertemplate";
}
}
```

You have now a getMembersXml method and a getMembersJson method; both are basically the same with the distinction that they return a different view name. Notice the produces attribute on the @RequestMapping annotation. This is used to determine which method to call: /members.xml will now produce XML, whereas /members.json will produce JSON.

Although this approach works, duplicating all the methods for the different supported view types isn't a feasible solution for enterprise applications. You could create a helper method to reduce the duplication, but you would still need a lot of boilerplate because of the differences in the @RequestMapping annotations.

Use @ResponseBody to Produce JSON

Using a MappingJackson2JsonView to produce JSON is one way of producing results; however, as mentioned in the previous section, it can be troublesome, especially with multiple supported view types. Instead, you can rely on the Spring MVC HttpMessageConverters to convert an object to the representation requested by the user. The following code shows the changes made to RestMemberController:

```
@Controller
public class RestMemberController {
...
    @RequestMapping("/members")
    @ResponseBody
    public Members getRestMembers() {
        Members members = new Members();
        members.addMembers(memberService.findAll());
        return members;
    }
}
```

The first change is that you have now, additionally, annotated the controller method with @ResponseBody. This annotation tells Spring MVC that the result of the method should be used as the body of the response. Because you want JSON, this marshalling is done by the Jackson2JsonMessageConverter class provided by Spring. The second change is that because of the @ResponseBody annotation, you don't need the view name anymore but can simply return the Members object.

■ **Tip** When using Spring 4 or higher instead of annotating the method with @ResponseBody, you can also annotate your controller with @RestController instead of @Controller, which would give the same result. This is especially convenient if you have a single controller with multiple methods.

These changes also allow you to clean up your configuration because you don't need MappingJackson2JsonView anymore.

```
package com.apress.springrecipes.court.web.config;

import org.springframework.context.annotation.Bean;
import org.springframework.context.annotation.ComponentScan;
import org.springframework.context.annotation.Configuration;
import org.springframework.web.servlet.config.annotation.EnableWebMvc;

@Configuration
@EnableWebMvc
@ComponentScan(basePackages = "com.apress.springrecipes.court")
public class CourtRestConfiguration {}
```

When the application is deployed and you request the members from http://localhost:8080/court/members.json, it will give the same results as before.

```
{
    "members" : {
        "members" : [ {
            "name" : "Marten Deinum",
            "phone" : "00-31-1234567890",
            "email" : "marten@deinum.biz"
        }, {
            "name" : "John Doe",
            "phone" : "1-800-800-800",
            "email" : "john@doe.com"
        }, {
            "name" : "Jane Doe",
            "phone" : "1-801-802-803",
            "email" : "jane@doe.com"
        } ]
    }
}
```

You probably noticed that RestMemberController and CourtRestConfiguration are now the same as in recipe 4-1. When calling http://localhost:8080/court/members.xml, you will get XML.

How is this possible without any additional configuration? Spring MVC will detect what is on the classpath; when it automatically detects JAXB 2, Jackson, and Rome (see recipe 4-4), it will register the appropriate HttpMessageConverter for the available technologies.

Use GSON to Produce JSON

Up until now you have been using Jackson to produce JSON from your objects; another popular library is GSON, and Spring has out-of-the-box support for it. To use GSON, you will need to add it to your classpath (instead of Jackson), and then it will be used to produce the JSON.

When using Maven, add the following dependency:

```
<dependency>
    <groupId>com.google.code.gson</groupId>
    <artifactId>gson</artifactId>
    <version>2.8.0</version>
</dependency>
```

When using Gradle, add the following:

```
compile 'com.google.code.gson:gson:2.8.0'
```

This, just like when using Jackson, is all you need to implement JSON serialization with GSON. If you start the application and call `http://localhost:8080/court/members.json`, you will still receive JSON but now through GSON instead.

4-3. Access a REST Service with Spring

Problem

You want to access a REST service from a third party (e.g., Google, Yahoo, or another business partner) and use its payload inside a Spring application.

Solution

Accessing a third-party REST service inside a Spring application revolves around the use of the Spring `RestTemplate` class. The `RestTemplate` class is designed on the same principles as many other Spring `*Template` classes (e.g., `JdbcTemplate`, `JmsTemplate`), providing a simplified approach with default behaviors for performing lengthy tasks. This means the processes of invoking a REST service and using its returning payload are streamlined in Spring applications.

How It Works

Before describing the particularities of the `RestTemplate` class, it's worth exploring the life cycle of a REST service so you're aware of the actual work the `RestTemplate` class performs. Exploring the life cycle of a REST service can best be done from a browser, so open your favorite browser on your workstation to get started. The first thing that's needed is a REST service endpoint. You are going to reuse the endpoint you created in recipe 4-2. This endpoint should be available at `http://localhost:8080/court/members.xml` (or `.json`). If you load this last REST service endpoint on your browser, the browser performs a GET request, which is one of the most popular HTTP requests supported by REST services. Upon loading the REST service, the browser displays a responding payload like the following:

```xml
<?xml version="1.0" encoding="UTF-8" standalone="yes"?>
<members>
    <member>
        <email>marten@deinum.biz</email>
        <name>Marten Deinum</name>
        <phone>00-31-1234567890</phone>
    </member>
    <member>
        <email>john@doe.com</email>
        <name>John Doe</name>
        <phone>1-800-800-800</phone>
    </member>
    <member>
        <email>jane@doe.com</email>
        <name>Jane Doe</name>
```

```
    <phone>1-801-802-803</phone>
  </member>
</members>
```

This last payload represents a well-formed XML fragment, which is in line with most REST services' responses. The actual meaning of the payload is highly dependent on a REST service. In this case, the XML tags (<members>, <member>, etc.) are definitions set forth by yourself, while the character data enclosed in each XML tag represents information related to a REST service's request.

It's the task of a REST service consumer (i.e., you) to know the payload structure—sometimes referred to as the *vocabulary*—of a REST service to appropriately process its information. Though this last REST service relies on what can be considered a custom vocabulary, a series of REST services often relies on standardized vocabularies (e.g., RSS), which make the processing of REST service payloads uniform. In addition, it's worth noting that some REST services provide Web Application Description Language (WADL) contracts to facilitate the discovery and consumption of payloads.

Now that you're familiar with a REST service's life cycle using your browser, you can take a look at how to use the Spring `RestTemplate` class to incorporate a REST service's payload into a Spring application. Given that the `RestTemplate` class is designed to call REST services, it should come as no surprise that its main methods are closely tied to REST's underpinnings, which are the HTTP protocol's methods: HEAD, GET, POST, PUT, DELETE, and OPTIONS. Table 4-1 contains the main methods supported by the `RestTemplate` class.

Table 4-1. RestTemplate Class Methods Based on HTTP Protocol's Request Methods

Method	Description
`headForHeaders(String, Object...)`	Performs an HTTP HEAD operation
`getForObject(String, Class, Object...)`	Performs an HTTP GET operation and returns the result as a type of the given class
`getForObject(String, Class, Object...)`	Performs an HTTP GET operation and returns a `ResponseEntity`
`postForLocation(String, Object, Object...)`	Performs an HTTP POST operation and returns the value of the location header
`postForObject(String, Object, Class, Object...)`	Performs an HTTP POST operation and returns the result as a type of the given class
`postForEntity(String, Object, Class, Object...)`	Performs an HTTP POST operation and returns a `ResponseEntity`
`put(String, Object, Object...)`	Performs an HTTP PUT operation
`delete(String, Object...)`	Performs an HTTP DELETE operation
`optionsForAllow(String, Object...)`	Performs an HTTP OPTIONS operation
`execute(String, HttpMethod, RequestCallback, ResponseExtractor, Object...)`	Can perform any HTTP operation with the exception of CONNECT

As you can observe in Table 4-1, the `RestTemplate` class methods are prefixed with a series of HTTP protocol methods that include HEAD, GET, POST, PUT, DELETE, and OPTIONS. In addition, the execute method serves as a general-purpose method that can perform any HTTP operation, including the more esoteric HTTP protocol TRACE method, except the CONNECT method, which is not supported by the underlying `HttpMethod` enum used by the execute method. Note that by far the most common HTTP method used in REST services is GET since it represents a safe operation to obtain information (i.e., it doesn't modify any data). On the other hand, HTTP methods such as PUT, POST, and DELETE are designed to modify a provider's information, which makes them less likely to be supported by a REST service provider. For cases in which data modification needs to take place, many providers opt for the SOAP protocol, which is an alternative mechanism to using REST services.

Now that you're aware of the RestTemplate class methods, you can move on to invoking the same REST service you did with your browser previously, except this time using Java code from the Spring Framework. The following code illustrates a class that accesses the REST service and returns its contents to System.out:

```java
package com.apress.springrecipes.court;

import org.springframework.web.client.RestTemplate;

public class Main {

    public static void main(String[] args) throws Exception {
        final String uri = "http://localhost:8080/court/members.json";
        RestTemplate restTemplate = new RestTemplate();
        String result = restTemplate.getForObject(uri, String.class);
        System.out.println(result);
    }
}
```

■ **Caution**   Some REST service providers restrict access to their data feeds depending on the requesting party. Access is generally denied by relying on data present in a request (e.g., HTTP headers or IP address). So, depending on the circumstances, a provider can return an access denied response even when a data feed appears to be working in another medium (e.g., you might be able to access a REST service in a browser but get an accessed denied response when attempting to access the same feed from a Spring application). This depends on the terms of use set forth by a REST provider.

The first line declares the import statement needed to access the RestTemplate class within a class's body. First you need to create an instance of the RestTemplate class. Next, you can find a call made to the getForObject method that belongs to the RestTemplate class, which as described in Table 4-1 is used to perform an HTTP GET operation—just like the one performed by a browser to obtain a REST service's payload. There are two important aspects related to this last method: its response and its parameters.

The response of calling the getForObject method is assigned to a String object. This means the same output you saw in your browser for this REST service (i.e., the XML structure) is assigned to a String. Even if you've never processed XML in Java, you're likely aware that extracting and manipulating data as a Java String is not an easy task. In other words, there are classes better suited for processing XML data (and with it a REST service's payload) than a String object. For the moment, just keep this in mind; other recipes in the chapter illustrate how to better extract and manipulate the data obtained from a REST service.

The parameters passed to the getForObject method consist of the actual REST service endpoint. The first parameter corresponds to the URL (i.e., endpoint) declaration. Notice the URL is identical to the one used when you relied on a browser to call it.

When you execute this, the output will be the same as in the browser except that it is now printed in the console.

Retrieve Data from a Parameterized URL

The previous section showed how you can call a URI to retrieve data, but what about a URI that requires parameters? You don't want to hard-code parameters into the URL. With the RestTemplate class, you can use a URL with placeholders, and these placeholders will be replaced with actual values upon execution. Placeholders are defined using { and }, just as with request mapping (see recipes 4-1 and 4-2).

The URI http://localhost:8080/court/member/{memberId} is an example of such a parameterized URI. To be able to call this method, you need to pass in a value for the placeholder. You can do this by using a Map and passing that as the third parameter to the getForObject method of the RestTemplate class.

```java
public class Main {

    public static void main(String[] args) throws Exception {
        final String uri = "http://localhost:8080/court/member/{memberId}";
        Map<String, String> params = new HashMap<>();
        params.put("memberId", "1");
        RestTemplate restTemplate = new RestTemplate();
        String result = restTemplate.getForObject(uri, String.class, params );
        System.out.println(result);
    }
}
```

This last snippet makes use of the HashMap class—part of the Java collections framework—and creates an instance with the corresponding REST service parameters, which is later passed to the getForObject method of the RestTemplate class. The results obtained by passing either a series of String parameters or a single Map parameter to the various RestTemplate methods are identical.

Retrieve Data as a Mapped Object

Instead of returning a String to be used in your application, you can also (re)use your Members and Member classes to map the result. Instead of passing in String.class as the second parameter, pass Members.class, and the response will be mapped onto this class.

```java
package com.apress.springrecipes.court;

import com.apress.springrecipes.court.domain.Members;
import org.springframework.web.client.RestTemplate;

public class Main {

    public static void main(String[] args) throws Exception {
        final String uri = "http://localhost:8080/court/members.xml";
        RestTemplate restTemplate = new RestTemplate();
        Members result = restTemplate.getForObject(uri, Members.class);
        System.out.println(result);
    }
}
```

The RestTemplate class makes use of the same HttpMessageConverter infrastructure as a controller with @ResponseBody marked methods. As JAXB 2 (as well as Jackson) is automatically detected, mapping to a JAXB-mapped object is quite easy.

4-4. Publish RSS and Atom Feeds

Problem

You want to publish an RSS or Atom feed in a Spring application.

Solution

RSS and Atom feeds have become a popular means by which to publish information. Access to these types of feeds is provided by means of a REST service, which means building a REST service is a prerequisite to publishing RSS and Atom feeds. In addition to relying on Spring's REST support, it's also convenient to rely on a third-party library especially designed to deal with the particularities of RSS and Atom feeds. This makes it easier for a REST service to publish this type of XML payload. For this last purpose, you will use Project Rome, an open source library available at `http://rometools.github.io/rome/`.

■ **Tip**   Even though RSS and Atom feeds are often categorized as news feeds, they have surpassed this initial usage scenario of providing just news. Nowadays, RSS and Atom feeds are used to publish information related to blogs, weather, travel, and many other things in a cross-platform manner (i.e., using XML). Hence, if you require publishing information of any sort that's to be accessible in a cross-platform manner, doing so as RSS or Atom feeds can be an excellent choice given their wide adoption (e.g., many applications support them, and many developers know their structure).

How It Works

The first thing you need to do is determine the information you want to publish as an RSS or Atom news feed. This information can be located in an RDBMS or text file, be accessed through JDBC or ORM, or inclusively be part of a Spring bean or some other type of construct. Describing how to obtain this information would go beyond the scope of this recipe, so we will assume you'll use whatever means you deem appropriate to access it. Once you've pinpointed the information you want to publish, it's necessary to structure it as an RSS or Atom feed, which is where Project Rome comes into the picture.

In case you're unfamiliar with an Atom feed's structure, the following snippet illustrates a fragment of this format:

```
<?xml version="1.0" encoding="utf-8"?>
<feed xmlns="http://www.w3.org/2005/Atom">
    <title>Example Feed</title>
    <link href="http://example.org/"/>
    <updated>2010-08-31T18:30:02Z</updated>
    <author>
        <name>John Doe</name>
    </author>
    <id>urn:uuid:60a76c80-d399-11d9-b93C-0003939e0af6</id>
    <entry>
        <title>Atom-Powered Robots Run Amok</title>
        <link href="http://example.org/2010/08/31/atom03"/>
        <id>urn:uuid:1225c695-cfb8-4ebb-aaaa-80da344efa6a</id>
```

```xml
        <updated>2010-08-31T18:30:02Z</updated>
        <summary>Some text.</summary>
    </entry>
</feed>
```

The following snippet illustrates a fragment of an RSS feed's structure:

```xml
<?xml version="1.0" encoding="utf-8"?>
<rss version="2.0">
    <channel>
        <title>RSS Example</title>
        <description>This is an example of an RSS feed</description>
        <link>http://www.example.org/link.htm</link>
        <lastBuildDate>Mon, 28 Aug 2006 11:12:55 -0400 </lastBuildDate>
        <pubDate>Tue, 31 Aug 2010 09:00:00 -0400</pubDate>
        <item>
            <title>Item Example</title>
            <description>This is an example of an Item</description>
            <link>http://www.example.org/link.htm</link>
            <guid isPermaLink="false"> 1102345</guid>
            <pubDate>Tue, 31 Aug 2010 09:00:00 -0400</pubDate>
        </item>
    </channel>
</rss>
```

As you can observe from these last two snippets, RSS and Atom feeds are just XML payloads that rely on a series of elements to publish information. Though going into the finer details of either an RSS or Atom feed structure would require a book in itself, both formats possess a series of common characteristics; chief among them are these:

- They have a metadata section to describe the contents of a feed (e.g., the <author> and <title> elements for the Atom format and the <description> and <pubDate> elements for the RSS format).

- They have recurring elements to describe information (e.g., the <entry> element for the Atom feed format and the <item> element for the RSS feed format). In addition, each recurring element has its own set of elements with which to further describe information.

- They have multiple versions. RSS versions include 0.90, 0.91 Netscape, 0.91 Userland, 0.92, 0.93, 0.94, 1.0, and 2.0. Atom versions include 0.3 and 1.0. Project Rome allows you to create a feed's metadata section, recurring elements, and any of the previously mentioned versions, from the information available in the Java code (e.g., Strings, Maps, or other such constructs).

Now that you're aware of the structure of RSS and Atom feeds, as well as the role Project Rome plays in this recipe, let's take a look at a Spring MVC controller charged with presenting a feed to an end user:

```java
//FINAL
package com.apress.springrecipes.court.web;

import com.apress.springrecipes.court.feeds.TournamentContent;
import org.springframework.stereotype.Controller;
import org.springframework.ui.Model;
import org.springframework.web.bind.annotation.RequestMapping;
```

```
import java.util.ArrayList;
import java.util.Date;
import java.util.List;

@Controller
public class FeedController {
    @RequestMapping("/atomfeed")
    public String getAtomFeed(Model model) {
        List<TournamentContent> tournamentList = new ArrayList<>();
        tournamentList.add(TournamentContent.of("ATP", new Date(), "Australian Open",
        "www.australianopen.com"));
        tournamentList.add(TournamentContent.of("ATP", new Date(), "Roland Garros",
        "www.rolandgarros.com"));
        tournamentList.add(TournamentContent.of("ATP", new Date(), "Wimbledon",
        "www.wimbledon.org"));
        tournamentList.add(TournamentContent.of("ATP", new Date(), "US Open",
        "www.usopen.org"));
        model.addAttribute("feedContent", tournamentList);

        return "atomfeedtemplate";
    }

    @RequestMapping("/rssfeed")
    public String getRSSFeed(Model model) {
        List<TournamentContent> tournamentList;
        tournamentList = new ArrayList<TournamentContent>();
        tournamentList.add(TournamentContent.of("FIFA", new Date(), "World Cup",
        "www.fifa.com/worldcup/"));
        tournamentList.add(TournamentContent.of("FIFA", new Date(), "U-20 World Cup",
        "www.fifa.com/u20worldcup/"));
        tournamentList.add(TournamentContent.of("FIFA", new Date(), "U-17 World Cup",
        "www.fifa.com/u17worldcup/"));
        tournamentList.add(TournamentContent.of("FIFA", new Date(), "Confederations Cup",
        "www.fifa.com/confederationscup/"));
        model.addAttribute("feedContent", tournamentList);

        return "rssfeedtemplate";
    }
}
```

This Spring MVC controller has two handler methods. One is called getAtomFeed(), which is mapped to a URL in the form http://[host_name]/[app-name]/atomfeed, and the other is called getRSSFeed(), which is mapped to a URL in the form http://[host_name]/[app-name]/rssfeed.

Each handler method defines a List of TournamentContent objects, where the backing class for a TournamentContent object is a POJO. This List is then assigned to the handler method's Model object for it to become accessible to the returning view. The returning logical views for each handler methods are atomfeedtemplate and rssfeedtemplate, respectively. These logical views are defined in the following manner inside a Spring configuration class:

```
package com.apress.springrecipes.court.web.config;

import com.apress.springrecipes.court.feeds.AtomFeedView;
import com.apress.springrecipes.court.feeds.RSSFeedView;
```

CHAPTER 4 ■ SPRING REST

```
import org.springframework.context.annotation.Bean;
import org.springframework.context.annotation.ComponentScan;
import org.springframework.context.annotation.Configuration;
import org.springframework.web.servlet.HandlerMapping;
import org.springframework.web.servlet.config.annotation.EnableWebMvc;
import org.springframework.web.servlet.handler.BeanNameUrlHandlerMapping;

@Configuration
@EnableWebMvc
@ComponentScan(basePackages = "com.apress.springrecipes.court")
public class CourtRestConfiguration {

    @Bean
    public AtomFeedView atomfeedtemplate() {
        return new AtomFeedView();
    }

    @Bean
    public RSSFeedView rssfeedtemplate() {
        return new RSSFeedView();
    }
...
}
```

As you can observe, each logical view is mapped to a class. Each of these classes is charged with implementing the necessary logic to build either an Atom or RSS view. If you recall from Chapter 3, you used an identical approach (i.e., using classes) for implementing PDF and Excel views.

In the case of Atom and RSS views, Spring comes equipped with two classes specially equipped and built on the foundations of Project Rome. These classes are AbstractAtomFeedView and AbstractRssFeedView. Such classes provide the foundations to build an Atom or RSS feed, without dealing in the finer details of each of these formats.

The following code illustrates the AtomFeedView class that implements the AbstractAtomFeedView class and is used to back the atomfeedtemplate logical view:

```
package com.apress.springrecipes.court.feeds;

import com.rometools.rome.feed.atom.Content;
import com.rometools.rome.feed.atom.Entry;
import com.rometools.rome.feed.atom.Feed;
import org.springframework.web.servlet.view.feed.AbstractAtomFeedView;

import javax.servlet.http.HttpServletRequest;
import javax.servlet.http.HttpServletResponse;
import java.util.List;
import java.util.Map;
import java.util.stream.Collectors;

public class AtomFeedView extends AbstractAtomFeedView {

    @Override
    protected void buildFeedMetadata(Map model, Feed feed, HttpServletRequest request) {
        feed.setId("tag:tennis.org");
        feed.setTitle("Grand Slam Tournaments");
```

```
        List<TournamentContent> tournamentList = (List<TournamentContent>)
        model.get("feedContent");

        feed.setUpdated(tournamentList.stream().map(TournamentContent::getPublicationDate).
        sorted().findFirst().orElse(null));

    }

    @Override
    protected List buildFeedEntries(Map model, HttpServletRequest request,
    HttpServletResponse response)
        throws Exception {
        List<TournamentContent> tournamentList = (List<TournamentContent>) model.
        get("feedContent");
        return tournamentList.stream().map(this::toEntry).collect(Collectors.toList());
    }

    private Entry toEntry(TournamentContent tournament) {
        Entry entry = new Entry();
        String date = String.format("%1$tY-%1$tm-%1$td", tournament.getPublicationDate());
        entry.setId(String.format("tag:tennis.org,%s:%d", date, tournament.getId()));
        entry.setTitle(String.format("%s - Posted by %s", tournament.getName(), tournament.
        getAuthor()));
        entry.setUpdated(tournament.getPublicationDate());

        Content summary = new Content();
        summary.setValue(String.format("%s - %s", tournament.getName(), tournament.
        getLink()));
        entry.setSummary(summary);
        return entry;
    }
}
```

The first thing to notice about this class is that it imports several Project Rome classes from the com.sun.syndication.feed.atom package, in addition to implementing the AbstractAtomFeedView class provided by the Spring Framework. In doing so, the only thing that's needed next is to provide a feed's implementation details for two methods inherited from the AbstractAtomFeedView class: buildFeedMetadata and buildFeedEntries.

buildFeedMetadata has three input parameters: a Map object that represents the data used to build the feed (i.e., data assigned inside the handler method, in this case a List of TournamentContent objects), a Feed object based on a Project Rome class that is used to manipulate the feed itself, and an HttpServletRequest object in case it's necessary to manipulate the HTTP request.

Inside the buildFeedMetadata method, you can observe several calls are made to the Feed object's setter methods (e.g., setId, setTitle, setUpdated). Two of these calls are made using hard-coded strings, while another is made with a value determined after looping over a feed's data (i.e., the Map object). All these calls represent the assignment of an Atom feed's metadata information.

■ **Note**   Consult Project Rome's API if you want to assign more values to an Atom feed's metadata section, as well as specify a particular Atom version. The default version is Atom 1.0.

The buildFeedEntries method also has three input parameters: a Map object that represents the data used to build the feed (i.e., data assigned inside the handler method, in this case a List of TournamentContent objects), an HttpServletRequest object in case it's necessary to manipulate the HTTP request, and an HttpServletResponse object in case it's necessary to manipulate the HTTP response. It's also important to note that the buildFeedEntries method returns a List of objects, which in this case corresponds to a List of Entry objects based on a Project Rome class and containing an Atom feed's recurring elements.

Inside the buildFeedEntries method, you can observe that the Map object is accessed to obtain the feedContent object assigned inside the handler method. Once this is done, an empty List of Entry objects is created. Next, a loop is performed on the feedContent object, which contains a list of a List of TournamentContent objects, and for each element, an Entry object is created that is assigned to the top-level List of Entry objects. Once the loop is finished, the method returns a filled List of Entry objects.

■ **Note**   Consult Project Rome's API if you want to assign more values to an Atom feed's recurring elements section.

Upon deploying the previous class, in addition to the previously cited Spring MVC controller, accessing a URL in the form http://[host_name]/[app-name]/atomfeed.atom (or http://[host_name]/atomfeed.xml) would result in the following response:

```xml
<?xml version="1.0" encoding="UTF-8"?>
<feed xmlns="http://www.w3.org/2005/Atom">
    <title>Grand Slam Tournaments</title>
    <id>tag:tennis.org</id>
    <updated>2017-04-19T01:32:52Z</updated>
    <entry>
        <title>Australian Open - Posted by ATP</title>
        <id>tag:tennis.org,2017-04-19:5</id>
        <updated>2017-04-19T01:32:52Z</updated>
        <summary>Australian Open - www.australianopen.com</summary>
    </entry>
    <entry>
        <title>Roland Garros - Posted by ATP</title>
        <id>tag:tennis.org,2017-04-19:6</id>
        <updated>2017-04-19T01:32:52Z</updated>
        <summary>Roland Garros - www.rolandgarros.com</summary>
    </entry>
    <entry>
        <title>Wimbledon - Posted by ATP</title>
        <id>tag:tennis.org,2017-04-19:7</id>
        <updated>2017-04-19T01:32:52Z</updated>
        <summary>Wimbledon - www.wimbledon.org</summary>
    </entry>
    <entry>
        <title>US Open - Posted by ATP</title>
        <id>tag:tennis.org,2017-04-19:8</id>
        <updated>2017-04-19T01:32:52Z</updated>
        <summary>US Open - www.usopen.org</summary>
    </entry>
</feed>
```

Turning your attention to the remaining handler method—getRSSFeed—from the previous Spring MVC controller charged with building an RSS feed, you'll see that the process is similar to the one just described for building Atom feeds. The handler methods also creates a List of TournamentContent objects, which is then assigned to the handler method's Model object for it to become accessible to the returning view. The returning logical view in this case, though, now corresponds to one named rssfeedtemplate. As described earlier, this logical view is mapped to a class named RssFeedView.

The following code illustrates the RssFeedView class, which implements the AbstractRssFeedView class:

```java
package com.apress.springrecipes.court.feeds;

import com.rometools.rome.feed.rss.Channel;
import com.rometools.rome.feed.rss.Item;
import org.springframework.web.servlet.view.feed.AbstractRssFeedView;

import javax.servlet.http.HttpServletRequest;
import javax.servlet.http.HttpServletResponse;
import java.util.List;
import java.util.Map;
import java.util.stream.Collectors;

public class RSSFeedView extends AbstractRssFeedView {

    @Override
    protected void buildFeedMetadata(Map model, Channel feed, HttpServletRequest request) {
        feed.setTitle("World Soccer Tournaments");
        feed.setDescription("FIFA World Soccer Tournament Calendar");
        feed.setLink("tennis.org");

        List<TournamentContent> tournamentList = (List<TournamentContent>) model.
        get("feedContent");
        feed.setLastBuildDate(tournamentList.stream().map( TournamentContent::getPublication
        Date).sorted().findFirst().orElse(null) );
    }

    @Override
    protected List<Item> buildFeedItems(Map model, HttpServletRequest request,
    HttpServletResponse response)
        throws Exception {
        List<TournamentContent> tournamentList = (List<TournamentContent>) model.
        get("feedContent");

        return tournamentList.stream().map(this::toItem).collect(Collectors.toList());
    }

    private Item toItem(TournamentContent tournament) {
        Item item = new Item();
        item.setAuthor(tournament.getAuthor());
        item.setTitle(String.format("%s - Posted by %s", tournament.getName(),
        tournament.getAuthor()));
        item.setPubDate(tournament.getPublicationDate());
        item.setLink(tournament.getLink());
        return item;
    }
}
```

The first thing to notice about this class is that it imports several Project Rome classes from the com.sun.syndication.feed.rss package, in addition to implementing the AbstractRssFeedView class provided by the Spring Framework. Once it does so, the only thing that's needed next is to provide a feed's implementation details for two methods inherited from the AbstractRssFeedView class: buildFeedMetadata and buildFeedItems. The buildFeedMetadata method is similar in nature to the one by the same name used in building an Atom feed. Notice the buildFeedMetadata method manipulates a Channel object based on a Project Rome class, which is used to build RSS feeds, instead of a Feed object, which is used to build Atom feeds. The setter method calls made on the Channel object (e.g., setTitle, setDescription, setLink) represent the assignment of an RSS feed's metadata information. The buildFeedItems method, which differs in name from its Atom counterpart buildFeedEntries, is so named because an Atom feed's recurring elements are called *entries* and an RSS feed's recurring elements are *items*. Naming conventions aside, their logic is similar.

Inside the buildFeedItems method, you can observe that the Map object is accessed to obtain the feedContent object assigned inside the handler method. Once this is done, an empty List of Item objects is created. Next, a loop is performed on the feedContent object, which contains a List of TournamentContent objects, and for each element, an Item object is created that is assigned to the top-level List of Item objects. Once the loop is finished, the method returns a filled List of x§x§ objects.

■ **Note** Consult Project Rome's API if you want to assign more values to an RSS feed's metadata and recurring element sections, as well as specify a particular RSS version. The default version is RSS 2.0.

When you deploy the previous class, in addition to the previously cited Spring MVC controller, accessing a URL in the form http://[host_name]/rssfeed.rss (or http://[host_name]/rssfeed.xml) results in the following response:

```xml
<?xml version="1.0" encoding="UTF-8"?>
<rss version="2.0">
    <channel>
        <title>World Soccer Tournaments</title>
        <link>tennis.org</link>
        <description>FIFA World Soccer Tournament Calendar</description>
        <lastBuildDate>Wed, 19 Apr 2017 01:32:31 GMT</lastBuildDate>
        <item>
            <title>World Cup - Posted by FIFA</title>
            <link>www.fifa.com/worldcup/</link>
            <pubDate>Wed, 19 Apr 2017 01:32:31 GMT</pubDate>
            314861_4_EnFIFA</author>
        </item>
        <item>
            <title>U-20 World Cup - Posted by FIFA</title>
            <link>www.fifa.com/u20worldcup/</link>
            <pubDate>Wed, 19 Apr 2017 01:32:31 GMT</pubDate>
            314861_4_EnFIFA</author>
        </item>
        <item>
            <title>U-17 World Cup - Posted by FIFA</title>
            <link>www.fifa.com/u17worldcup/</link>
            <pubDate>Wed, 19 Apr 2017 01:32:31 GMT</pubDate>
            314861_4_EnFIFA</author>
```

```
        </item>
        <item>
            <title>Confederations Cup - Posted by FIFA</title>
            <link>www.fifa.com/confederationscup/</link>
            <pubDate>Wed, 19 Apr 2017 01:32:31 GMT</pubDate>
            314861_4_EnFIFA</author>
        </item>
    </channel>
</rss>
```

Summary

In this chapter, you learned how to develop and access REST services using Spring. REST services are closely tied to Spring MVC, whereby a controller acts to dispatch requests made to REST services, as well as access third-party REST services to use this information for application content.

You learned how REST services leverage annotations used in Spring MVC controllers, which included @RequestMapping to indicate service endpoints, as well as @PathVariable to specify access parameters for filtering a service's payload. In addition, you learned about Spring's XML marshallers, such as Jaxb2Marshaller, which allow application objects to be transformed into XML and be output as a REST service's payload. You also learned about Spring's RestTemplate class and how it supports the series of HTTP methods that include HEAD, GET, POST, PUT, and DELETE—all of which allow you to access and perform operations on third-party REST services directly from the context of a Spring application.

Finally, you explored how to publish Atom and RSS feeds in a Spring application by leveraging the Project Rome API.

CHAPTER 5

■ ■ ■

Spring MVC: Async Processing

When the Servlet API was released, the majority of the implementing containers used one thread per request. This meant a thread was blocked until the request processing had finished and the response was sent to the client.

However, in those early days, there weren't as many devices connected to the Internet as today. Because of the increased number of devices, the number of HTTP requests being handled has grown significantly, and because of this increase, for lots of web applications, keeping a thread blocked isn't feasible anymore. As of the Servlet 3 specification, it is possible to handle an HTTP request asynchronously and release the thread that initially handled HTTP request. The new thread will run in the background, and as soon as the result is available, it will be written to the client. This, when done right, can all take place in a nonblocking way on a Servlet 3.1–compliant servlet container. Of course, all resources being used also would have to be nonblocking.

In the past couple of years, there has also been an uptick in reactive programming, and as of Spring 5, it is possible to write reactive web applications. A reactive Spring project utilizes Project Reactor (just like Spring, it is maintained by Pivotal) as an implementation of the Reactive Streams API. It goes beyond the scope of this book to do a full dive into reactive programming, but in short it is a way of doing nonblocking functional programming.

Traditionally, when working with web applications, there would be a request; HTML would be rendered on the server and then get sent back to the client. The last couple of years, the job of rendering HTML moved to the client, and communication was done not through HTML but by returning JSON, XML, or another representation to the client. This was traditionally still a request-and-response cycle although it was driven by an async call from the client through the XMLHttpRequest object. However, there are also other ways of communicating between the client and server; you could utilize server-sent events to have one-way communication from the server to the client, and for full-duplex communication, you could use the WebSocket protocol.

5-1. Handle Requests Asynchronously with Controllers and TaskExecutor

Problem

To reduce the load on the servlet container, you want to asynchronously handle a request.

Solution

When a request comes in, it is handled synchronously, which blocks the HTTP request-handling thread. The response stays open and is available to be written to. This is useful when a call, for instance, takes some time to finish. Instead of blocking threads, you can have this processed in the background and return a value to the user when finished.

© Marten Deinum, Daniel Rubio, and Josh Long 2017
M. Deinum et al., *Spring 5 Recipes*, DOI 10.1007/978-1-4842-2790-9_5

How It Works

As mentioned in recipe 3-1, Spring MVC supports a number of return types from methods. In addition to the return types, the types in Table 5-1 are processed in an asynchronous way.

Table 5-1. *Asynchronous Return Types*

Type	Description
DeferredResult	Async result produced later from another thread
ListenableFuture<?>	Async result produced later from another thread; an equivalent alternative for DeferredResult
CompletableStage<?> / CompletableFuture<?>	Async result produced later from another thread; an equivalent alternative for DeferredResult
Callable<?>	Async computation with the result produced after the computation finishes
ResponseBodyEmitter	Can be used to write multiple objects to the response asynchronously
SseEmitter	Can be used to write a server-sent event asynchronously
StreamingResponseBody	Can be used to write to OutputStream asynchronously

The generic async return types can hold any of the return types for the controller, including an object to be added to the model, the name of the view, or even a ModelAndView object.

Configure Async Processing

To use the async processing features of Spring MVC, you first have to enable them. Async request-handling support has been added to the Servlet 3.0 specification, and to enable it, you have to tell all your filters and servlets to behave asynchronously. To do this, you can call the setAsyncSupported() method when registering a filter or servlet.

When writing a WebApplicationInitializer, you have to do the following:

```
public class CourtWebApplicationInitializer implements WebApplicationInitializer {

    public void onStartup(ServletContext ctx) {

        DispatcherServlet servlet = new DispatcherServlet();
        ServletRegistration.Dynamic registration = ctx.addServlet("dispatcher", servlet);
        registration.setAsyncSupported(true);
    }

}
```

■ **Note** When doing async processing, *all* the servlet filters and servlets in your app should have this property switched to true or async processing won't work!

Luckily, Spring helps you with this, and when using the AbstractAnnotationConfigDispatcherServlet Initializer as a superclass, this property is enabled by default for the registered DispatcherServlet and filters. To change it, override isAsyncSupported() and implement the logic to determine whether it should be on or off.

Depending on your needs, you probably also need to configure an AsyncTaskExecutor and wire that in the MVC configuration.

```
package com.apress.springrecipes.court.config;

import org.springframework.context.annotation.Bean;
import org.springframework.context.annotation.Configuration;
import org.springframework.core.task.AsyncTaskExecutor;
import org.springframework.scheduling.concurrent.ThreadPoolTaskExecutor;
import org.springframework.web.servlet.config.annotation.AsyncSupportConfigurer;
import org.springframework.web.servlet.config.annotation.WebMvcConfigurationSupport;

@Configuration
public class AsyncConfiguration extends WebMvcConfigurationSupport {

    @Override
    protected void configureAsyncSupport(AsyncSupportConfigurer configurer) {
        configurer.setDefaultTimeout(5000);
        configurer.setTaskExecutor(mvcTaskExecutor());
    }

    @Bean
    public ThreadPoolTaskExecutor mvcTaskExecutor() {
        ThreadPoolTaskExecutor taskExecutor = new ThreadPoolTaskExecutor();
        taskExecutor.setThreadGroupName("mvc-executor");
        return taskExecutor;
    }
}
```

To configure async processing, you need to override the configureAsyncSupport method of WebMvcConfigurationSupport; overriding this method gives you access to the AsyncSupportConfigurer and allows you to set the defaultTimeout and AsyncTaskExecutor values. The timeout is set to five seconds, and for an executor, you will use a ThreadPoolTaskExecutor (see also recipe 2-23).

Write an Asynchronous Controller

Writing a controller and having it handle the request asynchronously is as simple as changing the return type of the controller's handler method. Let's imagine that the call to ReservationService.query takes quite some time, but you don't want to block the server for that.

Use a Callable

Here's how to use a callable:

```java
package com.apress.springrecipes.court.web;

import com.apress.springrecipes.court.Delayer;
import com.apress.springrecipes.court.domain.Reservation;
import com.apress.springrecipes.court.service.ReservationService;
import org.springframework.stereotype.Controller;
import org.springframework.ui.Model;
import org.springframework.web.bind.annotation.GetMapping;
import org.springframework.web.bind.annotation.PostMapping;
import org.springframework.web.bind.annotation.RequestMapping;
import org.springframework.web.bind.annotation.RequestParam;

import java.util.List;
import java.util.concurrent.Callable;

@Controller
@RequestMapping("/reservationQuery")
public class ReservationQueryController {

    private final ReservationService reservationService;

    public ReservationQueryController(ReservationService reservationService) {
        this.reservationService = reservationService;
    }

    @GetMapping
    public void setupForm() {}

    @PostMapping
    public Callable<String> sumbitForm(@RequestParam("courtName") String courtName, Model model) {
        return () -> {
            List<Reservation> reservations = java.util.Collections.emptyList();
            if (courtName != null) {
                Delayer.randomDelay(); // Simulate a slow service
                reservations = reservationService.query(courtName);
            }
            model.addAttribute("reservations", reservations);
            return "reservationQuery";
        };
    }
}
```

If you look at the submitForm method, it now returns a Callable<String> instead of returning a String directly. Inside the newly constructed Callable<String>, there is a random wait to simulate a delay before calling the query method.

Now when making a reservation, you will see something like this in the logs:

```
2017-06-20 10:37:04,836 [nio-8080-exec-2] DEBUG o.s.w.c.request.async.WebAsyncManager   :
Concurrent handling starting for POST [/court/reservationQuery]
2017-06-20 10:37:04,838 [nio-8080-exec-2] DEBUG o.s.web.servlet.DispatcherServlet       :
Leaving response open for concurrent processing
2017-06-20 10:37:09,954 [mvc-executor-1 ] DEBUG o.s.w.c.request.async.WebAsyncManager   :
Concurrent result value [reservationQuery] - dispatching request to resume processing
2017-06-20 10:37:09,959 [nio-8080-exec-3] DEBUG o.s.web.servlet.DispatcherServlet       :
DispatcherServlet with name 'dispatcher' resumed processing POST request for [/court/
reservationQuery]
```

Notice that request handling is handled on a certain thread (here nio-8080-exec-2), which is released, and then another thread does the processing and returns the result (here mvc-executor-1). Finally, the request is dispatched to the DispatcherServlet again to handle the result on yet another thread.

Use a DeferredResult

Instead of a Callable<String>, you could have used a DeferredResult<String>. When using a DeferredResult, you need to construct an instance of this class, submit a task to be async processed, and in that task fill the result of the DeferredResult using the setResult method. When an exception occurs, you can pass this exception to the setErrorResult method of the DeferredResult.

```
package com.apress.springrecipes.court.web;

import com.apress.springrecipes.court.Delayer;
import com.apress.springrecipes.court.domain.Reservation;
import com.apress.springrecipes.court.service.ReservationService;

import org.springframework.core.task.AsyncTaskExecutor;
import org.springframework.core.task.TaskExecutor;
import org.springframework.stereotype.Controller;
import org.springframework.ui.Model;
import org.springframework.web.bind.annotation.GetMapping;
import org.springframework.web.bind.annotation.PostMapping;
import org.springframework.web.bind.annotation.RequestMapping;
import org.springframework.web.bind.annotation.RequestParam;
import org.springframework.web.context.request.async.DeferredResult;

import java.util.List;

@Controller
@RequestMapping("/reservationQuery")
public class ReservationQueryController {

    private final ReservationService reservationService;
    private final TaskExecutor taskExecutor;
```

```
    public ReservationQueryController(ReservationService reservationService,
                                      AsyncTaskExecutor taskExecutor) {
        this.reservationService = reservationService;
        this.taskExecutor = taskExecutor;
    }

    @GetMapping
    public void setupForm() {}

    @PostMapping
    public DeferredResult<String> sumbitForm(@RequestParam("courtName") String courtName,
    Model model) {
        final DeferredResult<String> result = new DeferredResult<>();

        taskExecutor.execute(() -> {
            List<Reservation> reservations = java.util.Collections.emptyList();
            if (courtName != null) {
                Delayer.randomDelay(); // Simulate a slow service
                reservations = reservationService.query(courtName);
            }
            model.addAttribute("reservations", reservations);
            result.setResult("reservationQuery");
        });
        return result;
    }
}
```

The method now returns a DeferredResult<String>, which is still the name of the view to render. The actual result is set through a Runnable, which is passed to the execute method of the injected TaskExecutor. The main difference between returning a DeferredResult and a Callable is that for a DeferredResult you have to create your own Thread (or delegate it to a TaskExecutor); for a Callable, that isn't needed.

Use a CompletableFuture

Change the signature of the method to return a CompletableFuture<String> and use the TaskExecutor to async execute the code.

```
package com.apress.springrecipes.court.web;

import com.apress.springrecipes.court.Delayer;
import com.apress.springrecipes.court.domain.Reservation;
import com.apress.springrecipes.court.service.ReservationService;

import org.springframework.core.task.TaskExecutor;
import org.springframework.stereotype.Controller;
import org.springframework.ui.Model;
import org.springframework.web.bind.annotation.GetMapping;
import org.springframework.web.bind.annotation.PostMapping;
import org.springframework.web.bind.annotation.RequestMapping;
import org.springframework.web.bind.annotation.RequestParam;
```

```
import java.util.List;
import java.util.concurrent.CompletableFuture;

@Controller
@RequestMapping("/reservationQuery")
public class ReservationQueryController {

    private final ReservationService reservationService;
    private final TaskExecutor taskExecutor;

    public ReservationQueryController(ReservationService reservationService,
    TaskExecutor taskExecutor) {
        this.reservationService = reservationService;
        this.taskExecutor = taskExecutor;
    }

    @GetMapping
    public void setupForm() {}

    @PostMapping
    public CompletableFuture<String> sumbitForm(@RequestParam("courtName")
    String courtName, Model model) {

        return CompletableFuture.supplyAsync(() -> {
            List<Reservation> reservations = java.util.Collections.emptyList();
            if (courtName != null) {
                Delayer.randomDelay(); // Simulate a slow service
                reservations = reservationService.query(courtName);
            }
            model.addAttribute("reservations", reservations);
            return "reservationQuery";
        }, taskExecutor);
    }
}
```

When calling supplyAsync (or when using void; you could use runAsync), you submit a task and get back a CompletableFuture. Here you use the supplyAsync method, which takes both a Supplier and an Executor so that you can reuse the TaskExecutor for async processing. If you use the supplyAsync method, which takes only a Supplier, it will be executed using the default fork/join pool available on the JVM.

When returning a CompletableFuture, you can take advantage of all the features of it, such as composing and chaining multiple CompletableFuture instances.

Use a ListenableFuture

Spring provides the ListenableFuture interface, which is a Future implementation that will do a callback when the Future has completed. To create a ListenableFuture, you would need to submit a task to an AsyncListenableTaskExecutor, which will return a ListenableFuture. The previously configured ThreadPoolTaskExecutor is an implementation of the AsyncListenableTaskExecutor interface.

```java
// FINAL
package com.apress.springrecipes.court.web;

import com.apress.springrecipes.court.Delayer;
import com.apress.springrecipes.court.domain.Reservation;
import com.apress.springrecipes.court.service.ReservationService;
import org.springframework.core.task.AsyncListenableTaskExecutor;
import org.springframework.stereotype.Controller;
import org.springframework.ui.Model;
import org.springframework.util.concurrent.ListenableFuture;
import org.springframework.web.bind.annotation.GetMapping;
import org.springframework.web.bind.annotation.PostMapping;
import org.springframework.web.bind.annotation.RequestMapping;
import org.springframework.web.bind.annotation.RequestParam;

import java.util.List;

@Controller
@RequestMapping("/reservationQuery")
public class ReservationQueryController {

    private final ReservationService reservationService;
    private final AsyncListenableTaskExecutor taskExecutor;

    public ReservationQueryController(ReservationService reservationService,
    AsyncListenableTaskExecutor taskExecutor) {
        this.reservationService = reservationService;
        this.taskExecutor = taskExecutor;
    }

    @GetMapping
    public void setupForm() {}

    @PostMapping
    public ListenableFuture<String> sumbitForm(@RequestParam("courtName")
    String courtName, Model model) {

        return taskExecutor.submitListenable(() -> {
```

```
            List<Reservation> reservations = java.util.Collections.emptyList();
            if (courtName != null) {
                Delayer.randomDelay(); // Simulate a slow service
                reservations = reservationService.query(courtName);
            }
            model.addAttribute("reservations", reservations);
            return "reservationQuery";
        });
    }
}
```

You submit a task to the taskExecutor using the submitListenable method; this returns a ListenableFuture, which in turn can be used as the result for the method.

You might wonder where the success and failure callbacks are for the created ListenableFuture. Spring MVC will adapt the ListenableFuture to a DeferredResult and upon successful completion will call DeferredResult.setResult and, when an error happens, DeferredResult.setErrorResult. This is all handled for you with one of the HandlerMethodReturnValueHandler implementations shipped with Spring; in this case, it is handled by DeferredResultMethodReturnValueHandler.

5-2. Use Response Writers

Problem

You have a service, or multiple calls, and want to send the response in chunks to the client.

Solution

Use a ResponseBodyEmitter (or its sibling SseEmitter) to send the response in chunks.

How It Works

Spring supports writing objects as plain objects using the HttpMessageConverter infrastructure, the result will be a chunked (or streaming) list to the client. Instead of objects you could also send them as events, so called Server-Sent Events.

Send Multiple Results in a Response

Spring MVC has class named ResponseBodyEmitter that is particularly useful if, instead of a single result (like a view name or ModelAndView), you want to return multiple objects to the client. When sending an object, the object is converted to a result using an HttpMessageConverter (see also recipe 4-2). To use the ResponseBodyEmitter, you have to return it from the request-handling method.

Modify the find method of the ReservationQueryController to return a ResponseBodyEmitter and send the results one by one to the client.

```
// FINAL
package com.apress.springrecipes.court.web;

import com.apress.springrecipes.court.Delayer;
import com.apress.springrecipes.court.domain.Reservation;
import com.apress.springrecipes.court.service.ReservationService;
```

```java
import org.springframework.core.task.TaskExecutor;
import org.springframework.http.MediaType;
import org.springframework.stereotype.Controller;
import org.springframework.ui.Model;
import org.springframework.web.bind.annotation.GetMapping;
import org.springframework.web.bind.annotation.PostMapping;
import org.springframework.web.bind.annotation.RequestMapping;
import org.springframework.web.bind.annotation.RequestParam;
import org.springframework.web.servlet.mvc.method.annotation.ResponseBodyEmitter;

import java.io.IOException;
import java.util.Collection;
import java.util.List;
import java.util.concurrent.Callable;

@Controller
@RequestMapping("/reservationQuery")
public class ReservationQueryController {

    private final ReservationService reservationService;
    private final TaskExecutor taskExecutor;

    ...

    @GetMapping(params = "courtName")
    public ResponseBodyEmitter find(@RequestParam("courtName") String courtName) {
        final ResponseBodyEmitter emitter = new ResponseBodyEmitter();
        taskExecutor.execute(() -> {
            Collection<Reservation> reservations = reservationService.query(courtName);
            try {
                for (Reservation reservation : reservations) {
                    emitter.send(reservation);
                }
                emitter.complete();
            } catch (IOException e) {
                emitter.completeWithError(e);
            }
        });
        return emitter;
    }
}
```

First, a ResponseBodyEmitter is created and in the end returned from this method. Next, a task is executed that will query the reservations using the ReservationService.query method. All the results from that call are returned one by one using the send method of the ResponseBodyEmitter. When all the objects have been sent, the complete() method needs to be called so that the thread responsible for sending the response can complete the request and be freed up for the next response to handle. When an exception occurs and you want to inform the user of this, you call the completeWithError. The exception will pass through the normal exception handling of Spring MVC (see also recipe 3-8), and after that the response is completed.

When using a tool like httpie or curl, calling the URL `http://localhost:8080/court/reservationQuery courtName=='Tennis #1'` will yield something like Figure 5-1. The result will be chunked and have a status of 200 (OK).

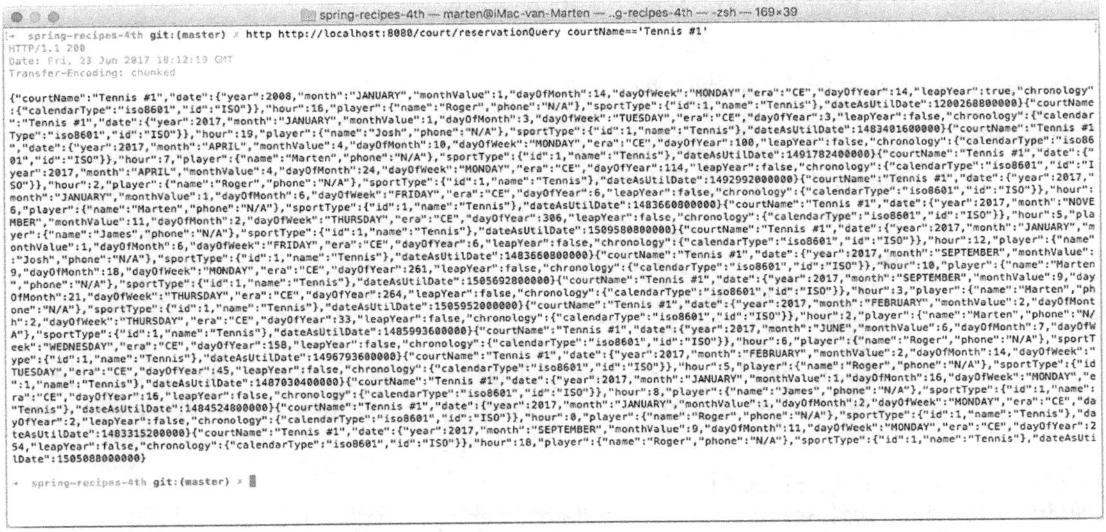

Figure 5-1. *Chunked result*

If you want to change the status code or add custom headers, you could also wrap the `ResponseBodyEmitter` in a `ResponseEntity`, which would allow for the customization of the return code, headers, and so on (see recipe 4-1).

```
@GetMapping(params = "courtName")
public ResponseEntity<ResponseBodyEmitter> find(@RequestParam("courtName") String courtName)
{
    final ResponseBodyEmitter emitter = new ResponseBodyEmitter();
    ....
    return ResponseEntity.status(HttpStatus.I_AM_A_TEAPOT)
        .header("Custom-Header", "Custom-Value")
        .body(emitter);
}
```

Now the status code will be changed to 418, and it will contain a custom header (see Figure 5-2).

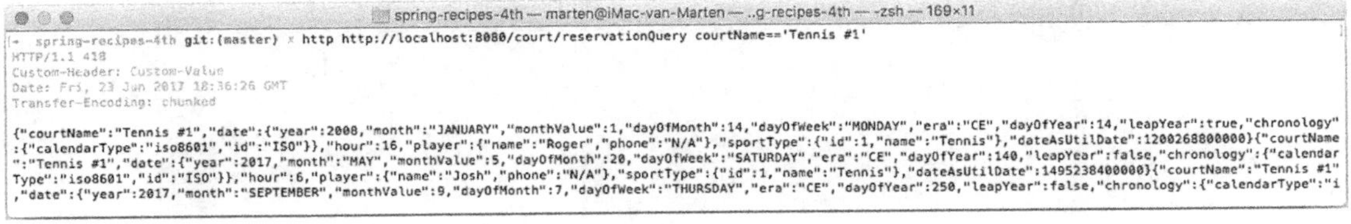

Figure 5-2. *Modified chunked result*

Send Multiple Results as Events

A sibling of the ResponseBodyEmitter is the SseEmitter, which can deliver events from the server to the client using server-sent events. Server-sent events are messages from the server side to the client, and they have a content type header of text/event-stream. They are quite lightweight and allow for four fields to be defined (see Table 5-2).

Table 5-2. *Allowed Fields for Server-Sent Events*

Field	Description
id	The ID of the event
event	The type of event
data	The event data
retry	Reconnection time for the event stream

To send events from a request-handling method, you need to create an instance of SseEmitter and return it from the request-handling method. Then you can use the send method to send individual elements to the client.

```
@GetMapping(params = "courtName")
public SseEmitter find(@RequestParam("courtName") String courtName) {
    final SseEmitter emitter = new SseEmitter();
    taskExecutor.execute(() -> {
        Collection<Reservation> reservations = reservationService.query(courtName);
        try {
            for (Reservation reservation : reservations) {
                Delayer.delay(125);
                emitter.send(reservation);
            }
            emitter.complete();
        } catch (IOException e) {
            emitter.completeWithError(e);
        }
    });
    return emitter;
}
```

■ **Note**   Here there is a delay in sending each item to the client, just so you can see the different events coming in. You wouldn't do this in real code.

Now when using something like curl to call the URL `http://localhost:8080/court/reservationQuery` `courtName=='Tennis #1'`, you will see events coming in one by one (Figure 5-3).

Figure 5-3. Result of server-sent events

Note that the Content-Type header has a value of text/event-stream to indicate that you get a stream of events. You could keep the stream open and keep receiving event notifications. You will also notice that each object written is converted to JSON; this is done with an HttpMessageConverter just like with a plain ResponseBodyEmitter. Each object is written in the data tag as the event data.

If you want to add more information to the event (in other words, fill in one of the other fields mentioned in Table 5-2), you can use the SseEventBuilder. To get an instance of that, you can call the event() factory method on the SseEmitter. Let's use it to fill in the id field with the hash code of the Reservation.

```java
@GetMapping(params = "courtName")
public SseEmitter find(@RequestParam("courtName") String courtName) {
    final SseEmitter emitter = new SseEmitter();
    taskExecutor.execute(() -> {
        Collection<Reservation> reservations = reservationService.query(courtName);
        try {
            for (Reservation reservation : reservations) {
                Delayer.delay(120);
                emitter.send(emitter.event().id(String.valueOf(reservation.hashCode())).
                    data(reservation));
            }
            emitter.complete();
        } catch (IOException e) {
            emitter.completeWithError(e);
        }
    });
    return emitter;
}
```

Now when using something like curl to call the URL `http://localhost:8080/court/reservationQuery courtName=='Tennis #1'`, you will see events coming in one by one, and they will contain both `id` and `data` fields.

5-3. Use Asynchronous Interceptors

Problem

Servlet filters defined by the Servlet API can pre-handle and post-handle every web request before and after it's handled by a servlet. You want to configure something with similar functions as filters in Spring's web application context to take advantage of the container features.

Moreover, sometimes you may want to pre-handle and post-handle web requests that are handled by Spring MVC handlers and manipulate the model attributes returned by these handlers before they are passed to the views.

Solution

Spring MVC allows you to intercept web requests for pre-handling and post-handling through handler interceptors. Handler interceptors are configured in Spring's web application context, so they can make use of any container features and refer to any beans declared in the container. A handler interceptor can be registered for particular URL mappings so that it only intercepts requests mapped to certain URLs.

As described in recipe 3-3, Spring provides the `HandlerInterceptor` interface, which contains three callback methods for you to implement: `preHandle()`, `postHandle()`, and `afterCompletion()`. The first and second methods are called before and after a request is handled by a handler. The second method also allows you to get access to the returned `ModelAndView` object so you can manipulate the model attributes in it. The last method is called after the completion of all request processing (i.e., after the view has been rendered).

For async processing, Spring provides the `AsyncHandlerInterceptor`, which contains an additional callback method for you to implement `afterConcurrentHandlingStarted`. This method is called as soon as the async handling starts, instead of calling `postHandle` and/or `afterCompletion`. When the async processing is done, the normal flow is called again.

How It Works

In recipe 3-3 you created a `MeasurementInterceptor` that measured each web request's handling time by each request handler and added it to the `ModelAndView`. Let's modify it to log the handling time for the request and response, including the thread that was used to handle the request.

```
package com.apress.springrecipes.court.web;

import org.springframework.web.servlet.AsyncHandlerInterceptor;
import org.springframework.web.servlet.ModelAndView;

import javax.servlet.http.HttpServletRequest;
import javax.servlet.http.HttpServletResponse;
```

```java
public class MeasurementInterceptor implements AsyncHandlerInterceptor {

    public static final String START_TIME = "startTime";

    public boolean preHandle(HttpServletRequest request, HttpServletResponse response,
        Object handler) throws Exception {

        if (request.getAttribute(START_TIME) == null) {
            request.setAttribute(START_TIME, System.currentTimeMillis());
        }
        return true;
    }

    public void postHandle(HttpServletRequest request, HttpServletResponse response,
        Object handler, ModelAndView modelAndView) throws Exception {

        long startTime = (Long) request.getAttribute(START_TIME);
        request.removeAttribute(START_TIME);
        long endTime = System.currentTimeMillis();
        System.out.println("Response-Processing-Time: " + (endTime - startTime) + "ms.");
        System.out.println("Response-Processing-Thread: " + Thread.currentThread().
        getName());
    }

    @Override
    public void afterConcurrentHandlingStarted(HttpServletRequest request,
        HttpServletResponse response, Object handler) throws Exception {

        long startTime = (Long) request.getAttribute(START_TIME);
        request.setAttribute(START_TIME, System.currentTimeMillis());
        long endTime = System.currentTimeMillis();

        System.out.println("Request-Processing-Time: " + (endTime - startTime) + "ms.");
        System.out.println("Request-Processing-Thread: " + Thread.currentThread().
        getName());
    }
}
```

In the preHandle() method of this interceptor, you record the start time and save it to a request attribute. This method should return true, allowing DispatcherServlet to proceed with request handling. Otherwise, DispatcherServlet assumes that this method has already handled the request, so DispatcherServlet returns the response to the user directly. Next, in afterConcurrentHandlingStarted, you get the time registered and calculate the time it took to start async processing. After that, you reset the start time and print the request-processing time and thread to the console.

Then, in the postHandle() method, you load the start time from the request attribute and compare it with the current time. You then calculate the total duration and print that, together with the current thread name to the console.

To register an interceptor, you need to modify the AsyncConfiguration, which was created in the first recipe. You need to have it implement WebMvcConfigurer and override the addInterceptors method. The method gives you access to InterceptorRegistry, which you can use to add interceptors. The modified class looks like this:

```
package com.apress.springrecipes.court.config;

import com.apress.springrecipes.court.web.MeasurementInterceptor;
import org.springframework.context.annotation.Bean;
import org.springframework.context.annotation.Configuration;
import org.springframework.scheduling.concurrent.ThreadPoolTaskExecutor;
import org.springframework.web.servlet.config.annotation.AsyncSupportConfigurer;
import org.springframework.web.servlet.config.annotation.InterceptorRegistry;
import org.springframework.web.servlet.config.annotation.WebMvcConfigurer;

import java.util.concurrent.TimeUnit;

@Configuration
public class AsyncConfiguration implements WebMvcConfigurer {

    ...

    @Override
    public void addInterceptors(InterceptorRegistry registry) {
        registry.addInterceptor(new MeasurementInterceptor());
    }
}
```

Now when running the application and when a request is handled, the logging looks something like Figure 5-4.

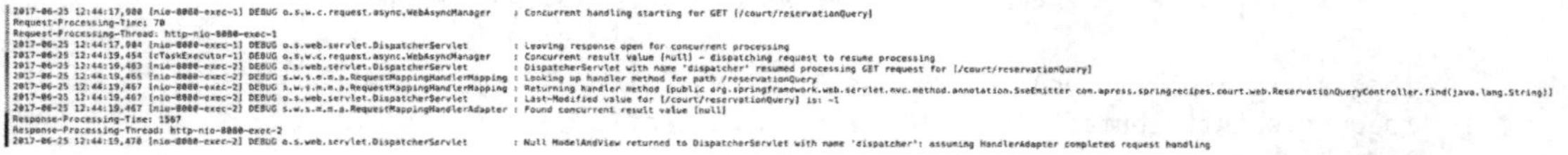

Figure 5-4. *Request/response processing times*

■ **Note**   Server-sent events aren't supported on Microsoft browsers (Internet Explorer or Edge). To make them work with a Microsoft browser, you would have to use a polyfill to add the support.

5-4. Use WebSockets

Problem

You want to use bidirectional communication from the client to the server over the Web.

Solution

Use WebSockets to communicate from the client to the server, and vice versa. The WebSocket technology provides a full-duplex communication, unlike HTTP.

How It Works

A full explanation of the WebSocket technology goes beyond the scope of this recipe; one thing worth mentioning, though, is that the relation between HTTP and the WebSocket technology is actually quite thin. The only usage of HTTP for the WebSocket technology is that the initial handshake uses HTTP. This upgrades the connection from plain HTTP to a TCP socket connection.

Configure WebSocket Support

Enabling the use of the WebSocket technology is just a matter of adding @EnableWebSocket to a configuration class.

```
@Configuration
@EnableWebSocket
public class WebSocketConfiguration {}
```

For further configuration of the WebSocket engine, you can add a ServletServerContainer FactoryBean object to configure things such as buffer size, timeouts, and so on.

```
@Bean
public ServletServerContainerFactoryBean configureWebSocketContainer() {
    ServletServerContainerFactoryBean factory = new ServletServerContainerFactoryBean();
    factory.setMaxBinaryMessageBufferSize(16384);
    factory.setMaxTextMessageBufferSize(16384);
    factory.setMaxSessionIdleTimeout(TimeUnit.MINUTES.convert(30, TimeUnit.MILLISECONDS));
    factory.setAsyncSendTimeout(TimeUnit.SECONDS.convert(5, TimeUnit.MILLISECONDS));
    return factory;
}
```

This will configure the text and binary buffer size to 16KB, set asyncSendTimeout to 5 seconds, and set the session timeout to 30 minutes.

Create a WebSocketHandler

To handle WebSocket messages and life-cycle events (handshake, connection established, etc.), you need to create a WebSocketHandler and register it to an endpoint URL.

WebSocketHandler defines five methods that you need to implement (see Table 5-3) if you want to implement this interface directly. However, Spring already provides a nice class hierarchy that you can use to your advantage. When writing your own custom handlers, it is often enough to extend one of TextWebSocketHandler or BinaryWebSocketHandler, which, as their names imply, can handle either text or binary messages.

Table 5-3. *WebSocketHandler Methods*

Method	Description
afterConnectionEstablished	Invoked when the WebSocket connection is open and ready for use.
handleMessage	Called when a WebSocket message arrives for this handler.
handleTransportError	Called when an error occurs.
afterConnectionClosed	Invoked after the WebSocket connection has been closed.
supportsPartialMessages	Invoked if this handler supports partial messages. If set to true, WebSocket messages can arrive over multiple calls.

Create EchoHandler by extending TextWebSocketHandler and then implement the afterConnectionEstablished and handleMessage methods.

```
package com.apress.springrecipes.websocket;

import org.springframework.web.socket.CloseStatus;
import org.springframework.web.socket.TextMessage;
import org.springframework.web.socket.WebSocketSession;
import org.springframework.web.socket.handler.TextWebSocketHandler;

public class EchoHandler extends TextWebSocketHandler {

    @Override
    public void afterConnectionEstablished(WebSocketSession session) throws Exception {
        session.sendMessage(new TextMessage("CONNECTION ESTABLISHED"));
    }

    @Override
    protected void handleTextMessage(WebSocketSession session, TextMessage message)
        throws Exception {
        String msg = message.getPayload();
        session.sendMessage(new TextMessage("RECEIVED: " + msg));
    }
}
```

When a connection is established, a TextMessage will be sent back to the client telling it that the connection was established. When a TextMessage is received, the payload (the actual message) is extracted and prefixed with RECEIVED: and sent back to the client.

Next you need to register this handler with a URI. To do so, you can create an @Configuration class that implements WebSocketConfigurer and register it in the registerWebSocketHandlers method. Let's add this interface to the WebSocketConfiguration class, as shown here:

```
package com.apress.springrecipes.websocket;

import org.springframework.context.annotation.Bean;
import org.springframework.context.annotation.Configuration;
import org.springframework.web.socket.config.annotation.EnableWebSocket;
import org.springframework.web.socket.config.annotation.WebSocketConfigurer;
import org.springframework.web.socket.config.annotation.WebSocketHandlerRegistry;
```

226

```java
import java.util.concurrent.TimeUnit;

@Configuration
@EnableWebSocket
public class WebSocketConfiguration implements WebSocketConfigurer {

    @Bean
    public EchoHandler echoHandler() {
        return new EchoHandler();
    }

    @Override
    public void registerWebSocketHandlers(WebSocketHandlerRegistry registry) {
        registry.addHandler(echoHandler(), "/echo");
    }
}
```

First you register the EchoHandler as a bean so that it can be used to attach it to a URI. In the registerWebSocketHandlers, you can use the WebSocketHandlerRegistry to register the handler. Using the addHandler method, you can register the handler to a URI, in this case /echo. With this configuration, you could use the ws://localhost:8080/echo-ws/echo URL to open a WebSocket connection from the client.

Now that the server is ready, you need a client to connect to your WebSocket endpoint. For this you will need some JavaScript and HTML. Write the following app.js:

```javascript
var ws = null;
var url = "ws://localhost:8080/echo-ws/echo";

function setConnected(connected) {
    document.getElementById('connect').disabled = connected;
    document.getElementById('disconnect').disabled = !connected;
    document.getElementById('echo').disabled = !connected;
}

function connect() {
    ws = new WebSocket(url);

    ws.onopen = function () {
        setConnected(true);
    };

    ws.onmessage = function (event) {
        log(event.data);
    };

    ws.onclose = function (event) {
        setConnected(false);
        log('Info: Closing Connection.');
    };
}
```

```
function disconnect() {
    if (ws != null) {
        ws.close();
        ws = null;
    }
    setConnected(false);
}
function echo() {
    if (ws != null) {
        var message = document.getElementById('message').value;
        log('Sent: ' + message);
        ws.send(message);
    } else {
        alert('connection not established, please connect.');
    }
}

function log(message) {
    var console = document.getElementById('logging');
    var p = document.createElement('p');
    p.appendChild(document.createTextNode(message));
    console.appendChild(p);
    while (console.childNodes.length > 12) {
        console.removeChild(console.firstChild);
    }
    console.scrollTop = console.scrollHeight;
}
```

There are a few functions here. The first connect will be invoked when clicking the Connect button. This will open a WebSocket connection to ws://localhost:8080/echo-ws/echo, which is the URL to the handler created and registered earlier. Connecting to the server will create a WebSocket JavaScript object, which gives you the ability to listen to messages and events on the client. Here the onopen, onmessage, and onclose callbacks are defined. The most important is the onmessage callback because that will be invoked whenever a message comes in from the server; this method simply calls the log function, which will add the received message to the logging element on the screen.

Next there is disconnect, which will close the WebSocket connection and clean up the JavaScript objects. Finally, there is the echo function, which will be invoked whenever the Echo Message button is clicked. The given message will be sent to the server (and eventually will be returned).

To use app.js, add the index.html file shown here:

```
<!DOCTYPE html>
<html>
<head>
    <link type="text/css" rel="stylesheet" href="https://cdnjs.cloudflare.com/ajax/libs/
    semantic-ui/2.2.10/semantic.min.css" />
    <script type="text/javascript" src="app.js"></script>
</head>
<body>
<div>
    <div id="connect-container" class="ui centered grid">
        <div class="row">
```

```
        <button id="connect" onclick="connect();" class="ui green button ">
        Connect</button>
        <button id="disconnect" disabled="disabled" onclick="disconnect();" class="ui
        red button">Disconnect</button>
    </div>
    <div class="row">
        <textarea id="message" style="width: 350px" class="ui input"
        placeholder="Message to Echo"></textarea>
    </div>
    <div class="row">
        <button id="echo" onclick="echo();" disabled="disabled" class="ui button">
        Echo message</button>
    </div>
</div>
<div id="console-container">
    <h3>Logging</h3>
    <div id="logging"></div>
</div>
</div>
</body>
</html>
```

Now when deploying the application, you can connect to the echo WebSocket service and send some messages and have them sent back (see Figure 5-5).

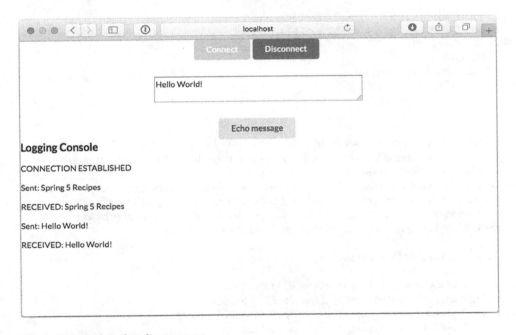

Figure 5-5. *WebSocket client output*

Use STOMP and MessageMapping

When using the WebSocket technology to create an application, that more or less implies messaging. Although you can use the WebSocket protocol as is, the protocol also allows you to use subprotocols. One of those protocols, supported by Spring WebSocket, is STOMP.

STOMP is a simple text-oriented protocol that was created for scripting languages like Ruby and Python to connect to message brokers. STOMP can be used over any reliable bidirectional network protocol like TCP and also WebSocket. The protocol itself is text-oriented, but the payload of the messages isn't strictly bound to this; it can also contain binary data.

When configuring and using STOMP with Spring WebSocket support, the WebSocket application acts as a broker for all connected clients. The broker can be an in-memory broker or an actual full-blown enterprise solution that supports the STOMP protocol (like RabbitMQ or ActiveMQ). In the latter case, the Spring WebSocket application will act as a relay for the actual broker. To add messaging over the WebSocket protocol, Spring uses Spring Messaging (see Chapter 14 for more recipes on messaging).

To be able to receive messages, you need to mark a method in an @Controller with @MessageMapping and tell it from which destination it will receive messages. Let's modify the EchoHandler to work with annotations.

```
package com.apress.springrecipes.websocket;

import org.springframework.messaging.handler.annotation.MessageMapping;
import org.springframework.messaging.handler.annotation.SendTo;
import org.springframework.stereotype.Controller;

@Controller
public class EchoHandler {

    @MessageMapping("/echo")
    @SendTo("/topic/echo")
    public String echo(String msg) {
        return "RECEIVED: " + msg;
    }
}
```

When a message is received on the /app/echo destination, it will be passed on to the @MessageMapping annotated method. Notice the @SendTo("/topic/echo") annotation on the method as well; this instructs Spring to put the result, a String, on said topic.

Now you need to configure the message broker and add an endpoint for receiving messages. For this, add @EnableWebSocketMessageBroker to the WebSocketConfiguration and let it extend the AbstractWebSocketMessageBrokerConfigurer (which implements the WebSocketMessageBroker Configurer, which is used to do further configuration for WebSocket messaging).

```
package com.apress.springrecipes.websocket;

import org.springframework.context.annotation.ComponentScan;
import org.springframework.context.annotation.Configuration;
import org.springframework.messaging.simp.config.MessageBrokerRegistry;
import org.springframework.web.socket.config.annotation.
AbstractWebSocketMessageBrokerConfigurer;
import org.springframework.web.socket.config.annotation.EnableWebSocketMessageBroker;
import org.springframework.web.socket.config.annotation.StompEndpointRegistry;
```

```
@Configuration
@EnableWebSocketMessageBroker
@ComponentScan
public class WebSocketConfiguration extends AbstractWebSocketMessageBrokerConfigurer {

    @Override
    public void configureMessageBroker(MessageBrokerRegistry registry) {
        registry.enableSimpleBroker("/topic");
        registry.setApplicationDestinationPrefixes("/app");
    }

    @Override
    public void registerStompEndpoints(StompEndpointRegistry registry) {
        registry.addEndpoint("/echo-endpoint");
    }
}
```

The @EnableWebSocketMessageBroker annotation will enable the use of STOMP over WebSocket. The broker is configured in the configureMessageBroker method; here we are using the simple message broker. To connect to an enterprise broker, use registry.enableStompBrokerRelay to connect to the actual broker. To distinquish between messages handled by the broker versus by the app, there are different prefixes. Anything on a destination starting with /topic will be passed on to the broker, and anything on a destination starting with /app will be sent to a message handler (i.e., the @MessageMapping annotated method).

The final part is the registration of a WebSocket endpoint that listens to incoming STOMP messages; in this case, the endpoint is mapped to /echo-endpoint. This registration is done in the registerStompEndpoints method, which can be overridden.

Finally, you need to modify the client to use STOMP instead of plain WebSocket. The HTML can remain pretty much the same; you need an additional library to be able to work with STOMP in the browser. This recipe uses webstomp-client (https://github.com/JSteunou/webstomp-client), but there are different libraries that you can use.

```html
<head>
    <link type="text/css" rel="stylesheet" href="https://cdnjs.cloudflare.com/ajax/
    libs/semantic-ui/2.2.10/semantic.min.css" />

    <script type="text/javascript" src="webstomp.js"></script>
    <script type="text/javascript" src="app.js"></script>

</head>
```

The biggest change is in the app.js file.

```javascript
var ws = null;
var url = "ws://localhost:8080/echo-ws/echo-endpoint";

function setConnected(connected) {
    document.getElementById('connect').disabled = connected;
    document.getElementById('disconnect').disabled = !connected;
    document.getElementById('echo').disabled = !connected;
}
```

231

```
function connect() {
    ws = webstomp.client(url);
    ws.connect({}, function(frame) {
        setConnected(true);
        log(frame);
        ws.subscribe('/topic/echo', function(message){
            log(message.body);
        })
    });
}

function disconnect() {
    if (ws != null) {
        ws.disconnect();
        ws = null;
    }
    setConnected(false);
}
function echo() {
    if (ws != null) {
        var message = document.getElementById('message').value;
        log('Sent: ' + message);
        ws.send("/app/echo", message);
    } else {
        alert('connection not established, please connect.');
    }
}

function log(message) {
    var console = document.getElementById('logging');
    var p = document.createElement('p');
    p.appendChild(document.createTextNode(message));
    console.appendChild(p);
    while (console.childNodes.length > 12) {
        console.removeChild(console.firstChild);
    }
    console.scrollTop = console.scrollHeight;
}
```

The connect function now uses webstomp.client to create a STOMP client connection to your broker. When connected, the client will subscribe to /topic/echo and receive the messages put on the topic. The echo function has been modified to use the send method of the client to send the message to the /app/echo destination, which in turn will be passed on to the @MessageMapping annotated method.

When starting the application and opening the client, you are still able to send and receive messages but now using the STOMP subprotocol. You could even connect multiple browsers, and each browser would see the messages on the /topic/echo destination as it acts like a topic.

When writing @MessageMapping annotated methods, you can use a variety of method arguments and annotations (see Table 5-4) to receive more or less information about the message. By default, it is assumed that a single argument will map to the payload of the message, and a MessageConverter will be used to convert the message payload to the desired type. (See recipe 14-2 for converting messages.)

Table 5-4. *Supported Method Arguments and Annotations*

Type	Description
Message	The actual underlying message including the headers and body
@Payload	The payload of the message (default); arguments can also be annotated with @ Validated to be validated
@Header	Gets the given header from Message
@Headers	Can be placed on a Map argument to get all Message headers
MessageHeaders	All the Message headers
Principal	The current user, if set

5-5. Develop a Reactive Application with Spring WebFlux

Problem

You want to develop a simple reactive web application with Spring WebFlux to learn the basic concepts and configurations of this framework.

Solution

The lowest component of Spring WebFlux is HttpHandler. This is an interface with a single handle method.

```
public interface HttpHandler {

    Mono<Void> handle(ServerHttpRequest request, ServerHttpResponse response);

}
```

The handle method returns Mono<Void>, which is the reactive way of saying it returns void. It takes both a ServerHttpRequest object and a ServerHttpResonse object from the org.springframework.http. server.reactive package. These are again interfaces, and depending on the container used for running an instance of the interface is created. For this, several adapters or bridges for containers exist. When running on a Servlet 3.1 container (supporting nonblocking I/O), ServletHttpHandlerAdapter (or one of its subclasses) is used to adapt from the plain servlet world to the reactive world. When running on a native reactive engine like Netty, ReactorHttpHandlerAdapter is used.

When a web request is sent to a Spring WebFlux application, HandlerAdapter first receives the request. Then it organizes the different components configured in Spring's application context that are needed to handle the request.

To define a controller class in Spring WebFlux, a class has to be marked with the @Controller or @RestController annotation (just like with Spring MVC; see Chapters 3 and 4).

When an @Controller annotated class (i.e., a controller class) receives a request, it looks for an appropriate handler method to handle the request. This requires that a controller class map each request to a handler method by one or more handler mappings. To do so, a controller class's methods are decorated with the @RequestMapping annotation, making them handler methods.

233

The signature for these handler methods—as you can expect from any standard class—is open ended. You can specify an arbitrary name for a handler method and define a variety of method arguments. Equally, a handler method can return any of a series of values (e.g., `String` or `void`), depending on the application logic it fulfills. The following is only a partial list of valid argument types, just to give you an idea.

- `ServerHttpRequest` or `ServerHttpResponse`

- Request parameters from the URL of arbitrary type, annotated with `@RequestParam`

- Model attributes of arbitrary type, annotated with `@ModelAttribute`

- Cookie values included in an incoming request, annotated with `@CookieValue`

- Request header values of arbitraty type, annotated with `@RequestHeader`

- Request attribute of arbitrary type, annotated with `@RequestAttribute`

- `Map` or `ModelMap`, for the handler method to add attributes to the model

- `Errors` or `BindingResult`, for the handler method to access the binding and validation result for the command object

- `WebSession`, for the session

Once the controller class has picked an appropriate handler method, it invokes the handler method's logic with the request. Usually, a controller's logic invokes back-end services to handle the request. In addition, a handler method's logic is likely to add or remove information from the numerous input arguments (e.g., `ServerHttpRequest`, `Map`, or `Errors`) that will form part of the ongoing flow.

After a handler method has finished processing the request, it delegates control to a view, which is represented as the handler method's return value. To provide a flexible approach, a handler method's return value doesn't represent a view's implementation (e.g., `user.html` or `report.pdf`) but rather a logical view (e.g., `user` or `report`)—note the lack of file extension.

A handler method's return value can be either a `String`, representing a logical view name, or `void`, in which case a default logical view name is determined on the basis of a handler method's or controller's name.

To pass information from a controller to a view, it's irrelevant that a handler's method returns a logical view name—`String` or a `void`—since the handler method input arguments will be available to a view.

For example, if a handler method takes `Map` and `Model` objects as input parameters—modifying their contents inside the handler method's logic—these same objects will be accessible to the view returned by the handler method.

When the controller class receives a view, it resolves the logical view name into a specific view implementation (e.g., `user.html` or `report.fmt`) by means of a view resolver. A *view resolver* is a bean configured in the web application context that implements the `ViewResolver` interface. Its responsibility is to return a specific view implementation for a logical view name.

Once the controller class has resolved a view name into a view implementation, per the view implementation's design, it renders the objects (e.g., `ServerHttpRequest`, `Map`, `Errors`, or `WebSession`) passed by the controller's handler method. The view's responsibility is to display the objects added in the handler method's logic to the user.

How It Works

Let's write a reactive version of the course reservation system mentioned in Chapter 3. First you write the following domain classes, which are regular classes (nothing reactive so far):

```
package com.apress.springrecipes.reactive.court;

public class Reservation {

    private String courtName;

    @DateTimeFormat(iso = DateTimeFormat.ISO.DATE)
    private LocalDate date;
    private int hour;
    private Player player;
    private SportType sportType;

    // Constructors, Getters and Setters
    ...
}
```

```
package com.apress.springrecipes.court.domain;

public class Player {

    private String name;
    private String phone;

    // Constructors, Getters and Setters
    ...
}
```

```
package com.apress.springrecipes.court.domain;

public class SportType {

    private int id;
    private String name;

    // Constructors, Getters and Setters
    ...
}
```

Then you define the following service interface to provide reservation services to the presentation layer:

```
package com.apress.springrecipes.reactive.court;

import reactor.core.publisher.Flux;

public interface ReservationService {

    Flux<Reservation> query(String courtName);
}
```

Notice the return type of the query method that returns a Flux<Reservation>, which means zero or more reservations.

In a production application, you should implement this interface with data store persistence and preferably one that has reactive support. But for simplicity's sake, you can store the reservation records in a list and hard-code several reservations for testing purposes.

```
package com.apress.springrecipes.reactive.court;

import reactor.core.publisher.Flux;

import java.time.LocalDate;
import java.util.ArrayList;
import java.util.List;
import java.util.Objects;

public class InMemoryReservationService implements ReservationService {
    public static final SportType TENNIS = new SportType(1, "Tennis");
    public static final SportType SOCCER = new SportType(2, "Soccer");

    private final List<Reservation> reservations = new ArrayList<>();

    public InMemoryReservationService() {

        reservations.add(new Reservation("Tennis #1", LocalDate.of(2008, 1, 14), 16,
            new Player("Roger", "N/A"), TENNIS));
        reservations.add(new Reservation("Tennis #2", LocalDate.of(2008, 1, 14), 20,
            new Player("James", "N/A"), TENNIS));
    }

    @Override
    public Flux<Reservation> query(String courtName) {
        return Flux.fromIterable(reservations)
            .filter(r -> Objects.equals(r.getCourtName(), courtName));
    }
}
```

The query method returns a Flux based on the embedded list of Reservations, and the Flux will filter the reservations that don't match.

Set Up a Spring WebFlux Application

To be able to handle request in a reactive way, you need to enable WebFlux. This is done by adding @EnableWebFlux to an @Configuration class (much like @EnableWebMvc for normal request processing).

```
package com.apress.springrecipes.websocket;

import org.springframework.context.annotation.ComponentScan;
import org.springframework.context.annotation.Configuration;
import org.springframework.web.reactive.config.EnableWebFlux;
import org.springframework.web.reactive.config.WebFluxConfigurer;
```

```
@Configuration
@EnableWebFlux
@ComponentScan
public class WebFluxConfiguration implements WebFluxConfigurer { ... }
```

The @EnableWebFlux annotation is what is turning on reactive processing. To do more WebFlux configuration, you can implement WebFluxConfigurer and add additional converters and so on.

Bootstrap the Application

Just as with a regular Spring MVC application, you need to bootstrap the application. How to bootstrap the application depends a little on the runtime you choose to run on. For all supported containers (see Table 5-5), there are different handler adapters so that the runtime can work with the HttpHandler abstraction for Spring WebFlux.

Table 5-5. *Supported Runtimes and HandlerAdapter*

Runtime	Adapter
Servlet 3.1 container	ServletHttpHandlerAdapter
Tomcat	ServletHttpHandlerAdapter or TomcatHttpHandlerAdapter
Jetty	ServletHttpHandlerAdapter or JettyHttpHandlerAdapter
Reactor Netty	ReactorHttpHandlerAdapter
RxNetty	RxNettyHttpHandlerAdapter
Undertow	UndertowHttpHandlerAdapter

Before adapting to the runtime, you would need to bootstrap the application using AnnotationConfig ApplicationContext and use that to configure a HttpHandler. You can create it using the WebHttpHandlerBuilder.applicationContext factory method. It will create a HttpHandler and configure it using the passed in ApplicationContext.

```
AnnotationConfigApplicationContext context =
    new AnnotationConfigApplicationContext(WebFluxConfiguration.class);
HttpHandler handler = WebHttpHandlerBuilder.applicationContext(context).build();
```

Next you would adapt HttpHandler to the runtime.
For Reactor Netty, it would be something like this:

```
ReactorHttpHandlerAdapter adapter = new ReactorHttpHandlerAdapter(handler);
HttpServer.create(host, port).newHandler(adapter).block();
```

First you create a ReactorHttpHandlerAdapter component, which is the component that knows how to adapt from the Reactor Netty handling to the internal HttpHandler. Next you register this adapter as a handler to the newly created Reactor Netty server.

When deploying an application to a servlet container, you can create a class implementing WebApplicationInitializer and do the setup manually.

```
public class WebFluxInitializer implements WebApplicationInitializer {

    public void onStartup(ServletContext servletContext) throws ServletException {}
        AnnotationConfigApplicationContext context =
            new AnnotationConfigApplicationContext(WebFluxConfiguration.class);
        HttpHandler handler = WebHttpHandlerBuilder.applicationContext(context).build();
        ServletHttpHandlerAdapter handlerAdapter = new ServletHttpHandlerAdapter(httpHandler)
        ServletRegistration.Dynamic registration =
            servletContext.addServlet("dispatcher-handler", handlerAdapter);
        registration.setLoadOnStartup(1);
        registration.addMapping("/");
        registration.setAsyncSupported(true);
    }
}
```

First you create an AnnotationConfigApplicationContext because you want to use annotations for configuration and pass that your WebFluxConfiguration class. Next you need an HttpHandler to handle and dispatch the request. This HttpHandler needs to be registered to the servlet container you are using as a servlet. For this, you wrap it in a ServletHttpHandlerAdapter. To be able to do reactive processing, asyncSupported needs to be true.

To make this configuration easier, Spring WebFlux provides a few convenience implementations for you to extend. In this case, you can use AbstractAnnotationConfigDispatcherHandlerInitializer as a base class. The configuration now looks like this:

```
package com.apress.springrecipes.websocket;

import org.springframework.web.reactive.support.AbstractAnnotationConfigDispatcherHandler
Initializer;

public class WebFluxInitializer extends AbstractAnnotationConfigDispatcherHandlerInitializer {

    @Override
    protected Class<?>[] getConfigClasses() {
        return new Class<?>[] {WebFluxConfiguration.class};
    }
}
```

The only thing required is the getConfigClasses method; all the moving parts are now handled by the base configuration provided by Spring WebFlux.

Now you are ready to run your application on a regular servlet container.

Create Spring WebFlux Controllers

An annotation-based controller class can be an arbitrary class that doesn't implement a particular interface or extend a particular base class. You can annotate it with the @Controller or @RestController annotation. There can be one or more handler methods defined in a controller to handle single or multiple actions. The signature of the handler methods is flexible enough to accept a range of arguments. (See also recipe 3-2 for more information on request mapping.)

The @RequestMapping annotation can be applied to the class level or the method level. The first mapping strategy is to map a particular URL pattern to a controller class and then a particular HTTP method to each handler method.

```
package com.apress.springrecipes.reactive.court.web;

import org.springframework.stereotype.Controller;
import org.springframework.ui.Model;
import org.springframework.web.bind.annotation.GetMapping;
import org.springframework.web.bind.annotation.RequestMapping;
import reactor.core.publisher.Mono;

import java.time.LocalDate;

@Controller
@RequestMapping("/welcome")
public class WelcomeController {

    @GetMapping
    public String welcome(Model model) {
        model.addAttribute("today", Mono.just(LocalDate.now()));
        return "welcome";
    }

}
```

This controller creates a java.util.Date object to retrieve the current date and then adds it to the input Model as an attribute so the target view can display it. Although this controller looks like a regular controller, the main difference is the way things are added to the model. Instead of directly adding it to the model, the current date will eventually appear in the model, due to the use of Mono.just(...).

Since you've already activated annotation scanning on the com.apress.springrecipes.reactive. court package, the annotations for the controller class are detected upon deployment.

The @Controller annotation defines the class as a controller. The @RequestMapping annotation is more interesting since it contains properties and can be declared at the class or handler method level. The first value in this class— ("/welcome")—is used to specify the URL on which the controller is actionable, meaning any request received on the /welcome URL is attended by the WelcomeController class.

Once a request is attended by the controller class, it delegates the call to the default HTTP GET handler method declared in the controller. The reason for this behavior is that every initial request made on a URL is of the HTTP GET kind. So when the controller attends to a request on the /welcome URL, it subsequently delegates to the default HTTP GET handler method for processing.

The annotation @GetMapping is used to decorate the welcome method as the controller's default HTTP GET handler method. It's worth mentioning that if no default HTTP GET handler method is declared, a ServletException is thrown. That's why it's important that a Spring MVC controller have at a minimum a URL route and default HTTP GET handler method.

Another variation to this approach can be declaring both values—URL route and default HTTP GET handler method—in the @GetMapping annotation used at the method level. This declaration is illustrated next:

```
@Controller
public class WelcomeController {

    @GetMapping("/welcome")
    public String welcome(Model model) { ... }

}
```

This last controller illustrates the basic principles of Spring MVC. However, a typical controller may invoke back-end services for business processing. For example, you can create a controller for querying reservations of a particular court as follows:

```
package com.apress.springrecipes.reactive.court.web;

import com.apress.springrecipes.reactive.court.Reservation;
import com.apress.springrecipes.reactive.court.ReservationService;
import org.springframework.stereotype.Controller;
import org.springframework.ui.Model;
import org.springframework.web.bind.annotation.GetMapping;
import org.springframework.web.bind.annotation.PostMapping;
import org.springframework.web.bind.annotation.RequestMapping;
import org.springframework.web.server.ServerWebExchange;
import reactor.core.publisher.Flux;

@Controller
@RequestMapping("/reservationQuery")
public class ReservationQueryController {

    private final ReservationService reservationService;

    public ReservationQueryController(ReservationService reservationService) {
        this.reservationService = reservationService;
    }

    @GetMapping
    public void setupForm() {
    }

    @PostMapping
    public String sumbitForm(ServerWebExchange serverWebExchange, Model model) {

        Flux<Reservation> reservations =
            serverWebExchange.getFormData()
                .map(form -> form.get("courtName"))
                .flatMapMany(Flux::fromIterable)
                .concatMap(courtName -> reservationService.query(courtName));
        model.addAttribute("reservations", reservations);
        return "reservationQuery";
    }
}
```

As outlined earlier, the controller then looks for a default HTTP GET handler method. Since the public void `setupForm()` method is assigned the necessary `@GetMapping` annotation for this purpose, it's called next.

Unlike the previous default HTTP GET handler method, notice that this method has no input parameters, has no logic, and has a void return value. This means two things. By having no input parameters and no logic, a view only displays data hard-coded in the implementation template (e.g., JSP) since no data is being added by the controller. By having a void return value, a default view name based on the request URL is used; therefore, since the requesting URL is `/reservationQuery`, a view named `reservationQuery` is assumed.

The remaining handler method is decorated with the `@PostMapping` annotation. At first sight, having two handler methods with only the class-level `/reservationQuery` URL statement can be confusing, but it's really simple. One method is invoked when HTTP GET requests are made on the `/reservationQuery` URL; the other is invoked when HTTP POST requests are made on the same URL.

The majority of requests in web applications are of the HTTP GET kind, whereas requests of the HTTP POST kind are generally made when a user submits an HTML form. So, revealing more of the application's view (which we will describe shortly), one method is called when the HTML form is initially loaded (i.e., HTTP GET), whereas the other is called when the HTML form is submitted (i.e., HTTP POST).

Looking closer at the HTTP POST default handler method, notice the two input parameters. First is the `ServerWebExchange` declaration, used to extract a request parameter named `courtName`. In this case, the HTTP POST request comes in the form `/reservationQuery?courtName=<value>`. This declaration makes said value available in the method under the variable named `courtName`. Second is the `Model` declaration, used to define an object in which to pass data onto the returning view. In a regular Spring MVC controller, you could have used `@RequestParam("courtName") String courtName` (see recipe 3-1) to obtain the parameter, but for Spring WebFlux that will not work for parameters passed as part of the form data; it will work only for parameters that are part of the URL. Hence, `ServerWebExchange` is needed to get the form data, obtain the parameter, and invoke the service.

The logic executed by the handler method consists of using the controller's `reservationService` to perform a query using the `courtName` variable. The results obtained from this query are assigned to the `Model` object, which will later become available to the returning view for display.

Finally, note that the method returns a view named `reservationQuery`. This method could have also returned void, just like the default HTTP GET, and have been assigned to the same `reservationQuery` default view on account of the requesting URL. Both approaches are identical.

Now that you are aware of how Spring MVC controllers are constituted, it's time to explore the views to which a controller's handler methods delegate their results.

Create Thymeleaf Views

Spring WebFlux supports several types of views for different presentation technologies. These include HTML, XML, JSON, Atom and RSS feeds, JasperReports, and other third-party view implementations. Here you will use Thymeleaf to write a few simple HTML-based templates. For this you need to add some additional configuration to the `WebFluxConfiguration` class to set up Thymeleaf and to register a `ViewResolver`, which will return the view name, returned from the controller, into the actual resource to load.

Here's the Thymeleaf configuration:

```
@Bean
public SpringResourceTemplateResolver thymeleafTemplateResolver() {

    final SpringResourceTemplateResolver resolver = new SpringResourceTemplateResolver();
    resolver.setPrefix("classpath:/templates/");
    resolver.setSuffix(".html");
    resolver.setTemplateMode(TemplateMode.HTML);
    return resolver;
}

@Bean
public ISpringWebFluxTemplateEngine thymeleafTemplateEngine(){

    final SpringWebFluxTemplateEngine templateEngine = new SpringWebFluxTemplateEngine();
    templateEngine.setTemplateResolver(thymeleafTemplateResolver());
    return templateEngine;
}
```

Thymeleaf uses a template engine to convert templates into actual HTML. Next you need to configure the ViewResolver, which knows how to work with Thymeleaf. ThymeleafReactiveViewResolver is the reactive implementation of ViewResolver. Finally, you need to make the WebFlux configuration aware of the new view resolver. This is done by overriding the configureViewResolvers method and adding it to ViewResolverRegistry.

```
@Bean
public ThymeleafReactiveViewResolver thymeleafReactiveViewResolver() {

    final ThymeleafReactiveViewResolver viewResolver = new ThymeleafReactiveViewResolver();
    viewResolver.setTemplateEngine(thymeleafTemplateEngine());
    viewResolver.setResponseMaxChunkSizeBytes(16384);
    return viewResolver;
}

@Override
public void configureViewResolvers(ViewResolverRegistry registry) {
    registry.viewResolver(thymeleafReactiveViewResolver());
}
```

The templates are resolved through a template resolver; here SpringResourceTemplateResolver uses the Spring resource-loading mechanism to load the templates. The templates are going to be in the src/main/resources/templates directory. For instance, for the welcome view, the actual src/main/resources/templates/welcome.html file will be loaded and parsed by the template engine.

Let's write the welcome.html template.

```html
<!DOCTYPE html>
<html lang="en" xmlns:th="http://www.thymeleaf.org">
<head>
    <meta charset="UTF-8">
    <title>Welcome</title>
</head>
<body>
<h2>Welcome to Court Reservation System</h2>
Today is <strong th:text="${#temporals.format(today, 'dd-MM-yyyy')}">21-06-2017</strong>
</body>
</html>
```

In this template, you make use of the temporals object in EL to format the today model attribute into the pattern dd-MM-yyyy.

Next, you can create another JSP template for the reservation query controller and name it reservationQuery.html to match the view name.

```html
<!DOCTYPE html>
<html lang="en" xmlns:th="http://www.thymeleaf.org">
<head>
    <meta charset="UTF-8">
    <title>Reservation Query</title>
</head>
<body>
<form method="post">
    Court Name
    <input type="text" name="courtName" value="${courtName}"/>
    <input type="submit" value="Query"/>
</form>

<table border="1">
    <thead>
    <tr>
        <th>Court Name</th>
        <th>Date</th>
        <th>Hour</th>
        <th>Player</th>
    </tr>
    </thead>
    <tbody>
    <tr th:each="reservation : ${reservations}">
        <td th:text="${reservation.courtName}">Court</td>
        <td th:text="${#temporals.format(reservation.date, 'dd-MM-yyyy')}">21-06-2017</td>
        <td th:text="${reservation.hour}">22</td>
        <td th:text="${reservation.player.name}">Player</td>
    </tr>
    </tbody>
</table>
</body>
</html>
```

In this template, you include a form for users to input the court name they want to query and then use the th:each tag to loop the reservations model attribute to generate the result table.

Run the Web Application

Depending on the runtime, either you can just run the application by executing the main method or you can build a WAR archive and deploy it to a servlet container. Here you will do the latter and use Apache Tomcat 8.5.*x* as the web container.

■ **Tip** The project can also create a Docker container with the app. Run ../gradlew buildDocker to get a container with Tomcat and the application. You can then start a Docker container to test the application (docker run -p 8080:8080 spring-recipes-4th/court-rx/welcome).

5-6. Handle Forms with Reactive Controllers

Problem

In a web application, you often have to deal with forms. A form controller has to show a form to a user and also handle the form submission. Form handling can be a complex and variable task.

Solution

When a user interacts with a form, it requires support for two operations from a controller. First, when a form is initially requested, it asks the controller to show a form with an HTTP GET request, which renders the form view to the user. Then, when the form is submitted, an HTTP POST request is made to handle things such as validation and business processing for the data present in the form. If the form is handled successfully, it renders the success view to the user. Otherwise, it renders the form view again with errors.

How It Works

Suppose you want to allow a user to make a court reservation by filling out a form. To give you a better idea of the data handled by a controller, we will introduce the controller's view (i.e., the form) first.

Create a Form's Views

Let's create the form view called reservationForm.html. The form relies on the Thymeleaf form tag library because this simplifies a form's data binding, display of error messages, and the redisplay of original values entered by the user in the case of errors.

```
<!DOCTYPE html>
<html lang="en" xmlns:th="http://www.thymeleaf.org">
<head>
    <title>Reservation Form</title>
    <style>
        .error {
            color: #ff0000;
            font-weight: bold;
        }
    </style>
</head>

<body>
<form method="post" th:object="${reservation}">

</form>
<table>
    <tr>
        <td>Court Name</td>
        <td><input type="text" th:field="*{courtName}" required/></td>
        <td><span class="error" th:if="${#fields.hasErrors('courtName')}"
        th:errors="*{courtName}"></span></td>
    </tr>
    <tr>
        <td>Date</td>
        <td><input type="date" th:field="*{date}" required/></td>
        <td><span class="error" th:if="${#fields.hasErrors('date')}" th:errors="*{date}">
        </span></td>
    </tr>
    <tr>
        <td>Hour</td>
        <td><input type="number" min="8" max="22" th:field="*{hour}" /></td>
        <td><span class="error" th:if="${#fields.hasErrors('hour')}" th:errors="*{hour}">
        </span></td>
    </tr>
    <tr>
        <td colspan="3"><input type="submit" /></td>
    </tr>
</table>

</form>
</body>
</html>
```

This form uses Thymeleaf to bind all form fields to a model attribute named reservation because of the th:object=${reservation} tag on the form tag. Each field will bind (and display the value) of the actual field on the Reservation object. This is what the th:field tag is used for. When there are errors on the field, those are displayed through the use of the th:errors tags.

Finally, you see the standard HTML tag <input type="submit" /> that generates a Submit button and triggers the sending of data to the server.

If the form and its data are processed correctly, you need to create a success view to notify the user of a successful reservation. The `reservationSuccess.html` file illustrated next serves this purpose:

```html
<html>
<head>
<title>Reservation Success</title>
</head>

<body>
Your reservation has been made successfully.
</body>
</html>
```

It's also possible for errors to occur because of invalid values being submitted in a form. For example, if the date is not in a valid format or an alphabetic character is presented for the hour field, the controller is designed to reject such field values. The controller will then generate a list of selective error codes for each error to be returned to the form view; these values are placed in the `th:errors` tag.

For example, for an invalid value input in the `date` field, the following error codes are generated by the data binding:

```
typeMismatch.command.date
typeMismatch.date
typeMismatch.java.time.LocalDate
typeMismatch
```

If you have a `ResourceBundleMessageSource` object defined, you can include the following error messages in your resource bundle for the appropriate locale (e.g., `messages.properties` for the default locale); see also recipe 3-5 on how to externalize localization concerns:

```
typeMismatch.date=Invalid date format
typeMismatch.hour=Invalid hour format
```

The corresponding error codes and their values are what are returned to a user if a failure occurs when processing form data.

Now that you know the structure of the views involved with a form, as well as the data handled by it, let's take a look at the logic that handles the submitted data (i.e., the reservation) in a form.

Create a Form's Service Processing

This is not the controller but rather the service used by the controller to process the form's data reservation. First define a `make()` method in the `ReservationService` interface.

```java
package com.apress.springrecipes.court.service;
...
public interface ReservationService {
    ...
    Mono<Reservation> make(Mono<Reservation> reservation)
        throws ReservationNotAvailableException;
}
```

Then you implement this make() method by adding a Reservation item to the list that stores the reservations. You throw a ReservationNotAvailableException in the case of a duplicate reservation.

```java
package com.apress.springrecipes.reactive.court;
...
public class InMemoryReservationService implements ReservationService {
    ...
    @Override
    public Mono<Reservation> make(Reservation reservation) {

        long cnt = reservations.stream()
            .filter(made -> Objects.equals(made.getCourtName(), reservation.getCourtName()))
            .filter(made -> Objects.equals(made.getDate(), reservation.getDate()))
            .filter(made -> made.getHour() == reservation.getHour())
            .count();

        if (cnt > 0) {
            return Mono.error(new ReservationNotAvailableException(reservation
                .getCourtName(), reservation.getDate(), reservation
                .getHour())));
        } else {
            reservations.add(reservation);
            return Mono.just(reservation);
        }
    }
}
```

Now that you have a better understanding of the two elements that interact with a controller—a form's views and the reservation service class—let's create a controller to handle the court reservation form.

Create a Form's Controller

A controller used to handle forms makes use of practically the same annotations you've already used in the previous recipes. So, let's get right to the code.

```java
package com.apress.springrecipes.reactive.court.web;
...

@Controller
@RequestMapping("/reservationForm")
public class ReservationFormController {

    private final ReservationService reservationService;

    @Autowired
    public ReservationFormController(ReservationService reservationService) {
        this.reservationService = reservationService;
    }
```

```
@RequestMapping(method = RequestMethod.GET)
public String setupForm(Model model) {
    Reservation reservation = new Reservation();
    model.addAttribute("reservation", reservation);
    return "reservationForm";
}

@RequestMapping(method = RequestMethod.POST)
public String submitForm(
    @ModelAttribute("reservation") Reservation reservation,
    BindingResult result) {
        reservationService.make(reservation);
        return "redirect:reservationSuccess";
}
}
```

The controller starts by using the standard @Controller annotation, as well as the @RequestMapping annotation that allows access to the controller through the following URL:

```
http://localhost:8080/court-rx/reservationForm
```

When you enter this URL in your browser, it will send an HTTP GET request to your web application. This in turn triggers the execution of the setupForm method, which is designated to attend to this type of request based on its @GetMapping annotation.

The setupForm method defines a Model object as an input parameter, which serves to send model data to the view (i.e., the form). Inside the handler method, an empty Reservation object is created that is added as an attribute to the controller's Model object. Then the controller returns the execution flow to the reservationForm view, which in this case is resolved to reservationForm.jsp (i.e., the form).

The most important aspect of this last method is the addition of an empty Reservation object. If you analyze the form reservationForm.html, you will notice the form tag declares the th:object="${reservation}" attribute. This means that upon rendering the view, the form expects an object named reservation to be available, which is achieved by placing it inside the handler method's Model. In fact, further inspection reveals that the th:field=*{expression} values for each input tag correspond to the field names belonging to the Reservation object. Since the form is being loaded for the first time, it should be evident that an empty Reservation object is expected.

Now turn your attention to submitting the form for the first time. After you have filled in the form fields, submitting the form triggers an HTTP POST request, which in turn invokes the submitForm method—on account of this method's @PostMapping value.

The input fields declared for the submitForm method are the @ModelAttribute("reservation") Reservation reservation used to reference the reservation object and the BindingResult object that contains newly submitted data by the user.

At this juncture, the handler method doesn't incorporate validation, which is the purpose of the BindingResult object.

The only operation performed by the handler method is reservationService.make(reservation);. This operation invokes the reservation service using the current state of the reservation object.

Generally, controller objects are first validated prior to performing this type of operation on them.

Finally, note the handler method returns a view named redirect:reservationSuccess. The actual name of the view in this case is reservationSuccess, which is resolved to the reservationSuccess.html page you created earlier.

The redirect: prefix in the view name is used to avoid a problem known as *duplicate form submission*.

When you refresh the web page in the form success view, the form you just submitted is resubmitted. To avoid this problem, you can apply the post/redirect/get design pattern, which recommends redirecting to another URL after a form submission is handled successfully, instead of returning an HTML page directly. This is the purpose of prefixing a view name with `redirect:`.

Initialize a Model Attribute Object and Prepopulate a Form with Values

The form is designed to let users make reservations. However, if you analyze the `Reservation` domain class, you will note the form is still missing two fields to create a complete reservation object. One of these fields is the `player` field, which corresponds to a `Player` object. Per the `Player` class definition, a `Player` object has both `name` and `phone` fields.

So, can the player field be incorporated into a form view and controller? Let's analyze the form view first, shown here:

```
<!DOCTYPE html>
<html lang="en" xmlns:th="http://www.thymeleaf.org">
<body>
<form method="post" th:object="${reservation}">

    <table>
    ...
      <tr>
          <td>Player Name</td>
          <td><input type="text" th:field="*{player.name}" required/></td>
          <td><span class="error" th:if="${#fields.hasErrors('player.name')}"
              th:errors="*{player.name}"></span></td>
      </tr>
      <tr>
          <td>Player Phone</td>
          <td><input type="text" th:field="*{player.phone}" required/></td>
          <td><span class="error" th:if="${#fields.hasErrors('player.phone')}"
              th:errors="*{player.phone}"></span>
          </td>
      </tr>
      <tr>
          <td colspan="3"><input type="submit"/></td>
      </tr>
    </table>

</form>
</body>
</html>
```

Using a straightforward approach, you add two additional `<input>` tags to represent the `Player` object's fields. Though these form declarations are simple, you also need to perform modifications to the controller. Recall that by using `<input>` tags, a view expects to have access to model objects passed by the controller, which match the path value for `<input>` tags.

Though the controller's HTTP GET handler method returns an empty Reservation object to this last view, the player property is null, so it causes an exception when rendering the form. To solve this problem, you have to initialize an empty Player object and assign it to the Reservation object returned to the view.

```
@RequestMapping(method = RequestMethod.GET)
public String setupForm(
@RequestParam(required = false, value = "username") String username, Model model) {
    Reservation reservation = new Reservation();
    reservation.setPlayer(new Player(username, null));
    model.addAttribute("reservation", reservation);
    return "reservationForm";
}
```

In this case, after creating the empty Reservation object, the setPlayer method is used to assign it an empty Player object. Further note that the creation of the Person object relies on the username value. This particular value is obtained from the @RequestParam input value, which was also added to the handler method. By doing so, the Player object can be created with a specific username value passed in as a request parameter, resulting in the username form field being prepopulated with this value.

So, for example, if a request to the form is made in the following manner:

```
http://localhost:8080/court/reservationForm?username=Roger
```

this allows the handler method to extract the username parameter to create the Player object, in turn prepopulating the form's username form field with a Roger value. It's worth noting that the @RequestParam annotation for the username parameter uses the property required=false; this allows a form request to be processed even if such a request parameter is not present.

Provide Form Reference Data

When a form controller is requested to render the form view, it may have some types of reference data to provide to the form (e.g., the items to display in an HTML selection). Now suppose you want to allow a user to select the sport type when reserving a court—which is the final unaccounted field for the Reservation class.

```
<!DOCTYPE html>
<html lang="en" xmlns:th="http://www.thymeleaf.org">
<body>
<form method="post" th:object="${reservation}">

    <table>
        ...
        <tr>
            <td>Sport Type</td>
            <td>
                <select th:field="*{sportType}">
                    <option th:each="sportType : ${sportTypes}" th:value="${sportType.id}"
                    th:text="${sportType.name}"/>
                </select>
            </td>
```

```
        <td><span class="error" th:if="${#fields.hasErrors('sportType')}"
           th:errors="*{sportType}"></span></td>
     </tr>
     <tr>
        <td colspan="3"><input type="submit"/></td>
     </tr>
  </table>

</form>
</body>
</html>
```

The <form:select> tag provides a way to generate a drop-down list of values passed to the view by the controller. Thus, the form represents the sportType field as a set of HTML <select> elements, instead of the previous open-ended fields—<input>—that require a user to introduce text values.

Next, let's take a look at how the controller assigns the sportType field as a model attribute; the process is a little different than the previous fields.

First let's define the getAllSportTypes() method in the ReservationService interface for retrieving all available sport types.

```
package com.apress.springrecipes.reactive.court;
...
public interface ReservationService {
    ...
    Flux<SportType> getAllSportTypes();
}
```

Then you can implement this method by returning a hard-coded list.

```
package com.apress.springrecipes.reactive.court;
...
public class InMemoryReservationService implements ReservationService {
    ...
    public static final SportType TENNIS = new SportType(1, "Tennis");
    public static final SportType SOCCER = new SportType(2, "Soccer");

    public Flux<SportType> getAllSportTypes() {
        return Flux.fromIterable(Arrays.asList(TENNIS, SOCCER));
    }
}
```

Now that you have an implementation that returns a hard-coded list of SportType objects, let's take a look at how the controller associates this list for it to be returned to the form view.

```
package com.apress.springrecipes.court.service;
.....
    @ModelAttribute("sportTypes")
    public Flux<SportType> populateSportTypes() {
        return reservationService.getAllSportTypes();
    }
```

```
@RequestMapping(method = RequestMethod.GET)
public String setupForm(
@RequestParam(required = false, value = "username") String username, Model model) {
    Reservation reservation = new Reservation();
    reservation.setPlayer(new Player(username, null));
    model.addAttribute("reservation", reservation);
    return "reservationForm";
}
```

Notice that the setupForm handler method charged with returning the empty Reservation object to the form view remains unchanged.

The new addition, which is responsible for passing a SportType list as a model attribute to the form view, is the method decorated with the @ModelAttribute("sportTypes") annotation. The @ModelAttribute annotation is used to define global model attributes, available to any returning view used in handler methods. In the same way, a handler method declares a Model object as an input parameter and assigns attributes that can be accessed in the returning view.

Since the method decorated with the @ModelAttribute("sportTypes") annotation has a return type of Flux<SportType> and makes a call to reservationService.getAllSportTypes(), the hard-coded TENNIS and SOCCER SportType objects are assigned to the model attribute named sportTypes. This last model attribute is used in the form view to populate a drop-down list (i.e., <select> tag).

Bind Properties of Custom Types

When a form is submitted, a controller binds the form field values to the model object's properties of the same name, in this case a Reservation object. However, for properties of custom types, a controller is not able to convert them unless you specify the corresponding property editors for them.

For example, the sport type selection field submits only the selected sport type ID—as this is the way HTML <select> fields operate. Therefore, you have to convert this ID into a SportType object with a property editor. First, you require the getSportType() method in ReservationService to retrieve a SportType object by its ID.

```
package com.apress.springrecipes.court.service;
...
public interface ReservationService {
    ...
    public SportType getSportType(int sportTypeId);
}
```

For testing purposes, you can implement this method with a switch/case statement.

```
package com.apress.springrecipes.court.service;
...
public class ReservationServiceImpl implements ReservationService {
    ...
    public SportType getSportType(int sportTypeId) {
        switch (sportTypeId) {
        case 1:
            return TENNIS;
```

```
        case 2:
            return SOCCER;
        default:
            return null;
        }
    }
}
```

Then you create the SportTypeConverter class to convert a sport type ID into a SportType object. This converter requires ReservationService to perform the lookup.

```
package com.apress.springrecipes.reactive.court.domain;

import com.apress.springrecipes.court.service.ReservationService;
import org.springframework.core.convert.converter.Converter;

public class SportTypeConverter implements Converter<String, SportType> {

    private final ReservationService reservationService;

    public SportTypeConverter(ReservationService reservationService) {
        this.reservationService = reservationService;
    }

    @Override
    public SportType convert(String source) {
        int sportTypeId = Integer.parseInt(source);
        SportType sportType = reservationService.getSportType(sportTypeId);
        return sportType;
    }
}
```

Now that you have the supporting SportTypeConverter class required to bind form properties to a custom class like SportType, you need to associate it with the controller. For this purpose, you can use the addFormatters method from the WebFluxConfigurer.

By overriding this method in your configuration class, custom types can be associated with a controller. This includes the SportTypeConverter class and other custom types like Date. Though we didn't mention the date field earlier, it suffers from the same problem as the sport type selection field. A user introduces date fields as text values. For the controller to assign these text values to the Reservation object's date field, this requires the date fields to be associated with a Date object. Given the Date class is part of the Java language, it won't be necessary to create a special class like SportTypeConverter for this purpose. The Spring Framework already includes a custom class for this purpose.

Knowing you need to bind both the SportTypeConverter class and a Date class to the underlying controller, the following code illustrates the modifications to the configuration class:

```
package com.apress.springrecipes.reactive.court;

import org.springframework.beans.factory.annotation.Autowired;
import org.springframework.context.annotation.Bean;
import org.springframework.context.annotation.ComponentScan;
import org.springframework.context.annotation.Configuration;
import org.springframework.format.FormatterRegistry;
```

253

```
import org.springframework.web.reactive.config.EnableWebFlux;
import org.springframework.web.reactive.config.ViewResolverRegistry;
import org.springframework.web.reactive.config.WebFluxConfigurer;
import org.thymeleaf.extras.java8time.dialect.Java8TimeDialect;
import org.thymeleaf.spring5.ISpringWebFluxTemplateEngine;
import org.thymeleaf.spring5.SpringWebFluxTemplateEngine;
import org.thymeleaf.spring5.templateresolver.SpringResourceTemplateResolver;
import org.thymeleaf.spring5.view.reactive.ThymeleafReactiveViewResolver;
import org.thymeleaf.templatemode.TemplateMode;

@Configuration
@EnableWebFlux
@ComponentScan
public class WebFluxConfiguration implements WebFluxConfigurer {

    @Autowired
    private ReservationService reservationService;

    ...

    @Override
    public void addFormatters(FormatterRegistry registry) {
        registry.addConverter(new SportTypeConverter(reservationService));
    }
}
```

The only field for this last class corresponds to reservationService, used to access the application's ReservationService bean. Note the use of the @Autowired annotation that enables the injection of the bean. Next, you can override the addFormatters method used to bind the Date and SportTypeConverter classes. You can then find two calls to register the converter and formatter. These methods belong to the FormatterRegistry object, which is passed as an input parameter to the addFormatters method.

The first call is used to bind a Date class to the DateFormatter class. The DateFormatter class is provided by the Spring Framework and offers functionality to parse and print Date objects.

The second call is used to register the SportTypeConverter class. Since you created the SportTypeConverter class, you should know that its only input parameter is a ReservationService bean. By using this approach, every annotation-based controller (i.e., classes using the @Controller annotation) can have access to the same custom converters and formatters in their handler methods.

Validate Form Data

When a form is submitted, it's standard practice to validate the data provided by a user before a submission is successful. Spring WebFlux, like Spring MVC, supports validation by means of a validator object that implements the Validator interface. You can write the following validator to check whether the required form fields are filled and whether the reservation hour is valid on holidays and weekdays:

```
package com.apress.springrecipes.reactive.court;

import org.springframework.stereotype.Component;
import org.springframework.validation.Errors;
import org.springframework.validation.ValidationUtils;
import org.springframework.validation.Validator;
```

```java
import java.time.DayOfWeek;
import java.time.LocalDate;

@Component
public class ReservationValidator implements Validator {

    public boolean supports(Class<?> clazz) {
        return Reservation.class.isAssignableFrom(clazz);
    }

    public void validate(Object target, Errors errors) {
        ValidationUtils.rejectIfEmptyOrWhitespace(errors, "courtName",
            "required.courtName", "Court name is required.");
        ValidationUtils.rejectIfEmpty(errors, "date",
            "required.date", "Date is required.");
        ValidationUtils.rejectIfEmpty(errors, "hour",
            "required.hour", "Hour is required.");
        ValidationUtils.rejectIfEmptyOrWhitespace(errors, "player.name",
            "required.playerName", "Player name is required.");
        ValidationUtils.rejectIfEmpty(errors, "sportType",
            "required.sportType", "Sport type is required.");

        Reservation reservation = (Reservation) target;
        LocalDate date = reservation.getDate();
        int hour = reservation.getHour();
        if (date != null) {
            if (date.getDayOfWeek() == DayOfWeek.SUNDAY) {
                if (hour < 8 || hour > 22) {
                    errors.reject("invalid.holidayHour", "Invalid holiday hour.");
                }
            } else {
                if (hour < 9 || hour > 21) {
                    errors.reject("invalid.weekdayHour", "Invalid weekday hour.");
                }
            }
        }
    }
}
```

In this validator, you use utility methods such as rejectIfEmptyOrWhitespace() and rejectIfEmpty() in the ValidationUtils class to validate the required form fields. If any of these form fields is empty, these methods will create a field error and bind it to the field. The second argument of these methods is the property name, while the third and fourth are the error code and default error message.

You also check whether the reservation hour is valid on holidays and weekdays. If it's invalid, you should use the reject() method to create an object error to be bound to the reservation object, not to a field.

Since the validator class is annotated with the @Component annotation, Spring attempts to instantiate the class as a bean in accordance with the class name, in this case reservationValidator.

255

Since validators may create errors during validation, you should define messages for the error codes for displaying to the user. If you have ResourceBundleMessageSource defined, you can include the following error messages in your resource bundle for the appropriate locale (e.g., messages.properties for the default locale); see also recipe 3-5:

```
required.courtName=Court name is required
required.date=Date is required
required.hour=Hour is required
required.playerName=Player name is required
required.sportType=Sport type is required
invalid.holidayHour=Invalid holiday hour
invalid.weekdayHour=Invalid weekday hour
```

To apply this validator, you need to perform the following modification to your controller:

```
package com.apress.springrecipes.court.service;
.....
    private final ReservationService reservationService;
    private final ReservationValidator reservationValidator;

    public ReservationFormController(ReservationService reservationService,
        ReservationValidator reservationValidator) {
        this.reservationService = reservationService;
        this.reservationValidator = reservationValidator;
    }

    @RequestMapping(method = RequestMethod.POST)
    public String submitForm(
        @ModelAttribute("reservation") @Validated Reservation reservation,
        BindingResult result, SessionStatus status) {
        if (result.hasErrors()) {
            return "reservationForm";
        } else {
            reservationService.make(reservation);
            return "redirect:reservationSuccess";
        }
    }

    @InitBinder
    public void initBinder(WebDataBinder binder) {
        binder.setValidator(reservationValidator);
    }
```

The first addition to the controller is the ReservationValidator field, which gives the controller access to an instance of the validator bean.

The next modification takes place in the HTTP POST handler method, which is always called when a user submits a form. Next to the @ModelAttribute annotation, there is now an @Validated annotation, which triggers validation of the object. After the validation, the result parameter—the BindingResult object—contains the results for the validation process. So next, a conditional based on the value of result. hasErrors() is made. If the validation class detects errors, this value is true.

If errors are detected in the validation process, the method handler returns the view reservationForm, which corresponds to the same form so that a user can resubmit information. If no errors are detected in the validation process, a call is made to perform the reservation— reservationService.make(reservation);— followed by a redirection to the success view reservationSuccess.

The registration of the validator is done in the @InitBinder annotated method, and the validator is set on the WebDataBinder so that it can be used after binding. To register the validator, you need to use the setValidator method. You can also register multiple validators using the addValidators method; this method takes a varargs argument for one or more Validator instances.

■ **Note**   The WebDataBinder object can also be used to register additional PropertyEditor, Converter, and Formatter instances for type conversion. This can be used instead of registering global PropertyEditors, Converters, or Formatters.

■ **Tip**   Instead of writing a custom Spring Validator instances, you could also utilize JSR-303 validation and annotate fields to have them validated.

5-7. Publish and Consume JSON with Reactive REST Services

Problem

You want to publish XML or JSON services in a reactive way.

Solution

Using the same declarations as described in recipes 4-1 and 4-2, you can write a reactive endpoint.

How It Works

To publish JSON you can use the @ResponseBody or a @RestController. By returning a reactive type, Mono or Flux, you can have a chunked response. How the result is handled depends on the requested representation. When consuming JSON you can annotate a reactive method argument, of type Mono or Flux, with @ResponseBody to have this reactivly consumed.

Publish JSON

By annotating the request-handling method with @ResponseBody, the output will be returned as JSON or XML (depending on the request return type and available libraries on the classpath). Instead of annotating the method with @ResponseBody, you could use the @RestController annotation on the class level, which automatically implies this for all request-handling methods.

Let's write a REST controller that returns all reservations in the system. You do this by annotating a class with @RestController and giving it an @GetMapping annotated method, which returns a Flux<Reservation> object.

```
package com.apress.springrecipes.reactive.court.web;

import com.apress.springrecipes.reactive.court.Reservation;
import com.apress.springrecipes.reactive.court.ReservationService;
import org.springframework.web.bind.annotation.GetMapping;
import org.springframework.web.bind.annotation.RequestMapping;
import org.springframework.web.bind.annotation.RestController;
import reactor.core.publisher.Flux;

@RestController
@RequestMapping("/reservations")
public class ReservationRestController {

    private final ReservationService reservationService;

    public ReservationRestController(ReservationService reservationService) {
        this.reservationService = reservationService;
    }

    @GetMapping
    public Flux<Reservation> listAll() {
        return reservationService.findAll();
    }
}
```

When you return a reactive type like this, it will be streamed to the client either as streaming JSON/XML or as server-sent events (see recipe 5-2). The result depends on the Accept-Header header from the client. Using httpie and doing http http://localhost:8080/court-rx/reservations --stream will get you JSON. When adding Accept:text/event-stream, the result will be published as server-sent events.

Consume JSON

In addition to producing JSON, you can also consume it. For this, add a method argument and annotate it with @RequestBody. The incoming JSON request body will be mapped onto the object. For a reactive controller, you can wrap it in a Mono or Flux for, respectively, single or multiple results.

First create a simple POJO that takes a courtName so you can query the reservations.

```
package com.apress.springrecipes.reactive.court.web;

public class ReservationQuery {

    private String courtName;

    public String getCourtName() {
        return courtName;
    }
```

```
public void setCourtName(String courtName) {
    this.courtName = courtName;
}
}
```

This is just a basic POJO, which will be filled through JSON. Now it's time for the controller. Add a method that takes `Mono<ReservationQuery>` as its argument.

```
@PostMapping
public Flux<Reservation> find(@RequestBody Mono<ReservationQuery> query) {
    return query.flatMapMany(q -> reservationService.query(q.getCourtName()));
}
```

Now when a request with a JSON body comes in, this will be deserialized into the `ReservationQuery` object. For this, Spring WebFlux uses (just like Spring MVC) a converter. The conversion is delegated to an instance of `HttpMessageReader`, in this case `DecoderHttpMessageReader`. This class will decode the reactive stream into the object. This again is delegated to a `Decoder` object. Because you want to use JSON (and have the Jackson 2 JSON library on the classpath), it will use `Jackson2JsonDecoder` for this. The `HttpMessageReader` and `Decoder` implementations are the reactive counterparts of `HttpMessageConverter` used by regular Spring MVC.

Using httpie and issuing the request `http POST http://localhost:8080/court-rx/reservations courtName="Tennis #1" --stream`, you will get back all the results for the court `Tennis #1`. This command will send the following JSON to the server:

```
{ courtName: "Tennis #1"}
```

5-8. Use an Asynchronous Web Client

Problem

You want to access a REST service from a third party (e.g., Google, Yahoo, or another business partner) and use its payload inside a Spring application.

Solution

Accessing a third-party REST service inside a Spring application revolves around the use of the Spring `WebClient` class. The `WebClient` class is designed on the same principles as the many other Spring `*Template` classes (e.g., `JdbcTemplate`, `JmsTemplate`), providing a simplified approach with default behaviors for performing lengthy tasks.

This means the processes of invoking a REST service and using its returning payload are streamlined in Spring applications.

■ **Note**   Prior to Spring 5, you would use `AsyncRestTemplate`; however, as of Spring 5, that has been deprecated in favor of `WebClient`.

How It Works

Before describing the particularities of the WebClient class, it's worth exploring the life cycle of a REST service so you're aware of the actual work the RestTemplate class performs. Exploring the life cycle of a REST service can best be done from a browser, so open your favorite browser on your workstation to get started.

The first thing that's needed is a REST service endpoint. You are going to reuse the endpoint you created in recipe 5-7. This endpoint should be available at http://localhost:8080/court-rx/reservations. If you load this REST service endpoint in your browser, the browser performs a GET request, which is one of the most popular HTTP requests supported by REST services. Upon loading the REST service, the browser displays a responding payload, as shown in Figure 5-6.

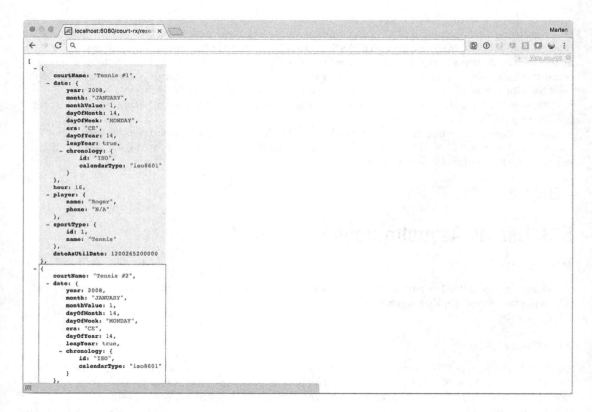

Figure 5-6. *Resulting JSON*

It's the task of a REST service consumer (i.e., you) to know the payload structure—sometimes referred to as the *vocabulary*—of a REST service to appropriately process its information. Though this last REST service relies on what can be considered a custom vocabulary, a series of REST services often relies on standardized vocabularies (e.g., RSS), which makes the processing of REST service payloads uniform. In addition, it's also worth noting that some REST services provide Web Application Description Language (WADL) contracts to facilitate the discovery and consumption of payloads.

Now that you're familiar with a REST service's life cycle using your browser, you can take a look at how to use the Spring WebClient class to incorporate a REST service's payload into a Spring application. Given that the WebClient class is designed to call REST services, it should come as no surprise that its main methods are closely tied to REST's underpinnings, which are the HTTP protocol's methods: HEAD, GET, POST, PUT, DELETE, and OPTIONS. Table 5-6 contains the main methods supported by the RestTemplate class.

Table 5-6. *WebClient Class Methods Based on HTTP's Request Methods*

Method	Description
create	Creates a WebClient; optionally you can give a default URL
head()	Prepares an HTTP HEAD operation
get()	Prepares an HTTP GET operation
post()	Prepares an HTTP POST operation
put()	Prepares an HTTP PUT operation
options()	Prepares an HTTP OPTIONS operation
patch()	Prepares an HTTP PATCH operation
delete()	Prepares an HTTP DELETE operation

As you can observe in Table 5-6, the WebClient class builder methods are modeled after HTTP protocol methods, which include HEAD, GET, POST, PUT, DELETE, and OPTIONS.

> ■ **Note** By far the most common HTTP method used in REST services is GET since it represents a safe operation to obtain information (i.e., it doesn't modify any data). On the other hand, HTTP methods such as PUT, POST, and DELETE are designed to modify a provider's information, which makes them less likely to be supported by a REST service provider. For cases in which data modification needs to take place, many providers opt for the SOAP protocol, which is an alternative mechanism to using REST services.

Now that you're aware of the WebClient basic builder methods, you can move on to invoking the same REST service you did with your browser previously, except this time using Java code from the Spring Framework. The following code illustrates a class that accesses the REST service and returns its contents to System.out:

```
package com.apress.springrecipes.reactive.court;

import org.springframework.http.MediaType;
import org.springframework.web.reactive.function.client.WebClient;

import java.io.IOException;

public class Main {

    public static void main(String[] args) throws IOException {
        final String url = "http://localhost:8080/court-rx";
```

```
        WebClient.create(url)
            .get()
            .uri("/reservations")
            .accept(MediaType.APPLICATION_STREAM_JSON)
            .exchange()
            .flatMapMany(cr -> cr.bodyToFlux(String.class)).subscribe(System.out::println);

        System.in.read();
    }
}
```

■ **Caution**   Some REST service providers restrict access to their data feeds depending on the requesting party. Access is generally denied by relying on data present in a request (e.g., HTTP headers or IP address). So, depending on the circumstances, a provider can return an access denied response even when a data feed appears to be working in another medium (e.g., you might be able to access a REST service in a browser but get an accessed denied response when attempting to access the same feed from a Spring application). This depends on the terms of use set forth by a REST provider.

The first line declares the `import` statement needed to access the `WebClient` class within a class's body. First you need to create an instance of the `WebClient` class using `WebClient.create`. Next, you can find a call made to the `get()` method that belongs to the `WebClient` class, which as described in Table 5-6 is used to prepare an HTTP GET operation—just like the one performed by a browser to obtain a REST service's payload. Next you extend the base URL to call because you want to call `http://localhost:8080/court-rx/reservations` and you want to have a stream of JSON, which is the reason for `accept(MediaType.APPLICATION_STREAM_JSON)`.

Next, the call to `exchange()` will switch the configuration from setting up the request to define the response handling. As you probably get zero or more elements, you need to convert the `ClientResponse` body to a `Flux`. For this you can call the `bodyToFlux` method on `ClientResponse` (there is also a plain body method that you could use if you need custom conversion or the `bodyToMono` method to convert to a single-element result). You want to write each element to `System.out`, so you subscribe to that.

When you execute the application, the output will be the same as in the browser except that it is now printed in the console.

Retrieve Data from a Parameterized URL

The previous section showed how you can call a URI to retrieve data, but what about a URI that requires parameters? You don't want to hard-code parameters into the URL. With the `WebClient` class, you can use a URL with placeholders; these placeholders will be replaced with actual values upon execution. Placeholders are defined using { and }, just as with a request mapping (see recipes 4-1 and 4-2).

The URI `http://localhost:8080/court-rx/reservations/{courtName}` is an example of such a parameterized URI. To be able to call this method, you need to pass in a value for the placeholder; you can do this by passing the parameters as arguments to the uri method of the WebClient class.

```java
public class Main {

    public static void main(String[] args) throws Exception {
        WebClient.create(url)
            .get()
            .uri("/reservations/{courtName}", "Tennis")
            .accept(MediaType.APPLICATION_STREAM_JSON)
            .exchange()
            .flatMapMany(cr -> cr.bodyToFlux(String.class))
            .subscribe(System.out::println);

        System.in.read();
    }
}
```

Retrieve Data as a Mapped Object

Instead of returning a String to be used in the application, you can also (re)use your Reservation, Player, and SportType classes to map the result. Instead of passing in String.class as a parameter to the bodyToFlux method, pass Reservation.class, and the response will be mapped onto this class.

```java
package com.apress.springrecipes.reactive.court;

import org.springframework.http.MediaType;
import org.springframework.web.reactive.function.client.WebClient;

import java.io.IOException;

public class Main {

    public static void main(String[] args) throws IOException {
        final String url = "http://localhost:8080/court-rx";

        WebClient.create(url)
            .get()
            .uri("/reservations")
            .accept(MediaType.APPLICATION_STREAM_JSON)
            .exchange()
            .flatMapMany(cr -> cr.bodyToFlux(Reservation.class))
            .subscribe(System.out::println);

        System.in.read();
    }
}
```

The WebClient class makes use of the same HttpMessageReader infrastructure as a controller with @ResponseBody marked methods. As JAXB 2 (as well as Jackson) is automatically detected, mapping to an object is quite easy.

5-9. Write a Reactive Handler Function

Problem

You want to write functions that react to incoming requests.

Solution

You can write a method that takes a ServerRequest, returns a Mono<ServerResponse>, and maps it as a router function.

How It Works

Instead of mapping requests to methods using @RequestMapping, you can also write functions that are essentially honoring the HandlerFunction interface.

```
package org.springframework.web.reactive.function.server;

import reactor.core.publisher.Mono;

@FunctionalInterface
public interface HandlerFunction<T extends ServerResponse> {

    Mono<T> handle(ServerRequest request);

}
```

A HandlerFunction, as shown in the previous code, is basically a method that takes a ServerRequest as an argument and returns a Mono<ServerResponse>. Both the ServerRequest and ServerResponse provide full reactive access to the underlying request and response; this is by exposing various parts of it as either Mono or Flux streams.

After a function has been written, it can be mapped to incoming requests using the RouterFunctions class. The mapping can be done on URLs, headers, methods, or custom-written RequestPredicate classes. The default available request predicates are accessible through the RequestPredicates class.

Write Handler Functions

Let's rewrite the ReservationRestController to simple request-handling functions instead of a controller.

To do so, remove all the request-mapping annotations and add a simple @Component to the class. Next rewrite the methods to adhere to the signature outlined by the HandlerFunction interface.

```
package com.apress.springrecipes.reactive.court.web;

import com.apress.springrecipes.reactive.court.Reservation;
import com.apress.springrecipes.reactive.court.ReservationService;
import org.springframework.stereotype.Component;
import org.springframework.web.bind.annotation.*;
import org.springframework.web.reactive.function.server.ServerRequest;
import org.springframework.web.reactive.function.server.ServerResponse;
```

```java
import reactor.core.publisher.Flux;
import reactor.core.publisher.Mono;

@Component
public class ReservationRestController {

    private final ReservationService reservationService;

    public ReservationRestController(ReservationService reservationService) {
        this.reservationService = reservationService;
    }

    public Mono<ServerResponse> listAll(ServerRequest request) {
        return ServerResponse.ok().body(reservationService.findAll(), Reservation.class);
    }

    public Mono<ServerResponse> find(ServerRequest request) {
        return ServerResponse
            .ok()
            .body(
                request.bodyToMono(ReservationQuery.class)
                    .flatMapMany(q -> reservationService.query(q.getCourtName())),
                    Reservation.class);
    }
}
```

The class still needs ReservationService as a dependency. Notice the change in the listAll and find methods. They now both return Mono<ServerResposne> and accept a ServerRequest as input. Because you want to return an HTTP status of OK (200), you can use ServerResponse.ok() to build that response. You need to add a body, Flux<Reservation> in this case, and you need to specify the type of elements, Reservation.class. The latter is needed because the reactive and generic nature type of information cannot be read when composing the function.

In the find method, something similar happens, but first you map the body of the incoming request to a ReservationQuery using bodyToMono. This result is then used to eventually call the query method on ReservationService.

Route Requests to Handler Functions

As you now have simple functions instead of annotation-based request-handling methods, routing needs to be done differently. You can use RouterFunctions to do the mapping instead.

```java
@Bean
public RouterFunction<ServerResponse> reservationsRouter(ReservationRestController handler)
{
    return RouterFunctions
        .route(GET("/*/reservations"), handler::listAll)
        .andRoute(POST("/*/reservations"), handler::find);
}
```

When an HTTP GET request comes in for /court-rx/reservations, the listAll method will be invoked for an HTTP POST the find method will be invoked.

Using RequestPredicates.GET is the same as writing RequestPredicates.method(HttpMethod.GET). and(RequestPredicates.path("/*/reservations")). You can combine as many RequestPredicate statements as you want. The methods in Table 5-7 are exposed through the RequestPredicates class.

Table 5-7. *Default Available RequestPredicates*

Method	Description
method	RequestPredicate for the HTTP METHOD
path	RequestPredicate for the URL or part of the URL
accept	RequestPredicate for the Accept header to match requested media types
queryParam	RequestPredicate to check for the existence of query parameters
headers	RequestPredicate to check for the existence of request headers

The RequestPredicates helper also provides shorthand methods for GET, POST, PUT, DELETE, HEAD, PATCH, and OPTIONS. This saves you from combining two expressions.

Summary

In this chapter, you looked at various ways to do async processing. The traditional way is to use the Servlet 3.*x* asynchronous support and have the controller return a DeferredResult or a Future.

For communication, you looked at server-sent events and WebSocket communication. This allowed you to communicate in an asynchronous way between the client and the server.

Then you moved on and learned how to write reactive controllers, which wasn't all that different from what you learned in Chapters 3 and 4. This also shows the power of Spring's abstractions; you can use almost the same programming model for a totally different technology. After writing reactive controllers, you looked at writing reactive handler functions, which can do much of the same stuff that reactive controllers can do in a more functional programming kind of way.

In between you also looked at the WebClient class to do asynchronous consumption of a REST API.

CHAPTER 6

Spring Social

Social networking is everywhere, and most Internet users have one or more social networking accounts. People tweet to share what they are doing or how they feel about a subject; they share pictures on Facebook and Instagram, and they write blogs using Tumblr. More and more social networks are appearing every day. As the owner of a web site, it can be beneficial to add integration with those social networks, allowing users to easily post links or to filter and show how people think.

Spring Social tries to have a unified API to connect to those different networks and an extension model. Spring Social itself provides integration for Facebook, Twitter, and LinkedIn; however, there are lots of community projects providing support for different social networks (such as Tumblr, Weibo, and Instagram, to name a few). Spring Social can be split into three parts. First there is the Connect Framework, which handles the authentication and connection flow with the underlying social network. Next is `ConnectController`, which is the controller doing the OAuth exchange between the service provider, the consumer (the application), and the user of the application. Finally, there is `SocialAuthenticationFilter`, which integrates Spring Social with Spring Security (see Chapter 8) to allow users to sign in with their social network account.

6-1. Set Up Spring Social

Problem

You want to use Spring Social in your application.

Solution

Add Spring Social to your dependencies and enable Spring Social in your configuration.

How It Works

Spring Social consists of several core modules and extension modules for each service provider (such as Twitter, Facebook, GitHub etc.). To be able to use Spring Social, you will need to add them to your application's dependencies. Table 6-1 shows the available modules.

© Marten Deinum, Daniel Rubio, and Josh Long 2017
M. Deinum et al., *Spring 5 Recipes*, DOI 10.1007/978-1-4842-2790-9_6

Table 6-1. *Overview of Spring Social Modules*

Module	Description
spring-social-core	Core module of Spring Social; contains the main and shared infrastructure classes
spring-social-config	Spring Social configuration module; makes it easier to configure (parts) of Spring Social
spring-social-web	Web integration for Spring Social contains filters and controllers for easy use
spring-social-security	Integration with Spring Security (see Chapter 7)

The dependencies are in the group org.springframework.social. This chapter will cover every module (core, config, web, and security) in different recipes. After adding the dependencies, you can set up Spring Social.

```
package com.apress.springrecipes.social.config;

import com.apress.springrecipes.social.StaticUserIdSource;
import org.springframework.context.annotation.*;
import org.springframework.core.env.Environment;
import org.springframework.social.config.annotation.EnableSocial;
import org.springframework.social.config.annotation.SocialConfigurerAdapter;

@Configuration
@EnableSocial
@PropertySource("classpath:/application.properties")
public class SocialConfig extends SocialConfigurerAdapter {

    @Override
    public StaticUserIdSource getUserIdSource() {
        return new StaticUserIdSource();
    }
}
```

To enable Spring Social, simply add the @EnableSocial annotation to an @Configuration annotated class. This annotation will trigger the loading of the configuration of Spring Social. It will detect any instance of SocialConfigurer beans, which are used for further configuration of Spring Social. Specifically, they are used to add the configuration for one or more service providers.

SocialConfig extends SocialConfigurerAdapter, which is an implementation of SocialConfigurer. As you can see, there is an overridden method called getUserIdSource, which returns a StaticUserIdSource object. Spring Social requires an instance of UserIdSource to determine the current user. This user is used to look up any connections with service providers. These connections are stored in a per-user ConnectionRepository. Which ConnectionRepository to use is determined by UsersConnectionRepository, which uses the current user. The default configured UsersConnectionRepository is InMemoryUsersConnectionRepository.

Finally, you load a properties file from the classpath. This properties file contains the API keys for your application to use for service providers. Instead of putting them in a properties file, you could also hard-code them into your code.

For the time being, you are going to use StaticUserIdSource to determine the current user.

```
package com.apress.springrecipes.social;

import org.springframework.social.UserIdSource;

public class StaticUserIdSource implements UserIdSource {

    private static final String DEFAULT_USERID = "anonymous";
    private String userId = DEFAULT_USERID;

    @Override
    public String getUserId() {
        return this.userId;
    }

    public void setUserId(String userId) {
        this.userId = userId;
    }
}
```

StaticUserIdSource implements UserIdSource and returns a preset userId. Although this works for now, in a real application, you would want to be able to store the connection information on a per-user basis.

6-2. Connect to Twitter

Problem

You want your application to have access to Twitter.

Solution

Register your application with Twitter and configure Spring Social to make use of the application credentials to get access to Twitter.

How It Works

Before you can have your application use Twitter, you need to register your application with Twitter. After this registration, you will have credentials (the API key and API secret) to identify your application.

Register an Application on Twitter

To register an application with Twitter, go to `https://dev.twitter.com` and look in the top-right corner for your avatar; from the drop-down menu, select "My apps" (see Figure 6-1).

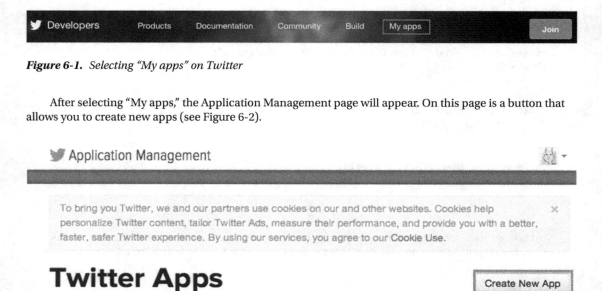

Figure 6-1. *Selecting "My apps" on Twitter*

After selecting "My apps," the Application Management page will appear. On this page is a button that allows you to create new apps (see Figure 6-2).

Figure 6-2. *Application Management page*

On this page, click the button to open a screen (see Figure 6-3) to register your application.

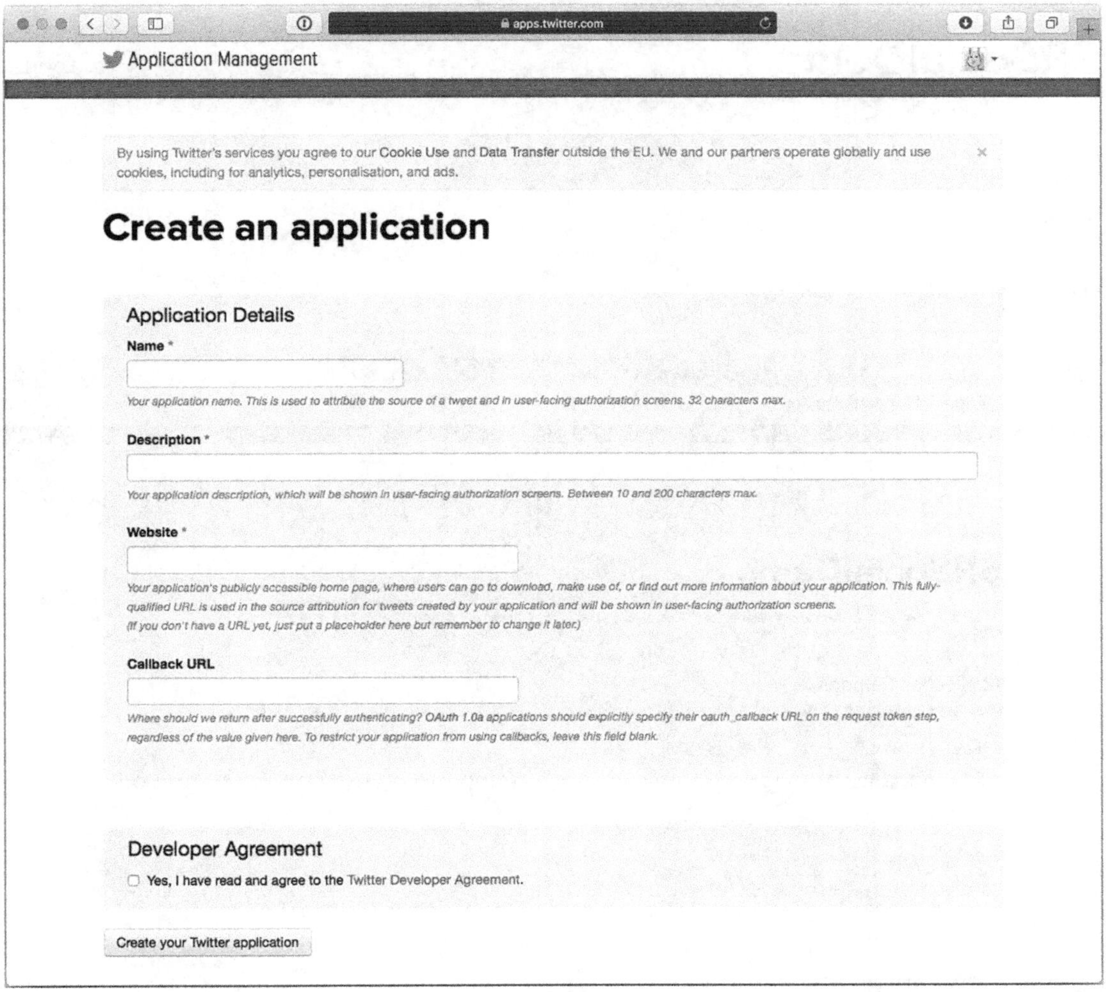

Figure 6-3. *Registering a new application*

On this screen, you must enter a name and description of your application and the URL of the web site on which this application is going to be used. When using Spring Social, it is also important that you fill out the callback URL field because you will need callbacks; the actual value doesn't really matter (unless you use a very old version of OAuth).

After accepting the terms and conditions and clicking the final create button, you will be taken to your application settings page. That means you have successfully created your application.

To be able to connect Spring Social to Twitter, you need to know your API key and API secret. You can find them on the API Keys tab of your application settings (see Figures 6-4 and 6-5).

Figure 6-4. *Application settings page*

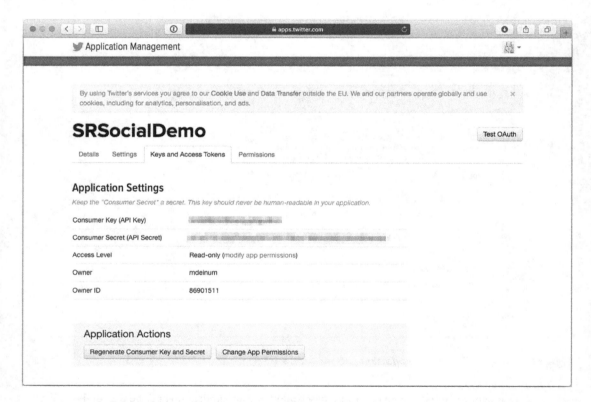

Figure 6-5. *API key and API secret needed to connect Spring Social*

Configure Spring Social to Connect with Twitter

Now that you have an API key and API secret, you can configure Spring Social to connect to Twitter. First create a properties file (for instance, application.properties) to hold your API key and API secret so that you can easily retrieve it when you need it.

```
twitter.appId=<your-twitter-API-key-here>
twitter.appSecret=<your-twitter-API-secret-here>
```

To connect to Twitter, you need to add a TwitterConnectionFactory, which will use the application ID and secret when requested to connect to Twitter.

```
package com.apress.springrecipes.social.config;

import org.springframework.core.env.Environment;
import org.springframework.social.config.annotation.ConnectionFactoryConfigurer;
import org.springframework.social.connect.Connection;
import org.springframework.social.connect.ConnectionRepository;
import org.springframework.social.twitter.api.Twitter;
import org.springframework.social.twitter.connect.TwitterConnectionFactory;

@Configuration
@EnableSocial
@PropertySource("classpath:/application.properties")
public class SocialConfig extends SocialConfigurerAdapter {
...
    @Configuration
    public static class TwitterConfigurer extends SocialConfigurerAdapter {

        @Override
        public void addConnectionFactories(
            ConnectionFactoryConfigurer connectionFactoryConfigurer,
            Environment env) {

            connectionFactoryConfigurer.addConnectionFactory(
                new TwitterConnectionFactory(
                    env.getRequiredProperty("twitter.appId"),
                    env.getRequiredProperty("twitter.appSecret")));
        }

        @Bean
        @Scope(value = "request", proxyMode = ScopedProxyMode.INTERFACES)
        public Twitter twitterTemplate(ConnectionRepository connectionRepository) {

            Connection<Twitter> connection = connectionRepository.
            findPrimaryConnection(Twitter.class);
            return connection != null ? connection.getApi() : null;
        }
    }
}
```

The SocialConfigurer interface has the callback method addConnectionFactories, which allows you to add ConnectionFactory instances to use Spring Social. For Twitter, there is the TwitterConnectionFactory, which takes two arguments. The first is the API key, and the second is the API secret. Both constructor arguments come from the properties file that is read. Of course, you could also hard-code the values into the configuration. The connection to Twitter has been made. Although you could use the raw underlying connection, it isn't really recommended to do so. Instead, use the TwitterTemplate, which makes it easier to work with the Twitter API. The previous configuration adds a TwitterTemplate to the application context.

273

Notice the @Scope annotation. It is important that this bean is request-scoped. For each request, the actual connection to Twitter might differ because potentially every request is for a different user, which is why you have the request-scoped bean. The ConnectionRepository that is injected into the method is determined based on the ID of the current user, which is retrieved using the UserIdSource you configured earlier.

■ **Note** Although the sample uses a separate configuration class to configure Twitter as a service provider, you can also add it to the main SocialConfig class. However, it can be desirable to separate the global Spring Social configuration from the specific service provider setup.

6-3. Connect to Facebook

Problem

You want your application to have access to Facebook.

Solution

Register your application with Facebook and configure Spring Social to make use of the application credentials to get access to Facebook.

How It Works

Before you can have your application use Facebook, you first need to register your application with Facebook. After this registration, you will have credentials (API key and API secret) to identify your application. To be able to register an application on Facebook, you need to have a Facebook account and have to be registered as a developer. (This recipe assumes you already have been registered as a developer with Facebook. If not, go to http://developers.facebook.com, click the Register Now button, and fill out the wizard.)

Register an Application on Facebook

Start by going to http://developers.facebook.com; click the Apps menu on top of the page and select Add a New App (see Figure 6-6).

Figure 6-6. *First steps in registering a new app*

This will open a screen (see Figure 6-7) that allows you to fill in some details about your application.

Create a New App ID

Get started integrating Facebook into your app or website

Display Name

The name you want to associate with this App ID

Contact Email

Used for important communication about your app

By proceeding, you agree to the **Facebook Platform Policies**   Cancel   Create App ID

Figure 6-7. Create a New App ID window

The name of your application can be anything as long as it doesn't contain the word *face* or *book*. It also needs an e-mail address so Facebook knows who to contact. After you've filled in the form, click the Create App ID button, which will take you to your application page (see Figure 6-8). On this page, navigate to the Settings tab.

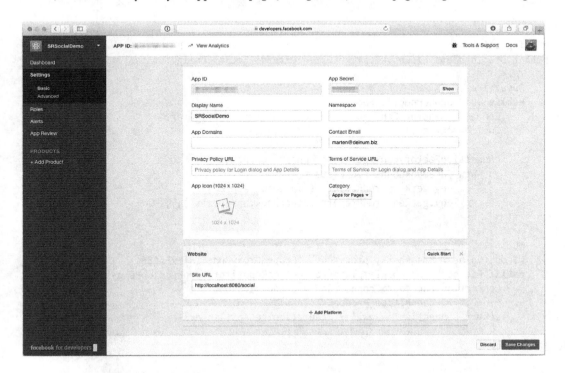

Figure 6-8. Facebook Settings page

On the Settings page, click the Add Platform button and select Website. Enter the URL of the site your app is going to be part of. In this exercise, that is http://localhost:8080/social. If this URL isn't present, authorization will not be granted, and the connection will be never made.

Configure Spring Social to Connect with Facebook

The Facebook Settings page also contains the application ID and secret needed by the application to connect to Facebook. Put them in the application.properties file.

```
facebook.appId=<your app-id here>
facebook.appSecret=<your app-secret here>
```

Assuming Spring Social is already set up (see recipe 6-1), it is a matter of adding a FacebookConnectionFactory and FacebookTemplate for easy access.

```
package com.apress.springrecipes.social.config;

import org.springframework.social.facebook.api.Facebook;
import org.springframework.social.facebook.connect.FacebookConnectionFactory;

@Configuration
@EnableSocial
@PropertySource("classpath:/application.properties")
public class SocialConfig extends SocialConfigurerAdapter {

...

    @Configuration
    public static class FacebookConfiguration extends SocialConfigurerAdapter {

        @Override
        public void addConnectionFactories(
            ConnectionFactoryConfigurer connectionFactoryConfigurer,
            Environment env) {

            connectionFactoryConfigurer.addConnectionFactory(
                new FacebookConnectionFactory(
                    env.getRequiredProperty("facebook.appId"),
                    env.getRequiredProperty("facebook.appSecret")));
        }

        @Bean
        @Scope(value = "request", proxyMode = ScopedProxyMode.INTERFACES)
        public Facebook facebookTemplate(ConnectionRepository connectionRepository) {
            Connection<Facebook> connection = connectionRepository.
            findPrimaryConnection(Facebook.class);
            return connection != null ? connection.getApi() : null;
        }
    }
}
```

The FacebookConnectionFactory needs the application ID and secret. Both properties are added to the application.properties file and are available through the Environment object.

The previous bean configuration adds a bean named facebookTemplate to the application context. Notice the @Scope annotation. It is important that this bean is request-scoped. For each request, the actual connection to Facebook might differ because potentially every request is for a different user, which is the reason for the request-scoped bean. Which ConnectionRepository is injected into the method is determined based on the ID of the current user, which is retrieved using the UserIdSource you configured earlier (see recipe 6-1).

> ■ **Note** Although the sample uses a separate configuration class to configure Facebook as a service provider, you can also add it to the main SocialConfig class. However, it can be desirable to separate the global Spring Social configuration from the specific service provider setup.

6-4. Show the Service Provider's Connection Status

Problem

You want to display the status of the connections of the used service providers.

Solution

Configure ConnectController and use it to show the status to the user.

How It Works

Spring Social comes with ConnectController, which takes care of connecting to and disconnecting from a service provider, but you can also show the status (connected or not) of the current user for the used service providers. ConnectController uses several REST URLs to either show, add, or remove the connection for the given user (see Table 6-2).

Table 6-2. *ConnectController URL Mapping*

URL	Method	Description
/connect	GET	Displays the connection status of all available service provides. Will return connect/status as the name of the view to render.
	POST	Starts the connection flow with the given provider.
	DELETE	Deletes all connections for the current user with the given provider.

To be able to use the controller, you first need to configure Spring MVC (see Chapter 4). For this, add the following configuration:

```java
package com.apress.springrecipes.social.config;

import org.springframework.context.annotation.Bean;
import org.springframework.context.annotation.ComponentScan;
import org.springframework.context.annotation.Configuration;
import org.springframework.web.servlet.ViewResolver;
import org.springframework.web.servlet.config.annotation.EnableWebMvc;
import org.springframework.web.servlet.config.annotation.ViewControllerRegistry;
import org.springframework.web.servlet.config.annotation.WebMvcConfigurer;
import org.springframework.web.servlet.view.InternalResourceViewResolver;

@Configuration
@EnableWebMvc
@ComponentScan({"com.apress.springrecipes.social.web"})
public class WebConfig implements WebMvcConfigurer {

    @Bean
    public ViewResolver internalResourceViewResolver() {
        InternalResourceViewResolver viewResolver = new InternalResourceViewResolver();
        viewResolver.setPrefix("/WEB-INF/views/");
        viewResolver.setSuffix(".jsp");
        return viewResolver;
    }

    @Override
    public void addViewControllers(ViewControllerRegistry registry) {
        registry.addViewController("/").setViewName("index");
        registry.addViewController("/signin").setViewName("signin");
    }
}
```

You need to enable Spring MVC using @EnableWebMvc and add a ViewResolver so the JSP pages can be picked up. Finally, you want to show the index.jsp page when the application starts up. Next add ConnectController to the WebConfig class. This controller needs ConnectionFactoryLocator and ConnectionRepository as constructor arguments. To access them, simply add them as method arguments.

```java
@Bean
public ConnectController connectController(
ConnectionFactoryLocator connectionFactoryLocator,
ConnectionRepository connectionRepository) {

    return new ConnectController(connectionFactoryLocator, connectionRepository);
}
```

ConnectController will listen to the URLs, as listed in Table 6-2. Now add two views in the /WEB-INF/views directory. The first is the main index, and the second is the status overview page. First create the index.jsp file.

```
<%@ taglib prefix="spring" uri="http://www.springframework.org/tags" %>
<html>
<head>
    <title>Hello Spring Social</title>
</head>
<body>

<h3>Connections</h3>
    Click <a href="<spring:url value='/connect'/>">here</a> to see your Social Network
    Connections.
</body>
</html>
```

Next create the status.jsp file in the /WEB-INF/views/connect directory.

```
<%@ taglib prefix="spring" uri="http://www.springframework.org/tags" %>
<%@ taglib prefix="c" uri="http://java.sun.com/jsp/jstl/core" %>
<html>
<head>
    <title>Spring Social - Connections</title>
</head>
<body>
<h3>Spring Social - Connections</h3>
<c:forEach items="${providerIds}" var="provider">
    <h4>${provider}</h4>
    <c:if test="${not empty connectionMap[provider]}">
        You are connected to ${provider} as ${connectionMap[provider][0].displayName}
    </c:if>

    <c:if test="${empty connectionMap[provider]}">
        <div>
            You are not yet connected to ${provider}. Click <a href="<spring:url
            value="/connect/${provider}"/>">here</a> to connect to ${provider}.
        </div>
    </c:if>
</c:forEach>
</body>
</html>
```

The status page will iterate over all available providers and will determine whether there is an existing connection for the current user for that service provider (Twitter, Facebook, etc.). ConnectController will make the list of providers available under the providerIds attribute, and connectionMap holds the connections of the current user. Now to bootstrap the application, you will need to create a WebApplicationInitializer that will register a ContextLoaderListener and DispatcherServlet to handle the requests.

```
package com.apress.springrecipes.social;

import com.apress.springrecipes.social.config.SocialConfig;
import com.apress.springrecipes.social.config.WebConfig;
import org.springframework.web.filter.DelegatingFilterProxy;
```

```
import org.springframework.web.servlet.support.
AbstractAnnotationConfigDispatcherServletInitializer;

import javax.servlet.Filter;

public class SocialWebApplicationInitializer extends
AbstractAnnotationConfigDispatcherServletInitializer {

    @Override
    protected Class<?>[] getRootConfigClasses() {

        return new Class<?>[]{SocialConfig.class};
    }

    @Override
    protected Class<?>[] getServletConfigClasses() {

        return new Class<?>[] {WebConfig.class, };
    }

    @Override
    protected String[] getServletMappings() {

        return new String[] {"/"};
    }
}
```

This will bootstrap the application. The SocialConfig class will be loaded by the ContextLoaderListener, and the WebConfig class will be loaded by the DispatcherServlet. To be able to handle requests, there needs to be a servlet mapping. For this, the mapping will be /.

Now that everything is configured, the application can be deployed and accessed by the URL http://localhost:8080/social. This will show the index page. Clicking the link will show the connection status page, which initially will show that the current user isn't connected.

Connect to a Service Provider

When clicking a link to connect to a service provider, the user will be sent to the /connect/{provider} URL. When there isn't a connection, the connect/{provider}Connect page will be rendered or the connect/{provider}Connected page will be shown. To be able to use ConnectController to connect to Twitter, you need to add the twitterConnect.jsp and twitterConnected.jsp pages. For Facebook, you need to add the facebookConnect.jsp and facebookConnected.jsp pages. The same pattern applies to all other service provider connectors for Spring Social (such as GitHub, FourSquare, LinkedIn, and so on). First add twitterConnect.jsp to the /WEB-INF/views/connect directory.

```
<%@ taglib prefix="spring" uri="http://www.springframework.org/tags" %>
<html>
<head>
    <title>Spring Social - Connect to Twitter</title>
</head>
<body>
<h3>Connect to Twitter</h3>
```

```
<form action="<spring:url value='/connect/twitter'/>" method="POST">
    <div class="formInfo">
        <p>You aren't connected to Twitter yet. Click the button to connect this application
        with your Twitter account.</p>
    </div>
    <p><button type="submit">Connect to Twitter</button></p>
</form>
</body>
</html>
```

Notice the form tag that POSTs the form back to the same URL. When clicking the Submit button, you will be redirected to Twitter, which will ask for your permission to allow this application to access your Twitter profile. (Replace this with facebook to connect to Facebook.)

Next add twitterConnected.jsp to the /WEB-INF/views/connect directory. This is the page that will be displayed when you are already connected to Twitter but also when you return from Twitter after authorizing the application.

```
<%@ taglib prefix="spring" uri="http://www.springframework.org/tags" %>
<html>
<head>
    <title>Spring Social - Connected to Twitter</title>
</head>

<body>
<h3>Connected to Twitter</h3>
<p>
    You are now connected to your Twitter account.
    Click <a href="<spring:url value='/connect'/>">here</a> to see your Connection Status.
</p>
</body>
</html>
```

When these pages are added, reboot the application and navigate to the status page. Now when clicking the Connect to Twitter link, you will be sent to the `twitterConnect.jsp` page. After clicking the Connect to Twitter button, you will be shown the Twitter authorize application page (see Figure 6-9).

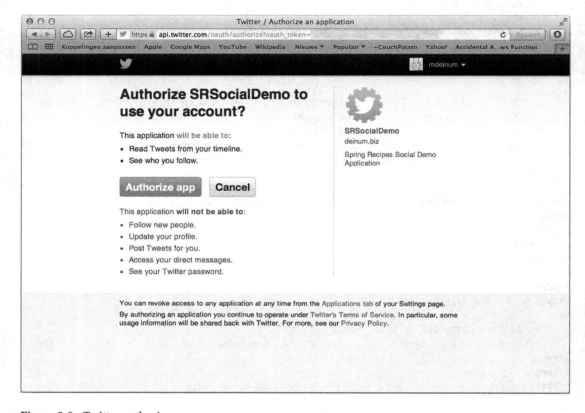

Figure 6-9. *Twitter authorize page*

After authorizing the application, you will be returned to the `twitterConnect.jsp` page telling you that you have successfully connected to Twitter. When returning to the status page, you will see that you are connected to Twitter with your nickname.

For Facebook or any other service provider, follow the same steps of adding the `{provider}Connect` and `{provider}Connected` pages, and Spring Social will be able to connect to that provider, given that you also added the correct service provider connector and configuration.

6-5. Use the Twitter API

Problem

You want to use the Twitter API.

Solution

Use the `Twitter` object to access the Twitter API.

How It Works

Each service provider has its own API using Twitter. There is an object implementing the Twitter interface, which represents the Twitter API in Java; for Facebook, an object implementing the Facebook interface is available. In recipe 6-2, you already set up the connection to Twitter and the TwitterTemplate. The TwitterTemplate exposes various parts of the Twitter API (see Table 6-3).

Table 6-3. Exposed Operations of the Twitter API

Operations	Description
blockOperations()	Blocking and unblocking users
directMessageOperations()	Reading and sending direct messages
friendOperations()	Retrieving a user's list of friends and followers and following/unfollowing users
geoOperations()	Working with locations
listOperations()	Maintaining, subscribing to, and unsubscribing from user lists
searchOperations()	Searching tweets and viewing search trends
streamingOperations()	Receiving tweets as they are created via Twitter's Streaming API
timelineOperations()	Reading timelines and posting tweets
userOperations()	Retrieving user profile data
restOperations()	The underlying RestTemplate if part of the API hasn't been exposed through the other APIs

It might be that for certain operations your application requires more access than read-only. If you want to send tweets or to be able to access direct messages, you need read-write access.

To post a status update, you would use the timelineOperations() method and then the updateStatus() method. Depending on your needs, the updateStatus method either takes a simple String, which is the status, or a value object called TweetData holding the status and other information such as location, whether it is a reply to another tweet, and optionally any resources such as images.

A simple controller could look like the following:

```
package com.apress.springrecipes.social.web;

import org.springframework.social.twitter.api.Twitter;
import org.springframework.stereotype.Controller;
import org.springframework.web.bind.annotation.RequestMapping;
import org.springframework.web.bind.annotation.RequestMethod;
import org.springframework.web.bind.annotation.RequestParam;

@Controller
@RequestMapping("/twitter")
public class TwitterController {

    private final Twitter twitter;
```

```
    public TwitterController(Twitter twitter) {
        this.twitter = twitter;
    }

    @RequestMapping(method = RequestMethod.GET)
    public String index() {
        return "twitter";
    }

    @RequestMapping(method = RequestMethod.POST)
    public String tweet(@RequestParam("status") String status) {
        twitter.timelineOperations().updateStatus(status);
        return "redirect:/twitter";
    }
}
```

The controller needs the Twitter API through the `TwitterTemplate`. The `TwitterTemplate` implements the `Twitter` interface. As you might recall from recipe 6-2, the API is request-scoped. You get a scoped proxy, which is the reason for using the `Twitter` interface. The tweet method receives a parameter and passes that on to Twitter.

6-6. Use a Persistent UsersConnectionRepository

Problem

You want to persist the users' connection data to survive server restarts.

Solution

Use the `JdbcUsersConnectionRepository` instead of the default `InMemoryUsersConnectionRepository`.

How It Works

By default Spring Social automatically configures an `InMemoryUsersConnectionRepository` for storing the connection information for a user. However, this doesn't work in a cluster nor does it survive server restarts. To solve this problem, it is possible to use a database to store the connection information. This is enabled by the `JdbcUsersConnectionRepository`.

The `JdbcUsersConnectionRepository` requires a database containing a table named `UserConnection` that has a certain number of columns. Luckily, Spring Social contains a DDL script, `JdbcUsersConnectionRepository.sql`, which you can use to create the table.

First add a data source to point to the database of your choice. In this case, Postgresql is used, but any database would do.

■ **Tip**   In the `bin` directory there is a `postgres.sh` file that will start a Dockerized PostgreSQL instance that you could use.

```
@Bean
public DataSource dataSource() {

    DriverManagerDataSource dataSource = new DriverManagerDataSource();
    dataSource.setUrl(env.getRequiredProperty("datasource.url"));
    dataSource.setUsername(env.getRequiredProperty("datasource.username"));
    dataSource.setPassword(env.getRequiredProperty("datasource.password"));
    dataSource.setDriverClassName(env.getProperty("datasource.driverClassName"));
    return dataSource;
}
```

Notice the dataSource.* properties, which are used to configure the URL, JDBC driver, and username/password. Add the properties to the application.properties file.

```
dataSource.password=app
dataSource.username=app
dataSource.driverClassName=org.apache.derby.jdbc.ClientDriver
dataSource.url=jdbc:derby://localhost:1527/social;create=true
```

If you want automatic creation of the desired database table, you will need to add a DataSourceInitializer and have it execute the JdbcUsersConnectionRepository.sql file.

```
@Bean
public DataSourceInitializer databasePopulator() {

    ResourceDatabasePopulator populator = new ResourceDatabasePopulator();
    populator.addScript(
        new ClassPathResource(
        "org/springframework/social/connect/jdbc/JdbcUsersConnectionRepository.sql"));
    populator.setContinueOnError(true);
    DataSourceInitializer initializer = new DataSourceInitializer();
    initializer.setDatabasePopulator(populator);
    initializer.setDataSource(dataSource());
    return initializer;
}
```

This DataSourceInitializer is executed at application startup and will execute all the scripts handed to it. By default it will stop application startup as soon as an error is encountered. To stop this, set the continueOnError property to true. Now that the data source is set up and configured, the final step is to add the JdbcUsersConnectionRepository to the SocialConfig class.

```
package com.apress.springrecipes.social.config;

import org.springframework.social.connect.jdbc.JdbcUsersConnectionRepository;
...

@Configuration
@EnableSocial
@PropertySource("classpath:/application.properties")
public class SocialConfig extends SocialConfigurerAdapter {
```

```
@Override
public UsersConnectionRepository getUsersConnectionRepository(ConnectionFactoryLocator
connectionFactoryLocator) {
    return new JdbcUsersConnectionRepository(dataSource(), connectionFactoryLocator,
    Encryptors.noOpText());
}

...
}
```

The JdbcUsersConnectionRepository takes three constructor arguments. The first is the data source, the second is the passed-in ConnectionFactoryLocator, and the last argument is a TextEncryptor. The TextEncryptor is a class from the Spring Security crypto module and is used to encrypt the access token, the secret, and (when available) the refresh token. The encryption is needed because when the data is stored as plain text, the data can be compromised. The tokens can be used to gain access to your profile information.

For testing, however, it can be handy to use the noOpText encryptor, which, as the name implies, does no encryption. For real production, you want to use a TextEncryptor, which uses a password and salt to encrypt the values.

When the JdbcUsersConnectionRepository is configured and the database has been started, you can restart the application. At first glance, nothing has changed; however, as soon as you grant access to, for instance, Twitter, this access will survive application restarts. You can also query the database and see that the information is stored in the USERCONNECTION table.

6-7. Integrate Spring Social and Spring Security

Problem

You want to allow users of your web site to connect their social network accounts.

Solution

Use the spring-social-security project to integrate both frameworks.

How It Works

Let's set up Spring Security. It goes beyond this recipe to discuss Spring Security in detail. For that, check Chapter 7. The setup for this recipe is as follows:

```
@Configuration
@EnableWebMvcSecurity
public class SecurityConfig extends WebSecurityConfigurerAdapter {

    @Override
    protected void configure(HttpSecurity http) throws Exception {

        http.authorizeRequests()
            .anyRequest().authenticated()
            .and()
                .formLogin()
```

```
            .loginPage("/signin")
            .failureUrl("/signin?param.error=bad_credentials")
            .loginProcessingUrl("/signin/authenticate").permitAll()
            .defaultSuccessUrl("/connect")
        .and()
            .logout().logoutUrl("/signout").permitAll();
}

@Bean
public UserDetailsManager userDetailsManager(DataSource dataSource) {
    JdbcUserDetailsManager userDetailsManager = new JdbcUserDetailsManager();
    userDetailsManager.setDataSource(dataSource);
    userDetailsManager.setEnableAuthorities(true);
    return userDetailsManager;
}

@Override
protected void configure(AuthenticationManagerBuilder auth) throws Exception {
    auth.userDetailsService(userDetailsManager(null));
}

}
```

The @EnableWebMvcSecurity annotation will enable security for Spring MVC applications. It registers beans needed for Spring Security to operate. To do further configuration, such as setting up security rules, one or more WebSecurityConfigurers can be added. To make it easier, there is a WebSecurityConfigurerAdapter that you can extend.

The configure(HttpSecurity http) method takes care of setting up security. This particular configuration wants a user to be authenticated for every call that is made. If a user isn't already authenticated (i.e., has logged in to the application), the user will be prompted with a login form. You will also notice that the loginPage, loginProcessingUrl, and logoutUrl are modified. This is done so that they match the default URLs from Spring Social.

■ **Note** If you want to keep the Spring Security defaults, configure the SocialAuthenticationFilter explicitly and set the signupUrl and defaultFailureUrl properties.

With the configure(AuthenticationManagerBuilder auth), you add a AuthenticationManager, which is used to determine whether a user exists and whether the correct credentials were entered. The UserDetailsService used is a JdbcUserDetailsManager, which, next to being a UserDetailsService, can also add and remove users from the repository. This will be needed when you add a Social sign-in page to the application.

The JdbcUserDetailsManager uses a DataSource to read and write the data, and the enableAuthorities properties is set to true so that any roles the user gets from the application are added to the database as well. To bootstrap the database, add the create_users.sql script to the database populator configured in the previous recipe.

```
@Bean
public DataSourceInitializer databasePopulator() {
    ResourceDatabasePopulator populator = new ResourceDatabasePopulator();
    populator.addScript(
    new ClassPathResource("org/springframework/social/connect/jdbc/JdbcUsersConnection
    Repository.sql"));
    populator.addScript(new ClassPathResource("sql/create_users.sql"));
    populator.setContinueOnError(true);

    DataSourceInitializer initializer = new DataSourceInitializer();
    initializer.setDatabasePopulator(populator);
    initializer.setDataSource(dataSource());
    return initializer;
}
```

Next, to be able to render the custom login or sign-in page, it needs to be added as a view controller to the WebConfig class. This tells that a request to /signin should render the signin.jsp page.

```
package com.apress.springrecipes.social.config;

import org.springframework.context.annotation.Bean;
import org.springframework.context.annotation.ComponentScan;
import org.springframework.context.annotation.Configuration;
import org.springframework.web.servlet.config.annotation.ViewControllerRegistry;
import org.springframework.web.servlet.config.annotation.WebMvcConfigurer;
...


@Configuration
@EnableWebMvc
@ComponentScan({"com.apress.springrecipes.social.web"})
public class WebConfig implements WebMvcConfigurer {

    @Override
    public void addViewControllers(ViewControllerRegistry registry) {
        registry.addViewController("/").setViewName("index");
        registry.addViewController("/signin").setViewName("signin");
    }
    ...
}
```

The signin.jsp page is a simple JSP page rendering a username and password input field and a Submit button.

```
<%@ taglib prefix="c" uri="http://java.sun.com/jsp/jstl/core" %>
<!DOCTYPE html>
<html>
<body>
    <c:url var="formLogin" value="/signin/authenticate" />
    <c:if test="${param.error eq 'bad_credentials'}">
        <div class="error">
            The login information was incorrect please try again.
        </div>
    </c:if>
```

```
<form method="post" action="${formLogin}">
    <input type="hidden" name="_csrf" value="${_csrf.token}" />
    <table>
        <tr>
            <td><label for="username">Username</label></td>
            <td><input type="text" name="username"/></td>
        </tr>
        <tr>
            <td><label for="password">Password</label></td>
            <td><input type="password" name="password"/></td>
        </tr>
        <tr><td colspan="2"><button>Login</button></td> </tr>
    </table>
</form>
</body>
</html>
```

Notice the hidden input, which contains a cross-site forgery request (CSFR) token. This is to prevent malicious web sites or JavaScript code to post to your URL. When using Spring Security, this is enabled by default. It can be disabled with `http.csrf().disable()` in the SecurityConfig class.

Two final configuration pieces are left. First, this configuration needs to be loaded, and second, a filter needs to be registered to apply the security to your request. For this, modify the SocialWebApplicationInitializer class.

```
package com.apress.springrecipes.social;

import com.apress.springrecipes.social.config.SecurityConfig;
import com.apress.springrecipes.social.config.SocialConfig;
import com.apress.springrecipes.social.config.WebConfig;
import org.springframework.web.filter.DelegatingFilterProxy;
import org.springframework.web.servlet.support.
AbstractAnnotationConfigDispatcherServletInitializer;

import javax.servlet.Filter;

public class SocialWebApplicationInitializer extends
AbstractAnnotationConfigDispatcherServletInitializer {

    @Override
    protected Class<?>[] getRootConfigClasses() {
        return new Class<?>[]{SecurityConfig.class, SocialConfig.class};
    }

    @Override
    protected Filter[] getServletFilters() {
        DelegatingFilterProxy springSecurityFilterChain = new DelegatingFilterProxy();
        springSecurityFilterChain.setTargetBeanName("springSecurityFilterChain");
        return new Filter[]{springSecurityFilterChain};
    }
...
}
```

First notice that the `SecurityConfig` class is added to the `getRootConfigClasses` method. This will take care of the configuration class being loaded. Next, the `getServletFilters` method is added. This method is used to register filters to requests that are going to be handled by the `DispatcherServlet`. Spring Security, by default, registers a `Filter` in the application context named `springSecurityFilterChain`. To have this executed, you need to add a `DelegatingFilterProxy`. The `DelegatingFilterProxy` will look up a bean of the type `Filter` for the specified `targetBeanName`.

Use Spring Security to Obtain the Username

In the previous recipes, you used a `UserIdSource` implementation that returned a static username. If you have an application that is already using Spring Security, you could use the `AuthenticationNameUserIdSource`, which uses the `SecurityContext` (from Spring Security) to obtain the username of the authenticated current user. That username in turn is used to store and look up the users' connections with the different service providers.

```
@Configuration
@EnableSocial
@PropertySource("classpath:/application.properties")
public class SocialConfig extends SocialConfigurerAdapter {

    @Override
    public UserIdSource getUserIdSource() {
        return new AuthenticationNameUserIdSource();
    }
    ...
}
```

■ **Tip** When using the `SpringsocialConfigurer`, you could omit this because the `AuthenticationNameUserIdSource` would be created and used by default.

Notice the construction of the `AuthenticationNameUserIdSource`. This is all that is needed to be able to retrieve the username from Spring Security. It will do a lookup of the `Authentication` object from the `SecurityContext` and return the name property of the `Authentication`. When restarting the application, you will be prompted with a login form. Now log in as `user1` with the password `user1`.

Use Spring Social for Signing In

Letting the current user connect to social networks is nice. It would be better if a user could use his or her social network account (or accounts) to sign in to the application. Spring Social provides tight integration with Spring Security to enable this. There are a couple of additional parts that need to be set up for this.

First Spring Social needs to be integrated with Spring Security. For this, the `SpringSocialConfigurer` can be used and applied to the Spring Security configuration.

```
@Configuration
@EnableWebMvcSecurity
public class SecurityConfig extends WebSecurityConfigurerAdapter {

    @Override
    protected void configure(HttpSecurity http) throws Exception {
        ...
        http.apply(new SpringSocialConfigurer());
    }
    ...
}
package com.apress.springrecipes.social.security;

import org.springframework.dao.DataAccessException;
import org.springframework.security.core.userdetails.UserDetails;
import org.springframework.security.core.userdetails.UserDetailsService;
import org.springframework.security.core.userdetails.UsernameNotFoundException;
import org.springframework.social.security.SocialUser;
import org.springframework.social.security.SocialUserDetails;
import org.springframework.social.security.SocialUserDetailsService;
import org.springframework.util.Assert;

public class SimpleSocialUserDetailsService implements SocialUserDetailsService {

    private final UserDetailsService userDetailsService;

    public SimpleSocialUserDetailsService(UserDetailsService userDetailsService) {
        Assert.notNull(userDetailsService, "UserDetailsService cannot be null.");
        this.userDetailsService = userDetailsService;    }

    @Override
    public SocialUserDetails loadUserByUserId(String userId) throws
    UsernameNotFoundException, DataAccessException {

        UserDetails user = userDetailsService.loadUserByUsername(userId);
        return new SocialUser(user.getUsername(), user.getPassword(), user.getAuthorities());
    }
}
```

Next add the links for your configured service providers to the sign-in page.

```
<%@ taglib prefix="c" uri="http://java.sun.com/jsp/jstl/core" %>
<!DOCTYPE html>
<html>
<body>

...

<!-- TWITTER SIGNIN -->

<c:url var="twitterSigin" value="/auth/twitter"/>

<p><a href="${twitterSigin}">Sign in with Twitter</a></p>
```

```
<!-- FACEBOOK SIGNIN -->
<c:url var="facebookSigin" value="/auth/facebook"/>
<p><a href="${facebookSigin}">Sign in with Facebook</a></p>
</body>
</html>
```

The SimpleSocialUserDetailsService delegates the actual lookup to a UserDetailsService, which is passed in through the constructor. When a user is retrieved, it uses the retrieved information to construct a SocialUser instance. Finally, this bean needs to be added to the configuration.

```
@Configuration
@EnableWebMvcSecurity
public class SecurityConfig extends WebSecurityConfigurerAdapter {

    @Bean
    public SocialUserDetailsService socialUserDetailsService(UserDetailsService
    userDetailsService) {
        return new SimpleSocialUserDetailsService(userDetailsService);
    }

    ...
}
```

This will allow users to sign in with their social networking accounts; however, the application needs to know which user the account belongs to. If a user cannot be located for the specific social network, a user needs to be created. Basically, the application needs a way for users to sign up for the application. By default the SocialAuthenticationFilter redirects the user to the /signup URL. You can create a controller that is attached to this URL and renders a form, allowing the user to create an account.

```
package com.apress.springrecipes.social.web;

import org.springframework.security.authentication.UsernamePasswordAuthenticationToken;
import org.springframework.security.core.GrantedAuthority;
import org.springframework.security.core.authority.SimpleGrantedAuthority;
import org.springframework.security.core.context.SecurityContextHolder;
import org.springframework.security.provisioning.UserDetailsManager;
import org.springframework.social.connect.Connection;
import org.springframework.social.connect.web.ProviderSignInUtils;
import org.springframework.social.security.SocialUser;
import org.springframework.stereotype.Controller;
import org.springframework.validation.BindingResult;
import org.springframework.validation.annotation.Validated;
import org.springframework.web.bind.annotation.GetMapping;
import org.springframework.web.bind.annotation.PostMapping;
import org.springframework.web.bind.annotation.RequestMapping;
import org.springframework.web.context.request.WebRequest;

import java.util.Collections;
import java.util.List;
```

```java
@Controller
@RequestMapping("/signup")
public class SignupController {

    private static final List<GrantedAuthority> DEFAULT_ROLES = Collections.
    singletonList(new SimpleGrantedAuthority("USER"));
    private final ProviderSignInUtils providerSignInUtils;
    private final UserDetailsManager userDetailsManager;

    public SignupController(ProviderSignInUtils providerSignInUtils,
                            UserDetailsManager userDetailsManager) {
        this.providerSignInUtils = providerSignInUtils;
        this.userDetailsManager = userDetailsManager;
    }

    @GetMapping
    public SignupForm signupForm(WebRequest request) {
        Connection<?> connection = providerSignInUtils.getConnectionFromSession(request);
        if (connection != null) {
            return SignupForm.fromProviderUser(connection.fetchUserProfile());
        } else {
            return new SignupForm();
        }
    }

    @PostMapping
    public String signup(@Validated SignupForm form, BindingResult formBinding,
                         WebRequest request) {
        if (!formBinding.hasErrors()) {
            SocialUser user = createUser(form);
            SecurityContextHolder.getContext().setAuthentication(new UsernamePassword
            AuthenticationToken(user.getUsername(), null, user.getAuthorities())));
            providerSignInUtils.doPostSignUp(user.getUsername(), request);
            return "redirect:/";
        }
        return null;
    }

    private SocialUser createUser(SignupForm form) {
        SocialUser user = new SocialUser(form.getUsername(), form.getPassword(),
        DEFAULT_ROLES);
        userDetailsManager.createUser(user);
        return user;
    }
}
```

First the signupForm method will be called because the initial request will be a GET request to the /signup URL. The signupForm method checks whether a connection attempt has been done. This is delegated to the ProviderSignInUtils provided by Spring Social. If that is the case, the retrieved UserProfile is used to prepopulate a SignupForm.

```
package com.apress.springrecipes.social.web;

import org.springframework.social.connect.UserProfile;

public class SignupForm {

    private String username;
    private String password;

    public String getUsername() {
        return username;
    }

    public void setUsername(String username) {
        this.username = username;
    }

    public String getPassword() {
        return password;
    }

    public void setPassword(String password) {
        this.password = password;
    }

    public static SignupForm fromProviderUser(UserProfile providerUser) {

        SignupForm form = new SignupForm();
        form.setUsername(providerUser.getUsername());
        return form;
    }
}
```

Here is the HTML form used for filling in the two fields:

```
<%@ taglib prefix="form" uri="http://www.springframework.org/tags/form" %>
<%@ page contentType="text/html;charset=UTF-8" language="java" %>
<html>
<head>
    <title>Sign Up</title>
</head>

<body>
<h3>Sign Up</h3>

<form:form modelAttribute="signupForm" method="POST">
    <table>
        <tr><td><form:label path="username" /></td><td><form:input path="username"/></td></tr>
        <tr><td><form:label path="password" /></td><td><form:password path="password"/>
        </td></tr>
```

```
<tr><td colspan="2"><button>Sign Up</button></td></tr>
    </table>
</form:form>
</body>
</html>
```

■ **Note**   There is no hidden input for the CSFR tag here. Spring Security integrates tightly with Spring MVC, and this field will be added automatically when using the Spring Framework form tags.

After the user fills out the form, the signup method will be called. This will create a user with the given username and password. After the user is created, a Connection is added for the entered username. Now that the connection has been made, the user is logged in to the application and on subsequent visits can use the social network connection to log in to the application.

The controller uses the ProviderSignInUtils to reuse the logic from Spring Social. You can create an instance in the SocialConfig class.

```
@Bean
public ProviderSignInUtils providerSignInUtils(ConnectionFactoryLocator
connectionFactoryLocator, UsersConnectionRepository usersConnectionRepository) {
    return new ProviderSignInUtils(connectionFactoryLocator, usersConnectionRepository);
}
```

The final piece of the configuration is to allow access to the /signup URL for all users. Add the following to the SecurityConfig class:

```
@Override
protected void configure(HttpSecurity http) throws Exception {

    http
        .authorizeRequests()
            .antMatchers("/signup").permitAll()
            .anyRequest().authenticated().and()
    ...
}
```

Summary

In this chapter, you explored Spring Social. The first step taken was to register an application with a service provider and use the generated API key and secret to connect the application to that service provider. Next you looked into connecting a user's account to the application so that it can be used to access user information; however, this will also allow you to use the service provider's API. For Twitter, you could query a timeline or look at someone's friends.

To make the connections to the service providers more useful, they are stored in JDBC-based storage.

Finally, you looked at how Spring Social can integrate with Spring Security and how it can be used to allow a service provider to sign in to your application.

CHAPTER 7

Spring Security

In this chapter, you will learn how to secure applications using the Spring Security framework, a subproject of the Spring Framework. Spring Security was initially known as Acegi Security, but its name was changed after joining with the Spring portfolio projects. Spring Security can be used to secure any Java application, but it's mostly used for web-based applications. Web applications, especially those that can be accessed through the Internet, are vulnerable to hacker attacks if they are not secured properly.

If you've never handled security in an application, there are several terms and concepts that you must understand first. *Authentication* is the process of verifying a principal's identity against what it claims to be. A *principal* can be a user, a device, or a system, but most typically, it's a user. A principal has to provide evidence of identity to be authenticated. This evidence is called a *credential*, which is usually a password when the target principal is a user.

Authorization is the process of granting authority to an authenticated user so that this user is allowed to access particular resources of the target application. The authorization process must be performed after the authentication process. Typically, authorities are granted in terms of roles.

Access control means controlling access to an application's resources. It entails making a decision on whether a user is allowed to access a resource. This decision is called an *access control decision*, and it's made by comparing the resource's access attributes with the user's granted authorities or other characteristics.

After finishing this chapter, you will understand basic security concepts and know how to secure your web applications at the URL access level, the method invocation level, the view-rendering level, and the domain object level.

■ **Note**   Before starting this chapter, take a look at the application for `recipe_7_1_i`. This is the initial unsecured application you will use in this chapter. It is a basic to-do app in which you can list, create, and mark to-dos completed. When you deploy the application, you will be greeted with the content, as shown in Figure 7-1.

© Marten Deinum, Daniel Rubio, and Josh Long 2017
M. Deinum et al., *Spring 5 Recipes*, DOI 10.1007/978-1-4842-2790-9_7

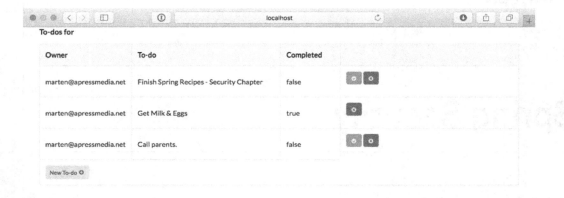

Figure 7-1. *Initial to-do application*

7-1. Secure URL Access

Problem

Many web applications have some particular URLs that are critically important and private. You must secure these URLs by preventing unauthorized access to them.

Solution

Spring Security enables you to secure a web application's URL access in a declarative way through simple configuration. It handles security by applying servlet filters to HTTP requests. To register a filter and detect the configuration, Spring Security provides a convenience base class to extend: `AbstractSecurityWebApplicationInitializer`.

Spring Security allows you to configure web application security through the various `configure` methods on the `WebSecurityConfigurerAdapter` configuration adapter. If your web application's security requirements are straightforward and typical, you can leave the configuration as is and use the default enabled security settings, including the following:

- *Form-based login service*: This provides a default page that contains a login form for users to log into this application.

- *HTTP Basic authentication*: This can process the HTTP Basic authentication credentials presented in HTTP request headers. It can also be used for authenticating requests made with remoting protocols and web services.

- *Logout service*: This provides a handler mapped with a URL for users to log out of this application.

- *Anonymous login*: This assigns a principal and grants authorities to an anonymous user so that you can handle an anonymous user like a normal user.

- *Servlet API integration*: This allows you to access security information in your web application via standard Servlet APIs, such as `HttpServletRequest.isUserInRole()` and `HttpServletRequest.getUserPrincipal()`.

- *CSFR*: This implements cross-site forgery request protection by creating a token and putting it in the `HttpSession`.

- *Security headers*: Like disabling caching for secured packages, this offers XSS protection, transport security, and X-Frame security.

With these security services registered, you can specify the URL patterns that require particular authorities to access. Spring Security will perform security checks according to your configurations. A user must log into an application before accessing the secure URLs, unless these URLs are opened for anonymous access. Spring Security provides a set of authentication providers for you to choose from. An authentication provider authenticates a user and returns the authorities granted to this user.

How It Works

First you need to register the filters used by Spring Security. The easiest way to do this is by extending the aforementioned `AbstractSecurityWebApplicationInitializer`.

```
package com.apress.springrecipes.board.security;

import org.springframework.security.web.context.AbstractSecurityWebApplicationInitializer;

public class TodoSecurityInitializer extends AbstractSecurityWebApplicationInitializer {

    public TodoSecurityInitializer() {
        super(TodoSecurityConfig.class);
    }
}
```

The `AbstractSecurityWebApplicationInitializer` class has a constructor that takes one or more configuration classes. These configuration classes are used to bootstrap the security.

■ **Note**   If you have a class that extends `AbstractAnnotationConfigDispatcherServletInitializer`, add the security configuration to that or you will get an exception during startup.

Although you can configure Spring Security in the same configuration class as the web and service layers, it's better to separate the security configurations in an isolated class (e.g., `TodoSecurityConfig`). Inside `WebApplicationInitializer` (e.g., `TodoWebInitializer`), you need to add that configuration class to the list of classes for the configuration.

First you need the security configuration. For this, you will create the TodoSecurityConfig class, as shown here:

```
package com.apress.springrecipes.board.security;

import org.springframework.context.annotation.Configuration;
import org.springframework.security.config.annotation.web.configuration.EnableWebSecurity;
import org.springframework.security.config.annotation.web.configuration.
WebSecurityConfigurerAdapter;

@Configuration
@EnableWebSecurity
public class TodoSecurityConfig extends WebSecurityConfigurerAdapter {}
```

When building and deploying the application and trying to access http://localhost:8080/todos/todos, you will now be greeted by the default Spring Security login page (see Figure 7-2).

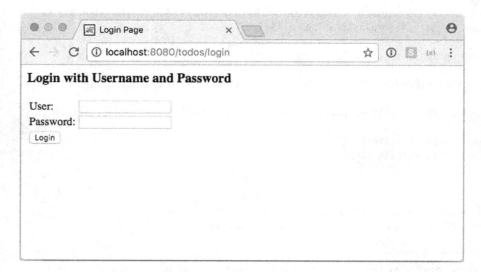

Figure 7-2. Default Spring Security login page

Secure URL Access

If you look at the configure method of the org.springframework.security.config.annotation.web.configuration.WebSecurityConfigurerAdapter class, you will see that it includes the anyRequest().authenticated() call. This tells Spring Security that for every request that comes in, you have to be authenticated with the system. You will also see that by default HTTP Basic authentication and form-based login are enabled. Form-based login also includes a default login page creator that will be used if you don't explicitly specify a login page.

```
protected void configure(HttpSecurity http) throws Exception {
    http
        .authorizeRequests()
            .anyRequest().authenticated()
            .and()
        .formLogin().and()
        .httpBasic();
}
```

Let's write a couple of security rules. Instead of only needing to be logged in, you can write some powerful access rules for the URLs.

```
package com.apress.springrecipes.board.security;

import org.springframework.context.annotation.Configuration;
import org.springframework.http.HttpMethod;
import org.springframework.security.config.annotation.authentication.builders.
AuthenticationManagerBuilder;
import org.springframework.security.config.annotation.web.builders.HttpSecurity;
import org.springframework.security.config.annotation.web.configuration.EnableWebSecurity;
import org.springframework.security.config.annotation.web.configuration.
WebSecurityConfigurerAdapter;

@Configuration
@EnableWebSecurity
public class TodoSecurityConfig extends WebSecurityConfigurerAdapter {

    @Override
    protected void configure(AuthenticationManagerBuilder auth) throws Exception {
        auth.inMemoryAuthentication()
            .withUser("marten@ya2do.io").password("user").authorities("USER")
            .and()
            .withUser("admin@ya2do.io").password("admin").authorities("USER", "ADMIN");
    }

    @Override
    protected void configure(HttpSecurity http) throws Exception {

        http.authorizeRequests()
            .antMatchers("/todos*").hasAuthority("USER")
            .antMatchers(HttpMethod.DELETE, "/todos*").hasAuthority("ADMIN")
            .and()
                .formLogin()
            .and()
                .csrf().disable();
    }
}
```

You can configure authorization rules and more by overriding the configure(HttpSecurity http) method (there are other configure methods as well).

With authorizeRequests(), you start securing your URLs. You can then use one of the matchers; in the previous code, you use antMatchers to define the matching rules and which authorities a user needs to have. Remember that you must always include a wildcard at the end of a URL pattern. Failing to do so will make the URL pattern unable to match a URL that has request parameters. As a result, hackers could easily skip the security check by appending an arbitrary request parameter. You have secured all access to /todos to users who have the authority USER. To be able to call /todos with a DELETE request, you need to be a user with the role ADMIN.

■ **Note**   Because you are now overriding the default access rules and login configuration, you need to enable formLogin again. There is also a call disabling CSFR protection for now, because CSFR protection would make the forms not work; this recipe will explain later how to enable it.

You can configure authentication services in the overridden configure(AuthenticationManagerBuil der auth) method. Spring Security supports several ways of authenticating users, including authenticating against a database or an LDAP repository. It also supports defining user details directly for simple security requirements. You can specify a username, a password, and a set of authorities for each user.

Now, you can redeploy this application to test its security configurations. You must log into this application with the correct username and password to see the to-dos. Finally, to delete a to-do, you must log in as an administrator.

Work with CSFR Protection

It is generally a good idea to leave the default for CSFR enabled because this will reduce the risk you have with a CSFR attack. It is enabled by default in Spring Security, and the line csfr().disable() can be removed from the configuration. When CSFR protection is enabled, Spring Security adds CsrfFilter to the list of filters it uses for protection. This filter in turn uses an implementation of CsrfTokenRepository to generate and store tokens; by default this is the HttpSessionCsrfTokenRepository class that, as the name implies, stores the generated token in the HttpSession interface. There is also a CookieCsrfTokenRepository class that stores the token information in a cookie. If you want to switch the CsrfTokenRepository class, you can use the csrfTokenRepository() configuration method to change it. You could also use this to configure an explicitly configured HttpSessionCsrfTokenRepository.

```
@Override
protected void configure(HttpSecurity http) throws Exception {

    HttpSessionCsrfTokenRepository repo = new HttpSessionCsrfTokenRepository();
    repo.setSessionAttributeName("csfr_token");
    repo.setParameterName("csfr_token")

    http.csrf().csrfTokenRepository(repo);
}
```

When CSFR is enabled, trying to complete or delete a to-do item after you log in will fail because of the absence of a CSFR token. To fix this, you need to pass the CSFR token back to the server on requests that modify content. You can easily do this with a hidden input in your form. The HttpSessionCsrfTokenRepository exposes the token in the session under the attribute _csfr (by default, unless you configured it explicitly). For a form you can use the parameterName and token properties to create the appropriate input tag.

Add the following to the two forms that complete and delete a to-do item:

```
<input type="hidden" name="${_csrf.parameterName}" value="${_csrf.token}"/>
```

Now when submitting the form, the token will be part of the request, and you will again be able to complete or delete a to-do item.

There is also a form in the `todo-create.jsp` page; however, because this is using the Spring MVC form tags, you don't need to modify this. When using the Spring MVC form tags, the CSFR token is added to the form automatically. To make this possible, Spring Security registers a `CsrfRequestDataValueProcessor` class, which takes care of adding the token to the form.

7-2. Log In to Web Applications

Problem

A secure application requires its users to log in before they can access certain secure functions. This is especially important for web applications running on the open Internet because hackers can easily reach them. Most web applications have to provide a way for users to input their credentials to log in.

Solution

Spring Security supports multiple ways for users to log into a web application. It supports form-based login by providing a default web page that contains a login form. You can also provide a custom web page as the login page. In addition, Spring Security supports HTTP Basic authentication by processing the Basic authentication credentials presented in HTTP request headers. HTTP Basic authentication can also be used for authenticating requests made with remoting protocols and web services.

Some parts of your application may allow for anonymous access (e.g., access to the welcome page). Spring Security provides an anonymous login service that can assign a principal and grant authorities to an anonymous user so that you can handle an anonymous user like a normal user when defining security policies.

Spring Security also supports "remember-me" login, which is able to remember a user's identity across multiple browser sessions so that a user doesn't need to log in again after logging in for the first time.

How It Works

To help you better understand the various login mechanisms in isolation, let's first disable the default security configuration.

■ **Caution**   You generally want to stick with the defaults and just disable what you don't want, such as `httpBasic().disable()`, instead of disabling all the security defaults!

```
@Configuration
@EnableWebSecurity
public class TodoSecurityConfig extends WebSecurityConfigurerAdapter {

    public TodoSecurityConfig() {
        super(true);
    }
}
```

Note that the login services introduced next will be registered automatically if you enable HTTP autoconfig. However, if you disable the default configuration or you want to customize these services, you have to configure the corresponding features explicitly.

Before enabling the authentication features, you will have to enable the basic Spring Security requirements you need to configure at least exception handling and security context integration.

```
protected void configure(HttpSecurity http) {

    http.securityContext()
        .and()
        .exceptionHandling();
}
```

Without these basics, Spring Security wouldn't store the user after logging in, and it wouldn't do proper exception translation for security-related exceptions (they would simply bubble up, which might expose some of your internals to the outside world). You also might want to enable the Servlet API integration so that you can use the methods on HttpServletRequest to do checks in your view.

```
protected void configure(HttpSecurity http) {
    http.servletApi();
}
```

Use HTTP Basic Authentication

The HTTP Basic authentication support can be configured via the httpBasic() method. When HTTP Basic authentication is required, a browser will typically display a login dialog or a specific login page for users to log in.

```
@Configuration
@EnableWebSecurity
public class TodoSecurityConfig extends WebSecurityConfigurerAdapter {

    @Override
    protected void configure(HttpSecurity http) throws Exception {
        http
            ...
            .httpBasic();
    }
}
```

> **■ Note** When HTTP Basic authentication and form-based login are enabled at the same time, the latter will be used. So, if you want your web application users to log in with this authentication type, you should not enable form-based login.

Use Form-Based Login

The form-based login service will render a web page that contains a login form for users to input their login details and process the login form submission. It's configured via the formLogin method.

```
@Configuration
@EnableWebSecurity
public class TodoSecurityConfig extends WebSecurityConfigurerAdapter {

    @Override
    protected void configure(HttpSecurity http) throws Exception {
        http
            ...
            .formLogin();
    }
}
```

By default, Spring Security automatically creates a login page and maps it to the URL /login. So, you can add a link to your application (e.g., in todos.jsp) referring to this URL for login.

```
<a href="<c:url value="/login" />">Login</a>
```

If you don't prefer the default login page, you can provide a custom login page of your own. For example, you can create the following login.jsp file in the root directory of the web application. Note that you shouldn't put this file inside WEB-INF, which would prevent users from accessing it directly.

```
<%@ taglib prefix="c" uri="http://java.sun.com/jsp/jstl/core" %>

<html>
<head>
    <title>Login</title>
    <link type="text/css" rel="stylesheet"
        href="https://cdnjs.cloudflare.com/ajax/libs/semantic-ui/2.2.10/semantic.min.css">
    <style type="text/css">
        body {
            background-color: #DADADA;
        }
        body > .grid {
            height: 100%;
        }
        .column {
            max-width: 450px;
        }
    </style>
</head>
```

305

```html
<body>
<div class="ui middle aligned center aligned grid">
    <div class="column">
        <h2 class="ui header">Log-in to your account</h2>
        <form method="POST" action="<c:url value="/login" />" class="ui large form">
            <input type="hidden" name="${_csrf.parameterName}" value="${_csrf.token}"/>
            <div class="ui stacked segment">
                <div class="field">
                    <div class="ui left icon input">
                        <i class="user icon"></i>
                        <input type="text" name="username" placeholder="E-mail address">
                    </div>
                </div>
                <div class="field">
                    <div class="ui left icon input">
                        <i class="lock icon"></i>
                        <input type="password" name="password" placeholder="Password">
                    </div>
                </div>
                <button class="ui fluid large submit green button">Login</button>
            </div>
        </form>
    </div>
</div>
</body>
</html>
```

For Spring Security to display your custom login page when a login is requested, you have to specify its URL in the loginPage configuration method.

```java
@Configuration
@EnableWebSecurity
public class TodoSecurityConfig extends WebSecurityConfigurerAdapter {

    @Override
    protected void configure(HttpSecurity http) throws Exception {
        http
            ...
            .formLogin().loginPage("/login.jsp");
    }
}
```

If the login page is displayed by Spring Security when a user requests a secure URL, the user will be redirected to the target URL once the login succeeds. However, if the user requests the login page directly via its URL, by default the user will be redirected to the context path's root (i.e., http://localhost:8080/todos/) after a successful login. If you have not defined a welcome page in your web deployment descriptor, you may want to redirect the user to a default target URL when the login succeeds.

```
@Configuration
@EnableWebSecurity
public class TodoSecurityConfig extends WebSecurityConfigurerAdapter {

    @Override
    protected void configure(HttpSecurity http) throws Exception {
        http
            ...
            .formLogin().loginPage("/login.jsp").defaultSuccessUrl("/todos");
    }
}
```

If you use the default login page created by Spring Security, then when a login fails, Spring Security will render the login page again with the error message. However, if you specify a custom login page, you will have to configure the authentication-failure-url value to specify which URL to redirect to on login error. For example, you can redirect to the custom login page again with the error request parameter, as shown here:

```
@Configuration
@EnableWebSecurity
public class TodoSecurityConfig extends WebSecurityConfigurerAdapter {

    @Override
    protected void configure(HttpSecurity http) throws Exception {
        http
            ...
            .formLogin()
                .loginPage("/login.jsp")
                .defaultSuccessUrl("/messageList")
                .failureUrl("login.jsp?error=true");
    }
}
```

Then your login page should test whether the error request parameter is present. If an error has occurred, you will have to display the error message by accessing the session scope attribute SPRING_SECURITY_LAST_EXCEPTION, which stores the last exception for the current user.

```
<form>
    ...
    <c:if test="${not empty param.error}">
        <div class="ui error message" style="display: block;">
            Authentication Failed<br/>
            Reason : ${sessionScope["SPRING_SECURITY_LAST_EXCEPTION"].message}
        </font>
    </div>
    </c:if>
</form>
```

Use the Logout Service

The logout service provides a handler to handle logout requests. It can be configured via the `logout()` configuration method.

```
@Configuration
@EnableWebSecurity
public class TodoSecurityConfig extends WebSecurityConfigurerAdapter {

    @Override
    protected void configure(HttpSecurity http) throws Exception {
        http
            ...
            .and()
                .logout();
    }
}
```

By default, it's mapped to the URL /logout and will react to POST requests only. You can add a small HTML form to your page to log out.

```
<form action="<c:url value="/logout"/>" method="post"><button>Logout</button><form>
```

■ **Note**   When using CSRF protection, don't forget to add the CSRF token to the form (see recipe 7-1) or the logout will fail.

By default, a user will be redirected to the context path's root when the logout succeeds, but sometimes you may want to direct the user to another URL, which you can do by using the `logoutSuccessUrl` configuration method.

```
@Configuration
@EnableWebSecurity
public class TodoSecurityConfig extends WebSecurityConfigurerAdapter {

    @Override
    protected void configure(HttpSecurity http) throws Exception {
        http
            ...
            .and()
                .logout().logoutSuccessUrl("/logout-success.jsp");
    }
}
```

After logout, you might notice that when using the browser's back button you will still be able to see the previous pages, even if your logout was successful. This has to do with the fact that the browser caches the pages. By enabling the security headers, with the `headers()` configuration method, the browser will be instructed to not cache the page.

```
@Configuration
@EnableWebSecurity
public class TodoSecurityConfig extends WebSecurityConfigurerAdapter {

    @Override
    protected void configure(HttpSecurity http) throws Exception {
        http
            ...
            .and()
                .headers();
    }
}
```

Next to the no-cache headers, this will also disable content sniffing and enable X-Frame protection (see recipe 7-1 for more information). With this enabled and using the browser's back button, you will be redirected to the login page.

Implement Anonymous Login

The anonymous login service can be configured via the anonymous() method in a Java config, where you can customize the username and authorities of an anonymous user, whose default values are anonymousUser and ROLE_ANONYMOUS.

```
@Configuration
@EnableWebSecurity
public class TodoSecurityConfig extends WebSecurityConfigurerAdapter {

    @Override
    protected void configure(HttpSecurity http) throws Exception {
        http
            ...
            .and()
                .anonymous().principal("guest").authorities("ROLE_GUEST");
    }
}
```

Implement Remember-Me Support

Remember-me support can be configured via the rememberMe() method in a Java config. By default, it encodes the username, the password, the remember-me expiration time, and a private key as a token and stores the token as a cookie in the user's browser. The next time the user accesses the same web application, this token will be detected so that the user can log in automatically.

```
@Configuration
@EnableWebSecurity
public class TodoSecurityConfig extends WebSecurityConfigurerAdapter {
```

```
    @Override
    protected void configure(HttpSecurity http) throws Exception {
        http
            ...
            .and()
                .rememberMe();
    }
}
```

However, static remember-me tokens can cause security issues because they may be captured by hackers. Spring Security supports rolling tokens for more advanced security needs, but this requires a database to persist the tokens. For details about rolling remember-me token deployment, please refer to the Spring Security reference documentation.

7-3. Authenticate Users

Problem

When a user attempts to log into your application to access its secure resources, you have to authenticate the user's principal and grant authorities to this user.

Solution

In Spring Security, authentication is performed by one or more `AuthenticationProviders`, connected as a chain. If any of these providers authenticates a user successfully, that user will be able to log into the application. If any provider reports that the user is disabled or locked or that the credential is incorrect or if no provider can authenticate the user, then the user will be unable to log into this application.

Spring Security supports multiple ways of authenticating users and includes built-in provider implementations for them. You can easily configure these providers with the built-in XML elements. Most common authentication providers authenticate users against a user repository storing user details (e.g., in an application's memory, a relational database, or an LDAP repository).

When storing user details in a repository, you should avoid storing user passwords in clear text because that makes them vulnerable to hackers. Instead, you should always store encrypted passwords in your repository. A typical way of encrypting passwords is to use a one-way hash function to encode the passwords. When a user enters a password to log in, you apply the same hash function to this password and compare the result with the one stored in the repository. Spring Security supports several algorithms for encoding passwords (including MD5 and SHA) and provides built-in password encoders for these algorithms.

If you retrieve a user's details from a user repository every time a user attempts to log in, your application may incur a performance impact. This is because a user repository is usually stored remotely, and it has to perform some kinds of queries in response to a request. For this reason, Spring Security supports caching user details in local memory and storage to save you the overhead of performing remote queries.

How It Works

Here you will explore different authentication mechanism, first you will look at the in-memory implemention, followed by the database driven one and finally you will take a look at LDAP. The final section will cover how to enable caching for the different authentication mechanisms.

Authenticate Users with In-Memory Definitions

If you have only a few users in your application and you seldom modify their details, you can consider defining the user details in Spring Security's configuration file so that they will be loaded into your application's memory.

```
@Configuration
@EnableWebSecurity
public class TodoSecurityConfig extends WebSecurityConfigurerAdapter {

...

    @Override
    protected void configure(AuthenticationManagerBuilder auth) throws Exception {
        auth.inMemoryAuthentication()
            .withUser("admin@ya2do.io").password("secret").authorities("ADMIN","USER").and()
            .withUser("marten@@ya2do.io").password("user").authorities("USER").and()
            .withUser("jdoe@does.net").password("unknown").disabled(true).
            authorities("USER");
    }
}
```

You can define user details with the inMemoryAuthentication() method. Using the withUser method, you can define the users. For each user, you can specify a username, a password, a disabled status, and a set of granted authorities. A disabled user cannot log into an application.

Authenticate Users Against a Database

More typically, user details should be stored in a database for easy maintenance. Spring Security has built-in support for querying the user details from a database. By default, it queries user details, including authorities, with the following SQL statements:

```
SELECT username, password, enabled
FROM   users
WHERE  username = ?

SELECT username, authority
FROM   authorities
WHERE  username = ?
```

For Spring Security to query user details with these SQL statements, you have to create the corresponding tables in your database. For example, you can create them in the todo schema with the following SQL statements:

```
CREATE TABLE USERS (
    USERNAME    VARCHAR(50)    NOT NULL,
    PASSWORD    VARCHAR(50)    NOT NULL,
    ENABLED     SMALLINT       NOT NULL,
    PRIMARY KEY (USERNAME)
);
```

```
CREATE TABLE AUTHORITIES (
    USERNAME    VARCHAR(50)    NOT NULL,
    AUTHORITY   VARCHAR(50)    NOT NULL,
    FOREIGN KEY (USERNAME) REFERENCES USERS
);
```

Next, you can input some user details into these tables for testing purposes. Tables 7-1 and 7-2 show the data for these two tables.

Table 7-1. *Testing User Data for the USERS Table*

USERNAME	PASSWORD	ENABLED
admin@ya2do.io	secret	1
marten@ya2do.io	user	1
jdoe@does.net	unknown	0

Table 7-2. *Testing User Data for the AUTHORITIES Table*

USERNAME	AUTHORITY
admin@ya2do.io	ADMIN
admin@ya2do.io	USER
marten@ya2do.io	USER
jdoe@does.net	USER

For Spring Security to access these tables, you have to declare a data source to be able to create connections to this database.

For a Java config, use the jdbcAuthentication() configuration method and pass it a DataSource.

```
@Configuration
@EnableWebSecurity
public class TodoSecurityConfig extends WebSecurityConfigurerAdapter {

    @Bean
    public DataSource dataSource() {
        return new EmbeddedDatabaseBuilder()
            .setType(EmbeddedDatabaseType.H2)
            .setName("board")
            .addScript("classpath:/schema.sql")
            .addScript("classpath:/data.sql")
            .build();
    }

    @Override
    protected void configure(AuthenticationManagerBuilder auth) throws Exception {
        auth.jdbcAuthentication().dataSource(dataSource());
    }
}
```

> **Note** The `@Bean` method used for the `DataSource` has been moved from the `TodoWebConfig` to the `TodoSecurityConfig`.

However, in some cases, you may already have your own user repository defined in a legacy database. For example, suppose that the tables are created with the following SQL statements and that all users in the MEMBER table have the enabled status:

```
CREATE TABLE MEMBER (
    ID          BIGINT          NOT NULL,
    USERNAME    VARCHAR(50)     NOT NULL,
    PASSWORD    VARCHAR(32)     NOT NULL,
    PRIMARY KEY (ID)
);

CREATE TABLE MEMBER_ROLE (
    MEMBER_ID   BIGINT          NOT NULL,
    ROLE        VARCHAR(10)     NOT NULL,
    FOREIGN KEY (MEMBER_ID)     REFERENCES MEMBER
);
```

Suppose you have legacy user data stored in these tables, as shown in Tables 7-3 and 7-4.

Table 7-3. Legacy User Data in the MEMBER Table

ID	USERNAME	PASSWORD
1	admin@ya2do.io	secret
2	marten@ya2do.io	user

Table 7-4. Legacy User Data in the MEMBER_ROLE Table

MEMBER_ID	ROLE
1	ROLE_ADMIN
1	ROLE_USER
2	ROLE_USER

Fortunately, Spring Security supports using custom SQL statements to query a legacy database for user details. You can specify the statements for querying a user's information and authorities using the `usersByUsernameQuery()` and `authoritiesByUsernameQuery()` configuration methods.

```
@Configuration
@EnableWebSecurity
public class TodoSecurityConfig extends WebSecurityConfigurerAdapter {

...

    @Override
    protected void configure(AuthenticationManagerBuilder auth) throws Exception {
        auth.jdbcAuthentication()
            .dataSource(dataSource)
            .usersByUsernameQuery(
                "SELECT username, password, 'true' as enabled FROM member WHERE username = ?")
            .authoritiesByUsernameQuery(
                "SELECT member.username, member_role.role as authorities " +
                "FROM member, member_role " +
                "WHERE  member.username = ? AND member.id = member_role.member_id");
    }
}
```

Encrypt Passwords

Until now, you have been storing user details with clear-text passwords. But this approach is vulnerable to hacker attacks, so you should encrypt the passwords before storing them. Spring Security supports several algorithms for encrypting passwords. For example, you can choose BCrypt, a one-way hash algorithm, to encrypt your passwords.

■ **Note**   You may need a helper to calculate BCrypt hashes for your passwords. You can do this online through, for example, `https://www.dailycred.com/article/bcrypt-calculator`, or you can simply create a class with a `main` method that uses Spring Security's `BCryptPasswordEncoder`.

Now, you can store the encrypted passwords in your user repository. For example, if you are using in-memory user definitions, you can specify the encrypted passwords in the password attributes. Then, you can specify the password encoder using the `passwordEncoder()` method on `AuthenticationManagerBuilder`.

```
@Configuration
@EnableWebSecurity
public class TodoSecurityConfig extends WebSecurityConfigurerAdapter {

...

    @Bean
    public BCryptPasswordEncoder passwordEncoder() {
        return new BCryptPasswordEncoder();
    }
```

```
    @Override
    protected void configure(AuthenticationManagerBuilder auth) throws Exception {
        auth
            .jdbcAuthentication()
                .passwordEncoder(passwordEncoder())
                .dataSource(dataSource());
    }
}
```

Of course, you have to store the encrypted passwords in the database tables, instead of the clear-text passwords, as shown in Table 7-5. To store BCrypt hashes in the password field, the length of the field has to be at least 60 characters long (which is the length of the BCrypt hash).

Table 7-5. Testing User Data with Encrypted Passwords for the USERS Table

USERNAME	PASSWORD	ENABLED
admin@ya2do.io	$2a$10$E3mPTZb50e7sSW15fDx8Ne7hDZpfDjrmMPTTUp8wVjLTu.G5oPYCO	1
marten@ya2do.io	$2a$10$5VWqjwoMYnFRTTmbWCRZT.iY3WW8ny27kQuUL9yPK1/WJcPcBLFWO	1
jdoe@does.net	$2a$10$cFKhO.XCUOA9L.in5smIiO2QIOT8.6ufQSwIIC.AVz26WctxhSWC6	0

Authenticate Users Against an LDAP Repository

Spring Security also supports accessing an LDAP repository for authenticating users. First, you have to prepare some user data for populating the LDAP repository. Let's prepare the user data in the LDAP Data Interchange Format (LDIF), a standard plain-text data format for importing and exporting LDAP directory data. For example, create the users.ldif file containing the following contents:

```
dn: dc=springrecipes,dc=com
objectClass: top
objectClass: domain
dc: springrecipes

dn: ou=groups,dc=springrecipes,dc=com
objectclass: top
objectclass: organizationalUnit
ou: groups

dn: ou=people,dc=springrecipes,dc=com
objectclass: top
objectclass: organizationalUnit
ou: people
```

```
dn: uid=admin,ou=people,dc=springrecipes,dc=com
objectclass: top
objectclass: uidObject
objectclass: person
uid: admin
cn: admin
sn: admin
userPassword: secret

dn: uid=user1,ou=people,dc=springrecipes,dc=com
objectclass: top
objectclass: uidObject
objectclass: person
uid: user1
cn: user1
sn: user1
userPassword: 1111

dn: cn=admin,ou=groups,dc=springrecipes,dc=com
objectclass: top
objectclass: groupOfNames
cn: admin
member: uid=admin,ou=people,dc=springrecipes,dc=com

dn: cn=user,ou=groups,dc=springrecipes,dc=com
objectclass: top
objectclass: groupOfNames
cn: user
member: uid=admin,ou=people,dc=springrecipes,dc=com
member: uid=user1,ou=people,dc=springrecipes,dc=com
```

Don't worry if you don't understand this LDIF file very well. You probably won't need to use this file format to define LDAP data often because most LDAP servers support GUI-based configuration. This users.ldif file includes the following contents:

- The default LDAP domain, dc=springrecipes,dc=com

- The groups and people organization units for storing groups and users

- The admin and user1 users with the passwords secret and 1111

- The admin group (including the admin user) and the user group (including the admin and user1 users)

For testing purposes, you can install an LDAP server on your local machine to host this user repository. For the sake of easy installation and configuration, we recommend installing OpenDS (www.opends.org/), a Java-based open source directory service engine that supports LDAP.

■ **Tip**   In the bin directory, there is an ldap.sh script that will start a Dockerized version of OpenDS and that will import the earlier mentioned users.ldif. Note that the root user and password for this LDAP server are cn=Directory Manager and ldap, respectively. Later, you will have to use this user to connect to this server.

CHAPTER 7 ■ SPRING SECURITY

After the LDAP server has started up, you can configure Spring Security to authenticate users against its repository.

You have to configure the LDAP repository using the ldapAuthentication() configuration method. You can specify the search filters and search bases for searching users and groups via several callback methods, whose values must be consistent with the repository's directory structure. With the preceding attribute values, Spring Security will search a user from the people organization unit with a particular user ID and search a user's groups from the groups organization unit. Spring Security will automatically insert the ROLE_ prefix to each group as an authority.

```
@Configuration
@EnableWebSecurity
public class TodoSecurityConfig extends WebSecurityConfigurerAdapter {
...
    @Override
    protected void configure(AuthenticationManagerBuilder auth) throws Exception {
        auth
            .ldapAuthentication()
                .contextSource()
                .url("ldap://localhost:1389/dc=springrecipes,dc=com")
                .managerDn("cn=Directory Manager").managerPassword("ldap")
            .and()
                .userSearchFilter("uid={0}").userSearchBase("ou=people")
                .groupSearchFilter("member={0}").groupSearchBase("ou=groups")

                .passwordEncoder(new LdapShaPasswordEncoder())
                .passwordCompare().passwordAttribute("userPassword");
    }
}
```

As OpenDS uses Salted Secure Hash Algorithm (SSHA) to encode user passwords by default, you have to specify the LdapShaPasswordEncoder as the password encoder. Note that this value is different from sha because it's specific to LDAP password encoding. You also need to specify the passwordAttribute value because the password encoder needs to know which field in LDAP is the password.

Finally, you have to refer to an LDAP server definition, which defines how to create connections to an LDAP server. You can specify the root user's username and password to connect to the LDAP server running on localhost by configuring the server using the contextSource method.

Cache User Details

Both <jdbc-user-service> and <ldap-user-service> support caching user details, but first you have to choose a cache implementation that provides a caching service. As Spring and Spring Security have built-in support for Ehcache (http://ehcache.sourceforge.net/), you can choose it as your cache implementation and create a configuration file for it (e.g., ehcache.xml in the classpath root) with the following contents:

```
<ehcache>
    <diskStore path="java.io.tmpdir"/>

    <defaultCache
        maxElementsInMemory="1000"
        eternal="false"
```

317

```
            timeToIdleSeconds="120"
            timeToLiveSeconds="120"
            overflowToDisk="true"
        />

    <cache name="userCache"
           maxElementsInMemory="100"
           eternal="false"
           timeToIdleSeconds="600"
           timeToLiveSeconds="3600"
           overflowToDisk="true"
        />
</ehcache>
```

This Ehcache configuration file defines two types of cache configurations. One is for the default, and the other is for caching user details. If the user cache configuration is used, a cache instance will cache the details of at most 100 users in memory. The cached users will overflow to disk when this limit is exceeded. A cached user will expire if it has been idle for 10 minutes or live for 1 hour after its creation.

Spring Security comes with two UserCache implementations: EhCacheBasedUserCache, which has to refer to an Ehcache instance, and SpringCacheBasedUserCache, which uses Spring's caching abstraction.

In a Java-based configuration, at the moment of this writing, only the jdbcAuthentication() method allows for easy configuration of a user cache. For a Spring caching-based cache solution (which still delegates to Ehcache), you need to configure a CacheManager instance and make this aware of Ehcache.

```
@Configuration
public class MessageBoardConfiguration {
...
    @Bean
    public EhCacheCacheManager cacheManager() {
        EhCacheCacheManager cacheManager = new EhCacheCacheManager();
        cacheManager.setCacheManager(ehCacheManager().getObject());
        return cacheManager;
    }

    @Bean
    public EhCacheManagerFactoryBean ehCacheManager() {
        return new EhCacheManagerFactoryBean();
    }
}
```

This is best added to the configuration of the services because the caching can also be used for other means (see the recipes regarding Spring caching). Now that you have the CacheManager instance set up, you need to configure a SpringCacheBasedUserCache class.

```
@Configuration
@EnableWebMvcSecurity
public class TodoSecurityConfig extends WebSecurityConfigurerAdapter {

    @Autowired
    private CacheManager cacheManager;
```

```
@Bean
public SpringCacheBasedUserCache userCache() throws Exception {
    Cache cache = cacheManager.getCache("userCache");
    return new SpringCacheBasedUserCache(cache);
}

@Override
protected void configure(AuthenticationManagerBuilder auth) throws Exception {
    auth.jdbcAuthentication()
        .userCache(userCache())
    ...
    }
}
```

Notice the autowiring of CacheManager into the configuration class. You need access to it because you need to retrieve a Cache instance that you pass into the constructor of SpringCacheBasedUseCache. You are going to use the cache named userCache (which you configured in the ehcache.xml file). Finally, you pass the configured UserCache into the jdbcAuthentications.userCache() method.

7-4. Make Access Control Decisions

Problem

In the authentication process, an application will grant a successfully authenticated user a set of authorities. When this user attempts to access a resource in the application, the application has to decide whether the resource is accessible with the granted authorities or other characteristics.

Solution

The decision of whether a user is allowed to access a resource in an application is called an *access control decision*. It is made based on the user's authentication status and the resource's nature and access attributes. In Spring Security, access control decisions are made by access decision managers, which have to implement the AccessDecisionManager interface. You are free to create your own access decision managers by implementing this interface, but Spring Security comes with three convenient access decision managers based on the voting approach. They are shown in Table 7-6.

Table 7-6. *Access Decision Managers That Come with Spring Security*

Access Decision Manager	Specifies when to grant access.
AffirmativeBased	At least one voter votes to grant access.
ConsensusBased	A consensus of voters votes to grant access.
UnanimousBased	All voters vote to abstain or grant access (no voter votes to deny access).

All these access decision managers require a group of voters to be configured for voting on access control decisions. Each voter has to implement the AccessDecisionVoter interface. A voter can vote to grant, abstain, or deny access to a resource. The voting results are represented by the ACCESS_GRANTED, ACCESS_DENIED, and ACCESS_ABSTAIN constant fields defined in the AccessDecisionVoter interface.

By default, if no access decision manager is specified explicitly, Spring Security will automatically configure an AffirmativeBased access decision manager with the following two voters configured:

- RoleVoter votes for an access control decision based on a user's role. It will only process access attributes that start with the ROLE_ prefix, but this prefix can be customized. It votes to grant access if the user has the same role as required to access the resource or to deny access if the user lacks any role required to access the resource. If the resource does not have an access attribute starting with ROLE_, it will abstain from voting.

- AuthenticatedVoter votes for an access control decision based on a user's authentication level. It will only process the access attributes IS_AUTHENTICATED_ FULLY, IS_AUTHENTICATED_REMEMBERED, and IS_AUTHENTICATED_ANONYMOUSLY. It votes to grant access if the user's authentication level is higher than the required attribute. From highest to lowest, authentication levels are fully authenticated, authentication remembered, and anonymously authenticated.

How It Works

By default, Spring Security will automatically configure an access decision manager if none is specified. This default access decision manager is equivalent to the one defined with the following configuration:

```
@Bean
public AffirmativeBased accessDecisionManager() {
    List<AccessDecisionVoter> decisionVoters = Arrays.asList(new RoleVoter(), new
    AuthenticatedVoter());
    return new AffirmativeBased(decisionVoters);
}

@Override
protected void configure(HttpSecurity http) throws Exception {

    http.authorizeRequests()
        .accessDecisionManager(accessDecisionManager())
    ...
}
```

This default access decision manager and its decision voters should satisfy most typical authorization requirements. However, if they don't satisfy yours, you can create your own. In most cases, you'll only need to create a custom voter. For example, you can create a voter to vote for a decision based on a user's IP address.

```
package com.apress.springrecipes.board.security;

import org.springframework.security.access.AccessDecisionVoter;
import org.springframework.security.access.ConfigAttribute;
import org.springframework.security.core.Authentication;
import org.springframework.security.web.authentication.WebAuthenticationDetails;

import java.util.Collection;
import java.util.Objects;

public class IpAddressVoter implements AccessDecisionVoter<Object> {

    private static final String IP_PREFIX = "IP_";
    private static final String IP_LOCAL_HOST = "IP_LOCAL_HOST";

    public boolean supports(ConfigAttribute attribute) {
        return (attribute.getAttribute() != null) && attribute.getAttribute().startsWith
        (IP_PREFIX);
    }

    @Override
    public boolean supports(Class<?> clazz) {
        return true;
    }

    public int vote(Authentication authentication, Object object,
    Collection<ConfigAttribute> configList) {
        if (!(authentication.getDetails() instanceof WebAuthenticationDetails)) {
            return ACCESS_DENIED;
        }

        WebAuthenticationDetails details = (WebAuthenticationDetails) authentication.
        getDetails();
        String address = details.getRemoteAddress();

        int result = ACCESS_ABSTAIN;

        for (ConfigAttribute config : configList) {
            result = ACCESS_DENIED;

            if (Objects.equals(IP_LOCAL_HOST, config.getAttribute())) {
                if (address.equals("127.0.0.1") || address.equals("0:0:0:0:0:0:0:1")) {
                    return ACCESS_GRANTED;
                }
            }
        }

        return result;
    }
}
```

Note that this voter will only process the access attributes that start with the IP_ prefix. At the moment, it only supports the IP_LOCAL_HOST access attribute. If the user is a web client whose IP address is equal to 127.0.0.1 or 0:0:0:0:0:0:0:1—the last value being returned by networkless Linux workstations—this voter will vote to grant access. Otherwise, it will vote to deny access. If the resource does not have an access attribute starting with IP_, it will abstain from voting.

Next, you have to define a custom access decision manager that includes this voter.

```
@Bean
public AffirmativeBased accessDecisionManager() {
    List<AccessDecisionVoter> decisionVoters = Arrays.asList(new RoleVoter(), new
    AuthenticatedVoter(), new IpAddressVoter());
    return new AffirmativeBased(decisionVoters);
}
```

Now, suppose you would like to allow users of the machine running the web container (i.e., the server administrators) to delete to-dos without logging in. You have to refer to this access decision manager from the configuration and add the access attribute IP_LOCAL_HOST to the delete URL mapping.

```
http.authorizeRequests()
    .accessDecisionManager()
    .antMatchers(HttpMethod.DELETE, "/todos*").access("ADMIN,IP_LOCAL_HOST");
```

When calling the URL directly, the to-do will be removed. To access it through the web interface, you still need to be logged in.

Use an Expression to Make Access Control Decisions

Although AccessDecisionVoters allow for a certain degree of flexibility, sometimes you want more complex access control rules to be more flexible. With Spring Security, it is possible to use Springs Expression Language (SpEL) to create powerful access control rules. Spring Security supports a couple of expressions out of the box (see Table 7-7 for a list). By using constructs such as and, or, and not, you can create very powerful and flexible expressions. Spring Security will automatically configure an access decision manager with WebExpressionVoter. This access decision manager is equivalent to the one defined with the following bean configuration:

```
@Bean
public AffirmativeBased accessDecisionManager() {
    List<AccessDecisionVoter> decisionVoters = Arrays.asList(new WebExpressionVoter());
    return new AffirmativeBased(decisionVoters);
}
```

Table 7-7. Spring Security Built-in Expressions

Expression	Description
hasRole(role) or hasAuthority(authority)	Returns true if the current user has the given role
hasAnyRole(role1,role2) / hasAnyAuthority(auth1,auth2)	Returns true if the current user has at least one of the given roles
hasIpAddress(ip-address)	Returns true if the current user has the given IP address
principal	The current user
Authentication	Access to the Spring Security authentication object
permitAll	Always evaluates to true
denyAll	Always evaluates to false
isAnonymous()	Returns true if the current user is anonymous
isRememberMe()	Returns true if the current user logged in by means of the remember-me functionality
isAuthenticated()	Returns true if this is not an anonymous user
isFullyAuthenticated()	Returns true if the user is not an anonymous or remember-me user

■ **Caution** Although the role and authority are almost the same, there is a slight, but important, difference in how they are processed. When using hasRole, the passed-in value for the role will be checked if it starts with ROLE_ (the default role prefix). If not, this will be added before checking the authority. So, hasRole('ADMIN') will actually check whether the current user has the authority ROLE_ADMIN. When using hasAuthority, it will check the value as is.

The previous expression would give access to delete a post if someone had the ADMIN role or was logged in on the local machine. In the previous section, you needed to create your own custom AccessDecisionVoter. Now you only have to write an expression. Writing expressions can be done through the access method instead of one of the has* methods when defining a matcher.

```
@Configuration
@EnableWebSecurity
public class TodoSecurityConfig extends WebSecurityConfigurerAdapter {

    @Override
    protected void configure(HttpSecurity http) throws Exception {
        http
            .authorizeRequests()
                .antMatchers("/messageList*").hasAnyRole("USER", "GUEST")
```

```
                 .antMatchers("/messagePost*").hasRole("USER")
                 .antMatchers("/messageDelete*")
             .access("hasRole('ROLE_ADMIN') or hasIpAddress('127.0.0.1') or
             hasIpAddress('0:0:0:0:0:0:0:1')")
                 ...
      }
  ...
  }
```

Although Spring Security has already several built-in functions that can be used when creating expressions, it is possible to extend the functions with your own. For this, you need to create a class that implements the SecurityExpressionOperations interface and register it with Spring Security. Although it would be possible to create a class that implements all the methods on this interface, it is in general easier to extend the default when you want to add expressions.

```
package com.apress.springrecipes.board.security;

import org.springframework.security.core.Authentication;
import org.springframework.security.web.FilterInvocation;
import org.springframework.security.web.access.expression.WebSecurityExpressionRoot;

public class ExtendedWebSecurityExpressionRoot extends WebSecurityExpressionRoot {

    public ExtendedWebSecurityExpressionRoot(Authentication a, FilterInvocation fi) {
        super(a, fi);
    }

    public boolean localAccess() {
        return hasIpAddress("127.0.0.1") || hasIpAddress("0:0:0:0:0:0:0:1");
    }

}
```

Here you extended WebSecurityExpressionRoot, which provides the default implementation, and you added the method localAccess(). This method checks whether you are logging in from the local machine. To make this class available for Spring Security, you need to create the SecurityExpressionHandler interface.

```
package com.apress.springrecipes.board.security;

import org.springframework.security.access.expression.SecurityExpressionOperations;
import org.springframework.security.authentication.AuthenticationTrustResolver;
import org.springframework.security.authentication.AuthenticationTrustResolverImpl;
import org.springframework.security.core.Authentication;
import org.springframework.security.web.FilterInvocation;
import org.springframework.security.web.access.expression.
DefaultWebSecurityExpressionHandler;
import org.springframework.security.web.access.expression.WebSecurityExpressionRoot;
```

```
public class ExtendedWebSecurityExpressionHandler extends
DefaultWebSecurityExpressionHandler {

    private AuthenticationTrustResolver trustResolver = new
    AuthenticationTrustResolverImpl();

    @Override
    protected SecurityExpressionOperations
        createSecurityExpressionRoot(Authentication authentication, FilterInvocation fi) {

        ExtendedWebSecurityExpressionRoot root =
            new ExtendedWebSecurityExpressionRoot(authentication, fi);
        root.setPermissionEvaluator(getPermissionEvaluator());
        root.setTrustResolver(trustResolver);
        root.setRoleHierarchy(getRoleHierarchy());
        return root;
    }

    @Override
    public void setTrustResolver(AuthenticationTrustResolver trustResolver) {
        this.trustResolver=trustResolver;
        super.setTrustResolver(trustResolver);
    }
}
```

You are extending DefaultWebSecurityExpressionHandler, which provides the default implementation. You override the createSecurityExpressionRoot method and let that create an instance of the ExtendedWebSecurityExpressionRoot class. As you need to add a couple of collaborators, you call the get methods of the superclass. As there isn't a getTrustResolver method, you need to create a new instance of that yourself and implement the setter method.

```
@Configuration
@EnableWebSecurity
public class TodoSecurityConfig extends WebSecurityConfigurerAdapter {

    @Override
    protected void configure(HttpSecurity http) throws Exception {
        http
            .authorizeRequests()
                .expressionHandler(new ExtendedWebSecurityExpressionHandler())
                .antMatchers("/todos*").hasAuthority("USER")
                .antMatchers(DELETE, "/todos*").access("hasRole('ROLE_ADMIN) or
                localAccess()")
    }
}
```

You set the custom expression handler with the expressionHandler method. Now you can rewrite your expression using your localAccess() expression.

325

Use an Expression to Make Access Control Decisions Using Spring Beans

Although you can extend Spring Security using these methods, it isn't the recommended approach. Instead, it is advises you to write a custom class and use that in the expression. Using the @ syntax in the expression, you can call any bean in the application context. So, you could write an expression like @accessChecker. hasLocalAccess(authentication) and provide a bean named accessChecker, which has a hasLocalAccess method that takes an Authentication object.

```
package com.apress.springrecipes.board.security;

import org.springframework.security.core.Authentication;
import org.springframework.security.web.authentication.WebAuthenticationDetails;

public class AccessChecker {

    public boolean hasLocalAccess(Authentication authentication) {
        boolean access = false;
        if (authentication.getDetails() instanceof WebAuthenticationDetails) {
            WebAuthenticationDetails details = (WebAuthenticationDetails) authentication.
            getDetails();
            String address = details.getRemoteAddress();
            access = address.equals("127.0.0.1") || address.equals("0:0:0:0:0:0:0:1");
        }
        return access;
    }
}
```

The AccessChecker still does the same checks as the earlier IpAddressVoter or custom expression handler but doesn't extend the Spring Security classes.

```
@Bean
public AccessChecker accessChecker() {
    return new AccessChecker();
}

@Override
protected void configure(HttpSecurity http) throws Exception {

    http.authorizeRequests()
        .antMatchers("/todos*").hasAuthority("USER")
        .antMatchers(HttpMethod.DELETE, "/todos*").access("hasAuthority('ADMIN') or
        @accessChecker.hasLocalAccess(authentication)")
    ...
}
```

7-5. Secure Method Invocations

Problem

As an alternative or a complement to securing URL access in the web layer, sometimes you may need to secure method invocations in the service layer. For example, in the case that a single controller has to invoke multiple methods in the service layer, you may want to enforce fine-grained security controls on these methods.

Solution

Spring Security enables you to secure method invocations in a declarative way. You annotate methods declared in a bean interface or an implementation class with the @Secured, @PreAuthorize /@PostAuthorize, or @PreFilter/@PostFilter annotations and then enable security for them using the @EnableGlobalMethodSecurity annotation.

How It Works

First you will explore how to secure method invocations using annotations and how to write security expression. Finally you will also see how you can use annotations and expression to filter input arguments and output of a method.

Secure Methods with Annotations

The approach to securing methods is by annotating them with @Secured. For example, you can annotate the methods in MessageBoardServiceImpl with the @Secured annotation and specify the access attributes as its value, whose type is String[] and which takes one or more authorities that will have access to the method.

```
package com.apress.springrecipes.board.service;
...
import org.springframework.security.access.annotation.Secured;

public class MessageBoardServiceImpl implements MessageBoardService {
    ...
    @Secured({"ROLE_USER", "ROLE_GUEST"})
    public List<Message> listMessages() {
        ...
    }

    @Secured("ROLE_USER")
    public synchronized void postMessage(Message message) {
        ...
    }

    @Secured({"ROLE_ADMIN", "IP_LOCAL_HOST"})
    public synchronized void deleteMessage(Message message) {
        ...
    }
```

```
@Secured({"ROLE_USER", "ROLE_GUEST"})
public Message findMessageById(Long messageId) {
    return messages.get(messageId);
}
}
```

Finally, you need to enable the method security. To do so, you have to add the @EnableGlobalMethodSecurity annotation to your configuration class. As you want to use @Secured, you have to set the securedEnabled attribute to true.

```
@Configuration
@EnableGlobalMethodSecurity(securedEnabled = true)
public class TodoWebConfiguration { ... }
```

■ **Note**   It is important that you add the @EnableGlobalMethodSecurity annotation to the application context configuration that contains the beans you want to secure!

Secure Methods with Annotations and Expressions

If you need more elaborate security rules, you can, just like with URL protection, use security expressions based on SpEL to secure your application. For this, you can use the @PreAuthorize and @PostAuthorize annotations. With them you can write security-based expressions just like with URL-based security. To enable the processing of those annotations, you have to set the prePostEnabled attribute on the @ EnableGlobalMethodSecurity annotation to true.

```
@Configuration
@EnableGlobalMethodSecurity(prePostEnabled = true)
public class TodoWebConfiguration { ... }
```

Now you can use the @PreAuthorize and @PostAuthorize annotations to secure your application.

```
package com.apress.springrecipes.board;

import org.springframework.security.access.prepost.PreAuthorize;
import org.springframework.stereotype.Service;

import javax.transaction.Transactional;
import java.util.List;

@Service
@Transactional
class TodoServiceImpl implements TodoService {

    private final TodoRepository todoRepository;

    TodoServiceImpl(TodoRepository todoRepository) {
        this.todoRepository = todoRepository;
    }
```

```java
@Override
@PreAuthorize("hasAuthority('USER')")
public List<Todo> listTodos() {
    return todoRepository.findAll();
}

@Override
@PreAuthorize("hasAuthority('USER')")
public void save(Todo todo) {
    this.todoRepository.save(todo);
}

@Override
@PreAuthorize("hasAuthority('USER')")
public void complete(long id) {
    Todo todo = findById(id);
    todo.setCompleted(true);
    todoRepository.save(todo);
}

@Override
@PreAuthorize("hasAnyAuthority('USER', 'ADMIN')")
public void remove(long id) {
    todoRepository.remove(id);
}

@Override
@PreAuthorize("hasAuthority('USER')")
@PostAuthorize("returnObject.owner == authentication.name")
public Todo findById(long id) {
    return todoRepository.findOne(id);
}
}
```

The @PreAuthorize annotation will be triggered before the actual method call, and the @PostAuthorize annotation will be triggered after the method call. You can also write a security expression and use the result of the method invocation using the returnObject expression. See the expression on the findById method; now if someone else as the owner tried to access the Todo object, a security exception would be thrown.

Filter with Annotations and Expressions

In addition to the @PreAuthorize and @PostAuthorize annotations, there are also the @PreFilter and @PostFilter annotations. The main difference between the two groups of annotations is that the @*Authorize ones will throw an exception if the security rules don't apply. The @*Filter annotations will simply filter the input and output variables of elements you don't have access to.

Currently, when calling listTodos, everything is returned from the database. You want to restrict the retrieval of all elements to the user with the authority ADMIN, and others can see only their own list of to-dos. This can be simply implemented with an @PostFilter annotation. Adding @PostFilter("hasAuthority ('ADMIN') or filterObject.owner == authentication.name") will implement this rule.

```
@PreAuthorize("hasAuthority('USER')")
@PostFilter("hasAnyAuthority('ADMIN') or filterObject.owner == authentication.name")
public List<Todo> listTodos() {
    return todoRepository.findAll();
}
```

When you redeploy the application and log in as a user, you will now only see your own to-dos, and when using a user with the ADMIN authority, you will still see all the available to-dos. See also recipe 7-7 for a more elaborate use of the @*Filter annotations.

■ **Caution**   Although @PostFilter and @PreFilter are a simple way of filtering the input/output of a method, use them with caution. When using them with large results, you can severely impact the performance of your application.

7-6. Handle Security in Views

Problem

Sometimes you may want to display a user's authentication information, such as the principal name and the granted authorities, in the views of your web application. In addition, you want to render the view contents conditionally according to the user's authorities.

Solution

Although you can write JSP scriptlets in your JSP files to retrieve authentication and authorization information through the Spring Security API, it's not an efficient solution. Spring Security provides a JSP tag library for you to handle security in JSP views. It includes tags that can display a user's authentication information and render the view contents conditionally according to the user's authorities.

How It Works

You will first learn how to use the Spring Security tags to display information of the currently authenticated user. Next you will learn how to conditionally hide parts of the page based on the authorities of the current authenticated user.

Display Authentication Information

Suppose you would like to display a user's principal name and grant authorities in the header of the to-do's listing page (i.e., todos.jsp). First, you have to import Spring Security's tag library definition.

```
<%@ taglib prefix="c" uri="http://java.sun.com/jsp/jstl/core" %>
<%@ taglib prefix="sec" uri="http://www.springframework.org/security/tags" %>
```

The `<sec:authentication>` tag exposes the current user's Authentication object for you to render its properties. You can specify a property name or property path in its property attribute. For example, you can render a user's principal name through the name property.

```
<h4>Todos for <sec:authentication property="name" /></h4>
```

In addition to rendering an authentication property directly, this tag supports storing the property in a JSP variable, whose name is specified in the var attribute. For example, you can store the authorities property, which contains the authorities granted to the user, in the JSP variable authorities and render them one by one with a `<c:forEach>` tag. You can further specify the variable scope with the scope ascope attribute.

```
<sec:authentication property="authorities" var="authorities" />
<ul>
    <c:forEach items="${authorities}" var="authority">
        <li>${authority.authority}</li>
    </c:forEach>
</ul>
```

Render View Contents Conditionally

If you want to render view contents conditionally according to a user's authorities, you can use the `<sec:authorize>` tag. For example, you can decide whether to render the message authors according to the user's authorities.

```
<td>
    <sec:authorize ifAllGranted="ROLE_ADMIN,ROLE_USER">${todo.owner}</sec:authorize>
</td>
```

If you want the enclosing content to be rendered only when the user has been granted certain authorities at the same time, you have to specify them in the ifAllGranted attribute. Otherwise, if the enclosing content can be rendered with any of the authorities, you have to specify them in the ifAnyGranted attribute.

```
<td>
    <sec:authorize ifAnyGranted="ROLE_ADMIN,ROLE_USER">${todo.owner}</sec:authorize>
</td>
```

You can also render the enclosing content when a user has not been granted any of the authorities specified in the ifNotGranted attribute.

```
<td>
    <sec:authorize ifNotGranted="ROLE_ADMIN,ROLE_USER">${todo.owner}</sec:authorize>
</td>
```

7-7. Handle Domain Object Security

Problem

Sometimes you may have complicated security requirements that require handling security at the domain object level. That means you have to allow each domain object to have different access attributes for different principals.

Solution

Spring Security provides a module named ACL that allows each domain object to have its own access control list (ACL). An ACL contains a domain object's object identity to associate with the object and also holds multiple access control entries (ACEs), each of which contains the following two core parts:

- *Permissions*: An ACE's permissions are represented by a particular bit mask, with each bit value for a particular type of permission. The BasePermission class predefines five basic permissions as constant values for you to use: READ (bit 0 or integer 1), WRITE (bit 1 or integer 2), CREATE (bit 2 or integer 4), DELETE (bit 3 or integer 8), and ADMINISTRATION (bit 4 or integer 16). You can also define your own using other unused bits.

- *Security identity (SID)*: Each ACE contains permissions for a particular SID. An SID can be a principal (PrincipalSid) or an authority (GrantedAuthoritySid) to associate with permissions. In addition to defining the ACL object model, Spring Security defines APIs for reading and maintaining the model, and it provides high-performance JDBC implementations for these APIs. To simplify ACL's usages, Spring Security also provides facilities, such as access decision voters and JSP tags, for you to use ACL consistently with other security facilities in your application.

How It Works

First you will see how to setup an ACL service and how to maintain the ACL permissions for your entities. Finally you will learn how to use security expressions to secure access to your entities using the stored ACL permissions.

Set Up an ACL Service

Spring Security provides built-in support for storing ACL data in a relational database and accessing it with JDBC. First, you have to create the following tables in your database for storing ACL data:

```
CREATE TABLE ACL_SID(
    ID          BIGINT        NOT NULL GENERATED BY DEFAULT AS IDENTITY,
    SID         VARCHAR(100)  NOT NULL,
    PRINCIPAL   SMALLINT      NOT NULL,
    PRIMARY KEY (ID),
    UNIQUE (SID, PRINCIPAL)
);

CREATE TABLE ACL_CLASS(
    ID      BIGINT        NOT NULL GENERATED BY DEFAULT AS IDENTITY,
    CLASS   VARCHAR(100)  NOT NULL,
    PRIMARY KEY (ID),
    UNIQUE (CLASS)
);
```

```
CREATE TABLE ACL_OBJECT_IDENTITY(
    ID                    BIGINT    NOT NULL GENERATED BY DEFAULT AS IDENTITY,
    OBJECT_ID_CLASS       BIGINT    NOT NULL,
    OBJECT_ID_IDENTITY    BIGINT    NOT NULL,
    PARENT_OBJECT         BIGINT,
    OWNER_SID             BIGINT,
    ENTRIES_INHERITING    SMALLINT  NOT NULL,
    PRIMARY KEY (ID),
    UNIQUE (OBJECT_ID_CLASS, OBJECT_ID_IDENTITY),
    FOREIGN KEY (PARENT_OBJECT)    REFERENCES ACL_OBJECT_IDENTITY,
    FOREIGN KEY (OBJECT_ID_CLASS)  REFERENCES ACL_CLASS,
    FOREIGN KEY (OWNER_SID)        REFERENCES ACL_SID
);

CREATE TABLE ACL_ENTRY(
    ID                    BIGINT    NOT NULL GENERATED BY DEFAULT AS IDENTITY,
    ACL_OBJECT_IDENTITY   BIGINT    NOT NULL,
    ACE_ORDER             INT       NOT NULL,
    SID                   BIGINT    NOT NULL,
    MASK                  INTEGER   NOT NULL,
    GRANTING              SMALLINT  NOT NULL,
    AUDIT_SUCCESS         SMALLINT  NOT NULL,
    AUDIT_FAILURE         SMALLINT  NOT NULL,
    PRIMARY KEY (ID),
    UNIQUE (ACL_OBJECT_IDENTITY, ACE_ORDER),
    FOREIGN KEY (ACL_OBJECT_IDENTITY) REFERENCES ACL_OBJECT_IDENTITY,
    FOREIGN KEY (SID)                 REFERENCES ACL_SID
);
```

Spring Security defines APIs and provides high-performance JDBC implementations for you to access ACL data stored in these tables, so you'll seldom have a need to access ACL data from the database directly. As each domain object can have its own ACL, there may be a large number of ACLs in your application. Fortunately, Spring Security supports caching ACL objects. You can continue to use Ehcache as your cache implementation and create a new configuration for ACL caching in ehcache.xml (located in the classpath root).

```
<ehcache>
    ...
    <cache name="aclCache"
        maxElementsInMemory="1000"
        eternal="false"
        timeToIdleSeconds="600"
        timeToLiveSeconds="3600"
        overflowToDisk="true"
        />
</ehcache>
```

Next, you have to set up an ACL service for your application. However, as Spring Security doesn't support configuring the ACL module with Java-based configuration yet, you have to configure this module with a group of normal Spring beans. For this reason, let's create a separate bean configuration class named TodoAclConfig, which will store ACL-specific configurations, and add its location in the deployment descriptor.

```
package com.apress.springrecipes.board.security;

import org.springframework.security.web.context.AbstractSecurityWebApplicationInitializer;

public class TodoSecurityInitializer extends AbstractSecurityWebApplicationInitializer {

    public TodoSecurityInitializer() {
        super(TodoSecurityConfig.class, TodoAclConfig.class);
    }
}
```

In an ACL configuration file, the core bean is an ACL service. In Spring Security, there are two interfaces that define operations of an ACL service: AclService and MutableAclService. AclService defines operations for you to read ACLs. MutableAclService is a subinterface of AclService that defines operations for you to create, update, and delete ACLs. If your application only needs to read ACLs, you can simply choose an AclService implementation, such as JdbcAclService. Otherwise, you should choose a MutableAclService implementation, such as JdbcMutableAclService.

```
package com.apress.springrecipes.board.security;

import org.springframework.cache.CacheManager;
import org.springframework.cache.ehcache.EhCacheManagerFactoryBean;
import org.springframework.context.annotation.Bean;
import org.springframework.context.annotation.Configuration;
import org.springframework.security.acls.AclEntryVoter;
import org.springframework.security.acls.domain.*;
import org.springframework.security.acls.jdbc.BasicLookupStrategy;
import org.springframework.security.acls.jdbc.JdbcMutableAclService;
import org.springframework.security.acls.jdbc.LookupStrategy;
import org.springframework.security.acls.model.AclCache;
import org.springframework.security.acls.model.AclService;
import org.springframework.security.acls.model.Permission;
import org.springframework.security.acls.model.PermissionGrantingStrategy;
import org.springframework.security.core.authority.SimpleGrantedAuthority;

import javax.sql.DataSource;

@Configuration
public class TodoAclConfig {

    private final DataSource dataSource;

    public TodoAclConfig(DataSource dataSource) {
        this.dataSource = dataSource;
    }

    @Bean
    public AclEntryVoter aclEntryVoter(AclService aclService) {
        return new AclEntryVoter(aclService, "ACL_MESSAGE_DELETE", new Permission[]
            {BasePermission.ADMINISTRATION, BasePermission.DELETE});
    }
```

```
@Bean
public EhCacheManagerFactoryBean ehCacheManagerFactoryBean() {
    return new EhCacheManagerFactoryBean();
}

@Bean
public AuditLogger auditLogger() {
    return new ConsoleAuditLogger();
}

@Bean
public PermissionGrantingStrategy permissionGrantingStrategy() {
    return new DefaultPermissionGrantingStrategy(auditLogger());
}

@Bean
public AclAuthorizationStrategy aclAuthorizationStrategy() {
    return new AclAuthorizationStrategyImpl(new SimpleGrantedAuthority("ADMIN"));
}

@Bean
public AclCache aclCache(CacheManager cacheManager) {
    return new SpringCacheBasedAclCache(cacheManager.getCache("aclCache"),
    permissionGrantingStrategy(), aclAuthorizationStrategy());
}

@Bean
public LookupStrategy lookupStrategy(AclCache aclCache) {
    return new BasicLookupStrategy(this.dataSource, aclCache,
    aclAuthorizationStrategy(), permissionGrantingStrategy());
}

@Bean
public AclService aclService(LookupStrategy lookupStrategy, AclCache aclCache) {
    return new JdbcMutableAclService(this.dataSource, lookupStrategy, aclCache);
}
}
```

The core bean definition in this ACL configuration file is the ACL service, which is an instance of
JdbcMutableAclService that allows you to maintain ACLs. This class requires three constructor arguments.
The first is a data source for creating connections to a database that stores ACL data. You should have a data
source defined beforehand so that you can simply refer to it here (assuming that you have created the ACL
tables in the same database). The third constructor argument is a cache instance to use with an ACL, which
you can configure using Ehcache as the back-end cache implementation.

The only implementation that comes with Spring Security is BasicLookupStrategy, which performs
basic lookup using standard and compatible SQL statements. If you want to make use of advanced database
features to increase lookup performance, you can create your own lookup strategy by implementing the
LookupStrategy interface. A BasicLookupStrategy instance also requires a data source and a cache
instance. Besides, it requires a constructor argument whose type is AclAuthorizationStrategy. This object
determines whether a principal is authorized to change certain properties of an ACL, usually by specifying
a required authority for each category of properties. For the preceding configurations, only a user who has

335

the ADMIN authority can change an ACL's ownership, an ACE's auditing details, or other ACL and ACE details, respectively. Finally, it needs a constructor argument whose type is PermissionGrantingStrategy. This object's responsibility is to check whether the ACL grants access to the given Sid with the Permissions value it has.

Finally, JdbcMutableAclService embeds standard SQL statements for maintaining ACL data in a relational database. However, those SQL statements may not be compatible with all database products. For example, you have to customize the identity query statement for Apache Derby.

Maintain ACLs for Domain Objects

In your back-end services and DAOs, you can maintain ACLs for domain objects with the previously defined ACL service via dependency injection. For your message board, you have to create an ACL for a to-do when it is posted and delete the ACL when this to-do is deleted.

```
package com.apress.springrecipes.board;

import org.springframework.security.access.prepost.PostFilter;
import org.springframework.security.access.prepost.PreAuthorize;
import org.springframework.security.acls.domain.*;
import org.springframework.security.acls.model.MutableAcl;
import org.springframework.security.acls.model.MutableAclService;
import org.springframework.security.acls.model.ObjectIdentity;
import org.springframework.stereotype.Service;

import javax.transaction.Transactional;
import java.util.List;

import static org.springframework.security.acls.domain.BasePermission.DELETE;
import static org.springframework.security.acls.domain.BasePermission.READ;
import static org.springframework.security.acls.domain.BasePermission.WRITE;

@Service
@Transactional
class TodoServiceImpl implements TodoService {

    private final TodoRepository todoRepository;
    private final MutableAclService mutableAclService;

    TodoServiceImpl(TodoRepository todoRepository, MutableAclService mutableAclService) {
        this.todoRepository = todoRepository;
        this.mutableAclService = mutableAclService;
    }

    @Override
    @PreAuthorize("hasAuthority('USER')")
    public void save(Todo todo) {

        this.todoRepository.save(todo);
```

```
        ObjectIdentity oid = new ObjectIdentityImpl(Todo.class, todo.getId());
        MutableAcl acl = mutableAclService.createAcl(oid);
        acl.insertAce(0, READ, new PrincipalSid(todo.getOwner()), true);
        acl.insertAce(1, WRITE, new PrincipalSid(todo.getOwner()), true);
        acl.insertAce(2, DELETE, new PrincipalSid(todo.getOwner()), true);

        acl.insertAce(3, READ, new GrantedAuthoritySid("ADMIN"), true);
        acl.insertAce(4, WRITE, new GrantedAuthoritySid("ADMIN"), true);
        acl.insertAce(5, DELETE, new GrantedAuthoritySid("ADMIN"), true);

    }

    @Override
    @PreAuthorize("hasAnyAuthority('USER', 'ADMIN')")
    public void remove(long id) {
        todoRepository.remove(id);

        ObjectIdentity oid = new ObjectIdentityImpl(Todo.class, id);
        mutableAclService.deleteAcl(oid, false);
    }

    ...
}
```

When a user creates a to-do, you create a new ACL for this message at the same time, using the ID as the ACL's object identity. When a user deletes a to-do, you delete the corresponding ACL as well. For a new to-do, you insert the following ACEs into its ACL:

- The owner of the to-do can READ, WRITE, and DELETE the to-do.

- A user who has the ADMIN authority can also READ, WRITE, and DELETE the to-dos.

JdbcMutableAclService requires that the calling methods have transactions enabled so that its SQL statements can run within transactions. So, you annotate the two methods involving ACL maintenance with the @Transactional annotation and then define a transaction manager and @EnableTransactionManagement on the TodoWebConfig. Also, don't forget to inject the ACL service into TodoService for it to maintain ACL.

```
package com.apress.springrecipes.board.web;

import org.springframework.context.annotation.Configuration;
import org.springframework.jdbc.datasource.DataSourceTransactionManager;
import org.springframework.transaction.annotation.EnableTransactionManagement;
...

import javax.sql.DataSource;

@Configuration
@EnableTransactionManagement
...
public class TodoWebConfig implements WebMvcConfigurer {

    ...
```

```
    @Bean
    public DataSourceTransactionManager transactionManager(DataSource dataSource) {
        return new DataSourceTransactionManager(dataSource);
    }
}
```

Make Access Control Decisions Using Expressions

With an ACL for each domain object, you can use an object's ACL to make access control decisions on methods that involve this object. For example, when a user attempts to delete a to-do, you can consult this message's ACL about whether the user is permitted to delete this to-do.

Configuring ACL can be a daunting task. Luckily, you can use annotations and expressions to make your life easier. You can use the @PreAuthorize and @PreFilter annotations to check whether someone is allowed to execute the method or use certain method arguments. The @PostAuthorize and @PostFilter annotations can be used to check whether a user is allowed to access the result or to filter results based on the ACL. To enable the processing of these annotations, you need to set the prePostEnabled attribute of the @EnableGlobalMethodSecurity annotation to true.

```
@EnableGlobalMethodSecurity(prePostEnabled=true)
```

In addition, you need to configure infrastructure components to be able to make decisions. You need to set up an AclPermissionEvaluator, which is needed to evaluate the permission for an object. This is done in TodoWebConfig and is needed here because that is the configuration class that enables the global method security, and as you want to use ACL to secure the methods using an expression, it needs the custom permission evaluator.

```
package com.apress.springrecipes.board.web.config;

import org.springframework.beans.factory.annotation.Autowired;
import org.springframework.cache.Cache;
import org.springframework.cache.CacheManager;
import org.springframework.context.annotation.Bean;
import org.springframework.context.annotation.Configuration;
import org.springframework.security.acls.AclPermissionEvaluator;
import org.springframework.security.acls.domain.AclAuthorizationStrategyImpl;
import org.springframework.security.acls.domain.ConsoleAuditLogger;
import org.springframework.security.acls.domain.DefaultPermissionGrantingStrategy;
import org.springframework.security.acls.domain.SpringCacheBasedAclCache;
import org.springframework.security.acls.jdbc.BasicLookupStrategy;
import org.springframework.security.acls.jdbc.JdbcMutableAclService;
import org.springframework.security.core.GrantedAuthority;
import org.springframework.security.core.authority.SimpleGrantedAuthority;

import javax.sql.DataSource;

@Configuration
public class TodoWebConfig {

    ...
```

```
    @Bean
    public AclPermissionEvaluator permissionEvaluator() {
        return new AclPermissionEvaluator(jdbcMutableAclService());
    }

}
```

The AclPermissionEvaluator requires an AclService to obtain the ACL for the objects it needs to check. When doing a Java-based configuration, this is enough because the PermissionEvaluator will be automatically detected and wired to the DefaultMethodSecurityExpressionHandler. Now everything is in place to use the annotations together with expressions to control access.

```
package com.apress.springrecipes.board;

...

@Service
@Transactional
class TodoServiceImpl implements TodoService {

    @Override
    @PreAuthorize("hasAuthority('USER')")
    @PostFilter("hasAnyAuthority('ADMIN') or hasPermission(filterObject, 'read')")
    public List<Todo> listTodos() { ... }

    @Override
    @PreAuthorize("hasAuthority('USER')")
    public void save(Todo todo) { ... }

    @Override
    @PreAuthorize("hasPermission(#id, 'com.apress.springrecipes.board.Todo', 'write')")
    public void complete(long id) { ... }

    @Override
    @PreAuthorize("hasPermission(#id, 'com.apress.springrecipes.board.Todo', 'delete')")
    public void remove(long id) { ... }

    @Override
    @PostFilter("hasPermission(filterObject, 'read')")
    public Todo findById(long id) { ... }
}
```

You probably noticed the different annotations and the expressions inside these annotations. The @PreAuthorize annotation can be used to check whether someone has the correct permissions to execute the method. The expression uses #message, which refers to the method argument with the name message. The hasPermission expression is a built-in expression from Spring Security (see Table 7-7).

The @PostFilter annotation allows you to filter the collection and remove the elements someone isn't allowed to read. In the expression, the keyword filterObject refers to an element in the collection. To remain in the collection, the logged-in user needs to have read permission.

@PostAuthorize can be used to check whether a single return value can be used (i.e., if the user has the right permissions). To use the return value in an expression, use the keyword returnObject.

7-8. Add Security to a WebFlux Application

Problem

You have an application built with Spring WebFlux (see Chapter 5), and you want to add security.

Solution

Enable security by adding @EnableWebFluxSecurity to your configuration and create a SecurityWebFilterChain containing the security configuration.

How It Works

A Spring WebFlux application is very different in nature than a regular Spring MVC application. Nonetheless, Spring Security strives to make the configuration as easy as possible, and it tries to be as similar to regular web configuration as possible.

Secure URL Access

First let's create a SecurityConfiguration class and put @EnableWebFluxSecurity on that class.

```
@Configuration
@EnableWebFluxSecurity
public class SecurityConfiguration { ... }
```

The @EnableWebFluxSecurity annotation registers a WebFluxConfigurer (see recipe 5-5) to add AuthenticationPrincipalArgumentResolver, which allows you to inject the Authentication object into a Spring WebFlux handler method. It also registers the WebFluxSecurityConfiguration class from Spring Security, which detects instances of SecurityWebFilterChain (containing the security configuration), which is wrapped as a WebFilter (comparable with a regular servlet filter), which in turn is used by WebFlux to add behavior to incoming requests (just like a normal servlet filter).

Your configuration now only enables security; let's add some security rules.

```
@Bean
SecurityWebFilterChain springWebFilterChain(HttpSecurity http) throws Exception {
    return http
        .authorizeExchange()
            .pathMatchers("/welcome", "/welcome/**").permitAll()
            .pathMatchers("/reservation*").hasRole("USER")
            .anyExchange().authenticated()
        .and()
        .build();
}
```

org.springframework.security.config.annotation.web.reactive.HttpSecurity should look familiar (see recipe 7-1) and is used to add security rules and do further configuration (such as adding/removing headers and configuring the login method). With the authorizeExchange, it is possible to write rules. Here you secure URLs; the /welcome URL is permitted for everyone, and the /reservation URLs are available only for the role USER. For other requests, you have to be authenticated. Finally, you need to call build() to actually build the SecurityWebFilterChain.

In addition to the authorizeExchange, it is also possible to use the headers() configuration method to add security headers to requests (see also recipe 7-2) such as cross-site scripting protection, cache headers, and so on.

Log in to WebFlux Applications

Currently, there is only the httpBasic() authentication mechanism supported by Spring Security WebFlux, and it is enabled by default. You could override parts of the default configuration by explicitly configuring them, and you could override the authentication manager used and the repository used to store the security context. The authentication manager is detected automatically; you just need to register a bean of type ReactiveAuthenticationManager or of type UserDetailsRepository.

You can also configure the location where the SecurityContext value is stored by configuring SecurityContextRepository. The default implementation used is the WebSessionSecurityContextRepository, which stores the context in the WebSession. The other default implementation the ServerWebExchangeAttributeSecurityContextRepository stores the SecurityContext as an attribute for the current exchange (i.e., request).

```
@Bean
SecurityWebFilterChain springWebFilterChain(HttpSecurity http) throws Exception {
    return http.httpBasic().
        .authenticationManager(new CustomReactiveAuthenticationManager())
        .securityContextRepository(new
        ServerWebExchangeAttributeSecurityContextRepository()).and().build();
}
```

This will override the defaults with a CustomReactiveAuthenticationManager and the stateless ServerWebExchangeAttributeSecurityContextRepository. However, for this application, you are going to stick with the defaults.

Authenticate Users

Authenticating users in a Spring WebFlux-based application is done through a ReactiveAuthenticationManager. This is an interface with a single authenticate method. You can either provide your own implementation or use one of the two provided implementations. The first is the UserDetailsRepositoryAuthenticationManager, which wraps an instance of UserDetailsRepository.

■ **Note** The UserDetailsRepository has only a single implementation, the MapUserDetailsRepository, which is an in-memory implementation. You could, of course, provide your own implementation based on a reactive data store (like MongoDB or Couchbase).

The other implementation, ReactiveAuthenticationManagerAdapter, is actually a wrapper for a regular AuthenticationManager (see recipe 7-3). It will wrap a regular instance, and because of that, you can use the blocking implementations in a reactive way. This doesn't make them reactive; they still block, but they are reusable in this way. With this, you could use JDBC, LDAP, and so on, for your reactive application.

When configuring Spring Security in a Spring WebFlux application, you can add an instance of either a ReactiveAuthenticationManager to your Java configuration class or a UserDetailsRepository. When the latter is detected, it will automatically be wrapped in a UserDetailsRepositoryAuthenticationManager.

```
@Bean
public MapUserDetailsRepository userDetailsRepository() {
    UserDetails marten = User.withUsername("marten").password("secret").roles("USER").build();
    UserDetails admin = User.withUsername("admin").password("admin").roles("USER","ADMIN").
    build();
    return new MapUserDetailsRepository(marten, admin);
}
```

When you now deploy the application (or run the ReactorNettyBootstrap class), you are free to access the /welcome page, but when accessing a URL starting with /reservation, you are greeted by a basic authentication prompt from the browser (Figure 7-3).

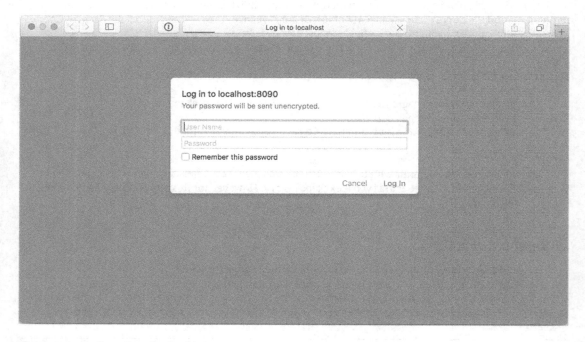

Figure 7-3. *Basic authentication login screen*

Make Access Control Decisions

Table 7-8 shows the Spring Security WebFlux built-in expressions.

Table 7-8. *Spring Security WebFlux Built-in Expressions*

Expression	Description
hasRole(role) or hasAuthority(authority)	Returns true if the current user has the given role
permitAll()	Always evaluates to true
denyAll()	Always evaluates to false
authenticated()	Returns true if the user is authenticated
access()	Use a function to determine whether access is granted

■ **Caution**   Although the role and authority are almost the same, there is a slight, but important, difference in how they are processed. When using hasRole, the passed-in value for the role will checked if it starts with ROLE_ (the default role prefix). If not, this will be added before checking the authority. So, hasRole('ADMIN') will actually check whether the current user has the authority ROLE_ADMIN. When using hasAuthority, it will check the value as is.

```
@Bean
SecurityWebFilterChain springWebFilterChain(HttpSecurity http) throws Exception {
    return http
        .authorizeExchange()
            .pathMatchers("/users/{user}/**").access(this::userEditAllowed)
            .anyExchange().authenticated()
        .and()
        .build();
}

private Mono<AuthorizationDecision> userEditAllowed(Mono<Authentication> authentication,
AuthorizationContext context) {
    return authentication
        .map( a -> context.getVariables().get("user").equals(a.getName()) ||
        a.getAuthorities().contains(new SimpleGrantedAuthority("ROLE_ADMIN")))
        .map( granted -> new AuthorizationDecision(granted));
}
```

The access() expression can be used to write powerful expressions. The previous snippet uses a path parameter in the URL {user}, and access is allowed if the current user is the actual user or if someone has the ROLE_ADMIN authority. AuthorizationContext contains the parsed variables that you could use to compare the name from the URI. Authentication contains the collection of GrantedAuthorities, which you can check for the ROLE_ADMIN authority. Of course, you can write as many complex expressions as you like; you could check for the IP address, request headers, and so on.

Summary

In this chapter, you learned how to secure applications using Spring Security. It can be used to secure any Java application, but it's mostly used for web applications. The concepts of authentication, authorization, and access control are essential in the security area, so you should have a clear understanding of them.

You often have to secure critical URLs by preventing unauthorized access to them. Spring Security can help you to achieve this in a declarative way. It handles security by applying servlet filters, which can be configured with a simple Java-based configuration. Spring Security will automatically configure the basic security services for you and tries to be as secure as possible by default.

Spring Security supports multiple ways for users to log into a web application, such as form-based login and HTTP Basic authentication. It also provides an anonymous login service that allows you to handle an anonymous user just like a normal user. Remember-me support allows an application to remember a user's identity across multiple browser sessions.

Spring Security supports multiple ways of authenticating users and has built-in provider implementations for them. For example, it supports authenticating users against in-memory definitions, a relational database, and an LDAP repository. You should always store encrypted passwords in your user repository because clear-text passwords are vulnerable to hacker attacks. Spring Security also supports caching user details locally to save you the overhead of performing remote queries.

Decisions on whether a user is allowed to access a given resource are made by access decision managers. Spring Security comes with three access decision managers that are based on the voting approach. All of them require a group of voters to be configured for voting on access control decisions.

Spring Security enables you to secure method invocations in a declarative way, either by embedding a security interceptor in a bean definition or by matching multiple methods with AspectJ pointcut expressions or annotations. Spring Security also allows you to display a user's authentication information in JSP views and render view contents conditionally according to a user's authorities.

Spring Security provides an ACL module that allows each domain object to have an ACL for controlling access. You can read and maintain an ACL for each domain object with Spring Security's high-performance APIs, which are implemented with JDBC. Spring Security also provides facilities such as access decision voters and JSP tags for you to use ACLs consistently with other security facilities.

Spring Security also has support for securing Spring WebFlux-based applications. In the previous recipe, you explored how you can add security to such an application.

CHAPTER 8

Spring Mobile

Today more mobile devices exist than ever before. Most of these mobile devices can access the Internet and can access web sites. However, some mobile devices might have a browser that lacks certain HTML or JavaScript features that you use on your web site; you also might want to show a different web site to your mobile users or maybe give them a choice of viewing a mobile version. In those cases, you could write all the device detection routines yourself, but Spring Mobile provides ways to detect the device being used.

8-1. Detect Devices Without Spring Mobile

Problem

You want to detect the type of device that connects to your web site.

Solution

Create a `Filter` that detects the `User-Agent` value of the incoming request and sets a request attribute so that it can be retrieved in a controller.

How It Works

Here is the `Filter` implementation you need to do device detection based on `User-Agent`:

```
package com.apress.springrecipes.mobile.web.filter;

import org.springframework.util.StringUtils;
import org.springframework.web.filter.OncePerRequestFilter;

import javax.servlet.FilterChain;
import javax.servlet.ServletException;
import javax.servlet.http.HttpServletRequest;
import javax.servlet.http.HttpServletResponse;
import java.io.IOException;
```

© Marten Deinum, Daniel Rubio, and Josh Long 2017
M. Deinum et al., *Spring 5 Recipes*, DOI 10.1007/978-1-4842-2790-9_8

```java
public class DeviceResolverRequestFilter extends OncePerRequestFilter {

    public static final String CURRENT_DEVICE_ATTRIBUTE = "currentDevice";

    public static final String DEVICE_MOBILE = "MOBILE";
    public static final String DEVICE_TABLET = "TABLET";
    public static final String DEVICE_NORMAL = "NORMAL";

    @Override
    protected void doFilterInternal(HttpServletRequest request, HttpServletResponse
    response,
                                    FilterChain filterChain) throws ServletException,
                                    IOException {
        String userAgent = request.getHeader("User-Agent");
        String device = DEVICE_NORMAL;

        if (StringUtils.hasText(userAgent)) {
            userAgent = userAgent.toLowerCase();
            if (userAgent.contains("android")) {
                device = userAgent.contains("mobile") ? DEVICE_NORMAL : DEVICE_TABLET;
            } else if (userAgent.contains("ipad") || userAgent.contains("playbook") ||
            userAgent.contains("kindle")) {
                device = DEVICE_TABLET;
            } else if (userAgent.contains("mobil") || userAgent.contains("ipod") ||
            userAgent.contains("nintendo DS")) {
                device = DEVICE_MOBILE;
            }
        }
        request.setAttribute(CURRENT_DEVICE_ATTRIBUTE, device);
        filterChain.doFilter(request, response);
    }
}
```

This implementation first retrieves the User-Agent header from the incoming request. When there is a value in there, the filter needs to check what is in the header. There are some if/else constructs in the header to do basic detection of the type of device. There is a special case for Android because that can be a tablet or mobile device. When the filter determines what the type of device is, the type is stored as a request attribute so that it is available to other components. Next, there is a controller and JSP page to display some information about what is going on. The controller simply directs to a home.jsp page, which is located in the WEB-INF/views directory. A configured InternalResourceViewResolver takes care of resolving the name to an actual JSP page (for more information, refer to the recipes in Chapter 4).

```java
package com.apress.springrecipes.mobile.web;

import org.springframework.stereotype.Controller;
import org.springframework.web.bind.annotation.RequestMapping;

import javax.servlet.http.HttpServletRequest;

@Controller
public class HomeController {
```

```
    @RequestMapping("/home")
    public String index(HttpServletRequest request) {
        return "home";
    }

}
```

Here's the home.jsp page:

```
<%@ taglib uri="http://java.sun.com/jsp/jstl/core" prefix="c" %>
<!doctype html>
<html>
<body>

<h1>Welcome</h1>
<p>
    Your User-Agent header: <c:out value="${header['User-Agent']}" />
</p>
<p>
    Your type of device: <c:out value="${requestScope.currentDevice}" />
</p>

</body>
</html>
```

The JSP shows the User-Agent header (if any) and the type of device, which has been determined by your own DeviceResolverRequestFilter.

Finally, here is the configuration and bootstrapping logic:

```
package com.apress.springrecipes.mobile.web.config;

import org.springframework.context.annotation.Bean;
import org.springframework.context.annotation.ComponentScan;
import org.springframework.context.annotation.Configuration;
import org.springframework.web.servlet.ViewResolver;
import org.springframework.web.servlet.config.annotation.EnableWebMvc;
import org.springframework.web.servlet.view.InternalResourceView;
import org.springframework.web.servlet.view.InternalResourceViewResolver;

@Configuration
@ComponentScan("com.apress.springrecipes.mobile.web")
public class MobileConfiguration {

    @Bean
    public ViewResolver viewResolver() {

        InternalResourceViewResolver viewResolver = new InternalResourceViewResolver();
        viewResolver.setPrefix("/WEB-INF/views/");
        viewResolver.setSuffix(".jsp");
        return viewResolver;
    }
}
```

The controller is picked up by the @ComponentScan annotation. For bootstrapping the application, there is the MobileApplicationInitializer, which bootstraps DispatcherServlet and optionally ContextLoaderListener.

```
package com.apress.springrecipes.mobile.web;

import com.apress.springrecipes.mobile.web.config.MobileConfiguration;
import com.apress.springrecipes.mobile.web.filter.DeviceResolverRequestFilter;
import org.springframework.web.servlet.support.
AbstractAnnotationConfigDispatcherServletInitializer;

import javax.servlet.Filter;

public class MobileApplicationInitializer extends
AbstractAnnotationConfigDispatcherServletInitializer {

    @Override
    protected Class<?>[] getRootConfigClasses() {
        return null;
    }

    @Override
    protected Class<?>[] getServletConfigClasses() {
        return new Class[] { MobileConfiguration.class };
    }

    @Override
    protected Filter[] getServletFilters() {
        return new Filter[] {new DeviceResolverRequestFilter()};
    }

    @Override
    protected String[] getServletMappings() {
        return new String[] {"/"};
    }
}
```

There are two things to notice here. First, the previously mentioned configuration class is passed to DispatcherServlet by implementing the getServletConfigClasses method. Second, the implementation of the getServletFilters method takes care of registering the filter and maps it to DispatcherServlet. When the application is deployed, using http://localhost:8080/mobile/home will show you the User-Agent value and what type the filter thinks it is (see Figure 8-1).

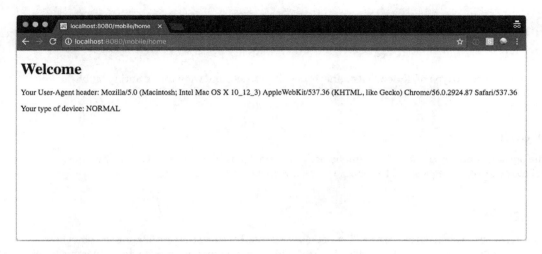

Figure 8-1. *Viewing the application in Chrome*

Using Chrome on an iMac produces the result shown in Figure 8-1. When using an iPhone, it looks something like Figure 8-2.

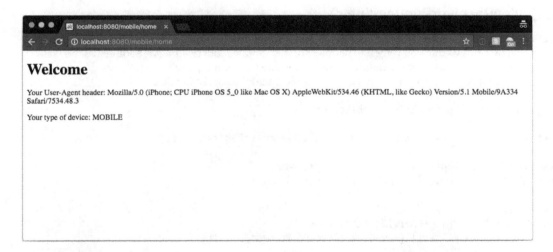

Figure 8-2. *Viewing the application using an iPhone 4*

■ **Note**   For testing different browsers, you can either use a tablet or mobile device on your internal network or use a browser plug-in such as User-Agent Switcher for Chrome or Firefox.

Although the filter does its job, it is far from complete. For instance, some mobile devices don't match the rules (the Kindle Fire has a different header than a regular Kindle device). It is also quite hard to maintain the list of rules and devices or to test with many devices. Using a library like Spring Mobile is much easier than doing this on your own.

8-2. Detect Devices with Spring Mobile

Problem

You want to detect the type of device that connects to your web site and want to use Spring Mobile to help you with this.

Solution

Use the Spring Mobile DeviceResolver and helper classes to determine the type of device by configuring either DeviceResolverRequestFilter or DeviceResolverHandlerInterceptor.

How It Works

Both DeviceResolverRequestFilter and DeviceResolverHandlerInterceptor delegate the detection of the type of device to a DeviceResolver class. Spring Mobile provides an implementation of that interface named LiteDeviceResolver. The DeviceResolver class returns a Device object, which indicates the type. This Device object is stored as a request attribute so that it can be used further down the chain. Spring Mobile comes with a single default implementation of the Device interface, LiteDevice.

Use DeviceResolverRequestFilter

Using DeviceResolverRequestFilter is a matter of adding it to the web application and mapping it to the servlet or requests that you want it to handle. For your application, that means adding it to the getServletFilters method. The advantage of using this filter is that it is possible to use it even outside a Spring-based application. It could be used in, for instance, a JSF-based application.

```
package com.apress.springrecipes.mobile.web;
...
import org.springframework.mobile.device.DeviceResolverRequestFilter;

public class MobileApplicationInitializer extends
AbstractAnnotationConfigDispatcherServletInitializer {
...
    @Override
    protected Filter[] getServletFilters() {
        return new Filter[] {new DeviceResolverRequestFilter()};
    }
}
```

This configuration registers DeviceResolverRequestFilter and will automatically attach it to requests handled by DispatcherServlet. To test this, issue a request to http://localhost:8080/mobile/home, which should display something like the following:

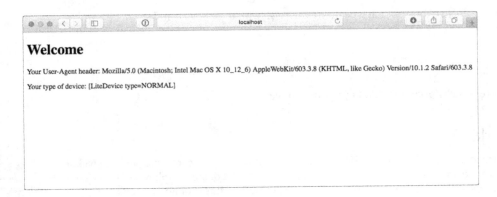

The output for the device is the text as created for the toString method on the LiteDevice class provided by Spring Mobile.

Use DeviceResolverHandlerInterceptor

When using Spring Mobile in a Spring MVC–based application, it is easier to work with DeviceResolverHandlerInterceptor. This needs to be configured in your configuration class and needs to be registered with the addInterceptors helper method.

```
package com.apress.springrecipes.mobile.web.config;

import org.springframework.mobile.device.DeviceResolverHandlerInterceptor;
import org.springframework.web.servlet.config.annotation.InterceptorRegistry;
import org.springframework.web.servlet.config.annotation.WebMvcConfigurerAdapter;

@Configuration
@EnableWebMvc
@ComponentScan("com.apress.springrecipes.mobile.web")
public class MobileConfiguration extends WebMvcConfigurerAdapter {
...
    @Override
    public void addInterceptors(InterceptorRegistry registry) {
        registry.addInterceptor(new DeviceResolverHandlerInterceptor());
    }
}
```

The MobileConfiguration class extends WebMvcConfigurerAdapter from this class, and you can override the addInterceptors method. All the interceptors added to the registry will be added to the HandlerMapping beans in the application context. When the application is deployed and a request is made to http://localhost:8080/mobile/home, the result should be the same as for the filter.

8-3. Use Site Preferences

Problem

You want to allow users to choose which type of site they visit with their device and store this for future reference.

Solution

Use the SitePreference support provided by Spring Mobile.

How It Works

Both SitePreferenceRequestFilter and SitePreferenceHandlerInterceptor delegate retrieval of the current SitePreference to a SitePreferenceHandler object. The default implementation uses a SitePreferenceRepository class to store the preferences; by default this is done in a cookie.

Use SitePreferenceRequestFilter

Using SitePreferenceRequestFilter is a matter of adding it to the web application and mapping it to the servlet or requests that you want it to handle. For your application, that means adding it to the getServletFilters method. The advantage of using a filter is that it is possible to use it even outside a Spring-based application. It could also be used in a JSF-based application.

```
package com.apress.springrecipes.mobile.web;

import org.springframework.mobile.device.site.SitePreferenceRequestFilter;
...

public class MobileApplicationInitializer extends
AbstractAnnotationConfigDispatcherServletInitializer {

    @Override
    protected Filter[] getServletFilters() {
        return new Filter[] {
            new DeviceResolverRequestFilter(),
            new SitePreferenceRequestFilter()};
    }

...
}
```

Now that SitePreferenceRequestFilter is registered, it will inspect incoming requests. If a request has a parameter named site_preference, it will use the passed-in value (NORMAL, MOBILE, or TABLET) to set the SitePreference value. The determined value is stored in a cookie and used for future reference; if a new value is detected, the cookie value will be reset. Modify the home.jsp pages to include the following in order to display the current SitePreference value:

```
<p>
    Your site preferences <c:out value="${requestScope.currentSitePreference}" />
</p>
```

Now opening the page using the URL http://localhost:8080/mobile/home?site_preference=TABLET will set the SitePreference value to TABLET.

Use SitePreferenceHandlerInterceptor

When using Spring Mobile in a Spring MVC-based application, it is easier to work with SitePreferenceHandlerInterceptor. This needs to be configured in your configuration class and needs to be registered with the addInterceptors helper method.

```
package com.apress.springrecipes.mobile.web.config;

import org.springframework.mobile.device.DeviceResolverHandlerInterceptor;
import org.springframework.mobile.device.site. SitePreferenceHandlerInterceptor;
import org.springframework.web.servlet.config.annotation.InterceptorRegistry;
import org.springframework.web.servlet.config.annotation.WebMvcConfigurerAdapter;

@Configuration
@EnableWebMvc
@ComponentScan("com.apress.springrecipes.mobile.web")
public class MobileConfiguration extends WebMvcConfigurerAdapter {
...
    @Override
    public void addInterceptors(InterceptorRegistry registry) {
        registry.addInterceptor(new DeviceResolverHandlerInterceptor());
        registry.addInterceptor(new SitePreferenceHandlerInterceptor());
    }
}
```

The MobileConfiguration class extends WebMvcConfigurerAdapter from this class, and you can override the addInterceptors method. All the interceptors added to the registry will be added to the HandlerMapping beans in the application context. When the application is deployed and a request is made to http://localhost:8080/mobile/home?site_preference=TABLET, the result should be the same as for the filter in the previous section.

8-4. Use the Device Information to Render Views

Problem

You want to render a different view based on the device or site preferences.

Solution

Use the current Device and SitePreferences objects to determine which view to render. This can be done manually or by using LiteDeviceDelegatingViewResolver.

How It Works

Now that the type of device is known, it can be used to your advantage. First let's create some additional views for each type of device supported and put them, respectively, in a mobile or tablet directory under WEB-INF/views. Here's the source for mobile/home.jsp:

```
<%@ taglib uri="http://java.sun.com/jsp/jstl/core" prefix="c" %>
<!doctype html>
<html>
<body>

<h1>Welcome Mobile User</h1>
<p>
    Your User-Agent header: <c:out value="${header['User-Agent']}" />
</p>
<p>
    Your type of device: <c:out value="${requestScope.currentDevice}" />
</p>
<p>
    Your site preferences <c:out value="${requestScope.currentSitePreference}" />
</p>
</body>
</html>
```

Here's the source for tablet/home.jsp:

```
<%@ taglib uri="http://java.sun.com/jsp/jstl/core" prefix="c" %>
<!doctype html>
<html>
<body>

<h1>Welcome Tablet User</h1>
<p>
    Your User-Agent header: <c:out value="${header['User-Agent']}" />
</p>
<p>
    Your type of device: <c:out value="${requestScope.currentDevice}" />
</p>
```

CHAPTER 8 ■ SPRING MOBILE

```
<p>
    Your site preferences <c:out value="${requestScope.currentSitePreference}" />
</p>
</body>
</html>
```

Now that the different views are in place, you need to find a way to render them based on the device value that has been detected. One way would be to manually get access to the current device from the request and use that to determine which view to render.

```java
package com.apress.springrecipes.mobile.web;

import org.springframework.mobile.device.Device;
import org.springframework.mobile.device.DeviceUtils;
import org.springframework.stereotype.Controller;
import org.springframework.web.bind.annotation.RequestMapping;

import javax.servlet.http.HttpServletRequest;

@Controller
public class HomeController {

    @RequestMapping("/home")
    public String index(HttpServletRequest request) {
        Device device = DeviceUtils.getCurrentDevice(request);
        if (device.isMobile()) {
            return "mobile/home";
        } else if (device.isTablet()) {
            return "tablet/home";
        } else {
            return "home";
        }
    }
}
```

Spring Mobile has a DeviceUtils class that can be used to retrieve the current device. The current device is retrieved from a request attribute (currentDevice), which has been set by the filter or interceptor. The device value can be used to determine which view to render.

Getting the device in each method that needs it isn't very convenient. It would be a lot easier if it could be passed into the controller method as a method argument. For this, you can use DeviceHandlerMethodArgumentResolver, which can be registered and will resolve the method argument to the current device. To retrieve the current SitePreference value, you can add a SitePreferenceHandlerMethodArgumentResolver class.

```java
package com.apress.springrecipes.mobile.web.config;

import org.springframework.mobile.device.DeviceHandlerMethodArgumentResolver;
...
import java.util.List;

@Configuration
@EnableWebMvc
```

355

```
@ComponentScan("com.apress.springrecipes.mobile.web")
public class MobileConfiguration extends WebMvcConfigurerAdapter {

...

    @Override
    public void addArgumentResolvers(List<HandlerMethodArgumentResolver> argumentResolvers)
{
        argumentResolvers.add(new DeviceHandlerMethodArgumentResolver());
        argumentResolvers.add(new SitePreferenceHandlerMethodArgumentResolver());
    }
}
```

Now that these have been registered, the controller method can be simplified, and the Device value can be passed in as a method argument.

```
package com.apress.springrecipes.mobile.web;

import org.springframework.mobile.device.Device;
import org.springframework.stereotype.Controller;
import org.springframework.web.bind.annotation.RequestMapping;

import javax.servlet.http.HttpServletRequest;

@Controller
public class HomeController {

    @RequestMapping("/home")
    public String index(Device device) {
        if (device.isMobile()) {
            return "mobile/home";
        } else if (device.isTablet()) {
            return "tablet/home";
        } else {
            return "home";
        }
    }
}
```

The method signature changed from having an HttpServletRequest value to a Device value. That takes care of the lookup and will pass in the current device. However, while this is more convenient than manual retrieval, it is still quite an antiquated way to determine which view to render. Currently, the preferences aren't taken into account, but this could be added to the method signature and could be used to determine the preference. However, it would complicate the detection algorithm. Imagine this code in multiple controller methods, which would soon become a maintenance nightmare.

Spring Mobile ships with a LiteDeviceDelegatingViewResolver class, which can be used to add additional prefixes and/or suffixes to the view name, before it is passed to the actual view resolver. It also takes into account the optional site preferences of the user.

```
package com.apress.springrecipes.mobile.web.config;

import org.springframework.mobile.device.view.LiteDeviceDelegatingViewResolver;
...
```

```
@Configuration
@EnableWebMvc
@ComponentScan("com.apress.springrecipes.mobile.web")
public class MobileConfiguration extends WebMvcConfigurerAdapter {
...
    @Bean
    public ViewResolver viewResolver() {
        InternalResourceViewResolver viewResolver = new InternalResourceViewResolver();
        viewResolver.setPrefix("/WEB-INF/views/");
        viewResolver.setSuffix(".jsp");
        viewResolver.setOrder(2);
        return viewResolver;
    }

    @Bean
    public ViewResolver mobileViewResolver() {
        LiteDeviceDelegatingViewResolver delegatingViewResolver =
            new LiteDeviceDelegatingViewResolver(viewResolver());
        delegatingViewResolver.setOrder(1);
        delegatingViewResolver.setMobilePrefix("mobile/");
        delegatingViewResolver.setTabletPrefix("tablet/");
        return delegatingViewResolver;

    }
}
```

LiteDeviceDelegatingViewResolver takes a delegate view resolver as a constructor argument; the earlier configured InternalResourceViewResolver is passed in as the delegate. Also, note the ordering of the view resolvers; you have to make sure that LiteDeviceDelegatingViewResolver executes before any other view resolver. This way, it has a chance to determine whether a custom view for a particular device exists. Next, notice in the configuration that the views for mobile devices are located in the mobile directory, and for the tablet they are in the tablet directory. To add these directories to the view names, the prefixes for those device types are set to their respective directories. Now when a controller returns home as the view name to select for a mobile device, it would be turned into mobile/home. This modified name is passed on to InternalResourceViewResolver, which turns it into /WEB-INF/views/mobile/home.jsp, the page you actually want to render.

```
package com.apress.springrecipes.mobile.web;

import org.springframework.stereotype.Controller;
import org.springframework.web.bind.annotation.RequestMapping;

@Controller
public class HomeController {

    @RequestMapping("/home")
    public String index() {
        return "home";
    }
}
```

The controller is quite clean now. Its only concern is to return the name of the view. The determination of which view to render is left to the configured view resolvers. `LiteDeviceDelegatingViewResolver` takes into account any `SitePreferences` values when found.

8-5. Implement Site Switching

Problem

Your mobile site is hosted on a different URL than your normal web site.

Solution

Use Spring Mobile's site switching support to redirect to the appropriate part of your web site.

How It Works

Spring Mobile comes with a `SiteSwitcherHandlerInterceptor` class, which you can use to switch to a mobile version of your site based on the detected `Device` value. To configure `SiteSwitcherHandlerInterceptor`, there are a couple of factory methods that provide ready-to-use settings (see Table 8-1).

Table 8-1. Overview of Factory Methods on SiteSwitcherHandlerInterceptor

Factory Method	Description
mDot	Redirects to a domain starting with `m.`; for instance, `http://www.yourdomain.com` would redirect to `http://m.yourdomain.com`.
dotMobi	Redirects to a domain ending with `.mobi`. A request to `http://www.yourdomain.com` would redirect to `http://www.yourdomain.mobi`.
urlPath	Sets up different context roots for different devices. This will redirect to the configured URL path for that device. For instance, `http://www.yourdomain.com` could be redirected to `http://www.yourdomain.com/mobile`.
standard	This is the most flexible configurable factory method, which allows you to specify a domain to redirect to for the mobile, tablet, and normal versions of your web site.

`SiteSwitcherHandlerInterceptor` also provides the ability to use site preferences. When using `SiteSwitcherHandlerInterceptor`, you don't need to register `SitePreferencesHandlerInterceptor` anymore because this is already taken care of. Configuration is as simple as adding it to the list of interceptors you want to apply; the only thing to remember is that you need to place it after `DeviceResolverHandlerInterceptor` because the device information is needed to calculate the redirection URL.

```
package com.apress.springrecipes.mobile.web.config;

...
import org.springframework.mobile.device.switcher.SiteSwitcherHandlerInterceptor;

@Configuration
@EnableWebMvc
@ComponentScan("com.apress.springrecipes.mobile.web")
public class MobileConfiguration extends WebMvcConfigurerAdapter {

    @Override
    public void addInterceptors(InterceptorRegistry registry) {
        registry.addInterceptor(new DeviceResolverHandlerInterceptor());
        registry.addInterceptor(siteSwitcherHandlerInterceptor());
    }

    @Bean
    public SiteSwitcherHandlerInterceptor siteSwitcherHandlerInterceptor() {
        return SiteSwitcherHandlerInterceptor.mDot("yourdomain.com", true);
    }
...
}
```

Notice in the bean declaration for SiteSwitcherHandlerInterceptor that the factory method mDot
is used to create an instance. The method takes two arguments. The first is the base domain name to use,
and the second is a boolean indicating whether tablets should be considered mobile devices. The default is
false. This configuration would lead to redirecting a request to the normal web site from mobile devices to
m.yourdomain.com.

```
@Bean
public SiteSwitcherHandlerInterceptor siteSwitcherHandlerInterceptor() {
    return SiteSwitcherHandlerInterceptor.dotMobi("yourdomain.com", true);
}
```

The previous configuration uses the dotMobi factory method, which takes two arguments. The first is
the base domain name to use, and the second is a Boolean indicating whether tablets are to be considered
mobile devices; the default is false. This would lead to redirecting requests to your normal web site from
mobile devices to yourdomain.mobi.

```
@Bean
public SiteSwitcherHandlerInterceptor siteSwitcherHandlerInterceptor() {
    return SiteSwitcherHandlerInterceptor.urlPath("/mobile", "/tablet", "/home");
}
```

The previous configuration uses the urlPath factory method with three arguments. The first argument
is the context root for mobile devices, and the second is the context root for tablets. The final argument is
the root path or your application. There are two more variations of the urlPath factory method: one that
takes only the path for mobile devices and another that takes a path for mobile devices and a root path. The
previous configuration will lead to requests from mobile devices being redirected to yourdomain.com/home/
mobile and for tablets to yourdomain.com/home/tablet.

Finally, there is the standard factory method, which is the most flexible and elaborate to configure.

```
@Bean
public SiteSwitcherHandlerInterceptor siteSwitcherHandlerInterceptor() {
    return SiteSwitcherHandlerInterceptor
        .standard("yourdomain.com", "mobile.yourdomain.com",
            "tablet.yourdomain.com", "*.yourdomain.com");
}
```

The previous configuration uses the standard factory method. It specifies a different domain for the normal, mobile, and tablet versions of the web site. Finally, it specifies the domain name of the cookie to use for storing the site preferences. This is needed because of the different subdomains specified.

There are several other variations of the standard factory method that allow for a subset of configuration of what was shown earlier.

Summary

In this chapter, you learned how to use Spring Mobile, which can detect the device that is requesting a page and can allow the user to select a certain page based on preferences. You learned how you can detect a user's device using DeviceResolverRequestFilter or DeviceResolverHandlerInterceptor. You also learned how you can use SitePreferences to allow the user to override the detected device. Next, you looked at how you can use the device information and preferences to render a view for that device. Finally, you learned how to redirect the user to a different part of your web site based on the user's device or site preferences.

CHAPTER 9

■ ■ ■

Data Access

In chapter, you will learn how Spring can simplify your database access tasks (Spring can also simplify your NoSQL and Big Data tasks, which are covered in Chapter 12). Data access is a common requirement for most enterprise applications, which usually require accessing data stored in relational databases. As an essential part of Java SE, Java Database Connectivity (JDBC) defines a set of standard APIs for you to access relational databases in a vendor-independent fashion.

The purpose of JDBC is to provide APIs through which you can execute SQL statements against a database. However, when using JDBC, you have to manage database-related resources by yourself and handle database exceptions explicitly. To make JDBC easier to use, Spring provides an abstraction framework for interfacing with JDBC. As the heart of the Spring JDBC framework, JDBC templates are designed to provide template methods for different types of JDBC operations. Each template method is responsible for controlling the overall process and allows you to override particular tasks of the process.

If raw JDBC doesn't satisfy your requirement or you feel your application would benefit from something slightly higher level, then Spring's support for object-relational mapping (ORM) solutions will interest you. In this chapter, you will also learn how to integrate ORM frameworks into your Spring applications. Spring supports most of the popular ORM (or data mapper) frameworks, including Hibernate, JDO, iBATIS, and the Java Persistence API (JPA). Classic TopLink isn't supported starting from Spring 3.0 (the JPA implementation is still supported, of course). However, the JPA support is varied with many implementations of JPA, including the Hibernate and TopLink-based versions. The focus of this chapter will be on Hibernate and JPA. However, Spring's support for ORM frameworks is consistent, so you can easily apply the techniques in this chapter to other ORM frameworks as well.

ORM is a modern technology for persisting objects into a relational database. An ORM framework persists your objects according to the mapping metadata you provide (XML- or annotation-based), such as the mappings between classes and tables, properties and columns, and so on. It generates SQL statements for object persistence at runtime, so you needn't write database-specific SQL statements unless you want to take advantage of database-specific features or provide optimized SQL statements of your own. As a result, your application will be database independent, and it can be easily migrated to another database in the future. Compared to the direct use of JDBC, an ORM framework can significantly reduce the data access effort of your applications.

Hibernate is a popular open source and high-performance ORM framework in the Java community. Hibernate supports most JDBC-compliant databases and can use specific dialects to access particular databases. Beyond the basic ORM features, Hibernate supports more advanced features such as caching, cascading, and lazy loading. It also defines a querying language called Hibernate Query Language (HQL) for you to write simple but powerful object queries.

JPA defines a set of standard annotations and APIs for object persistence in both the Java SE and Java EE platforms. JPA is defined as part of the EJB specification in JSR-220. JPA is just a set of standard APIs that require a JPA-compliant engine to provide persistence services. You can compare JPA with the JDBC API and a JPA engine with a JDBC driver. Hibernate can be configured as a JPA-compliant engine through an extension module called Hibernate EntityManager. This chapter will mainly demonstrate JPA with Hibernate as the underlying engine.

© Marten Deinum, Daniel Rubio, and Josh Long 2017
M. Deinum et al., *Spring 5 Recipes*, DOI 10.1007/978-1-4842-2790-9_9

Problems with Direct JDBC

Suppose you are going to develop an application for vehicle registration, whose major functions are the basic create, read, update, and delete (CRUD) operations on vehicle records. These records will be stored in a relational database and accessed with JDBC. First, you design the following Vehicle class, which represents a vehicle in Java:

```
package com.apress.springrecipes.vehicle;

public class Vehicle {

    private String vehicleNo;
    private String color;
    private int wheel;
    private int seat;

    // Constructors, Getters and Setters
    ...
}
```

Setting Up the Application Database

Before developing your vehicle registration application, you have to set up the database for it.
We have chosen PostgreSQL as our database engine. PostgreSQL is an open source relational database engine (See Table 9-1 for the connection properties).

■ **Note**   The sample code for this chapter provides scripts in the bin directory to start and connect to a Docker-based PostgreSQL instance. To start the instance and create the database, follow these steps:

1.   Execute bin\postgres.sh; this will download and start the Postgres Docker container.

2.   Execute bin\psql.sh; this will connect to the running Postgres container.

3.   Execute CREATE DATABASE vehicle to create the database to use for the samples.

4.   Next, you have to create the VEHICLE table for storing vehicle records with the following SQL statement.

```
CREATE TABLE VEHICLE (
    VEHICLE_NO    VARCHAR(10)    NOT NULL,
    COLOR         VARCHAR(10),
    WHEEL         INT,
    SEAT          INT,
    PRIMARY KEY (VEHICLE_NO)
);
```

Table 9-1. *JDBC Properties for Connecting to the Application Database*

Property	Value
Driver class	org.postgresql.Driver
URL	jdbc:postgresql://localhost:5432/vehicle
Username	postgres
Password	password

Understanding the Data Access Object Design Pattern

A typical design mistake is to mix different types of logic (e.g., presentation logic, business logic, and data access logic) in a single large module. This reduces the module's reusability and maintainability because of the tight coupling it introduces. The general purpose of the Data Access Object (DAO) pattern is to avoid these problems by separating data access logic from business logic and presentation logic. This pattern recommends that data access logic be encapsulated in independent modules called *data access objects*.

For your vehicle registration application, you can abstract the data access operations to insert, update, delete, and query a vehicle. These operations should be declared in a DAO interface to allow for different DAO implementation technologies.

```
package com.apress.springrecipes.vehicle;

import java.util.List;

public interface VehicleDao {

    void insert(Vehicle vehicle);
    void insert(Iterable<Vehicle> vehicles);
    void update(Vehicle vehicle);
    void delete(Vehicle vehicle);
    Vehicle findByVehicleNo(String vehicleNo);
    List<Vehicle> findAll();
}
```

Most parts of the JDBC APIs declare throwing java.sql.SQLException. But because this interface aims to abstract the data access operations only, it should not depend on the implementation technology. So, it's unwise for this general interface to declare throwing the JDBC-specific SQLException. A common practice when implementing a DAO interface is to wrap this kind of exception with a runtime exception (either your own business Exception subclass or a generic one).

Implementing the DAO with JDBC

To access the database with JDBC, you create an implementation for this DAO interface (e.g., JdbcVehicleDao). Because your DAO implementation has to connect to the database to execute SQL statements, you may establish database connections by specifying the driver class name, database URL, username, and password. However, you can obtain database connections from a preconfigured javax.sql.DataSource object without knowing about the connection details.

```java
package com.apress.springrecipes.vehicle;

import javax.sql.DataSource;
import java.sql.Connection;
import java.sql.PreparedStatement;
import java.sql.ResultSet;
import java.sql.SQLException;
import java.util.ArrayList;
import java.util.Collection;
import java.util.List;

public class PlainJdbcVehicleDao implements VehicleDao {

    private static final String INSERT_SQL     = "INSERT INTO VEHICLE (COLOR, WHEEL,
SEAT, VEHICLE_NO) VALUES (?, ?, ?, ?)";
    private static final String UPDATE_SQL     = "UPDATE VEHICLE SET COLOR=?,WHEEL=?,SEAT=?
WHERE VEHICLE_NO=?";
    private static final String SELECT_ALL_SQL = "SELECT * FROM VEHICLE";
    private static final String SELECT_ONE_SQL = "SELECT * FROM VEHICLE WHERE VEHICLE_NO = ?";
    private static final String DELETE_SQL     = "DELETE FROM VEHICLE WHERE VEHICLE_NO=?";

    private final DataSource dataSource;

    public PlainJdbcVehicleDao(DataSource dataSource) {
        this.dataSource = dataSource;
    }

    @Override
    public void insert(Vehicle vehicle) {
        try (Connection conn = dataSource.getConnection();
            PreparedStatement ps = conn.prepareStatement(INSERT_SQL)) {
            prepareStatement(ps, vehicle);
            ps.executeUpdate();
        } catch (SQLException e) {
            throw new RuntimeException(e);
        }
    }

    @Override
    public void insert(Collection<Vehicle> vehicles) {
        vehicles.forEach(this::insert);
    }
```

```java
    @Override
    public Vehicle findByVehicleNo(String vehicleNo) {
        try (Connection conn = dataSource.getConnection();
            PreparedStatement ps = conn.prepareStatement(SELECT_ONE_SQL)) {
            ps.setString(1, vehicleNo);

            Vehicle vehicle = null;
            try (ResultSet rs = ps.executeQuery()) {
                if (rs.next()) {
                    vehicle = toVehicle(rs);
                }
            }
            return vehicle;
        } catch (SQLException e) {
            throw new RuntimeException(e);
        }
    }

    @Override
    public List<Vehicle> findAll() {
        try (Connection conn = dataSource.getConnection();
            PreparedStatement ps = conn.prepareStatement(SELECT_ALL_SQL);
            ResultSet rs = ps.executeQuery()) {

            List<Vehicle> vehicles = new ArrayList<>();
            while (rs.next()) {
                vehicles.add(toVehicle(rs));
            }
            return vehicles;
        } catch (SQLException e) {
            throw new RuntimeException(e);
        }
    }

    private Vehicle toVehicle(ResultSet rs) throws SQLException {
        return new Vehicle(rs.getString("VEHICLE_NO"),
            rs.getString("COLOR"), rs.getInt("WHEEL"),
            rs.getInt("SEAT"));
    }

    private void prepareStatement(PreparedStatement ps, Vehicle vehicle) throws SQLException {
        ps.setString(1, vehicle.getColor());
        ps.setInt(2, vehicle.getWheel());
        ps.setInt(3, vehicle.getSeat());
        ps.setString(4, vehicle.getVehicleNo());
    }

    @Override
    public void update(Vehicle vehicle) { ... }

    @Override
    public void delete(Vehicle vehicle) { ... }
}
```

The vehicle insert operation is a typical JDBC update scenario. Each time this method is called, you obtain a connection from the data source and execute the SQL statement on this connection. Your DAO interface doesn't declare throwing any checked exceptions, so if a SQLException occurs, you have to wrap it with an unchecked RuntimeException. (There is a detailed discussion on handling exceptions in your DAOs later in this chapter.) The code shown here uses a so-called try-with-resources mechanism that will automatically close the used resources (i.e., Connection, PreparedStatement, and ResultSet). If you don't use a try-with-resources block, you have to remember to correctly close the used resources; failing to do so will lead to connection leaks.

Here, the update and delete operations will be skipped because they are much the same as the insert operation from a technical point of view. For the query operation, you have to extract the data from the returned result set to build a vehicle object in addition to executing the SQL statement. The toVehicle method is a simple helper method to be able to reuse the mapping logic, as well as a prepareStatement method to help set the parameters for the insert and update methods.

Configuring a Data Source in Spring

The javax.sql.DataSource interface is a standard interface defined by the JDBC specification that factories Connection instances. There are many data source implementations provided by different vendors and projects; HikariCP and Apache Commons DBCP are popular open source options, and most application servers will provide their own implementation. It is easy to switch between different data source implementations because they implement the common DataSource interface. As a Java application framework, Spring also provides several convenient but less powerful data source implementations. The simplest one is DriverManagerDataSource, which opens a new connection every time one is requested.

```
package com.apress.springrecipes.vehicle.config;

import com.apress.springrecipes.vehicle.PlainJdbcVehicleDao;
import com.apress.springrecipes.vehicle.VehicleDao;
import org.apache.derby.jdbc.ClientDriver;
import org.springframework.context.annotation.Bean;
import org.springframework.context.annotation.Configuration;
import org.springframework.jdbc.datasource.DriverManagerDataSource;

import javax.sql.DataSource;

@Configuration
public class VehicleConfiguration {

    @Bean
    public VehicleDao vehicleDao() {
        return new PlainJdbcVehicleDao(dataSource());
    }

    @Bean
    public DataSource dataSource() {
        DriverManagerDataSource dataSource = new DriverManagerDataSource();
        dataSource.setDriverClassName(ClientDriver.class.getName());
        dataSource.setUrl("jdbc:derby://localhost:1527/vehicle;create=true");
```

```
    dataSource.setUsername("app");
    dataSource.setPassword("app");
    return dataSource;

    }
}
```

DriverManagerDataSource is not an efficient data source implementation because it opens a new connection for the client every time it's requested. Another data source implementation provided by Spring is SingleConnectionDataSource (a DriverManagerDataSource subclass). As its name indicates, this maintains only a single connection that's reused all the time and never closed. Obviously, it is not suitable in a multithreaded environment.

Spring's own data source implementations are mainly used for testing purposes. However, many production data source implementations support connection pooling. For example, HikariCP provides HikariDataSource, which accepts the same connection properties as DriverManagerDataSource and allows you to specify, among other information, the minimum pool size and maximum active connections for the connection pool.

```
@Bean
public DataSource dataSource() {
    HikariDataSource dataSource = new HikariDataSource();
    dataSource.setUsername("postgres");
    dataSource.setPassword("password");
    dataSource.setJdbcUrl("jdbc:postgresql://localhost:5432/vehicle");
    dataSource.setMinimumIdle(2);
    dataSource.setMaximumPoolSize(5);
    return dataSource;
}
```

■ **Note**   To use the data source implementations provided by HikariCP, you have to add them to your CLASSPATH. If you are using Maven, add the following dependency to your project:

```
<dependency>
    <groupId>com.zaxxer</groupId>
    <artifactId>HikariCP</artifactId>
    <version>2.6.1</version>
</dependency>
```

If you're using Gradle, use the following:

```
compile 'com.zaxxer:HikariCP:2.6.1'
```

Many Java EE application servers build in data source implementations that you can configure from the server console or in configuration files. If you have a data source configured in an application server and exposed for JNDI lookup, you can use JndiDataSourceLookup to look it up.

```
@Bean
public DataSource dataSource() {
    return new JndiDataSourceLookup().getDataSource("jdbc/VehicleDS");
}
```

Running the DAO

The following Main class tests your DAO by using it to insert a new vehicle to the database. If it succeeds, you can query the vehicle from the database immediately.

```
package com.apress.springrecipes.vehicle;

import org.springframework.context.ApplicationContext;
import org.springframework.context.support.ClassPathXmlApplicationContext;

public class Main {

    public static void main(String[] args) {
        ApplicationContext context =
            new AnnotationConfigApplicationContext(VehicleConfiguration.class);

        VehicleDao vehicleDao = context.getBean(VehicleDao.class);
        Vehicle vehicle = new Vehicle("TEM0001", "Red", 4, 4);
        vehicleDao.insert(vehicle);

        vehicle = vehicleDao.findByVehicleNo("TEM0001");
        System.out.println(vehicle);
    }
}
```

Now you can implement a DAO using JDBC directly. However, as you can see from the preceding DAO implementation, most of the JDBC code is similar and needs to be repeated for each database operation. Such redundant code will make your DAO methods much longer and less readable.

Taking It a Step Further

An alternative approach is to use an object-relational mapping (ORM) tool, which lets you code the logic specifically for mapping an entity in your domain model to a database table. The ORM will, in turn, figure out how to write the logic to usefully persist your class's data to the database. This can be very liberating: you are suddenly beholden only to your business and domain model, not to the whims of your database's SQL parser. The flip side, of course, is that you are also divesting yourself from having complete control over the communication between your client and the database—you have to trust that the ORM layer will do the right thing.

9-1. Use a JDBC Template to Update a Database
Problem

Using JDBC is tedious and fraught with redundant API calls, many of which could be managed for you. To implement a JDBC update operation, you have to perform the following tasks, most of which are redundant:

1. Obtain a database connection from the data source.

2. Create a PreparedStatement object from the connection.

3. Bind the parameters to the PreparedStatement object.

4. Execute the PreparedStatement object.

5. Handle SQLException.

6. Clean up the statement object and connection.

JDBC is a very low-level API, but with the JDBC template, the surface area of the API that you need to work with becomes more expressive (you spend less time in the weeds and more time working on your application logic) and is simpler to work with safely.

Solution

The org.springframework.jdbc.core.JdbcTemplate class declares a number of overloaded update() template methods to control the overall update process. Different versions of the update() method allow you to override different task subsets of the default process. The Spring JDBC framework predefines several callback interfaces to encapsulate different task subsets. You can implement one of these callback interfaces and pass its instance to the corresponding update() method to complete the process.

How It Works

You will explore the different ways to update a database using the various options with the JdbcTemplate. You will look at PreparedStatementCreators, PreparedStatementSetters and finally the update methods on the JdbcTemplate itself.

Update a Database with a Statement Creator

The first callback interface to introduce is PreparedStatementCreator. You implement this interface to override the statement creation task (task 2) and the parameter binding task (task 3) of the overall update process. To insert a vehicle into the database, you implement the PreparedStatementCreator interface as follows:

```
package com.apress.springrecipes.vehicle;

import java.sql.Connection;
import java.sql.PreparedStatement;
import java.sql.SQLException;

import org.springframework.jdbc.core.PreparedStatementCreator;

public class JdbcVehicleDao implements VehicleDao {

    private class InsertVehicleStatementCreator implements PreparedStatementCreator {

        private final Vehicle vehicle;

        InsertVehicleStatementCreator(Vehicle vehicle) {
            this.vehicle = vehicle;
        }

        public PreparedStatement createPreparedStatement(Connection con) throws SQLException {
            PreparedStatement ps = con.prepareStatement(INSERT_SQL);
            prepareStatement(ps, this.vehicle);
            return ps;
        }
    }
}
```

369

When implementing the PreparedStatementCreator interface, you will get the database connection as the createPreparedStatement() method's argument. All you have to do in this method is to create a PreparedStatement object on this connection and bind your parameters to this object. Finally, you have to return the PreparedStatement object as the method's return value. Notice that the method signature declares throwing SQLException, which means you don't need to handle this kind of exception yourself. As you are creating this class as an inner class for the DAO, you can call the prepareStatement helper method from your implementation.

Now, you can use this statement creator to simplify the vehicle insert operation. First, you have to create an instance of the JdbcTemplate class and pass in the data source for this template to obtain a connection from it. Then, you just make a call to the update() method and pass in your statement creator for the template to complete the update process.

```
package com.apress.springrecipes.vehicle;
...
import org.springframework.jdbc.core.JdbcTemplate;

public class JdbcVehicleDao implements VehicleDao {
    ...
    public void insert(Vehicle vehicle) {
        JdbcTemplate jdbcTemplate = new JdbcTemplate(dataSource);
        jdbcTemplate.update(new InsertVehicleStatementCreator(vehicle));
    }
}
```

Typically, it is better to implement the PreparedStatementCreator interface and other callback interfaces as inner classes if they are used within one method only. This is because you can get access to the local variables and method arguments directly from the inner class, instead of passing them as constructor arguments. When using local variables, they have to be marked as final.

```
package com.apress.springrecipes.vehicle;
...
import org.springframework.jdbc.core.JdbcTemplate;
import org.springframework.jdbc.core.PreparedStatementCreator;

public class JdbcVehicleDao implements VehicleDao {
    ...
    public void insert(Vehicle vehicle) {
        JdbcTemplate jdbcTemplate = new JdbcTemplate(dataSource);

        jdbcTemplate.update(new PreparedStatementCreator() {

            public PreparedStatement createPreparedStatement(Connection conn)
                throws SQLException {
                PreparedStatement ps = conn.prepareStatement(INSERT_SQL);
                prepareStatement(ps, vehicle);
                return ps;
            }
        });
    }
}
```

With Java 8 this could also be implemented as a lambda expression.

```
@Override
public void insert(final Vehicle vehicle) {
    JdbcTemplate jdbcTemplate = new JdbcTemplate(this.dataSource);
    jdbcTemplate.update(con -> {
        PreparedStatement ps = con.prepareStatement(INSERT_SQL);
        prepareStatement(ps, vehicle);
        return ps;
    });
}
```

Now you can delete the preceding InsertVehicleStatementCreator inner class because it will not be used anymore.

Update a Database with a Statement Setter

The second callback interface, PreparedStatementSetter, as its name indicates, performs only the parameter binding task (task 3) of the overall update process.

Another version of the update() template method accepts a SQL statement and a PreparedStatementSetter object as arguments. This method will create a PreparedStatement object for you from your SQL statement. All you have to do with this interface is to bind your parameters to the PreparedStatement object (and for this you can delegate to the prepareStatement method again).

```
package com.apress.springrecipes.vehicle;
...
import org.springframework.jdbc.core.JdbcTemplate;
import org.springframework.jdbc.core.PreparedStatementSetter;

public class JdbcVehicleDao implements VehicleDao {
    ...
    public void insert(final Vehicle vehicle) {
        JdbcTemplate jdbcTemplate = new JdbcTemplate(dataSource);

        jdbcTemplate.update(INSERT_SQL, new PreparedStatementSetter() {

            public void setValues(PreparedStatement ps)
                throws SQLException {
                prepareStatement(ps, vehicle);
            }
        });
    }
}
```

It's even more compact as a Java 8 lambda, shown here:

```
@Override
public void insert(Vehicle vehicle) {
    JdbcTemplate jdbcTemplate = new JdbcTemplate(this.dataSource);
    jdbcTemplate.update(INSERT_SQL, ps -> prepareStatement(ps, vehicle));
}
```

Update a Database with a SQL Statement and Parameter Values

Finally, the simplest version of the update() method accepts a SQL statement and an object array as statement parameters. It will create a PreparedStatement object from your SQL statement and bind the parameters for you. Therefore, you don't have to override any of the tasks in the update process.

```
package com.apress.springrecipes.vehicle;
...
import org.springframework.jdbc.core.JdbcTemplate;

public class JdbcVehicleDao implements VehicleDao {
    ...
    public void insert(final Vehicle vehicle) {
        JdbcTemplate jdbcTemplate = new JdbcTemplate(dataSource);

        jdbcTemplate.update(INSERT_SQL, vehicle.getColor(),vehicle.getWheel(),
            vehicle.getSeat(),vehicle.getVehicleNo() );
    }
}
```

Of the three different versions of the update() method introduced, the last is the simplest because you don't have to implement any callback interfaces. Additionally, we've managed to remove all setX (setInt, setString, and so on)–style methods for parameterizing the query. In contrast, the first is the most flexible because you can do any preprocessing of the PreparedStatement object before its execution. In practice, you should always choose the simplest version that meets all your needs.

There are also other overloaded update() methods provided by the JdbcTemplate class. Please refer to the Javadoc for details.

Batch Update a Database

Suppose you want to insert a batch of vehicles into the database. If you call the update() method multiple times, the update will be very slow as the SQL statement will be compiled repeatedly. So, it would be better to implement it using batch updates to insert a batch of vehicles.

The JdbcTemplate class also offers a few batchUpdate() template methods for batch update operations. The one you are going to set takes a SQL statement, a collection of items, a batch size, and a ParameterizedPreparedStatementSetter.

```
package com.apress.springrecipes.vehicle;
...
import org.springframework.jdbc.core.BatchPreparedStatementSetter;
import org.springframework.jdbc.core.JdbcTemplate;

public class JdbcVehicleDao implements VehicleDao {
    ...
    @Override
    public void insert(Collection<Vehicle> vehicles) {
        JdbcTemplate jdbcTemplate = new JdbcTemplate(this.dataSource);
        jdbcTemplate.batchUpdate(INSERT_SQL, vehicles, vehicles.size(), new Parameterized
        PreparedStatementSetter<Vehicle>() {
```

```
        @Override
        public void setValues(PreparedStatement ps, Vehicle argument) throws
        SQLException {
            prepareStatement(ps, argument);
        }
    });
}

}
```

Here it is as a Java 8 lambda:

```
@Override
public void insert(Collection<Vehicle> vehicles) {
    JdbcTemplate jdbcTemplate = new JdbcTemplate(this.dataSource);
    jdbcTemplate.batchUpdate(INSERT_SQL, vehicles, vehicles.size(), this::prepareStatement);
}
```

You can test your batch insert operation with the following code snippet in the Main class:

```
package com.apress.springrecipes.vehicle;
...
public class Main {

    public static void main(String[] args) {
        ...
        VehicleDao vehicleDao = (VehicleDao) context.getBean("vehicleDao");
        Vehicle vehicle1 = new Vehicle("TEM0022", "Blue", 4, 4);
        Vehicle vehicle2 = new Vehicle("TEM0023", "Black", 4, 6);
        Vehicle vehicle3 = new Vehicle("TEM0024", "Green", 4, 5);
        vehicleDao.insertBatch(Arrays.asList(vehicle1, vehicle2, vehicle3));
    }
}
```

9-2. Use a JDBC Template to Query a Database

Problem

To implement a JDBC query operation, you have to perform the following tasks, two of which (tasks 5 and 6) are extra compared to an update operation:

1. Obtain a database connection from the data source.

2. Create a PreparedStatement object from the connection.

3. Bind the parameters to the PreparedStatement object.

4. Execute the PreparedStatement object.

5. Iterate the returned result set.

6. Extract data from the result set.

7. Handle SQLException.

8. Clean up the statement object and connection.

The only steps relevant to your business logic, however, are the definition of the query and the extraction of the results from the result set! The rest is better handled by the JDBC template.

Solution

The JdbcTemplate class declares a number of overloaded query() template methods to control the overall query process. You can override the statement creation (task 2) and the parameter binding (task 3) by implementing the PreparedStatementCreator and PreparedStatementSetter interfaces, just as you did for the update operations. Moreover, the Spring JDBC framework supports multiple ways for you to override the data extraction (task 6).

How It Works

Spring provided the RowCallbackHandler as well as the RowMapper interface to handle results in one of the query methods. You will first explore both interfaces and discover the different use-cases for both. Next you will explore how to use different query methods for retrieval of multiple and also single results.

Extract Data with Row Callback Handler

RowCallbackHandler is the primary interface that allows you to process the current row of the result set. One of the query() methods iterates the result set for you and calls your RowCallbackHandler for each row. So, the processRow() method will be called once for each row of the returned result set.

```
package com.apress.springrecipes.vehicle;
...
import org.springframework.jdbc.core.JdbcTemplate;
import org.springframework.jdbc.core.RowCallbackHandler;

public class JdbcVehicleDao implements VehicleDao {
    ...
    @Override
    public Vehicle findByVehicleNo(String vehicleNo) {
        JdbcTemplate jdbcTemplate = new JdbcTemplate(dataSource);

        final Vehicle vehicle = new Vehicle();
        jdbcTemplate.query(SELECT_ONE_SQL,
            new RowCallbackHandler() {
                public void processRow(ResultSet rs) throws SQLException {
                    vehicle.setVehicleNo(rs.getString("VEHICLE_NO"));
                    vehicle.setColor(rs.getString("COLOR"));
                    vehicle.setWheel(rs.getInt("WHEEL"));
                    vehicle.setSeat(rs.getInt("SEAT"));
                }
            }, vehicleNo);
        return vehicle;
    }
}
```

It's a bit more compact when using a Java 8 lambda.

```java
@Override
public Vehicle findByVehicleNo(String vehicleNo) {
    JdbcTemplate jdbcTemplate = new JdbcTemplate(dataSource);

    final Vehicle vehicle = new Vehicle();
    jdbcTemplate.query(SELECT_ONE_SQL,
        rs -> {
            vehicle.setVehicleNo(rs.getString("VEHICLE_NO"));
            vehicle.setColor(rs.getString("COLOR"));
            vehicle.setWheel(rs.getInt("WHEEL"));
            vehicle.setSeat(rs.getInt("SEAT"));
        }, vehicleNo);
    return vehicle;
}
```

As there will be one row returned for the SQL query at maximum, you can create a vehicle object as a local variable and set its properties by extracting data from the result set. For a result set with more than one row, you should collect the objects as a list.

Extract Data with a Row Mapper

The RowMapper<T> interface is more general than RowCallbackHandler. Its purpose is to map a single row of the result set to a customized object so it can be applied to a single-row result set as well as a multiple-row result set.

From the viewpoint of reuse, it's better to implement the RowMapper<T> interface as a normal class than as an inner class. In the mapRow() method of this interface, you have to construct the object that represents a row and return it as the method's return value.

```java
package com.apress.springrecipes.vehicle;

import java.sql.ResultSet;
import java.sql.SQLException;

import org.springframework.jdbc.core.RowMapper;

public class JdbcVehicleDao implements VehicleDao {

    private class VehicleRowMapper implements RowMapper<Vehicle> {
        @Override
        public Vehicle mapRow(ResultSet rs, int rowNum) throws SQLException {
            return toVehicle(rs);
        }
    }
}
```

As mentioned, RowMapper<T> can be used for either a single-row or multiple-row result set. When querying for a unique object like in findByVehicleNo(), you have to make a call to the queryForObject() method of JdbcTemplate.

```
package com.apress.springrecipes.vehicle;
...
import org.springframework.jdbc.core.JdbcTemplate;

public class JdbcVehicleDao implements VehicleDao {
    ...
    public Vehicle findByVehicleNo(String vehicleNo) {

        JdbcTemplate jdbcTemplate = new JdbcTemplate(dataSource);
        return jdbcTemplate.queryForObject(SELECT_ONE_SQL, new VehicleRowMapper(),
        vehicleNo);
    }
}
```

Spring comes with a convenient RowMapper<T> implementation, BeanPropertyRowMapper<T>, which can automatically map a row to a new instance of the specified class. Note that the specified class must be a top-level class and must have a default or no-argument constructor. It first instantiates this class and then maps each column value to a property by matching their names. It supports matching a property name (e.g., vehicleNo) to the same column name or the column name with underscores (e.g., VEHICLE_NO).

```
package com.apress.springrecipes.vehicle;
...
import org.springframework.jdbc.core.BeanPropertyRowMapper;
import org.springframework.jdbc.core.JdbcTemplate;

public class JdbcVehicleDao implements VehicleDao {

    ...

    public Vehicle findByVehicleNo(String vehicleNo) {

        JdbcTemplate jdbcTemplate = new JdbcTemplate(dataSource);
        return jdbcTemplate.queryForObject(SELECT_ONE_SQL, BeanPropertyRowMapper.
        newInstance(Vehicle.class), vehicleNo);
    }
}
```

Query for Multiple Rows

Now, let's look at how to query for a result set with multiple rows. For example, suppose that you need a findAll() method in the DAO interface to get all vehicles.

```
package com.apress.springrecipes.vehicle;
...
public interface VehicleDao {
    ...
    public List<Vehicle> findAll();
}
```

Without the help of RowMapper<T>, you can still call the queryForList() method and pass in a SQL statement. The returned result will be a list of maps. Each map stores a row of the result set with the column names as the keys.

```
package com.apress.springrecipes.vehicle;
...
import org.springframework.jdbc.core.JdbcTemplate;

public class JdbcVehicleDao implements VehicleDao {
    ...
    @Override
    public List<Vehicle> findAll() {
        JdbcTemplate jdbcTemplate = new JdbcTemplate(dataSource);

        List<Map<String, Object>> rows = jdbcTemplate.queryForList(SELECT_ALL_SQL);
        return rows.stream().map(row -> {
            Vehicle vehicle = new Vehicle();
            vehicle.setVehicleNo((String) row.get("VEHICLE_NO"));
            vehicle.setColor((String) row.get("COLOR"));
            vehicle.setWheel((Integer) row.get("WHEEL"));
            vehicle.setSeat((Integer) row.get("SEAT"));
            return vehicle;
        }).collect(Collectors.toList());
    }
}
```

You can test your findAll() method with the following code snippet in the Main class:

```
package com.apress.springrecipes.vehicle;
...
public class Main {

    public static void main(String[] args) {
        ...
        VehicleDao vehicleDao = (VehicleDao) context.getBean("vehicleDao");
        List<Vehicle> vehicles = vehicleDao.findAll();
        vehicles.forEach(System.out::println);
    }
}
```

If you use a RowMapper<T> object to map the rows in a result set, you will get a list of mapped objects from the query() method.

```
package com.apress.springrecipes.vehicle;
...
import org.springframework.jdbc.core.BeanPropertyRowMapper;
import org.springframework.jdbc.core.JdbcTemplate;
```

```java
public class JdbcVehicleDao implements VehicleDao {
    ...
  public List<Vehicle> findAll() {
     JdbcTemplate jdbcTemplate = new JdbcTemplate(dataSource);
     return jdbcTemplate.query (SELECT_ALL_SQL,
                                BeanPropertyRowMapper.newInstance(Vehicle.class));
  }
}
```

Query for a Single Value

Finally, let's consider a query for a single-row and single-column result set. As an example, add the following operations to the DAO interface:

```java
package com.apress.springrecipes.vehicle;
...
public interface VehicleDao {
    ...
    public String getColor(String vehicleNo);
    public int countAll();
}
```

To query for a single string value, you can call the overloaded queryForObject() method, which requires an argument of java.lang.Class type. This method will help you to map the result value to the type you specified.

```java
package com.apress.springrecipes.vehicle;
...
import org.springframework.jdbc.core.JdbcTemplate;

public class JdbcVehicleDao implements VehicleDao {

    private static final String COUNT_ALL_SQL = "SELECT COUNT(*) FROM VEHICLE";
    private static final String SELECT_COLOR_SQL = "SELECT COLOR FROM VEHICLE WHERE
    VEHICLE_NO=?";

    ...
    public String getColor(String vehicleNo) {

        JdbcTemplate jdbcTemplate = new JdbcTemplate(dataSource);
        return jdbcTemplate.queryForObject(SELECT_COLOR_SQL, String.class, vehicleNo);
    }

    public int countAll() {

        JdbcTemplate jdbcTemplate = new JdbcTemplate(dataSource);
        return jdbcTemplate.queryForObject(COUNT_ALL_SQL, Integer.class);
    }
}
```

You can test these two methods with the following code snippet in the `Main` class:

```
package com.apress.springrecipes.vehicle;
...
public class Main {

    public static void main(String[] args) {
        ...
        VehicleDao vehicleDao = context.getBean(VehicleDao.class);
        int count = vehicleDao.countAll();
        System.out.println("Vehicle Count: " + count);
        String color = vehicleDao.getColor("TEM0001");
        System.out.println("Color for [TEM0001]: " + color);
    }
}
```

9-3. Simplify JDBC Template Creation

Problem

It's not efficient to create a new instance of `JdbcTemplate` every time you need it because you have to repeat the creation statement and incur the cost of creating a new object.

Solution

The `JdbcTemplate` class is designed to be thread-safe, so you can declare a single instance of it in the IoC container and inject this instance into all your DAO instances. Furthermore, the Spring JDBC framework offers a convenient class, `org.springframework.jdbc.core.support.JdbcDaoSupport`, to simplify your DAO implementation. This class declares a `jdbcTemplate` property, which can be injected from the IoC container or created automatically from a data source, for example, `JdbcTemplate jdbcTemplate = new JdbcTemplate(dataSource)`. Your DAO can extend this class to have this property inherited.

How It Works

Instead of creating a new `JdbcTemplate` when you need you could either create a single instance as a bean and reuse that instance by injecting it into the DAO's that need one. Another option is to extend the Spring `JdbcDaoSupport` class which provides accessor methods for a `JdbcTemplate`.

Inject a JDBC Template

Until now, you have created a new instance of `JdbcTemplate` in each DAO method. Actually, you can have it injected at the class level and use this injected instance in all DAO methods. For simplicity's sake, the following code shows only the change to the `insert()` method:

```
package com.apress.springrecipes.vehicle;
...
import org.springframework.jdbc.core.JdbcTemplate;
```

```java
public class JdbcVehicleDao implements VehicleDao {

    private final JdbcTemplate jdbcTemplate;

    public JdbcVehicleDao (JdbcTemplate jdbcTemplate) {
        this.jdbcTemplate = jdbcTemplate;
    }

    public void insert(final Vehicle vehicle) {
        jdbcTemplate.update(INSERT_SQL, vehicle.getVehicleNo(), vehicle.getColor(),
            vehicle.getWheel(), vehicle.getSeat());
    }
    ...
}
```

A JDBC template requires a data source to be set. You can inject this property using either a setter method or a constructor argument. Then, you can inject this JDBC template into your DAO.

```java
@Configuration
public class VehicleConfiguration {

    @Bean
    public VehicleDao vehicleDao(JdbcTemplate jdbcTemplate) {
        return new JdbcVehicleDao(jdbcTemplate);
    }

    @Bean
    public JdbcTemplate jdbcTemplate(DataSource dataSource) {
        return new JdbcTemplate(dataSource);
    }
}
```

Extend the JdbcDaoSupport Class

The org.springframework.jdbc.core.support.JdbcDaoSupport class has a setDataSource() method and a setJdbcTemplate() method. Your DAO class can extend this class to have these methods inherited. Then, you can either inject a JDBC template directly or inject a data source for it to create a JDBC template. The following code fragment is taken from Spring's JdbcDaoSupport class:

```java
package org.springframework.jdbc.core.support;
...
public abstract class JdbcDaoSupport extends DaoSupport {

    private JdbcTemplate jdbcTemplate;

    public final void setDataSource(DataSource dataSource) {
        if( this.jdbcTemplate == null || dataSource != this.jdbcTemplate.getDataSource() ){
            this.jdbcTemplate = createJdbcTemplate(dataSource);
            initTemplateConfig();
        }
    }
    ...
```

```
    public final void setJdbcTemplate(JdbcTemplate jdbcTemplate) {
        this.jdbcTemplate = jdbcTemplate;
        initTemplateConfig();
    }

    public final JdbcTemplate getJdbcTemplate() {
        return this.jdbcTemplate;
    }
    ...
}
```

In your DAO methods, you can simply call the getJdbcTemplate() method to retrieve the JDBC template. You also have to delete the dataSource and jdbcTemplate properties, as well as their setter methods, from your DAO class, because they have already been inherited. Again, for simplicity's sake, only the change to the insert() method is shown here:

```
package com.apress.springrecipes.vehicle;
...
import org.springframework.jdbc.core.support.JdbcDaoSupport;

public class JdbcVehicleDao extends JdbcDaoSupport implements VehicleDao {

    public void insert(final Vehicle vehicle) {

        getJdbcTemplate().update(INSERT_SQL, vehicle.getVehicleNo(),
            vehicle.getColor(), vehicle.getWheel(), vehicle.getSeat());
    }
    ...
}
```

By extending JdbcDaoSupport, your DAO class inherits the setDataSource() method. You can inject a data source into your DAO instance for it to create a JDBC template.

```
@Configuration
public class VehicleConfiguration {
...
    @Bean
    public VehicleDao vehicleDao(DataSource dataSource) {
        JdbcVehicleDao vehicleDao = new JdbcVehicleDao();
        vehicleDao.setDataSource(dataSource);
        return vehicleDao;
    }
}
```

9-4. Use Named Parameters in a JDBC Template

Problem

In classic JDBC usage, SQL parameters are represented by the placeholder ? and are bound by position. The trouble with positional parameters is that whenever the parameter order is changed, you have to change the parameter bindings as well. For a SQL statement with many parameters, it is very cumbersome to match the parameters by position.

Solution

Another option when binding SQL parameters in the Spring JDBC framework is to use named parameters. As the term implies, named SQL parameters are specified by name (starting with a colon) rather than by position. Named parameters are easier to maintain and also improve readability. At runtime, the framework classes replace named parameters with placeholders. Named parameters are supported by the NamedParameterJdbcTemplate.

How It Works

When using named parameters in your SQL statement, you can provide the parameter values in a map with the parameter names as the keys.

```
package com.apress.springrecipes.vehicle;
...
import org.springframework.jdbc.core.namedparam.NamedParameterJdbcDaoSupport;

public class JdbcVehicleDao extends NamedParameterJdbcDaoSupport implements
    VehicleDao {

    private static final String INSERT_SQL = "INSERT INTO VEHICLE (COLOR, WHEEL, SEAT,
    VEHICLE_NO) VALUES (:color, :wheel, :seat, :vehicleNo)";

    public void insert(Vehicle vehicle) {

        getNamedParameterJdbcTemplate().update(INSERT_SQL, toParameterMap(vehicle));
    }

    private Map<String, Object> toParameterMap(Vehicle vehicle) {
        Map<String, Object> parameters = new HashMap<>();
        parameters.put("vehicleNo", vehicle.getVehicleNo());
        parameters.put("color", vehicle.getColor());
        parameters.put("wheel", vehicle.getWheel());
        parameters.put("seat", vehicle.getSeat());
        return parameters;
    }

    ...
}
```

You can also provide a SQL parameter source, whose responsibility is to offer SQL parameter values for named SQL parameters. There are three implementations of the SqlParameterSource interface. The basic one is MapSqlParameterSource, which wraps a map as its parameter source. In this example, this is a net loss compared to the previous example, as you've introduced one extra object—the SqlParameterSource.

```
package com.apress.springrecipes.vehicle;
...
import org.springframework.jdbc.core.namedparam.MapSqlParameterSource;
import org.springframework.jdbc.core.namedparam.SqlParameterSource;
import org.springframework.jdbc.core.namedparam.NamedParameterJdbcDaoSupport;

public class JdbcVehicleDao extends NamedParameterJdbcDaoSupport implements
    VehicleDao {

    public void insert(Vehicle vehicle) {

        SqlParameterSource parameterSource =
            new MapSqlParameterSource(toParameterMap(vehicle));

        getNamedParameterJdbcTemplate().update(INSERT_SQL, parameterSource);
    }
    ...
}
```

The power comes when you need an extra level of indirection between the parameters passed into the update method and the source of their values. For example, what if you want to get properties from a JavaBean? Here is where the SqlParameterSource intermediary starts to benefit you! SqlParameterSource is a BeanPropertySqlParameterSource, which wraps a normal Java object as a SQL parameter source. For each of the named parameters, the property with the same name will be used as the parameter value.

```
package com.apress.springrecipes.vehicle;

import org.springframework.jdbc.core.namedparam.BeanPropertySqlParameterSource;
import org.springframework.jdbc.core.namedparam.SqlParameterSource;
import org.springframework.jdbc.core.namedparam.NamedParameterJdbcDaoSupport;

public class JdbcVehicleDao extends NamedParameterJdbcDaoSupport implements
    VehicleDao {

    public void insert(Vehicle vehicle) {

        SqlParameterSource parameterSource =
            new BeanPropertySqlParameterSource(vehicle);

        getNamedParameterJdbcTemplate ().update(INSERT_SQL, parameterSource);
    }
}
```

Named parameters can also be used in batch update. You can provide either a `Map`, an array, or a `SqlParameterSource` array for the parameter values.

```
package com.apress.springrecipes.vehicle;
...
import org.springframework.jdbc.core.namedparam.BeanPropertySqlParameterSource;
import org.springframework.jdbc.core.namedparam.SqlParameterSource;
import org.springframework.jdbc.core.namedparam.NamedParameterJdbcDaoSupport;

public class JdbcVehicleDao extends NamedParameterJdbcDaoSupport implements VehicleDao {
    ...
    @Override
    public void insert(Collection<Vehicle> vehicles) {

        SqlParameterSource[] sources = vehicles.stream()
            .map(v -> new BeanPropertySqlParameterSource(v))
            .toArray(size -> new SqlParameterSource[size]);
        getNamedParameterJdbcTemplate().batchUpdate(INSERT_SQL, sources);
    }
}
```

9-5. Handle Exceptions in the Spring JDBC Framework

Problem

Many of the JDBC APIs declare throwing `java.sql.SQLException`, a checked exception that must be caught. It's very troublesome to handle this kind of exception every time you perform a database operation. You often have to define your own policy to handle this kind of exception. Failure to do so may lead to inconsistent exception handling.

Solution

The Spring Framework offers a consistent data access exception-handling mechanism for its data access module, including the JDBC framework. In general, all exceptions thrown by the Spring JDBC framework are subclasses of `org.springframework.dao.DataAccessException`, a type of `RuntimeException` that you are not forced to catch. It's the root exception class for all exceptions in Spring's data access module.

Figure 9-1 shows only part of the `DataAccessException` hierarchy in Spring's data access module. In total, there are more than 30 exception classes defined for different categories of data access exceptions.

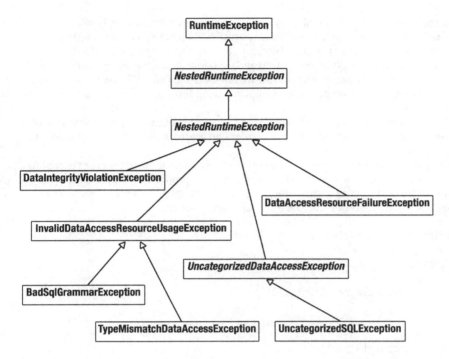

Figure 9-1. *Common exception classes in the DataAccessException hierarchy*

How It Works

First you will take a look at how the exception handling works in Spring JDBC and following that you will learn how to utilize it to your benefit by creating custom exceptions and mappings.

Understand Exception Handling in the Spring JDBC Framework

Until now, you haven't handled JDBC exceptions explicitly when using a JDBC template or when using JDBC operation objects. To help you understand the Spring JDBC framework's exception-handling mechanism, let's consider the following code fragment in the Main class, which inserts a vehicle. What happens if you insert a vehicle with a duplicate vehicle number?

```
package com.apress.springrecipes.vehicle;
...
public class Main {

    public static void main(String[] args) {
        ...
        VehicleDao vehicleDao = context.getBean(VehicleDao.class);
        Vehicle vehicle = new Vehicle("EX0001", "Green", 4, 4);
        vehicleDao.insert(vehicle);
    }
}
```

If you run the method twice or the vehicle has already been inserted into the database, it will throw a `DuplicateKeyException`, an indirect subclass of `DataAccessException`. In your DAO methods, you neither need to surround the code with a `try`/`catch` block nor declare throwing an exception in the method signature. This is because `DataAccessException` (and therefore its subclasses, including `DuplicateKeyException`) is an unchecked exception that you are not forced to catch. The direct parent class of `DataAccessException` is `NestedRuntimeException`, a core Spring exception class that wraps another exception in a `RuntimeException`.

When you use the classes of the Spring JDBC framework, they will catch `SQLException` for you and wrap it with one of the subclasses of `DataAccessException`. As this exception is a `RuntimeException`, you are not required to catch it.

But how does the Spring JDBC framework know which concrete exception in the `DataAccessException` hierarchy should be thrown? It's by looking at the `errorCode` and `SQLState` properties of the caught `SQLException`. As a `DataAccessException` wraps the underlying `SQLException` as the root cause, you can inspect the `errorCode` and `SQLState` properties with the following catch block:

```
package com.apress.springrecipes.vehicle;
...
import java.sql.SQLException;

import org.springframework.dao.DataAccessException;

public class Main {

    public static void main(String[] args) {
        ...
        VehicleDao vehicleDao = context.getBean(VehicleDao.class);
        Vehicle vehicle = new Vehicle("EX0001", "Green", 4, 4);
        try {
            vehicleDao.insert(vehicle);
        } catch (DataAccessException e) {
            SQLException sqle = (SQLException) e.getCause();
            System.out.println("Error code: " + sqle.getErrorCode());
            System.out.println("SQL state: " + sqle.getSQLState());
        }
    }
}
```

When you insert the duplicate vehicle again, notice that PostgreSQL returns the following error code and SQL state:

```
Error code : 0
SQL state : 23505
```

If you refer to the PostgreSQL reference manual, you will find the error code description shown in Table 9-2.

Table 9-2. PostgreSQL Error Code Description

SQL State	Message Text
23505	unique_violation

How does the Spring JDBC framework know that state 23505 should be mapped to DuplicateKeyException? The error code and SQL state are database specific, which means different database products may return different codes for the same kind of error. Moreover, some database products will specify the error in the errorCode property, while others (like PostgreSQL) will do so in the SQLState property.

As an open Java application framework, Spring understands the error codes of most popular database products. Because of the large number of error codes, however, it can only maintain mappings for the most frequently encountered errors. The mapping is defined in the sql-error-codes.xml file, located in the org.springframework.jdbc.support package. The following snippet for PostgreSQL is taken from this file:

```xml
<?xml version="1.0" encoding="UTF-8"?>
<!DOCTYPE beans PUBLIC "-//SPRING//DTD BEAN 3.0//EN"
    "http://www.springframework.org/dtd/spring-beans-3.0.dtd">

<beans>
    ...

    <bean id="PostgreSQL" class="org.springframework.jdbc.support.SQLErrorCodes">
        <property name="useSqlStateForTranslation">
            <value>true</value>
        </property>
        <property name="badSqlGrammarCodes">
            <value>03000,42000,42601,42602,42622,42804,42P01</value>
        </property>
        <property name="duplicateKeyCodes">
            <value>23505</value>
        </property>
        <property name="dataIntegrityViolationCodes">
            <value>23000,23502,23503,23514</value>
        </property>
        <property name="dataAccessResourceFailureCodes">
            <value>53000,53100,53200,53300</value>
        </property>
        <property name="cannotAcquireLockCodes">
            <value>55P03</value>
        </property>
        <property name="cannotSerializeTransactionCodes">
            <value>40001</value>
        </property>
        <property name="deadlockLoserCodes">
            <value>40P01</value>
        </property>
    </bean>
    ...
</beans>
```

The useSqlStateForTranslation property means that the SQLState property, rather than the errorCode property, should be used to match the error code. Finally, the SQLErrorCodes class defines several categories for you to map database error codes. The code 23505 lies in the dataIntegrityViolationCodes cdataIntegrityViolationCodes category.

Customize Data Access Exception Handling

The Spring JDBC framework only maps well-known error codes. Sometimes you may want to customize the mapping yourself. For example, you might decide to add more codes to an existing category or define a custom exception for particular error codes.

In Table 9-2, the error code 23505 indicates a duplicate key error in PostgreSQL. It is mapped by default to DataIntegrityViolationException. Suppose that you want to create a custom exception type, MyDuplicateKeyException, for this kind of error. It should extend DataIntegrityViolationException because it is also a kind of data integrity violation error. Remember that for an exception to be thrown by the Spring JDBC framework, it must be compatible with the root exception class DataAccessException.

```
package com.apress.springrecipes.vehicle;

import org.springframework.dao.DataIntegrityViolationException;

public class MyDuplicateKeyException extends DataIntegrityViolationException {

    public MyDuplicateKeyException(String msg) {
        super(msg);
    }

    public MyDuplicateKeyException(String msg, Throwable cause) {
        super(msg, cause);
    }
}
```

By default, Spring will look up an exception from the sql-error-codes.xml file located in the org. springframework.jdbc.support package. However, you can override some of the mappings by providing a file with the same name in the root of the classpath. If Spring can find your custom file, it will look up an exception from your mapping first. However, if it does not find a suitable exception there, Spring will look up the default mapping.

For example, suppose you want to map your custom DuplicateKeyException type to error code 23505. You have to add the binding via a CustomSQLErrorCodesTranslation bean and then add this bean to the customTranslations category.

```
<?xml version="1.0" encoding="UTF-8"?>
<!DOCTYPE beans PUBLIC "-//SPRING//DTD BEAN 2.0//EN"
    "http://www.springframework.org/dtd/spring-beans-2.0.dtd">

<beans>
    <bean id="PostgreSQL"
        class="org.springframework.jdbc.support.SQLErrorCodes">
        <property name="useSqlStateForTranslation">
            <value>true</value>
        </property>
        <property name="customTranslations">
            <list>
                <ref bean="myDuplicateKeyTranslation" />
            </list>
        </property>
    </bean>
```

```
<bean id="myDuplicateKeyTranslation"
    class="org.springframework.jdbc.support.CustomSQLErrorCodesTranslation">
    <property name="errorCodes">
        <value>23505</value>
    </property>
    <property name="exceptionClass">
        <value>
            com.apress.springrecipes.vehicle.MyDuplicateKeyException
        </value>
    </property>
</bean>
</beans>
```

Now, if you remove the `try/catch` block surrounding the vehicle insert operation and insert a duplicate vehicle, the Spring JDBC framework will throw a `MyDuplicateKeyException` instead.

However, if you are not satisfied with the basic code-to-exception mapping strategy used by the `SQLErrorCodes` class, you may further implement the `SQLExceptionTranslator` interface and inject its instance into a JDBC template via the `setExceptionTranslator()` method.

9-6. Avoid Problems by Using ORM Frameworks Directly

Problem

You've decided to go to the next level—you have a sufficiently complex domain model, and manually writing all the code for each entity is getting tedious, so you begin to investigate a few alternatives, such as Hibernate. You're stunned to find that while they're powerful, they can be anything but simple!

Solution

Let Spring lend a hand; it has facilities for dealing with ORM layers that rival those available for plain ol' JDBC access.

How It Works

Suppose you are developing a course management system for a training center. The first class you create for this system is Course. This class is called an *entity class* or a *persistent class* because it represents a real-world entity and its instances will be persisted to a database. Remember that for each entity class to be persisted by an ORM framework, a default constructor with no argument is required.

```
package com.apress.springrecipes.course;
...
public class Course {

    private Long id;
    private String title;
    private Date beginDate;
    private Date endDate;
    private int fee;

    // Constructors, Getters and Setters
    ...
}
```

For each entity class, you must define an identifier property to uniquely identify an entity. It's a best practice to define an autogenerated identifier because this has no business meaning and thus won't be changed under any circumstances. Moreover, this identifier will be used by the ORM framework to determine an entity's state. If the identifier value is null, this entity will be treated as a new and unsaved entity. When this entity is persisted, an insert SQL statement will be issued; otherwise, an update statement will be issued. To allow the identifier to be null, you should choose a primitive wrapper type like java.lang.Integer and java.lang.Long for the identifier.

In your course management system, you need a DAO interface to encapsulate the data access logic. Let's define the following operations in the CourseDao interface:

```
package com.apress.springrecipes.course;
...
public interface CourseDao {

    Course store(Course course);
    void delete(Long courseId);
    Course findById(Long courseId);
    List<Course> findAll();
}
```

Usually, when using ORM for persisting objects, the insert and update operations are combined into a single operation (e.g., store). This is to let the ORM framework (not you) decide whether an object should be inserted or updated. For an ORM framework to persist your objects to a database, it must know the mapping metadata for the entity classes. You have to provide mapping metadata to it in its supported format. Historically, Hibernate used XML to provide the mapping metadata. However, because each ORM framework may have its own format for defining mapping metadata, JPA defines a set of persistent annotations for you to define mapping metadata in a standard format that is more likely to be reusable in other ORM frameworks.

Hibernate also supports the use of JPA annotations to define mapping metadata, so there are essentially three different strategies for mapping and persisting your objects with Hibernate and JPA.

- Using the Hibernate API to persist objects with Hibernate XML mappings

- Using the Hibernate API to persist objects with JPA annotations

- Using JPA to persist objects with JPA annotations

The core programming elements of Hibernate, JPA, and other ORM frameworks resemble those of JDBC. They are summarized in Table 9-3.

Table 9-3. *Core Programming Elements for Different Data Access Strategies*

Concept	JDBC	Hibernate	JPA
Resource	Connection	Session	EntityManager
Resource factory	DataSource	SessionFactory	EntityManagerFactory
Exception	SQLException	HibernateException	PersistenceException

In Hibernate, the core interface for object persistence is Session, whose instances can be obtained from a SessionFactory instance. In JPA, the corresponding interface is EntityManager, whose instances can be obtained from an EntityManagerFactory instance. The exceptions thrown by Hibernate are of type HibernateException, while those thrown by JPA may be of type PersistenceException or other Java SE exceptions like IllegalArgumentException and IllegalStateException. Note that all these exceptions are subclasses of RuntimeException, which you are not forced to catch and handle.

Persist Objects Using the Hibernate API with Hibernate XML Mappings

To map entity classes with Hibernate XML mappings, you can provide a single mapping file for each class or a large file for several classes. Practically, you should define one for each class by joining the class name with .hbm.xml as the file extension for ease of maintenance. The middle extension hbm stands for "Hibernate metadata."

The mapping file for the Course class should be named Course.hbm.xml and put in the same package as the entity class.

```
<!DOCTYPE hibernate-mapping
    PUBLIC "-//Hibernate/Hibernate Mapping DTD 3.0//EN"
    "http://hibernate.sourceforge.net/hibernate-mapping-3.0.dtd">

<hibernate-mapping package="com.apress.springrecipes.course">
    <class name="Course" table="COURSE">
        <id name="id" type="long" column="ID">
            <generator class="identity" />
        </id>
        <property name="title" type="string">
            <column name="TITLE" length="100" not-null="true" />
        </property>
        <property name="beginDate" type="date" column="BEGIN_DATE" />
        <property name="endDate" type="date" column="END_DATE" />
        <property name="fee" type="int" column="FEE" />
    </class>
</hibernate-mapping>
```

In the mapping file, you can specify a table name for this entity class and a table column for each simple property. You can also specify the column details such as column length, not-null constraints, and unique constraints. In addition, each entity must have an identifier defined, which can be generated automatically or assigned manually. In this example, the identifier will be generated using a table identity column.

Now, let's implement the DAO interface in the hibernate subpackage using the plain Hibernate API. Before you call the Hibernate API for object persistence, you have to initialize a Hibernate session factory (e.g., in the constructor).

```
package com.apress.springrecipes.course.hibernate;

import com.apress.springrecipes.course.Course;
import com.apress.springrecipes.course.CourseDao;
import org.hibernate.Session;
import org.hibernate.SessionFactory;
import org.hibernate.Transaction;
import org.hibernate.cfg.AvailableSettings;
import org.hibernate.cfg.Configuration;
import org.hibernate.dialect.PostgreSQL95Dialect;

import java.util.List;
```

```java
public class HibernateCourseDao implements CourseDao {

    private final SessionFactory sessionFactory;

    public HibernateCourseDao() {

        Configuration configuration = new Configuration()
            .setProperty(AvailableSettings.URL, "jdbc:postgresql://localhost:5432/course")
            .setProperty(AvailableSettings.USER, "postgres")
            .setProperty(AvailableSettings.PASS, "password")
            .setProperty(AvailableSettings.DIALECT, PostgreSQL95Dialect.class.getName())
            .setProperty(AvailableSettings.SHOW_SQL, String.valueOf(true))
            .setProperty(AvailableSettings.HBM2DDL_AUTO, "update")
            .addClass(Course.class);
        sessionFactory = configuration.buildSessionFactory();
    }

    @Override
    public Course store(Course course) {
        Session session = sessionFactory.openSession();
        Transaction tx = session.getTransaction();
        try {
            tx.begin();
            session.saveOrUpdate(course);
            tx.commit();
            return course;
        } catch (RuntimeException e) {
            tx.rollback();
            throw e;
        } finally {
            session.close();
        }

    }

    @Override
    public void delete(Long courseId) {
        Session session = sessionFactory.openSession();
        Transaction tx = session.getTransaction();
        try {
            tx.begin();
            Course course = session.get(Course.class, courseId);
            session.delete(course);
            tx.commit();
        } catch (RuntimeException e) {
            tx.rollback();
            throw e;
        } finally {
            session.close();
        }
    }
```

```
    @Override
    public Course findById(Long courseId) {
        Session session = sessionFactory.openSession();
        try {
            return session.get(Course.class, courseId);
        } finally {
            session.close();
        }
    }

    @Override
    public List<Course> findAll() {
        Session session = sessionFactory.openSession();
        try {
            return session.createQuery("SELECT c FROM Course c", Course.class).list();
        } finally {
            session.close();
        }
    }
}
```

The first step in using Hibernate is to create a `Configuration` object and to configure properties such as the database settings (either JDBC connection properties or a data source's JNDI name), the database dialect, the mapping metadata's locations, and so on. When using XML mapping files to define mapping metadata, you use the `addClass` method to tell Hibernate what classes it has to manage; it will then by convention load the `Course.hbm.xml` file. Then, you build a Hibernate session factory from this `Configuration` object. The purpose of a session factory is to produce sessions for you to persist your objects.

Before you can persist your objects, you have to create tables in a database schema to store the object data. When using an ORM framework like Hibernate, you usually needn't design the tables by yourself. If you set the `hibernate.hbm2ddl.auto` property to `update`, Hibernate can help you to update the database schema and create the tables when necessary.

■ **Tip**   Naturally, you shouldn't enable this in production, but it can be a great speed boost for development.

In the preceding DAO methods, you first open a session from the session factory. For any operation that involves database update, such as `saveOrUpdate()` and `delete()`, you must start a Hibernate transaction on that session. If the operation completes successfully, you commit the transaction. Otherwise, you roll it back if any `RuntimeException` happens. For read-only operations such as `get()` and HQL queries, there's no need to start a transaction. Finally, you must remember to close a session to release the resources held by this session.

You can create the following `Main` class to test run all the DAO methods. It also demonstrates an entity's typical life cycle.

```
package com.apress.springrecipes.course;

import com.apress.springrecipes.course.hibernate.HibernateCourseDao;

import java.util.GregorianCalendar;
```

```
public class Main {
    public static void main(String[] args) {

        CourseDao courseDao = new HibernateCourseDao();

        Course course = new Course();
        course.setTitle("Core Spring");
        course.setBeginDate(new GregorianCalendar(2007, 8, 1).getTime());
        course.setEndDate(new GregorianCalendar(2007, 9, 1).getTime());
        course.setFee(1000);

        System.out.println("\nCourse before persisting");
        System.out.println(course);

        courseDao.store(course);

        System.out.println("\nCourse after persisting");
        System.out.println(course);

        Long courseId = course.getId();
        Course courseFromDb = courseDao.findById(courseId);

        System.out.println("\nCourse fresh from database");
        System.out.println(courseFromDb);

        courseDao.delete(courseId);

        System.exit(0);
    }
}
```

Persist Objects Using the Hibernate API with JPA Annotations

JPA annotations are standardized in the JSR-220 specification, so they're supported by all JPA-compliant ORM frameworks, including Hibernate. Moreover, the use of annotations will be more convenient for you to edit mapping metadata in the same source file.

The following Course class illustrates the use of JPA annotations to define mapping metadata:

```
package com.apress.springrecipes.course;
...
import javax.persistence.Column;
import javax.persistence.Entity;
import javax.persistence.GeneratedValue;
import javax.persistence.GenerationType;
import javax.persistence.Id;
import javax.persistence.Table;
```

```
@Entity
@Table(name = "COURSE")
public class Course {

    @Id
    @GeneratedValue(strategy = GenerationType.IDENTITY)
    @Column(name = "ID")
    private Long id;

    @Column(name = "TITLE", length = 100, nullable = false)
    private String title;

    @Column(name = "BEGIN_DATE")
    private Date beginDate;

    @Column(name = "END_DATE")
    private Date endDate;

    @Column(name = "FEE")
    private int fee;

    // Constructors, Getters and Setters
    ...
}
```

Each entity class must be annotated with the @Entity annotation. You can assign a table name for an entity class in this annotation. For each property, you can specify a column name and column details using the @Column annotation.

Each entity class must have an identifier defined by the @Id annotation. You can choose a strategy for identifier generation using the @GeneratedValue annotation. Here, the identifier will be generated by a table identity column.

The DAO is almost the same as the one used in the previous code sample with one minor change in the configuration.

```
public HibernateCourseDao() {

    Configuration configuration = new Configuration()
        .setProperty(AvailableSettings.URL, "jdbc:postgresql://localhost:5432/course")
        .setProperty(AvailableSettings.USER, "postgres")
        .setProperty(AvailableSettings.PASS, "password")
        .setProperty(AvailableSettings.DIALECT, PostgreSQL95Dialect.class.getName())
        .setProperty(AvailableSettings.SHOW_SQL, String.valueOf(true))
        .setProperty(AvailableSettings.HBM2DDL_AUTO, "update")
        .addAnnotatedClass(Course.class);
    sessionFactory = configuration.buildSessionFactory();
}
```

Because you are now using annotations to specify the metadata, you need to use the addAnnotatedClass method instead of the addClass. This instructs Hibernate to read the mapping metadata from the class itself instead of trying to locate an hbm.xml file. You can use the same Main class again to run this sample.

Persist Objects Using JPA with Hibernate as the Engine

In addition to persistent annotations, JPA defines a set of programming interfaces for object persistence. However, JPA is not a persistence implementation; you have to pick up a JPA-compliant engine to provide persistence services. Hibernate can be JPA-compliant through the Hibernate EntityManager module. With this, Hibernate can work as an underlying JPA engine to persist objects. This lets you both retain the valuable investment in Hibernate (perhaps it's faster or handles certain operations more to your satisfaction) and write code that is JPA-compliant and portable among other JPA engines. This can also be a useful way to transition a code base to JPA. New code is written strictly against the JPA APIs, and older code is transitioned to the JPA interfaces.

In a Java EE environment, you can configure the JPA engine in a Java EE container. But in a Java SE application, you have to set up the engine locally. The configuration of JPA is through the central XML file persistence.xml, located in the META-INF directory of the classpath root. In this file, you can set any vendor-specific properties for the underlying engine configuration. When using Spring to configure the EntityManagerFactory, this isn't needed, and the configuration can be done through Spring.

Now, let's create the JPA configuration file persistence.xml in the META-INF directory of the classpath root. Each JPA configuration file contains one or more <persistence-unit> elements. A persistence unit defines a set of persistent classes and how they should be persisted. Each persistence unit requires a name for identification. Here, you assign the name course to this persistence unit.

```
<persistence xmlns="http://xmlns.jcp.org/xml/ns/persistence"
    xmlns:xsi="http://www.w3.org/2001/XMLSchema-instance"
    xsi:schemaLocation="http://xmlns.jcp.org/xml/ns/persistence
    http://xmlns.jcp.org/xml/ns/persistence/persistence_2_1.xsd"
    version="2.1">

    <persistence-unit name="course" transaction-type="RESOURCE_LOCAL">
        <class>com.apress.springrecipes.course.Course</class>

        <properties>
            <property name="javax.persistence.jdbc.url"
                    value="jdbc:postgresql://localhost:5432/course" />
            <property name="javax.persistence.jdbc.user" value="postgres" />
            <property name="javax.persistence.jdbc.password" value="password" />

            <property name="hibernate.dialect"
                    value="org.hibernate.dialect.PostgreSQL95Dialect" />
            <property name="hibernate.show_sql" value="true" />
            <property name="hibernate.hbm2ddl.auto" value="update" />
        </properties>
    </persistence-unit>
</persistence>
```

In this JPA configuration file, you configure Hibernate as your underlying JPA engine. Notice that there are a few generic javax.persistence properties to configure the location of the database and username/password combination to use. Next there are some Hibernate-specific properties to configure the dialect and again the hibernate.hbm2ddl.auto property. Finally, there is a <class> element to specify which classes to use for mapping.

In a Java EE environment, a Java EE container is able to manage the entity manager for you and inject it into your EJB components directly. But when you use JPA outside of a Java EE container (e.g., in a Java SE application), you have to create and maintain the entity manager by yourself.

Now, let's implement the CourseDao interface using JPA in a Java SE application. Before you call JPA for object persistence, you have to initialize an entity manager factory. The purpose of an entity manager factory is to produce entity managers for you to persist your objects.

```java
package com.apress.springrecipes.course.jpa;
...
import javax.persistence.EntityManager;
import javax.persistence.EntityManagerFactory;
import javax.persistence.EntityTransaction;
import javax.persistence.Persistence;
import javax.persistence.Query;

public class JpaCourseDao implements CourseDao {

    private EntityManagerFactory entityManagerFactory;

    public JpaCourseDao() {
        entityManagerFactory = Persistence.createEntityManagerFactory("course");
    }

    public void store(Course course) {
        EntityManager manager = entityManagerFactory.createEntityManager();
        EntityTransaction tx = manager.getTransaction();
        try {
            tx.begin();
            manager.merge(course);
            tx.commit();
        } catch (RuntimeException e) {
            tx.rollback();
            throw e;
        } finally {
            manager.close();
        }
    }

    public void delete(Long courseId) {
        EntityManager manager = entityManagerFactory.createEntityManager();
        EntityTransaction tx = manager.getTransaction();
        try {
            tx.begin();
            Course course = manager.find(Course.class, courseId);
            manager.remove(course);
            tx.commit();
        } catch (RuntimeException e) {
            tx.rollback();
            throw e;
        } finally {
            manager.close();
        }
    }
```

```java
    public Course findById(Long courseId) {
        EntityManager manager = entityManagerFactory.createEntityManager();
        try {
            return manager.find(Course.class, courseId);
        } finally {
            manager.close();
        }
    }

    public List<Course> findAll() {
        EntityManager manager = entityManagerFactory.createEntityManager();
        try {
            Query query = manager.createQuery("select course from Course course");
            return query.getResultList();
        } finally {
            manager.close();
        }
    }
}
```

The entity manager factory is built by the static method createEntityManagerFactory() of the javax.persistence.Persistence class. You have to pass in a persistence unit name defined in persistence.xml for an entity manager factory.

In the preceding DAO methods, you first create an entity manager from the entity manager factory. For any operation that involves database update, such as merge() and remove(), you must start a JPA transaction on the entity manager. For read-only operations such as find() and JPA queries, there's no need to start a transaction. Finally, you must close an entity manager to release the resources.

You can test this DAO with the similar Main class, but this time, you instantiate the JPA DAO implementation instead.

```java
package com.apress.springrecipes.course;
...
public class Main {

    public static void main(String[] args) {
        CourseDao courseDao = new JpaCourseDao();
        ...
    }
}
```

In the preceding DAO implementations for both Hibernate and JPA, there are only one or two lines that are different for each DAO method. The rest of the lines are boilerplate routine tasks that you have to repeat. Moreover, each ORM framework has its own API for local transaction management.

9-7. Configure ORM Resource Factories in Spring

Problem

When using an ORM framework on its own, you have to configure its resource factory with its API. For Hibernate and JPA, you have to build a session factory and an entity manager factory from the native Hibernate API and JPA. You have no choice but to manage these objects manually, without Spring's support.

Solution

Spring provides several factory beans for you to create a Hibernate session factory or a JPA entity manager factory as a singleton bean in the IoC container. These factories can be shared between multiple beans via dependency injection. Moreover, this allows the session factory and the entity manager factory to integrate with other Spring data access facilities, such as data sources and transaction managers.

How It Works

For Hibernate Spring provides a `LocalSessionFactoryBean` to create a plain Hibernate `SessionFactory`, for JPA Spring has several options for constructing an `EntityManagerFactory`. You will explore how to retrieve the `EntityManagerFactory` from JNDI and how to use the `LocalEntityManagerFactoryBean` and `LocalContainerEntityManagerFactoryBean` and the differences between each option.

Configure a Hibernate Session Factory in Spring

First, let's modify `HibernateCourseDao` to accept a session factory via dependency injection, instead of creating it directly with the native Hibernate API in the constructor.

```
package com.apress.springrecipes.course.hibernate;
...
import org.hibernate.SessionFactory;

public class HibernateCourseDao implements CourseDao {

    private final SessionFactory sessionFactory;

    public HibernateCourseDao(SessionFactory sessionFactory) {
        this.sessionFactory = sessionFactory;
    }

    ...
}
```

Then, you create a configuration class for using Hibernate as the ORM framework. You can also declare a `HibernateCourseDao` instance under Spring's management.

```
package com.apress.springrecipes.course.config;

import com.apress.springrecipes.course.Course;
import com.apress.springrecipes.course.CourseDao;
import com.apress.springrecipes.course.hibernate.HibernateCourseDao;
import org.hibernate.SessionFactory;
import org.hibernate.cfg.AvailableSettings;
import org.hibernate.dialect.PostgreSQL95Dialect;
import org.springframework.context.annotation.Bean;
import org.springframework.context.annotation.Configuration;
import org.springframework.orm.hibernate5.LocalSessionFactoryBean;

import java.util.Properties;
```

399

```java
@Configuration
public class CourseConfiguration {

    @Bean
    public CourseDao courseDao(SessionFactory sessionFactory) {
        return new HibernateCourseDao(sessionFactory);
    }

    @Bean
    public LocalSessionFactoryBean sessionFactory() {

        LocalSessionFactoryBean sessionFactoryBean = new LocalSessionFactoryBean();
        sessionFactoryBean.setHibernateProperties(hibernateProperties());
        sessionFactoryBean.setAnnotatedClasses(Course.class);
        return sessionFactoryBean;
    }

    private Properties hibernateProperties() {

        Properties properties = new Properties();
        properties.setProperty(AvailableSettings.URL,
                            "jdbc:postgresql://localhost:5432/course");
        properties.setProperty(AvailableSettings.USER, "postgres");
        properties.setProperty(AvailableSettings.PASS, "password");
        properties.setProperty(AvailableSettings.DIALECT,
                            PostgreSQL95Dialect.class.getName());
        properties.setProperty(AvailableSettings.SHOW_SQL, String.valueOf(true));
        properties.setProperty(AvailableSettings.HBM2DDL_AUTO, "update");
        return properties;
    }
}
```

All the properties that were set earlier on the Configuration object are now translated to a Properties object and added to the LocalSessionFactoryBean. The annotated class is passed in through the setAnnotatedClasses method so that eventually Hibernate knowns about the annotated class. The constructed SessionFactory is passed to the HibernateCourseDao through its constructor.

If you are in a project that still uses Hibernate mapping files, you can use the mappingLocations property to specify the mapping files. LocalSessionFactoryBean also allows you take advantage of Spring's resource-loading support to load mapping files from various types of locations. You can specify the resource paths of the mapping files in the mappingLocations property, whose type is Resource[].

```java
@Bean
public LocalSessionFactoryBean sessionfactory() {
    LocalSessionFactoryBean sessionFactoryBean = new LocalSessionFactoryBean();
    sessionFactoryBean.setDataSource(dataSource());
    sessionFactoryBean.setMappingLocations(
        new ClassPathResource("com/apress/springrecipes/course/Course.hbm.xml"));
    sessionFactoryBean.setHibernateProperties(hibernateProperties());
    return sessionFactoryBean;
}
```

With Spring's resource-loading support, you can also use wildcards in a resource path to match multiple mapping files so that you don't need to configure their locations every time you add a new entity class. For this to work, you need a ResourcePatternResolver in your configuration class. You can get this by using ResourcePatternUtils and the ResourceLoaderAware interface. You implement the latter and use the getResourcePatternResolver method to get a ResourcePatternResolver based on the ResourceLoader.

```
@Configuration
public class CourseConfiguration implements ResourceLoaderAware {

    private ResourcePatternResolver resourcePatternResolver;
...
    @Override
    public void setResourceLoader(ResourceLoader resourceLoader) {
        this.resourcePatternResolver =
            ResourcePatternUtils.getResourcePatternResolver(resourceLoader);
    }
}
```

Now you can use the ResourcePatternResolver to resolve resource patterns to resources.

```
@Bean
public LocalSessionFactoryBean sessionfactory() throws IOException {
    LocalSessionFactoryBean sessionFactoryBean = new LocalSessionFactoryBean();
    Resource[] mappingResources =
        resourcePatternResolver.getResources("classpath:com/apress/springrecipes/course/*.
        hbm.xml");
    sessionFactoryBean.setMappingLocations(mappingResources);
    ...
    return sessionFactoryBean;
}
```

Now, you can modify the Main class to retrieve the HibernateCourseDao instance from the Spring IoC container.

```
package com.apress.springrecipes.course;
...
import org.springframework.context.ApplicationContext;
import org.springframework.context.support.ClassPathXmlApplicationContext;

public class Main {

    public static void main(String[] args) {
        ApplicationContext context =
            new AnnotationConfigApplicationContext(CourseConfiguration.class);
        CourseDao courseDao = context.getBean(CourseDao.class);
        ...
    }
}
```

The preceding factory bean creates a session factory by loading the Hibernate configuration file, which includes the database settings (either JDBC connection properties or a data source's JNDI name). Now, suppose you have a data source defined in the Spring IoC container. If you want to use this data source for your session factory, you can inject it into the dataSource property of LocalSessionFactoryBean. The data source specified in this property will override the database settings of the Hibernate configuration. If this is set, the Hibernate settings should not define a connection provider to avoid meaningless double configuration.

```
@Configuration
public class CourseConfiguration {
    ...
    @Bean
    public DataSource dataSource() {

        HikariDataSource dataSource = new HikariDataSource();
        dataSource.setUsername("postgres");
        dataSource.setPassword("password");
        dataSource.setJdbcUrl("jdbc:postgresql://localhost:5432/course");
        dataSource.setMinimumIdle(2);
        dataSource.setMaximumPoolSize(5);
        return dataSource;
    }

    @Bean
    public LocalSessionFactoryBean sessionFactory(DataSource dataSource) {

        LocalSessionFactoryBean sessionFactoryBean = new LocalSessionFactoryBean();
        sessionFactoryBean.setDataSource(dataSource);
        sessionFactoryBean.setHibernateProperties(hibernateProperties());
        sessionFactoryBean.setAnnotatedClasses(Course.class);
        return sessionFactoryBean;
    }

    private Properties hibernateProperties() {

        Properties properties = new Properties();
        properties.setProperty(AvailableSettings.DIALECT,
                            PostgreSQL95Dialect.class.getName());
        properties.setProperty(AvailableSettings.SHOW_SQL, String.valueOf(true));
        properties.setProperty(AvailableSettings.HBM2DDL_AUTO, "update");
        return properties;
    }}
```

Or you can even ignore the Hibernate configuration file by merging all the configurations into LocalSessionFactoryBean. For example, you can specify the packages containing the JPA annotated classes in the packagesToScan property and other Hibernate properties such as the database dialect in the hibernateProperties property.

```
@Configuration
public class CourseConfiguration {
...
    @Bean
    public LocalSessionFactoryBean sessionfactory() {
        LocalSessionFactoryBean sessionFactoryBean = new LocalSessionFactoryBean();
        sessionFactoryBean.setDataSource(dataSource());
        sessionFactoryBean.setPackagesToScan("com.apress.springrecipes.course");
        sessionFactoryBean.setHibernateProperties(hibernateProperties());
        return sessionFactoryBean;
    }

    private Properties hibernateProperties() {
        Properties properties = new Properties();
        properties.put("hibernate.dialect",
                        org.hibernate.dialect.DerbyTenSevenDialect.class.getName());
        properties.put("hibernate.show_sql", true);
        properties.put("hibernate.hbm2dll.auto", "update");
        return properties;
    }
}
```

You can now delete the Hibernate configuration file (i.e., `hibernate.cfg.xml`) because its configurations have been ported to Spring.

Configure a JPA Entity Manager Factory in Spring

First, let's modify `JpaCourseDao` to accept an entity manager factory via dependency injection, instead of creating it directly in the constructor.

```
package com.apress.springrecipes.course;
...
import javax.persistence.EntityManagerFactory;
import javax.persistence.Persistence;

public class JpaCourseDao implements CourseDao {

    private final EntityManagerFactory entityManagerFactory;

    public JpaCourseDao (EntityManagerFactory entityManagerFactory) {
        this.entityManagerFactory = entityManagerFactory;
    }
    ...
}
```

The JPA specification defines how you should obtain an entity manager factory in Java SE and Java EE environments. In a Java SE environment, an entity manager factory is created manually by calling the `createEntityManagerFactory()` static method of the `Persistence` class.

Let's create a bean configuration file for using JPA. Spring provides a factory bean,
LocalEntityManagerFactoryBean, for you to create an entity manager factory in the IoC container. You must
specify the persistence unit name defined in the JPA configuration file. You can also declare a JpaCourseDao
instance under Spring's management.

```java
package com.apress.springrecipes.course.config;

import com.apress.springrecipes.course.CourseDao;
import com.apress.springrecipes.course.jpa.JpaCourseDao;
import org.springframework.context.annotation.Bean;
import org.springframework.context.annotation.Configuration;
import org.springframework.orm.jpa.LocalEntityManagerFactoryBean;

import javax.persistence.EntityManagerFactory;

@Configuration
public class CourseConfiguration {

    @Bean
    public CourseDao courseDao(EntityManagerFactory entityManagerFactory) {
        return new JpaCourseDao(entityManagerFactory);
    }

    @Bean
    public LocalEntityManagerFactoryBean entityManagerFactory() {

        LocalEntityManagerFactoryBean emf = new LocalEntityManagerFactoryBean();
        emf.setPersistenceUnitName("course");
        return emf;
    }
}
```

Now, you can test this JpaCourseDao instance with the Main class by retrieving it from the Spring IoC
container.

```java
package com.apress.springrecipes.course;
...
import org.springframework.context.ApplicationContext;
import org.springframework.context.support.ClassPathXmlApplicationContext;

public class Main {

    public static void main(String[] args) {
        ApplicationContext context =
            new AnnotationConfigApplicationContext(CourseConfiguration.class);
        CourseDao courseDao = context.getBean(CourseDao.class);
        ...
    }
}
```

In a Java EE environment, you can look up an entity manager factory from a Java EE container with JNDI. In Spring, you can perform a JNDI lookup by using the JndiLocatorDelegate object (which is simpler than constructing a JndiObjectFactoryBean, which would also work).

```
@Bean
public EntityManagerFactory entityManagerFactory() throws NamingException {
    return JndiLocatorDelegate.createDefaultResourceRefLocator()
        .lookup("jpa/coursePU", EntityManagerFactory.class);
}
```

LocalEntityManagerFactoryBean creates an entity manager factory by loading the JPA configuration file (i.e., persistence.xml). Spring supports a more flexible way to create an entity manager factory by another factory bean, LocalContainerEntityManagerFactoryBean. It allows you to override some of the configurations in the JPA configuration file, such as the data source and database dialect. So, you can take advantage of Spring's data access facilities to configure the entity manager factory.

```
@Configuration
public class CourseConfiguration {
    ...
    @Bean
    public LocalContainerEntityManagerFactoryBean entityManagerFactory(DataSource
    dataSource) {

        LocalContainerEntityManagerFactoryBean emf =
            new LocalContainerEntityManagerFactoryBean();
        emf.setPersistenceUnitName("course");
        emf.setDataSource(dataSource);
        emf.setJpaVendorAdapter(jpaVendorAdapter());
        return emf;
    }

    private JpaVendorAdapter jpaVendorAdapter() {

        HibernateJpaVendorAdapter jpaVendorAdapter = new HibernateJpaVendorAdapter();
        jpaVendorAdapter.setShowSql(true);
        jpaVendorAdapter.setGenerateDdl(true);
        jpaVendorAdapter.setDatabasePlatform(PostgreSQL95Dialect.class.getName());
        return jpaVendorAdapter;
    }

    @Bean
    public DataSource dataSource() {

        HikariDataSource dataSource = new HikariDataSource();
        dataSource.setUsername("postgres");
        dataSource.setPassword("password");
        dataSource.setJdbcUrl("jdbc:postgresql://localhost:5432/course");
        dataSource.setMinimumIdle(2);
        dataSource.setMaximumPoolSize(5);
        return dataSource;
    }
}
```

In the preceding bean configurations, you inject a data source into this entity manager factory. It will override the database settings in the JPA configuration file. You can set a JPA vendor adapter to LocalContainerEntityManagerFactoryBean to specify JPA engine–specific properties. With Hibernate as the underlying JPA engine, you should choose HibernateJpaVendorAdapter. Other properties that are not supported by this adapter can be specified in the jpaProperties property.

Now your JPA configuration file (i.e., persistence.xml) can be simplified as follows because its configurations have been ported to Spring:

```
<persistence xmlns="http://xmlns.jcp.org/xml/ns/persistence"
    xmlns:xsi="http://www.w3.org/2001/XMLSchema-instance"
    xsi:schemaLocation="http://xmlns.jcp.org/xml/ns/persistence
    http://xmlns.jcp.org/xml/ns/persistence/persistence_2_1.xsd"
    version="2.1">

    <persistence-unit name="course" transaction-type="RESOURCE_LOCAL">
        <class>com.apress.springrecipes.course.Course</class>
    </persistence-unit>

</persistence>
```

Spring also makes it possible to configure the JPA EntityManagerFactory *without* a persistence.xml file. If you want, you can fully configure it in a Spring configuration file. Instead of a persistenceUnitName, you need to specify the packagesToScan property. After this, you can remove the persistence.xml file completely.

```
@Bean
public LocalContainerEntityManagerFactoryBean entityManagerFactory() {
    LocalContainerEntityManagerFactoryBean emf =
        new LocalContainerEntityManagerFactoryBean();
    emf.setDataSource(dataSource());
    emf.setPackagesToScan("com.apress.springrecipes.course");
    emf.setJpaVendorAdapter(jpaVendorAdapter());
    return emf;
}
```

9-8. Persist Objects with Hibernate's Contextual Sessions

Problem

You want to write a DAO based on the plain Hibernate API but still rely on Spring managed transactions.

Solution

As of Hibernate 3, a session factory can manage contextual sessions for you and allows you to retrieve them by the getCurrentSession() method on org.hibernate.SessionFactory. Within a single transaction, you will get the same session for each getCurrentSession() method call. This ensures that there will be only one Hibernate session per transaction, so it works nicely with Spring's transaction management support.

How It Works

To use the contextual session approach, your DAO methods require access to the session factory, which can be injected via a setter method or a constructor argument. Then, in each DAO method, you get the contextual session from the session factory and use it for object persistence.

```java
package com.apress.springrecipes.course.hibernate;

import com.apress.springrecipes.course.Course;
import com.apress.springrecipes.course.CourseDao;
import org.hibernate.Query;
import org.hibernate.Session;
import org.hibernate.SessionFactory;
import org.springframework.transaction.annotation.Transactional;

import java.util.List;

public class HibernateCourseDao implements CourseDao {

    private final SessionFactory sessionFactory;

    public HibernateCourseDao(SessionFactory sessionFactory) {
        this.sessionFactory=sessionFactory;
    }

    @Transactional
    public Course store(Course course) {
        Session session = sessionFactory.getCurrentSession();
        session.saveOrUpdate(course);
        return course;
    }

    @Transactional
    public void delete(Long courseId) {
        Session session = sessionFactory.getCurrentSession();
        Course course = session.get(Course.class, courseId);
        session.delete(course);
    }

    @Transactional(readOnly=true)
    public Course findById(Long courseId) {
        Session session = sessionFactory.getCurrentSession();
        return session.get(Course.class, courseId);
    }

    @Transactional(readOnly=true)
    public List<Course> findAll() {
        Session session = sessionFactory.getCurrentSession();
        return session.createQuery("from Course", Course.class).list();
    }
}
```

Note that all your DAO methods must be made transactional. This is required because Spring integrates with Hibernate through Hibernate's contextual session support. Spring has its own implementation of the CurrentSessionContext interface from Hibernate. It will attempt to find a transaction and then fail, complaining that no Hibernate sessions been bound to the thread. You can achieve this by annotating each method or the entire class with @Transactional. This ensures that the persistence operations within a DAO method will be executed in the same transaction and hence by the same session. Moreover, if a service layer component's method calls multiple DAO methods and it propagates its own transaction to these methods, then all these DAO methods will run within the same session as well.

■ **Caution**   When configuring Hibernate with Spring, make sure *not* to set the hibernate.current_session_ context_class property because that will interfere with Spring's ability to properly manage the transactions. You should set this property only when you are in need of JTA transactions.

In the bean configuration file, you have to declare a HibernateTransactionManager instance for this application and enable declarative transaction management via @EnableTransactionManagement.

```
@Configuration
@EnableTransactionManagement
public class CourseConfiguration {

    @Bean
    public CourseDao courseDao(SessionFactory sessionFactory) {
        return new HibernateCourseDao(sessionFactory);
    }
    @Bean
    public HibernateTransactionManager transactionManager(SessionFactory sessionFactory) {
        return new HibernateTransactionManager(sessionFactory);
    }
}
```

However, when calling the native methods on a Hibernate session, the exceptions thrown will be of native type HibernateException. If you want the Hibernate exceptions to be translated into Spring's DataAccessException for consistent exception handling, you have to apply the @Repository annotation to your DAO class that requires exception translation.

```
package com.apress.springrecipes.course.hibernate;
...
import org.springframework.stereotype.Repository;

@Repository
public class HibernateCourseDao implements CourseDao {
    ...
}
```

A PersistenceExceptionTranslationPostProcessor takes care of translating the native Hibernate exceptions into data access exceptions in Spring's DataAccessException hierarchy. This bean post-processor will only translate exceptions for beans annotated with @Repository. When using Java-based configuration, this bean is automatically registered in the AnnotationConfigApplicationContext; hence, there is no need to explicitly declare a bean for it.

In Spring, @Repository is a stereotype annotation. By annotating it, a component class can be autodetected through component scanning. You can assign a component name in this annotation and have the session factory autowired by the Spring IoC container.

```
package com.apress.springrecipes.course.hibernate;
...
import org.hibernate.SessionFactory;
import org.springframework.beans.factory.annotation.Autowired;
import org.springframework.stereotype.Repository;

@Repository("courseDao")
public class HibernateCourseDao implements CourseDao {

    private final SessionFactory sessionFactory;

    public HibernateCourseDao (SessionFactory sessionFactory) {
        this.sessionFactory = sessionFactory;
    }
    ...
}
```

Then, you can simply add the @ComponentScan annotation and delete the original HibernateCourseDao bean declaration.

```
@Configuration
@EnableTransactionManagement
@ComponentScan("com.apress.springrecipes.course")
public class CourseConfiguration { ... }
```

9-9. Persist Objects with JPA's Context Injection

Problem

In a Java EE environment, a Java EE container can manage entity managers for you and inject them into your EJB components directly. An EJB component can simply perform persistence operations on an injected entity manager without caring much about the entity manager creation and transaction management.

Solution

Originally, the @PersistenceContext annotation is used for entity manager injection in EJB components. Spring can also interpret this annotation by means of a bean post-processor. It will inject an entity manager into a property with this annotation. Spring ensures that all your persistence operations within a single transaction will be handled by the same entity manager.

How It Works

To use the context injection approach, you can declare an entity manager field in your DAO and annotate it with the @PersistenceContext annotation. Spring will inject an entity manager into this field for you to persist your objects.

```
package com.apress.springrecipes.course.jpa;

import com.apress.springrecipes.course.Course;
import com.apress.springrecipes.course.CourseDao;
import org.springframework.transaction.annotation.Transactional;

import javax.persistence.EntityManager;
import javax.persistence.PersistenceContext;
import javax.persistence.TypedQuery;
import java.util.List;

public class JpaCourseDao implements CourseDao {

    @PersistenceContext
    private EntityManager entityManager;

    @Transactional
    public Course store(Course course) {
        return entityManager.merge(course);
    }

    @Transactional
    public void delete(Long courseId) {
        Course course = entityManager.find(Course.class, courseId);
        entityManager.remove(course);
    }

    @Transactional(readOnly = true)
    public Course findById(Long courseId) {
        return entityManager.find(Course.class, courseId);
    }

    @Transactional(readOnly = true)
    public List<Course> findAll() {
        TypedQuery<Course> query =
            entityManager.createQuery("select c from Course c", Course.class);
        return query.getResultList();
    }
}
```

You can annotate each DAO method or the entire DAO class with @Transactional to make all these methods transactional. It ensures that the persistence operations within a single method will be executed in the same transaction and hence by the same entity manager.

In the bean configuration file, you have to declare a JpaTransactionManager instance and enable declarative transaction management via @EnableTransactionManagement. A PersistenceAnnotationBeanPostProcessor instance is registered automatically when using a Java-based config to inject entity managers into properties annotated with @PersistenceContext.

```java
package com.apress.springrecipes.course.config;

import com.apress.springrecipes.course.CourseDao;
import com.apress.springrecipes.course.JpaCourseDao;
import org.apache.derby.jdbc.ClientDriver;
import org.hibernate.dialect.DerbyTenSevenDialect;
import org.springframework.context.annotation.Bean;
import org.springframework.context.annotation.Configuration;
import org.springframework.jdbc.datasource.SimpleDriverDataSource;
import org.springframework.orm.jpa.JpaTransactionManager;
import org.springframework.orm.jpa.JpaVendorAdapter;
import org.springframework.orm.jpa.LocalContainerEntityManagerFactoryBean;
import org.springframework.orm.jpa.vendor.HibernateJpaVendorAdapter;
import org.springframework.transaction.PlatformTransactionManager;
import org.springframework.transaction.annotation.EnableTransactionManagement;

import javax.sql.DataSource;

@Configuration
@EnableTransactionManagement
public class CourseConfiguration {

    @Bean
    public CourseDao courseDao() {
        return new JpaCourseDao();
    }

    @Bean
    public LocalContainerEntityManagerFactoryBean entityManagerFactory() {
        LocalContainerEntityManagerFactoryBean emf =
            new LocalContainerEntityManagerFactoryBean();
        emf.setDataSource(dataSource());
        emf.setJpaVendorAdapter(jpaVendorAdapter());
        return emf;
    }

    private JpaVendorAdapter jpaVendorAdapter() {
        HibernateJpaVendorAdapter jpaVendorAdapter = new HibernateJpaVendorAdapter();
        jpaVendorAdapter.setShowSql(true);
        jpaVendorAdapter.setGenerateDdl(true);
        jpaVendorAdapter.setDatabasePlatform(DerbyTenSevenDialect.class.getName());
        return jpaVendorAdapter;
    }

    @Bean
    public JpaTransactionManager transactionManager(EntityManagerFactory
    entityManagerFactory) {
        return new JpaTransactionManager(entityManagerFactory);
    }

    @Bean
    public DataSource dataSource() { ... }

}
```

The PersistenceAnnotationBeanPostProcessor can also inject the entity manager factory into a property with the @PersistenceUnit annotation. This allows you to create entity managers and manage transactions by yourself. It's no different from injecting the entity manager factory via a setter method.

```
package com.apress.springrecipes.course;
...
import javax.persistence.EntityManagerFactory;
import javax.persistence.PersistenceUnit;

public class JpaCourseDao implements CourseDao {
    @PersistenceContext
    private EntityManager entityManager;

    @PersistenceUnit
    private EntityManagerFactory entityManagerFactory;
    ...
}
```

When calling native methods on a JPA entity manager, the exceptions thrown will be of the native type PersistenceException or other Java SE exceptions such as IllegalArgumentException and IllegalStateException. If you want JPA exceptions to be translated into Spring's DataAccessException, you have to apply the @Repository annotation to your DAO class.

```
package com.apress.springrecipes.course;
...
import org.springframework.stereotype.Repository;

@Repository("courseDao")
public class JpaCourseDao implements CourseDao {
    ...
}
```

A PersistenceExceptionTranslationPostProcessor instance will translate the native JPA exceptions into exceptions in Spring's DataAccessException hierarchy. When using Java-based configuration, this bean is automatically registered in the AnnotationConfigApplicationContext; hence, there is no need to explicitly declare a bean for it.

9-10. Simplify JPA with Spring Data JPA

Problem

Writing data access code, even with JPA, can be a tedious and repetitive task. You often need access to EntityManager or EntityManagerFactory and have to create queries—not to mention the repetitive declaration of findById and findAll methods for all different entities when you have lots of DAOs.

Solution

Spring Data JPA allows you, just like Spring itself does, to focus on the parts that are important and not on the boilerplate needed to accomplish this. It also provides default implementations for the most commonly used data access methods (i.e., findAll, delete, save, etc.).

How It Works

To use Spring Data JPA, you have to extend one of its interfaces. These interfaces are detected, and a default implementation of that repository is generated at runtime. In most cases, it is enough to extend the CrudRepository<T, ID> interface.

```
package com.apress.springrecipes.course;

import com.apress.springrecipes.course.Course;
import org.springframework.data.repository.CrudRepository;

public interface CourseRepository extends CrudRepository<Course, Long>{}
```

This is enough to be able to do all necessary CRUD actions for the Course entity. When extending the Spring Data interfaces, you have to specify the type, Course, and the type of the primary key, Long. This information is needed to generate the repository at runtime.

■ **Note** You could also extend JpaRepository, which adds some JPA-specific methods (flush, saveAndFlush) and provides query methods with paging/sorting capabilities.

Next you need to enable detection of the Spring Data–enabled repositories. For this you can use the @EnableJpaRepositories annotation provided by Spring Data JPA.

```
@Configuration
@EnableTransactionManagement
@EnableJpaRepositories("com.apress.springrecipes.course")
public class CourseConfiguration { ... }
```

This will bootstrap Spring Data JPA and will construct a usable repository. By default all repository methods are marked with @Transactional, so no additional annotations are needed.

Now, you can test this CourseRepository instance with the Main class by retrieving it from the Spring IoC container.

```
package com.apress.springrecipes.course.datajpa;
...
import org.springframework.context.ApplicationContext;
import org.springframework.context.support.ClassPathXmlApplicationContext;

public class Main {

    public static void main(String[] args) {
        ApplicationContext context =
            new AnnotationConfigApplicationContext(CourseConfiguration.class);

        CourseRepository repository = context.getBean(CourseRepository.class);
        ...
    }
}
```

All other things such as exception translation, transaction management, and easy configuration of your `EntityManagerFactory` still apply to Spring Data JPA–based repositories. It just makes your life a lot easier and lets you focus on what is important.

Summary

This chapter discussed how to use Spring's support for JDBC, Hibernate, and JPA. You learned how to configure a `DataSource` object to connect to a database and how to use Spring's `JdbcTemplate` and `NamedParameterJdbcTemplate` objects to rid your code of tedious boilerplate handling. You saw how to use the utility base classes to build DAO classes with JDBC and Hibernate, as well as how to use Spring's support for stereotype annotations and component scanning to easily build new DAOs and services. The final recipe showed you how to simplify your data access code even more by using the power of Spring Data JPA. In the next chapter, you will learn how to use transactions (i.e., for JMS or a database) with Spring to help ensure a consistent state in your services.

CHAPTER 10

Spring Transaction Management

In this chapter, you will learn about the basic concept of transactions and Spring's capabilities in the area of transaction management. Transaction management is an essential technique in enterprise applications to ensure data integrity and consistency. Spring, as an enterprise application framework, provides an abstract layer on top of different transaction management APIs. As an application developer, you can use Spring's transaction management facilities without having to know much about the underlying transaction management APIs.

Like the bean-managed transaction (BMT) and container-managed transaction (CMT) approaches in EJB, Spring supports both programmatic and declarative transaction management. The aim of Spring's transaction support is to provide an alternative to EJB transactions by adding transaction capabilities to POJOs.

Programmatic transaction management is achieved by embedding transaction management code in your business methods to control the commit and rollback of transactions. You usually commit a transaction if a method completes normally and roll back a transaction if a method throws certain types of exceptions. With programmatic transaction management, you can define your own rules to commit and roll back transactions.

However, when managing transactions programmatically, you have to include transaction management code in each transactional operation. As a result, the boilerplate transaction code is repeated in each of these operations. Moreover, it's hard for you to enable and disable transaction management for different applications. If you have a solid understanding of AOP, you may already have noticed that transaction management is a kind of crosscutting concern.

Declarative transaction management is preferable to programmatic transaction management in most cases. It's achieved by separating transaction management code from your business methods via declarations. Transaction management, as a kind of crosscutting concern, can be modularized with the AOP approach. Spring supports declarative transaction management through the Spring AOP framework. This can help you to enable transactions for your applications more easily and define a consistent transaction policy. Declarative transaction management is less flexible than programmatic transaction management.

Programmatic transaction management allows you to control transactions through your code—explicitly starting, committing, and joining them as you see fit. You can specify a set of transaction attributes to define your transactions at a fine level of granularity. The transaction attributes supported by Spring include the propagation behavior, isolation level, rollback rules, transaction timeout, and whether or not the transaction is read-only. These attributes allow you to further customize the behavior of your transactions.

Upon finishing this chapter, you will be able to apply different transaction management strategies in your application. Moreover, you will be familiar with different transaction attributes to finely define your transactions.

Programmatic transaction management is a good idea in certain cases where you don't feel the addition of Spring proxies is worth the trouble or negligible performance loss. Here, you might access the native transaction yourself and control the transaction manually. A more convenient option that avoids the overhead of Spring proxies is the `TransactionTemplate` class, which provides a template method around which a transactional boundary is started and then committed.

10-1. Avoid Problems with Transaction Management

Transaction management is an essential technique in enterprise application development to ensure data integrity and consistency. Without transaction management, your data and resources may be corrupted and left in an inconsistent state. Transaction management is particularly important for recovering from unexpected errors in a concurrent and distributed environment.

In simple words, a transaction is a series of actions treated as a single unit of work. These actions should either complete entirely or take no effect at all. If all the actions go well, the transaction should be committed permanently. In contrast, if any of them goes wrong, the transaction should be rolled back to the initial state as if nothing had happened.

The concept of transactions can be described with four key properties: atomicity, consistency, isolation, and durability (ACID).

- *Atomicity*: A transaction is an atomic operation that consists of a series of actions. The atomicity of a transaction ensures that the actions either complete entirely or take no effect at all.

- *Consistency*: Once all actions of a transaction have completed, the transaction is committed. Then your data and resources will be in a consistent state that conforms to business rules.

- *Isolation*: Because there may be many transactions processing with the same data set at the same time, each transaction should be isolated from others to prevent data corruption.

- *Durability*: Once a transaction has completed, its result should be durable to survive any system failure (imagine if the power to your machine was cut right in the middle of a transaction's commit). Usually, the result of a transaction is written to persistent storage.

To understand the importance of transaction management, let's begin with an example about purchasing books from an online bookshop. First, you have to create a new schema for this application in your database. We have chosen to use PostgreSQL as the database to use for these samples. The source code for this chapter contains a bin directory with two scripts: one (postgres.sh) to download a Docker container and start a default Postgres instance and a second one (psql.sh) to connect to the running Postgres instance. See Table 10-1 for the connection properties to use in your Java application.

■ **Note**   The sample code for this chapter provides scripts in the bin directory to start and connect to a Docker-based PostgreSQL instance. To start the instance and create the database, follow these steps:

1. Execute bin\postgres.sh, which will download and start the Postgres Docker container.

2. Execute bin\psql.sh, which will connect to the running Postgres container.

3. Execute CREATE DATABASE bookstore to create the database to use for the samples.

Table 10-1. *JDBC Properties for Connecting to the Application Database*

Property	Value
Driver class	org.postgresql.Driver
URL	jdbc:postgresql://localhost:5432/bookstore
Username	postgres
Password	password

For your bookshop application, you need a place to store the data. You'll create a simple database to manage books and accounts.

The entity relational (ER) diagram for the tables looks like Figure 10-1.

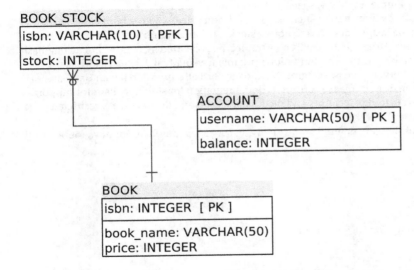

Figure 10-1. *BOOK_STOCK describes how many given BOOKs exist.*

Now, let's create the SQL for the preceding model. Execute the bin\psql.sh command to connect to the running container and open the psql tool.

Paste the following SQL into the shell and verify its success:

```
CREATE TABLE BOOK (
    ISBN        VARCHAR(50)     NOT NULL,
    BOOK_NAME   VARCHAR(100)    NOT NULL,
    PRICE       INT,
    PRIMARY KEY (ISBN)
);
```

```sql
CREATE TABLE BOOK_STOCK (
    ISBN     VARCHAR(50)     NOT NULL,
    STOCK    INT             NOT NULL,
    PRIMARY KEY (ISBN),
    CONSTRAINT positive_stock CHECK (STOCK >= 0)
);

CREATE TABLE ACCOUNT (
    USERNAME    VARCHAR(50)     NOT NULL,
    BALANCE     INT             NOT NULL,
    PRIMARY KEY (USERNAME),
    CONSTRAINT positive_balance CHECK (BALANCE >= 0)
);
```

A real-world application of this type would probably feature a price field with a decimal type, but using an int makes the programming simpler to follow, so leave it as an int.

The BOOK table stores basic book information such as the name and price, with the book ISBN as the primary key. The BOOK_STOCK table keeps track of each book's stock. The stock value is restricted by a CHECK constraint to be a positive number. Although the CHECK constraint type is defined in SQL-99, not all database engines support it. At the time of this writing, this limitation is mainly true of MySQL because Sybase, Derby, HSQL, Oracle, DB2, SQL Server, Access, PostgreSQL, and FireBird all support it. If your database engine doesn't support CHECK constraints, please consult its documentation for similar constraint support. Finally, the ACCOUNT table stores customer accounts and their balances. Again, the balance is restricted to be positive.

The operations of your bookshop are defined in the following BookShop interface. For now, there is only one operation: purchase().

```java
package com.apress.springrecipes.bookshop;

public interface BookShop {

    void purchase(String isbn, String username);
}
```

Because you will implement this interface with JDBC, you need to create the following JdbcBookShop class. To better understand the nature of transactions, let's implement this class without the help of Spring's JDBC support.

```java
package com.apress.springrecipes.bookshop;

import java.sql.Connection;
import java.sql.PreparedStatement;
import java.sql.ResultSet;
import java.sql.SQLException;

import javax.sql.DataSource;

public class JdbcBookShop implements BookShop {
```

```java
    private DataSource dataSource;

    public void setDataSource(DataSource dataSource) {
        this.dataSource = dataSource;
    }

    public void purchase(String isbn, String username) {
        Connection conn = null;
        try {
            conn = dataSource.getConnection();

            PreparedStatement stmt1 = conn.prepareStatement(
                "SELECT PRICE FROM BOOK WHERE ISBN = ?");
            stmt1.setString(1, isbn);
            ResultSet rs = stmt1.executeQuery();
            rs.next();
            int price = rs.getInt("PRICE");
            stmt1.close();

            PreparedStatement stmt2 = conn.prepareStatement(
                "UPDATE BOOK_STOCK SET STOCK = STOCK - 1 "+
                "WHERE ISBN = ?");
            stmt2.setString(1, isbn);
            stmt2.executeUpdate();
            stmt2.close();

            PreparedStatement stmt3 = conn.prepareStatement(
                "UPDATE ACCOUNT SET BALANCE = BALANCE - ? "+
                "WHERE USERNAME = ?");
            stmt3.setInt(1, price);
            stmt3.setString(2, username);
            stmt3.executeUpdate();
            stmt3.close();
        } catch (SQLException e) {
            throw new RuntimeException(e);
        } finally {
            if (conn != null) {
                try {
                    conn.close();
                } catch (SQLException e) {}
            }
        }
    }
}
```

For the purchase() operation, you have to execute three SQL statements in total. The first is to query the book price. The second and third update the book stock and account balance accordingly. Then, you can declare a bookshop instance in the Spring IoC container to provide purchasing services. For simplicity's sake, you can use DriverManagerDataSource, which opens a new connection to the database for every request.

■ **Note**   To access a PostgreSQL database, you have to add the Postgres client library to your CLASSPATH.

```
package com.apress.springrecipes.bookshop.config;

import com.apress.springrecipes.bookshop.BookShop;
import com.apress.springrecipes.bookshop.JdbcBookShop;
import org.springframework.context.annotation.Bean;
import org.springframework.context.annotation.Configuration;
import org.springframework.jdbc.datasource.DriverManagerDataSource;

import javax.sql.DataSource;

@Configuration
public class BookstoreConfiguration {

    @Bean
    public DataSource dataSource() {
        DriverManagerDataSource dataSource = new DriverManagerDataSource();
        dataSource.setDriverClassName(org.postgresql.Driver.class.getName());
        dataSource.setUrl("jdbc:postgresql://localhost:5432/bookstore");
        dataSource.setUsername("postgres");
        dataSource.setPassword("password");
        return dataSource;
    }

    @Bean
    public BookShop bookShop() {
        JdbcBookShop bookShop = new JdbcBookShop();
        bookShop.setDataSource(dataSource());
        return bookShop;
    }
}
```

To demonstrate the problems that can arise without transaction management, suppose you have the data shown in Tables 10-2, 10-3, and 10-4 entered in your bookshop database.

Table 10-2. Sample Data in the BOOK Table for Testing Transactions

ISBN	BOOK_NAME	PRICE
0001	The First Book	30

Table 10-3. Sample Data in the BOOK_STOCK Table for Testing Transactions

ISBN	STOCK
0001	10

Table 10-4. Sample Data in the ACCOUNT Table for Testing Transactions

USERNAME	BALANCE
user1	20

Then, write the following `Main` class for purchasing the book with ISBN 0001 by the user `user1`. Because that user's account has only $20, the funds are not sufficient to purchase the book.

```
package com.apress.springrecipes.bookshop;

import com.apress.springrecipes.bookshop.config.BookstoreConfiguration;
import org.springframework.context.ApplicationContext;
import org.springframework.context.annotation.AnnotationConfigApplicationContext;

public class Main {

    public static void main(String[] args) throws Throwable {

        ApplicationContext context =
            new AnnotationConfigApplicationContext(BookstoreConfiguration.class);

        BookShop bookShop = context.getBean(BookShop.class);
        bookShop.purchase("0001", "user1");

    }
}
```

When you run this application, you will encounter a SQLException, because the CHECK constraint of the ACCOUNT table has been violated. This is an expected result because you were trying to debit more than the account balance.

However, if you check the stock for this book in the BOOK_STOCK table, you will find that it was accidentally deducted by this unsuccessful operation! The reason is that you executed the second SQL statement to deduct the stock before you got an exception in the third statement.

As you can see, the lack of transaction management causes your data to be left in an inconsistent state. To avoid this inconsistency, your three SQL statements for the purchase() operation should be executed within a single transaction. Once any of the actions in a transaction fail, the entire transaction should be rolled back to undo all changes made by the executed actions.

Manage Transactions with JDBC Commit and Rollback

When using JDBC to update a database, by default each SQL statement will be committed immediately after its execution. This behavior is known as *autocommit*. However, it does not allow you to manage transactions for your operations. JDBC supports the primitive transaction management strategy of explicitly calling the commit() and rollback() methods on a connection. But before you can do that, you must turn off autocommit, which is turned on by default.

```
package com.apress.springrecipes.bookshop;
...
public class JdbcBookShop implements BookShop {
    ...
    public void purchase(String isbn, String username) {
        Connection conn = null;
        try {
            conn = dataSource.getConnection();
            conn.setAutoCommit(false);
            ...
            conn.commit();
        } catch (SQLException e) {
            if (conn != null) {
                try {
                    conn.rollback();
                } catch (SQLException e1) {}
            }
            throw new RuntimeException(e);
        } finally {
            if (conn != null) {
                try {
                    conn.close();
                } catch (SQLException e) {}
            }
        }
    }
}
```

The autocommit behavior of a database connection can be altered by calling the setAutoCommit() method. By default, autocommit is turned on to commit each SQL statement immediately after its execution. To enable transaction management, you must turn off this default behavior and commit the connection only when all the SQL statements have been executed successfully. If any of the statements go wrong, you must roll back all changes made by this connection.

Now, if you run your application again, the book stock will not be deducted when the user's balance is insufficient to purchase the book.

Although you can manage transactions by explicitly committing and rolling back JDBC connections, the code required for this purpose is boilerplate code that you have to repeat for different methods. Moreover, this code is JDBC specific, so once you have chosen another data access technology, it needs to be changed also. Spring's transaction support offers a set of technology-independent facilities, including transaction managers (e.g., org.springframework.transaction.PlatformTransactionManager), a transaction template (e.g., org.springframework.transaction.support.TransactionTemplate), and transaction declaration support, to simplify your transaction management tasks.

10-2. Choose a Transaction Manager Implementation

Problem

Typically, if your application involves only a single data source, you can simply manage transactions by calling the commit() and rollback() methods on a database connection. However, if your transactions extend across multiple data sources or you prefer to make use of the transaction management capabilities provided by your Java EE application server, you may choose the Java Transaction API (JTA). In addition, you may have to call different proprietary transaction APIs for different object-relational mapping frameworks such as Hibernate and JPA.

As a result, you have to deal with different transaction APIs for different technologies. It would be hard for you to switch from one set of APIs to another.

Solution

Spring abstracts a general set of transaction facilities from different transaction management APIs. As an application developer, you can simply utilize Spring's transaction facilities without having to know much about the underlying transaction APIs. With these facilities, your transaction management code will be independent of any specific transaction technology.

Spring's core transaction management abstraction is based on the interface PlatformTransactionManager. It encapsulates a set of technology-independent methods for transaction management. Remember that a transaction manager is needed no matter which transaction management strategy (programmatic or declarative) you choose in Spring. The PlatformTransactionManager interface provides three methods for working with transactions:

- `TransactionStatus getTransaction(TransactionDefinition definition) throws TransactionException`

- `void commit(TransactionStatus status) throws TransactionException;`

- `void rollback(TransactionStatus status) throws TransactionException;`

How It Works

PlatformTransactionManager is a general interface for all Spring transaction managers. Spring has several built-in implementations of this interface for use with different transaction management APIs.

- If you have to deal with only a single data source in your application and access it with JDBC, DataSourceTransactionManager should meet your needs.

- If you are using JTA for transaction management on a Java EE application server, you should use JtaTransactionManager to look up a transaction from the application server. Additionally, JtaTransactionManager is appropriate for distributed transactions (transactions that span multiple resources). Note that while it's common to use a JTA transaction manager to integrate the application server's transaction manager, there's nothing stopping you from using a stand-alone JTA transaction manager such as Atomikos.

- If you are using an object-relational mapping framework to access a database, you should choose a corresponding transaction manager for this framework, such as HibernateTransactionManager or JpaTransactionManager.

Figure 10-2 shows the common implementations of the PlatformTransactionManager interface in Spring.

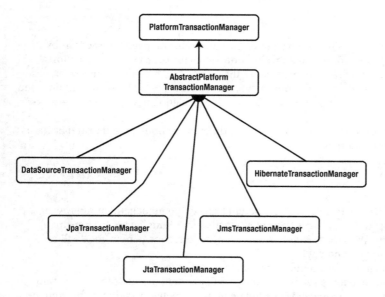

Figure 10-2. *Common implementations of the PlatformTransactionManager interface*

A transaction manager is declared in the Spring IoC container as a normal bean. For example, the following bean configuration declares a DataSourceTransactionManager instance. It requires the dataSource property to be set so that it can manage transactions for connections made by this data source.

```
@Bean
public DataSourceTransactionManager transactionManager() {
    DataSourceTransactionManager transactionManager = new DataSourceTransactionManager()
    transactionManager.setDataSource(dataSource());
    return transactionManager;
}
```

10-3. Manage Transactions Programmatically with the Transaction Manager API

Problem

You need to precisely control when to commit and roll back transactions in your business methods, but you don't want to deal with the underlying transaction API directly.

Solution

Spring's transaction manager provides a technology-independent API that allows you to start a new transaction (or obtain the currently active transaction) by calling the getTransaction() method and manage it by calling the commit() and rollback() methods. Because PlatformTransactionManager is an abstract unit for transaction management, the methods you called for transaction management are guaranteed to be technology independent.

How It Works

To demonstrate how to use the transaction manager API, let's create a new class, TransactionalJdbcBookShop, which will make use of the Spring JDBC template. Because it has to deal with a transaction manager, you add a property of type PlatformTransactionManager and allow it to be injected via a setter method.

```
package com.apress.springrecipes.bookshop;

import org.springframework.dao.DataAccessException;
import org.springframework.jdbc.core.support.JdbcDaoSupport;
import org.springframework.transaction.PlatformTransactionManager;
import org.springframework.transaction.TransactionDefinition;
import org.springframework.transaction.TransactionStatus;
import org.springframework.transaction.support.DefaultTransactionDefinition;

public class TransactionalJdbcBookShop extends JdbcDaoSupport implements BookShop {

    private PlatformTransactionManager transactionManager;

    public void setTransactionManager(PlatformTransactionManager transactionManager) {
        this.transactionManager = transactionManager;
    }

    public void purchase(String isbn, String username) {
        TransactionDefinition def = new DefaultTransactionDefinition();
        TransactionStatus status = transactionManager.getTransaction(def);

        try {
            int price = getJdbcTemplate().queryForObject(
                "SELECT PRICE FROM BOOK WHERE ISBN = ?", Integer.class, isbn);

            getJdbcTemplate().update(
                "UPDATE BOOK_STOCK SET STOCK = STOCK - 1 WHERE ISBN = ?", isbn);

            getJdbcTemplate().update(
                "UPDATE ACCOUNT SET BALANCE = BALANCE - ? WHERE USERNAME = ?",
                price, username);
```

```
            transactionManager.commit(status);
        } catch (DataAccessException e) {
            transactionManager.rollback(status);
            throw e;
        }
    }
}
```

Before you start a new transaction, you have to specify the transaction attributes in a transaction definition object of type TransactionDefinition. For this example, you can simply create an instance of DefaultTransactionDefinition to use the default transaction attributes.

Once you have a transaction definition, you can ask the transaction manager to start a new transaction with that definition by calling the getTransaction() method. Then, it will return a TransactionStatus object to keep track of the transaction status. If all the statements execute successfully, you ask the transaction manager to commit this transaction by passing in the transaction status. Because all exceptions thrown by the Spring JDBC template are subclasses of DataAccessException, you ask the transaction manager to roll back the transaction when this kind of exception is caught.

In this class, you have declared the transaction manager property of the general type PlatformTransactionManager. Now, you have to inject an appropriate transaction manager implementation. Because you are dealing with only a single data source and accessing it with JDBC, you should choose DataSourceTransactionManager. Here, you also wire a dataSource object because the class is a subclass of Spring's JdbcDaoSupport, which requires it.

```
@Configuration
public class BookstoreConfiguration {
...
    @Bean
    public DataSourceTransactionManager transactionManager() {
        DataSourceTransactionManager transactionManager =
            new DataSourceTransactionManager();
        transactionManager.setDataSource(dataSource());
        return transactionManager;
    }

    @Bean
    public BookShop bookShop() {
        TransactionalJdbcBookShop bookShop = new TransactionalJdbcBookShop();
        bookShop.setDataSource(dataSource());
        bookShop.setTransactionManager(transactionManager());
        return bookShop;
    }
}
```

10-4. Manage Transactions Programmatically with a Transaction Template

Problem

Suppose that you have a code block, but not the entire body, of a business method that has the following transaction requirements:

- Start a new transaction at the beginning of the block.

- Commit the transaction after the block completes successfully.

- Roll back the transaction if an exception is thrown in the block.

If you call Spring's transaction manager API directly, the transaction management code can be generalized in a technology-independent manner. However, you may not want to repeat the boilerplate code for each similar code block.

Solution

As with the JDBC template, Spring also provides a TransactionTemplate to help you control the overall transaction management process and transaction exception handling. You just have to encapsulate your code block in a callback class that implements the TransactionCallback<T> interface and pass it to the TransactionTemplate's execute method for execution. In this way, you don't need to repeat the boilerplate transaction management code for this block. The template objects that Spring provides are lightweight and usually can be discarded or re-created with no performance impact. A JDBC template can be re-created on the fly with a DataSource reference, for example, and so too can a TransactionTemplate be re-created by providing a reference to a transaction manager. You can, of course, simply create one in your Spring application context, too.

How It Works

A TransactionTemplate is created on a transaction manager just as a JDBC template is created on a data source. A transaction template executes a transaction callback object that encapsulates a transactional code block. You can implement the callback interface either as a separate class or as an inner class. If it's implemented as an inner class, you have to make the method arguments final for it to access.

```
package com.apress.springrecipes.bookshop;

import org.springframework.jdbc.core.support.JdbcDaoSupport;
import org.springframework.transaction.PlatformTransactionManager;
import org.springframework.transaction.TransactionStatus;
import org.springframework.transaction.support.TransactionCallbackWithoutResult;
import org.springframework.transaction.support.TransactionTemplate;

public class TransactionalJdbcBookShop extends JdbcDaoSupport implements BookShop {

    private PlatformTransactionManager transactionManager;

    public void setTransactionManager(PlatformTransactionManager transactionManager) {
        this.transactionManager = transactionManager;
    }
}
```

```java
public void purchase(final String isbn, final String username) {

    TransactionTemplate transactionTemplate =
        new TransactionTemplate(transactionManager);

    transactionTemplate.execute(new TransactionCallbackWithoutResult() {

        protected void doInTransactionWithoutResult(
            TransactionStatus status) {

            int price = getJdbcTemplate().queryForObject(
                "SELECT PRICE FROM BOOK WHERE ISBN = ?", Integer.class, isbn);

            getJdbcTemplate().update(
                "UPDATE BOOK_STOCK SET STOCK = STOCK - 1 WHERE ISBN = ?", isbn );

            getJdbcTemplate().update(
                "UPDATE ACCOUNT SET BALANCE = BALANCE - ? WHERE USERNAME = ?",
                price, username);
        }
    });
}
```

A TransactionTemplate can accept a transaction callback object that implements either the TransactionCallback<T> or an instance of the one implementer of that interface provided by the framework, the TransactionCallbackWithoutResult class. For the code block in the purchase() method for deducting the book stock and account balance, there's no result to be returned, so TransactionCallbackWithoutResult is fine. For any code blocks with return values, you should implement the TransactionCallback<T> interface instead. The return value of the callback object will finally be returned by the template's T execute() method. The main benefit is that the responsibility of starting, rolling back, or committing the transaction has been removed.

During the execution of the callback object, if it throws an unchecked exception (e.g., RuntimeException and DataAccessException fall into this category) or if you explicitly called setRollbackOnly() on the TransactionStatus argument in the doInTransactionWithoutResult method, the transaction will be rolled back. Otherwise, it will be committed after the callback object completes.

In the bean configuration file, the bookshop bean still requires a transaction manager to create a TransactionTemplate.

```java
@Configuration
public class BookstoreConfiguration {
...
    @Bean
    public DataSourceTransactionManager transactionManager() {
        DataSourceTransactionManager transactionManager =
            new DataSourceTransactionManager();
        transactionManager.setDataSource(dataSource());
        return transactionManager;
    }
```

```
    @Bean
    public BookShop bookShop() {
        TransactionalJdbcBookShop bookShop = new TransactionalJdbcBookShop();
        bookShop.setDataSource(dataSource());
        bookShop.setTransactionManager(transactionManager());
        return bookShop;
    }
}
```

You can also have the IoC container inject a transaction template instead of creating it directly. Because a transaction template handles all transactions, there's no need for your class to refer to the transaction manager anymore.

```
package com.apress.springrecipes.bookshop;
...
import org.springframework.transaction.support.TransactionTemplate;

public class TransactionalJdbcBookShop extends JdbcDaoSupport implements
    BookShop {

    private TransactionTemplate transactionTemplate;

    public void setTransactionTemplate(
        TransactionTemplate transactionTemplate) {
        this.transactionTemplate = transactionTemplate;
    }

    public void purchase(final String isbn, final String username) {
        transactionTemplate.execute(new TransactionCallbackWithoutResult() {
            protected void doInTransactionWithoutResult(TransactionStatus status) {
                ...
            }
        });
    }
}
```

Then you define a transaction template in the bean configuration file and inject it, instead of the transaction manager, into your bookshop bean. Notice that the transaction template instance can be used for more than one transactional bean because it is a thread-safe object. Finally, don't forget to set the transaction manager property for your transaction template.

```
package com.apress.springrecipes.bookshop.config;
...
import org.springframework.transaction.support.TransactionTemplate;

@Configuration
public class BookstoreConfiguration {
...
    @Bean
    public DataSourceTransactionManager transactionManager() { ... }
```

```
    @Bean
    public TransactionTemplate transactionTemplate() {
        TransactionTemplate transactionTemplate = new TransactionTemplate();
        transactionTemplate.setTransactionManager(transactionManager());
        return transactionTemplate;
    }

    @Bean
    public BookShop bookShop() {
        TransactionalJdbcBookShop bookShop = new TransactionalJdbcBookShop();
        bookShop.setDataSource(dataSource());
        bookShop.setTransactionTemplate(transactionTemplate());
        return bookShop;
    }
}
```

10-5. Manage Transactions Declaratively with the @Transactional Annotation

Problem

Declaring transactions in the bean configuration file requires knowledge of AOP concepts such as pointcuts, advices, and advisors. Developers who lack this knowledge might find it hard to enable declarative transaction management.

Solution

Spring allows you to declare transactions simply by annotating your transactional methods with @Transactional and adding the @EnableTransactionManegement annotation to your configuration class.

How It Works

To define a method as transactional, you can simply annotate it with @Transactional. Note that you should only annotate public methods because of the proxy-based limitations of Spring AOP.

```
package com.apress.springrecipes.bookshop;

import org.springframework.jdbc.core.support.JdbcDaoSupport;
import org.springframework.transaction.annotation.Transactional;

public class JdbcBookShop extends JdbcDaoSupport implements BookShop {

    @Transactional
    public void purchase(final String isbn, final String username) {

        int price = getJdbcTemplate().queryForObject(
            "SELECT PRICE FROM BOOK WHERE ISBN = ?", Integer.class, isbn);
```

```
        getJdbcTemplate().update(
            "UPDATE BOOK_STOCK SET STOCK = STOCK - 1 WHERE ISBN = ?", isbn);

        getJdbcTemplate().update(
            "UPDATE ACCOUNT SET BALANCE = BALANCE - ? WHERE USERNAME = ?", price, username);
    }
}
```

Note that because you are extending JdbcDaoSupport, you no longer need the setter for the DataSource; remove it from your DAO class.

You may apply the @Transactional annotation at the method level or the class level. When applying this annotation to a class, all the public methods within this class will be defined as transactional. Although you can apply @Transactional to interfaces or method declarations in an interface, it's not recommended because it may not work properly with class-based proxies (i.e., CGLIB proxies).

In the Java configuration class, you only have to add the @EnableTransactionManagement annotation. That's all you need to make it work. Spring will advise methods with @Transactional, or methods in a class with @Transactional, from beans declared in the IoC container. As a result, Spring can manage transactions for these methods.

```
@Configuration
@EnableTransactionManagement
public class BookstoreConfiguration {  ... }
```

10-6. Set the Propagation Transaction Attribute

Problem

When a transactional method is called by another method, it is necessary to specify how the transaction should be propagated. For example, the method may continue to run within the existing transaction, or it may start a new transaction and run within its own transaction.

Solution

A transaction's propagation behavior can be specified by the propagation transaction attribute. Spring defines seven propagation behaviors, as shown in Table 10-5. These behaviors are defined in the org. springframework.transaction.TransactionDefinition interface. Note that not all types of transaction managers support all of these propagation behaviors. Their behavior is contingent on the underlying resource. Databases, for example, may support varying isolation levels, which constrains what propagation behaviors the transaction manager can support.

Table 10-5. *Propagation Behaviors Supported by Spring*

Propagation	Description
REQUIRED	If there's an existing transaction in progress, the current method should run within this transaction. Otherwise, it should start a new transaction and run within its own transaction.
REQUIRES_NEW	The current method must start a new transaction and run within its own transaction. If there's an existing transaction in progress, it should be suspended.
SUPPORTS	If there's an existing transaction in progress, the current method can run within this transaction. Otherwise, it is not necessary to run within a transaction.
NOT_SUPPORTED	The current method should not run within a transaction. If there's an existing transaction in progress, it should be suspended.
MANDATORY	The current method must run within a transaction. If there's no existing transaction in progress, an exception will be thrown.
NEVER	The current method should not run within a transaction. If there's an existing transaction in progress, an exception will be thrown.
NESTED	If there's an existing transaction in progress, the current method should run within the nested transaction (supported by the JDBC 3.0 savepoint feature) of this transaction. Otherwise, it should start a new transaction and run within its own transaction. This feature is unique to Spring (whereas the previous propagation behaviors have analogs in Java EE transaction propagation). The behavior is useful for situations such as batch processing, in which you've got a long-running process (imagine processing 1 million records) and you want to chunk the commits on the batch. So, you commit every 10,000 records. If something goes wrong, you roll back the nested transaction and you've lost only 10,000 records worth of work (as opposed to the entire 1 million).

How It Works

Transaction propagation happens when a transactional method is called by another method. For example, suppose a customer would like to check out all books to purchase at the bookshop cashier. To support this operation, you define the Cashier interface as follows:

```
package com.apress.springrecipes.bookshop;
...
public interface Cashier {

    public void checkout(List<String> isbns, String username);
}
```

You can implement this interface by delegating the purchases to a bookshop bean by calling its purchase() method multiple times. Note that the checkout() method is made transactional by applying the @Transactional annotation.

```
package com.apress.springrecipes.bookshop;
...
import org.springframework.transaction.annotation.Transactional;

public class BookShopCashier implements Cashier {

    private BookShop bookShop;

    public void setBookShop(BookShop bookShop) {
        this.bookShop = bookShop;
    }

    @Transactional
    public void checkout(List<String> isbns, String username) {
        for (String isbn : isbns) {
            bookShop.purchase(isbn, username);
        }
    }
}
```

Then define a cashier bean in your bean configuration file and refer to the bookshop bean for purchasing books.

```
@Configuration
@EnableTransactionManagement()
public class BookstoreConfiguration {
...

    @Bean
    public Cashier cashier() {
        BookShopCashier cashier = new BookShopCashier();
        cashier.setBookShop(bookShop());
        return cashier;
    }
}
```

To illustrate the propagation behavior of a transaction, enter the data shown in Tables 10-6, 10-7, and 10-8 in your bookshop database.

Table 10-6. Sample Data in the BOOK Table for Testing Propagation Behaviors

ISBN	BOOK_NAME	PRICE
0001	The First Book	30
0002	The Second Book	50

Table 10-7. *Sample Data in the BOOK_STOCK Table for Testing Propagation Behaviors*

ISBN	STOCK
0001	10
0002	10

Table 10-8. *Sample Data in the ACCOUNT Table for Testing Propagation Behaviors*

USERNAME	BALANCE
user1	40

Use the REQUIRED Propagation Behavior

When the user user1 checks out two books from the cashier, the balance is sufficient to purchase the first book but not the second.

```
package com.apress.springrecipes.bookshop.spring;
...
public class Main {

    public static void main(String[] args) {
        ...
        Cashier cashier = context.getBean(Cashier.class);
        List<String> isbnList = Arrays.asList(new String[] { "0001", "0002"});
        cashier.checkout(isbnList, "user1");
    }
}
```

When the bookshop's purchase() method is called by another transactional method, such as checkout(), it will run within the existing transaction by default. This default propagation behavior is called REQUIRED. That means there will be only one transaction whose boundary is the beginning and ending of the checkout() method. This transaction will be committed only at the end of the checkout() method. As a result, the user can purchase none of the books.

Figure 10-3 illustrates the REQUIRED propagation behavior.

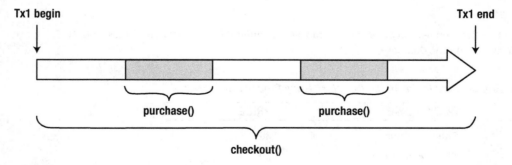

Figure 10-3. *The REQUIRED transaction propagation behavior*

However, if the purchase() method is called by a nontransactional method and there's no existing transaction in progress, it will start a new transaction and run within its own transaction. The propagation transaction attribute can be defined in the @Transactional annotation. For example, you can set the REQUIRED behavior for this attribute as follows. In fact, this is unnecessary, because it's the default behavior.

```
package com.apress.springrecipes.bookshop.spring;
...
import org.springframework.transaction.annotation.Propagation;
import org.springframework.transaction.annotation.Transactional;

public class JdbcBookShop extends JdbcDaoSupport implements BookShop {
    @Transactional(propagation = Propagation.REQUIRED)
    public void purchase(String isbn, String username) {
        ...
    }
}
package com.apress.springrecipes.bookshop.spring;
...
import org.springframework.transaction.annotation.Propagation;
import org.springframework.transaction.annotation.Transactional;

public class BookShopCashier implements Cashier {
    ...
    @Transactional(propagation = Propagation.REQUIRED)
    public void checkout(List<String> isbns, String username) {
        ...
    }
}
```

Use the REQUIRES_NEW Propagation Behavior

Another common propagation behavior is REQUIRES_NEW. This indicates that the method must start a new transaction and run within its new transaction. If there's an existing transaction in progress, it should be suspended first (for example, with the checkout method on BookShopCashier, with a propagation of REQUIRED).

```
package com.apress.springrecipes.bookshop.spring;
...
import org.springframework.transaction.annotation.Propagation;
import org.springframework.transaction.annotation.Transactional;

public class JdbcBookShop extends JdbcDaoSupport implements BookShop {
    @Transactional(propagation = Propagation.REQUIRES_NEW)
    public void purchase(String isbn, String username) {
        ...
    }
}
```

In this case, there will be three transactions started in total. The first transaction is started by the checkout() method, but when the first purchase() method is called, the first transaction will be suspended, and a new transaction will be started. At the end of the first purchase() method, the new transaction completes and commits. When the second `purchase()` method is called, another new transaction will be started. However, this transaction will fail and roll back. As a result, the first book will be purchased successfully, while the second will not. Figure 10-4 illustrates the `REQUIRES_NEW` propagation behavior.

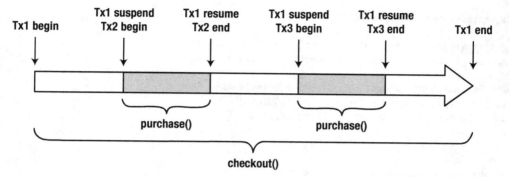

Figure 10-4. The REQUIRES_NEW transaction propagation behavior

10-7. Set the Isolation Transaction Attribute

Problem

When multiple transactions of the same application or different applications are operating concurrently on the same data set, many unexpected problems may arise. You must specify how you expect your transactions to be isolated from one another.

Solution

The problems caused by concurrent transactions can be categorized into four types.

- *Dirty read*: For the two transactions T1 and T2, T1 reads a field that has been updated by T2 but not yet committed. Later, if T2 rolls back, the field read by T1 will be temporary and invalid.

- *Nonrepeatable read*: For the two transactions T1 and T2, T1 reads a field and then T2 updates the field. Later, if T1 reads the same field again, the value will be different.

- *Phantom read*: For the two transactions T1 and T2, T1 reads some rows from a table, and then T2 inserts new rows into the table. Later, if T1 reads the same table again, there will be additional rows.

- *Lost updates*: For the two transactions T1 and T2, they both select a row for update and, based on the state of that row, make an update to it. Thus, one overwrites the other when the second transaction to commit should have waited until the first one committed before performing its selection.

In theory, transactions should be completely isolated from each other (i.e., serializable) to avoid all the mentioned problems. However, this isolation level will have great impact on performance because transactions have to run in serial order. In practice, transactions can run in lower isolation levels in order to improve performance.

A transaction's isolation level can be specified by the isolation transaction attribute. Spring supports five isolation levels, as shown in Table 10-9. These levels are defined in the org.springframework.transaction. TransactionDefinition interface.

Table 10-9. *Isolation Levels Supported by Spring*

Isolation	Description
DEFAULT	Uses the default isolation level of the underlying database. For most databases, the default isolation level is READ_COMMITTED.
READ_UNCOMMITTED	Allows a transaction to read uncommitted changes by other transactions. The dirty read, nonrepeatable read, and phantom read problems may occur.
READ_COMMITTED	Allows a transaction to read only those changes that have been committed by other transactions. The dirty read problem can be avoided, but the nonrepeatable read and phantom read problems may still occur.
REPEATABLE_READ	Ensures that a transaction can read identical values from a field multiple times. For the duration of this transaction, updates made by other transactions to this field are prohibited. The dirty read and nonrepeatable read problems can be avoided, but the phantom read problem may still occur.
SERIALIZABLE	Ensures that a transaction can read identical rows from a table multiple times. For the duration of this transaction, inserts, updates, and deletes made by other transactions to this table are prohibited. All the concurrency problems can be avoided, but the performance will be low.

■ **Note** Transaction isolation is supported by the underlying database engine but not an application or a framework. However, not all database engines support all these isolation levels. You can change the isolation level of a JDBC connection by calling the setTransactionIsolation() method on the java.sql.Connection interface.

How It Works

To illustrate the problems caused by concurrent transactions, let's add two new operations to your bookshop for increasing and checking the book stock.

```
package com.apress.springrecipes.bookshop;

public interface BookShop {
    ...
    public void increaseStock(String isbn, int stock);
    public int checkStock(String isbn);
}
```

Then, you implement these operations as follows. Note that these two operations should also be declared as transactional.

```
package com.apress.springrecipes.bookshop;

import org.springframework.jdbc.core.support.JdbcDaoSupport;
import org.springframework.transaction.annotation.Isolation;
import org.springframework.transaction.annotation.Transactional;

public class JdbcBookShop extends JdbcDaoSupport implements BookShop {

    @Transactional
    public void purchase(String isbn, String username) {
        int price = getJdbcTemplate().queryForObject(
            "SELECT PRICE FROM BOOK WHERE ISBN = ?", Integer.class, isbn);

        getJdbcTemplate().update(
            "UPDATE BOOK_STOCK SET STOCK = STOCK - 1 WHERE ISBN = ?", isbn );

        getJdbcTemplate().update(
            "UPDATE ACCOUNT SET BALANCE = BALANCE - ? WHERE USERNAME = ?",
            price, username);
    }

    @Transactional
    public void increaseStock(String isbn, int stock) {
        String threadName = Thread.currentThread().getName();
        System.out.println(threadName + " - Prepare to increase book stock");

        getJdbcTemplate().update("UPDATE BOOK_STOCK SET STOCK = STOCK + ?
        WHERE ISBN = ?", stock, isbn);

        System.out.println(threadName + " - Book stock increased by " + stock);
        sleep(threadName);

        System.out.println(threadName + " - Book stock rolled back");
        throw new RuntimeException("Increased by mistake");
    }

    @Transactional(isolation = Isolation.READ_UNCOMMITTED)
    public int checkStock(String isbn) {
        String threadName = Thread.currentThread().getName();
        System.out.println(threadName + " - Prepare to check book stock");

        int stock = getJdbcTemplate().queryForObject("SELECT STOCK FROM BOOK_STOCK
        WHERE ISBN = ?", Integer.class, isbn);

        System.out.println(threadName + " - Book stock is " + stock);
        sleep(threadName);

        return stock;
    }
```

```
private void sleep(String threadName) {
    System.out.println(threadName + " - Sleeping");

    try {
        Thread.sleep(10000);
    } catch (InterruptedException e) {
    }

    System.out.println(threadName + " - Wake up");
    }
}
```

To simulate concurrency, your operations need to be executed by multiple threads. You can track the current status of the operations through the println statements. For each operation, you print a couple of messages to the console around the SQL statement's execution. The messages should include the thread name for you to know which thread is currently executing the operation.

After each operation executes the SQL statement, you ask the thread to sleep for ten seconds. As you know, the transaction will be committed or rolled back immediately once the operation completes. Inserting a sleep statement can help to postpone the commit or rollback. For the increase() operation, you eventually throw a RuntimeException to cause the transaction to roll back. Let's look at a simple client that runs these examples.

Before you start with the isolation-level examples, enter the data from Tables 10-10 and 10-11 into your bookshop database. (Note that the ACCOUNT table isn't needed in this example.)

Table 10-10. Sample Data in the BOOK Table for Testing Isolation Levels

ISBN	BOOK_NAME	PRICE
0001	The First Book	30

Table 10-11. Sample Data in the BOOK_STOCK Table for Testing Isolation Levels

ISBN	STOCK
0001	10

Use the READ_UNCOMMITTED and READ_COMMITTED Isolation Levels

READ_UNCOMMITTED is the lowest isolation level that allows a transaction to read uncommitted changes made by other transactions. You can set this isolation level in the @Transaction annotation of your checkStock() method.

```
package com.apress.springrecipes.bookshop.spring;
...
import org.springframework.transaction.annotation.Isolation;
import org.springframework.transaction.annotation.Transactional;
```

439

```java
public class JdbcBookShop extends JdbcDaoSupport implements BookShop {
    ...
    @Transactional(isolation = Isolation.READ_UNCOMMITTED)
    public int checkStock(String isbn) {
        ...
    }
}
```

You can create some threads to experiment on this transaction isolation level. In the following Main class, there are two threads you are going to create. Thread 1 increases the book stock, while thread 2 checks the book stock. Thread 1 starts 5 seconds before thread 2.

```java
package com.apress.springrecipes.bookshop.spring;
...
public class Main {

    public static void main(String[] args) {
        ...
        final BookShop bookShop = context.getBean(BookShop.class);

        Thread thread1 = new Thread(() -> {
            try {
                bookShop.increaseStock("0001", 5);
            } catch (RuntimeException e) {}
        }, "Thread 1");

        Thread thread2 = new Thread(() -> {
            bookShop.checkStock("0001");
        }, "Thread 2");

        thread1.start();
        try {
            Thread.sleep(5000);
        } catch (InterruptedException e) {}
            thread2.start();
    }
}
```

If you run the application, you will get the following result:

```
Thread 1—Prepare to increase book stock
Thread 1—Book stock increased by 5
Thread 1—Sleeping
Thread 2—Prepare to check book stock
Thread 2—Book stock is 15
Thread 2—Sleeping
Thread 1—Wake up
Thread 1—Book stock rolled back
Thread 2—Wake up
```

First, thread 1 increased the book stock and then went to sleep. At that time, thread 1's transaction had not yet been rolled back. While thread 1 was sleeping, thread 2 started and attempted to read the book stock. With the READ_UNCOMMITTED isolation level, thread 2 would be able to read the stock value that had been updated by an uncommitted transaction.

However, when thread 1 wakes up, its transaction will be rolled back because of a RuntimeException, so the value read by thread 2 is temporary and invalid. This problem is known as a *dirty read* because a transaction may read values that are "dirty."

To avoid the dirty read problem, you should raise the isolation level of checkStock() to READ_COMMITTED.

```
package com.apress.springrecipes.bookshop.spring;
...
import org.springframework.transaction.annotation.Isolation;
import org.springframework.transaction.annotation.Transactional;

public class JdbcBookShop extends JdbcDaoSupport implements BookShop {
    ...
    @Transactional(isolation = Isolation.READ_COMMITTED)
    public int checkStock(String isbn) {
        ...
    }
}
```

If you run the application again, thread 2 won't be able to read the book stock until thread 1 has rolled back the transaction. In this way, the dirty read problem can be avoided by preventing a transaction from reading a field that has been updated by another uncommitted transaction.

```
Thread 1—Prepare to increase book stock
Thread 1—Book stock increased by 5
Thread 1—Sleeping
Thread 2—Prepare to check book stock
Thread 1—Wake up
Thread 1—Book stock rolled back
Thread 2—Book stock is 10
Thread 2—Sleeping
Thread 2—Wake up
```

For the underlying database to support the READ_COMMITTED isolation level, it may acquire an update lock on a row that was updated but not yet committed. Then, other transactions must wait to read that row until the update lock is released, which happens when the locking transaction commits or rolls back.

Use the REPEATABLE_READ Isolation Level

Now, let's restructure the threads to demonstrate another concurrency problem. Swap the tasks of the two threads so that thread 1 checks the book stock before thread 2 increases the book stock.

```
package com.apress.springrecipes.bookshop.spring;
...
public class Main {

    public static void main(String[] args) {
        ...
        final BookShop bookShop = (BookShop) context.getBean("bookShop");

        Thread thread1 = new Thread(() -> {
            public void run() {
                bookShop.checkStock("0001");
            }
        }, "Thread 1");

        Thread thread2 = new Thread(() -> {
            try {
                bookShop.increaseStock("0001", 5);
            } catch (RuntimeException e) {}
        }, "Thread 2");

        thread1.start();
        try {
            Thread.sleep(5000);
        } catch (InterruptedException e) {}
            thread2.start();
    }
}
```

If you run the application, you will get the following result:

```
Thread 1—Prepare to check book stock
Thread 1—Book stock is 10
Thread 1—Sleeping
Thread 2—Prepare to increase book stock
Thread 2—Book stock increased by 5
Thread 2—Sleeping
Thread 1—Wake up
Thread 2—Wake up
Thread 2—Book stock rolled back
```

First, thread 1 read the book stock and then went to sleep. At that time, thread 1's transaction had not yet been committed. While thread 1 was sleeping, thread 2 started and attempted to increase the book stock. With the READ_COMMITTED isolation level, thread 2 would be able to update the stock value that was read by an uncommitted transaction.

However, if thread 1 reads the book stock again, the value will be different from its first read. This problem is known as a *nonrepeatable read* because a transaction may read different values for the same field.

To avoid the nonrepeatable read problem, you should raise the isolation level of checkStock() to REPEATABLE_READ.

```
package com.apress.springrecipes.bookshop.spring;
...
import org.springframework.transaction.annotation.Isolation;
import org.springframework.transaction.annotation.Transactional;

public class JdbcBookShop extends JdbcDaoSupport implements BookShop {
    ...
    @Transactional(isolation = Isolation.REPEATABLE_READ)
    public int checkStock(String isbn) {
        ...
    }
}
```

If you run the application again, thread 2 won't be able to update the book stock until thread 1 has committed the transaction. In this way, the nonrepeatable read problem can be avoided by preventing a transaction from updating a value that has been read by another uncommitted transaction.

```
Thread 1—Prepare to check book stock
Thread 1—Book stock is 10
Thread 1—Sleeping
Thread 2—Prepare to increase book stock
Thread 1—Wake up
Thread 2—Book stock increased by 5
Thread 2—Sleeping
Thread 2—Wake up
Thread 2—Book stock rolled back
```

For the underlying database to support the REPEATABLE_READ isolation level, it may acquire a read lock on a row that was read but not yet committed. Then, other transactions must wait to update the row until the read lock is released, which happens when the locking transaction commits or rolls back.

Use the SERIALIZABLE Isolation Level

After a transaction has read several rows from a table, another transaction inserts new rows into the same table. If the first transaction reads the same table again, it will find additional rows that are different from the first read. This problem is known as a *phantom read*. Actually, a phantom read is very similar to a nonrepeatable read but involves multiple rows.

To avoid the phantom read problem, you should raise the isolation level to the highest: SERIALIZABLE. Notice that this isolation level is the slowest because it may acquire a read lock on the full table. In practice, you should always choose the lowest isolation level that can satisfy your requirements.

10-8. Set the Rollback Transaction Attribute

Problem

By default, only unchecked exceptions (i.e., of type RuntimeException and Error) will cause a transaction to roll back, while checked exceptions will not. Sometimes, you may want to break this rule and set your own exceptions for rolling back.

Solution

The exceptions that cause a transaction to roll back or not can be specified by the rollback transaction attribute. Any exceptions not explicitly specified in this attribute will be handled by the default rollback rule (i.e., rolling back for unchecked exceptions and not rolling back for checked exceptions).

How It Works

A transaction's rollback rule can be defined in the @Transactional annotation via the rollbackFor and noRollbackFor attributes. These two attributes are declared as Class[], so you can specify more than one exception for each attribute.

```
package com.apress.springrecipes.bookshop.spring;
...
import org.springframework.transaction.annotation.Propagation;
import org.springframework.transaction.annotation.Transactional;
import java.io.IOException;

public class JdbcBookShop extends JdbcDaoSupport implements BookShop {
    ...
    @Transactional(
        propagation = Propagation.REQUIRES_NEW,
        rollbackFor = IOException.class,
        noRollbackFor = ArithmeticException.class)
    public void purchase(String isbn, String username) throws Exception {
        throw new ArithmeticException();
    }
}
```

10-9. Set the Timeout and Read-Only Transaction Attributes

Problem

Because a transaction may acquire locks on rows and tables, a long transaction will tie up resources and have an impact on overall performance. Besides, if a transaction only reads but does not update data, the database engine could optimize this transaction. You can specify these attributes to increase the performance of your application.

Solution

The timeout transaction attribute (an integer that describes seconds) indicates how long your transaction can survive before it is forced to roll back. This can prevent a long transaction from tying up resources. The read-only attribute indicates that this transaction will only read but not update data. The read-only flag is just a hint to enable a resource to optimize the transaction, and a resource might not necessarily cause a failure if a write is attempted.

How It Works

The timeout and read-only transaction attributes can be defined in the @Transactional annotation. Note that the timeout is measured in seconds.

```
package com.apress.springrecipes.bookshop.spring;
...
import org.springframework.transaction.annotation.Isolation;
import org.springframework.transaction.annotation.Transactional;

public class JdbcBookShop extends JdbcDaoSupport implements BookShop {
    ...
    @Transactional(
        isolation = Isolation.REPEATABLE_READ,
        timeout = 30,
        readOnly = true)
    public int checkStock(String isbn) {
        ...
    }
}
```

10-10. Manage Transactions with Load-Time Weaving

Problem

By default, Spring's declarative transaction management is enabled via its AOP framework. However, as Spring AOP can only advise public methods of beans declared in the IoC container, you are restricted to managing transactions within this scope using Spring AOP. Sometimes you may want to manage transactions for nonpublic methods, or methods of objects created outside the Spring IoC container (e.g., domain objects).

Solution

Spring provides an AspectJ aspect named AnnotationTransactionAspect that can manage transactions for any methods of any objects, even if the methods are nonpublic or the objects are created outside the Spring IoC container. This aspect will manage transactions for any methods with the @Transactional annotation. You can choose either AspectJ's compile-time weaving or load-time weaving to enable this aspect.

How It Works

To weave this aspect into your domain classes at load time, you have to put the @EnableLoadTimeWeaving annotation on your configuration class. To enable Spring's AnnotationTransactionAspect for transaction management, you just define the @EnableTransactionManagement annotation and set its mode attribute to ASPECTJ. The @EnableTransactionManagement annotation takes two values for the mode attribute: ASPECTJ and PROXY. ASPECTJ stipulates that the container should use load-time or compile-time weaving to enable the transaction advice. This requires the spring-instrument JAR to be on the classpath, as well as the appropriate configuration at load time or compile time.

Alternatively, PROXY stipulates that the container should use the Spring AOP mechanisms. It's important to note that the ASPECTJ mode doesn't support the configuration of the @Transactional annotation on interfaces. Then the transaction aspect will automatically get enabled. You also have to provide a transaction manager for this aspect. By default, it will look for a transaction manager whose name is transactionManager.

```
package com.apress.springrecipes.bookshop;

Configuration
@EnableTransactionManagement(mode = AdviceMode.ASPECTJ)
@EnableLoadTimeWeaving
public class BookstoreConfiguration { ... }
```

■ **Note**   To use the Spring aspect library for AspectJ, you have to include the spring-aspects module on your CLASSPATH. To enable load-time weaving, you also have to include a Java agent, which is available in the spring-instrument module.

For a simple Java application, you can weave this aspect into your classes at load time with the Spring agent specified as a VM argument.

```
java -javaagent:lib/spring-instrument-5.0.0.RELEASE.jar -jar recipe_10_10_i.jar
```

Summary

This chapter discussed transactions and why you should use them. You explored the approach taken for transaction management historically in Java EE and then learned how the approach the Spring framework offers differs. You explored the explicit use of transactions in your code as well as the implicit use with annotation-driven aspects. You set up a database and used transactions to enforce valid state in the database.

In the next chapter, you will explore Spring Batch. Spring Batch provides infrastructure and components that can be used as the foundation for batch processing jobs.

CHAPTER 11

■ ■ ■

Spring Batch

Batch processing has been around for decades. The earliest widespread applications of technology for managing information (information technology) were applications of batch processing. These environments didn't have interactive sessions and usually didn't have the capability to load multiple applications in memory. Computers were expensive and bore no resemblance to today's servers. Typically, machines were multiuser and in use during the day (time-shared). During the evening, however, the machines would sit idle, which was a tremendous waste. Businesses invested in ways to utilize the offline time to do work aggregated through the course of the day. Out of this practice emerged batch processing.

Batch processing solutions typically run offline, unaware of events in the system. In the past, batch processes ran offline out of necessity. Today, however, most batch processes are run offline because having work done at a predictable time and having chunks of work done are requirements for lots of architectures. A batch processing solution doesn't usually respond to requests, although there's no reason it couldn't be started as a consequence of a message or request. Batch processing solutions tend to be used on large data sets where the duration of the processing is a critical factor in its architecture and implementation. A process might run for minutes, hours, or days! Jobs may have unbounded durations (i.e., run until all work is finished, even if this means running for a few days), or they may be strictly bounded (jobs must proceed in constant time, with each row taking the same amount of time regardless of bound, which lets you, say, predict that a given job will finish in a certain time window).

Batch processing has had a long history that informs even modern batch processing solutions.

Mainframe applications used batch processing, and one of the largest modern-day environments for batch processing, CICS on z/OS, is still fundamentally a mainframe operating system. Customer Information Control System (CICS) is very well suited to a particular type of task: take input, process it, and write it to output. CICS is a transaction server used most in financial institutions and government that runs programs in a number of languages (COBOL, C, PLI, and so on). It can easily support thousands of transactions per second. CICS was one of the first containers, a concept familiar to Spring and Java EE users, even though CICS itself debuted in 1969! A CICS installation is very expensive, and although IBM still sells and installs CICS, many other solutions have come along since then. These solutions are usually specific to a particular environment: COBOL/CICS on mainframes, C on Unix, and, today, Java on any number of environments. The problem is that there's very little standardized infrastructure for dealing with these types of batch processing solutions. Few people are even aware of what they're missing because there's very little native support on the Java platform for batch processing. Businesses that need a solution typically end up writing it in-house, resulting in fragile, domain-specific code.

The pieces are there, however: transaction support, fast I/O, schedulers such as Quartz, and solid threading support, as well as a very powerful concept of an application container in Java EE and Spring. It was only natural that Dave Syer and his team would come along and build Spring Batch, a batch processing solution for the Spring platform.

It's important to think about the kinds of problems this framework solves before diving into the details. A technology is defined by its solution space. A typical Spring Batch application typically reads in a lot of data and then writes it back out in a modified form. Decisions about transactional barriers, input size, concurrency, and order of steps in processing are all dimensions of a typical integration.

© Marten Deinum, Daniel Rubio, and Josh Long 2017
M. Deinum et al., *Spring 5 Recipes*, DOI 10.1007/978-1-4842-2790-9_11

A common requirement is loading data from a comma-separated value (CSV) file, perhaps as a business-to-business (B2B) transaction or perhaps as an integration technique with an older legacy application. Another common application is nontrivial processing on records in a database. Perhaps the output is an update of the database record itself. An example might be resizing images on the file system whose metadata is stored in a database or needing to trigger another process based on some condition.

■ **Note**   Fixed-width data is a format of rows and cells, quite like a CSV file. CSV file cells are separated by commas or tabs, however, and fixed-width data works by presuming certain lengths for each value. The first value might be the first nine characters, the second value the next four characters after that, and so on.

Fixed-width data that is often used with legacy or embedded systems is a fine candidate for batch processing. Processing that deals with a resource that's fundamentally nontransactional (e.g., a web service or a file) begs for batch processing because batch processing provides retry/skip/fail functionality that most web services will not.

It's also important to understand what Spring Batch doesn't do. Spring Batch is a flexible but not all-encompassing solution. Just as Spring doesn't reinvent the wheel when it can be avoided, Spring Batch leaves a few important pieces to the discretion of the implementer. Case in point: Spring Batch provides a generic mechanism by which to launch a job, be it by the command line, a Unix cron, an operating system service, Quartz (discussed in Chapter 13), or in response to an event on an enterprise service bus (for example, the Mule ESB or Spring's own ESB-like solution, Spring Integration, which is discussed in Chapter 15). Another example is the way Spring Batch manages the state of batch processes. Spring Batch requires a durable store. The only useful implementation of a JobRepository (an interface provided by Spring Batch for storing batch metadata entities) requires a database because a database is transactional and there's no need to reinvent it. To which database you should deploy, however, is largely unspecified, although there are useful defaults provided for you, of course.

■ **Note**   The JEE7 specification includes JSR-352 (Batch Applications for the Java Platform). Spring Batch is the reference implementation of this specification.

Runtime Metadata Model

Spring Batch works with a JobRepository, which is the keeper of all the knowledge and metadata for each job (including component parts such as JobInstances, JobExecution, and StepExecution). Each job is composed of one or more steps, one after another. With Spring Batch, a step can conditionally follow another step, allowing for primitive workflows.

These steps can also be concurrent; two steps can run at the same time.

When a job is run, it's often coupled with JobParameter to parameterize the runtime behavior of the Job itself. For example, a job might take a date parameter to determine which records to process. To identify a job run, a JobInstance is created. A JobInstance is unique because of the JobParameters associated with it. Each time the same JobInstance (i.e., the same Job and JobParameters) is run, it's called a JobExecution. This is a runtime context for a version of the Job. Ideally, for every JobInstance there'd be only one JobExecution: the JobExecution that was created the first time the JobInstance ran. However, if there were any errors, the JobInstance should be restarted; the subsequent run would create another JobExecution. For every step in the original job, there is a StepExecution in the JobExecution.

Thus, you can see that Spring Batch has a mirrored object graph—one reflecting the design/build time view of a job and another reflecting the runtime view of a job. This split between the prototype and the instance is similar to the way many workflow engines, including jBPM, work.

For example, suppose that a daily report is generated at 2 a.m. The parameter to the job would be the date (most likely the previous day's date). The job, in this case, would model a loading step, a summary step, and an output step. Each day the job is run, a new `JobInstance` and `JobExecution` would be created. If there are any retries of the same `JobInstance`, conceivably many `JobExecutions` would be created.

11-1. Set Up Spring Batch's Infrastructure

Problem

Spring Batch provides a lot of flexibility and guarantees to your application, but it cannot work in a vacuum. To do its work, the `JobRepository` requires data storage (could be a SQL database or other means of storing data). Additionally, there are several collaborators required for Spring Batch to do its work. This configuration is mostly boilerplate.

Solution

In this recipe, you'll set up the Spring Batch database and also create a Spring application configuration that can be imported by subsequent solutions. This configuration is repetitive and largely uninteresting. It will also tell Spring Batch what database to use for the metadata it stores.

How It Works

The `JobRepository` interface is the first thing that you'll have to deal with when setting up a Spring Batch process. You usually don't deal with it in code, but in a Spring configuration, it is key to getting everything else working. There's only one really useful implementation of the `JobRepository` interface called `SimpleJobRepository`, which stores information about the state of the batch processes in a data store. Creation is done through a `JobRepositoryFactoryBean`. Another standard factory, `MapJobRepositoryFactoryBean`, is useful mainly for testing because its state is not durable—it's an in-memory implementation. Both factories create an instance of `SimpleJobRepository`.

Because this `JobRepository` instance works on your database, you need to set up the schema for Spring Batch to work with. The schemas for different databases are in the Spring Batch distribution. The simplest way to initialize your database is to use a `DataSourceInitializer` in a Java config. The files can be found in the `org/springframework/batch/core` directory; there are several `.sql` files, each containing the data definition language (DDL, the subset of SQL used for defining and examining the structure of a database) for the required schema for the database of your choice. These examples will use H2 (an in-memory database), so you will use the DDL for H2: `schema-h2.sql`. Make sure you configure it and tell Spring Batch about it, as in the following configurations:

```
@Configuration
@ComponentScan("com.apress.springrecipes.springbatch")
@PropertySource("classpath:batch.properties")
public class BatchConfiguration {

    @Autowired
    private Environment env;

    @Bean
    public DataSource dataSource() {
        DriverManagerDataSource dataSource = new DriverManagerDataSource();
```

```java
        dataSource.setUrl(env.getRequiredProperty("dataSource.url"));
        dataSource.setUsername(env.getRequiredProperty("dataSource.username"));
        dataSource.setPassword(env.getRequiredProperty("dataSource.password"));
        return dataSource;
    }

    @Bean
    public DataSourceInitializer dataSourceInitializer() {
        DataSourceInitializer initializer = new DataSourceInitializer();
        initializer.setDataSource(dataSource());
        initializer.setDatabasePopulator(databasePopulator());
        return initializer;
    }

    private DatabasePopulator databasePopulator() {
        ResourceDatabasePopulator databasePopulator = new ResourceDatabasePopulator();
        databasePopulator.setContinueOnError(true);
        databasePopulator.addScript(
            new ClassPathResource("org/springframework/batch/core/schema-h2.sql"));
        databasePopulator.addScript(
            new ClassPathResource("sql/reset_user_registration.sql"));
        return databasePopulator;
    }

    @Bean
    public DataSourceTransactionManager transactionManager() {
        return new DataSourceTransactionManager(dataSource());
    }

    @Bean
    public JobRepositoryFactoryBean jobRepository() {
        JobRepositoryFactoryBean jobRepositoryFactoryBean = new JobRepositoryFactoryBean();
        jobRepositoryFactoryBean.setDataSource(dataSource());
        jobRepositoryFactoryBean.setTransactionManager(transactionManager());
        return jobRepositoryFactoryBean;
    }

    @Bean
    public JobLauncher jobLauncher() throws Exception {
        SimpleJobLauncher jobLauncher = new SimpleJobLauncher();
        jobLauncher.setJobRepository(jobRepository().getObject());
        return jobLauncher;
    }

    @Bean
    public JobRegistryBeanPostProcessor jobRegistryBeanPostProcessor() {
        JobRegistryBeanPostProcessor jobRegistryBeanPostProcessor =
            new JobRegistryBeanPostProcessor();
        jobRegistryBeanPostProcessor.setJobRegistry(jobRegistry());
        return jobRegistryBeanPostProcessor;
    }
```

```java
@Bean
public JobRegistry jobRegistry() {
    return new MapJobRegistry();
}
}
```

The first few beans are related strictly to configuration. There's nothing particularly novel or peculiar to Spring Batch: a data source, a transaction manager, and a data source initializer.

Eventually, you get to the declaration of a MapJobRegistry instance. This is critical—it is the central store for information regarding a given job, and it controls the "big picture" about all jobs in the system. Everything else works with this instance.

Next, you have a SimpleJobLauncher, whose sole purpose is to give you a mechanism to launch batch jobs, where a "job" in this case is your batch solution. The jobLauncher is used to specify the name of the batch solution to run as well as any parameters required. I'll follow up more on that in the next recipe.

Next, you define a JobRegistryBeanPostProcessor. This bean scans your Spring context file and associates any configured jobs with the MapJobRegistry.

Finally, you get to the SimpleJobRepository (that is, in turn, factoried by the JobRepositoryFactoryBean). The JobRepository is an implementation of a "repository" (in the Patterns of Enterprise Application Architecture sense of the word): it handles persistence and retrieval for the domain models surrounding steps and jobs.

The @PropertySource annotation will instruct Spring to load your batch.properties file (located in src/main/resource). You are going to retrieve the properties you need using the Environment class.

■ **Tip** You could have also used an @Value annotation to inject all individual properties, but when needing multiple properties in a configuration class, it is easier to use the Environment object.

The batch.properties file contains the following:

```
dataSource.password=sa
dataSource.username=
dataSource.url= jdbc:h2:~/batch
```

Although this works, Spring Batch also has support to configure these defaults out of the box using the @EnableBatchProcessing annotation. This makes things a little easier.

```java
package com.apress.springrecipes.springbatch.config;

import org.apache.commons.dbcp2.BasicDataSource;
import org.springframework.batch.core.configuration.annotation.EnableBatchProcessing;
import org.springframework.beans.factory.annotation.Autowired;
import org.springframework.context.annotation.Bean;
import org.springframework.context.annotation.ComponentScan;
import org.springframework.context.annotation.Configuration;
import org.springframework.context.annotation.PropertySource;
import org.springframework.core.env.Environment;
import org.springframework.core.io.ClassPathResource;
import org.springframework.jdbc.datasource.init.DataSourceInitializer;
import org.springframework.jdbc.datasource.init.ResourceDatabasePopulator;
```

```java
import javax.sql.DataSource;

@Configuration
@EnableBatchProcessing
@ComponentScan("com.apress.springrecipes.springbatch")
@PropertySource("classpath:/batch.properties")
public class BatchConfiguration {

    @Autowired
    private Environment env;

    @Bean
    public DataSource dataSource() {
        BasicDataSource dataSource = new BasicDataSource();
        dataSource.setUrl(env.getRequiredProperty("dataSource.url"));
        dataSource.setDriverClassName(
            env.getRequiredProperty("dataSource.driverClassName"));
        dataSource.setUsername(env.getProperty("dataSource.username"));
        dataSource.setPassword(env.getProperty("dataSource.password"));
        return dataSource;
    }

    @Bean
    public DataSourceInitializer databasePopulator() {
        ResourceDatabasePopulator populator = new ResourceDatabasePopulator();
        populator.addScript(
            new ClassPathResource("org/springframework/batch/core/schema-derby.sql"));
        populator.addScript(new ClassPathResource("sql/reset_user_registration.sql"));
        populator.setContinueOnError(true);
        populator.setIgnoreFailedDrops(true);

        DataSourceInitializer initializer = new DataSourceInitializer();
        initializer.setDatabasePopulator(populator);
        initializer.setDataSource(dataSource());
        return initializer;
    }
}
```

This class contains only two bean definitions: one for the data source and one for initializing the database; everything else has been taken care of because of the @EnableBatchProcessing annotation. The previous configuration class will bootstrap Spring Batch with some sensible defaults.

The default configuration will configure a JobRepository, JobRegistry, and JobLauncher.

If there are multiple data sources in your application, you need to add an explicit BatchConfigurer to select the data source to use for the batch part of your application.

The following Main class will use the Java-based configuration for running the batch application:

```java
package com.apress.springrecipes.springbatch;

import com.apress.springrecipes.springbatch.config.BatchConfiguration;
import org.springframework.batch.core.configuration.JobRegistry;
import org.springframework.batch.core.launch.JobLauncher;
import org.springframework.batch.core.repository.JobRepository;
```

```java
import org.springframework.context.ApplicationContext;
import org.springframework.context.annotation.AnnotationConfigApplicationContext;

public class Main {
    public static void main(String[] args) throws Throwable {
        ApplicationContext context =
            new AnnotationConfigApplicationContext(BatchConfiguration.class);

        JobRegistry jobRegistry = context.getBean("jobRegistry", JobRegistry.class);
        JobLauncher jobLauncher = context.getBean("jobLauncher", JobLauncher.class);
        JobRepository jobRepository = context.getBean("jobRepository", JobRepository.class);

        System.out.println("JobRegistry: " + jobRegistry);
        System.out.println("JobLauncher: " + jobLauncher);
        System.out.println("JobRepository: " + jobRepository);

    }
}
```

11-2. Read and Write Data

Problem

You want to insert data from a CSV file into a database. This solution will be one of the simplest solutions and will give you a chance to explore the moving pieces of a typical solution.

Solution

You'll build a solution that does a minimal amount of work, while being a viable application of the technology. The solution will read in a file of arbitrary length and write out the data into a database. The end result will be almost 100 percent code free. You will rely on an existing model class and write one class (a class containing the public static void main(String [] args) method) to round out the example. There's no reason why the model class couldn't be a Hibernate class or something from your DAO layer; however, in this case it's a brainless POJO. This solution will use the components you configured in recipe 11-1.

How It Works

This example demonstrates the simplest possible use of Spring Batch: to provide scalability. This program will do nothing but read data from a CSV file, with fields delimited by commas and rows delimited by newlines. It then inserts the records into a table. You are exploiting the intelligent infrastructure that Spring Batch provides to avoid worrying about scaling. This application could easily be done manually. You will not exploit any of the smart transactional functionality made available to you, nor will you worry about retries for the time being.

This solution is as simple as Spring Batch solutions get. Spring Batch models solutions using XML schema. The abstractions and terms are in the spirit of classical batch processing solutions so will be portable from previous technologies and perhaps to subsequent technologies. Spring Batch provides useful default classes that you can override or selectively adjust. In the following example, you'll use a lot of the utility implementations provided by Spring Batch. Fundamentally, most solutions look about the same and feature a combination of the same set of interfaces. It's usually just a matter of picking and choosing the right ones.

When I ran this program, it worked on files with 20,000 rows, and it worked on files with 1 million rows. I experienced no increase in memory, which indicates there were no memory leaks. Naturally, it took a lot longer! (The application ran for several hours with the 1-million-row insert.)

■ **Tip**   Of course, it would be catastrophic if you worked with a million rows and it failed on the penultimate record. You'd lose all your work when the transaction rolled back! Read on for examples on chunking. Additionally, you might want to read Chapter 10 to brush up on transactions.

```
create table USER_REGISTRATION (
    ID BIGINT NOT NULL PRIMARY KEY GENERATED ALWAYS AS IDENTITY (START WITH 1, INCREMENT BY 1),
    FIRST_NAME VARCHAR(255) not null,
    LAST_NAME VARCHAR(255) not null,
    COMPANY VARCHAR(255) not null,
    ADDRESS VARCHAR(255) not null,
    CITY VARCHAR(255) not null,
    STATE VARCHAR(255) not null,
    ZIP VARCHAR(255) not null,
    COUNTY VARCHAR(255) not null,
    URL VARCHAR(255) not null,
    PHONE_NUMBER VARCHAR(255) not null,
    FAX VARCHAR(255) not null
) ;
```

I didn't tune the table at all. For example, there are no indexes on any of the columns besides the primary key. This is to avoid complicating the example. Great care should be taken with a table like this one in a nontrivial, production-bound application.

Spring Batch applications are workhorse applications and have the potential to reveal bottlenecks in your application you didn't know you had. Imagine suddenly being able to achieve 1 million new database insertions every 10 minutes. Would your database grind to a halt? Insert speed can be a critical factor in the speed of your application. Software developers will (ideally) think about their database schema in terms of how well it enforces the constraints of the business logic and how well it serves the overall business model. However, it's important to wear another hat, that of a DBA, when writing applications such as this one. A common solution is to create a denormalized table whose contents can be coerced into valid data once inside the database, perhaps by a trigger on inserts. This is typical in data warehousing. Later, you'll explore using Spring Batch to do processing on a record before insertion. This lets the developer verify or override the input into the database. This processing, in tandem with a conservative application of constraints that are best expressed in the database, can make for applications that are very robust and quick.

The Job Configuration

The configuration for the job is as follows:

```
package com.apress.springrecipes.springbatch.config;

import com.apress.springrecipes.springbatch.UserRegistration;
import org.springframework.batch.core.Job;
import org.springframework.batch.core.Step;
```

```java
import org.springframework.batch.core.configuration.annotation.JobBuilderFactory;
import org.springframework.batch.core.configuration.annotation.StepBuilderFactory;
import org.springframework.batch.item.ItemReader;
import org.springframework.batch.item.ItemWriter;
import org.springframework.batch.item.database.BeanPropertyItemSqlParameterSourceProvider;
import org.springframework.batch.item.database.JdbcBatchItemWriter;
import org.springframework.batch.item.file.FlatFileItemReader;
import org.springframework.batch.item.file.LineMapper;
import org.springframework.batch.item.file.mapping.BeanWrapperFieldSetMapper;
import org.springframework.batch.item.file.mapping.DefaultLineMapper;
import org.springframework.batch.item.file.transform.DelimitedLineTokenizer;
import org.springframework.beans.factory.annotation.Autowired;
import org.springframework.beans.factory.annotation.Value;
import org.springframework.context.annotation.Bean;
import org.springframework.context.annotation.Configuration;
import org.springframework.core.io.Resource;

import javax.sql.DataSource;

@Configuration
public class UserJob {

    private static final String INSERT_REGISTRATION_QUERY =
        "insert into USER_REGISTRATION (FIRST_NAME, LAST_NAME, COMPANY, ADDRESS,CITY,
        STATE,ZIP,COUNTY,URL,PHONE_NUMBER,FAX)" +
        " values " +
        "(:firstName,:lastName,:company,:address,:city,:state,:zip,:county,:url,:
        phoneNumber,:fax)";

    @Autowired
    private JobBuilderFactory jobs;

    @Autowired
    private StepBuilderFactory steps;

    @Autowired
    private DataSource dataSource;

    @Value("file:${user.home}/batches/registrations.csv")
    private Resource input;

    @Bean
    public Job insertIntoDbFromCsvJob() {
        return jobs.get("User Registration Import Job")
            .start(step1())
            .build();
    }

    @Bean
    public Step step1() {
        return steps.get("User Registration CSV To DB Step")
            .<UserRegistration,UserRegistration>chunk(5)
```

455

```
        .reader(csvFileReader())
        .writer(jdbcItemWriter())
        .build();
}

@Bean
public FlatFileItemReader<UserRegistration> csvFileReader() {
    FlatFileItemReader<UserRegistration> itemReader = new FlatFileItemReader<>();
    itemReader.setLineMapper(lineMapper());
    itemReader.setResource(input);
    return itemReader;
}

@Bean
public JdbcBatchItemWriter<UserRegistration> jdbcItemWriter() {
    JdbcBatchItemWriter<UserRegistration> itemWriter = new JdbcBatchItemWriter<>();
    itemWriter.setDataSource(dataSource);
    itemWriter.setSql(INSERT_REGISTRATION_QUERY);
    itemWriter.setItemSqlParameterSourceProvider(new BeanPropertyItemSql
    ParameterSourceProvider<>());
    return itemWriter;
}

@Bean
public DefaultLineMapper<UserRegistration> lineMapper() {
    DefaultLineMapper<UserRegistration> lineMapper = new DefaultLineMapper<>();
    lineMapper.setLineTokenizer(tokenizer());
    lineMapper.setFieldSetMapper(fieldSetMapper());
    return lineMapper;
}

@Bean
public BeanWrapperFieldSetMapper<UserRegistration> fieldSetMapper() {
    BeanWrapperFieldSetMapper<UserRegistration> fieldSetMapper = new
    BeanWrapperFieldSetMapper<>();
    fieldSetMapper.setTargetType(UserRegistration.class);
    return fieldSetMapper;
}

@Bean
public DelimitedLineTokenizer tokenizer() {
    DelimitedLineTokenizer tokenizer = new DelimitedLineTokenizer();
    tokenizer.setDelimiter(",");
    tokenizer.setNames(new String[]{"firstName","lastName","company","address",
    "city","state","zip","county","url","phoneNumber","fax"});
    return tokenizer;
}
}
```

As described earlier, a job consists of steps, which are the real workhorse of a given job. The steps can be as complex or as simple as you like. Indeed, a step could be considered the smallest unit of work for a job. Input (what's read) is passed to the step and potentially processed; then output (what's written) is created from the step. This processing is spelled out using a `Tasklet` (which is another interface provided by Spring Batch). You can provide your own `Tasklet` implementation or simply use some of the preconfigured configurations for different processing scenarios. These implementations are made available in terms of configuration methods. One of the most important aspects of batch processing is chunk-oriented processing, which is employed here using the `chunk()` configuration method.

In chunk-oriented processing, input is read from a reader, optionally processed, and then aggregated. Finally, at a configurable interval—as specified by the commit-interval attribute to configure how many items will be processed before the transaction is committed—all the input is sent to the writer. If there is a transaction manager in play, the transaction is also committed. Right before a commit, the metadata in the database is updated to mark the progress of the job.

There are some nuances surrounding the aggregation of the input (read) values when a transaction-aware writer (or processor) rolls back. Spring Batch caches the values it reads and writes them to the writer. If the writer component is transactional, like a database, and the reader is not, there's nothing inherently wrong with caching the read values and perhaps retrying or taking some alternative approach. If the reader itself is also transactional, then the values read from the resource will be rolled back and could conceivably change, rendering the in-memory cached values stale. If this happens, you can configure the chunk to not cache the values using `reader-transactional-queue="true"` on the chunk element.

Input

The first responsibility is reading a file from the file system. You use a provided implementation for the example. Reading CSV files is a common scenario, and Spring Batch's support does not disappoint. The `org.springframework.batch.item.file.FlatFileItemReader<T>` class delegates the task of delimiting fields and records within a file to a `LineMapper<T>`, which in turn delegates the task of identifying the fields within that record to `LineTokenizer`. You use an `org.springframework.batch.item.file.transform.DelimitedLineTokenizer`, which is configured to delineate fields separated by a comma (`,`) character.

The `DefaultLineMapper` also declares a `fieldSetMapper` attribute that requires an implementation of `FieldSetMapper`. This bean is responsible for taking the input name-value pairs and producing a type that will be given to the writer component.

In this case, you use a `BeanWrapperFieldSetMapper` that will create a JavaBean POJO of type `UserRegistration`. You name the fields so that you can reference them later in the configuration. These names don't have to be the values of some header row in the input file; they just have to correspond to the order in which the fields are found in the input file. These names are also used by the `FieldSetMapper` to match properties on a POJO. As each record is read, the values are applied to an instance of a POJO, and that POJO is returned.

```
@Bean
public FlatFileItemReader<UserRegistration> csvFileReader() {
    FlatFileItemReader<UserRegistration> itemReader = new FlatFileItemReader<>();
    itemReader.setLineMapper(lineMapper());
    itemReader.setResource(input);
    return itemReader;
}

@Bean
public DefaultLineMapper<UserRegistration> lineMapper() {
    DefaultLineMapper<UserRegistration> lineMapper = new DefaultLineMapper<>();
    lineMapper.setLineTokenizer(tokenizer());
```

```
        lineMapper.setFieldSetMapper(fieldSetMapper());
        return lineMapper;
}

@Bean
public BeanWrapperFieldSetMapper<UserRegistration> fieldSetMapper() {
    BeanWrapperFieldSetMapper<UserRegistration> fieldSetMapper =
        new BeanWrapperFieldSetMapper<>();
    fieldSetMapper.setTargetType(UserRegistration.class);
    return fieldSetMapper;
}

@Bean
public DelimitedLineTokenizer tokenizer() {
    DelimitedLineTokenizer tokenizer = new DelimitedLineTokenizer();
    tokenizer.setDelimiter(",");
    tokenizer.setNames(new String[]{"firstName","lastName","company","address","city",
    "state","zip","county","url","phoneNumber","fax"});
    return tokenizer;
}
```

The class returned from the reader, UserRegistration, is a rather plain JavaBean.

```
package com.apress.springrecipes.springbatch;

public class UserRegistration implements Serializable {

    private String firstName;
    private String lastName;
    private String company;
    private String address;
    private String city;
    private String state;
    private String zip;
    private String county;
    private String url;
    private String phoneNumber;
    private String fax;

    //... accessor / mutators omitted for brevity ...

}
```

Output

The next component to do work is the writer, which is responsible for taking the aggregated collection of items read from the reader. In this case, you might imagine that a new collection (java.util. List<UserRegistration>) is created, then written, and then reset each time the collection exceeds the commit-interval attribute on the chunk element. Because you're trying to write to a database, you use Spring Batch's org.springframework.batch.item.database.JdbcBatchItemWriter. This class contains support for taking input and writing it to a database. It is up to the developer to provide the input and to specify what SQL should be run for the input. It will run the SQL specified by the sql property, in essence reading from the database, as many times as specified by the chunk element's commit-interval and then commit the whole transaction. Here, you're doing a simple insert. The names and values for the named parameters are being created by the bean configured for the itemSqlParameterSourceProvider property, which is an instance of BeanPropertyItemSqlParameterSourceProvider, whose sole job it is to take JavaBean properties and make them available as named parameters corresponding to the property name on the JavaBean.

```
@Bean
public JdbcBatchItemWriter<UserRegistration> jdbcItemWriter() {
    JdbcBatchItemWriter<UserRegistration> itemWriter = new JdbcBatchItemWriter<>();
    itemWriter.setDataSource(dataSource);
    itemWriter.setSql(INSERT_REGISTRATION_QUERY);
    itemWriter.setItemSqlParameterSourceProvider(
        new BeanPropertyItemSqlParameterSourceProvider<>());
    return itemWriter;
}
```

That's it! A working solution. With little configuration and no custom code, you've built a solution for taking large CSV files and reading them into a database. This solution is bare-bones and leaves a lot of edge cases uncared for. You might want to do processing on the item as it's read (before it's inserted), for example.

This exemplifies a simple job. It's important to remember that there are similar classes for doing the exact opposite transformation: reading from a database and writing to a CSV file.

```
@Bean
public Job insertIntoDbFromCsvJob() {
    return jobs.get("User Registration Import Job")
        .start(step1())
        .build();
}
```

```
@Bean
public Step step1() {
    return steps.get("User Registration CSV To DB Step")
        .<UserRegistration,UserRegistration>chunk(5)
        .reader(csvFileReader())
        .writer(jdbcItemWriter())
        .build();
}
```

To configure the step, you give it the name User Registration CSV To DB Step. You are using chunk-based processing, and you need to tell it that you want a chunk size of 5. Next you supply it with a reader and writer, and finally you tell the factory to build to the step. The configured step is finally wired as a starting point to your job, named User Registration Import Job, which consists only of this step.

Simplify the ItemReader and ItemWriter Configuration

Configuring the ItemReader and ItemWriter can be a daunting task. You need to know a quite a lot of the internals of Spring Batch (which classes to use, etc.). As of Spring Batch 4, configuring the readers and writers has become easier as there are now specific builders for the different readers and writers.

To configure the FlatFileItemReader, you could use the FlatFileItemReaderBuilder and instead of configuring four individual beans, it is now six lines of code (mainly because the formatting in the sample).

```
@Bean
public FlatFileItemReader<UserRegistration> csvFileReader() throws Exception {

    return new FlatFileItemReaderBuilder<UserRegistration>()
        .name(ClassUtils.getShortName(FlatFileItemReader.class))
        .resource(input)
        .targetType(UserRegistration.class)
        .delimited()
        .names(new String[]{"firstName","lastName","company","address","city","state",
        "zip","county","url","phoneNumber","fax"})
        .build();
}
```

This builder will automatically create the DefaultLineMapper, BeanWrapperFieldSetMapper, and DelimitedLineTokenizer, and you don't have to know that they are used internally. You can now basically describe your configuration rather than explicitly configuring all the different items.

The same can be applied to the JdbcBatchItemWriter using the JdbcBatchItemWriterBuilder.

```
@Bean
public JdbcBatchItemWriter<UserRegistration> jdbcItemWriter() {
    return new JdbcBatchItemWriterBuilder<UserRegistration>()
        .dataSource(dataSource)
        .sql(INSERT_REGISTRATION_QUERY)
        .beanMapped()
        .build();
}
```

11-3. Write a Custom ItemWriter and ItemReader

Problem

You want to talk to a resource (you might imagine an RSS feed or any other custom data format) that Spring Batch doesn't know how to connect to.

Solution

You can easily write your own ItemWriter or ItemReader. The interfaces are drop-dead simple, and there's not a lot of responsibility placed on the implementations.

How It Works

As easy and trivial as this process is to do, it's still not better than just reusing any of the numerous provided options. If you look, you'll likely find something. There's support for writing JMS (JmsItemWriter<T>), JPA (JpaItemWriter<T>), JDBC (JdbcBatchItemWriter<T>), files (FlatFileItemWriter<T>), Hibernate (HibernateItemWriter<T>), and more. There's even support for writing by invoking a method on a bean (PropertyExtractingDelegatingItemWriter<T>) and passing to it as arguments the properties on the Item to be written! One of the more useful writers lets you write to a set of files that are numbered. This implementation—MultiResourceItemWriter<T>—delegates to the other proper ItemWriter<T> implementation for the work but lets you write to multiple files, not just one very large one. There's a slightly smaller but impressive set of implementations for ItemReader implementations. If it doesn't exist, look again. If you still can't find one, consider writing your own. In this recipe, you will do just that.

Write a Custom ItemReader

The ItemReader example is trivial. Here, an ItemReader is created that knows how to retrieve
UserRegistration objects from a remote procedure call (RPC) endpoint:

```
package com.apress.springrecipes.springbatch;

import org.springframework.batch.item.ItemReader;

import java.util.Collection;
import java.util.Date;

public class UserRegistrationItemReader implements ItemReader<UserRegistration> {

    private final UserRegistrationService userRegistrationService;

    public UserRegistrationItemReader(UserRegistrationService userRegistrationService) {
        this.userRegistrationService = userRegistrationService;
    }

    public UserRegistration read() throws Exception {
        final Date today = new Date();
        Collection<UserRegistration> registrations =
            userRegistrationService.getOutstandingUserRegistrationBatchForDate(1, today);
        return registrations.stream().findFirst().orElse(null);
    }
}
```

As you can see, the interface is trivial. In this case, you defer most work to a remote service to provide you
with the input. The interface requires that you return one record. The interface is parameterized to the type of
object (the "item") to be returned. All the read items will be aggregated and then passed to the ItemWriter.

Write a Custom ItemWriter

The ItemWriter example is also trivial. Imagine wanting to write by invoking a remote service using any
of the numerous options for remoting that Spring provides. The ItemWriter<T> interface is parameterized
by the type of item you're expecting to write. Here, you expect a UserRegistration object from the
ItemReader<T>. The interface consists of one method, which expects a List of the class's parameterized
type. These are the objects read from ItemReader<T> and aggregated. If your commit-interval were ten, you
might expect ten or fewer items in the List.

```
package com.apress.springrecipes.springbatch;

import org.slf4j.Logger;
import org.slf4j.LoggerFactory;
import org.springframework.batch.item.ItemWriter;

import java.util.List;
```

```
public class UserRegistrationServiceItemWriter implements ItemWriter<UserRegistration> {

    private static final Logger logger = LoggerFactory.getLogger(UserRegistrationService
    ItemWriter.class);

    private final UserRegistrationService userRegistrationService;

    public UserRegistrationServiceItemWriter(UserRegistrationService userRegistrationService) {
        this.userRegistrationService = userRegistrationService;
    }

    public void write(List<? extends UserRegistration> items) throws Exception {
        items.forEach(this::write);
    }

    private void write(UserRegistration userRegistration) {
        UserRegistration registeredUserRegistration =
            userRegistrationService.registerUser(userRegistration);
        logger.debug("Registered: {}", registeredUserRegistration);

    }
}
```

Here, you've wired in the service's client interface. You simply loop through the UserRegistration objects and invoke the service, which in turn hands you back an identical instance of UserRegistration. If you remove the gratuitous spacing, curly brackets, and logging output, it becomes two lines of code to satisfy the requirement.

The interface for UserRegistrationService follows:

```
package com.apress.springrecipes.springbatch;

import java.util.Collection;
import java.util.Date;

public interface UserRegistrationService {

    Collection<UserRegistration> getOutstandingUserRegistrationBatchForDate(
        int quantity, Date date);

    UserRegistration registerUser(UserRegistration userRegistrationRegistration);

}
```

In this example, you have no particular implementation for the interface, as it is irrelevant: it could be any interface that Spring Batch doesn't know about already.

11-4. Process Input Before Writing

Problem

While transferring data directly from a spreadsheet or CSV dump might be useful, you can imagine having to do some sort of processing on the data before it's written. Data in a CSV file, and more generally from any source, is not usually exactly the way you expect it to be or immediately suitable for writing. Just because Spring Batch can coerce it into a POJO on your behalf, that doesn't mean the state of the data is correct. There may be additional data that you need to infer or fill in from other services before the data is suitable for writing.

Solution

Spring Batch will let you do processing on reader output. This processing can do virtually anything to the output before it gets passed to the writer, including changing the type of the data.

How It Works

Spring Batch gives the implementer a chance to perform any custom logic on the data read from the reader. The processor attribute on the chunk configuration expects a reference to a bean of the interface org.springframework.batch.item.ItemProcessor<I,O>. Thus, the revised definition for the job from the previous recipe looks like this:

```
@Bean
public Step step1() {
    return steps.get("User Registration CSV To DB Step")
        .<UserRegistration,UserRegistration>chunk(5)
        .reader(csvFileReader())
        .processor(userRegistrationValidationItemProcessor())
        .writer(jdbcItemWriter())
        .build();
}
```

The goal is to do certain validations on the data before you authorize it to be written to the database. If you determine the record is invalid, you can stop further processing by returning null from the ItemProcessor<I,O>. This is crucial and provides a necessary safeguard. One thing that you want to do is ensure that the data is the right format (for example, the schema may require a valid two-letter state name instead of the longer full state name). Telephone numbers are expected to follow a certain format, and you can use this processor to strip the telephone number of any extraneous characters, leaving only a valid (in the United States) ten-digit phone number. The same applies for U.S. zip codes, which consist of five characters and optionally a hyphen followed by a four-digit code. Finally, while a constraint guarding against duplicates is best implemented in the database, there may very well be some other eligibility criteria for a record that can be met only by querying the system before insertion.

Here's the configuration for the ItemProcessor:

```
@Bean
public ItemProcessor<UserRegistration, UserRegistration>
userRegistrationValidationItemProcessor() {
    return new UserRegistrationValidationItemProcessor();
}
```

In the interest of keeping this class short, I won't reprint it in its entirety, but the salient bits should be obvious.

```java
package com.apress.springrecipes.springbatch;
import java.util.Arrays;
import java.util.Collection;

import org.apache.commons.lang3.StringUtils;
import org.springframework.batch.core.StepExecution;
import org.springframework.batch.item.ItemProcessor;
import com.apress.springrecipes.springbatch.UserRegistration;

public class UserRegistrationValidationItemProcessor
    implements ItemProcessor<UserRegistration, UserRegistration> {

    private String stripNonNumbers(String input) { /* ... */ }

    private boolean isTelephoneValid(String telephone) { /* ... */ }

    private boolean isZipCodeValid(String zip) { /* ... */ }

    private boolean isValidState(String state) { /* ... */ }

    public UserRegistration process(UserRegistration input) throws Exception {
        String zipCode = stripNonNumbers(input.getZip());
        String telephone = stripNonNumbers(input.getPhoneNumber());
        String state = StringUtils.defaultString(input.getState());
        if (isTelephoneValid(telephone) && isZipCodeValid(zipCode) &&
        isValidState(state)) {
            input.setZip(zipCode);
            input.setPhoneNumber(telephone );
            return input;
        }
        return null;
    }
}
```

The class is a parameterized type. The type information is the type of the input, as well as the type of the output. The input is what's given to the method for processing, and the output is the returned data from the method. Because you're not transforming anything in this example, the two parameterized types are the same. Once this process has completed, there's a lot of useful information to be had in the Spring Batch metadata tables. Issue the following query on your database:

```sql
select * from BATCH_STEP_EXECUTION;
```

Among other things, you'll get back the exit status of the job, how many commits occurred, how many items were read, and how many items were filtered. So if the preceding job was run on a batch with 100 rows, each item was read and passed through the processor, and it found 10 items invalid (it returned null 10 times), the value for the filter_count column would be 10. You could see that a 100 items were read from the read_count. The write_count column would reflect that 10 items didn't make it and would show 90.

Chain Processors Together

Sometimes you might want to add extra processing that isn't congruous with the goals of the processor you've already set up. Spring Batch provides a convenience class, CompositeItemProcessor<I,O>, that forwards the output of the filter to the input of the successive filter. In this way, you can write many, singly focused ItemProcessor<I,O> s and then reuse them and chain them as necessary.

```
@Bean
public CompositeItemProcessor<Customer, Customer> compositeBankCustomerProcessor() {
    List<ItemProcessor<Customer, Customer>> delegates = Arrays.asList(creditScoreValidation
    Processor(), salaryValidationProcessor(), customerEligibilityProcessor());
    CompositeItemProcessor<Customer, Customer> processor = new CompositeItemProcessor<>();
    processor.setDelegates(delegates);
    return processor;
}
```

The example created a simple workflow. The first ItemProcessor<T> will take an input of whatever's coming from the ItemReader<T> configured for this job, presumably a Customer object. It will check the credit score of the Customer and, if approved, forward the Customer to the salary and income validation processor. If everything checks out there, the Customer will be forwarded to the eligibility processor, where the system is checked for duplicates or any other invalid data. It will finally be forwarded to the writer to be added to the output. If at any point in the three processors the Customer fails a check, the executing ItemProcessor can simply return null and arrest processing.

11-5. Achieve Better Living Through Transactions

Problem

You want your reads and writes to be robust. Ideally, they'll use transactions where appropriate and correctly react to exceptions.

Solution

Transaction capabilities are built on top of the first-class support already provided by the core Spring framework. Where relevant, Spring Batch surfaces the configuration so that you can control it. Within the context of chunk-oriented processing, it also exposes a lot of control over the frequency of commits, rollback semantics, and so on.

How It Works

First you explore how to make a step (or chunk) transactional followed by the configuration of retry logic on a step.

Transactions

Spring's core framework provides first-class support for transactions. You simply wire up a PlatformTransactionManager and give Spring Batch a reference, just as you would in any regular JdbcTemplate or HibernateTemplate solution. As you build your Spring Batch solutions, you'll be given opportunities to control how steps behave in a transaction. You've already seen some of the support for transactions baked right in.

The configuration used in all these examples established a `DriverManagerDataSource` and a `DataSourceTransactionManager` bean. The `PlatformTransactionManager` and `DataSource` were then wired to the `JobRepository`, which was in turn wired to the `JobLauncher`, which you used to launch all jobs thus far. This enabled all the metadata your jobs created to be written to the database in a transactional way.

You might wonder why there is no explicit mention of the transaction manager when you configured the `JdbcItemWriter` with a reference to `dataSource`. The transaction manager reference can be specified, but in your solutions, it wasn't required because Spring Batch will, by default, try to pluck the `PlatformTransactionManager` named `transactionManager` from the context and use it. If you want to explicitly configure this, you can specify the `transactionManager` property on the `tasklet` configuration method. A simple transaction manager for JDBC work might look like this:

```
@Bean
protected Step step1() {
    return steps.get("step1")
        .<UserRegistration,UserRegistration>chunk(5)
        .reader(csvFileReader())
        .processor(userRegistrationValidationItemProcessor())
        .writer(jdbcItemWriter())
        .transactionManager(new DataSourceTransactionManager(dataSource))
        .build();
}
```

Items read from an `ItemReader<T>` are normally aggregated. If a commit on the `ItemWriter<T>` fails, the aggregated items are kept and then resubmitted. This process is efficient and works most of the time. One place where it breaks semantics is when reading from a transactional resource (like a JMS queue or database). Reads from a message queue can and should be rolled back if the transaction they participate in (in this case, the transaction for the writer) fails.

```
@Bean
protected Step step1() {
    return steps.get("step1")
        .<UserRegistration,UserRegistration>chunk(5)
        .reader(csvFileReader()).readerIsTransactionalQueue()
        .processor(userRegistrationValidationItemProcessor())
        .writer(jdbcItemWriter())
        .transactionManager(new DataSourceTransactionManager(dataSource))
        .build();
}
```

Rollbacks

Handling the simple case ("read X items, and every Y items, commit a database transaction every Y items") is easy. Spring Batch excels in the robustness it surfaces as simple configuration options for the edge and failure cases.

If a write fails on an `ItemWriter`, or some other exception occurs in processing, Spring Batch will roll back the transaction. This is valid handling for a majority of the cases. There may be some scenarios when you want to control which exceptional cases cause the transaction to roll back.

When using Java-based configuration to enable rollbacks, the first step needs to be a fault-tolerant step, which in turn can be used to specify the no-rollback exceptions. First use `faultTolerant()` to obtain a fault-tolerant step, next the `skipLimit()` method can be used to specify the number of ignored rollbacks before actually stopping the job execution, and finally the `noRollback()` method can be used to specify the exceptions that don't trigger a rollback. To specify multiple exceptions, you can simply chain calls to the `noRollback()` method.

```
@Bean
protected Step step1() {
    return steps.get("step1")
        .<UserRegistration,UserRegistration>chunk(10)
            .faultTolerant()
                .noRollback(com.yourdomain.exceptions.YourBusinessException.class)
        .reader(csvFileReader())
        .processor(userRegistrationValidationItemProcessor())
        .writer(jdbcItemWriter())
        .build();
}
```

11-6. Retry

Problem

You are dealing with a requirement for functionality that may fail but is not transactional. Perhaps it is transactional but unreliable. You want to work with a resource that may fail when you try to read from or write to it. It may fail because of networking connectivity because an endpoint is down or for any other number of reasons. You know that it will likely be back up soon, though, and that it should be retried.

Solution

Use Spring Batch's retry capabilities to systematically retry the read or write.

How It Works

As you saw in the previous recipe, it's easy to handle transactional resources with Spring Batch. When it comes to transient or unreliable resources, a different tack is required. Such resources tend to be distributed or manifest problems that eventually resolve themselves. Some (such as web services) cannot inherently participate in a transaction because of their distributed nature. There are products that can start a transaction on one server and propagate the transactional context to a distributed server and complete it there, although this tends to be very rare and inefficient. Alternatively, there's good support for distributed ("global" or XA) transactions if you can use it. Sometimes, however, you may be dealing with a resource that isn't either of those. A common example might be a call made to a remote service, such as an RMI service or a REST endpoint. Some invocations will fail but may be retried with some likelihood of success in a transactional scenario. For example, an update to the database resulting in `org.springframework.dao.DeadlockLoserDataAccessException` might be usefully retried.

Configure a Step

When using Java-based configuration to enable retrying, the first step needs to be a fault-tolerant step, which in turn can be used to specify the retry limit and retryable exceptions. First use `faultTolerant()` to obtain a fault-tolerant step, next the `retryLimit()` method can be used to specify the number of retry attempts, and finally the `retry()` method can be used to specify the exceptions that trigger a retry. To specify multiple exceptions, you can simply chain calls to the `retry()` method.

```
@Bean
public Step step1() {
    return steps.get("User Registration CSV To DB Step")
        .<UserRegistration,UserRegistration>chunk(10)
            .faultTolerant()
                .retryLimit(3).retry(DeadlockLoserDataAccessException.class)
        .reader(csvFileReader())
        .writer(jdbcItemWriter())
        .transactionManager(transactionManager)
        .build();
}
```

Retry Template

Alternatively, you can leverage Spring Retry support for retries and recovery in your own code. For example, you can have a custom `ItemWriter<T>` in which retry functionality is desired or even an entire service interface for which retry support is desired.

Spring Batch supports these scenarios through the `RetryTemplate` that (much like its various other `Template` cousins) isolates your logic from the nuances of retries and instead enables you to write the code as though you were going to attempt it only once. Let Spring Batch handle everything else through declarative configuration.

The `RetryTemplate` supports many use cases, with convenient APIs to wrap otherwise tedious retry/fail/recover cycles in concise, single-method invocations.

Let's take a look at the modified version of a simple `ItemWriter<T>` from recipe 11-4 on how to write a custom `ItemWriter<T>`. The solution was simple enough and would ideally work all the time. It fails to handle the error cases for the service, however. When dealing with RPC, always proceed as if it's almost impossible for things to go right; the service itself may surface a semantic or system violation. An example might be a duplicate database key, invalid credit card number, and so on. This is true whether the service is distributed or in-VM, of course.

Next, the RPC layer below the system may also fault. Here's the rewritten code, this time allowing for retries:

```
ppackage com.apress.springrecipes.springbatch;

import org.slf4j.Logger;
import org.slf4j.LoggerFactory;
import org.springframework.batch.item.ItemWriter;
import org.springframework.retry.RetryCallback;
import org.springframework.retry.support.RetryTemplate;
```

```java
import java.util.List;

public class RetryableUserRegistrationServiceItemWriter implements
ItemWriter<UserRegistration> {

    private static final Logger logger = LoggerFactory.getLogger(RetryableUserRegistration
    ServiceItemWriter.class);

    private final UserRegistrationService userRegistrationService;
    private final RetryTemplate retryTemplate;

    public RetryableUserRegistrationServiceItemWriter(UserRegistrationService
    userRegistrationService, RetryTemplate retryTemplate) {
        this.userRegistrationService = userRegistrationService;
        this.retryTemplate = retryTemplate;
    }

    public void write(List<? extends UserRegistration> items)
        throws Exception {
        for (final UserRegistration userRegistration : items) {
            UserRegistration registeredUserRegistration = retryTemplate.execute(
                (RetryCallback<UserRegistration, Exception>) context ->
                userRegistrationService.registerUser(userRegistration));

            logger.debug("Registered: {}", registeredUserRegistration);
        }
    }
}
```

As you can see, the code hasn't changed much, and the result is much more robust. The RetryTemplate itself is configured in the Spring context, although it's trivial to create in code. I declare it in the Spring context only because there is some surface area for configuration when creating the object, and I try to let Spring handle the configuration.

One of the more useful settings for the RetryTemplate is the BackOffPolicy in use. The BackOffPolicy dictates how long the RetryTemplate should back off between retries. Indeed, there's even support for growing the delay between retries after each failed attempt to avoid lock stepping with other clients attempting the same invocation. This is great for situations in which there are potentially many concurrent attempts on the same resource and a race condition may ensue. There are other BackOffPolicy settings, including one that delays retries by a fixed amount called FixedBackOffPolicy.

```java
@Bean
public RetryTemplate retryTemplate() {
    RetryTemplate retryTemplate = new RetryTemplate();
    retryTemplate.setBackOffPolicy(backOffPolicy());
    return retryTemplate;
}

@Bean
public ExponentialBackOffPolicy backOffPolicy() {
    ExponentialBackOffPolicy backOffPolicy = new ExponentialBackOffPolicy();
    backOffPolicy.setInitialInterval(1000);
```

```
    backOffPolicy.setMaxInterval(10000);
    backOffPolicy.setMultiplier(2);
    return backOffPolicy;
}
```

You have configured a RetryTemplate's backOffPolicy so that backOffPolicy will wait 1 second (1,000 milliseconds) before the initial retry. Subsequent attempts will double that value (the growth is influenced by the multiplier). It'll continue until the maxInterval is met, at which point all subsequent retry intervals will level off, retrying at a consistent interval.

AOP-Based Retries

An alternative is an AOP adviser provided by Spring Batch that will wrap invocations of methods whose success is not guaranteed in retries, as you did with the RetryTemplate. In the previous example, you rewrote an ItemWriter<T> to make use of the template. Another approach might be to merely advise the entire userRegistrationService proxy with this retry logic. In this case, the code could go back to the way it was in the original example, with no RetryTemplate!

To do so, you would annotate the method (or methods) to be retryable with the @Retryable annotation. To achieve the same as in the code with an explicit RetryTemplate, you would need to add the following.

```
@Retryable(backoff = @Backoff(delay = 1000, maxDelay = 10000, multiplier = 2))
public UserRegistration registerUser(UserRegistration userRegistrationRegistration) { ... }
```

Only adding this annotation isn't enough; you would also need to enable annotation processing for this with the @EnableRetry annotation on your configuration.

```
@Configuration
@EnableBatchProcessing
@EnableRetry
@ComponentScan("com.apress.springrecipes.springbatch")
@PropertySource("classpath:/batch.properties")
public class BatchConfiguration { ... }
```

11-7. Control Step Execution

Problem

You want to control how steps are executed, perhaps to eliminate a needless waste of time by introducing concurrency or by executing steps only if a condition is true.

Solution

There are different ways to change the runtime profile of your jobs, mainly by exerting control over the way steps are executed: concurrent steps, decisions, and sequential steps.

How It Works

Thus far, you have explored running one step in a job. Typical jobs of almost any complexity will have multiple steps, however. A step provides a boundary (transactional or not) to the beans and logic it encloses. A step can have its own reader, writer, and processor. Each step helps decide what the next step will be. A step is isolated and provides focused functionality that can be assembled using the updated schema and configuration options in Spring Batch in sophisticated workflows. In fact, some of the concepts and patterns you're about to see will be familiar if you have an interest in business process management (BPM) systems and workflows. BPM provides many constructs for process or job control that are similar to what you're seeing here. A step often corresponds to a bullet point when you outline the definition of a job on paper. For example, a batch job to load the daily sales and produce a report might be proposed as follows:

1. Load customers from the CSV file into the database.

2. Calculate daily statistics and write to a report file.

3. Send messages to the message queue to notify an external system of the successful registration for each of the newly loaded customers.

Sequential Steps

In the previous example, there's an implied sequence between the first two steps; the audit file can't be written until all the registrations have completed. This sort of relationship is the default relationship between two steps. One occurs after the other. Each step executes with its own execution context and shares only a parent job execution context and an order.

```
@Bean
public Job nightlyRegistrationsJob () {
    return jobs.get("nightlyRegistrationsJob ")
        .start(loadRegistrations())
        .next(reportStatistics())
        .next(...)
        .build();
    }
}
```

Concurrency

The first version of Spring Batch was oriented toward batch processing inside the same thread and, with some alteration, perhaps inside the virtual machine. There were workarounds, of course, but the situation was less than ideal.

In the outline for this example job, the first step had to come before the second two because the second two are dependent on the first. The second two, however, do not share any such dependencies. There's no reason why the audit log couldn't be written at the same time as the JMS messages are being delivered. Spring Batch provides the capability to fork processing to enable just this sort of arrangement.

```
@Bean
public Job insertIntoDbFromCsvJob() {
    JobBuilder builder = jobs.get("insertIntoDbFromCsvJob");
    return builder
        .start(loadRegistrations())
        .split(taskExecutor())
```

```
        .add(
            builder.flow(reportStatistics()),
            builder.flow(sendJmsNotifications()))
      .build();
}
```

You can use the `split()` method on the job builder. To make a step into a flow, the `flow()` method of the job builder can be used; then, to add more steps to the flow, these can be added with the `next()` method. The `split()` method requires a `TaskExecutor` to be set; see recipe 2-23 for more information on scheduling and concurrency.

In this example, there's nothing to prevent you from having many steps within the flow elements, nor was there anything preventing you from having more steps after the split element. The split element, like the step elements, takes a next attribute as well.

Spring Batch provides a mechanism to offload processing to another process. This distribution requires some sort of durable, reliable connection. This is a perfect use of JMS because it's rock-solid and transactional, fast, and reliable. Spring Batch support is modeled at a slightly higher level, on top of the Spring Integration abstractions for Spring Integration channels. This support is not in the main Spring Batch code; it can be found in the spring-batch-integration project. Remote chunking lets individual steps read and aggregate items as usual in the main thread. This step is called the *master*. Items read are sent to the `ItemProcessor<I,O>/ItemW riter<T>` running in another process (this is called the *slave*). If the slave is an aggressive consumer, you have a simple, generic mechanism to scale: work is instantly farmed out over as many JMS clients as you can throw at it. The aggressive-consumer pattern refers to the arrangement of multiple JMS clients all consuming the same queue's messages. If one client consumes a message and is busy processing, other idle queues will get the message instead. As long as there's a client that's idle, the message will be processed instantly.

Additionally, Spring Batch supports implicitly scaling out using a feature called *partitioning*. This feature is interesting because it's built in and generally very flexible. You replace your instance of a step with a subclass, `PartitionStep`, which knows how to coordinate distributed executors and maintains the metadata for the execution of the step, thus eliminating the need for a durable medium of communication as in the "remote chunking" technology.

The functionality here is also very generic. It could, conceivably, be used with any sort of grid fabric technology such as GridGain or Hadoop. Spring Batch ships with only a `TaskExecutorPartitionHandler`, which executes steps in multiple threads using a `TaskExecutor` strategy. This simple improvement might be enough of a justification for this feature! If you're really hurting, however, you can extend it.

Conditional Steps with Statuses

Using the `ExitStatus` of a given job or step to determine the next step is the simplest example of a conditional flow. Spring Batch facilitates this through the use of the stop, next, fail, and end elements. By default, assuming no intervention, a step will have an `ExitStatus` that matches its `BatchStatus`, which is a property whose values are defined in an enum and may be any of the following: COMPLETED, STARTING, STARTED, STOPPING, STOPPED, FAILED, ABANDONED, or UNKNOWN.

Let's look at an example that executes one of two steps based on the success of a preceding step:

```
@Bean
public Job insertIntoDbFromCsvJob() {
    return jobs.get("User Registration Import Job")
        .start(step1())
            .on("COMPLETED").to(step2())
            .on("FAILED").to(failureStep())
        .build();
}
```

It's also possible to provide a wildcard. This is useful if you want to ensure a certain behavior for any number of BatchStatus values, perhaps in tandem with a more specific next element that matches only one BatchStatus.

```
@Bean
public Job insertIntoDbFromCsvJob() {
    return jobs.get("User Registration Import Job")
        .start(step1())
            .on("COMPLETED").to(step2())
            .on("*").to(failureStep())
        .build();
}
```

In this example, you are instructing Spring Batch to perform some step based on any unaccounted-for ExitStatus. Another option is to just stop processing altogether with a BatchStatus of FAILED. You can do this using the fail element. A less aggressive rewrite of the preceding example might be the following:

```
@Bean
public Job insertIntoDbFromCsvJob() {
    return jobs.get("User Registration Import Job")
        .start(step1())
            .on("COMPLETED").to(step2())
            .on("FAILED").fail()
        .build();
}
```

In all these examples, you're reacting to the standard BatchStatus values that the Spring Batch framework provides. But it's also possible to raise your own ExitStatus. If, for example, you wanted the whole job to fail with a custom ExitStatus of MAN DOWN, you might do something like this:

```
@Bean
public Job insertIntoDbFromCsvJob() {
    return jobs.get("User Registration Import Job")
        .start(step1())
            .on("COMPLETED").to(step2())
            .on("FAILED").end("MAN DOWN")
        .build();
}
```

Finally, if all you want to do is end processing with a BatchStatus of COMPLETED, you can use the end() method. This is an explicit way of ending a flow as if it had run out of steps and incurred no errors.

```
@Bean
public Job insertIntoDbFromCsvJob() {
    return jobs.get("User Registration Import Job")
        .start(step1())
            .on("COMPLETED").end()
            .on("FAILED").to(errorStep())
        .build();
}
```

Conditional Steps with Decisions

If you want to vary the execution flow based on some logic more complex than a job's ExitStatus values, you may give Spring Batch a helping hand by using a decision element and providing it with an implementation of a JobExecutionDecider.

```
package com.apress.springrecipes.springbatch;

import org.springframework.batch.core.JobExecution;
import org.springframework.batch.core.StepExecution;
import org.springframework.batch.core.job.flow.FlowExecutionStatus;
import org.springframework.batch.core.job.flow.JobExecutionDecider;

public class HoroscopeDecider implements JobExecutionDecider {

    private boolean isMercuryIsInRetrograde () { return Math.random() > .9 ; }

    public FlowExecutionStatus decide(JobExecution jobExecution,
                                      StepExecution stepExecution) {
        if (isMercuryIsInRetrograde()) {
            return new FlowExecutionStatus("MERCURY_IN_RETROGRADE");
        }
        return FlowExecutionStatus.COMPLETED;
    }
}
```

All that remains is the configuration, shown here:

```
@Bean
public Job insertIntoDbFromCsvJob() {
    JobBuilder builder = jobs.get("insertIntoDbFromCsvJob");
    return builder
        .start(step1())
        .next((horoscopeDecider())
            .on("MERCURY_IN_RETROGRADE").to(step2())
            .on(("COMPLETED ").to(step3())
        .build();
}
```

11-8. Launch a Job

Problem

What deployment scenarios does Spring Batch support? How does Spring Batch launch? How does Spring Batch work with a system scheduler, such as cron or autosys, or from a web application? You want to understand all this.

Solution

Spring Batch works well in all environments that Spring runs: your public static void main, OSGi, a web application—anywhere! Some use cases are uniquely challenging, though: it is rarely practical to run Spring Batch in the same thread as an HTTP response because it might end up stalling execution, for example. Spring Batch supports asynchronous execution for just this scenario. Spring Batch also provides a convenience class that can be readily used with cron or autosys to support launching jobs. Additionally, Spring's excellent scheduler namespace provides a great mechanism to schedule jobs.

How It Works

Before you get into creating a solution, it's important to know what options are available for deploying and running these solutions. All solutions require, at minimum, a job and a JobLauncher. You already configured these components in the previous recipe. The job is configured in your Spring application context, as you'll see later. The simplest example of launching a Spring Batch solution from Java code is about five lines of Java code (three if you've already got a handle to the ApplicationContext)!

```
package com.apress.springrecipes.springbatch;

import org.springframework.batch.core.Job;
import org.springframework.batch.core.JobParameters;
import org.springframework.batch.core.JobParametersBuilder;
import org.springframework.batch.core.launch.JobLauncher;
import org.springframework.context.support.ClassPathXmlApplicationContext;

import java.util.Date;

public class Main {
    public static void main(String[] args) throws Throwable {
        ClassPathXmlApplicationContext ctx = new ClassPathXmlApplicationContext("solution2.xml");

        JobLauncher jobLauncher = ctx.getBean("jobLauncher", JobLauncher.class);
        Job job = ctx.getBean("myJobName", Job.class);
        JobExecution jobExecution = jobLauncher.run(job, new JobParameters());
    }
}
```

As you can see, the JobLauncher reference you configured previously is obtained and used to then launch an instance of a Job. The result is a JobExecution. You can interrogate the JobExecution for information on the state of the Job, including its exit status and runtime status.

```
JobExecution jobExecution = jobLauncher.run(job, jobParameters);
BatchStatus batchStatus = jobExecution.getStatus();
while(batchStatus.isRunning()) {
    System.out.println( "Still running...");
    Thread.sleep( 10 * 1000 ); // 10 seconds
}
```

You can also get the ExitStatus.

```
System.out.println( "Exit code: "+ jobExecution.getExitStatus().getExitCode());
```

The JobExecution also provides a lot of other useful information such as the create time of the Job, the start time, the last updated date, and the end time—all as java.util.Date instances. If you want to correlate the job back to the database, you'll need the job instance and the ID.

```
JobInstance jobInstance = jobExecution.getJobInstance();
System.out.println( "job instance Id: "+ jobInstance.getId());
```

In this simple example, you use an empty JobParameters instance. In practice, this will work only once. Spring Batch builds a unique key based on the parameters and will use that to keep uniquely identifying one run of a given Job from another. You'll learn about parameterizing a Job in detail in the next recipe.

Launch from a Web Application

Launching a job from a web application requires a slightly different approach because the client thread (presumably an HTTP request) can't usually wait for a batch job to finish. The ideal solution is to have the job execute asynchronously when launched from a controller or action in the web tier, unattended by the client thread. Spring Batch supports this scenario through the use of a Spring TaskExecutor. This requires a simple change to the configuration for the JobLauncher, although the Java code can stay the same. Here, you will use a SimpleAsyncTaskExecutor that will spawn a thread of execution and manage that thread without blocking:

```
package com.apress.springrecipes.springbatch.config;

@Configuration
@EnableBatchProcessing
@ComponentScan("com.apress.springrecipes.springbatch")
@PropertySource("classpath:/batch.properties")
public class BatchConfiguration {

    @Bean
    public SimpleAsyncTaskExecutor taskExecutor() {
        return new SimpleAsyncTaskExecutor();
    }
}
```

As you cannot use the default settings anymore, you need to add your own implementation of a BatchConfigurer to configure the TaskExecutor and add it to the SimpleJobLauncher. For this implementation, you used the DefaultBatchConfigurer as a reference; you only override the createJobLauncher method to add the TaskExecutor.

```
package com.apress.springrecipes.springbatch.config;

import org.springframework.batch.core.configuration.annotation.DefaultBatchConfigurer;
import org.springframework.batch.core.launch.JobLauncher;
import org.springframework.batch.core.launch.support.SimpleJobLauncher;
import org.springframework.core.task.TaskExecutor;
import org.springframework.stereotype.Component;
```

```
@Component
public class CustomBatchConfigurer extends DefaultBatchConfigurer {

    private final TaskExecutor taskExecutor;

    public CustomBatchConfigurer(TaskExecutor taskExecutor) {
        this.taskExecutor = taskExecutor;
    }

    @Override
    protected JobLauncher createJobLauncher() throws Exception {
        SimpleJobLauncher jobLauncher = new SimpleJobLauncher();
        jobLauncher.setJobRepository(getJobRepository());
        jobLauncher.setTaskExecutor(this.taskExecutor);
        jobLauncher.afterPropertiesSet();
        return jobLauncher;
    }
}
```

Run from the Command Line

Another common use case is deployment of a batch process from a system scheduler such as cron or autosys, or even Window's event scheduler. Spring Batch provides a convenience class that takes as its parameters the name of the XML application context (that contains everything required to run a job) as well as the name of the job bean itself. Additional parameters may be provided and used to parameterize the job. These parameters must be in the form name=value. An example invocation of this class on the command line (on a Linux/Unix system), assuming that you set up the classpath, might look like this:

```
java CommandLineJobRunner jobs.xml hourlyReport date=`date +%m/%d/%Y time=date +%H`
```

The CommandLineJobRunner will even return system error codes (0 for success, 1 for failure, and 2 for an issue with loading the batch job) so that a shell (such as used by most system schedulers) can react or do something about the failure. More complicated return codes can be returned by creating and declaring a top-level bean that implements the interface ExitCodeMapper, in which you can specify a more useful translation of exit status messages to integer-based error codes that the shell will see on process exit.

Run on a Schedule

Spring has support for a scheduling framework (see also recipe 3-22). This framework lends itself perfectly to running Spring Batch. First, let's modify the existing application context configuration to enable scheduling by using the @EnableScheduling annotation and by adding a ThreadPoolTaskScheduler.

```
package com.apress.springrecipes.springbatch.config;

@Configuration
@EnableBatchProcessing
@ComponentScan("com.apress.springrecipes.springbatch")
@PropertySource("classpath:/batch.properties")
```

```java
@EnableScheduling
@EnableAsync
public class BatchConfiguration {

    @Bean
    public ThreadPoolTaskScheduler taskScheduler() {
        ThreadPoolTaskScheduler taskScheduler = new ThreadPoolTaskScheduler();
        taskScheduler.setThreadGroupName("batch-scheduler");
        taskScheduler.setPoolSize(10);
        return taskScheduler;
    }

}
```

These imports enable the simplest possible support for scheduling. The preceding annotations ensure that any bean under the package com.apress.springrecipes.springbatch will be configured and scheduled as required. The scheduler bean is as follows:

```java
package com.apress.springrecipes.springbatch.scheduler;

import org.springframework.batch.core.Job;
import org.springframework.batch.core.JobExecution;
import org.springframework.batch.core.JobParameters;
import org.springframework.batch.core.JobParametersBuilder;
import org.springframework.batch.core.launch.JobLauncher;
import org.springframework.scheduling.annotation.Scheduled;
import org.springframework.stereotype.Component;

import java.util.Date;

@Component
public class JobScheduler {

    private final JobLauncher jobLauncher;
    private final Job job;

    public JobScheduler(JobLauncher jobLauncher, Job job) {
        this.jobLauncher = jobLauncher;
        this.job = job;
    }

    public void runRegistrationsJob(Date date) throws Throwable {
        System.out.println("Starting job at " + date.toString());

        JobParametersBuilder jobParametersBuilder = new JobParametersBuilder();
        jobParametersBuilder.addDate("date", date);
        jobParametersBuilder.addString("input.file", "registrations");
```

```
        JobParameters jobParameters = jobParametersBuilder.toJobParameters();

        JobExecution jobExecution = jobLauncher.run(job, jobParameters);

        System.out.println("jobExecution finished, exit code: " + jobExecution.
        getExitStatus().getExitCode());
    }

    @Scheduled(fixedDelay = 1000 * 10)
    public void runRegistrationsJobOnASchedule() throws Throwable {
        runRegistrationsJob(new Date());
    }
}
```

There is nothing particularly novel here; it's a good study of how the different components of the Spring Framework work well together. The bean is recognized and becomes part of the application context because of the @Component annotation, which you enabled with the @ComponentScan annotation in your configuration class. There's only one Job in the UserJob class and only one JobLauncher, so you simply have those autowired into your bean. Finally, the logic for kicking off a batch run is inside the runRegistrationsJob(java.util.Date date) method. This method could be called from anywhere. Your only client for this functionality is the scheduled method runRegistrationsJobOnASchedule. The framework will invoke this method for you, according to the timeline dictated by the @Scheduled annotation.

There are other options for this sort of thing; traditionally in the Java and Spring world, this sort of problem would be a good fit for Quartz. It might still be, as the Spring scheduling support isn't designed to be as extensible as Quartz. If you are in an environment requiring more traditional, ops-friendly scheduling tools, there are of course old standbys like cron, autosys, and BMC, too.

11-9. Parameterize a Job

Problem

The previous examples work well enough, but they leave something to be desired in terms of flexibility. To apply the batch code to some other file, you'd have to edit the configuration and hard-code the name in there. The ability to parameterize the batch solution would be very helpful.

Solution

Use JobParameters to parameterize a job, which is then available to your steps through Spring Batch's expression language or via API calls.

How It Works

First you will see how to launch a job using JobParameters and after that you will learn how to use and access the JobParameters in a Job and the configuration.

Launch a Job with Parameters

A job is a prototype of a JobInstance. JobParameters are used to provide a way of identifying a unique run of a job (a JobInstance). These JobParameters allow you to give input to your batch process, just as you would with a method definition in Java. You've seen the JobParameters in previous examples but not in detail. The JobParameters object is created as you launch the job using the JobLauncher. To launch a job called dailySalesFigures, with the date for the job to work with, you would write something like this:

```
package com.apress.springrecipes.springbatch;

import com.apress.springrecipes.springbatch.config.BatchConfiguration;
import org.springframework.batch.core.*;
import org.springframework.batch.core.launch.JobLauncher;
import org.springframework.context.ApplicationContext;
import org.springframework.context.annotation.AnnotationConfigApplicationContext;

import java.util.Date;

public class Main {
    public static void main(String[] args) throws Throwable {

        ApplicationContext context =
            new AnnotationConfigApplicationContext(BatchConfiguration.class);

        JobLauncher jobLauncher = context.getBean(JobLauncher.class);
        Job job = context.getBean("dailySalesFigures", Job.class);

        jobLauncher.run(job, new JobParametersBuilder()
            .addDate( "date", new Date() ).toJobParameters());
    }
}
```

Access JobParameters

Technically, you can get at JobParameters via any of the ExecutionContexts (step and job). Once you have it, you can access the parameters in a type-safe way by calling getLong(), getString(), and so on. A simple way to do this is to bind to the @BeforeStep event, save the StepExecution, and iterate over the parameters this way. From here, you can inspect the parameters and do anything you want with them. Let's look at that in terms of the ItemProcessor<I,O> you wrote earlier.

```
// ...
private StepExecution stepExecution;

@BeforeStep
public void saveStepExecution(StepExecution stepExecution) {
    this.stepExecution = stepExecution;
}

public UserRegistration process(UserRegistration input) throws Exception {

    Map<String, JobParameter> params = stepExecution.getJobParameters().getParameters();
```

```
for (String jobParameterKey : params.keySet()) {
    System.out.println(String.format("%s=%s", jobParameterKey,
params.get(jobParameterKey).getValue().toString()));
}

Date date = stepExecution.getJobParameters().getDate("date");
// etc ...
}
```

This turns out to be of limited value. The 80 percent case is that you'll need to bind parameters from the job's launch to the Spring beans in the application context. These parameters are available only at runtime, whereas the steps in the XML application context are configured at design time. This happens in many places. Previous examples demonstrated ItemWriters<T> and ItemReaders<T> with hard-coded paths. That works fine unless you want to parameterize the file name. This is hardly acceptable unless you plan on using a job just once!

The core Spring Framework features an enhanced expression language that Spring Batch uses to defer binding of the parameter until the correct time (or, in this case, until the bean is in the correct scope). Spring Batch has the "step" scope for just this purpose. Let's take a look at how you'd rework the previous example to use a parameterized file name for the ItemReader's resource:

```
@Bean
@StepScope
public ItemReader<UserRegistration> csvFileReader(@Value("file:${user.home}/
batches/#{jobParameters['input.fileName']}.csv") Resource input) { ... }
```

All you did is scope the bean (the FlatFileItemReader<T>) to the life cycle of a step (at which point those JobParameters will resolve correctly) and then used the EL syntax to parameterize the path to work off of.

Summary

This chapter introduced you to the concepts of batch processing, some of its history, and why it fits in a modern-day architecture. You learned about Spring Batch, the batch processing from SpringSource, and how to do reading and writing with ItemReader<T> and ItemWriter<T> implementations in your batch jobs. You wrote your own ItemReader<T> and ItemWriter <T> implementations as needed and saw how to control the execution of steps inside a job.

CHAPTER 12

Spring with NoSQL

Most applications use a relational database such as Oracle, MySQL, or PostgreSQL; however, there is more to data storage than just SQL databases. There are

- Relational databases (Oracle, MySQL, PostgreSQL, etc.)

- Document stores (MongoDB, Couchbase)

- Key-value stores (Redis, Volgemort)

- Column stores (Cassandra)

- Graph stores (Neo4j, Giraph)

Each of these technologies (and all of the implementations) works in a different way, so you have to spend time learning each one you want to use. Additionally, it might feel that you have to write a lot of duplicated plumbing code for handling transactions and error translation.

The Spring Data project can help make life easier; it can help configure the different technologies with the plumbing code. Each of the integration modules will have support for exception translation to Spring's consistent DataAccessException hierarchy and the use of Spring's templating approach. Spring Data also provides a cross-storage solution for some technologies, which means part of your model can be stored in a relational database with JPA and the other part can be stored in a graph or document store.

Tip Each section in this chapter describes how to download and install the needed persistence store. However, the bin directory contains scripts that set up Docker containers for each persistence store.

12-1. Use MongoDB

Problem

You want to use MongoDB to store and retrieve documents.

Solution

Download and configure MongoDB.

© Marten Deinum, Daniel Rubio, and Josh Long 2017
M. Deinum et al., *Spring 5 Recipes*, DOI 10.1007/978-1-4842-2790-9_12

How It Works

Before you can start using MongoDB you need to have an instance installed and up and running. When you have it running you will need to connect to it to be able to use the datastore for actual storage. You will start with plain MongoDB how to store and retrieve documents and gradually move to Spring Data MongoDB to close with a reactive version of the repository.

Download and Start MongoDB

Download MongoDB from www.mongodb.org. Select the version that is applicable for the system in use and follow the installation instructions in the manual (http://docs.mongodb.org/manual/installation/). When the installation is complete, MongoDB can be started. To start MongoDB, execute the mongodb command on the command line (see Figure 12-1). This will start a MongoDB server on port 27017. If a different port is required, this can be done by specifying the --port option on the command line when starting the server.

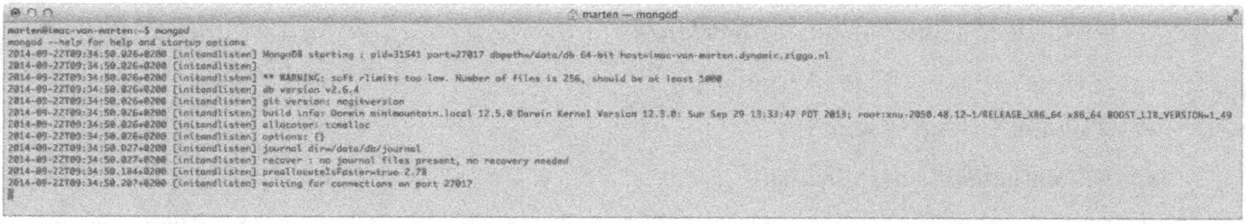

Figure 12-1. *Output after initial start of MongoDB*

The default location for storing data is \data\db (for Windows users, this is from the root of the disk where MongoDB was installed!). To change the path, use the --dbpath option on the command line. Make sure that the directory exists and is writable for MongoDB.

Connect to MongoDB

For a connection to MongoDB, you need an instance of Mongo. You can use this instance to get the database to use and the actual underlying collection (or collections). Let's create a small system that uses MongoDB to create an object to use for storage.

```
package com.apress.springrecipes.nosql;

public class Vehicle {

    private String vehicleNo;
    private String color;
    private int wheel;
    private int seat;

    public Vehicle() {
    }
```

```
    public Vehicle(String vehicleNo, String color, int wheel, int seat) {
        this.vehicleNo = vehicleNo;
        this.color = color;
        this.wheel = wheel;
        this.seat = seat;
    }
    /// Getters and Setters have been omitted for brevity.
}
```

To work with this object, create a repository interface.

```
package com.apress.springrecipes.nosql;

public interface VehicleRepository {

    long count();
    void save(Vehicle vehicle);
    void delete(Vehicle vehicle);
    List<Vehicle> findAll()
    Vehicle findByVehicleNo(String vehicleNo);
}
```

For MongoDB, create the MongoDBVehicleRepository implementation of the VehicleRepository.

```
package com.apress.springrecipes.nosql;

import com.mongodb.*;

import java.util.ArrayList;
import java.util.List;

public class MongoDBVehicleRepository implements VehicleRepository {

    private final Mongo mongo;
    private final String collectionName;
    private final String databaseName;

    public MongoDBVehicleRepository(Mongo mongo, String databaseName, String collectionName) {
        this.mongo = mongo;
        this.databaseName=databaseName;
        this.collectionName = collectionName;
    }

    @Override
    public long count() {
        return getCollection().count();
    }

    @Override
    public void save(Vehicle vehicle) {
        BasicDBObject query = new BasicDBObject("vehicleNo", vehicle.getVehicleNo());
        DBObject dbVehicle = transform(vehicle);
```

```
        DBObject fromDB = getCollection().findAndModify(query, dbVehicle);
        if (fromDB == null) {
            getCollection().insert(dbVehicle);
        }
    }

    @Override
    public void delete(Vehicle vehicle) {
        BasicDBObject query = new BasicDBObject("vehicleNo", vehicle.getVehicleNo());
        getCollection().remove(query);
    }

    @Override
    public List<Vehicle> findAll() {
        DBCursor cursor = getCollection().find(null);
        List<Vehicle> vehicles = new ArrayList<>(cursor.size());
        for (DBObject dbObject : cursor) {
            vehicles.add(transform(dbObject));
        }
        return vehicles;
    }

    @Override
    public Vehicle findByVehicleNo(String vehicleNo) {
        BasicDBObject query = new BasicDBObject("vehicleNo", vehicleNo);
        DBObject dbVehicle = getCollection().findOne(query);
        return transform(dbVehicle);
    }

    private DBCollection getCollection() {
        return mongo.getDB(databaseName).getCollection(collectionName);
    }

    private Vehicle transform(DBObject dbVehicle) {
        return new Vehicle(
            (String) dbVehicle.get("vehicleNo"),
            (String) dbVehicle.get("color"),
            (int) dbVehicle.get("wheel"),
            (int) dbVehicle.get("seat"));
    }

    private DBObject transform(Vehicle vehicle) {
        BasicDBObject dbVehicle = new BasicDBObject("vehicleNo", vehicle.getVehicleNo())
            .append("color", vehicle.getColor())
            .append("wheel", vehicle.getWheel())
            .append("seat", vehicle.getSeat());
        return dbVehicle;
    }
}
```

First notice the constructor takes three arguments. The first is the actual MongoDB client, the second is the name of the database that is going to be used, and the last is the name of the collection in which the objects are stored. Documents in MongoDB are stored in collections, and a collection belongs to a database.

For easy access to the DBCollection used, there is the getCollection method that gets a connection to the database and returns the configured DBCollection. This DBCollection can then be used to execute operations such as storing, deleting, or updating documents.

The save method will first try to update an existing document. If this fails, a new document for the given Vehicle will be created. To store objects, start by transforming the domain object Vehicle into a DBObject, in this case a BasicDBObject. The BasicDBObject takes key-value pairs of the different properties of your Vehicle object. When querying for a document, the same DBObject is used, and the key-value pairs that are present on the given object are used to look up documents; you can find an example in the findByVehicleNo method in the repository. Conversion from and to Vehicle objects is done through the two transform methods.

To use this class, create the following Main class:

```java
package com.apress.springrecipes.nosql;

import com.mongodb.MongoClient;

import java.util.List;

public class Main {

    public static final String DB_NAME = "vehicledb";

    public static void main(String[] args) throws Exception {
        // Default monogclient for localhost and port 27017
        MongoClient mongo = new MongoClient();

        VehicleRepository repository = new MongoDBVehicleRepository(mongo, DB_NAME,
        "vehicles");

        System.out.println("Number of Vehicles: " + repository.count());

        repository.save(new Vehicle("TEM0001", "RED", 4, 4));
        repository.save(new Vehicle("TEM0002", "RED", 4, 4));

        System.out.println("Number of Vehicles: " + repository.count());

        Vehicle v = repository.findByVehicleNo("TEM0001");

        System.out.println(v);

        List<Vehicle> vehicleList = repository.findAll();

        System.out.println("Number of Vehicles: " + vehicleList.size());
        vehicleList.forEach(System.out::println);
        System.out.println("Number of Vehicles: " + repository.count());
```

```
        // Cleanup and close
        mongo.dropDatabase(DB_NAME);
        mongo.close();
    }
}
```

The main class constructs an instance of the MongoClient that will try to connect to port 27017 on localhost for a MongoDB instance. If another port or host is needed, there is also a constructor that takes a host and port as parameters: new MongoClient("mongodb-server.local", 28018). Next an instance of the MongoDBVehicleRepository class is constructed; the earlier constructed MongoClient is passed as well as the name of the database, which is vehicledb, and the name of the collection, which is vehicles.

The next lines of code will insert two vehicles into the database, try to find them, and finally delete them. The last lines in the Main class will close the MongoClient and before doing so will drop the database. The latter is something you don't want to do when using a production database.

Use Spring for Configuration

The setup and configuration of the MongoClient and MongoDBVehicleRepository can easily be moved to the Spring configuration.

```java
package com.apress.springrecipes.nosql.config;

import com.apress.springrecipes.nosql.MongoDBVehicleRepository;
import com.apress.springrecipes.nosql.VehicleRepository;
import com.mongodb.Mongo;
import com.mongodb.MongoClient;
import org.springframework.context.annotation.Bean;
import org.springframework.context.annotation.Configuration;

import java.net.UnknownHostException;

@Configuration
public class MongoConfiguration {

    public static final String DB_NAME = "vehicledb";

    @Bean
    public Mongo mongo() throws UnknownHostException {
        return new MongoClient();
    }

    @Bean
    public VehicleRepository vehicleRepository(Mongo mongo) {
        return new MongoDBVehicleRepository(mongo, DB_NAME, " vehicles");
    }
}
```

The following @PreDestroy annotated method has been added to the MongoDBVehicleRepository to take care of the cleanup of the database.

```
@PreDestroy
public void cleanUp() {
    mongo.dropDatabase(databaseName);
}
```

Finally, the Main program needs to be updated to reflect the changes.

```
package com.apress.springrecipes.nosql;

...
import org.springframework.context.ApplicationContext;
import org.springframework.context.annotation.AnnotationConfigApplicationContext;
import org.springframework.context.support.AbstractApplicationContext;

import java.util.List;

public class Main {

    public static final String DB_NAME = "vehicledb";

    public static void main(String[] args) throws Exception {
        ApplicationContext ctx =
            new AnnotationConfigApplicationContext(MongoConfiguration.class);
        VehicleRepository repository = ctx.getBean(VehicleRepository.class);

        ...

        ((AbstractApplicationContext) ctx).close();

    }
}
```

The configuration is loaded by an AnnotationConfigApplicationContext. From this context, the VehicleRepository bean is retrieved and used to execute the operations. When the code that has run the context is closed, it triggers the cleanUp method in the MongoDBVehicleRepository.

Use a MongoTemplate to Simplify MongoDB Code

At the moment, the MongoDBVehicleRepository class uses the plain MongoDB API. Although it's not very complex, it still requires knowledge about the API. In addition, there are some repetitive tasks like mapping from and to a Vehicle object. Using a MongoTemplate can simplify the repository considerably.

■ **Note** Before using Spring Data Mongo, the relevant JARs need to be added to the classpath. When using Maven, add the following dependency:

```
<dependency>
    <groupId>org.springframework.data</groupId>
    <artifactId>spring-data-mongodb</artifactId>
    <version>1.10.1.RELEASE</version>
</dependency>
```

When using Gradle, use the following:

```
compile 'org.springframework.data:spring-data-mongodb:1.10.1.RELEASE'
```

```java
package com.apress.springrecipes.nosql;

import org.springframework.data.mongodb.core.MongoTemplate;
import org.springframework.data.mongodb.core.query.Query;

import javax.annotation.PreDestroy;
import java.util.List;

import static org.springframework.data.mongodb.core.query.Criteria.where;

public class MongoDBVehicleRepository implements VehicleRepository {

    private final MongoTemplate mongo;
    private final String collectionName;

    public MongoDBVehicleRepository(MongoTemplate mongo, String collectionName) {
        this.mongo = mongo;
        this.collectionName = collectionName;
    }

    @Override
    public long count() {
        return mongo.count(null, collectionName);
    }

    @Override
    public void save(Vehicle vehicle) {
        mongo.save(vehicle, collectionName);
    }

    @Override
    public void delete(Vehicle vehicle) {
        mongo.remove(vehicle, collectionName);
    }
```

```
    @Override
    public List<Vehicle> findAll() {
        return mongo.findAll(Vehicle.class, collectionName);
    }

    @Override
    public Vehicle findByVehicleNo(String vehicleNo) {
        return mongo.findOne(new Query(where("vehicleNo").is(vehicleNo)), Vehicle.class,
        collectionName);
    }

    @PreDestroy
    public void cleanUp() {
        mongo.execute(db -> {
            db.drop();
            return null;
        });
    }
}
```

The code looks a lot cleaner when using a MongoTemplate. It has convenience methods for almost every operation: save, update, and delete. Additionally, it has a nice query builder approach (see the findByVehicleNo method). There are no more mappings to and from the MongoDB classes, so there is no need to create a DBObject anymore. That burden is now handled by the MongoTemplate. To convert the Vehicle object to the MongoDB classes, a MongoConverter is used. By default a MappingMongoConverter is used. This mapper maps properties to attribute names, and vice versa, and while doing so, also tries to convert from and to the correct data type. If a specific mapping is needed, it is possible to write your own implementation of a MongoConverter and register it with the MongoTemplate.

Because of the use of the MongoTemplate, the configuration needs to be modified.

```
package com.apress.springrecipes.nosql.config;

import com.apress.springrecipes.nosql.MongoDBVehicleRepository;
import com.apress.springrecipes.nosql.VehicleRepository;
import com.mongodb.Mongo;
import org.springframework.context.annotation.Bean;
import org.springframework.context.annotation.Configuration;
import org.springframework.data.mongodb.core.MongoClientFactoryBean;
import org.springframework.data.mongodb.core.MongoTemplate;

@Configuration
public class MongoConfiguration {

    public static final String DB_NAME = "vehicledb";

    @Bean
    public MongoTemplate mongo(Mongo mongo) throws Exception {
        return new MongoTemplate(mongo, DB_NAME);
    }
```

```
    @Bean
    public MongoClientFactoryBean mongoFactoryBean() {
        return new MongoClientFactoryBean();
    }

    @Bean
    public VehicleRepository vehicleRepository(MongoTemplate mongo) {
        return new MongoDBVehicleRepository(mongo, "vehicles");
    }
}
```

Notice the use of the `MongoClientFactoryBean`. It allows for easy setup of the `MongoClient`. It isn't a requirement for using the `MongoTemplate`, but it makes it easier to configure the client. Another benefit is that there is no more `java.net.UnknownHostException` thrown that is handled internally by the `MongoClientFactoryBean`.

The `MongoTemplate` has various constructors. The one used here takes a `Mongo` instance and the name of the database to use. To resolve the database, an instance of a `MongoDbFactory` is used; by default, it's the `SimpleMongoDbFactory`. In most cases, this is sufficient, but if some special case arises, like encrypted connections, it is quite easy to extend the default implementation. Finally, the `MongoTemplate` is injected, together with the name of the collection, into the `MongoDBVehicleRepository`.

A final addition needs to be made to the `Vehicle` object. It is required that a field is available for storing the generated ID. This can be either a field with the name `id` or a field with the `@Id` annotation.

```
public class Vehicle {

    private String id;

...
}
```

Use Annotations to Specify Mapping Information

Currently the `MongoDBVehicleRepository` needs to know the name of the collection you want to access. It would be easier and more flexible if this could be specified on the `Vehicle` object, just as with a JPA `@Table` annotation. With Spring Data Mongo, this is possible using the `@Document` annotation.

```
package com.apress.springrecipes.nosql;

import org.springframework.data.mongodb.core.mapping.Document;

@Document(collection = "vehicles")
public class Vehicle { ... }
```

The `@Document` annotation can take two attributes: `collection` and `language`. The `collection` property is for specifying the name of the collection to use, and the `language` property is for specifying the language for this object. Now that the mapping information is on the `Vehicle` class, the collection name can be removed from the `MongoDBVehicleRepository`.

```java
public class MongoDBVehicleRepository implements VehicleRepository {

    private final MongoTemplate mongo;

    public MongoDBVehicleRepository(MongoTemplate mongo) {
        this.mongo = mongo;
    }

    @Override
    public long count() {
        return mongo.count(null, Vehicle.class);
    }

    @Override
    public void save(Vehicle vehicle) {
        mongo.save(vehicle);
    }

    @Override
    public void delete(Vehicle vehicle) {
        mongo.remove(vehicle);
    }

    @Override
    public List<Vehicle> findAll() {
        return mongo.findAll(Vehicle.class);
    }

    @Override
    public Vehicle findByVehicleNo(String vehicleNo) {
        return mongo.findOne(new Query(where("vehicleNo").is(vehicleNo)), Vehicle.class);
    }
}
```

Of course, the collection name can be removed from the configuration of the
MongoDBVehicleRepository as well.

```java
@Configuration
public class MongoConfiguration {
...
    @Bean
    public VehicleRepository vehicleRepository(MongoTemplate mongo) {
        return new MongoDBVehicleRepository(mongo);
    }
}
```

When running the Main class, the result should still be the same as it was before.

Create a Spring Data MongoDB Repository

Although the code has been reduced a lot in that there is no more mapping from and to MongoDB classes and no more collection names passing around, it can still be reduced even further. Leveraging another feature of Spring Data Mongo, the complete implementation of the MongoDBVehicleRepository could be removed.

First the configuration needs to be modified.

```java
package com.apress.springrecipes.nosql.config;

import com.mongodb.Mongo;
import org.springframework.context.annotation.Bean;
import org.springframework.context.annotation.Configuration;
import org.springframework.data.mongodb.core.MongoClientFactoryBean;
import org.springframework.data.mongodb.core.MongoTemplate;
import org.springframework.data.mongodb.repository.config.EnableMongoRepositories;

@Configuration
@EnableMongoRepositories(basePackages = "com.apress.springrecipes.nosql")
public class MongoConfiguration {

    public static final String DB_NAME = "vehicledb";

    @Bean
    public MongoTemplate mongoTemplate(Mongo mongo) throws Exception {
        return new MongoTemplate(mongo, DB_NAME);
    }

    @Bean
    public MongoClientFactoryBean mongoFactoryBean() {
        return new MongoClientFactoryBean();
    }
}
```

First, notice the removal of the @Bean method that constructed the MongoDBVehicleRepository. Second, notice the addition of the @EnableMongoRepositories annotation. This enables detection of interfaces that extend the Spring Data CrudRepository and are used for domain objects annotated with @Document.

To have your VehicleRepository detected by Spring Data, you need to let it extend CrudRepository or one of its subinterfaces like MongoRepository.

```java
package com.apress.springrecipes.nosql;

import org.springframework.data.mongodb.repository.MongoRepository;

public interface VehicleRepository extends MongoRepository<Vehicle, String> {

    public Vehicle findByVehicleNo(String vehicleNo);

}
```

You might wonder where all the methods have gone. They are already defined in the super interfaces and as such can be removed from this interface. The findByVehicleNo method is still there. This method will still be used to look up a Vehicle by its vehicleNo property. All the findBy methods are converted into a MongoDB query. The part after the findBy is interpreted as a property name. It is also possible to write more complex queries using different operators such as and, or, and between.

Now running the Main class again should still result in the same output; however, the actual code written to work with MongoDB has been minimized.

Create a Reactive Spring Data MongoDB Repository

Instead of creating a traditional MongoDB repository, it is possible to create a reactive repository, which is done by extending the ReactiveMongoRepository class (or one of the other reactive repository interfaces). This will change the return types for methods that return a single value into Mono<T> (or Mono<Void> for nonreturning methods) and Flux<T> for zero or more elements.

■ **Note**   If you want to use RxJava instead Project Reactor, extend one of the RxJava2*Repository interfaces and use a Single or Observable instead of Mono and Flux.

To be able to use a reactive repository implementation, you first have to use a reactive implementation of the MongoDB driver and configure Spring Data to use that driver. To make it easier, you can extend AbstractReactiveMongoConfiguration and implement the two required methods getDatabaseName and mongoClient.

```
@Configuration
@EnableReactiveMongoRepositories(basePackages = "com.apress.springrecipes.nosql")
public class MongoConfiguration extends AbstractReactiveMongoConfiguration {

    public static final String DB_NAME = "vehicledb";

    @Bean
    @Override
    public MongoClient reactiveMongoClient() {
        return MongoClients.create();
    }

    @Override
    protected String getDatabaseName() {
        return DB_NAME;
    }
}
```

Another thing that has changed is the use of @EnableReactiveMongoRepositories instead of @EnableMongoRepositories. The database name is still needed, and you need to connect with a reactive driver to the MongoDB instance. For this you can use one of the MongoClients.create methods; here you can simply use the default.

Next change VehicleRepository to extend ReactiveMongoRepository so it will become reactive; you also need to change the return type of the findByVehicleNo method to Mono<Vehicle> instead of a plain Vehicle.

```
package com.apress.springrecipes.nosql;

import org.springframework.data.mongodb.repository.ReactiveMongoRepository;
import reactor.core.publisher.Mono;

public interface VehicleRepository extends ReactiveMongoRepository<Vehicle, String> {

    Mono<Vehicle> findByVehicleNo(String vehicleNo);

}
```

The final piece that would need to change is the Main class to test all this. Instead of blocking calls, you want to use a stream of methods to be called.

```
package com.apress.springrecipes.nosql;

import com.apress.springrecipes.nosql.config.MongoConfiguration;
import org.springframework.context.ApplicationContext;
import org.springframework.context.annotation.AnnotationConfigApplicationContext;
import org.springframework.context.support.AbstractApplicationContext;
import reactor.core.publisher.Flux;

import java.util.concurrent.CountDownLatch;

public class Main {

    public static void main(String[] args) throws Exception {
        ApplicationContext ctx =
            new AnnotationConfigApplicationContext(MongoConfiguration.class);
        VehicleRepository repository = ctx.getBean(VehicleRepository.class);

        CountDownLatch countDownLatch = new CountDownLatch(1);

        repository.count().doOnSuccess(cnt -> System.out.println("Number of Vehicles: " + cnt))
            .thenMany(repository.saveAll(
                Flux.just(
                    new Vehicle("TEM0001", "RED", 4, 4),
                    new Vehicle("TEM0002", "RED", 4, 4)))).last()
        .then(repository.count()).doOnSuccess(cnt -> System.out.println("Number of
         Vehicles: " + cnt))
        .then(repository.findByVehicleNo("TEM0001")).doOnSuccess(System.out::println)
        .then(repository.deleteAll())
            .doOnSuccess(x -> countDownLatch.countDown())
            .doOnError(t -> countDownLatch.countDown())
        .then(repository.count()).subscribe(cnt -> System.out.println
        ("Number of Vehicles: " + cnt.longValue())));

        countDownLatch.await();
        ((AbstractApplicationContext) ctx).close();

    }
}
```

The flow starts with a count, and when that succeeds, the Vehicle instances are put into MongoDB. When the last() vehicle has been added, a count is done again, followed by a query that in turn is followed by a deleteAll. All these methods are called in a reactive fashion one after the other, triggered by an event. Because you don't want to block using the block() method, you wait for the code to execute using a CountDownLatch, and the counter is decremented after the deletion of all records, after which the program will continue execution. Granted, this is still blocking. When using this in a full reactive stack, you would probably return the Mono from the last then and do further composition or give the output a Spring WebFlux controller (see Chapter 5).

12-2. Use Redis

Problem

You want to utilize Redis to store data.

Solution

Download and install Redis and use Spring and Spring Data to access the Redis instance.

How It Works

Redis is a key-value cache or store, and it will hold only simple data types such as strings and hashes. When storing more complex data structures, conversion from and to that data structure is needed.

Download and Start Redis

You can download Redis sources from http://redis.io/download. At the time of writing, version 3.2.8 is the most recently released stable version. You can find a compiled version for Windows at https://github.com/MSOpenTech/redis/releases. The official download site only provides Unix binaries. Mac users can use Homebrew (http://brew.sh) to install Redis.

After downloading and installing Redis, start it using the redis-server command from the command line. When started, the output should be similar to that in Figure 12-2. It will output the process ID (PID) and the port number (default 6379) it listens on.

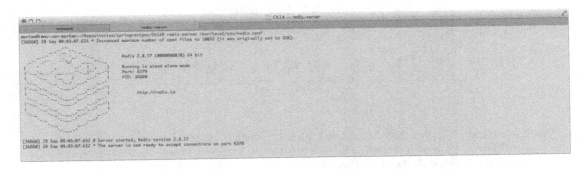

Figure 12-2. *Output after starting Redis*

Connect to Redis

To be able to connect to Redis, a client is needed, much like a JDBC driver to connect to a database. Several clients are available. You can find a full list on the Redis web site (http://redis.io/clients). For this recipe, the Jedis client will be used because it is quite active and recommended by the Redis team.

Let's start with a simple Hello World sample to see whether a connection to Redis can be made.

```
package com.apress.springrecipes.nosql;

import redis.clients.jedis.Jedis;

public class Main {

    public static void main(String[] args) {
        Jedis jedis = new Jedis("localhost");
        jedis.set("msg", "Hello World, from Redis!");
        System.out.println(jedis.get("msg"));
    }
}
```

A Jedis client is created and passed the name of the host to connect to, in this case simply localhost. The set method on the Jedis client will put a message in the store, and with get the message is retrieved again. Instead of a simple object, you could also have Redis mimic a List or a Map.

```
package com.apress.springrecipes.nosql;

import redis.clients.jedis.Jedis;

public class Main {

    public static void main(String[] args) {
        Jedis jedis = new Jedis("localhost");
        jedis.rpush("authors", "Marten Deinum", "Josh Long", "Daniel Rubio", "Gary Mak");
        System.out.println("Authors: " + jedis.lrange("authors",0,-1));

        jedis.hset("sr_3", "authors", "Gary Mak, Danial Rubio, Josh Long, Marten Deinum");
        jedis.hset("sr_3", "published", "2014");

        jedis.hset("sr_4", "authors", "Josh Long, Marten Deinum");
        jedis.hset("sr_4", "published", "2017");

        System.out.println("Spring Recipes 3rd: " + jedis.hgetAll("sr_3"));
        System.out.println("Spring Recipes 4th: " + jedis.hgetAll("sr_4"));
    }
}
```

With rpush and lpush, you can add elements to a List. rpush adds the elements to the end of the list, and lpush adds them to the start of the list. To retrieve them, the lrange or rrange method can be used. The lrange starts from the left and takes a start and end index. The sample uses -1, which indicates everything.

To add elements to a Map, use hset. This takes a key and a field and a value. Another option is to use hmset (multiset), which takes a Map<String, String> or Map<byte[], byte[]> as an argument.

Store Objects with Redis

Redis is a key-value store and can handle only String or byte[]. The same goes for the keys. So, storing an object in Redis isn't as straightforward as with other technologies. The object needs to be serialized to a String or a byte[] before storing.

Let's reuse the Vehicle class from recipe 12-1 and store and retrieve that using a Jedis client.

```
package com.apress.springrecipes.nosql;

import java.io.Serializable;

public class Vehicle implements Serializable{

    private String vehicleNo;
    private String color;
    private int wheel;
    private int seat;

    public Vehicle() {
    }

    public Vehicle(String vehicleNo, String color, int wheel, int seat) {
        this.vehicleNo = vehicleNo;
        this.color = color;
        this.wheel = wheel;
        this.seat = seat;
    }
    // getters/setters omitted
}
```

Notice the implements Serializable for the Vehicle class. This is needed to make the object serializable for Java. Before storing the object, it needs to be converted into a byte[] in Java. The ObjectOutputStream can write objects, and the ByteArrayOutputStream can write to a byte[]. To transform a byte[] into an object again, ObjectInputStream and ByteArrayInputStream are of help. Spring has a helper class for this called org.springframework.util.SerializationUtils, which provides serialize and deserialize methods.

Now in the Main class, let's create a Vehicle and store it using Jedis.

```
package com.apress.springrecipes.nosql;

import org.springframework.util.SerializationUtils;
import redis.clients.jedis.Jedis;

public class Main {

    public static void main(String[] args) throws Exception {
        Jedis jedis = new Jedis("localhost");

        final String vehicleNo = "TEM0001";
        Vehicle vehicle = new Vehicle(vehicleNo, "RED", 4,4);
```

```
        jedis.set(vehicleNo.getBytes(), SerializationUtils.serialize(vehicle));

        byte[] vehicleArray = jedis.get(vehicleNo.getBytes());

        System.out.println("Vehicle: " + SerializationUtils.deserialize(vehicleArray));
    }
}
```

First, an instance of the Vehicle is created. Next, the earlier mentioned SerializationUtils is used to convert the object into a byte[ ]. When storing a byte[ ], the key also needs to be a byte[ ]; hence, the key, here vehicleNo, is converted too. Finally, the same key is used to read the serialized object from the store again and convert it back into an object again. The drawback of this approach is that every object that is stored needs to implement the Serializable interface. If this isn't the case, the object might be lost, or an error during serialization might occur. In addition, the byte[ ] is a representation of the class. Now if this class is changed, there is a great chance that converting it back into an object will fail.

Another option is to use a String representation of the object. Convert the Vehicle object into XML or JSON, which would be more flexible than a byte[ ]. Let's take a look at converting the object into JSON using the excellent Jackson JSON library:

```
package com.apress.springrecipes.nosql;

import com.fasterxml.jackson.databind.ObjectMapper;
import redis.clients.jedis.Jedis;

public class Main {

    public static void main(String[] args) throws Exception {
        Jedis jedis = new Jedis("localhost");
        ObjectMapper mapper = new ObjectMapper();
        final String vehicleNo = "TEM0001";
        Vehicle vehicle = new Vehicle(vehicleNo, "RED", 4,4);

        jedis.set(vehicleNo, mapper.writeValueAsString(vehicle));

        String vehicleString = jedis.get(vehicleNo);

        System.out.println("Vehicle: " + mapper.readValue(vehicleString, Vehicle.class));
    }
}
```

First, an instance of the ObjectMapper is needed. This object is used to convert from and to JSON. When writing, the writeValueAsString method is used as it will transform the object into a JSON String. This String is then stored in Redis. Next, the String is read again and passed to the readValue method of the ObjectMapper. Based on the type argument, Vehicle.class here, an object is constructed, and the JSON is mapped to an instance of the given class.

Storing objects when using Redis isn't straightforward, and some argue that this isn't how Redis was intended to be used (storing complex object structures).

Configure and Use the RedisTemplate

Depending on the client library used to connect to Redis, it might be harder to use the Redis API. To unify this, there is the RedisTemplate. It can work with most Redis Java clients out there. Next to providing a unified approach, it also takes care of translating any exceptions into the Spring's DataAccessException hierarchy. This lets it integrate nicely with any already existing data access and allows it to use Spring's transactions support.

The RedisTemplate requires a RedisConnectionFactory to be able to get a connection. The RedisConnectionFactory is an interface, and several implementations are available. In this case, the JedisConnectionFactory is needed.

```
package com.apress.springrecipes.nosql.config;

import com.apress.springrecipes.nosql.Vehicle;
import org.springframework.context.annotation.Bean;
import org.springframework.context.annotation.Configuration;
import org.springframework.data.redis.connection.RedisConnectionFactory;
import org.springframework.data.redis.connection.jedis.JedisConnectionFactory;
import org.springframework.data.redis.core.RedisTemplate;

@Configuration
public class RedisConfig {

    @Bean
    public RedisTemplate<String, Vehicle> redisTemplate(RedisConnectionFactory
    connectionFactory) {
        RedisTemplate template = new RedisTemplate();
        template.setConnectionFactory(connectionFactory);
        return template;
    }

    @Bean
    public RedisConnectionFactory redisConnectionFactory() {
        return new JedisConnectionFactory();
    }
}
```

Notice the return type of the redisTemplate bean method. RedisTemplate is a generic class and requires a key and value type to be specified. In this case, String is the type of key, and Vehicle is the type of value. When storing and retrieving objects, RedisTemplate will take care of the conversion. Conversion is done using a RedisSerializer interface, which is an interface for which several implementations exist (see Table 12-1). The default RedisSerializer, JdkSerializationRedisSerializer, uses standard Java serialization to convert objects to byte[ ] and back.

Table 12-1. Default RedisSerializer Implementations

Name	Description
GenericToStringSerializer	String to byte[] serializer; uses the Spring ConversionService to convert objects to String before converting to byte[]
Jackson2JsonRedisRedisSerializer	Reads and writes JSON using a Jackson 2 ObjectMapper
JacksonJsonRedisRedisSerializer	Reads and writes JSON using a Jackson ObjectMapper
JdkSerializationRedisSerializer	Uses default Java serialization and deserialization and is the default implementation used
OxmSerializer	Reads and writes XML using Spring's Marshaller and Unmarshaller
StringRedisSerializer	Simple String to byte[] converter

To be able to use the RedisTemplate, the Main class needs to be modified. The configuration needs to be loaded and the RedisTemplate retrieved from it.

```
package com.apress.springrecipes.nosql;

import com.apress.springrecipes.nosql.config.RedisConfig;
import org.springframework.context.ApplicationContext;
import org.springframework.context.annotation.AnnotationConfigApplicationContext;
import org.springframework.data.redis.core.RedisTemplate;

public class Main {

    public static void main(String[] args) throws Exception {
        ApplicationContext context = new AnnotationConfigApplicationContext(RedisConfig.class);
        RedisTemplate<String, Vehicle> template = context.getBean(RedisTemplate.class);

        final String vehicleNo = "TEM0001";
        Vehicle vehicle = new Vehicle(vehicleNo, "RED", 4,4);
        template.opsForValue().set(vehicleNo, vehicle);
        System.out.println("Vehicle: " + template.opsForValue().get(vehicleNo));
    }
}
```

When the RedisTemplate template has been retrieved from ApplicationContext, it can be used. The biggest advantage here is that you can use objects, and the template handles the hard work of converting from and to objects. Notice how the set method takes a String and Vehicle as arguments instead of only String or byte[]. This makes code more readable and easier to maintain. By default JDK serialization is used. To use Jackson, a different RedisSerializer needs to be configured.

```
package com.apress.springrecipes.nosql.config;
...
import org.springframework.data.redis.serializer.Jackson2JsonRedisSerializer;

@Configuration
public class RedisConfig {
```

```
@Bean
public RedisTemplate<String, Vehicle> redisTemplate() {
    RedisTemplate template = new RedisTemplate();
    template.setConnectionFactory(redisConnectionFactory());
    template.setDefaultSerializer(new Jackson2JsonRedisSerializer(Vehicle.class));
    return template;
}
...
}
```

The RedisTemplate template will now use a Jackson ObjectMapper object to perform the serialization and deserialization. The remainder of the code can remain the same. When running the main program again, it still works, and the object will be stored using JSON. When Redis is used inside a transaction, it can also participate in that same transaction. For this, set the enableTransactionSupport property on the RedisTemplate template to true. This will take care of executing the Redis operation inside the transaction when the transaction commits.

12-3. Use Neo4j

Problem

You want to use Neo4j in your application.

Solution

Use the Spring Data Neo4j library to access Neo4j.

How It Works

Before you can start using Neo4J you need to have an instance installed and up and running. When you have it running you will need to connect to it to be able to use the datastore for actual storage. You will start with a plain Neo4J based repository to show how to store and retrieve objects and gradually move to Spring Data Neo4J based repositories.

Download and Run Neo4J

You can download Neo4J from the Neo4j web site (http://neo4j.com/download/). For this recipe, it is enough to download the community edition; however, it should also work with the commercial version of Neo4j. Windows users can run the installer to install Neo4j. Mac and Linux users can extract the archive and, from inside the directory created, start with bin/neo4j. Mac users can also use Homebrew (http://brew.sh) to install Neo4j with brew install neo4j. Starting can then be done with neo4j start on the command line.

After starting on the command line, the output should be similar to that of Figure 12-3.

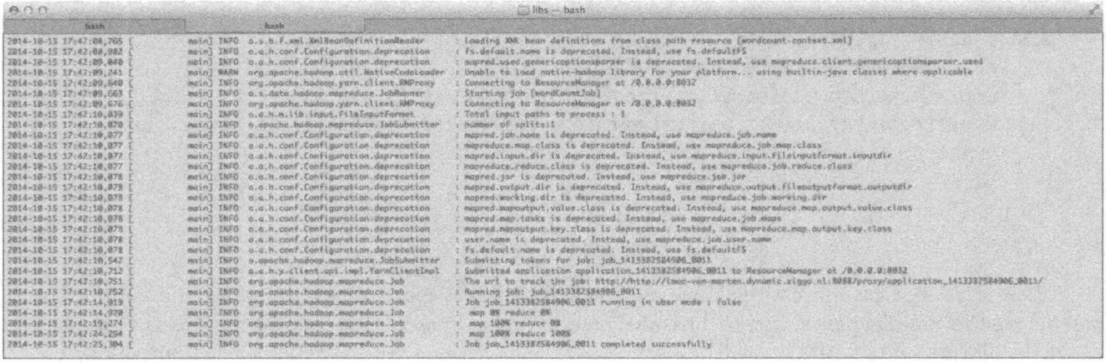

Figure 12-3. *Output after initial start of Neo4j*

Start Neo4j

Let's start by creating a simple Hello World program with an embedded Neo4j server. Create a `Main` class that starts an embedded server, adds some data to Neo4j, and retrieves it again.

```java
package com.apress.springrecipes.nosql;

import org.neo4j.graphdb.GraphDatabaseService;
import org.neo4j.graphdb.Node;
import org.neo4j.graphdb.Transaction;
import org.neo4j.graphdb.factory.GraphDatabaseFactory;

import java.nio.file.Paths;

public class Main {

    public static void main(String[] args) {
        final String DB_PATH = System.getProperty("user.home") + "/friends";

        GraphDatabaseService db = new GraphDatabaseFactory()
            .newEmbeddedDatabase(Paths.get(DB_PATH).toFile());

        Transaction tx1 = db.beginTx();

        Node hello = db.createNode();
        hello.setProperty("msg", "Hello");

        Node world = db.createNode();
        world.setProperty("msg", "World");
        tx1.success();

        db.getAllNodes().stream()
            .map(n -> n.getProperty("msg"))
            .forEach(m -> System.out.println("Msg: " + m));

        db.shutdown();
    }
}
```

This Main class will start an embedded Neo4j server. Next it will start a transaction and create two nodes. Next all nodes are retrieved, and the value of the msg property is printed to the console. Neo4j is good at traversing relations between nodes. It is especially optimized for that (just like other Graph data stores).

Let's create some nodes that have a relationship between them.

```
package com.apress.springrecipes.nosql;

import org.neo4j.graphdb.*;
import org.neo4j.graphdb.factory.GraphDatabaseFactory;

import java.nio.file.Paths;

import static com.apress.springrecipes.nosql.Main.RelationshipTypes.*;

public class Main {

    enum RelationshipTypes implements RelationshipType {FRIENDS_WITH, MASTER_OF, SIBLING,
    LOCATION}

    public static void main(String[] args) {
        final String DB_PATH = System.getProperty("user.home") + "/friends";
        final GraphDatabaseService db = new GraphDatabaseFactory()
            .newEmbeddedDatabase(Paths.get(DB_PATH).toFile());
        final Label character = Label.label("character");
        final Label planet = Label.label("planet");

        try (Transaction tx1 = db.beginTx()) {

            // Planets
            Node dagobah = db.createNode(planet);
            dagobah.setProperty("name", "Dagobah");

            Node tatooine = db.createNode(planet);
            tatooine.setProperty("name", "Tatooine");

            Node alderaan = db.createNode(planet);
            alderaan.setProperty("name", "Alderaan");

            // Characters
            Node yoda = db.createNode(character);
            yoda.setProperty("name", "Yoda");

            Node luke = db.createNode(character);
            luke.setProperty("name", "Luke Skywalker");

            Node leia = db.createNode(character);
            leia.setProperty("name", "Leia Organa");

            Node han = db.createNode(character);
            han.setProperty("name", "Han Solo");
```

```
        // Relations
        yoda.createRelationshipTo(luke, MASTER_OF);
        yoda.createRelationshipTo(dagobah, LOCATION);
        luke.createRelationshipTo(leia, SIBLING);
        luke.createRelationshipTo(tatooine, LOCATION);
        luke.createRelationshipTo(han, FRIENDS_WITH);
        leia.createRelationshipTo(han, FRIENDS_WITH);
        leia.createRelationshipTo(alderaan, LOCATION);

        tx1.success();
    }

    Result result = db.execute("MATCH (n) RETURN n.name as name");
    result.stream()
        .flatMap(m -> m.entrySet().stream())
        .map(row -> row.getKey() + " : " + row.getValue() + ";")
        .forEach(System.out::println);

    db.shutdown();
    }
}
```

The code reflects a tiny part of the Star Wars universe. It has characters and their locations, which are actually planets. There are also relations between people (see Figure 12-4 for the relationship diagram).

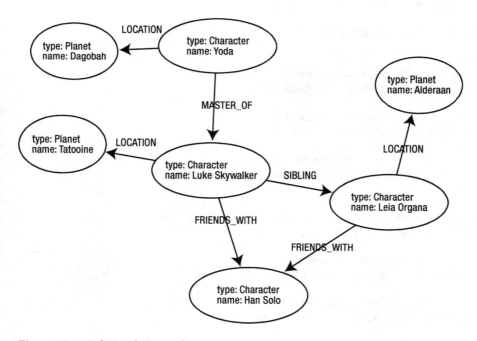

Figure 12-4. *Relationship sample*

The relationships in the code are enabled by using an enum that implements a Neo4j interface called RelationshipType. This is, as the name suggests, needed to differentiate between the different types of relationships. The type of node is differentiated by putting a label on the node. The name is set as a basic property on the node. When running the code, it will execute the cypher query MATCH (n) RETURN n.name as name. This selects all nodes and returns the name property of all the nodes.

Map Objects with Neo4j

The code until now is quite low level and bound to plain Neo4j. Creating and manipulating nodes is cumbersome. Ideally, you would use a Planet class and a Character class and have them stored/retrieved from Neo4j. First create the Planet and Character classes.

```java
package com.apress.springrecipes.nosql;

public class Planet {

    private long id = -1;
    private String name;
    // Getters and Setters omitted
}
package com.apress.springrecipes.nosql;

import java.util.ArrayList;
import java.util.Collections;
import java.util.List;

public class Character {

    private long id = -1;
    private String name;

    private Planet location;
    private final List<Character> friends = new ArrayList<>();
    private Character apprentice;

    public void addFriend(Character friend) {
        friends.add(friend);
    }

    // Getters and Setters omitted
}
```

The Planet class is quite straightforward. It has id and name properties. The Character class is a bit more complicated. It also has the id and name properties along with some additional properties for the relationships. There is the location value for the LOCATION relationship, a collection of Characters for the FRIENDS_WITH relationship, and also an apprentice for the MASTER_OF relationship.

To be able to store these classes, let's create a StarwarsRepository interface to hold the save operations.

```
package com.apress.springrecipes.nosql;

public interface StarwarsRepository {

    Planet save(Planet planet);
    Character save(Character character);

}
```

Here's the implementation for Neo4j:

```
package com.apress.springrecipes.nosql;

import org.neo4j.graphdb.GraphDatabaseService;
import org.neo4j.graphdb.Label;
import org.neo4j.graphdb.Node;
import org.neo4j.graphdb.Transaction;

import static com.apress.springrecipes.nosql.RelationshipTypes.*;

public class Neo4jStarwarsRepository implements StarwarsRepository {

    private final GraphDatabaseService db;

    public Neo4jStarwarsRepository(GraphDatabaseService db) {
        this.db = db;
    }

    @Override
    public Planet save(Planet planet) {
        if (planet.getId() != null) {
            return planet;
        }
        try (Transaction tx = db.beginTx()) {
            Label label = Label.label("planet");
            Node node = db.createNode(label);
            node.setProperty("name", planet.getName());
            tx.success();
            planet.setId(node.getId());
            return planet;
        }
    }

    @Override
    public Character save(Character character) {
        if (character.getId() != null) {
            return character;
        }
```

```
try (Transaction tx = db.beginTx()) {
    Label label = Label.label("character");
    Node node = db.createNode(label);
    node.setProperty("name", character.getName());

    if (character.getLocation() != null) {
        Planet planet = character.getLocation();
        planet = save(planet);
        node.createRelationshipTo(db.getNodeById(planet.getId()), LOCATION);
    }

    for (Character friend : character.getFriends()) {
        friend = save(friend);
        node.createRelationshipTo(db.getNodeById(friend.getId()), FRIENDS_WITH);
    }

    if (character.getApprentice() != null) {
        save(character.getApprentice());
        node.createRelationshipTo(db.getNodeById(character.getApprentice().getId()),
        MASTER_OF);
    }

    tx.success();
    character.setId(node.getId());
    return character;
    }
  }
}
```

There is a whole lot going on here to convert the objects into a Node object. For the Planet object, it is pretty easy. First check whether it has already been persisted (the ID is greater than -1 in that case); if not, start a transaction, create a node, set the name property, and transfer the id value to the Planet object. However, for the Character class, it is a bit more complicated as all the relationships need to be taken into account.

The Main class needs to be modified to reflect the changes to the classes.

```
package com.apress.springrecipes.nosql;

import org.neo4j.graphdb.GraphDatabaseService;
import org.neo4j.graphdb.Result;
import org.neo4j.graphdb.Transaction;
import org.neo4j.graphdb.factory.GraphDatabaseFactory;

import java.nio.file.Paths;

public class Main {

    public static void main(String[] args) {
        final String DB_PATH = System.getProperty("user.home") + "/starwars";
        final GraphDatabaseService db = new GraphDatabaseFactory().
        newEmbeddedDatabase(Paths.get(DB_PATH).toFile());
```

```
    StarwarsRepository repository = new Neo4jStarwarsRepository(db);

    try (Transaction tx = db.beginTx()) {

        // Planets
        Planet dagobah = new Planet();
        dagobah.setName("Dagobah");

        Planet alderaan = new Planet();
        alderaan.setName("Alderaan");

        Planet tatooine = new Planet();
        tatooine.setName("Tatooine");

        dagobah = repository.save(dagobah);
        repository.save(alderaan);
        repository.save(tatooine);

        // Characters
        Character han = new Character();
        han.setName("Han Solo");

        Character leia = new Character();
        leia.setName("Leia Organa");
        leia.setLocation(alderaan);
        leia.addFriend(han);

        Character luke = new Character();
        luke.setName("Luke Skywalker");
        luke.setLocation(tatooine);
        luke.addFriend(han);
        luke.addFriend(leia);

        Character yoda = new Character();
        yoda.setName("Yoda");
        yoda.setLocation(dagobah);
        yoda.setApprentice(luke);

        repository.save(han);
        repository.save(luke);
        repository.save(leia);
        repository.save(yoda);

        tx.success();
    }

    Result result = db.execute("MATCH (n) RETURN n.name as name");
    result.stream()
        .flatMap(m -> m.entrySet().stream())
```

```
        .map(row -> row.getKey() + " : " + row.getValue() + ";")
        .forEach(System.out::println);

    db.shutdown();

  }
}
```

When executing, the result should still be the same as before. However, the main difference is now that the code is using domain objects instead of working directly with nodes. Storing the objects as nodes in Neo4j is quite cumbersome. Luckily, Spring Data Neo4j can help to make it a lot easier.

Map Objects Using Neo4j OGM

In the conversion to nodes and relationships, properties can be quite cumbersome. Wouldn't it be nice if you could simply specify what to store where using annotations, just as is done using JPA? Neo4j OGM offers those annotations. To make an object a Neo4j mapped entity, use the @NodeEntity annotation on the type. Relationships can be modeled with the @Relationship annotation. To identify the field used for the ID, add the @GraphId annotation. Applying these to the Planet and Character classes would make them look like the following:

```
package com.apress.springrecipes.nosql;

import org.neo4j.ogm.annotation.GraphId;
import org.neo4j.ogm.annotation.NodeEntity;

@NodeEntity
public class Planet {

    @GraphId
    private Long id;
    private String name;

    // Getters/setters omitted
}
```

Here's the Character class:

```
package com.apress.springrecipes.nosql;

import org.neo4j.ogm.annotation.GraphId;
import org.neo4j.ogm.annotation.NodeEntity;
import org.neo4j.ogm.annotation.Relationship;

import java.util.Collections;
import java.util.HashSet;
import java.util.Objects;
import java.util.Set;
```

```
@NodeEntity
public class Character {

    @GraphId
    private Long id;
    private String name;

    @Relationship(type = "LOCATION")
    private Planet location;
    @Relationship(type="FRIENDS_WITH")
    private final Set<Character> friends = new HashSet<>();
    @Relationship(type="MASTER_OF")
    private Character apprentice;

    // Getters / Setters omitted

}
```

Now that the entities are annotated, the repository can be rewritten to use SessionFactory and Session for easier access.

```
package com.apress.springrecipes.nosql;

import org.neo4j.ogm.model.Result;
import org.neo4j.ogm.session.Session;
import org.neo4j.ogm.session.SessionFactory;
import org.neo4j.ogm.transaction.Transaction;
import org.springframework.beans.factory.annotation.Autowired;
import org.springframework.stereotype.Repository;

import javax.annotation.PreDestroy;
import java.util.Collections;

@Repository
public class Neo4jStarwarsRepository implements StarwarsRepository {

    private final SessionFactory sessionFactory;

    @Autowired
    public Neo4jStarwarsRepository(SessionFactory sessionFactory) {
        this.sessionFactory = sessionFactory;
    }

    @Override
    public Planet save(Planet planet) {

        Session session = sessionFactory.openSession();
        try (Transaction tx = session.beginTransaction()) {
            session.save(planet);
            return planet;
        }
    }
```

```java
@Override
public Character save(Character character) {

    Session session = sessionFactory.openSession();
    try (Transaction tx = session.beginTransaction()) {
        session.save(character);
        return character;
    }
}

@Override
public void printAll() {

    Session session = sessionFactory.openSession();
    Result result = session.query("MATCH (n) RETURN n.name as name",
        Collections.emptyMap(), true);
    result.forEach(m -> m.entrySet().stream()
        .map(row -> row.getKey() + " : " + row.getValue() + ";")
        .forEach(System.out::println));
}

}
```

There are a couple of things to notice: the code is a lot cleaner when using SessionFactory and Session as a lot of the plumping is done for you, especially mapping from and to nodes. The final thing to note is the addition of the printAll method. It has been added to move the code from the Main class to the repository.

The next class to modify is the Main class as it now needs to construct a SessionFactory. To construct a SessionFactory, you need to specify which packages it needs to scan for @NodeEntity annotated classes.

```java
package com.apress.springrecipes.nosql;

import org.neo4j.ogm.session.SessionFactory;

public class Main {

    public static void main(String[] args) {
        SessionFactory sessionFactory = new SessionFactory("com.apress.springrecipes.nosql");

        StarwarsRepository repository = new Neo4jStarwarsRepository(sessionFactory);

        // Planets
        Planet dagobah = new Planet();
        dagobah.setName("Dagobah");

        Planet alderaan = new Planet();
        alderaan.setName("Alderaan");

        Planet tatooine = new Planet();
        tatooine.setName("Tatooine");

        dagobah = repository.save(dagobah);
        repository.save(alderaan);
        repository.save(tatooine);
```

```
    // Characters
    Character han = new Character();
    han.setName("Han Solo");

    Character leia = new Character();
    leia.setName("Leia Organa");
    leia.setLocation(alderaan);
    leia.addFriend(han);

    Character luke = new Character();
    luke.setName("Luke Skywalker");
    luke.setLocation(tatooine);
    luke.addFriend(han);
    luke.addFriend(leia);

    Character yoda = new Character();
    yoda.setName("Yoda");
    yoda.setLocation(dagobah);
    yoda.setApprentice(luke);

    repository.save(han);
    repository.save(luke);
    repository.save(leia);
    repository.save(yoda);

    repository.printAll();

    sessionFactory.close();
    }
}
```

A SessionFactory is created and used to construct a Neo4jStarwarsRepository. Next the data is being set up, and the printAll method is called. The code that was there initially is now in that method. The end result should still be similar to what you got until now.

Use Spring for Configuration

Up until now everything was manually configured and wired. Let's create a Spring configuration class.

```
package com.apress.springrecipes.nosql;

import org.neo4j.ogm.session.SessionFactory;
import org.springframework.context.annotation.Bean;
import org.springframework.context.annotation.Configuration;

@Configuration
public class StarwarsConfig {

    @Bean
    public SessionFactory sessionFactory() {
        return new SessionFactory("com.apress.springrecipes.nosql");
    }
}
```

```
    @Bean
    public Neo4jStarwarsRepository starwarsRepository(SessionFactory sessionFactory) {
        return new Neo4jStarwarsRepository(sessionFactory);
    }
}
```

Both SessionFactory and Neo4jStarwarsRepository are Spring managed beans now. You can now let the Main class use this configuration to bootstrap an ApplicationContext and retrieve the StarwarsRepository from it.

```
package com.apress.springrecipes.nosql;

import org.springframework.context.annotation.AnnotationConfigApplicationContext;

public class Main {

    public static void main(String[] args) {
        AnnotationConfigApplicationContext context =
            new AnnotationConfigApplicationContext(StarwarsConfig.class);

        StarwarsRepository repository = context.getBean(StarwarsRepository.class);

        // Planets
        Planet dagobah = new Planet();
        dagobah.setName("Dagobah");

        Planet alderaan = new Planet();
        alderaan.setName("Alderaan");

        Planet tatooine = new Planet();
        tatooine.setName("Tatooine");

        dagobah = repository.save(dagobah);
        repository.save(alderaan);
        repository.save(tatooine);

        // Characters
        Character han = new Character();
        han.setName("Han Solo");

        Character leia = new Character();
        leia.setName("Leia Organa");
        leia.setLocation(alderaan);
        leia.addFriend(han);

        Character luke = new Character();
        luke.setName("Luke Skywalker");
        luke.setLocation(tatooine);
        luke.addFriend(han);
        luke.addFriend(leia);
```

```
        Character yoda = new Character();
        yoda.setName("Yoda");
        yoda.setLocation(dagobah);
        yoda.setApprentice(luke);

        repository.save(han);
        repository.save(luke);
        repository.save(leia);
        repository.save(yoda);

        repository.printAll();

        context.close();
    }
}
```

It is still largely the same. The main difference is that now Spring is in control of the life cycle of the beans.

Spring Data Neo4j also provides a Neo4jTransactionManager implementation, which takes care of starting and stopping a transaction for you, just like the other PlatformTransactionManager implementations do. First let's modify the configuration to include it and to add @EnableTransactionManagement.

```
package com.apress.springrecipes.nosql;

import org.neo4j.ogm.session.SessionFactory;
import org.springframework.context.annotation.Bean;
import org.springframework.context.annotation.Configuration;
import org.springframework.data.neo4j.transaction.Neo4jTransactionManager;
import org.springframework.transaction.annotation.EnableTransactionManagement;

@Configuration
@EnableTransactionManagement
public class StarwarsConfig {

    @Bean
    public SessionFactory sessionFactory() {
        return new SessionFactory("com.apress.springrecipes.nosql");
    }

    @Bean
    public Neo4jStarwarsRepository starwarsRepository(SessionFactory sessionFactory) {
        return new Neo4jStarwarsRepository(sessionFactory);
    }

    @Bean
    public Neo4jTransactionManager transactionManager(SessionFactory sessionFactory) {
        return new Neo4jTransactionManager(sessionFactory);
    }
}
```

With this in place, you can now further clean up the Neo4jStarwarsRepository class.

```java
package com.apress.springrecipes.nosql;

import org.neo4j.ogm.model.Result;
import org.neo4j.ogm.session.Session;
import org.neo4j.ogm.session.SessionFactory;
import org.springframework.beans.factory.annotation.Autowired;
import org.springframework.stereotype.Repository;
import org.springframework.transaction.annotation.Transactional;

import javax.annotation.PreDestroy;
import java.util.Collections;

@Repository
@Transactional
public class Neo4jStarwarsRepository implements StarwarsRepository {

    private final SessionFactory sessionFactory;

    @Autowired
    public Neo4jStarwarsRepository(SessionFactory sessionFactory) {
        this.sessionFactory = sessionFactory;
    }

    @Override
    public Planet save(Planet planet) {
        Session session = sessionFactory.openSession();
        session.save(planet);
        return planet;
    }

    @Override
    public Character save(Character character) {
        Session session = sessionFactory.openSession();
        session.save(character);
        return character;
    }

    @Override
    public void printAll() {

        Session session = sessionFactory.openSession();
        Result result = session.query("MATCH (n) RETURN n.name as name",
            Collections.emptyMap(), true);
        result.forEach(m -> m.entrySet().stream()
            .map(row -> row.getKey() + " : " + row.getValue() + ";")
            .forEach(System.out::println));
    }
```

```
    @PreDestroy
    public void cleanUp() {
        Session session = sessionFactory.openSession();
        session.query("MATCH (n) OPTIONAL MATCH (n)-[r]-() DELETE n,r", null);
    }
}
```

The Main class can remain as is, and storing and querying should still work as before.

Use Spring Data Neo4j Repositories

The code has been simplified considerably. The usage of the SessionFactory and Session made it a lot easier to work with entities with Neo4j. It can be even easier. As with the JPA or Mongo version of Spring Data, it can generate repositories for you. The only thing you need to do is write an interface. Let's create PlanetRepository and CharacterRepository classes to operate on the entities.

```
package com.apress.springrecipes.nosql;

import org.springframework.data.repository.CrudRepository;

public interface CharacterRepository extends CrudRepository<Character, Long> {}
```

Here's PlanetRepository:

```
package com.apress.springrecipes.nosql;

import org.springframework.data.repository.CrudRepository;

public interface PlanetRepository extends CrudRepository<Planet, Long> {}
```

The repositories all extend CrudRepository, but it could also have been PagingAndSortingRepository or the special Neo4jRepository interface. For the recipe, CrudRepository is sufficient.

Next, rename StarwarsRepository and its implementation to StarwarsService because it isn't really a repository anymore; the implementation also needs to change to operate on the repositories instead of the SessionFactory.

```
package com.apress.springrecipes.nosql;

import org.springframework.stereotype.Service;
import org.springframework.transaction.annotation.Transactional;

import javax.annotation.PreDestroy;

@Service
@Transactional
public class Neo4jStarwarsService implements StarwarsService {
```

```java
    private final PlanetRepository planetRepository;
    private final CharacterRepository characterRepository;

    Neo4jStarwarsService(PlanetRepository planetRepository,
                         CharacterRepository characterRepository) {
        this.planetRepository=planetRepository;
        this.characterRepository=characterRepository;
    }

    @Override
    public Planet save(Planet planet) {
        return planetRepository.save(planet);
    }

    @Override
    public Character save(Character character) {
        return characterRepository.save(character);
    }

    @Override
    public void printAll() {
        planetRepository.findAll().forEach(System.out::println);
        characterRepository.findAll().forEach(System.out::println);
    }

    @PreDestroy
    public void cleanUp() {
        characterRepository.deleteAll();
        planetRepository.deleteAll();
    }
}
```

Now all operations are done on the specific repository interfaces. Those interfaces don't create instances themselves. To enable the creation, the @EnableNeo4jRepositories annotations need to be added to the configuration class. Also, add an @ComponentScan to have StarwarsService detected and autowired.

```java
@Configuration
@EnableTransactionManagement
@EnableNeo4jRepositories
@ComponentScan
public class StarwarsConfig { ... }
```

Notice the @EnableNeo4jRepositories annotation. This annotation will scan the configured base packages for repositories. When one is found, a dynamic implementation is created, and this implementation eventually delegates to SessionFactory.

Finally, modify the Main class to use the refactored StarwarsService.

```
package com.apress.springrecipes.nosql;

import com.apress.springrecipes.nosql.config.StarwarsConfig;
import org.springframework.context.annotation.AnnotationConfigApplicationContext;

public class Main {

    public static void main(String[] args) {
        AnnotationConfigApplicationContext context =
            new AnnotationConfigApplicationContext(StarwarsConfig.class);

        StarwarsService service = context.getBean(StarwarsService.class);
        ...
    }
}
```

Now all the components have been changed to use the dynamically created Spring Data Neo4j repositories.

Connect to a Remote Neo4j Database

Until now all the coding for Neo4j has been done to an embedded Neo4j instance; however, at the beginning, you downloaded and installed Neo4j. Let's change the configuration to connect to that remote Neo4j instance.

```
package com.apress.springrecipes.nosql;

import org.neo4j.ogm.session.SessionFactory;
import org.springframework.context.annotation.Bean;
import org.springframework.context.annotation.ComponentScan;
import org.springframework.context.annotation.Configuration;
import org.springframework.data.neo4j.repository.config.EnableNeo4jRepositories;
import org.springframework.data.neo4j.transaction.Neo4jTransactionManager;
import org.springframework.transaction.annotation.EnableTransactionManagement;

@Configuration
@EnableTransactionManagement
@EnableNeo4jRepositories
@ComponentScan
public class StarwarsConfig {

    @Bean
    public org.neo4j.ogm.config.Configuration configuration() {
        return new org.neo4j.ogm.config.Configuration.Builder().uri("bolt://localhost").
        build();
    }
```

```
@Bean
public SessionFactory sessionFactory() {
    return new SessionFactory(configuration(),"com.apress.springrecipes.nosql");
}

@Bean
public Neo4jTransactionManager transactionManager(SessionFactory sessionFactory) {
    return new Neo4jTransactionManager(sessionFactory);
}
}
```

There is now a Configuration object that is used by SessionFactory; you can either use new Configuration or use a Builder to construct the Configuration object. You need to specify the URI of the Neo4j server. In this case, that is localhost. The default driver is the Bolt driver, which uses a binary protocol to transfer data. HTTP(S) could also be used, but another dependency is needed for that. The created Configuration object is used by SessionFactory to configure itself.

12-4. Use Couchbase

Problem

You want to use Couchbase in your application to store documents.

Solution

First download, install, and set up Couchbase; then use the Spring Data Couchbase project to store and retrieve documents from the data store.

How It Works

Before you can start using Couchbase you need to have an instance installed and up and running. When you have it running you will need to connect to it to be able to use the datastore for actual storage. You will start with a plain Couchbase based repository to show how to store and retrieve documents and gradually move to Spring Data Couchbase and to close with a reactive version of the repository.

Download, Install, and Set Up Couchbase

After downloading and starting Couchbase, open your browser and go to http://localhost:8091. You should be greeted with a page similar to Figure 12-5. On that page, simply click the Setup button.

Figure 12-5. Installing Couchbase

On the next screen (see Figure 12-6), you can configure the cluster. You can either start a new one or join an existing cluster. For this recipe you will start a new cluster. Specify the memory limits and optionally the paths for the disk storage. For this recipe, it is enough to leave them to the defaults. Then click Next.

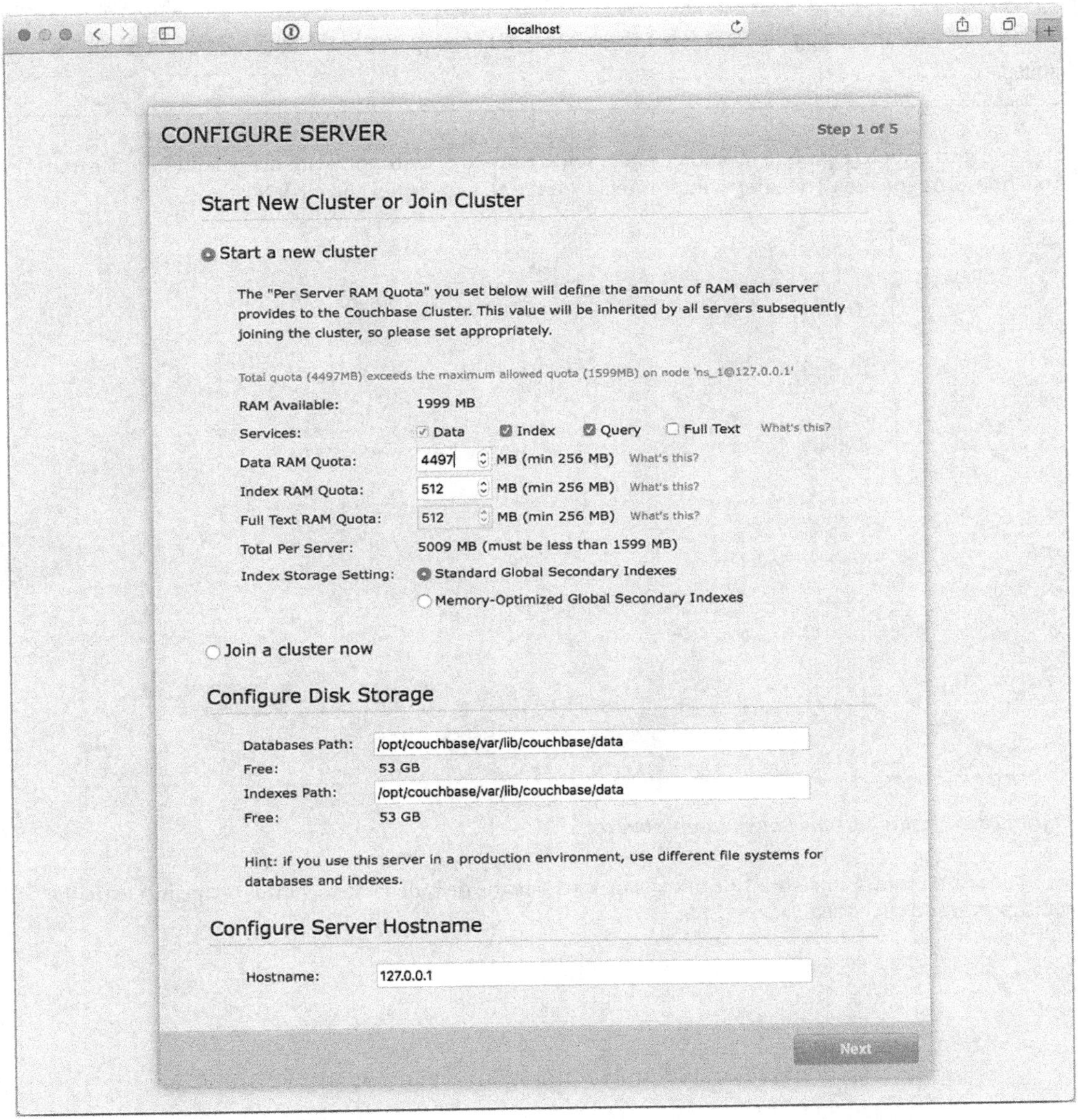

CONFIGURE SERVER   Step 1 of 5

Start New Cluster or Join Cluster

● Start a new cluster

The "Per Server RAM Quota" you set below will define the amount of RAM each server provides to the Couchbase Cluster. This value will be inherited by all servers subsequently joining the cluster, so please set appropriately.

Total quota (4497MB) exceeds the maximum allowed quota (1599MB) on node 'ns_1@127.0.0.1'

RAM Available:	1999 MB
Services:	☑ Data ☑ Index ☑ Query ☐ Full Text What's this?
Data RAM Quota:	4497 ⟳ MB (min 256 MB) What's this?
Index RAM Quota:	512 ⟳ MB (min 256 MB) What's this?
Full Text RAM Quota:	512 ⟳ MB (min 256 MB) What's this?
Total Per Server:	5009 MB (must be less than 1599 MB)
Index Storage Setting:	● Standard Global Secondary Indexes
	○ Memory-Optimized Global Secondary Indexes

○ Join a cluster now

Configure Disk Storage

Databases Path:	/opt/couchbase/var/lib/couchbase/data
Free:	53 GB
Indexes Path:	/opt/couchbase/var/lib/couchbase/data
Free:	53 GB

Hint: if you use this server in a production environment, use different file systems for databases and indexes.

Configure Server Hostname

Hostname:	127.0.0.1

Next

Figure 12-6. Installing Couchbase, cluster settings

523

■ **Note** If you are running the Dockerized Couchbase, you need to reduce the data RAM quota as that is limited.

The next screen (Figure 12-7) allows you to select sample data to work with the default samples from Couchbase. As you aren't needing it for this recipe, leave all unselected and click Next.

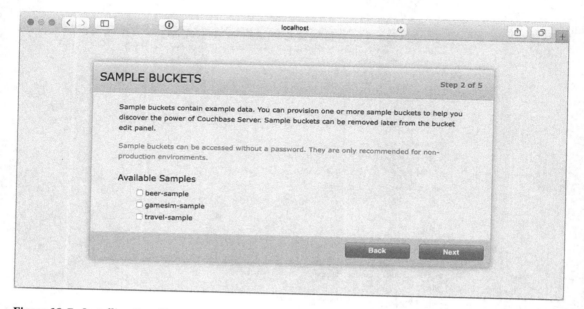

Figure 12-7. *Installing Couchbase, sample buckets*

The screen shown in Figure 12-8 allows you to create the default bucket. For this recipe just leave the settings as is and click Next.

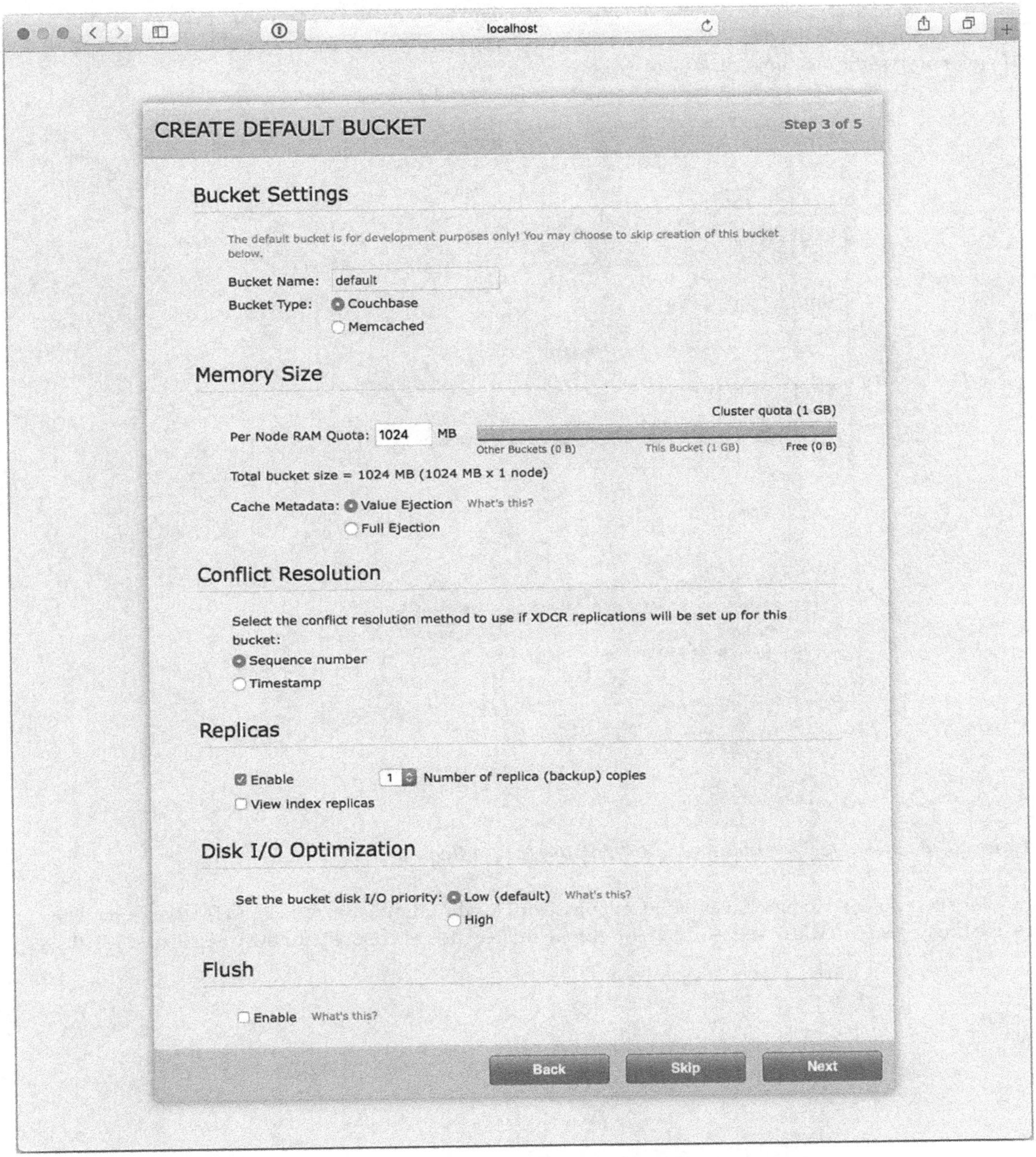

Figure 12-8. *Installing Couchbase, creating a default bucket*

If you want to register the product, fill out the form and decide whether you want to be notified of software updates. You need to at least select the box to agree with the terms and conditions (Figure 12-9). Then for almost the last time, click Next.

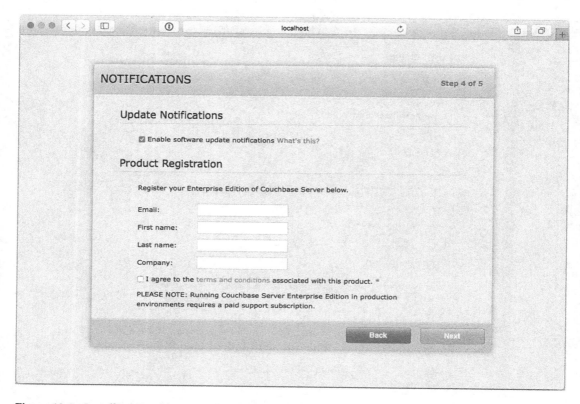

Figure 12-9. *Installing Couchbase, notifications and registration*

Finally, you need to pick a username and password for the administrator account for the server. This recipe is using *admin* with a password of *sr4-admin*, but feel free to choose your own. See Figure 12-10.

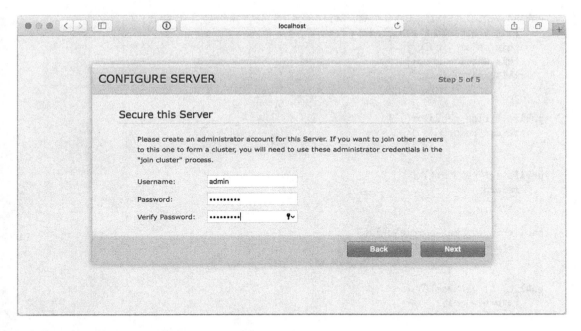

Figure 12-10. *Installing Couchbase, setting up an admin user*

Store and Retrieve Documents with Couchbase

To store an object in Couchbase, you need to create a Document that can hold various types of content, like serializable objects, JSON, strings, dates, or binary data in the form of a Netty ByteBuf. However, the primary type of content is JSON. This way you can use it with other technologies as well. When using a SerializableDocument, you are restricting yourself to the usage of Java-based solutions.

However, before storing an object in Couchbase, you need to make a connection to the cluster. To connect to Couchbase, you need a Cluster to be able to access the Bucket you created while doing the setup for Couchbase. You can use the CouchbaseCluster class to create a connection to the earlier setup cluster. The resulting Cluster can be used to open a Bucket with the openBucket() method. For this recipe, you are going to use the default bucket and simplest cluster setup.

First, create a Vehicle class (or reuse the one from recipe 12-1), which you are going to store in Couchbase.

```
package com.apress.springrecipes.nosql;

import java.io.Serializable;

public class Vehicle implements Serializable {

    private String vehicleNo;
    private String color;
    private int wheel;
    private int seat;

    public Vehicle() {
    }
```

```java
    public Vehicle(String vehicleNo, String color, int wheel, int seat) {
        this.vehicleNo = vehicleNo;
        this.color = color;
        this.wheel = wheel;
        this.seat = seat;
    }

    public String getColor() {
        return color;
    }

    public int getSeat() {
        return seat;
    }

    public String getVehicleNo() {
        return vehicleNo;
    }

    public int getWheel() {
        return wheel;
    }

    public void setColor(String color) {
        this.color = color;
    }

    public void setSeat(int seat) {
        this.seat = seat;
    }

    public void setVehicleNo(String vehicleNo) {
        this.vehicleNo = vehicleNo;
    }

    public void setWheel(int wheel) {
        this.wheel = wheel;
    }

    @Override
    public String toString() {
        return "Vehicle [" +
                "vehicleNo='" + vehicleNo + '\'' +
                ", color='" + color + '\'' +
                ", wheel=" + wheel +
                ", seat=" + seat +
                ']';
    }
}
```

Notice this part: implements Serializable. This is needed because you will use, at first, the SerializableDocument class from Couchbase to store the object.

To communicate with Couchbase, you will create a repository. First define the interface.

```
package com.apress.springrecipes.nosql;

public interface VehicleRepository {

    void save(Vehicle vehicle);

    void delete(Vehicle vehicle);

    Vehicle findByVehicleNo(String vehicleNo);

}
```

Here's the implementation, which will store the Vehicle value using SerializableDocument:

```
package com.apress.springrecipes.nosql;

import com.couchbase.client.java.Bucket;
import com.couchbase.client.java.document.SerializableDocument;

class CouchBaseVehicleRepository implements VehicleRepository {

    private final Bucket bucket;

    public CouchBaseVehicleRepository(Bucket bucket) {
        this.bucket=bucket;
    }

    @Override
    public void save(Vehicle vehicle) {
        SerializableDocument vehicleDoc = SerializableDocument
            .create(vehicle.getVehicleNo(), vehicle);
        bucket.upsert(vehicleDoc);
    }

    @Override
    public void delete(Vehicle vehicle) {
        bucket.remove(vehicle.getVehicleNo());
    }

    @Override
    public Vehicle findByVehicleNo(String vehicleNo) {
        SerializableDocument doc = bucket.get(vehicleNo, SerializableDocument.class);
        if (doc != null) {
            return (Vehicle) doc.content();
        }
        return null;
    }
}
```

The repository needs a Bucket for storing the documents; it is like the table of a database (a Bucket is like the table, and the Cluster more like the whole database). When storing the Vehicle, it is wrapped in a SerializableDocument, and the vehicleNo value is used as the ID; after that, the upsert method is called. This will either update or insert the document depending on whether it already exists.

Let's create a Main class that stores and retrieves the data for a Vehicle in the bucket.

```
package com.apress.springrecipes.nosql;

import com.couchbase.client.java.Bucket;
import com.couchbase.client.java.Cluster;
import com.couchbase.client.java.CouchbaseCluster;

public class Main {

    public static void main(String[] args) {

        Cluster cluster = CouchbaseCluster.create();
        Bucket bucket = cluster.openBucket();

        CouchBaseVehicleRepository vehicleRepository = new CouchBaseVehicleRepository(bucket);
        vehicleRepository.save(new Vehicle("TEM0001", "GREEN", 3, 1));
        vehicleRepository.save(new Vehicle("TEM0004", "RED", 4, 2));

        System.out.println("Vehicle: " + vehicleRepository.findByVehicleNo("TEM0001"));
        System.out.println("Vehicle: " + vehicleRepository.findByVehicleNo("TEM0004"));

        bucket.remove("TEM0001");
        bucket.remove("TEM0004");

        bucket.close();
        cluster.disconnect();
    }
}
```

First, a connection is made to the Cluster using the CouchbaseCluster.create() method. This will, by default, connect to the cluster on localhost. When using Couchbase in a production environment, you probably want to use one of the other create methods and pass in a list of hosts to connect to or to set even more properties using a CouchbaseEnvironment (to set things like queryTimeout, searchTimeout, etc.). For this recipe, it is enough to use the default Cluster. Next you need to specify the Bucket to use for storing and retrieving documents. As you will use the defaults, using cluster.openBucket() is enough. There are several other overloaded methods to specify a specific Bucket to use and to specify properties for the connection to the bucket (such as timeout settings, username/password, etc.).

The Bucket is used to create an instance of CouchbaseVehicleRepository. After that, two Vehicles are stored, retrieved, and removed again (as to leave no clutter from this recipe). Finally, the connections are closed.

Although you are now storing documents in CouchBase, there is one drawback: you are doing that using SerializableDocument, which is something CouchBase cannot use for indexing. In addition, it will only be readable from other Java-based clients and not using different languages (like JavaScript). Instead, it is recommended to use JsonDocument instead. Let's rewrite CouchbaseVehicleRepository to reflect this.

```java
package com.apress.springrecipes.nosql;

import com.couchbase.client.java.Bucket;
import com.couchbase.client.java.document.JsonDocument;
import com.couchbase.client.java.document.json.JsonObject;

class CouchbaseVehicleRepository implements VehicleRepository {

    private final Bucket bucket;

    public CouchbaseVehicleRepository(Bucket bucket) {
        this.bucket=bucket;
    }

    @Override
    public void save(Vehicle vehicle) {

        JsonObject vehicleJson = JsonObject.empty()
            .put("vehicleNo", vehicle.getVehicleNo())
            .put("color", vehicle.getColor())
            .put("wheels", vehicle.getWheel())
            .put("seat", vehicle.getSeat());

        JsonDocument vehicleDoc = JsonDocument.create(vehicle.getVehicleNo(), vehicleJson);
        bucket.upsert(vehicleDoc);
    }

    @Override
    public void delete(Vehicle vehicle) {
        bucket.remove(vehicle.getVehicleNo());
    }

    @Override
    public Vehicle findByVehicleNo(String vehicleNo) {

        JsonDocument doc = bucket.get(vehicleNo, JsonDocument.class);
        if (doc != null) {
            JsonObject result = doc.content();
            return new Vehicle(result.getString("vehicleNo"), result.getString("color"),
                result.getInt("wheels"), result.getInt("seat"));
        }
        return null;
    }
}
```

Notice this code uses a JsonObject object and converts Vehicle to a JsonObject object, and vice versa. Running the Main class again should store, retrieve, and remove two documents from Couchbase again.

Converting to/from JSON can become quite cumbersome for larger object graphs, so instead of doing things manually, you could use a JSON library, like Jackson, to convert to/from JSON.

```java
package com.apress.springrecipes.nosql;

import com.couchbase.client.java.Bucket;
import com.couchbase.client.java.document.JsonDocument;
import com.couchbase.client.java.document.json.JsonObject;
import com.fasterxml.jackson.core.JsonProcessingException;
import com.fasterxml.jackson.databind.ObjectMapper;

import java.io.IOException;

class CouchbaseVehicleRepository implements VehicleRepository {

    private final Bucket bucket;
    private final ObjectMapper mapper;

    public CouchbaseVehicleRepository(Bucket bucket, ObjectMapper mapper) {
        this.bucket=bucket;
        this.mapper=mapper;
    }

    @Override
    public void save(Vehicle vehicle) {

        String json = null;
        try {
            json = mapper.writeValueAsString(vehicle);
        } catch (JsonProcessingException e) {
            throw new RuntimeException("Error encoding JSON.", e);
        }
        JsonObject vehicleJson = JsonObject.fromJson(json);
        JsonDocument vehicleDoc = JsonDocument.create(vehicle.getVehicleNo(), vehicleJson);
        bucket.upsert(vehicleDoc);
    }

    @Override
    public void delete(Vehicle vehicle) {
        bucket.remove(vehicle.getVehicleNo());
    }

    @Override
    public Vehicle findByVehicleNo(String vehicleNo) {
        JsonDocument doc = bucket.get(vehicleNo, JsonDocument.class);
        if (doc != null) {
            JsonObject result = doc.content();
            try {
                return mapper.readValue(result.toString(), Vehicle.class);
            } catch (IOException e) {
                throw new RuntimeException("Error decoding JSON.", e);
            }
        }
        return null;
    }
}
```

Now you use the powerful Jackson library for converting from/to JSON.

Use Spring

At the moment, everything is configured in the Main class. Let's move the configuration parts to a CouchbaseConfiguration class and use it to bootstrap an application.

```
package com.apress.springrecipes.nosql;

import com.couchbase.client.java.Bucket;
import com.couchbase.client.java.Cluster;
import com.couchbase.client.java.CouchbaseCluster;
import com.fasterxml.jackson.databind.ObjectMapper;
import org.springframework.context.annotation.Bean;
import org.springframework.context.annotation.Configuration;

@Configuration
public class CouchbaseConfiguration {

    @Bean(destroyMethod = "disconnect")
    public Cluster cluster() {
        return CouchbaseCluster.create();
    }

    @Bean
    public Bucket bucket(Cluster cluster) {
        return cluster.openBucket();
    }

    @Bean
    public ObjectMapper mapper() {
        return new ObjectMapper();
    }

    @Bean
    public CouchbaseVehicleRepository vehicleRepository(Bucket bucket, ObjectMapper mapper) {
        return new CouchbaseVehicleRepository(bucket, mapper);
    }
}
```

Notice the destroyMethod method on the Cluster bean. This method will be invoked when the application shuts down. The close method on the Bucket will be called automatically as that is one of the predefined methods that is automatically detected. The construction of the CouchbaseVehicleRepository is still the same, but you now pass two Spring managed beans to it.

Modify the `Main` class to use `CouchbaseConfiguration`.

```java
package com.apress.springrecipes.nosql;

import org.springframework.context.ApplicationContext;
import org.springframework.context.annotation.AnnotationConfigApplicationContext;

public class Main {

    public static void main(String[] args) {

        ApplicationContext context =
            new AnnotationConfigApplicationContext(CouchbaseConfiguration.class);
        VehicleRepository vehicleRepository =context.getBean(VehicleRepository.class);

        vehicleRepository.save(new Vehicle("TEM0001", "GREEN", 3, 1));
        vehicleRepository.save(new Vehicle("TEM0004", "RED", 4, 2));

        System.out.println("Vehicle: " + vehicleRepository.findByVehicleNo("TEM0001"));
        System.out.println("Vehicle: " + vehicleRepository.findByVehicleNo("TEM0004"));

        vehicleRepository.delete(vehicleRepository.findByVehicleNo("TEM0001"));
        vehicleRepository.delete(vehicleRepository.findByVehicleNo("TEM0004"));
    }
}
```

`VehicleRepository` is retrieved from the constructed `ApplicationContext`, and still there are `Vehicle` instances stored, retrieved, and removed from the Couchbase cluster.

Use Spring Data's CouchbaseTemplate

Although using Couchbase from Java with Jackson for mapping JSON is pretty straightforward, it can become quite cumbersome with larger repositories or when using specific indexes and N1QL queries, not to mention if you want to integrate this in an application that has other means of storing data. The Spring Data Couchbase project contains a `CouchbaseTemplate` template, which takes away part of the plumbing you are now doing in the repository, such as mapping to/from JSON but also converting exceptions into a `DataAccessException`. This makes it easier to integrate it with other data access technologies that are utilized with Spring.

First rewrite the repository to use `CouchbaseTemplate`.

```java
package com.apress.springrecipes.nosql;

import org.springframework.data.couchbase.core.CouchbaseTemplate;

public class CouchbaseVehicleRepository implements VehicleRepository {

    private final CouchbaseTemplate couchbase;

    public CouchbaseVehicleRepository(CouchbaseTemplate couchbase) {
        this.couchbase = couchbase;
    }
```

```
    @Override
    public void save(Vehicle vehicle) {
        couchbase.save(vehicle);
    }

    @Override
    public void delete(Vehicle vehicle) {
        couchbase.remove(vehicle);
    }

    @Override
    public Vehicle findByVehicleNo(String vehicleNo) {
        return couchbase.findById(vehicleNo, Vehicle.class);
    }
}
```

Now the repository is reduced to just a couple of lines of code. To be able to store the Vehicle object, you need to annotate Vehicle; it needs to know which field to use for the ID.

```
package com.apress.springrecipes.nosql;

import com.couchbase.client.java.repository.annotation.Field;
import com.couchbase.client.java.repository.annotation.Id;

import java.io.Serializable;

public class Vehicle implements Serializable{

    @Id
    private String vehicleNo;
    @Field
    private String color;
    @Field
    private int wheel;
    @Field
    private int seat;

    // getters/setters omitted.
}
```

The field vehicleNo has been annotated with the @Id annotation and the other fields with @Field. Although the latter isn't required to do, it is recommended to specify it. You can also use the @Field annotation to specify a different name for the name of the JSON property, which can be nice if you need to map existing documents to Java objects.

Finally, you need to configure a CouchbaseTemplate template in the configuration class.

```
package com.apress.springrecipes.nosql;

import com.couchbase.client.java.Bucket;
import com.couchbase.client.java.Cluster;
import com.couchbase.client.java.CouchbaseCluster;
```

```java
import org.springframework.context.annotation.Bean;
import org.springframework.context.annotation.Configuration;
import org.springframework.data.couchbase.core.CouchbaseTemplate;

@Configuration
public class CouchbaseConfiguration {

    @Bean(destroyMethod = "disconnect")
    public Cluster cluster() {
        return CouchbaseCluster.create();
    }

    @Bean
    public Bucket bucket(Cluster cluster) {
        return cluster.openBucket();
    }

    @Bean
    public CouchbaseVehicleRepository vehicleRepository(CouchbaseTemplate couchbaseTemplate) {
        return new CouchbaseVehicleRepository(couchbaseTemplate);
    }

    @Bean
    public CouchbaseTemplate couchbaseTemplate(Cluster cluster, Bucket bucket) {
        return new CouchbaseTemplate(cluster.clusterManager("default","").info(), bucket);
    }
}
```

A CouchbaseTemplate object needs a Bucket, and it needs access to ClusterInfo, which can be obtained through ClusterManager; here you pass the name of the Bucket, which is default, and no password. Instead, you could have passed *admin/sr4-admin* as the username/password combination. Finally, the configured CouchbaseVehicleRepository instance is created with this configured template.

When running the Main class, access is still provided, and storing, retrieving, and removing still work.

To make configuration a little easier, Spring Data Couchbase provides a base configuration class, AbstractCouchbaseConfiguration, which you can extend so you don't need to configure the Cluster, Bucket, or CouchbaseTemplate objects anymore.

```java
package com.apress.springrecipes.nosql;

import org.springframework.context.annotation.Bean;
import org.springframework.context.annotation.Configuration;
import org.springframework.data.couchbase.config.AbstractCouchbaseConfiguration;
import org.springframework.data.couchbase.core.CouchbaseTemplate;

import java.util.Collections;
import java.util.List;
```

```
@Configuration
public class CouchbaseConfiguration extends AbstractCouchbaseConfiguration {

    @Override
    protected List<String> getBootstrapHosts() {
        return Collections.singletonList("localhost");
    }

    @Override
    protected String getBucketName() {
        return "default";
    }

    @Override
    protected String getBucketPassword() {
        return "";
    }

    @Bean
    public CouchbaseVehicleRepository vehicleRepository(CouchbaseTemplate couchbaseTemplate) {
        return new CouchbaseVehicleRepository(couchbaseTemplate);
    }
}
```

The configuration now extends the AbstractCouchbaseConfiguration base class, and you only need to provide the name of the bucket, an optional password, and the list of hosts. The base configuration class provides CouchbaseTemplate and all the objects it needs.

Use Spring Data's Couchbase Repositories

As with other technologies, Spring Data Couchbase provides the option to specify an interface and have an actual repository implementation available at runtime. This way, you only need to create an interface and not the concrete implementation. For this, like with other Spring Data projects, you need to extend CrudRepository. Note you could also extend CouchbaseRepository or CouchbasePagingAndSortingRepository if you need that functionality. For this recipe, you are going to use CrudRepository.

```
package com.apress.springrecipes.nosql;

import org.springframework.data.repository.CrudRepository;

public interface VehicleRepository extends CrudRepository<Vehicle, String> {}
```

As you can see, the interface has no more methods, as all the CRUD methods are provided already. Next, an @EnableCouchbaseRepositories annotation is needed on the configuration class.

```
package com.apress.springrecipes.nosql;

import org.springframework.context.annotation.Configuration;
import org.springframework.data.couchbase.config.AbstractCouchbaseConfiguration;
import org.springframework.data.couchbase.repository.config.EnableCouchbaseRepositories;
```

```
import java.util.Collections;
import java.util.List;

@Configuration
@EnableCouchbaseRepositories(
public class CouchbaseConfiguration extends AbstractCouchbaseConfiguration { ... }
```

Finally, the Main class needs a minor modification because instead of findByVehicleNo, you need to use the findById method.

```
package com.apress.springrecipes.nosql;

import org.springframework.context.ApplicationContext;
import org.springframework.context.annotation.AnnotationConfigApplicationContext;

public class Main {

    public static void main(String[] args) {

        ApplicationContext context =
            new AnnotationConfigApplicationContext(CouchbaseConfiguration.class);
        VehicleRepository vehicleRepository =context.getBean(VehicleRepository.class);

        vehicleRepository.save(new Vehicle("TEM0001", "GREEN", 3, 1));
        vehicleRepository.save(new Vehicle("TEM0004", "RED", 4, 2));

        vehicleRepository.findById("TEM0001").ifPresent(System.out::println);
        vehicleRepository.findById("TEM0004").ifPresent(System.out::println);

        vehicleRepository.deleteById("TEM0001");
        vehicleRepository.deleteById("TEM0004");
    }
}
```

The findById method returns a java.util.Optional object, and as such you can use the ifPresent method to print it to the console.

Use Spring Data's Reactive Couchbase Repositories

In addition to the blocking repositories, it is possible to utilize ReactiveCouchbaseRepository to get a reactive repository. It will now return a Mono for zero or one returning methods such as findById, and it will return a Flux for methods returning zero or more elements, such as findAll. The default Couchbase driver already has reactive support built in. To be able to use this, you need to have the RxJava and RxJava reactive streams on your classpath. To be able to use the reactive types from ReactiveCouchbaseRepository, you also need Pivotal Reactor on your classpath.

To configure reactive repositories for Couchbase, modify CouchbaseConfiguration. Let it extend AbstractReactiveCouchbaseConfiguration, and instead of @EnableCouchbaseRepositories, use @EnableReactiveCouchbaseRepositories.

```
package com.apress.springrecipes.nosql;

import org.springframework.context.annotation.Configuration;
import org.springframework.data.couchbase.config.AbstractReactiveCouchbaseConfiguration;
import org.springframework.data.couchbase.repository.config.
EnableReactiveCouchbaseRepositories;

import java.util.Collections;
import java.util.List;

@Configuration
@EnableReactiveCouchbaseRepositories
public class CouchbaseConfiguration extends AbstractReactiveCouchbaseConfiguration {

    @Override
    protected List<String> getBootstrapHosts() {
        return Collections.singletonList("localhost");
    }

    @Override
    protected String getBucketName() {
        return "default";
    }

    @Override
    protected String getBucketPassword() {
        return "";
    }
}
```

The remainder of the configuration remains the same as compared to the regular Couchbase configuration; you still need to connect to the same Couchbase server and use the same Bucket.

Next, the VehicleRepository should extend ReactiveCrudRepository instead of CrudRepository.

```
package com.apress.springrecipes.nosql;

import org.springframework.data.repository.reactive.ReactiveCrudRepository;

public interface VehicleRepository extends ReactiveCrudRepository<Vehicle, String> {}
```

This is basically all that is needed to get a reactive repository. To be able to test this, you also need to modify the Main class.

```
package com.apress.springrecipes.nosql;

import org.springframework.context.ApplicationContext;
import org.springframework.context.annotation.AnnotationConfigApplicationContext;
import reactor.core.publisher.Flux;
import reactor.core.publisher.Mono;
```

```java
import java.util.Arrays;
import java.util.concurrent.CountDownLatch;

public class Main {

    public static void main(String[] args) throws InterruptedException {

        ApplicationContext context =
            new AnnotationConfigApplicationContext(CouchbaseConfiguration.class);
        VehicleRepository repository =context.getBean(VehicleRepository.class);

        CountDownLatch countDownLatch = new CountDownLatch(1);

        repository.saveAll(Flux.just(new Vehicle("TEM0001", "GREEN", 3, 1), //
            new Vehicle("TEM0004", "RED", 4, 2)))
            .last().log()
            .then(repository.findById("TEM0001")).doOnSuccess(System.out::println)
            .then(repository.findById("TEM0004")).doOnSuccess(System.out::println)
            .then(repository.deleteById(Flux.just("TEM0001", "TEM00004")))
                .doOnSuccess(x -> countDownLatch.countDown())
                .doOnError(t -> countDownLatch.countDown())
            .subscribe();

        countDownLatch.await();
    }
}
```

Creating the `ApplicationContext` and obtaining the `VehicleRepository` isn't any different. However, after that, you have a chain of method calls, one following the other. First you add two `Vehicle` instances to the data store. When the last one has been saved, you will query the repository for each instance. When that is done, everything is deleted again. For everything to be able to complete, you could either block with `block()` or wait yourself. Generally, using `block()` in a reactive system is something you want to avoid. That is why you are using `CountDownLatch`; when the `deleteById` method completes, the `CountDownLatch` value is decremented. The `countDownLatch.await()` method waits until the counter reaches zero and then finishes the program.

Summary

In this recipe, you took an introductory journey into different types of data stores, including how to use them and how to make using them easier with different modules of the Spring Data family. You started out by looking at document-driven stores in the form of MongoDB and the usage of the Spring Data MongoDB module. Next the journey took you to key-value stores; you used Redis as an implementation and used the Spring Data Redis module. The final data store was a graph-based one called Neo4j, for which you explored the embedded Neo4j, how to use it, and how to build a repository for storing entities.

For two of the data stores, you also explored the reactive features by extending the reactive version of the interface as well as configuring the reactive drivers for those data stores.

CHAPTER 13

■ ■ ■

Spring Java Enterprise Services and Remoting Technologies

In this chapter, you will learn about Spring's support for the most common Java enterprise services: using Java Management Extensions (JMX), sending e-mail with JavaMail, and scheduling tasks with Quartz. In addition, you'll learn about Spring's support for various remoting technologies, such as RMI, Hessian, HTTP Invoker, and SOAP web services.

JMX is part of Java SE and is a technology for managing and monitoring system resources such as devices, applications, objects, and service-driven networks. These resources are represented as managed beans (MBeans). Spring supports JMX by exporting any Spring beans as model MBeans without programming against the JMX API. In addition, Spring can easily access remote MBeans.

JavaMail is the standard API and implementation for sending e-mail in Java. Spring further provides an abstract layer to send e-mail in an implementation-independent fashion.

There are two main options for scheduling tasks on the Java platform: JDK Timer and Quartz Scheduler (http://quartz-scheduler.org/). JDK Timer offers simple task scheduling features that are bundled with the JDK. Compared with JDK Timer, Quartz offers more powerful job scheduling features. For both options, Spring supplies utility classes to configure scheduling tasks in a bean configuration file, without using either API directly.

Remoting is a key technology to develop distributed applications, especially multitier enterprise applications. It allows different applications or components, running in different JVMs or on different machines, to communicate with each other using a specific protocol. Spring's remoting support is consistent across different remoting technologies. On the server side, Spring allows you to expose an arbitrary bean as a remote service through a service exporter. On the client side, Spring provides various proxy factory beans for you to create a local proxy for a remote service so that you can use the remote service like you would local beans.

You'll learn how to use a series of remoting technologies that include RMI, Hessian, HTTP Invoker, and SOAP web services using Spring Web Services (Spring-WS).

13-1. Register Spring POJOs as JMX MBeans

Problem

You want to register an object in your Java application as a JMX MBean to get the ability to look at services that are running and manipulate their state at runtime. This will allow you to run tasks such as rerun batch jobs, invoke methods, and change configuration metadata.

© Marten Deinum, Daniel Rubio, and Josh Long 2017
M. Deinum et al., *Spring 5 Recipes*, DOI 10.1007/978-1-4842-2790-9_13

Solution

Spring supports JMX by allowing you to export any beans in its IoC container as model MBeans. This can be done simply by declaring an `MBeanExporter` instance. With Spring's JMX support, you don't need to deal with the JMX API directly. In addition, Spring enables you to declare JSR-160 (Java Management Extensions Remote API) connectors to expose MBeans for remote access over a specific protocol by using a factory bean. Spring provides factory beans for both servers and clients.

Spring's JMX support comes with other mechanisms by which you can assemble an MBean's management interface. These options include using exporting beans by method names, interfaces, and annotations. Spring can also detect and export MBeans automatically from beans declared in the IoC container and annotated with JMX-specific annotations defined by Spring.

How It Works

Suppose you're developing a utility for replicating files from one directory to another. Let's design the interface for this utility:

```
package com.apress.springrecipes.replicator;
...
public interface FileReplicator {

    public String getSrcDir();
    public void setSrcDir(String srcDir);

    public String getDestDir();
    public void setDestDir(String destDir);

    public FileCopier getFileCopier();
    public void setFileCopier(FileCopier fileCopier);

    public void replicate() throws IOException;
}
```

The source and destination directories are designed as properties of a replicator object, not method arguments. That means each file replicator instance replicates files only for a particular source and destination directory. You can create multiple replicator instances in your application.

But before you implement this replicator, let's create another interface that copies a file from one directory to another, given its name.

```
package com.apress.springrecipes.replicator;
...
public interface FileCopier {

    public void copyFile(String srcDir, String destDir, String filename)
        throws IOException;
}
```

There are many strategies for implementing this file copier. For instance, you can make use of the FileCopyUtils class provided by Spring.

```
package com.apress.springrecipes.replicator;
...
import org.springframework.util.FileCopyUtils;

public class FileCopierJMXImpl implements FileCopier {

    public void copyFile(String srcDir, String destDir, String filename)
        throws IOException {
        File srcFile = new File(srcDir, filename);
        File destFile = new File(destDir, filename);
        FileCopyUtils.copy(srcFile, destFile);
    }
}
```

With the help of a file copier, you can implement the file replicator, as shown in the following code:

```
package com.apress.springrecipes.replicator;

import java.io.File;
import java.io.IOException;

public class FileReplicatorJMXImpl implements FileReplicator {

    private String srcDir;
    private String destDir;
    private FileCopier fileCopier;

    // getters ommited for brevity

    public void setSrcDir(String srcDir) {
        this.srcDir = srcDir;
    }

    public void setDestDir(String destDir) {
        this.destDir = destDir;
    }

    public void setFileCopier(FileCopier fileCopier) {
        this.fileCopier = fileCopier;
    }

    public synchronized void replicate() throws IOException {
        File[] files = new File(srcDir).listFiles();
        for (File file : files) {
            if (file.isFile()) {
                fileCopier.copyFile(srcDir, destDir, file.getName());
            }
        }
    }
}
```

Each time you call the `replicate()` method, all files in the source directory are replicated to the destination directory. To avoid unexpected problems caused by concurrent replication, you declare this method as synchronized.

Now, you can configure one or more file replicator instances in a Java config class. The documentReplicator instance needs references to two directories: a source directory from which files are read and a target directory to which files are backed up. The code in this example attempts to read from a directory called docs in your operating system user's home directory and then copy to a folder called docs_backup in your operating system user's home directory.

When this bean starts up, it creates the two directories if they don't already exist there.

■ **Tip**   The "home directory" is different for each operating system, but typically on Unix it's the directory that ~ resolves to. On a Linux box, the folder might be /home/user. On macOS, the folder might be /Users/user, and on Windows it might be similar to C:\Documents and Settings\user.

```java
package com.apress.springrecipes.replicator.config;
...

@Configuration
public class FileReplicatorConfig {

    @Value("#{systemProperties['user.home']}/docs")
    private String srcDir;
    @Value("#{systemProperties['user.home']}/docs_backup")
    private String destDir;

    @Bean
    public FileCopier fileCopier() {
        FileCopier fCop = new FileCopierJMXImpl();
        return fCop;
    }

    @Bean
    public FileReplicator documentReplicator() {
        FileReplicator fRep = new FileReplicatorJMXImpl();
        fRep.setSrcDir(srcDir);
        fRep.setDestDir(destDir);
        fRep.setFileCopier(fileCopier());
        return fRep;
    }

    @PostConstruct
    public void verifyDirectoriesExist() {
        File src = new File(srcDir);
        File dest = new File(destDir);
        if (!src.exists())
            src.mkdirs();
        if (!dest.exists())
            dest.mkdirs();
    }
}
```

Initially two fields are declared using the @Value annotations to gain access to the user's home directory and define the source and destination directories. Next, two bean instances are created using the @Bean annotation. Notice the @PostConstuct annotation on the verifyDirectoriesExist() method, which ensures the source and destination directories exist.

Now that you have the application's core beans, let's take look at how to register and access the beans as an MBean.

Register MBeans Without Spring's Support

First, let's see how to register a model MBean using the JMX API directly. In the following Main class, you get the FileReplicator bean from the IoC container and register it as an MBean for management and monitoring. All properties and methods are included in the MBean's management interface.

```
package com.apress.springrecipes.replicator;
...
import java.lang.management.ManagementFactory;

import javax.management.Descriptor;
import javax.management.JMException;
import javax.management.MBeanServer;
import javax.management.ObjectName;
import javax.management.modelmbean.DescriptorSupport;
import javax.management.modelmbean.InvalidTargetObjectTypeException;
import javax.management.modelmbean.ModelMBeanAttributeInfo;
import javax.management.modelmbean.ModelMBeanInfo;
import javax.management.modelmbean.ModelMBeanInfoSupport;
import javax.management.modelmbean.ModelMBeanOperationInfo;
import javax.management.modelmbean.RequiredModelMBean;

import org.springframework.context.ApplicationContext;
import org.springframework.context.support.GenericXmlApplicationContext;

public class Main {

    public static void main(String[] args) throws IOException {
        ApplicationContext context =
            new AnnotationConfigApplicationContext("com.apress.
            springrecipes.replicator.config");

        FileReplicator documentReplicator = context.getBean(FileReplicator.class);
        try {
            MBeanServer mbeanServer = ManagementFactory.getPlatformMBeanServer();
            ObjectName objectName = new ObjectName("bean:name=documentReplicator");

            RequiredModelMBean mbean = new RequiredModelMBean();
            mbean.setManagedResource(documentReplicator, "objectReference");

            Descriptor srcDirDescriptor = new DescriptorSupport(new String[] {
                "name=SrcDir", "descriptorType=attribute",
                "getMethod=getSrcDir", "setMethod=setSrcDir" });
            ModelMBeanAttributeInfo srcDirInfo = new ModelMBeanAttributeInfo(
                "SrcDir", "java.lang.String", "Source directory",
                true, true, false, srcDirDescriptor);
```

```
            Descriptor destDirDescriptor = new DescriptorSupport(new String[] {
                "name=DestDir", "descriptorType=attribute",
                "getMethod=getDestDir", "setMethod=setDestDir" });
            ModelMBeanAttributeInfo destDirInfo = new ModelMBeanAttributeInfo(
                "DestDir", "java.lang.String", "Destination directory",
                true, true, false, destDirDescriptor);

            ModelMBeanOperationInfo getSrcDirInfo = new ModelMBeanOperationInfo(
                "Get source directory",
                FileReplicator.class.getMethod("getSrcDir"));
            ModelMBeanOperationInfo setSrcDirInfo = new ModelMBeanOperationInfo(
                "Set source directory",
                FileReplicator.class.getMethod("setSrcDir", String.class));
            ModelMBeanOperationInfo getDestDirInfo = new ModelMBeanOperationInfo(
                "Get destination directory",
                FileReplicator.class.getMethod("getDestDir"));
            ModelMBeanOperationInfo setDestDirInfo = new ModelMBeanOperationInfo(
                "Set destination directory",
                FileReplicator.class.getMethod("setDestDir", String.class));
            ModelMBeanOperationInfo replicateInfo = new ModelMBeanOperationInfo(
                "Replicate files",
                FileReplicator.class.getMethod("replicate"));

            ModelMBeanInfo mbeanInfo = new ModelMBeanInfoSupport(
                "FileReplicator", "File replicator",
                new ModelMBeanAttributeInfo[] { srcDirInfo, destDirInfo },
                null,
                new ModelMBeanOperationInfo[] { getSrcDirInfo, setSrcDirInfo,
                    getDestDirInfo, setDestDirInfo, replicateInfo },
                null);
            mbean.setModelMBeanInfo(mbeanInfo);

            mbeanServer.registerMBean(mbean, objectName);
        } catch (JMException e) {
            ...
        } catch (InvalidTargetObjectTypeException e) {
            ...
        } catch (NoSuchMethodException e) {
            ...
        }

        System.in.read();
    }
}
```

To register an MBean, you need an instance of the interface javax.managment.MBeanServer. You can call the static method ManagementFactory.getPlatformMBeanServer() to locate a platform MBean server. It will create an MBean server if none exists and then register this server instance for future use. Each MBean requires an MBean object name that includes a domain. The preceding MBean is registered under the domain bean with the name documentReplicator.

From the preceding code, you can see that for each MBean attribute and MBean operation, you need to create a ModelMBeanAttributeInfo object and a ModelMBeanOperationInfo object for describing it. After those, you have to create a ModelMBeanInfo object for describing the MBean's management interface by assembling the preceding information. For details about using these classes, you can consult their Javadocs. Moreover, you have to handle the JMX-specific exceptions when calling the JMX API. These exceptions are checked exceptions that you must handle. Note that you must prevent your application from terminating before you look inside it with a JMX client tool. Requesting a key from the console using System.in.read() is a good choice.

Finally, you have to add the VM argument -Dcom.sun.management.jmxremote to enable local monitoring of this application. If you're using the book's source code, you can use the following:

```
java -Dcom.sun.management.jmxremote -jar  Recipe_13_1_i-4.0.0.jar
```

Now, you can use any JMX client tools to monitor your MBeans locally. The simplest one is JConsole, which comes with JDK. To start JConsole, just execute the jconsole executable file located in the bin directory of the JDK installation.

When JConsole starts, you can see a list of JMX-enabled applications on the Local tab of the connection window. Select the process that corresponds to the running Spring app (i.e., Recipe_13_1_i-1.0-SNAPSHOT.jar). This is illustrated in Figure 13-1.

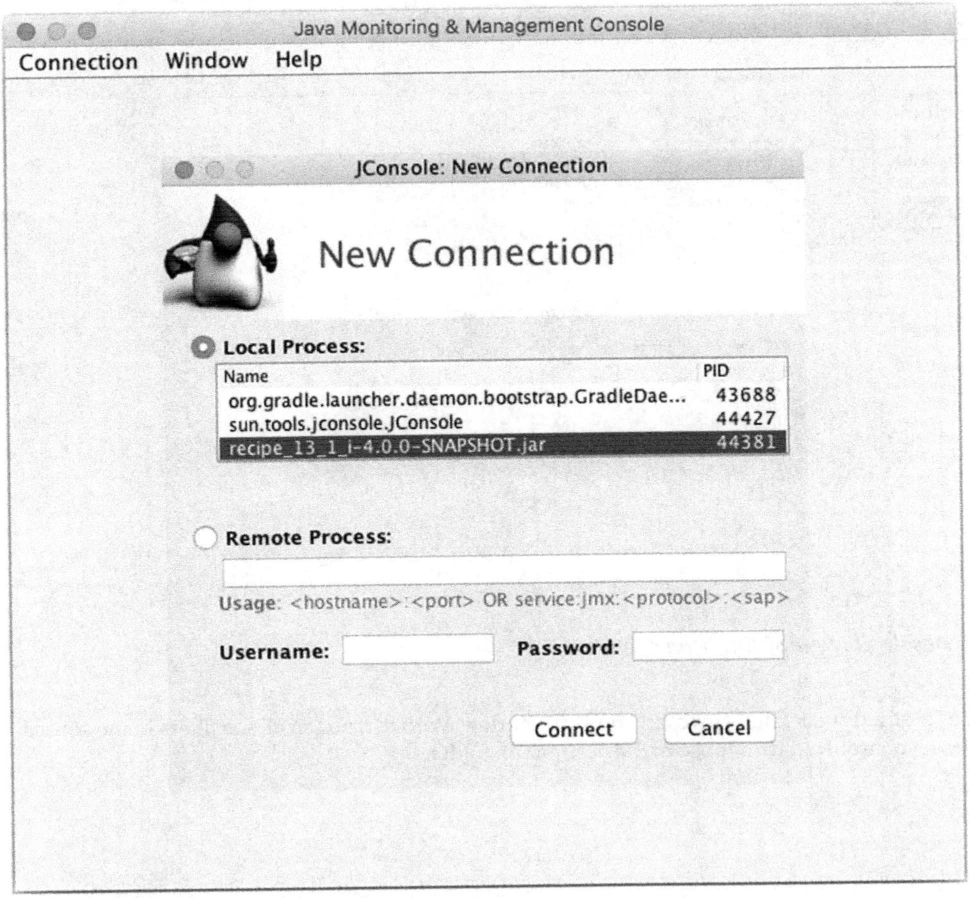

Figure 13-1. JConsole startup window

■ **Caution** If you're on Windows, you may not see any processes in JConsole. This is a known bug where JConsole isn't able to detect running Java processes. To solve this issue, you'll need to ensure the user has the hsperfdata folder in the temp folder. This folder is used by Java and JConsole to keep track of running processes, and it may not exist. For example, if you're running the application as user John.Doe, ensure the following path exists: C:\Users\John.Doe\AppData\Local\Temp\hsperfdata_John.Doe\.

After connecting to the replicator application, go to the MBeans tab. Next, click the Bean folder in the tree on the left, followed by the operations section. In the main screen you'll see a series of buttons to invoke the bean's operations. To invoke replicate(), simply click the replicate button. This screen is illustrated in Figure 13-2.

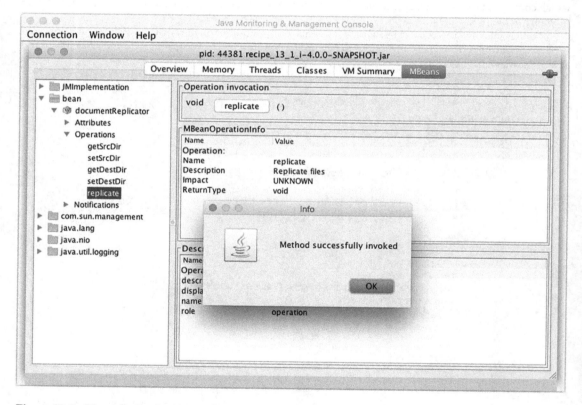

Figure 13-2. JConsole simulate Spring bean operation

You'll see a "Method successfully invoked" pop-up window. With this action all the filters in the source folder are copied/synchronized with those in the destination folder.

Register MBean with Spring Support

The prior application relied on the use of the JMX API directly. As you saw in the Main application class, there's a lot of code that can be difficult to write, manage, and sometimes understand. To export beans configured in the Spring IoC container as MBeans, you simply create an MBeanExporter instance and specify the beans to export, with their MBean object names as the keys. This can be done by adding the following configuration class. Note that the key entry in the beansToExport map is used as the ObjectName for the bean referenced by the corresponding entry value.

```
package com.apress.springrecipes.replicator.config;

import com.apress.springrecipes.replicator.FileReplicator;
import org.springframework.beans.factory.annotation.Autowired;
import org.springframework.context.annotation.Bean;
import org.springframework.context.annotation.Configuration;
import org.springframework.jmx.export.MBeanExporter;

import java.util.HashMap;
import java.util.Map;

@Configuration
public class JmxConfig {

    @Autowired
    private FileReplicator fileReplicator;

    @Bean
    public MBeanExporter mbeanExporter() {
        MBeanExporter mbeanExporter = new MBeanExporter();
        mbeanExporter.setBeans(beansToExport());
        return mbeanExporter;
    }

    private Map<String, Object> beansToExport() {
        Map<String, Object> beansToExport = new HashMap<>();
        beansToExport.put("bean:name=documentReplicator", fileReplicator);
        return beansToExport;
    }
}
```

The preceding configuration exports the FileReplicator bean as an MBean, under the domain bean and with the name documentReplicator. By default, all public properties are included as attributes, and all public methods (with the exception of those from java.lang.Object) are included as operations in the MBean's management interface. With the help of this, Spring JMX MBeanExporter the main class in the application can be cut down to the following lines:

```
package com.apress.springrecipes.replicator;
...
import org.springframework.context.annotation.AnnotationConfigApplicationContext;

public class Main {

    public static void main(String[] args) throws IOException {
        new AnnotationConfigApplicationContext("com.apress.springrecipes.replicator.config");
        System.in.read();
    }
}
```

Work with Multiple MBean Server Instances

The Spring MBeanExporter approach can locate an MBean server instance and register MBeans with it implicitly. The JDK creates an MBean server the first time when you locate it, so there's no need to create an MBean server explicitly. The same case applies if an application is running in an environment that provides an MBean server (e.g., a Java application server).

However, if you have multiple MBean servers running, you need to tell the mbeanServer bean to which server it should bind. You do this by specifying the agentId value of the server. To figure out the agentId value of a given server in JConsole, go to the MBeans tab and in the left tree and go to JMImplementation/MBeanServerDelegate/Attributes/MBeanServerId. There, you'll see the string value. On our local machine, the value is workstation_1253860476443. To enable it, configure the agentId property of the MBeanServer.

```
@Bean
public MBeanServerFactoryBean mbeanServer() {
    MBeanServerFactoryBean mbeanServer = new MBeanServerFactoryBean();
    mbeanServer.setLocateExistingServerIfPossible(true);
    mbeanServer.setAgentId("workstation_1253860476443");
    return mbeanServer;
}
```

If you have multiple MBean server instances in your context, you can explicitly specify a specific MBean server for MBeanExporter to export your MBeans to. In this case, MBeanExporter will not locate an MBean server; it will use the specified MBean server instance. This property is for you to specify a particular MBean server when more than one is available.

```
@Bean
public MBeanExporter mbeanExporter() {
    MBeanExporter mbeanExporter = new MBeanExporter();
    mbeanExporter.setBeans(beansToExport());
    mbeanExporter.setServer(mbeanServer().getObject());
    return mbeanExporter;
}
```

```
@Bean
public MBeanServerFactoryBean mbeanServer() {
    MBeanServerFactoryBean mbeanServer = new MBeanServerFactoryBean();
    mbeanServer.setLocateExistingServerIfPossible(true);
    return mbeanServer;
}
```

Register MBeans for Remote Access with RMI

If you want your MBeans to be accessed remotely, you need to enable a remoting protocol for JMX. JSR-160 defines a standard for JMX remoting through a JMX connector. Spring allows you to create a JMX connector server through ConnectorServerFactoryBean. By default, ConnectorServerFactoryBean creates and starts a JMX connector server bound to the service URL service:jmx:jmxmp://localhost:9875, which exposes the JMX connector through the JMX Messaging Protocol (JMXMP). However, most JMX implementations don't support JMXMP. Therefore, you should choose a widely supported remoting protocol for your JMX connector, such as RMI. To expose your JMX connector through a specific protocol, you just provide the service URL for it.

```
@Bean
public FactoryBean<Registry> rmiRegistry() {
    return new RmiRegistryFactoryBean();
}
```

```
@Bean
@DependsOn("rmiRegistry")
public FactoryBean<JMXConnectorServer> connectorServer() {
    ConnectorServerFactoryBean connectorServerFactoryBean =
        new ConnectorServerFactoryBean();
    connectorServerFactoryBean
.setServiceUrl("service:jmx:rmi://localhost/jndi/rmi://localhost:1099/replicator");
    return connectorServerFactoryBean;
}
```

You specify the preceding URL to bind your JMX connector to an RMI registry listening on port 1099 of localhost. If no RMI registry has been created externally, you should create one by using RmiRegistryFactoryBean. The default port for this registry is 1099, but you can specify another one in its port property. Note that ConnectorServerFactoryBean must create the connector server after the RMI registry is created and ready. You can set the depends-on attribute for this purpose.

Now, your MBeans can be accessed remotely via RMI. Note there's no need to start an RMI-enabled app with the JMX -Dcom.sun.management.jmxremote flag, as you did in previous apps. When JConsole starts, you can enter service:jmx:rmi://localhost/jndi/rmi://localhost:1099/replicator in the service URL in the Remote Processes section of the connection window. This is illustrated in Figure 13-3.

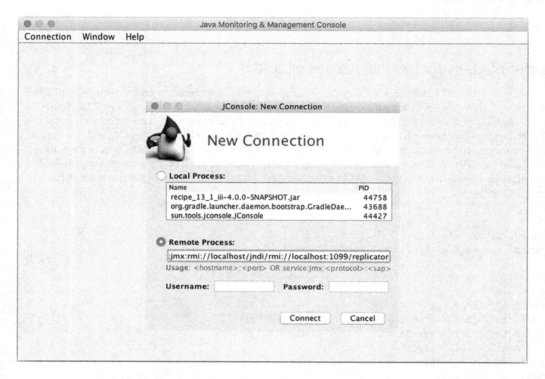

Figure 13-3. *JConsole connection to MBean through RMI*

Once the connection is established, you can invoke bean methods just as you did with previous examples.

Assemble the Management Interface of MBeans

By default, the Spring MBeanExporter exports all public properties of a bean as MBean attributes and all public methods as MBean operations. But you can assemble the management interface of MBeans using an MBean assembler. The simplest MBean assembler in Spring is MethodNameBasedMBeanInfoAssembler, which allows you to specify the names of the methods to export.

```
@Configuration
public class JmxConfig {
    ...
    @Bean
    public MBeanExporter mbeanExporter() {
        MBeanExporter mbeanExporter = new MBeanExporter();
        mbeanExporter.setBeans(beansToExport());
        mbeanExporter.setAssembler(assembler());
        return mbeanExporter;
    }

    @Bean
    public MBeanInfoAssembler assembler() {
        MethodNameBasedMBeanInfoAssembler assembler;
        assembler = new MethodNameBasedMBeanInfoAssembler();
        assembler.setManagedMethods(new String[] {"getSrcDir","setSrcDir","getDestDir",
        "setDestDir","replicate"});
        return assembler;
    }
}
```

Another MBean assembler is `InterfaceBasedMBeanInfoAssembler`, which exports all methods defined in the interfaces you specified.

```
@Bean
public MBeanInfoAssembler assembler() {
    InterfaceBasedMBeanInfoAssembler assembler = new InterfaceBasedMBeanInfoAssembler();
    assembler.setManagedInterfaces(new Class[] {FileReplicator.class});
    return assembler;
}
```

Spring also provides `MetadataMBeanInfoAssembler` to assemble an MBean's management interface based on the metadata in the bean class. It supports two types of metadata: JDK annotations and Apache Commons attributes (behind the scenes, this is accomplished using a strategy interface called `JmxAttributeSource`). For a bean class annotated with JDK annotations, you specify an `AnnotationJmxAttributeSource` instance as the attribute source of `MetadataMBeanInfoAssembler`.

```
@Bean
public MBeanInfoAssembler assembler() {
    MetadataMBeanInfoAssembler assembler = new MetadataMBeanInfoAssembler();
    assembler.setAttributeSource(new AnnotationJmxAttributeSource());
    return assembler;
}
```

Then, you annotate your bean class and methods with the annotations @ManagedResource, @ManagedAttribute, and @ManagedOperation for `MetadataMBeanInfoAssembler` to assemble the management interface for this bean. The annotations are easily interpreted. They expose the element that they annotate. If you have a JavaBeans-compliant property, JMX will use the term *attribute*. Classes themselves are referred to as *resources*. In JMX, methods will be called *operations*. Knowing that, it's easy to see what the following code does:

```java
package com.apress.springrecipes.replicator;
...
import org.springframework.jmx.export.annotation.ManagedAttribute;
import org.springframework.jmx.export.annotation.ManagedOperation;
import org.springframework.jmx.export.annotation.ManagedResource;

@ManagedResource(description = "File replicator")
public class FileReplicatorJMXImpl implements FileReplicator {
    ...
    @ManagedAttribute(description = "Get source directory")
    public String getSrcDir() {
        ...
    }

    @ManagedAttribute(description = "Set source directory")
    public void setSrcDir(String srcDir) {
        ...
    }

    @ManagedAttribute(description = "Get destination directory")
    public String getDestDir() {
        ...
    }

    @ManagedAttribute(description = "Set destination directory")
    public void setDestDir(String destDir) {
        ...
    }

    ...

    @ManagedOperation(description = "Replicate files")
    public synchronized void replicate() throws IOException {
        ...
    }
}
```

Register MBeans with Annotations

In addition to exporting a bean explicitly with MBeanExporter, you can simply configure its subclass AnnotationMBeanExporter to autodetect MBeans from beans declared in the IoC container. You don't need to configure an MBean assembler for this exporter because it uses MetadataMBeanInfoAssembler with AnnotationJmxAttributeSource by default. You can delete the previous beans and assembler properties for this registration and simply leave the following:

```
@Configuration
public class JmxConfig {

    @Bean
    public MBeanExporter mbeanExporter() {
        AnnotationMBeanExporter mbeanExporter = new AnnotationMBeanExporter();
        return mbeanExporter;
    }
}
```

AnnotationMBeanExporter detects any beans configured in the IoC container with the @ManagedResource annotation and exports them as MBeans. By default, this exporter exports a bean to the domain whose name is the same as its package name. Also, it uses the bean's name in the IoC container as its MBean name and uses the bean's short class name as its type. So, the documentReplicator bean will be exported under the following MBean object name: com.apress.springrecipes.replicator:name=documentReplicator, type=FileReplicatorJMXImpl.

If you don't want to use the package name as the domain name, you can set the default domain for the exporter by adding the defaultDomain property:

```
@Bean
public MBeanExporter mbeanExporter() {
    AnnotationMBeanExporter mbeanExporter = new AnnotationMBeanExporter();
    mbeanExporter.setDefaultDomain("bean");
    return mbeanExporter;
}
```

After setting the default domain to bean, the documentReplicator bean is exported under the following MBean object name:

```
bean:name=documentReplicator,type=FileReplicatorJMXImpl
```

In addition, you can specify a bean's MBean object name in the objectName attribute of the @ManagedResource annotation. For example, you can export the file copier as an MBean by annotating it with the following annotations:

```
package com.apress.springrecipes.replicator;
...
import org.springframework.jmx.export.annotation.ManagedOperation;
import org.springframework.jmx.export.annotation.ManagedOperationParameter;
import org.springframework.jmx.export.annotation.ManagedOperationParameters;
import org.springframework.jmx.export.annotation.ManagedResource;
```

```
@ManagedResource(
    objectName = "bean:name=fileCopier,type=FileCopierJMXImpl",
    description = "File Copier")
public class FileCopierImpl implements FileCopier {

    @ManagedOperation(
        description = "Copy file from source directory to destination directory")
    @ManagedOperationParameters( {
        @ManagedOperationParameter(
            name = "srcDir", description = "Source directory"),
        @ManagedOperationParameter(
            name = "destDir", description = "Destination directory"),
        @ManagedOperationParameter(
            name = "filename", description = "File to copy") })
    public void copyFile(String srcDir, String destDir, String filename)
        throws IOException {
        ...
    }
}
```

However, specifying the object name in this way works only for classes that you're going to create a single instance of in the IoC container (e.g., file copier), not for classes that you may create multiple instances of (e.g., file replicator). This is because you can only specify a single object name for a class. As a result, you shouldn't try to run the same server multiple times without changing the names.

Finally, another possibility is to rely on Spring class scanning to export MBeans decorated with @ManagedResource. If the beans are initialized in a Java config class, you can decorate the configuration class with the @EnableMBeanExport annotation. This tells Spring to export any beans created with the @Bean annotation that are decorated with the @EnableMBeanSupport annotation.

```
package com.apress.springrecipes.replicator.config;

...

import org.springframework.context.annotation.EnableMBeanExport;

@Configuration
@EnableMBeanExport
public class FileReplicatorConfig {
    ....
    @Bean
    public FileReplicatorJMXImpl documentReplicator() {
        FileReplicatorJMXImpl fRep = new FileReplicatorJMXImpl();
        fRep.setSrcDir(srcDir);
        fRep.setDestDir(destDir);
        fRep.setFileCopier(fileCopier());
        return fRep;
    }
    ...
}
```

Because of the presence of the @EnableMBeanExport annotation, the bean documentReplicatior of the type FileReplicatorJMXImpl gets exported as an MBean because its source is decorated with the @ManagedResource annotation.

■ **Caution**   The use of the @EnableMBeanExport annotation is done on @Bean instances with concrete classes, not interfaces like previous examples. Interface-based beans *hide* the target class, as well as the JMX managed resource annotations, and the MBean is not exported.

13-2. Publish and Listen to JMX Notifications

Problem

You want to publish JMX notifications from your MBeans and listen to them with JMX notification listeners.

Solution

Spring allows your beans to publish JMX notifications through the NotificationPublisher interface. You can also register standard JMX notification listeners in the IoC container to listen to JMX notifications.

How It Works

To publish event you need access to the NotificationPublisher you can get access through Spring by implementing the NotificationPublisherAware interface. To listen to events you can use the default JMX constructs of implementing the NotificationListener interface and register this implementation with JMX.

Publish JMX Notifications

The Spring IoC container supports the beans that are going to be exported as MBeans to publish JMX notifications. These beans must implement the NotificationPublisherAware interface to get access to NotificationPublisher so that they can publish notifications.

```
package com.apress.springrecipes.replicator;
...
import javax.management.Notification;

import org.springframework.jmx.export.notification.NotificationPublisher;
import org.springframework.jmx.export.notification.NotificationPublisherAware;

@ManagedResource(description = "File replicator")
public class FileReplicatorImpl implements FileReplicator,
    NotificationPublisherAware {

    ...
    private int sequenceNumber;
    private NotificationPublisher notificationPublisher;
```

```java
    public void setNotificationPublisher(
        NotificationPublisher notificationPublisher) {
        this.notificationPublisher = notificationPublisher;
    }

    @ManagedOperation(description = "Replicate files")
    public void replicate() throws IOException {
        notificationPublisher.sendNotification(
            new Notification("replication.start", this, sequenceNumber));
        ...
        notificationPublisher.sendNotification(
            new Notification("replication.complete", this, sequenceNumber));
        sequenceNumber++;
    }
}
```

In this file replicator, you send a JMX notification whenever a replication starts or completes. The notification is visible both in the standard output in the console and in the JConsole Notifications menu on the MBeans tab, as illustrated in Figure 13-4.

Figure 13-4. *MBean events reported in JConsole*

To see notifications in Jconsole, you must first click the Subscribe button that appears toward the bottom, as illustrated in Figure 13-4. Then, when you invoke the `replicate()` method using the JConsole button in the MBean operations section, you'll see two new notifications arrive. The first argument in the Notification constructor is the notification type, while the second is the notification source.

Listen to JMX Notifications

Now, let's create a notification listener to listen to JMX notifications. Because a listener will be notified of many different types of notifications, such as `javax.management.AttributeChangeNotification` when an MBean's attribute has changed, you have to filter those notifications that you are interested in handling.

```
package com.apress.springrecipes.replicator;

import javax.management.Notification;
import javax.management.NotificationListener;

public class ReplicationNotificationListener implements NotificationListener {

    public void handleNotification(Notification notification, Object handback) {
        if (notification.getType().startsWith("replication")) {
            System.out.println(
                notification.getSource() + " " +
                notification.getType() + " #" +
                notification.getSequenceNumber());
        }
    }
}
```

Then, you can register this notification listener with your MBean exporter to listen to notifications emitted from certain MBeans.

```
@Bean
public AnnotationMBeanExporter mbeanExporter() {
    AnnotationMBeanExporter mbeanExporter = new AnnotationMBeanExporter();
    mbeanExporter.setDefaultDomain("bean");
    mbeanExporter.setNotificationListenerMappings(notificationMappings());
    return mbeanExporter;
}

public Map<String, NotificationListener> notificationMappings() {
    Map<String, NotificationListener> mappings = new HashMap<>();
    mappings.put("bean:name=documentReplicator,type=FileReplicatorJMXImpl",
        new ReplicationNotificationListener());
    return mappings;
}
```

13-3. Access Remote JMX MBeans in Spring

Problem

You want to access JMX MBeans running on a remote MBean server exposed by a JMX connector. When accessing remote MBeans directly with the JMX API, you have to write complex JMX-specific code.

Solution

Spring offers two approaches to simplify remote MBean access. First, it provides a factory bean to create an MBean server connection declaratively. With this server connection, you can query and update an MBean's attributes, as well as invoke its operations. Second, Spring provides another factory bean that allows you to create a proxy for a remote MBean. With this proxy, you can operate a remote MBean as if it were a local bean.

How It Works

To make it easier to work with JMX Spring provides two approaches one is to make it easier to work with plain JMX by helping configuring the connection to the MBean server. Another is more like the other remoting technologies from Spring by providing a proxy to a remote MBean.

Access Remote MBeans Through an MBean Server Connection

A JMX client requires an MBean server connection to access MBeans running on a remote MBean server. Spring provides org.springframework.jmx.support.MBeanServerConnectionFactoryBean for you to create a connection to a remote JSR-160–enabled MBean server declaratively. You only have to provide the service URL for it to locate the MBean server. Now let's declare this factory bean in your client bean configuration class.

```
package com.apress.springrecipes.replicator.config;

import org.springframework.beans.factory.FactoryBean;
import org.springframework.context.annotation.Bean;
import org.springframework.context.annotation.Configuration;
import org.springframework.jmx.support.MBeanServerConnectionFactoryBean;

import javax.management.MBeanServerConnection;
import java.net.MalformedURLException;

@Configuration
public class JmxClientConfiguration {

    @Bean
    public FactoryBean<MBeanServerConnection> mbeanServerConnection()
    throws MalformedURLException {
        MBeanServerConnectionFactoryBean mBeanServerConnectionFactoryBean =
            new MBeanServerConnectionFactoryBean();
        mBeanServerConnectionFactoryBean
            .setServiceUrl("service:jmx:rmi://localhost/jndi/rmi://localhost:1099/
            replicator");
        return mBeanServerConnectionFactoryBean;
    }
}
```

With the MBean server connection created by this factory bean, you can access and operate the MBeans running on the RMI server that's running on port 1099.

■ **Tip**   You can use the RMI server presented in recipe 13-1, which exposes MBeans. If you're using the book's source code, after you build the application with Gradle, you can start the server with the following command: `java -jar Recipe_14_1_iii-1.0-SNAPSHOT.jar`.

With the connection established between both points, you can query and update an MBean's attributes through the getAttribute() and setAttribute() methods, giving the MBean's object name and attribute name. You can also invoke an MBean's operations by using the invoke() method.

```java
package com.apress.springrecipes.replicator;

import javax.management.Attribute;
import javax.management.MBeanServerConnection;
import javax.management.ObjectName;

import org.springframework.context.ApplicationContext;
import org.springframework.context.support.Generic XmlApplicationContext;

public class Client {

    public static void main(String[] args) throws Exception {
        ApplicationContext context =
            new AnnotationConfigApplicationContext("com.apress.springrecipes.
            replicator.config");

        MBeanServerConnection mbeanServerConnection =
            context.getBean(MBeanServerConnection.class);

        ObjectName mbeanName = new ObjectName("bean:name=documentReplicator");

        String srcDir = (String) mbeanServerConnection.getAttribute(mbeanName, "SrcDir");

        mbeanServerConnection.setAttribute(mbeanName,
            new Attribute("DestDir", srcDir + "_backup"));

        mbeanServerConnection.invoke(mbeanName, "replicate", new Object[] {}, new String[] {});
    }
}
```

In addition, let's create a JMX notification listener so you can listen in on file replication notifications.

```java
package com.apress.springrecipes.replicator;

import javax.management.Notification;
import javax.management.NotificationListener;

public class ReplicationNotificationListener implements NotificationListener {

    public void handleNotification(Notification notification, Object handback) {
        if (notification.getType().startsWith("replication")) {
            System.out.println(
                notification.getSource() + " " +
                notification.getType() + " #" +
                notification.getSequenceNumber());
        }
    }
}
```

You can register this notification listener to the MBean server connection to listen to notifications emitted from this MBean server.

```
package com.apress.springrecipes.replicator;
...
import javax.management.MBeanServerConnection;
import javax.management.ObjectName;

public class Client {

    public static void main(String[] args) throws Exception {
        ...
        MBeanServerConnection mbeanServerConnection =
            (MBeanServerConnection) context.getBean("mbeanServerConnection");

        ObjectName mbeanName = new ObjectName(
            "bean:name=documentReplicator");

        mbeanServerConnection.addNotificationListener(
            mbeanName, new ReplicationNotificationListener(), null, null);
        ...
    }
}
```

After you run this application client, check JConsole for the RMI server application—using a Remote Process setting of service:jmx:rmi://localhost/jndi/rmi://localhost:1099/replicator. Under the Notifications menu of the MBeans tab, you'll see new notification of type jmx.attribute.change, as illustrated in Figure 13-5.

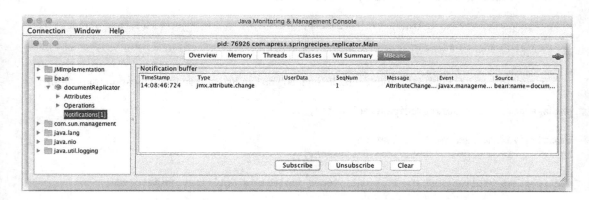

Figure 13-5. *JConsole notification event invoked through RMI*

Access Remote MBeans Through an MBean Proxy

Another approach that Spring offers for remote MBean access is through `MBeanProxy`, which can be created by `MBeanProxyFactoryBean`.

```
package com.apress.springrecipes.replicator.config;

...
import org.springframework.beans.factory.FactoryBean;
import org.springframework.jmx.access.MBeanProxyFactoryBean;
import org.springframework.jmx.support.MBeanServerConnectionFactoryBean;

import javax.management.MBeanServerConnection;
import java.net.MalformedURLException;

@Configuration
public class JmxClientConfiguration {

...

    @Bean
    public MBeanProxyFactoryBean fileReplicatorProxy() throws Exception {
        MBeanProxyFactoryBean fileReplicatorProxy = new MBeanProxyFactoryBean();
        fileReplicatorProxy.setServer(mbeanServerConnection().getObject());
        fileReplicatorProxy.setObjectName("bean:name=documentReplicator");
        fileReplicatorProxy.setProxyInterface(FileReplicator.class);
        return fileReplicatorProxy;
    }
}
```

You need to specify the object name and the server connection for the MBean you are going to proxy. The most important is the proxy interface, whose local method calls will be translated into remote MBean calls behind the scenes. Now, you can operate the remote MBean through this proxy as if it were a local bean. The preceding MBean operations invoked on the MBean server connection directly can be simplified as follows:

```
package com.apress.springrecipes.replicator;
...
public class Client {

    public static void main(String[] args) throws Exception {
        ...
        FileReplicator fileReplicatorProxy = context.getBean(FileReplicator.class);
        String srcDir = fileReplicatorProxy.getSrcDir();
        fileReplicatorProxy.setDestDir(srcDir + "_backup");
        fileReplicatorProxy.replicate();
    }
}
```

13-4. Send E-mail with Spring's E-mail Support

Problem

Many applications need to send e-mail. In a Java application, you can send e-mail with the JavaMail API. However, when using JavaMail, you have to handle JavaMail-specific mail sessions and exceptions. As a result, an application becomes JavaMail dependent and hard to switch to another e-mail API.

Solution

Spring's e-mail support makes it easier to send e-mail by providing an abstract and implementation-independent API for sending e-mail. The core interface of Spring's e-mail support is `MailSender`. The `JavaMailSender` interface is a subinterface of `MailSender` that includes specialized JavaMail features such as Multipurpose Internet Mail Extensions (MIME) message support. To send an e-mail message with HTML content, inline images, or attachments, you have to send it as a MIME message.

How It Works

Suppose you want the file replicator application from the previous recipes to notify the administrator of any error. First, you create the following `ErrorNotifier` interface, which includes a method for notifying of a file copy error:

```
package com.apress.springrecipes.replicator;

public interface ErrorNotifier {

    public void notifyCopyError(String srcDir, String destDir, String filename);
}
```

■ **Note** Invoking this notifier in case of error is left for you to accomplish. Because you can consider error handling a crosscutting concern, AOP would be an ideal solution to this problem. You can write an after throwing advice to invoke this notifier.

Next, you can implement this interface to send a notification in a way of your choice. The most common way is to send e-mail. Before you implement the interface in this way, you may need a local e-mail server that supports the Simple Mail Transfer Protocol (SMTP) for testing purposes. We recommend installing Apache James Server (`http://james.apache.org/server/index.html`), which is easy to install and configure.

■ **Note** You can download Apache James Server (e.g., version 2.3.2) from the Apache James web site and extract it to a directory of your choice to complete the installation. To start it, just execute the run script (located in the `bin` directory).

Let's create two user accounts for sending and receiving e-mail with this server. By default, the remote manager service of James listens on port 4555. You can telnet, using a console, to this port and run the following commands to add the users *system* and *admin*, whose passwords are *12345*:

```
> telnet 127.0.0.1 4555
JAMES Remote Administration Tool 2.3.2
Please enter your login and password
Login id:
root
Password:
itroot
Welcome root. HELP for a list of commands
adduser system 12345
User system added
adduser admin 12345
User admin added
listusers
Existing accounts 2
user: admin
user: system
quit
Bye
```

Send E-mail Using the JavaMail API

Now, let's take a look at how to send e-mail using the JavaMail API. You can implement the `ErrorNotifier` interface to send e-mail notifications in case of errors.

```java
package com.apress.springrecipes.replicator;

import java.util.Properties;

import javax.mail.Message;
import javax.mail.MessagingException;
import javax.mail.Session;
import javax.mail.Transport;
import javax.mail.internet.InternetAddress;
import javax.mail.internet.MimeMessage;

public class EmailErrorNotifier implements ErrorNotifier {

    public void notifyCopyError(String srcDir, String destDir, String filename) {
        Properties props = new Properties();
        props.put("mail.smtp.host", "localhost");
        props.put("mail.smtp.port", "25");
        props.put("mail.smtp.username", "system");
        props.put("mail.smtp.password", "12345");
        Session session = Session.getDefaultInstance(props, null);
        try {
```

```
            Message message = new MimeMessage(session);
            message.setFrom(new InternetAddress("system@localhost"));
            message.setRecipients(Message.RecipientType.TO,
                    InternetAddress.parse("admin@localhost"));
            message.setSubject("File Copy Error");
            message.setText(
                "Dear Administrator,\n\n" +
                "An error occurred when copying the following file :\n" +
                "Source directory : " + srcDir + "\n" +
                "Destination directory : " + destDir + "\n" +
                "Filename : " + filename);
            Transport.send(message);
        } catch (MessagingException e) {
            throw new RuntimeException(e);
        }
    }
}
```

You first open a mail session connecting to an SMTP server by defining the properties. Then, you create a message from this session for constructing your e-mail. After that, you send the e-mail by making a call to Transport.send(). When dealing with the JavaMail API, you have to handle the checked exception MessagingException. Note that all of these classes, interfaces, and exceptions are defined by JavaMail.

Next, declare an instance of EmailErrorNotifier in the Spring IoC container for sending e-mail notifications in case of file replication errors.

```
package com.apress.springrecipes.replicator.config;

import com.apress.springrecipes.replicator.EmailErrorNotifier;
import com.apress.springrecipes.replicator.ErrorNotifier;
import org.springframework.context.annotation.Bean;
import org.springframework.context.annotation.Configuration;

@Configuration
public class MailConfiguration {

    @Bean
    public ErrorNotifier errorNotifier() {
        return new EmailErrorNotifier();
    }
}
```

You can write the following Main class to test EmailErrorNotifier. After running it, you can configure your e-mail application to receive the e-mail from your James server via POP3.

```
package com.apress.springrecipes.replicator;

import org.springframework.context.ApplicationContext;
import org.springframework.context.support.GenericXmlApplicationContext;

public class Main {
```

```
public static void main(String[] args) {
    ApplicationContext context =
        new AnnotationConfigApplicationContext("com.apress.springrecipes.replicator.
        config");

    ErrorNotifier errorNotifier = context.getBean(ErrorNotifier.class);
    errorNotifier.notifyCopyError("c:/documents", "d:/documents", "spring.doc");
}
}
```

To verify the e-mail was sent, you can log in to the POP server included with Apache James. You can telnet, using a console, to port 110 and run the following commands to view the e-mail for user *admin*, whose password is the same as you set on creation:

```
> telnet 127.0.0.1 110
OK workstation POP3 server <JAMES POP3 Server 2.3.2> ready
USER admin
+OK
PASS 12345
+OK Welcome admin
LIST
+ OK 1 698
RETR 1
+OK Message follows
...
```

Send E-mail with Spring's MailSender

Now, let's look at how to send e-mail with the help of Spring's MailSender interface, which can send SimpleMailMessage in its send() method. With this interface, your code is no longer JavaMail specific, and now it's easier to test.

```
package com.apress.springrecipes.replicator;

import org.springframework.mail.MailSender;
import org.springframework.mail.SimpleMailMessage;

public class EmailErrorNotifier implements ErrorNotifier {

    private MailSender mailSender;

    public void setMailSender(MailSender mailSender) {
        this.mailSender = mailSender;
    }

    public void notifyCopyError(String srcDir, String destDir, String filename) {
        SimpleMailMessage message = new SimpleMailMessage();
        message.setFrom("system@localhost");
        message.setTo("admin@localhost");
        message.setSubject("File Copy Error");
```

```
        message.setText(
            "Dear Administrator,\n\n" +
            "An error occurred when copying the following file :\n" +
            "Source directory : " + srcDir + "\n" +
            "Destination directory : " + destDir + "\n" +
            "Filename : " + filename);
        mailSender.send(message);
    }
}
```

Next, you have to configure a MailSender implementation in the bean configuration file and inject it into EmailErrorNotifier. In Spring, the unique implementation of this interface is JavaMailSenderImpl, which uses JavaMail to send e-mail.

```
@Configuration
public class MailConfiguration {

    @Bean
    public ErrorNotifier errorNotifier() {
        EmailErrorNotifier errorNotifier = new EmailErrorNotifier();
        errorNotifier.setMailSender(mailSender());
        return errorNotifier;
    }

    @Bean
    public JavaMailSenderImpl mailSender() {
        JavaMailSenderImpl mailSender = new JavaMailSenderImpl();
        mailSender.setHost("localhost");
        mailSender.setPort(25);
        mailSender.setUsername("system");
        mailSender.setPassword("12345");
        return mailSender;
    }
}
```

The default port used by JavaMailSenderImpl is the standard SMTP port 25, so if your e-mail server listens on this port for SMTP, you can simply omit this property. Also, if your SMTP server doesn't require user authentication, you needn't set the username and password.

If you have a JavaMail session configured in your Java app server, you can first look it up with the help of JndiLocatorDelegate.

```
@Bean
public Session mailSession() throws NamingException {
    return JndiLocatorDelegate
        .createDefaultResourceRefLocator()
        .lookup("mail/Session", Session.class);
}
```

You can inject the JavaMail session into JavaMailSenderImpl for its use. In this case, you no longer need to set the host, port, username, or password.

```
@Bean
public JavaMailSenderImpl mailSender() {
    JavaMailSenderImpl mailSender = new JavaMailSenderImpl();
    mailSender.setSession(mailSession());
    return mailSender;
}
```

Define an E-mail Template

Constructing an e-mail message from scratch in the method body is not efficient because you have to hard-code the e-mail properties. Also, you may have difficulty in writing the e-mail text in terms of Java strings. You can consider defining an e-mail message template in the bean configuration file and constructing a new e-mail message from it.

```
@Configuration
public class MailConfiguration {
...
    @Bean
    public ErrorNotifier errorNotifier() {
        EmailErrorNotifier errorNotifier = new EmailErrorNotifier();
        errorNotifier.setMailSender(mailSender());
        errorNotifier.setCopyErrorMailMessage(copyErrorMailMessage());
        return errorNotifier;
    }

    @Bean
    public SimpleMailMessage copyErrorMailMessage() {
        SimpleMailMessage message = new SimpleMailMessage();
        message.setFrom("system@localhost");
        message.setTo("admin@localhost");
        message.setSubject("File Copy Error");
        message.setText("Dear Administrator,\n" +
            "\n" +
            "                    An error occurred when copying the following file :\n" +
            "\t\t       Source directory : %s\n" +
            "\t\t       Destination directory : %s\n" +
            "\t\t       Filename : %s");
        return message;
    }
}
```

Note that in the preceding message text, you include the placeholders %s, which will be replaced by message parameters through String.format(). Of course, you can also use a powerful templating language such as Velocity or FreeMarker to generate the message text according to a template. It's also a good practice to separate mail message templates from bean configuration files.

Each time you send e-mail, you can construct a new `SimpleMailMessage` instance from this injected template. Then you can generate the message text using `String.format()` to replace the %s placeholders with your message parameters.

```
package com.apress.springrecipes.replicator;
...
import org.springframework.mail.SimpleMailMessage;

public class EmailErrorNotifier implements ErrorNotifier {
    ...
    private SimpleMailMessage copyErrorMailMessage;

    public void setCopyErrorMailMessage(SimpleMailMessage copyErrorMailMessage) {
        this.copyErrorMailMessage = copyErrorMailMessage;
    }

    public void notifyCopyError(String srcDir, String destDir, String filename) {
        SimpleMailMessage message = new SimpleMailMessage(copyErrorMailMessage);
        message.setText(String.format(
            copyErrorMailMessage.getText(), srcDir, destDir, filename));
        mailSender.send(message);
    }
}
```

Send E-mail with Attachments (MIME Messages)

So far, the `SimpleMailMessage` class you used can send only a simple plain-text e-mail message. To send e-mail that contains HTML content, inline images, or attachments, you have to construct and send a MIME message instead. MIME is supported by JavaMail through the `Javax.mail.internet.MimeMessage` class.

First, you have to use the `JavaMailSender` interface instead of its parent interface `MailSender`. The `JavaMailSenderImpl` instance you injected does implement this interface, so you needn't modify your bean configurations. The following notifier sends Spring's bean configuration file as an e-mail attachment to the administrator:

```
package com.apress.springrecipes.replicator;

import javax.mail.MessagingException;
import javax.mail.internet.MimeMessage;

import org.springframework.core.io.ClassPathResource;
import org.springframework.mail.MailParseException;
import org.springframework.mail.SimpleMailMessage;
import org.springframework.mail.javamail.JavaMailSender;
import org.springframework.mail.javamail.MimeMessageHelper;

public class EmailErrorNotifier implements ErrorNotifier {

    private JavaMailSender mailSender;
    private SimpleMailMessage copyErrorMailMessage;
```

```java
    public void setMailSender(JavaMailSender mailSender) {
        this.mailSender = mailSender;
    }

    public void setCopyErrorMailMessage(SimpleMailMessage copyErrorMailMessage) {
        this.copyErrorMailMessage = copyErrorMailMessage;
    }

    public void notifyCopyError(String srcDir, String destDir, String filename) {
        MimeMessage message = mailSender.createMimeMessage();
        try {
            MimeMessageHelper helper = new MimeMessageHelper(message, true);
            helper.setFrom(copyErrorMailMessage.getFrom());
            helper.setTo(copyErrorMailMessage.getTo());

            helper.setSubject(copyErrorMailMessage.getSubject());
            helper.setText(String.format(
                copyErrorMailMessage.getText(), srcDir, destDir, filename));

            ClassPathResource config = new ClassPathResource("beans.xml");
            helper.addAttachment("beans.xml", config);
        } catch (MessagingException e) {
            throw new MailParseException(e);
        }
        mailSender.send(message);
    }
}
```

Unlike `SimpleMailMessage`, the `MimeMessage` class is defined by JavaMail, so you can only instantiate it by calling `mailSender.createMimeMessage()`. Spring provides the helper class `MimeMessageHelper` to simplify the operations of `MimeMessage`. It allows you to add an attachment from a Spring `Resource` object. However, the operations of this helper class can still throw JavaMail's `MessagingException`. You have to convert this exception into Spring's mail runtime exception for consistency. Spring offers another method for you to construct a MIME message, which is through implementing the `MimeMessagePreparator` interface.

```java
package com.apress.springrecipes.replicator;
...
import javax.mail.internet.MimeMessage;

import org.springframework.mail.javamail.MimeMessagePreparator;

public class EmailErrorNotifier implements ErrorNotifier {
    ...
    public void notifyCopyError(
            final String srcDir, final String destDir, final String filename) {
        MimeMessagePreparator preparator = new MimeMessagePreparator() {

            public void prepare(MimeMessage mimeMessage) throws Exception {
                MimeMessageHelper helper =
                    new MimeMessageHelper(mimeMessage, true);
                helper.setFrom(copyErrorMailMessage.getFrom());
```

```
                helper.setTo(copyErrorMailMessage.getTo());
                helper.setSubject(copyErrorMailMessage.getSubject());
                helper.setText(String.format(
                    copyErrorMailMessage.getText(), srcDir, destDir, filename));

                ClassPathResource config = new ClassPathResource("beans.xml");
                helper.addAttachment("beans.xml", config);
            }
        };
        mailSender.send(preparator);
    }
}
```

In the prepare() method, you can prepare the MimeMessage object, which is precreated for
JavaMailSender. If there is any exception thrown, it will be converted into Spring's mail runtime exception
automatically.

13-5. Schedule Tasks with Spring's Quartz Support

Problem

Your application has an advanced scheduling requirement that you want to fulfill using Quartz Scheduler.
Such a requirement might be something seemingly complex like the ability to run at arbitrary times or at
strange intervals ("every other Thursday, but only after 10 a.m. and before 2 p.m."). Moreover, you want to
configure scheduling jobs in a declarative way.

Solution

Spring provides utility classes for Quartz to enable scheduling jobs without programming against the
Quartz API.

How It Works

First you will take a look at how to use Quartz with Spring without the Spring utility classes followed by the
approach which does use the Spring utility classes for Quartz.

Use Quartz Without Spring's Support

To use Quartz for scheduling, you first need to create a job by implementing the Job interface. For example,
the following job executes the replicate() method of the file replicator designed in the previous recipes.
It retrieves a job data map—which is a Quartz concept to define jobs—through the JobExecutionContext
object.

```
package com.apress.springrecipes.replicator;
...
import org.quartz.Job;
import org.quartz.JobExecutionContext;
import org.quartz.JobExecutionException;
```

```java
public class FileReplicationJob implements Job {

    public void execute(JobExecutionContext context)
        throws JobExecutionException {
        Map dataMap = context.getJobDetail().getJobDataMap();
        FileReplicator fileReplicator =
            (FileReplicator) dataMap.get("fileReplicator");
        try {
            fileReplicator.replicate();
        } catch (IOException e) {
            throw new JobExecutionException(e);
        }
    }
}
```

After creating the job, you configure and schedule it with the Quartz API. For instance, the following scheduler runs your file replication job every 60 seconds with a 5-second delay for the first time of execution:

```java
package com.apress.springrecipes.replicator;
...
import org.quartz.JobDetail;
import org.quartz.JobDataMap;
import org.quartz.JobBuilder;
import org.quartz.Trigger;
import org.quartz.TriggerBuilder;
import org.quartz.SimpleScheduleBuilder;
import org.quartz.DateBuilder.IntervalUnit.*;
import org.quartz.Scheduler;
import org.quartz.impl.StdSchedulerFactory;

import org.springframework.context.ApplicationContext;
import org.springframework.context.support.GenericXmlApplicationContext;

public class Main {

    public static void main(String[] args) throws Exception {
        ApplicationContext context =
            new AnnotationConfigApplicationContext("com.apress.springrecipes.
            replicator.config");

        FileReplicator documentReplicator = context.getBean(FileReplicator.class);

        JobDataMap jobDataMap = new JobDataMap();
        jobDataMap.put("fileReplicator", documentReplicator);

        JobDetail job = JobBuilder.newJob(FileReplicationJob.class)
                                .withIdentity("documentReplicationJob")
                                .storeDurably()
                                .usingJobData(jobDataMap)
                                .build();
```

```
        Trigger trigger = TriggerBuilder.newTrigger()
    .withIdentity("documentReplicationTrigger")
    .startAt(new Date(System.currentTimeMillis() + 5000))
    .forJob(job)
    .withSchedule(SimpleScheduleBuilder.simpleSchedule()
.withIntervalInSeconds(60)
.repeatForever())
.build();

        Scheduler scheduler = new StdSchedulerFactory().getScheduler();
        scheduler.start();
        scheduler.scheduleJob(job, trigger);
    }
}
```

In the Main class, you first create a job map. In this case it's a single job, where the key is a descriptive name and the value is an object reference for the job. Next, you define the job details for the file replication job in a JobDetail object and prepare job data in its jobDataMap property. Next, you create a SimpleTrigger object to configure the scheduling properties. Finally, you create a scheduler to run your job using this trigger.

Quartz supports various types of schedules to run jobs at different intervals. Schedules are defined as part of triggers. In the most recent release, Quartz schedules are SimpleScheduleBuilder, CronScheduleBuilder, CalendarIntervalScheduleBuilder, and DailyTimeIntervalScheduleBuilder. SimpleScheduleBuilder allows you to schedule jobs setting properties such as start time, end time, repeat interval, and repeat count. CronScheduleBuilder accepts a Unix cron expression for you to specify the times to run your job. For example, you can replace the preceding SimpleScheduleBuilder with the following CronScheduleBuilder to run a job at 17:30 every day: .withSchedule(CronScheduleBuilder. cronSchedule(" 0 30 17 * * ?")). A cron expression consists of seven fields (the last field is optional), separated by spaces. Table 13-1 shows the field description for a cron expression.

Table 13-1. *Field Description for a cron Expression*

Position	Field Name	Range
1	Second	0–59
2	Minute	0–59
3	Hour	0–23
4	Day of month	1–31
5	Month	1–12 or JAN–DEC
6	Day of week	1–7 or SUN–SAT
7	Year (optional)	1970–2099

Each part of a cron expression can be assigned a specific value (e.g., 3), a range (e.g., 1–5), a list (e.g., 1,3,5), a wildcard (* matches all values), or a question mark (? is used in either of the "Day of month" and "Day of week" fields for matching one of these fields but not both). CalendarIntervalScheduleBuilder allows you to schedule jobs based on calendar times (day, week, month, year), whereas DailyTimeIntervalScheduleBuilder provides convenience utilities to set a job's end time (e.g., methods like endingDailyAt() and endingDailyAfterCount()).

Use Quartz with Spring's Support

When using Quartz, you can create a job by implementing the Job interface and retrieve job data from the job data map through JobExecutionContext. To decouple your job class from the Quartz API, Spring provides QuartzJobBean, which you can extend to retrieve job data through setter methods. QuartzJobBean converts the job data map into properties and injects them via the setter methods.

```
package com.apress.springrecipes.replicator;
...
import org.quartz.JobExecutionContext;
import org.quartz.JobExecutionException;
import org.springframework.scheduling.quartz.QuartzJobBean;

public class FileReplicationJob extends QuartzJobBean {

    private FileReplicator fileReplicator;

    public void setFileReplicator(FileReplicator fileReplicator) {
        this.fileReplicator = fileReplicator;
    }

    protected void executeInternal(JobExecutionContext context)
        throws JobExecutionException {
        try {
            fileReplicator.replicate();
        } catch (IOException e) {
            throw new JobExecutionException(e);
        }
    }
}
```

Then, you can configure a Quartz JobDetail object in Spring's bean configuration file through JobDetailBean. By default, Spring uses this bean's name as the job name. You can modify it by setting the name property.

```
@Bean
@Autowired
public JobDetailFactoryBean documentReplicationJob(FileReplicator fileReplicator) {
    JobDetailFactoryBean documentReplicationJob = new JobDetailFactoryBean();
    documentReplicationJob.setJobClass(FileReplicationJob.class);
    documentReplicationJob.setDurability(true);
    documentReplicationJob.setJobDataAsMap(
        Collections.singletonMap("fileReplicator", fileReplicator));
    return documentReplicationJob;
}
```

Spring also offers MethodInvokingJobDetailFactoryBean for you to define a job that executes a single method of a particular object. This saves you the trouble of creating a job class. You can use the following job detail to replace the previous:

```
@Bean
@Autowired
public MethodInvokingJobDetailFactoryBean documentReplicationJob(FileReplicator
fileReplicator) {
    MethodInvokingJobDetailFactoryBean documentReplicationJob =
        new MethodInvokingJobDetailFactoryBean();
    documentReplicationJob.setTargetObject(fileReplicator);
    documentReplicationJob.setTargetMethod("replicatie");
    return documentReplicationJob;
}
```

Once you define a job, you can configure a Quartz trigger. Spring supports SimpleTriggerFactoryBean and CronTriggerFactoryBean. SimpleTriggerFactoryBean requires a reference to a JobDetail object and provides common values for schedule properties, such as start time and repeat count.

```
@Bean
@Autowired
public SimpleTriggerFactoryBean documentReplicationTrigger(JobDetail documentReplicationJob)
{
    SimpleTriggerFactoryBean documentReplicationTrigger = new SimpleTriggerFactoryBean();
    documentReplicationTrigger.setJobDetail(documentReplicationJob);
    documentReplicationTrigger.setStartDelay(5000);
    documentReplicationTrigger.setRepeatInterval(60000);
    return documentReplicationTrigger;
}
```

You can also use the CronTriggerFactoryBean bean to configure a cron-like schedule.

```
@Bean
@Autowired
public CronTriggerFactoryBean documentReplicationTrigger(JobDetail documentReplicationJob) {
    CronTriggerFactoryBean documentReplicationTrigger = new CronTriggerFactoryBean();
    documentReplicationTrigger.setJobDetail(documentReplicationJob);
    documentReplicationTrigger.setStartDelay(5000);
    documentReplicationTrigger.setCronExpression("0/60 * * * * ?");
    return documentReplicationTrigger;
}
```

Finally, once you have the Quartz job and trigger, you can configure a SchedulerFactoryBean instance to create a Scheduler object for running your trigger. You can specify multiple triggers in this factory bean.

```
@Bean
@Autowired
public SchedulerFactoryBean scheduler(Trigger[] triggers) {
    SchedulerFactoryBean scheduler = new SchedulerFactoryBean();
    scheduler.setTriggers(triggers);
    return scheduler;
}
```

Now, you can simply start your scheduler with the following `Main` class. In this way, you don't require a single line of code for scheduling jobs.

```
package com.apress.springrecipes.replicator;

import org.springframework.context.annotation.AnnotationConfigApplicationContext;

public class Main {

    public static void main(String[] args) throws Exception {
        new AnnotationConfigApplicationContext("com.apress.springrecipes.replicator.config");
    }
}
```

13-6. Schedule Tasks with Spring's Scheduling

Problem

You want to schedule a method invocation in a consistent manner, using either a `cron` expression, an interval, or a rate, and you don't want to have to go through Quartz just to do it.

Solution

Spring has support to configure `TaskExecutors` and `TaskSchedulers`. This capability, coupled with the ability to schedule method execution using the `@Scheduled` annotation, makes Spring scheduling support work with a minimum of fuss: all you need are a method and an annotation and to have switched on the scanner for annotations.

How It Works

Let's revisit the example in the previous recipe: you want to schedule a call to the replication method on the bean using a `cron` expression. The configuration class looks like the following:

```
package com.apress.springrecipes.replicator.config;

import org.springframework.context.annotation.Bean;
import org.springframework.context.annotation.Configuration;
import org.springframework.scheduling.annotation.EnableScheduling;
import org.springframework.scheduling.annotation.SchedulingConfigurer;
import org.springframework.scheduling.config.ScheduledTaskRegistrar;

import java.util.concurrent.Executor;
import java.util.concurrent.Executors;

@Configuration
@EnableScheduling
public class SchedulingConfiguration implements SchedulingConfigurer {
```

```
@Override
public void configureTasks(ScheduledTaskRegistrar taskRegistrar) {
    taskRegistrar.setScheduler(scheduler());
}

@Bean
public Executor scheduler() {
    return Executors.newScheduledThreadPool(10);
}

}
```

You enable the annotation-driven scheduling support by specifying @EnableScheduling. This will register a bean that scans the beans in the application context for the @Scheduled annotation. You also implemented the interface SchedulingConfigurer because you wanted to do some additional configuration of your scheduler. You want to give it a pool of ten threads to execute your scheduled tasks.

```
package com.apress.springrecipes.replicator;

import org.springframework.scheduling.annotation.Scheduled;

import java.io.File;
import java.io.IOException;

public class FileReplicatorImpl implements FileReplicator {

    @Scheduled(fixedDelay = 60 * 1000)
    public synchronized void replicate() throws IOException {
        File[] files = new File(srcDir).listFiles();

        for (File file : files) {
            if (file.isFile()) {
                fileCopier.copyFile(srcDir, destDir, file.getName());
            }
        }
    }
}
```

Note that you've annotated the replicate() method with the @Scheduled annotation. Here, you've told the scheduler to execute the method every 60 seconds. Alternatively, you might specify a fixedRate value for the @Scheduled annotation, which would measure the time between successive starts and then trigger another run.

```
@Scheduled(fixedRate = 60 * 1000)
public synchronized void replicate() throws IOException {
    File[] files = new File(srcDir).listFiles();

    for (File file : files) {
        if (file.isFile()) {
            fileCopier.copyFile(srcDir, destDir, file.getName());
        }
    }
}
```

Finally, you might want more complex control over the execution of the method. In this case, you can use a cron expression, just as you did in the Quartz example.

```
@Scheduled( cron = "0/60 * * * * ? " )
public synchronized void replicate() throws IOException {
    File[] files = new File(srcDir).listFiles();

    for (File file : files) {
        if (file.isFile()) {
            fileCopier.copyFile(srcDir, destDir, file.getName());
        }
    }
}
```

There is support for configuring all of this in Java too. This might be useful if you didn't want to, or couldn't, add an annotation to an existing bean method. Here's a look at how you might re-create the preceding annotation-centric examples using the Spring ScheduledTaskRegistrar:

```
package com.apress.springrecipes.replicator.config;

import com.apress.springrecipes.replicator.FileReplicator;
import org.springframework.beans.factory.annotation.Autowired;
import org.springframework.context.annotation.Bean;
import org.springframework.context.annotation.Configuration;
import org.springframework.scheduling.annotation.EnableScheduling;
import org.springframework.scheduling.annotation.SchedulingConfigurer;
import org.springframework.scheduling.config.ScheduledTaskRegistrar;

import java.io.IOException;
import java.util.concurrent.Executor;
import java.util.concurrent.Executors;

@Configuration
@EnableScheduling
public class SchedulingConfiguration implements SchedulingConfigurer {

    @Autowired
    private FileReplicator fileReplicator;
```

```
    @Override
    public void configureTasks(ScheduledTaskRegistrar taskRegistrar) {
        taskRegistrar.setScheduler(scheduler());
        taskRegistrar.addFixedDelayTask(() -> {
            try {
                fileReplicator.replicate();
            } catch (IOException e) {
                e.printStackTrace();
            }
        }, 60000);
    }

    @Bean
    public Executor scheduler() {
        return Executors.newScheduledThreadPool(10);
    }

}
```

13-7. Expose and Invoke Services Through RMI

Problem

You want to expose a service from your Java application for other Java-based clients to invoke remotely. Because both parties are running on the Java platform, you can choose a pure Java-based solution without considering cross-platform portability.

Solution

Remote Method Invocation (RMI) is a Java-based remoting technology that allows two Java applications running in different JVMs to communicate with each other. With RMI, an object can invoke the methods of a remote object. RMI relies on object serialization to marshal and unmarshal method arguments and return values.

To expose a service through RMI, you have to create the service interface that extends java.rmi. Remote and whose methods declare throwing java.rmi.RemoteException. Then, you create the service implementation for this interface. After that, you start an RMI registry and register your service to it. So, there are quite a lot of steps required for exposing a simple service.

To invoke a service through RMI, you first look up the remote service reference in an RMI registry, and then you can call the methods on it. However, to call the methods on a remote service, you must handle java.rmi.RemoteException in case any exception is thrown by the remote service.

Spring's remoting facilities can significantly simplify the RMI usage on both the server and client sides. On the server side, you can use RmiServiceExporter to export a Spring POJO as an RMI service whose methods can be invoked remotely. It's just several lines of bean configuration without any programming. Beans exported in this way don't need to implement java.rmi.Remote or throw java.rmi.RemoteException. On the client side, you can simply use RmiProxyFactoryBean to create a proxy for the remote service. It allows you to use the remote service as if it were a local bean. Again, it requires no additional programming at all.

How It Works

Suppose you're going to build a weather web service for clients running on different platforms. This service includes an operation for querying a city's temperatures on multiple dates. First, let's create the TemperatureInfo class representing the minimum, maximum, and average temperatures of a particular city and date.

```
package com.apress.springrecipes.weather;
...
public class TemperatureInfo implements Serializable {

    private String city;
    private Date date;
    private double min;
    private double max;
    private double average;

    // Constructors, Getters and Setters
    ...
}
```

Next, let's define the service interface that includes the getTemperatures() operation, which returns a city's temperatures on multiple dates.

```
package com.apress.springrecipes.weather;
...
public interface WeatherService {

    List<TemperatureInfo> getTemperatures(String city, List<Date> dates);
}
```

You have to provide an implementation for this interface. In a production application, you would implement this service interface by querying the database. Here, you'll hard-code the temperatures for testing purposes.

```
package com.apress.springrecipes.weather;
...
public class WeatherServiceImpl implements WeatherService {

    public List<TemperatureInfo> getTemperatures(String city, List<Date> dates) {
        List<TemperatureInfo> temperatures = new ArrayList<TemperatureInfo>();
        for (Date date : dates) {
            temperatures.add(new TemperatureInfo(city, date, 5.0, 10.0, 8.0));
        }
        return temperatures;
    }
}
```

Expose an RMI Service

Next, let's expose the weather service as an RMI service. To use Spring's remoting facilities, you'll create a Java config class to create the necessary beans and export the weather service as an RMI service by using RmiServiceExporter.

```
package com.apress.springrecipes.weather.config;

...
import com.apress.springrecipes.weather.WeatherService;
import com.apress.springrecipes.weather.WeatherServiceImpl;

import org.springframework.remoting.rmi.RmiServiceExporter;

@Configuration
public class WeatherConfig {

    @Bean
    public WeatherService weatherService() {
        return new WeatherServiceImpl();
    }

    @Bean
    public RmiServiceExporter rmiService() {
        RmiServiceExporter rmiService = new RmiServiceExporter();
        rmiService.setServiceName("WeatherService");
        rmiService.setServiceInterface(com.apress.springrecipes.weather.
        WeatherService.class);
        rmiService.setService(weatherService());
        return rmiService;
    }
}
```

There are several properties you must configure for an RmiServiceExporter instance, including the service name, the service interface, and the service object to export. You can export any bean configured in the IoC container as an RMI service. RmiServiceExporter will create an RMI proxy to wrap this bean and bind it to the RMI registry. When the proxy receives an invocation request from the RMI registry, it will invoke the corresponding method on the bean. By default, RmiServiceExporter attempts to look up an RMI registry at localhost port 1099. If it can't find the RMI registry, it will start a new one. However, if you want to bind your service to another running RMI registry, you can specify the host and port of that registry in the registryHost and registryPort properties. Note that once you specify the registry host, RmiServiceExporter will not start a new registry, even if the specified registry doesn't exist. Run the following RmiServer class to create an application context:

```
package com.apress.springrecipes.weather;

import com.apress.springrecipes.weather.config.WeatherConfigServer;
import org.springframework.context.annotation.AnnotationConfigApplicationContext;
```

```java
public class RmiServer {

    public static void main(String[] args) {
        new AnnotationConfigApplicationContext(WeatherConfigServer.class);
    }
}
```

In this configuration, the server will launch; in the output, you should see a message indicating that an existing RMI registry could not be found.

Invoke an RMI Service

By using Spring's remoting facilities, you can invoke a remote service just like a local bean. For example, you can create a client that refers to the weather service by its interface.

```java
package com.apress.springrecipes.weather;

import java.util.Arrays;
import java.util.Date;
import java.util.List;

public class WeatherServiceClient {

    private final WeatherService weatherService;

    public WeatherServiceClient(WeatherService weatherService) {
        this.weatherService = weatherService;
    }

    public TemperatureInfo getTodayTemperature(String city) {
        List<Date> dates = Arrays.asList(new Date());
        List<TemperatureInfo> temperatures =
            weatherService.getTemperatures(city, dates);
        return temperatures.get(0);
    }
}
```

Notice the weatherService field is being wired through the constructor, so you'll need to create an instance of this bean. The weatherService will use RmiProxyFactoryBean to create a proxy for the remote service. Then, you can use this service as if it were a local bean. The following Java config class illustrates the necessary beans for the RMI client:

```java
package com.apress.springrecipes.weather.config;

import com.apress.springrecipes.weather.WeatherService;
import com.apress.springrecipes.weather.WeatherServiceClient;

import org.springframework.context.annotation.Bean;
import org.springframework.context.annotation.Configuration;
import org.springframework.remoting.rmi.RmiProxyFactoryBean;
```

```
@Configuration
public class WeatherConfigClient {

    @Bean
    public RmiProxyFactoryBean weatherService() {
        RmiProxyFactoryBean rmiProxy = new RmiProxyFactoryBean();
        rmiProxy.setServiceUrl("rmi://localhost:1099/WeatherService");
        rmiProxy.setServiceInterface(WeatherService.class);
        return rmiProxy;
    }

    @Bean
    public WeatherServiceClient weatherClient(WeatherService weatherService) {
        return new WeatherServiceClient(weatherService);
    }
}
```

There are two properties you must configure for an RmiProxyFactoryBean instance. The service URL property specifies the host and port of the RMI registry, as well as the service name. The service interface allows this factory bean to create a proxy for the remote service against a known, shared Java interface. The proxy will transfer the invocation requests to the remote service transparently. In addition to the RmiProxyFactoryBean instance, you also create an instance of the WeatherServiceClient called weatherClient.

Next, run the following RmiClient main class:

```
package com.apress.springrecipes.weather;

import com.apress.springrecipes.weather.config.WeatherConfigClient;
import org.springframework.context.ApplicationContext;
import org.springframework.context.annotation.AnnotationConfigApplicationContext;

public class RmiClient {

    public static void main(String[] args) {
        ApplicationContext context =
            new AnnotationConfigApplicationContext(WeatherConfigClient.class);

        WeatherServiceClient client = context.getBean(WeatherServiceClient.class);

        TemperatureInfo temperature = client.getTodayTemperature("Houston");
        System.out.println("Min temperature : " + temperature.getMin());
        System.out.println("Max temperature : " + temperature.getMax());
        System.out.println("Average temperature : " + temperature.getAverage());
    }
}
```

13-8. Expose and Invoke Services Through HTTP

Problem

RMI communicates through its own protocol, which may not pass through firewalls. Ideally, you'd like to communicate over HTTP.

Solution

Hessian is a simple lightweight remoting technology developed by Caucho Technology (www.caucho.com/). It communicates using proprietary messages over HTTP and has its own serialization mechanism, but it is much simpler than RMI. The message format of Hessian is also supported on other platforms besides Java, such as PHP, Python, C#, and Ruby. This allows your Java applications to communicate with applications running on the other platforms.

In addition to the preceding technology, the Spring Framework offers a remoting technology called HTTP Invoker. It also communicates over HTTP but uses Java's object serialization mechanism to serialize objects. Unlike Hessian, HTTP Invoker requires both sides of a service to be running on the Java platform and using the Spring Framework. However, it can serialize all kinds of Java objects, some of which may not be serialized by Hessian's proprietary mechanism.

Spring's remoting facilities are consistent in exposing and invoking remote services with these technologies. On the server side, you can create a service exporter such as HessianServiceExporter or HttpInvokerServiceExporter to export a Spring bean as a remote service whose methods can be invoked remotely. It's just a few lines of bean configurations without any programming. On the client side, you can also configure a proxy factory bean such as HessianProxyFactoryBean or HttpInvokerProxyFactoryBean to create a proxy for a remote service. It allows you to use the remote service as if it were a local bean. Again, it requires no additional programming at all.

How It Works

To export a service you need a service exported here you will learn about the HessianServiceExporter and the HttpInvokerServiceExporter. To consume the exposed services there are some helper classes respectivly the HessianProxyFactoryBean and the HttpInvokerProxyFactorybean. Both the solutions for Hessian and HTTP will be explored here.

Expose a Hessian Service

You'll use the same weather service from the previous RMI recipe and expose it as a Hessian service with Spring. You'll create a simple web application using Spring MVC to deploy the service. First, let's create a WeatherServiceInitializer class to bootstrap the web application and Spring application context.

```
package com.apress.springrecipes.weather.config;

import org.springframework.web.servlet.support.
AbstractAnnotationConfigDispatcherServletInitializer;

public class WeatherServiceInitializer extends
AbstractAnnotationConfigDispatcherServletInitializer {

    @Override
    protected String[] getServletMappings() {
        return new String[] {"/*"};
    }

    @Override
    protected Class<?>[] getRootConfigClasses() {
        return null;
    }
```

```
    @Override
    protected Class<?>[] getServletConfigClasses() {
        return new Class[] {WeatherConfigHessianServer.class};
    }
}
```

The WeatherServiceInitializer class creates a DispatcherServlet servlet to map all URLs under the root path (/*) and will use the WeatherConfigHessianServer class for the configuration.

```
package com.apress.springrecipes.weather.config;

import com.apress.springrecipes.weather.WeatherService;
import com.apress.springrecipes.weather.WeatherServiceImpl;
import org.springframework.context.annotation.Bean;
import org.springframework.context.annotation.Configuration;
import org.springframework.remoting.caucho.HessianServiceExporter;

@Configuration
public class WeatherConfigHessianServer {

    @Bean
    public WeatherService weatherService() {
        WeatherService wService = new WeatherServiceImpl();
        return wService;
    }

    @Bean(name = "/weather")
    public HessianServiceExporter exporter() {
        HessianServiceExporter exporter = new HessianServiceExporter();
        exporter.setService(weatherService());
        exporter.setServiceInterface(WeatherService.class);
        return exporter;
    }
}
```

The scanning component allows Spring to inspect a Java config class that instantiates the weatherService bean, which contains the operations that are to be exposed by the HessianServiceExporter instance. The weatherService bean in this case is identical to the one used in the previous RMI recipe. You can also consult the book's source code to get the prebuilt application.

For a HessianServiceExporter instance, you have to configure a service object to export and its service interface. You can export any Spring bean as a Hessian service. The HessianServiceExporter creates a proxy to wrap this bean.

When the proxy receives an invocation request, it invokes the corresponding method on that bean. By default, BeanNameUrlHandlerMapping is preconfigured for Spring MVC applications, so this means beans are mapped to URL patterns specified as bean names. The preceding configuration maps the URL pattern /weather to this exporter. Next, you can deploy this web application to a web container (e.g., Apache Tomcat). By default, Tomcat listens on port 8080, so if you deploy your application to the Hessian context path, you can access this service with the following URL: http://localhost:8080/hessian/weather.

Invoke a Hessian Service

By using Spring's remoting facilities, you can invoke a remote service just like a local bean. In a client application, you can create a HessianProxyFactoryBean instance in a Java config class to create a proxy for the remote Hessian service. Then you can use this service as if it were a local bean.

```
@Bean
public HessianProxyFactoryBean weatherService() {
    HessianProxyFactoryBean factory = new HessianProxyFactoryBean();
    factory.setServiceUrl("http://localhost:8080/hessian/weather");
    factory.setServiceInterface(WeatherService.class);
    return factory;
}
```

For a HessianProxyFactoryBean instance, you have to configure two properties. The service URL property specifies the URL for the target service. The service interface property is for this factory bean to create a local proxy for the remote service. The proxy will send the invocation requests to the remote service transparently.

Expose an HTTP Invoker Service

Similarly, the configuration for exposing a service using HTTP Invoker is similar to that of Hessian, except you have to use HttpInvokerServiceExporter instead.

```
@Bean(name = "/weather")
public HttpInvokerServiceExporter exporter() {
    HttpInvokerServiceExporter exporter = new HttpInvokerServiceExporter();
    exporter.setService(weatherService());
    exporter.setServiceInterface(WeatherService.class);
    return exporter;
}
```

Invoke an HTTP Invoker Service

Invoking a service exposed by HTTP Invoker is also similar to Hessian and Burlap. This time, you have to use HttpInvokerProxyFactoryBean.

```
@Bean
public HttpInvokerProxyFactoryBean weatherService() {
    HttpInvokerProxyFactoryBean factory = new HttpInvokerProxyFactoryBean();
    factory.setServiceUrl("http://localhost:8080/httpinvoker/weather");
    factory.setServiceInterface(WeatherService.class);
    return factory;
}
```

13-9. Expose and Invoke SOAP Web Services with JAX-WS

Problem

SOAP is an enterprise standard and cross-platform application communication technology. Most modern and mission-critical software remoting tasks (e.g., banking services, inventory applications) typically use this standard. You want to be able to invoke third-party SOAP web services from your Java applications, as well as expose web services from your Java applications so third parties on different platforms can invoke them via SOAP.

Solution

Use the JAX-WS @WebService and @WebMethod annotations, as well as Spring's SimpleJaxWsServiceExporter to allow access to bean business logic via SOAP. You can also leverage Apache CXF with Spring to expose SOAP services in a Java server like Tomcat. To access SOAP services, you can use Apache CXF with Spring or leverage Spring's JaxWsPortProxyFactoryBean.

How It Works

JAX-WS 2.0 is the successor of JAX-RPC 1.1—the Java API for XML-based web services. So, if you're going to use SOAP in the context of Java, JAX-WS is the most recent standard that enjoys support in both Java EE and the standard JDK.

Expose a Web Service Using the JAX-WS Endpoint Support in the JDK

You can rely on Java's JDK JAX-WS runtime support to expose JAX-WS services. This means you don't necessarily need to deploy JAX-WS services as part of a Java web application. By default, the JAX-WS support in the JDK is used if you have no other runtime. Let's implement the weather service application from previous recipes with JAX-WS using the JDK. You need to annotate the weather service to indicate that it should be exposed to clients. The revised WeatherServiceImpl implementation needs to be decorated with the @WebService and @WebMethod annotations. The Main class is decorated with @WebService, and the method that will be exposed by the service is decorated with @WebMethod.

```
package com.apress.springrecipes.weather;

import javax.jws.WebMethod;
import javax.jws.WebService;
import java.util.ArrayList;
import java.util.Date;
import java.util.List;

@WebService(serviceName = "weather", endpointInterface = " com.apress.springrecipes.weather.
WeatherService ")
public class WeatherServiceImpl implements WeatherService {

    @WebMethod(operationName = "getTemperatures")
    public List<TemperatureInfo> getTemperatures(String city, List<Date> dates) {
        List<TemperatureInfo> temperatures = new ArrayList<TemperatureInfo>();
```

```java
    for (Date date : dates) {
        temperatures.add(new TemperatureInfo(city, date, 5.0, 10.0, 8.0));
    }

    return temperatures;
    }
}
```

Note you don't need to provide any parameters to the annotations, like endpointInterface or serviceName, but you are here to make the resulting SOAP contract more readable. Similarly, you don't need to provide an operationName on the @WebMethod annotation. This is generally good practice, though, because it insulates clients of the SOAP endpoint from any refactoring you may do on the Java implementation.

Next, so that Spring is able to detect beans with @WebService annotations, you rely on Spring's SimpleHttpServerJaxWsServiceExporter. This is the @Bean definition of this class in a Java config class:

```java
@Bean
public SimpleHttpServerJaxWsServiceExporter jaxWsService() {
    SimpleHttpServerJaxWsServiceExporter simpleJaxWs =
        new SimpleHttpServerJaxWsServiceExporter();
    simpleJaxWs.setPort(8888);
    simpleJaxWs.setBasePath("/jaxws/");
    return simpleJaxWs;
}
```

Notice the bean definition calls setPort and setBasePath and sets them to 8888 and /jaxws/. This is the endpoint for the application's JAX-WS service. Under this address—which is a stand-alone server spun by the JDK—is where all the beans defined with @WebService annotations will reside. So, if there's an @Webservice name called weather, it will become accessible under http://localhost:8888/jaxws/weather.

■ **Note** If you are using this as part of a web deployment, use SimpleJaxWsServiceExporter instead because SimpleHttpServerJaxWsServiceExporter will start an embedded HTTP server, which generally isn't doable in a web deployment.

If you launch a browser and inspect the results at http://localhost:8888/jaxws/weather?wsdl, you'll see the generated SOAP WSDL contract, as follows:

```xml
<?xml version="1.0" encoding="UTF-8"?>
<!--
 Published by JAX-WS RI (http://jax-ws.java.net). RI's version is JAX-WS RI 2.2.9-
b130926.1035 svn-revision#5f6196f2b90e9460065a4c2f4e30e065b245e51e.
-->
<!--
 Generated by JAX-WS RI (http://jax-ws.java.net). RI's version is JAX-WS RI 2.2.9-
b130926.1035 svn-revision#5f6196f2b90e9460065a4c2f4e30e065b245e51e.
-->
<definitions xmlns="http://schemas.xmlsoap.org/wsdl/" xmlns:soap="http://schemas.xmlsoap.
org/wsdl/soap/" xmlns:tns="http://weather.springrecipes.apress.com/" xmlns:wsam="http://
www.w3.org/2007/05/addressing/metadata" xmlns:wsp="http://www.w3.org/ns/ws-policy"
```

```
xmlns:wsp1_2="http://schemas.xmlsoap.org/ws/2004/09/policy" xmlns:wsu="http://docs.oasis-
open.org/wss/2004/01/oasis-200401-wss-wssecurity-utility-1.0.xsd" xmlns:xsd="http://
www.w3.org/2001/XMLSchema" targetNamespace="http://weather.springrecipes.apress.com/"
name="weather">
    <types>
        <xsd:schema>
            <xsd:import namespace="http://weather.springrecipes.apress.com/"
                schemaLocation="http://localhost:8888/jaxws/weather?xsd=1" />
        </xsd:schema>
    </types>
    <message name="getTemperatures">
        <part name="parameters" element="tns:getTemperatures" />
    </message>
    <message name="getTemperaturesResponse">
        <part name="parameters" element="tns:getTemperaturesResponse" />
    </message>
    <portType name="WeatherService">
        <operation name="getTemperatures">
            <input wsam:Action="http://weather.springrecipes.apress.com/WeatherService/
                getTemperaturesRequest" message="tns:getTemperatures" />
            <output wsam:Action="http://weather.springrecipes.apress.com/WeatherService/
                getTemperaturesResponse" message="tns:getTemperaturesResponse" />
        </operation>
    </portType>
    <binding name="WeatherServiceImplPortBinding" type="tns:WeatherService">
        <soap:binding transport="http://schemas.xmlsoap.org/soap/http" style="document" />
        <operation name="getTemperatures">
            <soap:operation soapAction="" />
            <input>
            <soap:body use="literal" />
            </input>
            <output>
            <soap:body use="literal" />
            </output>
        </operation>
    </binding>
    <service name="weather">
        <port name="WeatherServiceImplPort" binding="tns:WeatherServiceImplPortBinding">
            <soap:address location="http://localhost:8888/jaxws/weather" />
        </port>
    </service>
</definitions>
```

The SOAP WSDL contract is used by clients to access the service. If you inspect the generated WSDL, you'll see it's pretty basic—describing the weather service method—but more importantly it's programming language neutral. This neutrality is the whole purpose of SOAP: to be able to access services across diverse platforms that can interpret SOAP.

Expose a Web Service Using CXF

Exposing a stand-alone SOAP endpoint using the JAX-WS service exporter and the JAX-WS JDK support is simple. However, this solution ignores the fact that most Java applications in real-world environments operate on Java app runtimes, such as Tomcat. Tomcat by itself doesn't support JAX-WS, so you'll need to equip the application with a JAX-WS runtime.

There are many choices, and you're free to take your pick. A popular choice is CXF, which is an Apache project. For this example, you'll embed CXF since it's robust, is fairly well tested, and provides support for other important standards such as JAX-RS, which is the API for RESTful endpoints.

First let's take a look at the Initializer class to bootstrap an application under a Servlet 3.1–compliant server like Apache Tomcat 8.5.

```
package com.apress.springrecipes.weather.config;

import org.springframework.web.WebApplicationInitializer;
import org.springframework.web.servlet.DispatcherServlet;
import org.springframework.web.context.ContextLoaderListener;

import org.springframework.web.context.support.XmlWebApplicationContext;

import org.apache.cxf.transport.servlet.CXFServlet;

import javax.servlet.ServletRegistration;

import javax.servlet.ServletContext;
import javax.servlet.ServletException;

public class Initializer implements WebApplicationInitializer {
    public void onStartup(ServletContext container) throws ServletException {
        XmlWebApplicationContext context = new XmlWebApplicationContext();
        context.setConfigLocation("/WEB-INF/appContext.xml");

        container.addListener(new ContextLoaderListener(context));

        ServletRegistration.Dynamic cxf = container.addServlet("cxf", new CXFServlet());
        cxf.setLoadOnStartup(1);
        cxf.addMapping("/*");
    }
}
```

This Initializer class will look pretty much like all Spring MVC applications do. The only exception here is that you've configured a CXFServlet, which handles a lot of the heavy lifting required to expose your service. In the Spring MVC configuration file, you'll be using the Spring namespace support that CXF provides for configuring services. The Spring context file is simple; most of it is boilerplate XML namespace and Spring context file imports. The only two salient stanzas are shown here, where you first configure the service itself as usual. Finally, you use the CXF jaxws:endpoint namespace to configure the endpoint.

```java
package com.apress.springrecipes.weather.config;

import com.apress.springrecipes.weather.WeatherService;
import com.apress.springrecipes.weather.WeatherServiceImpl;
import org.apache.cxf.Bus;
import org.apache.cxf.jaxws.EndpointImpl;
import org.springframework.context.annotation.Bean;
import org.springframework.context.annotation.Configuration;
import org.springframework.context.annotation.ImportResource;

@Configuration
@ImportResource("classpath:META-INF/cxf/cxf.xml")
public class WeatherConfig {

    @Bean
    public WeatherService weatherService() {
        return new WeatherServiceImpl();
    }

    @Bean(initMethod = "publish")
    public EndpointImpl endpoint(Bus bus) {
        EndpointImpl endpoint = new EndpointImpl(bus, weatherService());
        endpoint.setAddress("/weather");
        return endpoint;
    }
}
```

You register an endpoint using the EndpointImp class. It requires the CXF Bus, which is configured in the imported cxf.xml file (which is provided by Apache CXF), and it uses the weatherService Spring bean as the implementation. You tell it at what address to publish the service using the address property. In this case, because the Initializer mounts the CXF servlet under the root directory (/), the CXF weatherService endpoint becomes accessible under /cxf/weather (as the application is deployed on /cxf).

Notice that the publish method is used as an initMethod. Instead of this and setAddress, you could use endpoint.publish("/weather"). However, using an initMethod allows for callbacks to be able to enhance/configure the actual EndpointImpl before the endpoint is being published. This can be handy if, for instance, you have multiple endpoints that need to be configured with SSL, and so on.

Note the Java code in weatherServiceImpl stays the same as before, with the @WebService and @WebMethod annotations in place. Launch the application and your web container and then bring up the application in your browser. In the book's source code, the application is built in a WAR called cxf.war, and given that CXF is deployed at /cxf, the SOAP WSDL contract is available at http://localhost:8080/cxf/weather. If you bring up the page at http://localhost:8080/cxf, you'll see a directory of the available services and their operations. Click the link for the service's WSDL—or simply append ?wsdl to the service endpoint—to see the WSDL for the service. The WSDL contract is pretty similar to the ones described in the previous section using JAX-WS JDK support. The only difference is the WSDL contract is generated with the help of CXF.

Invoke a Web Service Using Spring's JaxWsPortProxyFactoryBean

Spring provides the functionality to access a SOAP WSDL contract and communicate with
the underlying services as if it were a regular Spring bean. This functionality is provided by
JaxWsPortProxyFactoryBean. The following is a sample bean definition to access the SOAP weather service
with JaxWsPortProxyFactoryBean:

```
@Bean
public JaxWsPortProxyFactoryBean weatherService() throws MalformedURLException {
    JaxWsPortProxyFactoryBean weatherService = new JaxWsPortProxyFactoryBean();
    weatherService.setServiceInterface(WeatherService.class);
    weatherService.setWsdlDocumentUrl(new URL("http://localhost:8080/cxf/weather?WSDL"));
    weatherService.setNamespaceUri("http://weather.springrecipes.apress.com/");
    weatherService.setServiceName("weather");
    weatherService.setPortName("WeatherServiceImplPort");
    return weatherService;
}
```

The bean instance is given the weatherService name. It's through this reference that you'll be able
to invoke the underlying SOAP service methods, as if they were running locally (e.g., weatherService.
getTemperatures(city, dates)). The JaxWsPortProxyFactoryBean requires several properties that are
described next.

The serviceInterface property defines the service interface for the SOAP call. In the case of the
weather service, you can use the server-side implementation code, which is the same. In case you're
accessing a SOAP service for which you don't have the server-side code, you can always create this Java
interface from the WSDL contract with a tool like java2wsdl. Note that serviceInterface used by the client
side needs to use the same JAX-WS annotation used by the server-side implementation
(i.e., @WebService).

The wsdlDocumentUrl property represents the location of the WSDL contract. In this case, it's pointing
toward the CXF SOAP endpoint from this recipe, but you can equally define this property to access the JAX-
WS JDK endpoint from this recipe or any WSDL contract for that matter.

The namesapceUrl, serviceName, and portName properties pertain to the WSDL contract itself. Since
there can be various namespaces, services, and ports in a WSDL contract, you need to tell Spring which
values to use for the purpose of accessing the service. The values presented here can easily be verified by
doing a manual inspection of the weather WSDL contract.

Invoke a Web Service Using CXF

Let's now use CXF to define a web service client. The client is the same as in previous recipes, and there
is no special Java configuration or coding to be done. You simply need the interface of the service on the
classpath. Once that's done, you can use CXF's namespace support to create a client.

```
package com.apress.springrecipes.weather.config;

import com.apress.springrecipes.weather.WeatherService;
import com.apress.springrecipes.weather.WeatherServiceClient;
import org.apache.cxf.jaxws.JaxWsProxyFactoryBean;
import org.springframework.context.annotation.Bean;
import org.springframework.context.annotation.Configuration;
import org.springframework.context.annotation.ImportResource;
```

```
@Configuration
@ImportResource("classpath:META-INF/cxf/cxf.xml")
public class WeatherConfigCxfClient {

    @Bean
    public WeatherServiceClient weatherClient(WeatherService weatherService) {
        return new WeatherServiceClient(weatherService);
    }

    @Bean
    public WeatherService weatherServiceProxy() {
        JaxWsProxyFactoryBean factory = new JaxWsProxyFactoryBean();
        factory.setServiceClass(WeatherService.class);
        factory.setAddress("http://localhost:8080/cxf/weather");
        return (WeatherService) factory.create();
    }
}
```

Notice the @ImportResource("classpath:META-INF/cxf/cxf.xml"), which imports and loads the infrastructure beans needed and provided by Apache CXF.

To create a client, you can use the JaxWsProxyFactoryBean and pass it the service class it needs to use and the address it needs to connect with. Then you use the create method to have a proxy created that acts like a regular WeatherService. That is all that's required. The examples from previous recipes work otherwise unchanged: here you inject the client into WeatherServiceClient and invoke it using the weatherService reference (e.g., weatherService.getTemperatures(city, dates)).

13-10. Use Contract-First SOAP Web Services

Problem

You want to develop a contract-first SOAP web service instead of a code-first SOAP web service as you did in the previous recipe.

Solution

There are two ways to develop SOAP web services. One is called *code first*, which means you start with a Java class and then build out toward a WSDL contract. The other method is called *contract first*, which means you start with an XML data contract—something simpler than WSDL—and build in toward a Java class to implement the service. To create a data contract for a contract-first SOAP web service, you'll need an XSD file or XML Schema file that describes the operations and data supported by the service. The requirement for an XSD file is because "under the hood" the communication between a SOAP service client and server takes place as XML defined in an XSD file. However, because an XSD file can be difficult to write correctly, it's preferable to start by creating sample XML messages and then generating the XSD file from them. Then with the XSD file, you can leverage something like Spring-WS to build the SOAP web service from the XSD file.

How It Works

The easiest way to start with a contract first web service is to write sample XML messages, when these are written you can use a tool to extract the contract, the XSD files, from them. When you have the XSD files you can use these with another tool to build the Web Services client.

Create Sample XML Messages

Let's do the same weather service presented in previous recipes, but this time using the SOAP contract-first approach. You're asked to write a SOAP service that is able to communicate weather information based on a city and date, returning the minimum, maximum, and average temperatures. Instead of writing code to support the previous functionality as you did in the previous recipe, let's describe the temperature of a particular city and date using a contract-first approach with an XML message like the following:

```
<TemperatureInfo city="Houston" date="2013-12-01">
    <min>5.0</min>
    <max>10.0</max>
    <average>8.0</average>
</TemperatureInfo>
```

This is the first step toward having a data contract in a SOAP contract-first way for the weather service. Now let's define some operations. You want to allow clients to query the temperatures of a particular city for multiple dates. Each request consists of a city element and multiple date elements. You'll also specify the namespace for this request to avoid naming conflicts with other XML documents. Let's create this XML message and save it into a file called request.xml.

```
<GetTemperaturesRequest
    xmlns="http://springrecipes.apress.com/weather/schemas">
    <city>Houston</city>
    <date>2013-12-01</date>
    <date>2013-12-08</date>
    <date>2013-12-15</date>
</GetTemperaturesRequest>
```

The response for a request of the previous type would consist of multiple TemperatureInfo elements, each of which represents the temperature of a particular city and date, in accordance with the requested dates. Let's create this XML message and save it to a file called response.xml.

```
<GetTemperaturesResponse
    xmlns="http://springrecipes.apress.com/weather/schemas">
    <TemperatureInfo city="Houston" date="2013-12-01">
        <min>5.0</min>
        <max>10.0</max>
        <average>8.0</average>
    </TemperatureInfo>
    <TemperatureInfo city="Houston" date="2007-12-08">
        <min>4.0</min>
        <max>13.0</max>
        <average>7.0</average>
    </TemperatureInfo>
    <TemperatureInfo city="Houston" date="2007-12-15">
        <min>10.0</min>
        <max>18.0</max>
        <average>15.0</average>
    </TemperatureInfo>
</GetTemperaturesResponse>
```

Generate an XSD File from Sample XML Messages

Now, you can generate the XSD file from the preceding sample XML messages. Most XML tools and enterprise Java IDEs can generate an XSD file from a couple of XML files. Here, you'll use Apache XMLBeans (http://xmlbeans.apache.org/) to generate the XSD file.

■ **Note**   You can download Apache XMLBeans (e.g., v2.6.0) from the Apache XMLBeans web site and extract it to a directory of your choice to complete the installation.

Apache XMLBeans provides a tool called inst2xsd to generate XSD files from XML files. It supports several design types for generating XSD files. The simplest is called *Russian doll design*, which generates local elements and local types for the target XSD file. Because there's no enumeration type used in your XML messages, you can disable the enumeration generation feature. You can execute the following command to generate the XSD file from the previous XML files:

```
inst2xsd -design rd -enumerations never request.xml response.xml
```

The generated XSD file will have the default name schema0.xsd, located in the same directory. Let's rename it to temperature.xsd.

```xml
<?xml version="1.0" encoding="UTF-8"?>
<xs:schema attributeFormDefault="unqualified"
    elementFormDefault="qualified"
    targetNamespace="http://springrecipes.apress.com/weather/schemas"
    xmlns:xs="http://www.w3.org/2001/XMLSchema">

    <xs:element name="GetTemperaturesRequest">
        <xs:complexType>
            <xs:sequence>
                <xs:element type="xs:string" name="city" />
                <xs:element type="xs:date" name="date"
                    maxOccurs="unbounded" minOccurs="0" />
            </xs:sequence>
        </xs:complexType>
    </xs:element>

    <xs:element name="GetTemperaturesResponse">
        <xs:complexType>
            <xs:sequence>
                <xs:element name="TemperatureInfo"
                    maxOccurs="unbounded" minOccurs="0">
                    <xs:complexType>
                        <xs:sequence>
                            <xs:element type="xs:float" name="min" />
                            <xs:element type="xs:float" name="max" />
                            <xs:element type="xs:float" name="average" />
                        </xs:sequence>
                        <xs:attribute type="xs:string" name="city"
                            use="optional" />
```

```
            <xs:attribute type="xs:date" name="date"
                    use="optional" />
            </xs:complexType>
          </xs:element>
        </xs:sequence>
      </xs:complexType>
    </xs:element>
</xs:schema>
```

Optimizing the Generated XSD File

As you can see, the generated XSD file allows clients to query temperatures for unlimited dates. If you want to add a constraint on the maximum and minimum query dates, you can modify the maxOccurs and minOccurs attributes.

```
<?xml version="1.0" encoding="UTF-8"?>
<xs:schema attributeFormDefault="unqualified"
    elementFormDefault="qualified"
    targetNamespace="http://springrecipes.apress.com/weather/schemas"
    xmlns:xs="http://www.w3.org/2001/XMLSchema">

    <xs:element name="GetTemperaturesRequest">
        <xs:complexType>
            <xs:sequence>
                <xs:element type="xs:string" name="city" />
                <xs:element type="xs:date" name="date"
                    maxOccurs="5" minOccurs="1" />
            </xs:sequence>
        </xs:complexType>
    </xs:element>

    <xs:element name="GetTemperaturesResponse">
        <xs:complexType>
            <xs:sequence>
                <xs:element name="TemperatureInfo"
                    maxOccurs="5" minOccurs="1">
                    ...
                </xs:element>
            </xs:sequence>
        </xs:complexType>
    </xs:element>
</xs:schema>
```

Preview the Generated WSDL File

As you will learn shortly and in full detail, Spring-WS is equipped to automatically generate a WSDL contract from an XSD file. The following snippet illustrates the Spring bean configuration for this purpose—we'll add context on how to use this snippet in the next recipe, which describes how to build SOAP web services with Spring-WS.

```
<sws:dynamic-wsdl id="temperature" portTypeName="Weather" locationUri="/">
    <sws:xsd location="/WEB-INF/temperature.xsd"/>
</sws:dynamic-wsdl>
```

Here, you'll preview the generated WSDL file to better understand the service contract. For simplicity's sake, the less important parts are omitted.

```
<?xml version="1.0" encoding="UTF-8" ?>
<wsdl:definitions ...
    targetNamespace="http://springrecipes.apress.com/weather/schemas">
    <wsdl:types>
        <!-- Copied from the XSD file -->
        ...
    </wsdl:types>
    <wsdl:message name="GetTemperaturesResponse">
        <wsdl:part element="schema:GetTemperaturesResponse"
            name="GetTemperaturesResponse">
        </wsdl:part>
    </wsdl:message>
    <wsdl:message name="GetTemperaturesRequest">
        <wsdl:part element="schema:GetTemperaturesRequest"
            name="GetTemperaturesRequest">
        </wsdl:part>
    </wsdl:message>
    <wsdl:portType name="Weather">
        <wsdl:operation name="GetTemperatures">
            <wsdl:input message="schema:GetTemperaturesRequest"
                name="GetTemperaturesRequest">
            </wsdl:input>
            <wsdl:output message="schema:GetTemperaturesResponse"
                name="GetTemperaturesResponse">
            </wsdl:output>
        </wsdl:operation>
    </wsdl:portType>
    ...
    <wsdl:service name="WeatherService">
        <wsdl:port binding="schema:WeatherBinding" name="WeatherPort">
            <soap:address
                location="http://localhost:8080/weather/services" />
        </wsdl:port>
    </wsdl:service>
</wsdl:definitions>
```

In the Weather port type, a GetTemperatures operation is defined whose name is derived from the prefix of the input and output messages (i.e., <GetTemperaturesRequest> and <GetTemperaturesResponse>). The definitions of these two elements are included in the <wsdl:types> part, as defined in the data contract.

Now with the WSDL contract in hand, you can generate the necessary Java interfaces and then write the backing code for each of the operations that started out as XML messages. This full technique is explored in the next recipe, which uses Spring-WS for the process.

13-11. Expose and Invoke SOAP Web Services with Spring-WS

Problem

You have an XSD file to develop a contract-first SOAP web service and don't know how or what to use to implement the contract-first SOAP service.

Spring-WS was designed from the outset to support contract-first SOAP web services. However, this does not mean Spring-WS is the only way to create SOAP web services in Java. JAX-WS implementations like CXF also support this technique. Nevertheless, Spring-WS is the more mature and natural approach to do contract-first SOAP web services in the context of Spring applications. Describing other contract-first SOAP Java techniques would lead you outside the scope of the Spring Framework.

Solution

Spring-WS provides a set of facilities to develop contract-first SOAP web services. The essential tasks for building a Spring-WS web service include the following:

1. Set up and configure a Spring MVC application for Spring-WS.

2. Map web service requests to endpoints.

3. Create service endpoints to handle the request messages and return the response messages.

4. Publish the WSDL file for the web service.

Set Up a Spring-WS Application

To implement a web service using Spring-WS, let's first create a web application initializer class to bootstrap a web application with a SOAP web service. You need to configure the `MessageDispatcherServlet` servlet, which is part of Spring-WS. This servlet specializes in dispatching web service messages to appropriate endpoints and detecting the framework facilities of Spring-WS.

```
package com.apress.springrecipes.weather.config;

import org.springframework.ws.transport.http.support.
AbstractAnnotationConfigMessageDispatcherServletInitializer;

public class Initializer extends AbstractAnnotationConfigMessageDispatcherServletInitializer
{

    @Override
    protected Class<?>[] getRootConfigClasses() {
        return null;
    }

    @Override
    protected Class<?>[] getServletConfigClasses() {
        return new Class<?>[] {SpringWsConfiguration.class};
    }

}
```

To make configuration easier, there is the `AbstractAnnotationConfigMessageDispatcherServlet Initializer` base class that you can extend. You need to supply it with the configuration classes that make up `rootConfig` and `servletConfig`. The first can be `null`, and the latter is required.

The previous configuration will bootstrap `MessageDispatcherServlet` using the `SpringWs Configuration` class and register it for the `/services/*` and `*.wsdl` URLs.

```
package com.apress.springrecipes.weather.config;

import org.springframework.context.annotation.Bean;
import org.springframework.context.annotation.ComponentScan;
import org.springframework.context.annotation.Configuration;
import org.springframework.core.io.ClassPathResource;
import org.springframework.ws.config.annotation.EnableWs;
import org.springframework.ws.wsdl.wsdl11.DefaultWsdl11Definition;
import org.springframework.xml.xsd.SimpleXsdSchema;
import org.springframework.xml.xsd.XsdSchema;

@Configuration
@EnableWs
@ComponentScan("com.apress.springrecipes.weather")
public class SpringWsConfiguration {

    ...
}
```

The SpringWsConfiguration class is annotated with @EnableWs that registers necessary beans to make MessageDispatcherServlet work. There is also the @ComponentScan annotation that scans for @Service and @Endpoint beans.

Create Service Endpoints

Spring-WS supports annotating an arbitrary class as a service endpoint by the @Endpoint annotation so it becomes accessible as a service. Besides the @Endpoint annotation, you need to annotate handler methods with the @PayloadRoot annotation to map service requests. And each handler method also relies on the @ResponsePayload and @RequestPayload annotations to handle the incoming and outgoing service data.

```
package com.apress.springrecipes.weather;

import org.dom4j.Document;
import org.dom4j.DocumentHelper;
import org.dom4j.Element;
import org.dom4j.XPath;
import org.dom4j.xpath.DefaultXPath;
import org.springframework.ws.server.endpoint.annotation.Endpoint;
import org.springframework.ws.server.endpoint.annotation.PayloadRoot;
import org.springframework.ws.server.endpoint.annotation.RequestPayload;
import org.springframework.ws.server.endpoint.annotation.ResponsePayload;

import java.text.DateFormat;
import java.text.SimpleDateFormat;
import java.util.*;

@Endpoint
public class TemperatureEndpoint {

    private static final String namespaceUri = "http://springrecipes.apress.com/weather/
    schemas";
    private XPath cityPath;
    private XPath datePath;

    private final WeatherService weatherService;

    public TemperatureEndpoint(WeatherService weatherService) {
        this.weatherService = weatherService;
        // Create the XPath objects, including the namespace
        Map<String, String> namespaceUris = new HashMap<String, String>();
        namespaceUris.put("weather", namespaceUri);
        cityPath = new DefaultXPath("/weather:GetTemperaturesRequest/weather:city");
        cityPath.setNamespaceURIs(namespaceUris);
        datePath = new DefaultXPath("/weather:GetTemperaturesRequest/weather:date");
        datePath.setNamespaceURIs(namespaceUris);
    }
```

```
@PayloadRoot(localPart = "GetTemperaturesRequest", namespace = namespaceUri)
@ResponsePayload
public Element getTemperature(@RequestPayload Element requestElement) throws Exception {
    DateFormat dateFormat = new SimpleDateFormat("yyyy-MM-dd");
    // Extract the service parameters from the request message
    String city = cityPath.valueOf(requestElement);
    List<Date> dates = new ArrayList<Date>();
    for (Object node : datePath.selectNodes(requestElement)) {
        Element element = (Element) node;
        dates.add(dateFormat.parse(element.getText()));
    }

    // Invoke the back-end service to handle the request
    List<TemperatureInfo> temperatures =
        weatherService.getTemperatures(city, dates);

    // Build the response message from the result of back-end service
    Document responseDocument = DocumentHelper.createDocument();
    Element responseElement = responseDocument.addElement(
        "GetTemperaturesResponse", namespaceUri);
    for (TemperatureInfo temperature : temperatures) {
        Element temperatureElement = responseElement.addElement(
            "TemperatureInfo");
        temperatureElement.addAttribute("city", temperature.getCity());
        temperatureElement.addAttribute(
            "date", dateFormat.format(temperature.getDate()));
        temperatureElement.addElement("min").setText(
            Double.toString(temperature.getMin()));
        temperatureElement.addElement("max").setText(
            Double.toString(temperature.getMax()));
        temperatureElement.addElement("average").setText(
            Double.toString(temperature.getAverage()));
    }
    return responseElement;
}
}
```

In the @PayloadRoot annotation, you specify the local name (getTemperaturesRequest) and namespace (http://springrecipes.apress.com/weather/schemas) of the payload root element to be handled. Next, the method is decorated with the @ResponsePayload annotation, indicating the method's return value is the service response data. In addition, the method's input parameter is decorated with the @RequestPayload annotation to indicate it's the service input value.

Then inside the handler method, you first extract the service parameters from the request message. Here, you use XPath to help locate the elements. The XPath objects are created in the constructor so that they can be reused for subsequent request handling. Note that you must also include the namespace in the XPath expressions, or else they will not be able to locate the elements correctly. After extracting the service parameters, you invoke the back-end service to handle the request. Because this endpoint is configured in the Spring IoC container, it can easily refer to other beans through dependency injection. Finally, you build the response message from the back-end service's result. In this case, you used the dom4j library that provides a rich set of APIs for you to build an XML message. But you can use any other XML processing API or Java parser you want (e.g., DOM).

Because you already defined the @ComponentScan annotation in the SpringWsConfiguration class, Spring automatically picks up all the Spring-WS annotations and deploys the endpoint to the servlet.

Publish the WSDL File

The last step to complete the SOAP web service is to publish the WSDL file. In Spring-WS, it's not necessary for you to write the WSDL file manually; you only need to add a bean to the SpringWsConfiguration class.

```
@Bean
public DefaultWsdl11Definition temperature() {
    DefaultWsdl11Definition temperature = new DefaultWsdl11Definition();
    temperature.setPortTypeName("Weather");
    temperature.setLocationUri("/");
    temperature.setSchema(temperatureSchema());
    return temperature;
}


@Bean
public XsdSchema temperatureSchema() {
    return new SimpleXsdSchema(new ClassPathResource("/META-INF/xsd/temperature.xsd"));
}
```

The DefaultWsdl11Definition class requires that you specify two properties: a portTypeName for the service, as well as a locationUri on which to deploy the final WSDL. In addition, it requires that you specify the location of the XSD file from which to create the WSDL—see the previous recipe for details on how to create and XSD file. In this case, the XSD file will be located inside the application's META-INF directory. Because you have defined <GetTemperaturesRequest> and <GetTemperaturesResponse> in your XSD file and you have specified the port type name as Weather, the WSDL builder will generate the following WSDL port type and operation for you. The following snippet is taken from the generated WSDL file:

```
<wsdl:portType name="Weather">
    <wsdl:operation name="GetTemperatures">
        <wsdl:input message="schema:GetTemperaturesRequest"
            name="GetTemperaturesRequest" />
        <wsdl:output message="schema:GetTemperaturesResponse"
            name="GetTemperaturesResponse" />
    </wsdl:operation>
</wsdl:portType>
```

Finally, you can access this WSDL file by joining its definition's bean name and the .wsdl suffix. Assuming the web application is packaged in a WAR file named springws, then the service is deployed in http://localhost:8080/springws/—because the Spring-WS servlet in the initializer is deployed on the / services directory—and the WSDL file's URL would be http://localhost:8080/springws/services/ weather/temperature.wsdl, given that the bean name of the WSDL definition is temperature.

Invoke SOAP Web Services with Spring-WS

Now, let's create a Spring-WS client to invoke the weather service according to the contract it publishes. You can create a Spring-WS client by parsing the request and response XML messages. As an example, you will use dom4j to implement it, but you are free to choose any other XML-parsing APIs for it.

603

To shield the client from the low-level invocation details, you'll create a local proxy to call the SOAP web service. This proxy also implements the WeatherService interface, and it translates local method calls into remote SOAP web service calls.

```
package com.apress.springrecipes.weather;

import org.dom4j.Document;
import org.dom4j.DocumentHelper;
import org.dom4j.Element;
import org.dom4j.io.DocumentResult;
import org.dom4j.io.DocumentSource;
import org.springframework.ws.client.core.WebServiceTemplate;

import java.text.DateFormat;
import java.text.ParseException;
import java.text.SimpleDateFormat;
import java.util.ArrayList;
import java.util.Date;
import java.util.List;

public class WeatherServiceProxy implements WeatherService {

    private static final String namespaceUri = "http://springrecipes.apress.com/weather/
    schemas";
    private final WebServiceTemplate webServiceTemplate;

    public WeatherServiceProxy(WebServiceTemplate webServiceTemplate) throws Exception {
        this.webServiceTemplate = webServiceTemplate;
    }

    public List<TemperatureInfo> getTemperatures(String city, List<Date> dates) {
        private DateFormat dateFormat = new SimpleDateFormat("yyyy-MM-dd");

        Document requestDocument = DocumentHelper.createDocument();
        Element requestElement = requestDocument.addElement(
                "GetTemperaturesRequest", namespaceUri);
        requestElement.addElement("city").setText(city);
        for (Date date : dates) {
            requestElement.addElement("date").setText(dateFormat.format(date));
        }

        DocumentSource source = new DocumentSource(requestDocument);
        DocumentResult result = new DocumentResult();
        webServiceTemplate.sendSourceAndReceiveToResult(source, result);
```

```
        Document responsetDocument = result.getDocument();
        Element responseElement = responsetDocument.getRootElement();
        List<TemperatureInfo> temperatures = new ArrayList<TemperatureInfo>();
        for (Object node : responseElement.elements("TemperatureInfo")) {
            Element element = (Element) node;
            try {
                Date date = dateFormat.parse(element.attributeValue("date"));
                double min = Double.parseDouble(element.elementText("min"));
                double max = Double.parseDouble(element.elementText("max"));
                double average = Double.parseDouble(
                    element.elementText("average"));
                temperatures.add(
                    new TemperatureInfo(city, date, min, max, average));
            } catch (ParseException e) {
                throw new RuntimeException(e);
            }
        }
        return temperatures;
    }
}
```

In the getTemperatures() method, you first build the request message using the dom4j API.
WebServiceTemplate provides a sendSourceAndReceiveToResult() method that accepts a java.xml.
transform.Source object and a java.xml.transform.Result object as arguments. You have to build a
dom4j DocumentSource object to wrap your request document and create a new dom4j DocumentResult
object for the method to write the response document to it. Finally, you get the response message and
extract the results from it.

With the service proxy written, you can declare it in a configuration class and later call it using a stand-
alone class.

```
package com.apress.springrecipes.weather.config;

import com.apress.springrecipes.weather.WeatherService;
import com.apress.springrecipes.weather.WeatherServiceClient;
import com.apress.springrecipes.weather.WeatherServiceProxy;
import org.springframework.context.annotation.Bean;
import org.springframework.context.annotation.Configuration;
import org.springframework.ws.client.core.WebServiceTemplate;

@Configuration
public class SpringWsClientConfiguration {

    @Bean
    public WeatherServiceClient weatherServiceClient(WeatherService weatherService)
    throws Exception {
        return new WeatherServiceClient(weatherService);
    }
```

```
    @Bean
    public WeatherServiceProxy weatherServiceProxy(WebServiceTemplate webServiceTemplate)
    throws Exception {
        return new WeatherServiceProxy(webServiceTemplate);
    }

    @Bean
    public WebServiceTemplate webServiceTemplate() {
        WebServiceTemplate webServiceTemplate = new WebServiceTemplate();
        webServiceTemplate.setDefaultUri("http://localhost:8080/springws/services");
        return webServiceTemplate;
    }
}
```

Note the webServiceTemplate has its defaultUri value set to the endpoint defined for the Spring-WS endpoint in the previous sections. Once the configuration is loaded by an application, you can call the SOAP service using the following class:

```
package com.apress.springrecipes.weather;

import org.springframework.context.ApplicationContext;
import org.springframework.context.support.GenericXmlApplicationContext;

public class SpringWSInvokerClient {

    public static void main(String[] args) {
        ApplicationContext context =
            new AnnotationConfigApplicationContext("com.apress.springrecipes.weather.config");

        WeatherServiceClient client = context.getBean(WeatherServiceClient.class);
        TemperatureInfo temperature = client.getTodayTemperature("Houston");
        System.out.println("Min temperature : " + temperature.getMin());
        System.out.println("Max temperature : " + temperature.getMax());
        System.out.println("Average temperature : " + temperature.getAverage());
    }
}
```

13-12. Develop SOAP Web Services with Spring-WS and XML Marshalling

Problem

To develop web services with the contract-first approach, you have to process request and response XML messages. If you parse the XML messages with XML parsing APIs directly, you'll have to deal with the XML elements one by one with low-level APIs, which is a cumbersome and inefficient task.

Solution

Spring-WS supports using XML marshalling technology to marshal and unmarshal objects to and from XML documents. In this way, you can deal with object properties instead of XML elements. This technology is also known as object/XML mapping (OXM), because you are actually mapping objects to and from XML documents. To implement endpoints with an XML marshalling technology, you can configure an XML marshaller for it. Table 13-2 lists the marshallers provided by Spring for different XML marshalling APIs.

Table 13-2. Marshallers for Different XML Marshalling APIs

API	Marshaller
JAXB 2.0	org.springframework.oxm.jaxb.Jaxb2Marshaller
Castor	org.springframework.oxm.castor.CastorMarshaller
XMLBeans	org.springframework.oxm.xmlbeans.XmlBeansMarshaller
JiBX	org.springframework.oxm.jibx.JibxMarshaller
XStream	org.springframework.oxm.xstream.XStreamMarshaller

Similarly, Spring WS clients can also use this same marshalling and unmarshalling technique to simplify XML data processing.

How It Works

You can use marshalling and unmarshalling for both the endpoints as well as clients. First you will see how to create an endpoint and utilize the Spring OXM marshallers followed by a client which utilizes the same.

Create Service Endpoints with XML Marshalling

Spring-WS supports various XML marshalling APIs, including JAXB 2.0, Castor, XMLBeans, JiBX, and XStream. As an example, you'll create a service endpoint using Castor (www.castor.org) as the marshaller. Using other XML marshalling APIs is similar. The first step in using XML marshalling is creating the object model according to the XML message formats. This model can usually be generated by the marshalling API. For some marshalling APIs, the object model must be generated by them so that they can insert marshalling-specific information. Because Castor supports marshalling between XML messages and arbitrary Java objects, you can start creating the following classes by yourself:

```
package com.apress.springrecipes.weather;
...
public class GetTemperaturesRequest {

    private String city;
    private List<Date> dates;

    // Constructors, Getters and Setters
    ...
}
```

```
package com.apress.springrecipes.weather;
...
public class GetTemperaturesResponse {

    private List<TemperatureInfo> temperatures;

    // Constructors, Getters and Setters
    ...
}
```

With the object model created, you can easily integrate marshalling on any endpoint. Let's apply this technique to the endpoint presented in the previous recipe.

```
package com.apress.springrecipes.weather;

import org.springframework.ws.server.endpoint.annotation.Endpoint;
import org.springframework.ws.server.endpoint.annotation.PayloadRoot;
import org.springframework.ws.server.endpoint.annotation.RequestPayload;
import org.springframework.ws.server.endpoint.annotation.ResponsePayload;

import java.util.List;

@Endpoint
public class TemperatureMarshallingEndpoint {

    private static final String namespaceUri = "http://springrecipes.apress.com/weather/
    schemas";

    private final WeatherService weatherService;

    public TemperatureMarshallingEndpoint(WeatherService weatherService) {
        this.weatherService = weatherService;
    }

    @PayloadRoot(localPart = "GetTemperaturesRequest", namespace = namespaceUri)
    public @ResponsePayload GetTemperaturesResponse getTemperature(@RequestPayload
    GetTemperaturesRequest request) {
        List<TemperatureInfo> temperatures =
            weatherService.getTemperatures(request.getCity(), request.getDates());
        return new GetTemperaturesResponse(temperatures);
    }
}
```

Notice that all you have to do in this new method endpoint is handle the request object and return the response object. Then, it will be marshalled to the response XML message. In addition to this endpoint modification, a marshalling endpoint also requires that both the marshaller and unmarshaller properties be set. Usually, you can specify a single marshaller for both properties. For Castor, you declare a CastorMarshaller bean as the marshaller. Next to the marshaller you also need to register MethodArgumentResolver and MethodReturnValueHandler to actually handle the marshalling of the method argument and return type. For this you extend WsConfigurerAdapter and override the addArgumentResolvers and addReturnValueHandlers methods and add MarshallingPayloadMethodProcessor to both lists.

```
@Configuration
@EnableWs
@ComponentScan("com.apress.springrecipes.weather")
public class SpringWsConfiguration extends WsConfigurerAdapter {

    @Bean
    public MarshallingPayloadMethodProcessor marshallingPayloadMethodProcessor() {
        return new MarshallingPayloadMethodProcessor(marshaller());
    }

    @Bean
    public Marshaller marshaller() {
        CastorMarshaller marshaller = new CastorMarshaller();
        marshaller.setMappingLocation(new ClassPathResource("/mapping.xml"));
        return marshaller;
    }

    @Override
    public void addArgumentResolvers(List<MethodArgumentResolver> argumentResolvers) {
        argumentResolvers.add(marshallingPayloadMethodProcessor());
    }

    @Override
    public void addReturnValueHandlers(List<MethodReturnValueHandler> returnValueHandlers) {
        returnValueHandlers.add(marshallingPayloadMethodProcessor());
    }
}
```

Note that Castor requires a mapping configuration file to know how to map objects to and from XML documents. You can create this file in the classpath root and specify it in the mappingLocation property (e.g., mapping.xml). The following Castor mapping file defines the mappings for the GetTemperaturesRequest, GetTemperaturesResponse, and TemperatureInfo classes:

```
<!DOCTYPE mapping PUBLIC "-//EXOLAB/Castor Mapping DTD Version 1.0//EN"
    "http://castor.org/mapping.dtd">

<mapping>
    <class name="com.apress.springrecipes.weather.GetTemperaturesRequest">
        <map-to xml="GetTemperaturesRequest"
            ns-uri="http://springrecipes.apress.com/weather/schemas" />
        <field name="city" type="string">
            <bind-xml name="city" node="element" />
        </field>
        <field name="dates" collection="arraylist" type="string"
            handler="com.apress.springrecipes.weather.DateFieldHandler">
            <bind-xml name="date" node="element" />
        </field>
    </class>
```

```
<class name="com.apress.springrecipes.weather.
GetTemperaturesResponse">
    <map-to xml="GetTemperaturesResponse"
        ns-uri="http://springrecipes.apress.com/weather/schemas" />
    <field name="temperatures" collection="arraylist"
        type="com.apress.springrecipes.weather.TemperatureInfo">
        <bind-xml name="TemperatureInfo" node="element" />
    </field>
</class>

<class name="com.apress.springrecipes.weather.TemperatureInfo">
    <map-to xml="TemperatureInfo"
        ns-uri="http://springrecipes.apress.com/weather/schemas" />
    <field name="city" type="string">
        <bind-xml name="city" node="attribute" />
    </field>
    <field name="date" type="string"
        handler="com.apress.springrecipes.weather.DateFieldHandler">
        <bind-xml name="date" node="attribute" />
    </field>
    <field name="min" type="double">
        <bind-xml name="min" node="element" />
    </field>
    <field name="max" type="double">
        <bind-xml name="max" node="element" />
    </field>
    <field name="average" type="double">
        <bind-xml name="average" node="element" />
    </field>
</class>
</mapping>
```

In addition, in all the date fields you have to specify a handler to convert the dates with a particular date format. This handler is shown next:

```
package com.apress.springrecipes.weather;
...
import org.exolab.castor.mapping.GeneralizedFieldHandler;

public class DateFieldHandler extends GeneralizedFieldHandler {

    private DateFormat format = new SimpleDateFormat("yyyy-MM-dd");

    public Object convertUponGet(Object value) {
        return format.format((Date) value);
    }
```

```
public Object convertUponSet(Object value) {
    try {
        return format.parse((String) value);
    } catch (ParseException e) {
        throw new RuntimeException(e);
    }
}

public Class getFieldType() {
    return Date.class;
}
}
```

Invoke Web Services with XML Marshalling

A Spring-WS client can also marshal and unmarshal the request and response objects to and from XML messages. As an example, you will create a client using Castor as the marshaller so that you can reuse the object models GetTemperaturesRequest, GetTemperaturesResponse, and TemperatureInfo, as well as the mapping configuration file, mapping.xml, from the service endpoint. Let's implement the service proxy with XML marshalling. WebServiceTemplate provides a marshalSendAndReceive() method that accepts a request object as the method argument, which will be marshalled to the request message. This method has to return a response object that will be unmarshalled from the response message.

```
package com.apress.springrecipes.weather;

import org.springframework.ws.client.core.WebServiceTemplate;

import java.util.Date;
import java.util.List;

public class WeatherServiceProxy implements WeatherService {

    private WebServiceTemplate webServiceTemplate;

    public WeatherServiceProxy(WebServiceTemplate webServiceTemplate) throws Exception {
        this.webServiceTemplate = webServiceTemplate;
    }

    public List<TemperatureInfo> getTemperatures(String city, List<Date> dates) {

        GetTemperaturesRequest request = new GetTemperaturesRequest(city, dates);
        GetTemperaturesResponse response = (GetTemperaturesResponse)
            this.webServiceTemplate.marshalSendAndReceive(request);
        return response.getTemperatures();
    }
}
```

When you are using XML marshalling, WebServiceTemplate requires both the marshaller and unmarshaller properties to be set. You can also set them to WebServiceGatewaySupport if you extend this class to have WebServiceTemplate autocreated. Usually, you can specify a single marshaller for both properties. For Castor, you declare a CastorMarshaller bean as the marshaller.

```
package com.apress.springrecipes.weather.config;

import com.apress.springrecipes.weather.WeatherService;
import com.apress.springrecipes.weather.WeatherServiceClient;
import com.apress.springrecipes.weather.WeatherServiceProxy;
import org.springframework.context.annotation.Bean;
import org.springframework.context.annotation.Configuration;
import org.springframework.core.io.ClassPathResource;
import org.springframework.oxm.castor.CastorMarshaller;
import org.springframework.ws.client.core.WebServiceTemplate;

@Configuration
public class SpringWsClientConfiguration {

    @Bean
    public WeatherServiceClient weatherServiceClient(WeatherService weatherService)
    throws Exception {
        return new WeatherServiceClient(weatherService);
    }

    @Bean
    public WeatherServiceProxy weatherServiceProxy(WebServiceTemplate webServiceTemplate)
    throws Exception {
        return new WeatherServiceProxy(webServiceTemplate);
    }

    @Bean
    public WebServiceTemplate webServiceTemplate() {
        WebServiceTemplate webServiceTemplate = new WebServiceTemplate(marshaller());
        webServiceTemplate.setDefaultUri("http://localhost:8080/springws/services");
        return webServiceTemplate;
    }

    @Bean
    public CastorMarshaller marshaller() {
        CastorMarshaller marshaller = new CastorMarshaller();
        marshaller.setMappingLocation(new ClassPathResource("/mapping.xml"));
        return marshaller;
    }
}
```

Summary

This chapter discussed JMX and a few of the surrounding specifications. You learned how to export Spring beans as JMX MBeans and how to use those MBeans from a client, both remotely and locally by using Spring's proxies. You published and listened to notification events on a JMX server from Spring. You also learned how to do e-mail tasks with the aid of Spring, including how to create e-mail templates and send e-mails with attachments (MIME messages). You also learned how to schedule tasks using the Quartz Scheduler, as well as Spring's task namespace. This chapter introduced you to the various remoting technologies supported by Spring. You learned how to both publish and consume an RMI service. We also discussed how to build services that operate through HTTP, using three different techniques/protocols: Burlap, Hessian, and HTTP Invoker. Next, we discussed SOAP web services and how to use JAX-WS, as well as the Apache CXF framework, to build and consume these types of services. Finally, we discussed contract-first SOAP web services and how to leverage Spring-WS to create and consume these types of services.

CHAPTER 14

Spring Messaging

In this chapter, you will learn about Spring's support for messaging. Messaging is a very powerful technique for scaling applications. It allows work that would otherwise overwhelm a service to be queued up. It also encourages a decoupled architecture. A component, for example, might only consume messages with a single java.util.Map-based key-value pair. This loose contract makes it a viable hub of communication for multiple, disparate systems.

In this chapter, we'll refer quite a bit to topics and queues. Messaging solutions are designed to solve two types of architecture requirements: messaging from one point in an application to another known point, and messaging from one point in an application to many other unknown points. These patterns are the middleware equivalents of telling somebody something face to face and saying something over a loud speaker to a room of people, respectively.

If you want messages sent on a message queue to be broadcast to an unknown set of clients who are "listening" for the message (as in the loud speaker analogy), you send the message on a *topic*. If you want the message sent to a single, known client, then you send it over a *queue*.

By the end of this chapter, you will be able to create and access message-based middleware using Spring. This chapter will also provide you with a working knowledge of messaging in general, which will help you when we discuss Spring Integration in the next chapter.

We will take a look at the messaging abstraction and how to use it to work with JMS, AMQP, and Apache Kafka. For each of the technologies, Spring simplifies the usage with a template-based approach for easy message sending and receiving. Moreover, Spring enables beans declared in its IoC container to listen for messages and react to them. It takes the same approach for each of these technologies.

■ **Note** In the ch14\bin directory there are several scripts for starting a Dockerized version of the different messaging providers: ActiveMQ for JMS, RabbitMQ for AMQP, and finally Apache Kafka.

14-1. Send and Receive JMS Messages with Spring

Problem

To send or receive a JMS message, you have to perform the following tasks:

1. Create a JMS connection factory on a message broker.

2. Create a JMS destination, which can be either a queue or a topic.

3. Open a JMS connection from the connection factory.

© Marten Deinum, Daniel Rubio, and Josh Long 2017
M. Deinum et al., *Spring 5 Recipes*, DOI 10.1007/978-1-4842-2790-9_14

4. Obtain a JMS session from the connection.

5. Send or receive the JMS message with a message producer or consumer.

6. Handle JMSException, which is a checked exception that must be handled.

7. Close the JMS session and connection.

As you can see, a lot of coding is required to send or receive a simple JMS message. In fact, most of these tasks are boilerplate and require you to repeat them each time when dealing with JMS.

Solution

Spring offers a template-based solution to simplify JMS code. With a JMS template (the Spring Framework class JmsTemplate), you can send and receive JMS messages with much less code. The template handles the boilerplate tasks and also converts the JMS API's JMSException hierarchy into Spring's runtime exception org.springframework.jms.JmsException hierarchy.

How It Works

Suppose you are developing a post-office system that includes two subsystems: the front-desk subsystem and the back-office subsystem. When the front desk receives mail, it passes the mail to the back office for categorizing and delivering. At the same time, the front-desk subsystem sends a JMS message to the back-office subsystem, notifying it of new mail. The mail information is represented by the following class:

```
package com.apress.springrecipes.post;
public class Mail {

    private String mailId;
    private String country;
    private double weight;

    // Constructors, Getters and Setters
    ...
}
```

The methods for sending and receiving mail information are defined in the FrontDesk and BackOffice interfaces as follows:

```
package com.apress.springrecipes.post;

public interface FrontDesk {

    public void sendMail(Mail mail);
}
package com.apress.springrecipes.post;

public interface BackOffice {

    public Mail receiveMail();
}
```

Send and Receive Messages Without Spring's JMS Template Support

Let's look at how to send and receive JMS messages without Spring's JMS template support. The following FrontDeskImpl class sends JMS messages with the JMS API directly.

```
package com.apress.springrecipes.post;

import javax.jms.Connection;
import javax.jms.ConnectionFactory;
import javax.jms.Destination;
import javax.jms.JMSException;
import javax.jms.MapMessage;
import javax.jms.MessageProducer;
import javax.jms.Session;

import org.apache.activemq.ActiveMQConnectionFactory;
import org.apache.activemq.command.ActiveMQQueue;

public class FrontDeskImpl implements FrontDesk {

    public void sendMail(Mail mail) {
        ConnectionFactory cf =
            new ActiveMQConnectionFactory("tcp://localhost:61616");
        Destination destination = new ActiveMQQueue("mail.queue");

        Connection conn = null;
        try {
            conn = cf.createConnection();
            Session session =
                conn.createSession(false, Session.AUTO_ACKNOWLEDGE);
            MessageProducer producer = session.createProducer(destination);

            MapMessage message = session.createMapMessage();
            message.setString("mailId", mail.getMailId());
            message.setString("country", mail.getCountry());
            message.setDouble("weight", mail.getWeight());
            producer.send(message);

            session.close();
        } catch (JMSException e) {
            throw new RuntimeException(e);
        } finally {
            if (conn != null) {
                try {
                    conn.close();
                } catch (JMSException e) {
                }
            }
        }
    }
}
```

In the preceding sendMail() method, you first create JMS-specific ConnectionFactory and Destination objects with the classes provided by ActiveMQ. The message broker URL is the default for ActiveMQ if you run it on localhost. In JMS, there are two types of destinations: queue and topic.

As explained at the start of the chapter, a *queue* is for the point-to-point communication model, while a *topic* is for the publish-subscribe communication model. Because you are sending JMS messages point to point from front desk to back office, you should use a message queue. You can easily create a topic as a destination using the ActiveMQTopic class.

Next, you have to create a connection, session, and message producer before you can send your message. There are several types of messages defined in the JMS API, including TextMessage, MapMessage, BytesMessage, ObjectMessage, and StreamMessage. MapMessage contains message content in key-value pairs like a map. All of them are interfaces, whose superclass is simply Message. In the meantime, you have to handle JMSException, which may be thrown by the JMS API. Finally, you must remember to close the session and connection to release system resources. Every time a JMS connection is closed, all its opened sessions will be closed automatically. So, you only have to ensure that the JMS connection is closed properly in the finally block.

On the other hand, the following BackOfficeImpl class receives JMS messages with the JMS API directly:

```
package com.apress.springrecipes.post;

import javax.jms.Connection;
import javax.jms.ConnectionFactory;
import javax.jms.Destination;
import javax.jms.JMSException;
import javax.jms.MapMessage;
import javax.jms.MessageConsumer;
import javax.jms.Session;

import org.apache.activemq.ActiveMQConnectionFactory;
import org.apache.activemq.command.ActiveMQQueue;

public class BackOfficeImpl implements BackOffice {

    public Mail receiveMail() {
        ConnectionFactory cf =
            new ActiveMQConnectionFactory("tcp://localhost:61616");
        Destination destination = new ActiveMQQueue("mail.queue");

        Connection conn = null;
        try {
            conn = cf.createConnection();
            Session session =
                conn.createSession(false, Session.AUTO_ACKNOWLEDGE);
            MessageConsumer consumer = session.createConsumer(destination);

            conn.start();
            MapMessage message = (MapMessage) consumer.receive();
            Mail mail = new Mail();
            mail.setMailId(message.getString("mailId"));
            mail.setCountry(message.getString("country"));
```

```
            mail.setWeight(message.getDouble("weight"));
            session.close();
            return mail;
        } catch (JMSException e) {
            throw new RuntimeException(e);
        } finally {
            if (conn != null) {
                try {
                    conn.close();
                } catch (JMSException e) {
                }
            }
        }
    }
}
```

Most of the code in this method is similar to that for sending JMS messages, except that you create a message consumer and receive a JMS message from it. Note that you used the connection's start() method here, although you didn't in the FrontDeskImpl example before.

When using a Connection to receive messages, you can add listeners to the connection that are invoked on receipt of a message, or you can block synchronously, waiting for a message to arrive. The container has no way of knowing which approach you will take and so it doesn't start polling for messages until you've explicitly called start(). If you add listeners or do any kind of configuration, you do so before you invoke start().

Finally, let's create two configuration class for the front-desk subsystem (e.g., FrontOfficeConfiguration) and one for the back-office subsystem (e.g., BackOfficeConfiguration).

```
package com.apress.springrecipes.post.config;

import com.apress.springrecipes.post.FrontDeskImpl;
import org.springframework.context.annotation.Bean;
import org.springframework.context.annotation.Configuration;

@Configuration
public class FrontOfficeConfiguration {

    @Bean
    public FrontDeskImpl frontDesk() {
        return new FrontDeskImpl();
    }
}
package com.apress.springrecipes.post.config;

import com.apress.springrecipes.post.BackOfficeImpl;
import org.springframework.context.annotation.Bean;
import org.springframework.context.annotation.Configuration;
```

```java
@Configuration
public class BackOfficeConfiguration {

    @Bean
    public BackOfficeImpl backOffice() {
        return new BackOfficeImpl();
    }
}
```

Now, the front-desk and back-office subsystems are almost ready to send and receive JMS messages. But before moving on to the final step, start up the ActiveMQ message broker (if not done already).

You can easily monitor the ActiveMQ messaging broker's activity. In a default installation, you can open http://localhost:8161/admin/queueGraph.jsp to see what's happening with mail.queue, the queue used in these examples. Alternatively, ActiveMQ exposes very useful beans and statistics from JMX. Simply run jconsole and drill down to org.apache.activemq in the MBeans tab.

Next, let's create a couple of main classes to run the message system: one for the front-desk subsystem (FrontDeskMain class) and another for the back-office subsystem (BackOfficeMain) class.

```java
package com.apress.springrecipes.post;

import com.apress.springrecipes.post.config.FrontOfficeConfiguration;
import org.springframework.context.ApplicationContext;
import org.springframework.context.annotation.AnnotationConfigApplicationContext;

public class FrontDeskMain {

    public static void main(String[] args) {

        ApplicationContext context =
            new AnnotationConfigApplicationContext(FrontOfficeConfiguration.class);

        FrontDesk frontDesk = context.getBean(FrontDesk.class);
        frontDesk.sendMail(new Mail("1234", "US", 1.5));
    }
}
```

```java
package com.apress.springrecipes.post;

import com.apress.springrecipes.post.config.BackOfficeConfiguration;
import org.springframework.context.ApplicationContext;
import org.springframework.context.annotation.AnnotationConfigApplicationContext;

public class BackOfficeMain {

    public static void main(String[] args) {

        ApplicationContext context =
            new AnnotationConfigApplicationContext(BackOfficeConfiguration.class);

        BackOffice backOffice = context.getBean(BackOffice.class);
        Mail mail = backOffice.receiveMail();
        System.out.println("Mail #" + mail.getMailId() + " received");
    }
}
```

Every time you run the front-desk application with the previous FrontDeskMain class, a message is sent to the broker, and every time you run the back-office application with the previous BackOfficeMain class, an attempt is made pick a message from the broker.

Send and Receive Messages with Spring's JMS Template

Spring offers a JMS template that can significantly simplify your JMS code. To send a JMS message with this template, you simply call the send() method and provide a message destination, as well as a MessageCreator object, which creates the JMS message you are going to send. The MessageCreator object is usually implemented as an anonymous inner class.

```
package com.apress.springrecipes.post;

import javax.jms.Destination;
import javax.jms.JMSException;
import javax.jms.MapMessage;
import javax.jms.Message;
import javax.jms.Session;

import org.springframework.jms.core.JmsTemplate;
import org.springframework.jms.core.MessageCreator;

public class FrontDeskImpl implements FrontDesk {

    private JmsTemplate jmsTemplate;
    private Destination destination;

    public void setJmsTemplate(JmsTemplate jmsTemplate) {
        this.jmsTemplate = jmsTemplate;
    }

    public void setDestination(Destination destination) {
        this.destination = destination;
    }

    public void sendMail(final Mail mail) {
        jmsTemplate.send(destination, new MessageCreator() {
            public Message createMessage(Session session) throws JMSException {
                MapMessage message = session.createMapMessage();
                message.setString("mailId", mail.getMailId());
                message.setString("country", mail.getCountry());
                message.setDouble("weight", mail.getWeight());
                return message;
            }
        });
    }
}
```

Note that an inner class can only access arguments or variables of the enclosing method that are declared as final. The MessageCreator interface declares only a createMessage() method for you to implement. In this method, you create and return your JMS message with the provided JMS session.

A JMS template helps you to obtain and release the JMS connection and session, and it sends the JMS message created by your `MessageCreator` object. Moreover, it converts the JMS API's `JMSException` hierarchy into Spring's JMS runtime exception hierarchy, whose base exception class is `org.springframework.jms.JmsException`. You can catch the `JmsException` thrown from `send` and the other `send` variants and then take action in the `catch` block if you want.

In the front-desk subsystem's bean configuration file, you declare a JMS template that refers to the JMS connection factory for opening connections. Then, you inject this template as well as the message destination into your front-desk bean.

```java
package com.apress.springrecipes.post.config;

import com.apress.springrecipes.post.FrontDeskImpl;
import org.apache.activemq.ActiveMQConnectionFactory;
import org.apache.activemq.command.ActiveMQQueue;
import org.springframework.context.annotation.Bean;
import org.springframework.context.annotation.Configuration;
import org.springframework.jms.core.JmsTemplate;

import javax.jms.ConnectionFactory;
import javax.jms.Queue;

@Configuration
public class FrontOfficeConfiguration {

    @Bean
    public ConnectionFactory connectionFactory() {
        return new ActiveMQConnectionFactory("tcp://localhost:61616");
    }

    @Bean
    public Queue destination() {
        return new ActiveMQQueue("mail.queue");
    }

    @Bean
    public JmsTemplate jmsTemplate() {
        JmsTemplate jmsTemplate = new JmsTemplate();
        jmsTemplate.setConnectionFactory(connectionFactory());
        return jmsTemplate;
    }

    @Bean
    public FrontDeskImpl frontDesk() {
        FrontDeskImpl frontDesk = new FrontDeskImpl();
        frontDesk.setJmsTemplate(jmsTemplate());
        frontDesk.setDestination(destination());
        return frontDesk;
    }
}
```

To receive a JMS message with a JMS template, you call the receive() method by providing a message destination. This method returns a JMS message, javax.jms.Message, whose type is the base JMS message type (that is, an interface), so you have to cast it into proper type before further processing.

```
package com.apress.springrecipes.post;

import javax.jms.Destination;
import javax.jms.JMSException;
import javax.jms.MapMessage;

import org.springframework.jms.core.JmsTemplate;
import org.springframework.jms.support.JmsUtils;

public class BackOfficeImpl implements BackOffice {

    private JmsTemplate jmsTemplate;
    private Destination destination;

    public void setJmsTemplate(JmsTemplate jmsTemplate) {
        this.jmsTemplate = jmsTemplate;
    }

    public void setDestination(Destination destination) {
        this.destination = destination;
    }

    public Mail receiveMail() {
        MapMessage message = (MapMessage) jmsTemplate.receive(destination);
        try {
            if (message == null) {
                return null;
            }
            Mail mail = new Mail();
            mail.setMailId(message.getString("mailId"));
            mail.setCountry(message.getString("country"));
            mail.setWeight(message.getDouble("weight"));
            return mail;
        } catch (JMSException e) {
            throw JmsUtils.convertJmsAccessException(e);
        }
    }
}
```

However, when extracting information from the received MapMessage object, you still have to handle the JMS API's JMSException. This is in stark contrast to the default behavior of the framework, where it automatically maps exceptions for you when invoking methods on JmsTemplate. To make the type of the exception thrown by this method consistent, you have to make a call to JmsUtils. convertJmsAccessException() to convert the JMS API's JMSException into Spring's JmsException.

In the back-office subsystem's bean configuration file, you declare a JMS template and inject it together with the message destination into your back-office bean.

```
package com.apress.springrecipes.post.config;

import com.apress.springrecipes.post.BackOfficeImpl;
import org.apache.activemq.ActiveMQConnectionFactory;
import org.apache.activemq.command.ActiveMQQueue;
import org.springframework.context.annotation.Bean;
import org.springframework.context.annotation.Configuration;
import org.springframework.jms.core.JmsTemplate;

import javax.jms.ConnectionFactory;
import javax.jms.Queue;

@Configuration
public class BackOfficeConfiguration {

    @Bean
    public ConnectionFactory connectionFactory() {
        return new ActiveMQConnectionFactory("tcp://localhost:61616");
    }

    @Bean
    public Queue destination() {
        return new ActiveMQQueue("mail.queue");
    }

    @Bean
    public JmsTemplate jmsTemplate() {
        JmsTemplate jmsTemplate = new JmsTemplate();
        jmsTemplate.setConnectionFactory(connectionFactory());
        jmsTemplate.setReceiveTimeout(10000);
        return jmsTemplate;
    }

    @Bean
    public BackOfficeImpl backOffice() {
        BackOfficeImpl backOffice = new BackOfficeImpl();
        backOffice.setDestination(destination());
        backOffice.setJmsTemplate(jmsTemplate());
        return backOffice;
    }
}
```

Pay special attention to the JMS template's receiveTimeout property, which specifies how long to wait in milliseconds. By default, this template waits for a JMS message at the destination forever, and the calling thread is blocked in the meantime. To avoid waiting for a message so long, you should specify a receive timeout for this template. If there's no message available at the destination in the duration, the JMS template's receive() method will return a null message.

In your applications, the main use of receiving a message might be because you're expecting a response to something or want to check for messages at an interval, handling the messages and then spinning down until the next interval. If you intend to receive messages and respond to them as a service, you're likely going to want to use the message-driven POJO functionality described later in this chapter. There, we discuss a mechanism that will constantly sit and wait for messages, handling them by calling back into your application as the messages arrive.

Send and Receive Messages to and from a Default Destination

Instead of specifying a message destination for each JMS template's send() and receive() method call, you can specify a default destination for a JMS template. Then, you no longer need to inject it into your message sender and receiver beans again.

```
@Configuration
public class FrontOfficeConfiguration {
...
    @Bean
    public JmsTemplate jmsTemplate() {
        JmsTemplate jmsTemplate = new JmsTemplate();
        jmsTemplate.setConnectionFactory(connectionFactory());
        jmsTemplate.setDefaultDestination(mailDestination());
        return jmsTemplate;
    }

    @Bean
    public FrontDeskImpl frontDesk() {
        FrontDeskImpl frontDesk = new FrontDeskImpl();
        frontDesk.setJmsTemplate(jmsTemplate());
        return frontDesk;
    }
}
```

For the back office, the configuration would look like this:

```
@Configuration
public class BackOfficeConfiguration {
...
    @Bean
    public JmsTemplate jmsTemplate() {
        JmsTemplate jmsTemplate = new JmsTemplate();
        jmsTemplate.setConnectionFactory(connectionFactory());
        jmsTemplate.setDefaultDestination(mailDestination());
        jmsTemplate.setReceiveTimeout(10000);
        return jmsTemplate;
    }

    @Bean
    public BackOfficeImpl backOffice() {
        BackOfficeImpl backOffice = new BackOfficeImpl();
        backOffice.setJmsTemplate(jmsTemplate());
        return backOffice;
    }
}
```

625

With the default destination specified for a JMS template, you can delete the setter method for a message destination from your message sender and receiver classes. Now, when you call the send() and receive() methods, you no longer need to specify a message destination.

```
package com.apress.springrecipes.post;
...
import org.springframework.jms.core.MessageCreator;

public class FrontDeskImpl implements FrontDesk {
    ...
    public void sendMail(final Mail mail) {
        jmsTemplate.send(new MessageCreator() {
            ...
        });
    }
}
package com.apress.springrecipes.post;
...
import javax.jms.MapMessage;
...

public class BackOfficeImpl implements BackOffice {
    ...
    public Mail receiveMail() {
        MapMessage message = (MapMessage) jmsTemplate.receive();
        ...
    }
}
```

In addition, instead of specifying an instance of the Destination interface for a JMS template, you can specify the destination name to let the JMS template resolve it for you, so you can delete the destination property declaration from both bean configuration classes. This is done by adding the defaultDestinationName property.

```
@Bean
    public JmsTemplate jmsTemplate() {
        JmsTemplate jmsTemplate = new JmsTemplate();
        ...
        jmsTemplate.setDefaultDestinationName("mail.queue");
        return jmsTemplate;
    }
```

Extend the JmsGatewaySupport Class

JMS sender and receiver classes can also extend JmsGatewaySupport to retrieve a JMS template. You have the following two options for classes that extend JmsGatewaySupport to create their JMS template:

- Inject a JMS connection factory for JmsGatewaySupport to create a JMS template on it automatically. However, if you do it this way, you won't be able to configure the details of the JMS template.

- Inject a JMS template for JmsGatewaySupport that is created and configured by you.

Of them, the second approach is more suitable if you have to configure the JMS template yourself. You can delete the private field jmsTemplate and its setter method from both your sender and receiver classes. When you need access to the JMS template, you just make a call to getJmsTemplate().

```
package com.apress.springrecipes.post;

import org.springframework.jms.core.support.JmsGatewaySupport;
...

public class FrontDeskImpl extends JmsGatewaySupport implements FrontDesk {
    ...
    public void sendMail(final Mail mail) {
        getJmsTemplate().send(new MessageCreator() {
            ...
        });
    }
}
package com.apress.springrecipes.post;
...

import org.springframework.jms.core.support.JmsGatewaySupport;

public class BackOfficeImpl extends JmsGatewaySupport implements BackOffice {
    public Mail receiveMail() {
        MapMessage message = (MapMessage) getJmsTemplate().receive();
        ...
    }
}
```

14-2. Convert JMS Messages

Problem

Your application receives messages from your message queue but needs to transform those messages from the JMS-specific type to a business-specific class.

Solution

Spring provides an implementation of SimpleMessageConverter to handle the translation of a JMS message received to a business object and the translation of a business object to a JMS message. You can leverage the default or provide your own.

How It Works

The previous recipes handled the raw JMS messages. Spring's JMS template can help you convert JMS messages to and from Java objects using a message converter. By default, the JMS template uses SimpleMessageConverter for converting TextMessage to or from a string, BytesMessage to or from a byte array, MapMessage to or from a map, and ObjectMessage to or from a serializable object.

For the front-desk and back-office classes of the previous recipe, you can send and receive a map using the `convertAndSend()` and `receiveAndConvert()` methods, where the map is converted to/from `MapMessage`.

```
package com.apress.springrecipes.post;
...
public class FrontDeskImpl extends JmsGatewaySupport implements FrontDesk {
    public void sendMail(Mail mail) {
        Map<String, Object> map = new HashMap<String, Object>();
        map.put("mailId", mail.getMailId());
        map.put("country", mail.getCountry());
        map.put("weight", mail.getWeight());
        getJmsTemplate().convertAndSend(map);
    }
}
package com.apress.springrecipes.post;
...
public class BackOfficeImpl extends JmsGatewaySupport implements BackOffice {
    public Mail receiveMail() {
        Map map = (Map) getJmsTemplate().receiveAndConvert();
        Mail mail = new Mail();
        mail.setMailId((String) map.get("mailId"));
        mail.setCountry((String) map.get("country"));
        mail.setWeight((Double) map.get("weight"));
        return mail;
    }
}
```

You can also create a custom message converter by implementing the `MessageConverter` interface for converting mail objects.

```
package com.apress.springrecipes.post;

import javax.jms.JMSException;
import javax.jms.MapMessage;
import javax.jms.Message;
import javax.jms.Session;

import org.springframework.jms.support.converter.MessageConversionException;
import org.springframework.jms.support.converter.MessageConverter;

public class MailMessageConverter implements MessageConverter {

    public Object fromMessage(Message message) throws JMSException,
        MessageConversionException {
        MapMessage mapMessage = (MapMessage) message;
        Mail mail = new Mail();
        mail.setMailId(mapMessage.getString("mailId"));
        mail.setCountry(mapMessage.getString("country"));
        mail.setWeight(mapMessage.getDouble("weight"));
        return mail;
    }
```

```java
    public Message toMessage(Object object, Session session) throws JMSException,
        MessageConversionException {
        Mail mail = (Mail) object;
        MapMessage message = session.createMapMessage();
        message.setString("mailId", mail.getMailId());
        message.setString("country", mail.getCountry());
        message.setDouble("weight", mail.getWeight());
        return message;
    }
}
```

To apply this message converter, you have to declare it in both bean configuration classes and inject it into the JMS template.

```java
@Configuration
public class BackOfficeConfiguration {
    ...
    @Bean
    public JmsTemplate jmsTemplate() {
        JmsTemplate jmsTemplate = new JmsTemplate();
        jmsTemplate.setMessageConverter(mailMessageConverter());
        ...
        return jmsTemplate;
    }

    @Bean
    public MailMessageConverter mailMessageConverter() {
        return new MailMessageConverter();
    }
}
```

When you set a message converter for a JMS template explicitly, it will override the default SimpleMessageConverter. Now, you can call the JMS template's convertAndSend() and receiveAndConvert() methods to send and receive mail objects.

```java
package com.apress.springrecipes.post;
...
public class FrontDeskImpl extends JmsGatewaySupport implements FrontDesk {
    public void sendMail(Mail mail) {
        getJmsTemplate().convertAndSend(mail);
    }
}
package com.apress.springrecipes.post;
...
public class BackOfficeImpl extends JmsGatewaySupport implements BackOffice {
    public Mail receiveMail() {
        return (Mail) getJmsTemplate().receiveAndConvert();
    }
}
```

14-3. Manage JMS Transactions

Problem

You want to participate in transactions with JMS so that the receipt and sending of messages are transactional.

Solution

You can use the same transactions strategy as you would for any Spring component. Leverage Spring's TransactionManager implementations as needed and wire the behavior into beans.

How It Works

When producing or consuming multiple JMS messages in a single method, if an error occurs in the middle, the JMS messages produced or consumed at the destination may be left in an inconsistent state. You have to surround the method with a transaction to avoid this problem.

In Spring, JMS transaction management is consistent with other data access strategies. For example, you can annotate the methods that require transaction management with the @Transactional annotation.

```
package com.apress.springrecipes.post;

import org.springframework.jms.core.support.JmsGatewaySupport;
import org.springframework.transaction.annotation.Transactional;
...
public class FrontDeskImpl extends JmsGatewaySupport implements FrontDesk {

    @Transactional
    public void sendMail(Mail mail) {
        ...
    }
}
package com.apress.springrecipes.post;

import org.springframework.jms.core.support.JmsGatewaySupport;
import org.springframework.transaction.annotation.Transactional;
...
public class BackOfficeImpl extends JmsGatewaySupport implements BackOffice {

    @Transactional
    public Mail receiveMail() {
        ...
    }
}
```

Then, in both Java configuration classes, add the @EnableTransactionManagement annotation and declare a transaction manager. The corresponding transaction manager for local JMS transactions is JmsTransactionManager, which requires a reference to the JMS connection factory.

```
package com.apress.springrecipes.post.config;
...
import org.springframework.jms.connection.JmsTransactionManager;
import org.springframework.transaction.annotation.EnableTransactionManagement;

import javax.jms.ConnectionFactory;

@Configuration
@EnableTransactionManagement
public class BackOfficeConfiguration {

    @Bean
    public ConnectionFactory connectionFactory() { ... }

    @Bean
    public PlatformTransactionManager transactionManager() {
        return new JmsTransactionManager(connectionFactory());
    }
}
```

If you require transaction management across multiple resources, such as a data source and an ORM resource factory, or if you need distributed transaction management, you have to configure JTA transaction in your app server and use JtaTransactionManager. Note that for multiple resource transaction support, the JMS connection factory must be XA compliant (i.e., it must support distributed transactions).

14-4. Create Message-Driven POJOs in Spring

Problem

When you call the receive() method on a JMS message consumer to receive a message, the calling thread is blocked until a message is available. The thread can do nothing but wait. This type of message reception is called *synchronous reception* because an application must wait for the message to arrive before it can finish its work. You can create a message-driven POJO (MDP) to support the asynchronous reception of JMS messages. An MDP is decorated with the @MessageDriven annotation.

■ **Note**   A message-driven POJO or MDP in the context of this recipe refers to a POJO that can listen for JMS messages without any particular runtime requirements. It does not refer to message-driven beans (MDBs) aligned to the EJB specification that require an EJB container.

Solution

Spring allows beans declared in its IoC container to listen for JMS messages in the same way as MDBs, which are based on the EJB spec. Because Spring adds message-listening capabilities to POJOs, they are called message-driven POJOs (MDPs).

How It Works

Suppose you want to add an electronic board to the post office's back office to display mail information in real time as it arrives from the front desk. As the front desk sends a JMS message along with mail, the back-office subsystem can listen for these messages and display them on the electronic board. For better system performance, you should apply the asynchronous JMS reception approach to avoid blocking the thread that receives these JMS messages.

Listen for JMS Messages with Message Listeners

First, you create a message listener to listen for JMS messages. The message listener provides an alternative to the approach taken in BackOfficeImpl in previous recipes with JmsTemplate. A listener can also consume messages from a broker. For example, the following MailListener listens for JMS messages that contain mail information:

```
package com.apress.springrecipes.post;

import javax.jms.JMSException;
import javax.jms.MapMessage;
import javax.jms.Message;
import javax.jms.MessageListener;

import org.springframework.jms.support.JmsUtils;

public class MailListener implements MessageListener {

    public void onMessage(Message message) {
        MapMessage mapMessage = (MapMessage) message;
        try {
            Mail mail = new Mail();
            mail.setMailId(mapMessage.getString("mailId"));
            mail.setCountry(mapMessage.getString("country"));
            mail.setWeight(mapMessage.getDouble("weight"));
            displayMail(mail);
        } catch (JMSException e) {
            throw JmsUtils.convertJmsAccessException(e);
        }
    }

    private void displayMail(Mail mail) {
        System.out.println("Mail #" + mail.getMailId() + " received");
    }
}
```

A message listener must implement the javax.jms.MessageListener interface. When a JMS message arrives, the onMessage() method will be called with the message as the method argument. In this sample, you simply display the mail information to the console. Note that when extracting message information from a MapMessage object, you need to handle the JMS API's JMSException. You can make a call to JmsUtils.convertJmsAccessException() to convert it into Spring's runtime exception JmsException.

Next, you have to configure this listener in the back office's configuration. Declaring this listener alone is not enough to listen for JMS messages. You need a message listener container to monitor JMS messages at a message destination and trigger your message listener on message arrival.

```
package com.apress.springrecipes.post.config;

import com.apress.springrecipes.post.MailListener;
import org.apache.activemq.ActiveMQConnectionFactory;
import org.springframework.context.annotation.Bean;
import org.springframework.context.annotation.Configuration;
import org.springframework.jms.listener.SimpleMessageListenerContainer;

import javax.jms.ConnectionFactory;

@Configuration
public class BackOfficeConfiguration {

    @Bean
    public ConnectionFactory connectionFactory() { ... }

    @Bean
    public MailListener mailListener() {
        return new MailListener();
    }

    @Bean
    public Object container() {
        SimpleMessageListenerContainer smlc = new SimpleMessageListenerContainer();
        smlc.setConnectionFactory(connectionFactory());
        smlc.setDestinationName("mail.queue");
        smlc.setMessageListener(mailListener());
        return smlc;
    }
}
```

Spring provides several types of message listener containers for you to choose from in the `org.springframework.jms.listener` package, of which `SimpleMessageListenerContainer` and `DefaultMessageListenerContainer` are the most commonly used. `SimpleMessageListenerContainer` is the simplest one that doesn't support transactions. If you have a transaction requirement in receiving messages, you have to use `DefaultMessageListenerContainer`.

Now, you can start the message listener. Since you won't need to invoke a bean to trigger message consumption—the listener will do it for you—the following main class, which only starts the Spring IoC container, is enough:

```
package com.apress.springrecipes.post;

import org.springframework.context.support.GenericXmlApplicationContext;

public class BackOfficeMain {

    public static void main(String[] args) {
        new AnnotationConfigApplicationContext(BackOfficeConfiguration.class);
    }
}
```

When you start this back-office application, it will listen for messages on the message broker (i.e., ActiveMQ). As soon as the front-desk application sends a message to the broker, the back-office application will react and display the message to the console.

Listen for JMS Messages with POJOs

A listener that implements the MessageListener interface can listen for messages, and so can an arbitrary bean declared in the Spring IoC container. Doing so means that beans are decoupled from the Spring Framework interfaces as well as the JMS MessageListener interface. For a method of this bean to be triggered on message arrival, it must accept one of the following types as its sole method argument:

- Raw JMS message type: For TextMessage, MapMessage, BytesMessage, and ObjectMessage
- String: For TextMessage only
- Map: For MapMessage only
- byte[]: For BytesMessage only
- Serializable: For ObjectMessage only

For example, to listen for MapMessage, you declare a method that accepts a Map as its argument and annotate it with @JmsListener. This class no longer needs to implement the MessageListener interface.

```
package com.apress.springrecipes.post;

import org.springframework.jms.annotation.JmsListener;

import java.util.Map;

public class MailListener {

    @JmsListener(destination = "mail.queue")
    public void displayMail(Map map) {
        Mail mail = new Mail();
        mail.setMailId((String) map.get("mailId"));
        mail.setCountry((String) map.get("country"));
        mail.setWeight((Double) map.get("weight"));
        System.out.println("Mail #" + mail.getMailId() + " received");
    }
}
```

To detect the @JmsListener annotations, you need to put the @EnableJms annotation on the configuration class, and you need to register a JmsListenerContainerFactory, which by default is detected with the name jmsListenerContainerFactory.

A POJO is registered to a listener container through a JmsListenerContainerFactory. This factory creates and configures a MessageListenerContainer and registers the annotated method as a message listener to it. You could implement your own version of the JmsListenerContainerFactory, but it is generally enough to use one of the provided classes. SimpleJmsListenerContainerFactory creates an instance of the SimpleMessageListenerContainer, whereas DefaultJmsListenerContainerFactory creates a DefaultMessageListenerContainer.

For now you will use a SimpleJmsListenerContainerFactory. If the need arises, you can quite easily switch to the DefaultMessageListenerContainer, for instance, when transactions or async processing with a TaskExecutor is needed.

```
package com.apress.springrecipes.post.config;

import com.apress.springrecipes.post.MailListener;
import org.apache.activemq.ActiveMQConnectionFactory;
import org.springframework.context.annotation.Bean;
import org.springframework.context.annotation.Configuration;
import org.springframework.jms.annotation.EnableJms;
import org.springframework.jms.config.SimpleJmsListenerContainerFactory;
import org.springframework.jms.listener.SimpleMessageListenerContainer;
import org.springframework.jms.listener.adapter.MessageListenerAdapter;

import javax.jms.ConnectionFactory;

@Configuration
@EnableJms
public class BackOfficeConfiguration {

    @Bean
    public ConnectionFactory connectionFactory() {
        return new ActiveMQConnectionFactory("tcp://localhost:61616");
    }

    @Bean
    public MailListener mailListener() {
        return new MailListener();
    }

    @Bean
    public SimpleJmsListenerContainerFactory jmsListenerContainerFactory() {
        SimpleJmsListenerContainerFactory listenerContainerFactory =
            new SimpleJmsListenerContainerFactory();
        listenerContainerFactory.setConnectionFactory(connectionFactory());
        return listenerContainerFactory;
    }
}
```

Convert JMS Messages

You can also create a message converter for converting mail objects from JMS messages that contain mail information. Because message listeners receive messages only, the method toMessage() will not be called, so you can simply return null for it. However, if you use this message converter for sending messages too, you have to implement this method. The following example reprints the `MailMessageConvertor` class written earlier:

```java
package com.apress.springrecipes.post;

import javax.jms.JMSException;
import javax.jms.MapMessage;
import javax.jms.Message;
import javax.jms.Session;

import org.springframework.jms.support.converter.MessageConversionException;
import org.springframework.jms.support.converter.MessageConverter;

public class MailMessageConverter implements MessageConverter {

    public Object fromMessage(Message message) throws JMSException,
        MessageConversionException {
        MapMessage mapMessage = (MapMessage) message;
        Mail mail = new Mail();
        mail.setMailId(mapMessage.getString("mailId"));
        mail.setCountry(mapMessage.getString("country"));
        mail.setWeight(mapMessage.getDouble("weight"));
        return mail;
    }

    public Message toMessage(Object object, Session session) throws JMSException,
        MessageConversionException {
        ...
    }
}
```

A message converter should be applied to the listener container factory for it to convert messages into objects before calling your POJO's methods.

```java
package com.apress.springrecipes.post.config;

import com.apress.springrecipes.post.MailListener;
import com.apress.springrecipes.post.MailMessageConverter;
import org.apache.activemq.ActiveMQConnectionFactory;
import org.springframework.context.annotation.Bean;
import org.springframework.context.annotation.Configuration;
import org.springframework.jms.annotation.EnableJms;
import org.springframework.jms.config.SimpleJmsListenerContainerFactory;

import javax.jms.ConnectionFactory;

@Configuration
@EnableJms
public class BackOfficeConfiguration {
```

```java
@Bean
public ConnectionFactory connectionFactory() {
    return new ActiveMQConnectionFactory("tcp://localhost:61616");
}

@Bean
public MailListener mailListener() {
    return new MailListener();
}

@Bean
public MailMessageConverter mailMessageConverter() {
    return new MailMessageConverter();
}

@Bean
public SimpleJmsListenerContainerFactory jmsListenerContainerFactory() {
    SimpleJmsListenerContainerFactory listenerContainerFactory =
        new SimpleJmsListenerContainerFactory();
    listenerContainerFactory.setConnectionFactory(connectionFactory());
    listenerContainerFactory.setMessageConverter(mailMessageConverter());
    return listenerContainerFactory;
}
}
```

With this message converter, the listener method of your POJO can accept a mail object as the method argument.

```java
package com.apress.springrecipes.post;

import org.springframework.jms.annotation.JmsListener;

public class MailListener {

    @JmsListener(destination = "mail.queue")
    public void displayMail(Mail mail) {
        System.out.println("Mail #" + mail.getMailId() + " received");
    }
}
```

Manage JMS Transactions

As mentioned, SimpleMessageListenerContainer doesn't support transactions. So, if you need transaction management for your message listener method, you have to use DefaultMessageListenerContainer instead. For local JMS transactions, you can simply enable its sessionTransacted property, and your listener method will run within a local JMS transaction (as opposed to XA transactions). To use a DefaultMessageListenerContainer, change the SimpleJmsListenerContainerFactory to a DefaultJmsListenerContainerFactory and configure said sessionTransacted property.

```
@Bean
public DefaultJmsListenerContainerFactory jmsListenerContainerFactory() {
    DefaultJmsListenerContainerFactory listenerContainerFactory =
        new DefaultJmsListenerContainerFactory();
    listenerContainerFactory.setConnectionFactory(cachingConnectionFactory());
    listenerContainerFactory.setMessageConverter(mailMessageConverter());
    listenerContainerFactory.setSessionTransacted(true);
    return listenerContainerFactory;
}
```

However, if you want your listener to participate in a JTA transaction, you need to declare a
JtaTransactionManager instance and inject it into your listener container factory.

14-5. Cache and Pool JMS Connections

Problem

Throughout this chapter, for the sake of simplicity, you've explored Spring's JMS support with a simple
instance of org.apache.activemq.ActiveMQConnectionFactory as the connection factory. This isn't the
best choice in practice. As with all things, there are performance considerations.

The crux of the issue it is that JmsTemplate closes sessions and consumers on each invocation. This
means that it tears down all those objects and frees the memory. This is "safe," but not performant, as some
of the objects created—like consumers—are meant to be long lived. This behavior stems from the use of
JmsTemplate in application server environments, where typically the application server's connection factory
is used, and it, internally, provides connection pooling. In this environment, restoring all the objects simply
returns it to the pool, which is the desirable behavior.

Solution

There's no "one-size-fits-all" solution to this. You need to weigh the qualities you're looking for and react
appropriately.

How It Works

Generally, you want a connection factory that provides pooling and caching of some sort when publishing
messages using JmsTemplate. The first place to look for a pooled connection factory might be your
application server. It may very well provide one by default.

In the examples in this chapter, you use ActiveMQ in a stand-alone configuration. ActiveMQ, like many
vendors, provides a pooled connection factory class alternative. ActiveMQ provides two, actually: one for
use consuming messages with a JCA connector and another one for use outside of a JCA container. You
can use these instead to handle caching producers and sessions when sending messages. The following
configuration pools a connection factory in a stand-alone configuration. It's a drop-in replacement for the
previous examples when publishing messages.

```
@Bean(destroyMethod = "stop")
public ConnectionFactory connectionFactory() {
    ActiveMQConnectionFactory connectionFactoryToUse =
        new ActiveMQConnectionFactory("tcp://localhost:61616");
```

```
PooledConnectionFactory connectionFactory = new PooledConnectionFactory();
connectionFactory.setConnectionFactory(connectionFactoryToUse);
return connectionFactory;
}
```

If you are receiving messages, you could still stand some more efficiency because the JmsTemplate constructs a new MessageConsumer each time as well. In this situation, you have a few alternatives: use Spring's various *MessageListenerContainer implementations (MDPs) because it caches consumers correctly, or use Spring's ConnectionFactory implementations. The first implementation, org.springframework.jms.connection.SingleConnectionFactory, returns the same underlying JMS connection each time (which is thread-safe according to the JMS API) and ignores calls to the close() method.

Generally, this implementation works well with the JMS API. A newer alternative is org.springframework.jms.connection.CachingConnectionFactory. First, the obvious advantage is that it provides the ability to cache multiple instances. Second, it caches sessions, message producers, and message consumers. Finally, it works regardless of your JMS connection factory implementation.

```
@Bean
public ConnectionFactory cachingConnectionFactory() {
    return new CachingConnectionFactory(connectionFactory());
}
```

14-6. Send and Receive AMQP Messages with Spring

Problem

You want to use RabbitMQ to send and receive messages.

Solution

The Spring AMQP project provides easy access to the AMQP protocol. It has support similar to that of Spring JMS. It comes with a RabbitTemplate, which provides basic send and receive options; it also comes with a MessageListenerContainer option that mimics Spring JMS.

How It Works

Let's look at how you can send a message using RabbitTemplate. To get access to RabbitTemplate, it is the simplest to extend RabbitGatewaySupport. You'll use FrontDeskImpl, which uses RabbitTemplate.

Send and Receive Message Without Spring's Template Support

Let's look at how to send and receive messages without Spring's template support. The following FrontDeskImpl class sends a message to RabbitMQ using the plain API:

```
package com.apress.springrecipes.post;

import com.fasterxml.jackson.databind.ObjectMapper;
import com.rabbitmq.client.Channel;
import com.rabbitmq.client.Connection;
```

```java
import com.rabbitmq.client.ConnectionFactory;
import org.springframework.scheduling.annotation.Scheduled;

import java.io.IOException;
import java.util.Locale;
import java.util.Random;
import java.util.concurrent.TimeoutException;

public class FrontDeskImpl implements FrontDesk {

    private static final String QUEUE_NAME = "mail.queue";

    public void sendMail(final Mail mail) {
        ConnectionFactory connectionFactory = new ConnectionFactory();
        connectionFactory.setHost("localhost");
        connectionFactory.setUsername("guest");
        connectionFactory.setPassword("guest");
        connectionFactory.setPort(5672);

        Connection connection = null;
        Channel channel = null;
        try {

            connection = connectionFactory.newConnection();
            channel = connection.createChannel();
            channel.queueDeclare(QUEUE_NAME, true, false, false, null);
            String message = new ObjectMapper().writeValueAsString(mail);
            channel.basicPublish("", QUEUE_NAME, null, message.getBytes("UTF-8"));

        } catch (IOException | TimeoutException e) {
            throw new RuntimeException(e);
        } finally {
            if (channel != null) {
                try {
                    channel.close();
                } catch (IOException | TimeoutException e) {
                }
            }

            if (connection != null) {
                try {
                    connection.close();
                } catch (IOException e) {
                }
            }
        }
    }
}
```

First you create a ConnectionFactory to obtain a connection to RabbitMQ; here we configured it for localhost and provided a username/password combination. Next you need to obtain a Channel to finally create a queue. Then the passed-in Mail message is converted to JSON using a Jackson ObjectMapper and finally sent to the queue. When creating connections and sending messages, you need to take care of the different exceptions that can occur, and after sending, you need to properly close and release Connection again, which also can throw an exception.

Before you can send and receive AMQP messages, you need to install an AMQP message broker.

■ **Note** In the bin directory is a rabbitmq.sh file, which downloads and starts a RabbitMQ broker in a Docker container.

The following BackOfficeImpl class receives messages using the plain RabbitMQ API:

```
package com.apress.springrecipes.post;

import com.fasterxml.jackson.databind.ObjectMapper;
import com.rabbitmq.client.*;
import org.springframework.stereotype.Service;

import javax.annotation.PreDestroy;
import java.io.IOException;
import java.util.concurrent.TimeoutException;

@Service
public class BackOfficeImpl implements BackOffice {

    private static final String QUEUE_NAME = "mail.queue";

    private MailListener mailListener = new MailListener();
    private Connection connection;

    @Override
    public Mail receiveMail() {

        ConnectionFactory connectionFactory = new ConnectionFactory();
        connectionFactory.setHost("localhost");
        connectionFactory.setUsername("guest");
        connectionFactory.setPassword("guest");
        connectionFactory.setPort(5672);

        Channel channel = null;
        try {

            connection = connectionFactory.newConnection();
            channel = connection.createChannel();
            channel.queueDeclare(QUEUE_NAME, true, false, false, null);
```

```
            Consumer consumer = new DefaultConsumer(channel) {
                @Override
                public void handleDelivery(String consumerTag, Envelope envelope,
                AMQP.BasicProperties properties, byte[] body)
                    throws IOException {
                    Mail mail = new ObjectMapper().readValue(body, Mail.class);
                    mailListener.displayMail(mail);
                }
            };
            channel.basicConsume(QUEUE_NAME, true, consumer);

    } catch (IOException | TimeoutException e) {
        throw new RuntimeException(e);
    }

    return null;
}

@PreDestroy
public void destroy() {
    if (this.connection != null) {
        try {
            this.connection.close();
        } catch (IOException e) {
        }
    }
}
}
```

This code is largely the same as FrontDeskImpl except that you now register a Consumer object to retrieve the messages. In this consumer, you use Jackson to map the message to the Mail object again and pass it to MailListener, which in turn prints the converted message to the console. When using a channel, you can add a consumer that will be invoked when a message is received. The consumer will be ready as soon as it is registered with the channel using the basicConsume method.

If you already have the FrontDeskImpl running, you will see the messages coming in quite quickly.

Send Messages with Spring's Template Support

The FrontDeskImpl class extends RabbitGatewaySupport, which configures a RabbitTemplate based on the configuration you pass in. To send a message, you use the getRabbitOperations method to get the template and next to convert and send the message. For this you use the convertAndSend method. This method will first use a MessageConverter to convert the message into JSON and then send it to the queue you have configured.

```
package com.apress.springrecipes.post;

import org.springframework.amqp.rabbit.core.RabbitGatewaySupport;

public class FrontDeskImpl extends RabbitGatewaySupport implements FrontDesk {

    public void sendMail(final Mail mail) {
        getRabbitOperations().convertAndSend(mail);
    }
}
```

Let's take a look at the configuration:

```
package com.apress.springrecipes.post.config;

import com.apress.springrecipes.post.FrontDeskImpl;
import org.springframework.amqp.rabbit.connection.CachingConnectionFactory;
import org.springframework.amqp.rabbit.connection.ConnectionFactory;
import org.springframework.amqp.rabbit.core.RabbitTemplate;
import org.springframework.amqp.support.converter.Jackson2JsonMessageConverter;
import org.springframework.context.annotation.Bean;
import org.springframework.context.annotation.Configuration;

@Configuration
public class FrontOfficeConfiguration {

    @Bean
    public ConnectionFactory connectionFactory() {
        CachingConnectionFactory connectionFactory =
            new CachingConnectionFactory("127.0.0.1");
        connectionFactory.setUsername("guest");
        connectionFactory.setPassword("guest");
        connectionFactory.setPort(5672);
        return connectionFactory;
    }

    @Bean
    public RabbitTemplate rabbitTemplate() {
        RabbitTemplate rabbitTemplate = new RabbitTemplate();
        rabbitTemplate.setConnectionFactory(connectionFactory());
        rabbitTemplate.setMessageConverter(new Jackson2JsonMessageConverter());
        rabbitTemplate.setRoutingKey("mail.queue");
        return rabbitTemplate;
    }

    @Bean
    public FrontDeskImpl frontDesk() {
        FrontDeskImpl frontDesk = new FrontDeskImpl();
        frontDesk.setRabbitOperations(rabbitTemplate());
        return frontDesk;
    }
}
```

The configuration is quite similar to the JMS configuration. You need a ConnectionFactory to connect to your RabbitMQ broker. You use a CachingConnectionFactory so that you can reuse your connections. Next there is the RabbitTemplate that uses the connection and has a MessageConverter to convert the message. The message is being converted into JSON using the Jackson2 library, which is the reason for the configuration of the Jackson2JsonMessageConverter. Finally, RabbitTemplate is passed into the FrontDeskImpl class so that it is available for usage.

```
package com.apress.springrecipes.post;

import com.apress.springrecipes.post.config.FrontOfficeConfiguration;
import org.springframework.context.ConfigurableApplicationContext;
import org.springframework.context.annotation.AnnotationConfigApplicationContext;

public class FrontDeskMain {

    public static void main(String[] args) throws Exception {
        ConfigurableApplicationContext context =
            new AnnotationConfigApplicationContext(FrontOfficeConfiguration.class);

        FrontDesk frontDesk = context.getBean(FrontDesk.class);
        frontDesk.sendMail(new Mail("1234", "US", 1.5));

        System.in.read();

        context.close();
    }
}
```

Listen for AMQP Messages with Message Listeners

Spring AMQP supports MessageListenerContainers for retrieving messages in the same way as it Spring JMS does for JMS. Spring AMQP has the @RabbitListener annotation to indicate an AMQP-based message listener. Let's take a look at the MessageListener that is used.

```
package com.apress.springrecipes.post;

import org.springframework.amqp.rabbit.annotation.RabbitListener;

public class MailListener {

    @RabbitListener(queues = "mail.queue")
    public void displayMail(Mail mail) {
        System.out.println("Received: " + mail);
    }
}
```

MailListener is exactly the same as the one created in recipe 14-4 for receiving JMS messages. The difference is in the configuration.

```
package com.apress.springrecipes.post.config;

import com.apress.springrecipes.post.MailListener;
import org.springframework.amqp.rabbit.annotation.EnableRabbit;
import org.springframework.amqp.rabbit.config.SimpleRabbitListenerContainerFactory;
import org.springframework.amqp.rabbit.connection.CachingConnectionFactory;
import org.springframework.amqp.rabbit.connection.ConnectionFactory;
```

```java
import org.springframework.amqp.rabbit.listener.RabbitListenerContainerFactory;
import org.springframework.amqp.support.converter.Jackson2JsonMessageConverter;
import org.springframework.context.annotation.Bean;
import org.springframework.context.annotation.Configuration;

@Configuration
@EnableRabbit
public class BackOfficeConfiguration {

    @Bean
    public RabbitListenerContainerFactory rabbitListenerContainerFactory() {
        SimpleRabbitListenerContainerFactory containerFactory =
            new SimpleRabbitListenerContainerFactory();
        containerFactory.setConnectionFactory(connectionFactory());
        containerFactory.setMessageConverter(new Jackson2JsonMessageConverter());
        return containerFactory;
    }

    @Bean
    public ConnectionFactory connectionFactory() {
        CachingConnectionFactory connectionFactory = new
        CachingConnectionFactory("127.0.0.1");
        connectionFactory.setUsername("guest");
        connectionFactory.setPassword("guest");
        connectionFactory.setPort(5672);
        return connectionFactory;
    }

    @Bean
    public MailListener mailListener() {
        return new MailListener();
    }

}
```

To enable AMQP annotation-based listeners, you add the @EnableRabbit annotation to the
configuration class. As each listener requires a MessageListenerContainer, you need to configure a
RabbitListenerContainerFactory, which takes care of creating those containers. The @EnableRabbit logic
will, by default, will look for a bean named rabbitListenerContainerFactory.

RabbitListenerContainerFactory needs a ConnectionFactory. For this you are using
CachingConnectionFactory. Before the MailListener.displayMail method is invoked by
MessageListenerContainer, it needs to convert the message payload, in JSON, into a Mail object using
Jackon2JsonMessageConverter.

To listen to messages, create a class with a main method that only needs to construct the application context.

```
package com.apress.springrecipes.post;

import com.apress.springrecipes.post.config.BackOfficeConfiguration;
import org.springframework.context.annotation.AnnotationConfigApplicationContext;

public class BackOfficeMain {

    public static void main(String[] args) {
        new AnnotationConfigApplicationContext(BackOfficeConfiguration.class);
    }
}
```

14-7. Send and Receive Messages with Spring Kafka

Problem

You want to use Apache Kafka to send and receive messages.

Solution

The Spring Kafka project provides easy access to Apache Kafka. It has support similar to that of Spring JMS using the Spring Messaging abstraction. It comes with KafkaTemplate, which provides basic send options; it also comes with a MessageListenerContainer option that mimics Spring JMS and can be enabled by @EnableKafka.

How It Works

First you will see how to setup the KafkaTemplate to send messages and how to listen to messages using a KafkaListener. Finally you will look at how to convert objects into message payloads using MessageConverters.

Send Messages with Spring's Template Support

Let's start by rewriting the FrontOfficeImpl class to use KafkaTemplate to send a message. To do so, you actually want an object that implements KafkaOperations, which is the interface implemented by KafkaTemplate.

```
package com.apress.springrecipes.post;

import com.fasterxml.jackson.core.JsonProcessingException;
import com.fasterxml.jackson.databind.ObjectMapper;
import org.springframework.kafka.core.KafkaOperations;
import org.springframework.kafka.support.SendResult;
import org.springframework.util.concurrent.ListenableFuture;
import org.springframework.util.concurrent.ListenableFutureCallback;
```

```java
public class FrontDeskImpl implements FrontDesk {

    private final KafkaOperations<Integer, String> kafkaOperations;

    public FrontDeskImpl(KafkaOperations<Integer, String> kafkaOperations) {
        this.kafkaOperations = kafkaOperations;
    }

    public void sendMail(final Mail mail) {

        ListenableFuture<SendResult<Integer, String>> future =
            kafkaOperations.send("mails", convertToJson(mail));
        future.addCallback(new ListenableFutureCallback<SendResult<Integer, String>>() {

            @Override
            public void onFailure(Throwable ex) {
                ex.printStackTrace();
            }

            @Override
            public void onSuccess(SendResult<Integer, String> result) {
                System.out.println("Result (success): " + result.getRecordMetadata());
            }
        });
    }

    private String convertToJson(Mail mail) {
        try {
            return new ObjectMapper().writeValueAsString(mail);
        } catch (JsonProcessingException e) {
            throw new IllegalArgumentException(e);
        }
    }
}
```

Notice the kafkaOperations field, which takes KafkaOperations<Integer, String>. This means you are sending a message with an Integer type as the key (generated when sending a message), and you will send a message of type String. This means you need to convert the incoming Mail instance to a String. This is taken care of by the convertToJson method using a Jackson2 ObjectMapper. The message will be sent to the mails topic, which is the first argument in the send method; the second one is the payload to send (the converted Mail message).

Sending a message using Kafka is generally an async operation, and the KafkaOperations.send methods reflect this in returning a ListenableFuture. It is a normal Future, so you could use the call to get() to make it a blocking operation or register ListenableFutureCallback to get notified of the success or failure of the operation.

Next you need to create a configuration class to configure KafkaTemplate to use in FrontDeskImpl.

```java
package com.apress.springrecipes.post.config;

import com.apress.springrecipes.post.FrontDeskImpl;
import org.apache.kafka.clients.producer.ProducerConfig;
```

```java
import org.apache.kafka.common.serialization.IntegerSerializer;
import org.apache.kafka.common.serialization.StringSerializer;
import org.springframework.context.annotation.Bean;
import org.springframework.context.annotation.Configuration;
import org.springframework.kafka.core.DefaultKafkaProducerFactory;
import org.springframework.kafka.core.KafkaTemplate;
import org.springframework.kafka.core.ProducerFactory;

import java.util.HashMap;
import java.util.Map;

@Configuration
public class FrontOfficeConfiguration {

    @Bean
    public KafkaTemplate<Integer, String> kafkaTemplate() {
        KafkaTemplate<Integer, String> kafkaTemplate = new KafkaTemplate<>(producerFactory());
        return kafkaTemplate;
    }

    @Bean
    public ProducerFactory<Integer, String> producerFactory() {
        DefaultKafkaProducerFactory producerFactory = new DefaultKafkaProducerFactory<>
        (producerFactoryProperties());
        return producerFactory;
    }

    @Bean
    public Map<String, Object> producerFactoryProperties() {
        Map<String, Object> properties = new HashMap<>();
        properties.put(ProducerConfig.BOOTSTRAP_SERVERS_CONFIG, "localhost:9092");
        properties.put(ProducerConfig.KEY_SERIALIZER_CLASS_CONFIG, IntegerSerializer.class);
        properties.put(ProducerConfig.VALUE_SERIALIZER_CLASS_CONFIG, StringSerializer.class);
        return properties;
    }

    @Bean
    public FrontDeskImpl frontDesk() {
        return new FrontDeskImpl(kafkaTemplate());
    }

}
```

The aforementioned configuration creates a minimally configured KafkaTemplate. You need to configure ProducerFactory used by KafkaTemplate; it requires at least the URL to connect to and needs to know which key and value types you want to serialize the messages to. The URL is specified by using ProducerConfig.BOOTSTRAP_SERVERS_CONFIG. This can take one or more servers to connect to. ProducerConfig.KEY_SERIALIZER_CLASS_CONFIG and ProducerConfig.VALUE_SERIALIZER_CLASS_CONFIG respectively configure the key and value serializers used. As you want to use an Integer for the key and String for the value, those are configured with IntegerSerializer and StringSerializer.

Finally, the constructed KafkaTemplate is passed to FrontDeskImpl. To run the front-desk application, the following Main class is all that is needed:

```
package com.apress.springrecipes.post;

import org.springframework.context.ConfigurableApplicationContext;
import org.springframework.context.annotation.AnnotationConfigApplicationContext;

import com.apress.springrecipes.post.config.FrontOfficeConfiguration;

public class FrontDeskMain {

    public static void main(String[] args) throws Exception {
        ConfigurableApplicationContext context =
            new AnnotationConfigApplicationContext(FrontOfficeConfiguration.class);
        context.registerShutdownHook();

        FrontDesk frontDesk = context.getBean(FrontDesk.class);
        frontDesk.sendMail(new Mail("1234", "US", 1.5));

        System.in.read();

    }
}
```

This will launch the front-desk application and send a message through Kafka.

Listen to Messages Using Spring Kafka

Spring Kafka also has message listener containers for listening to messages on topics just like Spring JMS and Spring AMQP. To enable the use of these containers, you need to put @EnableKafka on your configuration class and create and configure your Kafka consumer using @KafkaListener.

First let's create the listener, which is as easy as annotating a method with a single argument with @KafkaListener.

```
package com.apress.springrecipes.post;

import org.springframework.kafka.annotation.KafkaListener;

public class MailListener {

    @KafkaListener(topics = "mails")
    public void displayMail(String mail) {
        System.out.println(" Received: " + mail);
    }
}
```

For now you are interested in the raw String-based payload as that is what is being sent.
Next you need to configure the listener container.

```java
package com.apress.springrecipes.post.config;

import com.apress.springrecipes.post.MailListener;
import org.apache.kafka.clients.consumer.ConsumerConfig;
import org.apache.kafka.common.serialization.IntegerDeserializer;
import org.apache.kafka.common.serialization.StringDeserializer;
import org.springframework.context.annotation.Bean;
import org.springframework.context.annotation.Configuration;
import org.springframework.kafka.annotation.EnableKafka;
import org.springframework.kafka.config.ConcurrentKafkaListenerContainerFactory;
import org.springframework.kafka.config.KafkaListenerContainerFactory;
import org.springframework.kafka.core.ConsumerFactory;
import org.springframework.kafka.core.DefaultKafkaConsumerFactory;
import org.springframework.kafka.listener.ConcurrentMessageListenerContainer;

import java.util.HashMap;
import java.util.Map;

@Configuration
@EnableKafka
public class BackOfficeConfiguration {

    @Bean
    KafkaListenerContainerFactory<ConcurrentMessageListenerContainer<Integer, String>>
    kafkaListenerContainerFactory() {
        ConcurrentKafkaListenerContainerFactory factory =
            new ConcurrentKafkaListenerContainerFactory();
        factory.setConsumerFactory(consumerFactory());
        return factory;
    }

    @Bean
    public ConsumerFactory<Integer, String> consumerFactory() {
        return new DefaultKafkaConsumerFactory<>(consumerConfiguration());
    }

    @Bean
    public Map<String, Object> consumerConfiguration() {
        Map<String, Object> properties = new HashMap<>();
        properties.put(ConsumerConfig.BOOTSTRAP_SERVERS_CONFIG, "localhost:9092");
        properties.put(ConsumerConfig.KEY_DESERIALIZER_CLASS_CONFIG, IntegerDeserializer.class);
        properties.put(ConsumerConfig.VALUE_DESERIALIZER_CLASS_CONFIG,
                    StringDeserializer.class);
        properties.put(ConsumerConfig.GROUP_ID_CONFIG, "group1");
        return properties;
    }
```

```java
@Bean
public MailListener mailListener() {
    return new MailListener();
}

}
```

The configuration is similar to the client; you need to pass the URL (or URLs) to connect to Apache Kafka, and as you want to deserialize messages, you need to specify a key and value deserializer. Finally, you need to add a group ID or you won't be able to connect to Kafka. The URL is passed by using ConsumerConfig.BOOTSTRAP_SERVERS_CONFIG; the key and value deserializers used are the IntegerDeserializer for the key (as that was an integer); and as the payload is a String, you need to use the StringDeserializer. Finally, the group property is set.

With these properties, you can configure KafkaListenerContainerFactory, which is a factory used to create a Kafka-based MessageListenerContainer. The container is internally used by the functionality enabled by adding the @EnableKafka annotation. For each method annotated with @KafkaListener, a MessageListenerContainer is created.

To run the back-office application, you would need to load this configuration and let it listen:

```java
package com.apress.springrecipes.post;

import com.apress.springrecipes.post.config.BackOfficeConfiguration;
import org.springframework.context.annotation.AnnotationConfigApplicationContext;

public class BackOfficeMain {

    public static void main(String[] args) {
        new AnnotationConfigApplicationContext(BackOfficeConfiguration.class);
    }
}
```

Now when the front-office application is started, the Mail message will be converted to a String and sent through Kafka to the back office, resulting in the following output:

```
Received: {"mailId":"1234","country":"US","weight":1.5}
```

Use a MessageConverter to Convert Payloads into Objects

The listener now receives a String, but it would be nicer if you could automatically convert this into a Mail object again. This is quite easily done with some tweaks in the configuration. The KafkaListenerContainerFactory used here accepts a MessageConverter, and to automatically turn a String into the desired object, you can pass it a StringJsonMessageConverter. This will take the String and convert it into the object as specified as argument in the @KafkaListener annotated method.

First update the configuration.

```
package com.apress.springrecipes.post.config;

import org.springframework.kafka.support.converter.StringJsonMessageConverter;

@Configuration
@EnableKafka
public class BackOfficeConfiguration {

    @Bean
    KafkaListenerContainerFactory<ConcurrentMessageListenerContainer<Integer, String>>
    kafkaListenerContainerFactory() {
        ConcurrentKafkaListenerContainerFactory factory =
            new ConcurrentKafkaListenerContainerFactory();
        factory.setMessageConverter(new StringJsonMessageConverter());
        factory.setConsumerFactory(consumerFactory());
        return factory;
    }
    ...
}
```

Next you need to modify the MailListener to use a Mail object instead of the plain String.

```
package com.apress.springrecipes.post;

import org.springframework.kafka.annotation.KafkaListener;

public class MailListener {

    @KafkaListener(topics = "mails")
    public void displayMail(Mail mail) {
        System.out.println("Mail #" + mail.getMailId() + " received");
    }
}
```

When running the back office and front office, the message will still be sent and received.

Convert Objects to Payloads

In the front office, the Mail instance is manually being converted to a JSON string. Although it's not hard, it would be nice if the framework could do this transparently. This is possible by configuring JsonSerializer instead of StringSerializer.

```
package com.apress.springrecipes.post.config;

import com.apress.springrecipes.post.FrontDeskImpl;
import org.apache.kafka.clients.producer.ProducerConfig;
import org.apache.kafka.common.serialization.IntegerSerializer;
import org.springframework.context.annotation.Bean;
import org.springframework.context.annotation.Configuration;
```

```
import org.springframework.kafka.core.DefaultKafkaProducerFactory;
import org.springframework.kafka.core.KafkaTemplate;
import org.springframework.kafka.core.ProducerFactory;
import org.springframework.kafka.support.serializer.JsonSerializer;

import java.util.HashMap;
import java.util.Map;

@Configuration
public class FrontOfficeConfiguration {

    @Bean
    public KafkaTemplate<Integer, Object> kafkaTemplate() {
        return new KafkaTemplate<>(producerFactory());
    }

    @Bean
    public ProducerFactory<Integer, Object> producerFactory() {
        return new DefaultKafkaProducerFactory<>(producerFactoryProperties());
    }

    @Bean
    public Map<String, Object> producerFactoryProperties() {
        Map<String, Object> properties = new HashMap<>();
        properties.put(ProducerConfig.BOOTSTRAP_SERVERS_CONFIG, "localhost:9092");
        properties.put(ProducerConfig.KEY_SERIALIZER_CLASS_CONFIG, IntegerSerializer.class);
        properties.put(ProducerConfig.VALUE_SERIALIZER_CLASS_CONFIG, JsonSerializer.class);
        return properties;
    }

    @Bean
    public FrontDeskImpl frontDesk() {
        return new FrontDeskImpl(kafkaTemplate());
    }
}
```

Instead of KafkaTemplate<Integer, String>, you now use KafkaTemplate<Integer, Object> because you will now be able to send objects serialized to a String to Kafka.

The FrontOfficeImpl class can also be cleaned up now because conversion to JSON is now handled by KafkaTemplate.

```
package com.apress.springrecipes.post;

import org.springframework.kafka.core.KafkaOperations;
import org.springframework.kafka.support.SendResult;
import org.springframework.util.concurrent.ListenableFuture;
import org.springframework.util.concurrent.ListenableFutureCallback;
```

```java
public class FrontDeskImpl implements FrontDesk {

    private final KafkaOperations<Integer, Object> kafkaOperations;

    public FrontDeskImpl(KafkaOperations<Integer, Object> kafkaOperations) {
        this.kafkaOperations = kafkaOperations;
    }

    public void sendMail(final Mail mail) {

        ListenableFuture<SendResult<Integer, Object>> future = kafkaOperations.send("mails",
        mail);
        future.addCallback(new ListenableFutureCallback<SendResult<Integer, Object>>() {

            @Override
            public void onFailure(Throwable ex) {
                ex.printStackTrace();
            }

            @Override
            public void onSuccess(SendResult<Integer, Object> result) {
                System.out.println("Result (success): " + result.getRecordMetadata());
            }
        });
    }
}
```

Summary

This chapter explored Spring's messaging support and how to use this to build message-oriented architectures. You learned how to produce and consume messages using different messaging solutions. For different messaging solutions, you looked at how to build message-driven POJOs using `MessageListenerContainer`.

You looked at JMS and AMQP with ActiveMQ, a reliable open source message queue, and you briefly looked at Apache Kafka.

The next chapter will explore Spring Integration, which is an ESB-like framework for building application integration solutions, similar to Mule ESB and ServiceMix. You will be able to leverage the knowledge gained in this chapter to take your message-oriented applications to new heights with Spring Integration.

CHAPTER 15

Spring Integration

In this chapter, you will learn the principles behind enterprise application integration (EAI), used by many modern applications to decouple dependencies between components. The Spring Framework provides a powerful and extensible framework called Spring Integration. Spring Integration provides the same level of decoupling for disparate systems and data that the core Spring Framework provides for components within an application. This chapter aims to give you all the required knowledge to understand the patterns involved in EAI to understand what an enterprise service bus (ESB) is and—ultimately—how to build solutions using Spring Integration. If you've used an EAI server or an ESB, you'll find that Spring Integration is markedly simpler than anything you're likely to have used before.

After finishing this chapter, you will be able to write fairly sophisticated Spring Integration solutions to integrate applications so that they can share services and data. You will learn Spring Integration's many options for configuration, too. Spring Integration can be configured entirely in a standard XML namespace, if you like, but you'll probably find that a hybrid approach, using annotations and XML, is more natural. You will also learn why Spring Integration is a very attractive alternative for people coming from a classic enterprise application integration background. If you've used an ESB before, such as Mule or ServiceMix, or a classical EAI server, such as Axway's Integrator or TIBCO's ActiveMatrix, the idioms explained here should be familiar and the configuration refreshingly straightforward.

15-1. Integrate One System with Another Using EAI

Problem

You have two applications that need to talk to each other through external interfaces. You need to establish a connection between the applications' services and/or their data.

Solution

You need to employ EAI, which is the discipline of integrating applications and data using a set of well-known patterns. These patterns are usefully summarized and embodied in a landmark book called *Enterprise Integration Patterns* by Gregor Hohpe and Bobby Woolf. Today the patterns are canonical and are the *lingua franca* of the modern-day ESB.

How It Works

There are several different integration styles which you can use, you could use the File system, the database, messaging or even do remote procedure calls. Next you will explore how you could implement or realise the different integration styles and what choices there are next to Spring Integration.

© Marten Deinum, Daniel Rubio, and Josh Long 2017
M. Deinum et al., *Spring 5 Recipes*, DOI 10.1007/978-1-4842-2790-9_15

Pick an Integration Style

There are multiple integration styles, each best suited for certain types of applications and requirements. The basic premise is simple: your application can't speak directly to the other system using the native mechanism in one system. So, you can devise a bridging connection, something to build on top of, abstract, or work around some characteristic about the other system in a way that's advantageous to the invoking system. What you abstract is different for each application. Sometimes it's the location, sometimes it's the synchronous or asynchronous nature of the call, and sometimes it's the messaging protocol. There are many criteria for choosing an integration style, related to how tightly coupled you want your application to be, to server affinity, to the demands of the messaging formats, and so on. In a way, TCP/IP is the most famous of all integration techniques because it decouples one application from another's server.

You have probably built applications that use some or all of the following integration styles (using Spring, no less!). A shared database, for example, is easily achieved using Spring's JDBC support; Remote Procedure Invocation is easily achieved using Spring's exporter functionality.

The four integration styles are as follows:

- *File transfer*: Have each application produce files of shared data for others to consume and to consume files that others have produced.

- *Shared database*: Have the applications store the data they want to share in a common database. This usually takes the form of a database to which different applications have access. This is not usually a favored approach because it means exposing your data to different clients that might not respect the constraints you have in place (but not codified). Using views and stored procedures can often make this option possible, but it's not ideal. There's no particular support for talking to a database, per se, but you can build an endpoint that deals with new results in a SQL database as message payloads. Integration with databases doesn't tend to be granular or message-oriented but batch-oriented instead. After all, a million new rows in a database isn't an event so much as a batch! It's no surprise then that Spring Batch (discussed in Chapter 11) included terrific support for JDBC-oriented input and output.

- *Remote Procedure Invocation*: Have each application expose some of its procedures so that they can be invoked remotely and have applications invoke them to initiate behavior and exchange data. There is specific support for optimizing RPC exchanges (which includes remote procedure calls such as SOAP, RMI, and HTTP Invoker) using Spring Integration.

- *Messaging*: Have each application connect to a common messaging system and exchange data and invoke behavior using messages. This style, mostly enabled by JMS in the JEE world, also describes other asynchronous or multicast publish-subscribe architectures. In a way, an ESB or an EAI container such as Spring Integration lets you handle most of the other styles as though you were dealing with a messaging queue: a request comes in on a queue and is managed, responded to, or forwarded to another queue.

Build on an ESB Solution

Now that you know how you want to approach the integration, it's all about implementing it. You have many choices in today's world. If the requirement is common enough, most middleware or frameworks will accommodate it in some way. JEE, .NET, and others handle common cases very well via SOAP,

XML-RPC, a binary layer such as EJB or binary remoting, JMS, or an MQ abstraction. If, however, the requirement is somewhat exotic or you have a lot of configuration to do, then perhaps an ESB is required. An ESB is middleware that provides a high-level approach to modeling integrations, in the spirit of the patterns described by EAI. The ESB provides a manageable configuration format for orchestrating the different pieces of an integration in a simple high-level format.

Spring Integration, an API in the SpringSource portfolio, provides a robust mechanism for modeling a lot of these integration scenarios that work well with Spring. Spring Integration has many advantages over a lot of other ESBs, especially the lightweight nature of the framework. The nascent ESB market is filled with choices. Some are former EAI servers, reworked to address the ESB-centric architectures. Some are genuine ESBs, built with that in mind. Some are little more than message queues with adapters.

Indeed, if you're looking for an extraordinarily powerful EAI server (with almost integration with the JEE platform and a very hefty price tag), you might consider Axway Integrator. There's very little it can't do. Vendors such as TIBCO and WebMethods made their marks (and were subsequently acquired) because they provided excellent tools for dealing with integration in the enterprise. These options, although powerful, are usually very expensive and middleware-centric; your integrations are deployed to the middleware.

Standardization attempts, such as Java Business Integration (JBI), have proven successful to an extent, and there are good compliant ESBs based on these standards (OpenESB and ServiceMix, for example). One of the thought leaders in the ESB market is the Mule ESB, which has a good reputation; it is free/open source friendly, community friendly, and lightweight. These characteristics also make Spring Integration attractive. Often, you simply need to talk to another open system, and you don't want to requisition a purchase approval for middleware that's more expensive than some houses!

Each Spring Integration application is completely embedded and needs no server infrastructure. In fact, you could deploy an integration inside another application, perhaps in your web application endpoint. Spring Integration flips the deployment paradigms of most ESBs on their head. You deploy Spring Integration into your application; you don't deploy your application into Spring Integration. There are no start and stop scripts and no ports to guard. The simplest possible working Spring Integration application is a simple Java `public static void main()` method to bootstrap a Spring context.

```
package com.apress.springrecipes.springintegration;

import org.springframework.context.annotation.AnnotationConfigApplicationContext;

public class Main {
    public static void main(String [] args){
        ApplicationContext applicationContext =
            new AnnotationConfigApplicationContext(IntegrationConfiguration.class);
    }
}
```

You created a standard Spring application context and started it. The contents of the Spring application context will be discussed in subsequent recipes, but it's helpful to see how simple it is. You might decide to hoist the context up in a web application, an EJB container, or anything else you want. Indeed, you can use Spring Integration to power the e-mail polling functionality in a Swing/JavaFX application! It's as lightweight as you want it to be. In subsequent examples, the configuration shown should be put in an XML file and that XML file referenced as the first parameter when running this class. When the main method runs to completion, your context will start up the Spring Integration bus and start responding to requests on the components configured in the application context's XML.

15-2. Integrate Two Systems Using JMS

Problem

You want to build an integration to connect one application to another using JMS, which provides locational and temporal decoupling on modern middleware for Java applications. You're interested in applying more sophisticated routing and want to isolate your code from the specifics of the origin of the message (in this case, the JMS queue or topic).

Solution

While you can do this by using regular JMS code or EJB's support for message-driven beans (MDBs) or by using core Spring's message-driven POJO (MDP) support, all are necessarily coded for handling messages coming specifically from JMS. Your code is tied to JMS. Using an ESB lets you hide the origin of the message from the code that's handling it. You'll use this solution as an easy way to see how a Spring Integration solution can be built. Spring Integration provides an easy way to work with JMS, just as you might use MDPs in the core Spring container. Here, however, you could conceivably replace the JMS middleware with an e-mail, and the code that reacts to the message could stay the same.

How It Works

As you might recall from Chapter 14, Spring can replace EJB's MDB functionality by using MDPs. This is a powerful solution for anyone wanting to build something that handles messages on a message queue. You'll build an MDP, but you will configure it using Spring Integration's more concise configuration and provide an example of a very rudimentary integration. All this integration will do is take an inbound JMS message (whose payload is of type `Map<String,Object>`) and write it to the log.

As with a standard MDP, a configuration for the `ConnectionFactory` class exists. Shown following is a configuration class. You can pass it in as a parameter to the Spring `ApplicationContext` instance on creation (as you did in the previous recipe, in the `Main` class).

```
package com.apress.springrecipes.springintegration;

import org.apache.activemq.ActiveMQConnectionFactory;
import org.springframework.context.annotation.Bean;
import org.springframework.context.annotation.ComponentScan;
import org.springframework.context.annotation.Configuration;
import org.springframework.integration.config.EnableIntegration;
import org.springframework.integration.dsl.IntegrationFlow;
import org.springframework.integration.dsl.IntegrationFlows;
import org.springframework.integration.jms.dsl.Jms;
import org.springframework.jms.connection.CachingConnectionFactory;
import org.springframework.jms.core.JmsTemplate;

import javax.jms.ConnectionFactory;

@Configuration
@EnableIntegration
```

```
@ComponentScan
public class IntegrationConfiguration {

    @Bean
    public CachingConnectionFactory connectionFactory() {
        ActiveMQConnectionFactory connectionFactory =
            new ActiveMQConnectionFactory("tcp://localhost:61616");
        return new CachingConnectionFactory(connectionFactory);
    }

    @Bean
    public JmsTemplate jmsTemplate(ConnectionFactory connectionFactory) {
        return new JmsTemplate(connectionFactory);
    }

    @Bean
    public InboundHelloWorldJMSMessageProcessor messageProcessor() {
        return new InboundHelloWorldJMSMessageProcessor();
    }

    @Bean
    public IntegrationFlow jmsInbound(ConnectionFactory connectionFactory) {
        return return IntegrationFlows
            .from(Jms.messageDrivenChannelAdapter(connectionFactory)
            .extractPayload(true)
            .destination("recipe-15-2"))
            .handle(messageProcessor())
            .get();
    }
}
```

As you can see, the most intimidating part is the schema import! The rest of the code is standard boilerplate. You define a connectionFactory exactly as if you were configuring a standard MDP.

Then, you define any beans specific to this solution, in this case, a bean that responds to messages coming in to the bus from the message queue, messageProcessor. A service activator is a generic endpoint in Spring Integration that's used to invoke functionality—whether it be an operation in a service, some routine in a regular POJO, or anything you want instead—in response to a message sent in on an input channel. Although this will be covered in some detail, it's interesting here only because you are using it to respond to messages. These beans taken together are the collaborators in the solution, and this example is fairly representative of how most integrations look. You define your collaborating components, and then you define the flow using the Spring Integration Java DSL that configures the solution itself.

■ **Tip**   There is also a Spring Integration Groovy DSL.

The configuration starts with IntegrationFlows, which is used to define how the messages flow through the system. The flow starts with the definition of messageDrivenChannelAdapter, which basically receives messages from the recipe-15-2 destination and passes it to a Spring Integration channel. messageDrivenChannelAdapter is, as the name suggests, an adapter. An adapter is a component that knows how to speak to a specific type of subsystem and translate messages on that subsystem into something

659

that can be used in the Spring Integration bus. Adapters also do the same in reverse, taking messages on the Spring Integration bus and translating them into something a specific subsystem will understand. This is different from a service activator (covered next) in that an adapter is meant to be a general connection between the bus and the foreign endpoint. A service activator, however, only helps you invoke your application's business logic on receipt of a message. What you do in the business logic, connecting to another system or not, is up to you.

The next component, a service activator, listens for messages coming into that channel and invokes the bean referenced through the handle method, which in this case is the messageProcessor bean defined previously. Because of the @ServiceActivator annotation on the method of the component, Spring Integration knows which method to invoke.

```
package com.apress.springrecipes.springintegration;

import org.slf4j.Logger;
import org.slf4j.LoggerFactory;
import org.springframework.integration.annotation.ServiceActivator;
import org.springframework.messaging.Message;

import java.util.Map;

public class InboundHelloWorldJMSMessageProcessor {

    private final Logger logger =
        LoggerFactory.getLogger(InboundHelloWorldJMSMessageProcessor.class);

    @ServiceActivator
    public void handleIncomingJmsMessage(Message<Map<String, Object>> inboundJmsMessage)
        throws Throwable {
        Map<String, Object> msg = inboundJmsMessage.getPayload();
        logger.info("firstName: {}, lastName: {}, id: {}", msg.get("firstName"),
                                                           msg.get("lastName"),
                                                           msg.get("id"));
    }
}
```

Notice that there is an annotation, @ServiceActivator, that tells Spring to configure this component, and this method as the recipient of the message payload from the channel, which is passed to the method as Message<Map<String, Object>> inboundJmsMessage. In the previous configuration, extract-payload="true" tells Spring Integration to take the payload of the message from the JMS queue (in this case, a Map<String,Object>) and extract it and pass that as the payload of the message that's being moved through Spring Integration's channels as a org.springframework.messaging.Message<T>. The Spring Message interface is not to be confused with the JMS Message interface, although they have some similarities. Had you not specified the extractPayload option, the type of payload on the Spring Message interface would have been javax.jms.Message. The onus of extracting the payload would have been on you, the developer, but sometimes getting access to that information is useful. Rewritten to handle unwrapping the javax.jms.Message interface, the example would look a little different, as shown here:

```java
package com.apress.springrecipes.springintegration;

import org.slf4j.Logger;
import org.slf4j.LoggerFactory;
import org.springframework.integration.annotation.ServiceActivator;
import org.springframework.messaging.Message;

import javax.jms.MapMessage;

public class InboundHelloWorldJMSMessageProcessor {

    private final Logger logger =
        LoggerFactory.getLogger(InboundHelloWorldJMSMessageProcessor.class);

    @ServiceActivator
    public void handleIncomingJmsMessageWithPayloadNotExtracted(
        Message<javax.jms.Message> msgWithJmsMessageAsPayload) throws Throwable {
        javax.jms.MapMessage jmsMessage =
            (MapMessage) msgWithJmsMessageAsPayload.getPayload();
        logger.debug("firstName: {}, lastName: {}, id: {}", jmsMessage.
                                                getString("firstName"),
                                                jmsMessage.
                                                getString("lastName"),
                                                jmsMessage.getLong("id"));
    }
}
```

You could have specified the payload type as the type of parameter passed into the method. If the payload of the message coming from JMS was of type Cat, for example, the method prototype could just as well have been public void handleIncomingJmsMessageWithPayloadNotExtracted(Cat inboundJmsMessage) throws Throwable. Spring Integration will figure out the right thing to do. In this case, we prefer access to Spring Message<T>, which has header values that can be useful to interrogate.

Also note that you don't need to specify throws Throwable. Error handling can be as generic or as specific as you want in Spring Integration.

In the example, you use the @ServiceActivator annotation to invoke the functionality where the integration ends. However, you can forward the response from the activation on to the next channel by returning a value from the method. The type of the return value is what will be used to determine the next message sent in the system. If you return a Message<T>, that will be sent directly. If you return something other than Message<T>, that value will be wrapped as a payload in a Message<T> instance, and that will become the next message that is ultimately sent to the next component in the processing pipeline. This Message<T> interface will be sent on the output channel that's configured on the service activator. There is no requirement to send a message on the output channel with the same type as the message that came on in the input channel; this is an effective way to transform the message type. A service activator is a very flexible component in which to put hooks to your system and to help mold the integration.

This solution is pretty straightforward, and in terms of configuration for one JMS queue, it's not really a win over straight MDPs because there's an extra level of indirection to overcome. The Spring Integration facilities make building complex integrations easier than Spring Core or EJB3 could because the configuration is centralized. You have a bird's-eye view of the entire integration, with routing and processing centralized, so you can better reposition the components in your integration. However, as you'll see, Spring Integration wasn't meant to compete with EJB and Spring Core; it shines at solutions that couldn't naturally be built using EJB3 or Spring Core.

15-3. Interrogate Spring Integration Messages for Context Information

Problem

You want more information about the message coming into the Spring Integration processing pipeline than the type of the message implicitly can give you.

Solution

Interrogate the Spring Integration `Message<T>` interface for header information specific to the message. These values are enumerated as header values in a map (of type `Map<String,Object>`).

How It Works

The Spring `Message<T>` interface is a generic wrapper that contains a pointer to the actual payload of the message as well as to headers that provide contextual message metadata. You can manipulate or augment this metadata to enable/enhance the functionality of components that are downstream, too; for example, when sending a message through e-mail, it's useful to specify the `TO/FROM` headers.

Any time you expose a class to the framework to handle some requirement (such as the logic you provide for the service activator component or a transformer component), there will be some chance to interact with `Message<T>` and with the message headers. Remember that Spring Integration pushes a `Message<T>` instance through a processing pipeline. Each component that interfaces with the `Message<T>` instance has to act on it, do something with it, or forward it on. One way of providing information to those components, and of getting information about what's happened in the components up until that point, is to interrogate `MessageHeaders`.

You should be aware of several values when working with Spring Integration (see Tables 15-1 and 15-2). These constants are exposed on the `org.springframework.messaging.MessageHeaders` interface and `org.springframework.integration.IntegrationMessageHeaderAccessor`.

Table 15-1. *Common Headers Found in Core Spring Messaging*

Constant	Description
ID	This is a unique value assigned to the message by the Spring Integration engine.
TIMESTAMP	This is the timestamp assigned to the message.
REPLY_CHANNEL	This is the `String` name of the channel to which the output of the current component should be sent. This can be overridden.
ERROR_CHANNEL	This is the `String` name of the channel to which the output of the current component should be sent if an exception bubbles up into the runtime. This can be overridden.
CONTENT_TYPE	This is the content type (MIME type) of the message, mainly used for Web Socket messages.

In addition to the headers defined by Spring Messaging, there are some commonly used headers in Spring Integration; these are defined in the org.springframework.integration.IntegrationMessageHeaderAccessor class (see Table 15-2).

Table 15-2. *Common Headers Found in Spring Integration*

Constant	Description
CORRELATION_ID	This is optional and used by some components (such as aggregators) to group messages together in some sort of processing pipeline.
EXPIRATION_DATE	This is used by some components as a threshold for processing after which a component can wait no longer in processing.
PRIORITY	This is the priority of the message; higher numbers indicate a higher priority.
SEQUENCE_NUMBER	This is the order in which the message is to be sequenced; it is typically used with a sequencer.
SEQUENCE_SIZE	This is the size of the sequence so that an aggregator can know when to stop waiting for more messages and move forward. This is useful in implementing join functionality.
ROUTING_SLIP	This is the header containing the information when the Routing Slip pattern is used.
CLOSEABLE_RESOURCE	This is optional and used by some components to determine if the message payload can/should be closed (like a File or InputStream).

Some header values are specific to the type of the source message's payload; for example, payloads sourced from a file on the file system are different from those coming in from a JMS queue, which are different from messages coming from an e-mail system. These different components are typically packaged in their own JARs, and there's usually some class that provides constants for accessing these headers. Component-specific headers are examples of the constants defined for files on org.springframework.integration.file.FileHeaders: FILENAME and PREFIX. Naturally, when in doubt, you can just enumerate the values manually because the headers are just a java.util.Map instance.

```
package com.apress.springrecipes.springintegration;

import org.slf4j.Logger;
import org.slf4j.LoggerFactory;
import org.springframework.integration.annotation.ServiceActivator;
import org.springframework.messaging.Message;
import org.springframework.messaging.MessageHeaders;

import java.io.File;
import java.util.Map;

public class InboundFileMessageServiceActivator {
    private final Logger logger = LoggerFactory.getLogger(InboundFileMessageService
    Activator.class);
```

```
@ServiceActivator
public void interrogateMessage(Message<File> message) {
    MessageHeaders headers = message.getHeaders();
    for (Map.Entry<String, Object> header : headers.entrySet()) {
        logger.debug("{} : {}", header.getKey(), header.getValue() );
    }
}
}
```

These headers let you interrogate the specific features of these messages without surfacing them as a concrete interface dependency if you don't want them. They can also be used to help processing and allow you to specify custom metadata to downstream components. The act of providing extra data for the benefit of a downstream component is called *message enrichment*. Message enrichment is when you take the headers of a given message and add to them, usually to the benefit of components in the processing pipeline downstream. You might imagine processing a message to add a customer to a customer relationship management (CRM) system that makes a call to a third-party web site to establish credit ratings. This credit is added to the headers so the component downstream, which is tasked with adding or rejecting customers, can make its decisions on these header values.

Another way to get access to header metadata is to simply have it passed as parameters to your component's method. You simply annotate the parameter with the @Header annotation, and Spring Integration will take care of the rest.

```
package com.apress.springrecipes.springintegration;

import java.io.File;

import org.slf4j.Logger;
import org.slf4j.LoggerFactory;
import org.springframework.integration.annotation.ServiceActivator;
import org.springframework.integration.file.FileHeaders;
import org.springframework.messaging.MessageHeaders;
import org.springframework.messaging.handler.annotation.Header;

public class InboundFileMessageServiceActivator {
    private final Logger logger = LoggerFactory.getLogger(InboundFileMessageService
    Activator.class);

    @ServiceActivator
    public void interrogateMessage(
        @Header(MessageHeaders.ID) String uuid,
        @Header(FileHeaders.FILENAME) String fileName, File file) {
        logger.debug("the id of the message is {}, and name of the file payload is {}",
        uuid, fileName);
    }
}
```

You can also have Spring Integration simply pass Map<String,Object>.

```
package com.apress.springrecipes.springintegration;

import java.io.File;
import java.util.Map;

import org.slf4j.Logger;
import org.slf4j.LoggerFactory;
import org.springframework.integration.annotation.ServiceActivator;
import org.springframework.integration.file.FileHeaders;
import org.springframework.messaging.MessageHeaders;
import org.springframework.messaging.handler.annotation.Header;

public class InboundFileMessageServiceActivator {
    private final Logger logger = LoggerFactory.getLogger(InboundFileMessageService
    Activator.class);

    @ServiceActivator
    public void interrogateMessage(
        @Header(MessageHeaders.ID) Map<String, Object> headers, File file) {
        logger.debug("the id of the message is {}, and name of the file payload is {}",
            headers.get(MessageHeaders.ID), headers.get(FileHeaders.FILENAME));
    }
}
```

15-4. Integrate Two Systems Using a File System

Problem

You want to build a solution that takes files on a well-known, shared file system and uses them as the conduit for integration with another system. An example might be that your application produces a comma-separated value (CSV) dump of all the customers added to a system every hour. The company's third-party financial system is updated with these sales by a process that checks a shared folder, mounted over a network file system, and processes the CSV records. What's required is a way to treat the presence of a new file as an event on the bus.

Solution

You have an idea of how this could be built by using standard techniques, but you want something more elegant. Let Spring Integration isolate you from the event-driven nature of the file system and from the file input/output requirements. Instead, let's use it to focus on writing the code that deals with the java.io.File payload itself. With this approach, you can write unit-testable code that accepts an input and responds by adding the customers to the financial system. When the functionality is finished, you configure it in the Spring Integration pipeline and let Spring Integration invoke your functionality whenever a new file is recognized on the file system. This is an example of an event-driven architecture (EDA). EDAs let you ignore how an event was generated and focus instead on reacting to them, in much the same way that event-driven GUIs let you change the focus of your code from controlling how a user triggers an action to actually reacting to the invocation itself. Spring Integration makes it a natural approach for loosely coupled solutions. In fact, this code should look similar to the solution you built for the JMS queue because it's just another class that takes a parameter (a Spring Integration Message<T> interface, a parameter of the same type as the payload of the message, and so on).

How It Works

Building a solution to talk to JMS is old hat. Instead, let's consider what building a solution using a shared file system might look like. Imagine how to build it without an ESB solution. You need some mechanism by which to poll the file system periodically and detect new files. Perhaps Quartz and some sort of cache? You need something to read in these files quickly and then pass the payload to your processing logic efficiently. Finally, your system needs to work with that payload.

Spring Integration frees you from all that infrastructure code; all you need to do is configure it. There are some issues with dealing with file system–based processing, however, that are up to you to resolve. Behind the scenes, Spring Integration is still dealing with polling the file system and detecting new files. It can't possibly have a semantically correct idea for your application of when a file is "completely" written, and thus providing a way around that is up to you.

Several approaches exist. You might write out a file and then write another zero-byte file. The presence of that file would mean it's safe to assume that the real payload is present. Configure Spring Integration to look for that file. If it finds it, it knows that there's another file (perhaps with the same name and a different file extension?) and that it can start reading it/working with it. Another solution along the same line is to have the client ("producer") write the file to the directory using a name that the glob pattern that Spring Integration is using to poll the directory won't detect. Then, when it's finished writing, issue an mv command if you trust your file system to do the right thing there.

Let's revisit the first solution, but this time with a file-based adapter. The configuration looks conceptually the same as before, except the configuration for the adapter has changed, and with that has gone a lot of the configuration for the JMS adapter, like the connection factory. Instead, you tell Spring Integration about a different source from whence messages will come: the file system.

```
package com.apress.springrecipes.springintegration;

import org.springframework.beans.factory.annotation.Value;
import org.springframework.context.annotation.Bean;
import org.springframework.context.annotation.ComponentScan;
import org.springframework.context.annotation.Configuration;
import org.springframework.integration.config.EnableIntegration;
import org.springframework.integration.dsl.IntegrationFlow;
import org.springframework.integration.dsl.IntegrationFlows;
import org.springframework.integration.dsl.Pollers;
import org.springframework.integration.file.dsl.Files;

import java.io.File;
import java.util.concurrent.TimeUnit;

@Configuration
@EnableIntegration
@ComponentScan
public class IntegrationConfiguration {

    @Bean
    public InboundHelloWorldFileMessageProcessor messageProcessor() {
        return new InboundHelloWorldFileMessageProcessor();
    }
```

```
@Bean
public IntegrationFlow inboundFileFlow(@Value("${user.home}/inboundFiles/new/") File
directory) {
    return IntegrationFlows
        .from(
            Files.inboundAdapter(directory).patternFilter("*.csv"),
            c -> c.poller(Pollers.fixedRate(10, TimeUnit.SECONDS)))
        .handle(messageProcessor())
        .get();
    }
}
```

This is nothing you haven't already seen, really. The code for `Files.inboundAdapter` is the only new element. The code for the `@ServiceActivator` annotation has changed to reflect the fact that you're expecting a message containing a message of type `Message<java.io.File>`.

```
package com.apress.springrecipes.springintegration;

import org.slf4j.Logger;
import org.slf4j.LoggerFactory;
import org.springframework.integration.annotation.ServiceActivator;
import org.springframework.messaging.Message;

import java.io.File;

public class InboundHelloWorldFileMessageProcessor {
    private final Logger logger = LoggerFactory.getLogger(InboundHelloWorldFileMessage
    Processor.class);

    @ServiceActivator
    public void handleIncomingFileMessage(Message<File> inboundJmsMessage)
        throws Throwable {
        File filePayload = inboundJmsMessage.getPayload();
        logger.debug("absolute path: {}, size: {}", filePayload.getAbsolutePath(),
        filePayload.length());
    }
}
```

15-5. Transform a Message from One Type to Another

Problem

You want to send a message into the bus and transform it before working with it further. Usually, this is done to adapt the message to the requirements of a component downstream. You might also want to transform a message by enriching it—adding extra headers or augmenting the payload so that components downstream in the processing pipeline can benefit from it.

Solution

Use a transformer component to take a Message<T> interface of a payload and send Message<T> out with a payload of a different type. You can also use the transformer to add extra headers or update the values of headers for the benefit of components downstream in the processing pipeline.

How It Works

Spring Integration provides a transformer message endpoint to permit the augmentation of the message headers or the transformation of the message itself. In Spring Integration, components are chained together, and output from one component is returned by way of the method invoked for that component. The return value of the method is passed out on the "reply channel" for the component to the next component, which receives it as an input parameter. A transformer component lets you change the type of the object being returned or add extra headers, and that updated object is what is passed to the next component in the chain.

Modify a Message's Payload

The configuration of a transformer component is very much in keeping with everything you've seen so far.

```
package com.apress.springrecipes.springintegration;

import org.springframework.integration.annotation.Transformer;
import org.springframework.messaging.Message;

import java.util.Map;

public class InboundJMSMessageToCustomerTransformer {

    @Transformer
    public Customer transformJMSMapToCustomer(
        Message<Map<String, Object>> inboundSprignIntegrationMessage) {
        Map<String, Object> jmsMessagePayload =
            inboundSprignIntegrationMessage.getPayload();
        Customer customer = new Customer();
        customer.setFirstName((String) jmsMessagePayload.get("firstName"));
        customer.setLastName((String) jmsMessagePayload.get("lastName"));
        customer.setId((Long) jmsMessagePayload.get("id"));
        return customer;
    }
}
```

Nothing terribly complex is happening here: a Message<T> interface of type Map<String,Object> is passed in. The values are manually extracted and used to build an object of type Customer. The Customer object is returned, which has the effect of passing it out on the reply channel for this component. The next component in the configuration will receive this object as its input Message<T>.

The solution is mostly the same as you've seen, but there is a new transformer element.

```java
package com.apress.springrecipes.springintegration;

import javax.jms.ConnectionFactory;

import org.apache.activemq.ActiveMQConnectionFactory;
import org.springframework.context.annotation.Bean;
import org.springframework.context.annotation.ComponentScan;
import org.springframework.context.annotation.Configuration;
import org.springframework.integration.config.EnableIntegration;
import org.springframework.integration.dsl.IntegrationFlow;
import org.springframework.integration.dsl.IntegrationFlows;
import org.springframework.integration.jms.dsl.Jms;
import org.springframework.jms.connection.CachingConnectionFactory;
import org.springframework.jms.core.JmsTemplate;

@Configuration
@EnableIntegration
@ComponentScan
public class IntegrationConfiguration {

    @Bean
    public CachingConnectionFactory connectionFactory() {
        ActiveMQConnectionFactory connectionFactory =
            new ActiveMQConnectionFactory("tcp://localhost:61616");
        return new CachingConnectionFactory(connectionFactory);
    }

    @Bean
    public JmsTemplate jmsTemplate(ConnectionFactory connectionFactory) {
        return new JmsTemplate(connectionFactory);
    }

    @Bean
    public InboundJMSMessageToCustomerTransformer customerTransformer() {
        return new InboundJMSMessageToCustomerTransformer();
    }

    @Bean
    public InboundCustomerServiceActivator customerServiceActivator() {
        return new InboundCustomerServiceActivator();
    }

    @Bean
    public IntegrationFlow jmsInbound(ConnectionFactory connectionFactory) {
        return IntegrationFlows
            .from(Jms.messageDrivenChannelAdapter(connectionFactory).
             extractPayload(true).destination("recipe-15-5"))
            .transform(customerTransformer())
            .handle(customerServiceActivator())
            .get();
    }
}
```

Here, you're specifying a `messageDrivenChannelAdapter` component that moves the incoming content to an `InboundJMSMessageToCustomerTransformer`, which transforms it into a `Customer`, and that `Customer` is sent to the `InboundCustomerServiceActivator`.

The code in the next component can now declare a dependency on the `Customer` interface with impunity. You can, with transformers, receive messages from any number of sources and transform them into a `Customer` so that you can reuse the `InboundCustomerServiceActivator` instance.

```
package com.apress.springrecipes.springintegration;

import org.slf4j.Logger;
import org.slf4j.LoggerFactory;
import org.springframework.integration.annotation.ServiceActivator;
import org.springframework.messaging.Message;

public class InboundCustomerServiceActivator {
    private static final Logger logger = LoggerFactory.getLogger(InboundCustomerService
    Activator.class);

    @ServiceActivator
    public void doSomethingWithCustomer(Message<Customer> customerMessage) {
        Customer customer = customerMessage.getPayload();
        logger.debug("id={}, firstName: {}, lastName: {}",
            customer.getId(), customer.getFirstName(), customer.getLastName());
    }
}
```

Modify a Message's Headers

Sometimes changing a message's payload isn't enough. Sometimes you want to update the payload as well as the headers. Doing this is slightly more interesting because it involves using the `MessageBuilder<T>` class, which allows you to create new `Message<T>` objects with any specified payload and any specified header data. The XML configuration is identical in this case.

```
package com.apress.springrecipes.springintegration;

import org.springframework.integration.annotation.Transformer;
import org.springframework.integration.core.Message;
import org.springframework.integration.message.MessageBuilder;

import java.util.Map;

public class InboundJMSMessageToCustomerTransformer {
    @Transformer
    public Message<Customer> transformJMSMapToCustomer(
        Message<Map<String, Object>> inboundSpringIntegrationMessage) {
        Map<String, Object> jmsMessagePayload =
            inboundSpringIntegrationMessage.getPayload();
        Customer customer = new Customer();
        customer.setFirstName((String) jmsMessagePayload.get("firstName"));
        customer.setLastName((String) jmsMessagePayload.get("lastName"));
        customer.setId((Long) jmsMessagePayload.get("id"));
```

```
    return MessageBuilder.withPayload(customer)
        .copyHeadersIfAbsent( inboundSpringIntegrationMessage.getHeaders())
        .setHeaderIfAbsent("randomlySelectedForSurvey", Math.random() > .5)
        .build();
    }
}
```

As before, this code is simply a method with an input and an output. The output is constructed dynamically using MessageBuilder<T> to create a message that has the same payload as the input message as well as copy the existing headers and adds an extra header: randomlySelectedForSurvey.

15-6. Handle Errors Using Spring Integration

Problem

Spring Integration brings together systems distributed across different nodes; computers; and services, protocol, and language stacks. Indeed, a Spring Integration solution might not even finish in remotely the same time period as when it started. Exception handling, then, can never be as simple as a language-level try/catch block in a single thread for any component with asynchronous behavior. This implies that many of the kinds of solutions you're likely to build, with channels and queues of any kind, need a way of signaling an error that is distributed and natural to the component that created the error. Thus, an error might get sent over a JMS queue on a different continent, or in process, on a queue in a different thread.

Solution

Use Spring Integration's support for an error channel, both implicitly and explicitly via code.

How It Works

Spring Integration provides the ability to catch exceptions and send them to an error channel of your choosing. By default, it's a global channel called errorChannel. By default Spring Integration registers a handler called LoggingHandler to this channel, which does nothing more than log the exception and stacktrace. To make this work, you have to tell the message-driven channel adapter that you want the error to be sent to errorChannel; you can do this by configuring the error channel attribute.

```
@Bean
public IntegrationFlow jmsInbound(ConnectionFactory connectionFactory) {
    return IntegrationFlows
        .from(Jms.messageDrivenChannelAdapter(connectionFactory).extractPayload(true).
        destination("recipe-15-6").errorChannel("errorChannel"))
        .transform(customerTransformer())
        .handle(customerServiceActivator())
        .get();
}
```

Use a Custom Handler to Handle Exceptions

Of course, you can also have components subscribe to messages from this channel to override the exception-handling behavior. You can create a class that will be invoked whenever a message comes in on the errorChannel channel.

```
@Bean
public IntegrationFlow errorFlow() {
    return IntegrationFlows
        .from("errorChannel")
        .handle(errorHandlingServiceActivator())
        .get();
}
```

The Java code is exactly as you'd expect it to be. Of course, the component that receives the error message from the errorChannel channel doesn't need to be a service activator. You are just using it for convenience here. The code for the following service activator depicts some of the machinations you might go through to build a handler for errorChannel:

```
package com.apress.springrecipes.springintegration;

import org.slf4j.Logger;
import org.slf4j.LoggerFactory;
import org.springframework.integration.annotation.ServiceActivator;
import org.springframework.messaging.Message;
import org.springframework.messaging.MessagingException;

public class DefaultErrorHandlingServiceActivator {
    private static final Logger logger = LoggerFactory.getLogger(DefaultErrorHandlingService
    Activator.class);

    @ServiceActivator
    public void handleThrowable(Message<Throwable> errorMessage)
        throws Throwable {
        Throwable throwable = errorMessage.getPayload();
        logger.debug("Message: {}", throwable.getMessage(), throwable);

        if (throwable instanceof MessagingException) {
            Message<?> failedMessage = ((MessagingException) throwable).getFailedMessage();

            if (failedMessage != null) {
                // do something with the original message
            }
        } else {
            // it's something that was thrown in the execution of code in some component you
            created
        }
    }
}
```

All errors thrown from Spring Integration components will be a subclass of MessagingException. MessagingException carries a pointer to the original Message that caused an error, which you can dissect for more context information. In the example, you're doing a nasty instanceof. Clearly, being able to delegate to custom exception handlers based on the type of exception would be useful.

Route to Custom Handlers Based on the Type of Exception

Sometimes more specific error handling is required. In the following code, this router is configured as an exception-type router, which in turn listens to errorChannel. It then splinters off, using the type of the exception as the predicate in determining which channel should get the results.

```
@Bean
public ErrorMessageExceptionTypeRouter exceptionTypeRouter() {
    ErrorMessageExceptionTypeRouter router = new ErrorMessageExceptionTypeRouter();
    router.setChannelMapping(MyCustomException.class.getName(), "customExceptionChannel");
    router.setChannelMapping(RuntimeException.class.getName(), "runtimeExceptionChannel");
    router.setChannelMapping(MessageHandlingException.class.getName(),
    "messageHandlingExceptionChannel");
    return router;
}

@Bean
public IntegrationFlow errorFlow() {
    return IntegrationFlows
        .from("errorChannel")
        .route(exceptionTypeRouter())
        .get();
}
```

Build a Solution with Multiple Error Channels

The preceding example might work fine for simple cases, but often different integrations require different error-handling approaches, which implies that sending all the errors to the same channel can eventually lead to a large switch-laden class that's too complex to maintain. Instead, it's better to selectively route error messages to the error channel most appropriate to each integration. This avoids centralizing all error handling. One way to do that is to explicitly specify on what channel errors for a given integration should go. The following example shows a component (service activator) that, upon receiving a message, adds a header indicating the name of the error channel. Spring Integration will use that header and forward errors encountered in the processing of this message to that channel.

```
package com.apress.springrecipes.springintegration;

import org.apache.log4j.Logger;
import org.springframework.integration.annotation.ServiceActivator;
import org.springframework.integration.core.Message;
import org.springframework.integration.core.MessageHeaders;
import org.springframework.integration.message.MessageBuilder;
```

```java
public class ServiceActivatorThatSpecifiesErrorChannel {
    private static final Logger logger = Logger.getLogger(
        ServiceActivatorThatSpecifiesErrorChannel.class);

    @ServiceActivator
    public Message<?> startIntegrationFlow(Message<?> firstMessage)
        throws Throwable {
        return MessageBuilder.fromMessage(firstMessage).
            setHeaderIfAbsent( MessageHeaders.ERROR_CHANNEL,
                "errorChannelForMySolution").build();
    }
}
```

Thus, all errors that come from the integration in which this component is used will be directed to customErrorChannel, to which you can subscribe any component you like.

15-7. Fork Integration Control: Splitters and Aggregators

Problem

You want to fork the process flow from one component to many, either all at once or to a single one based on a predicate condition.

Solution

You can use a splitter component (and maybe its cohort, the aggregator component) to fork and join (respectively) control of processing.

How It Works

One of the fundamental cornerstones of an ESB is routing. You've seen how components can be chained together to create sequences in which progression is mostly linear. Some solutions require the capability to split a message into many constituent parts. One reason this might be is that some problems are parallel in nature and don't depend on each other in order to complete. You should strive to achieve the efficiencies of parallelism wherever possible.

Use a Splitter

It's often useful to divide large payloads into separate messages with separate processing flows. In Spring Integration, this is accomplished by using a splitter component. A splitter takes an input message and asks you, the user of the component, on what basis it should split Message<T>: you're responsible for providing the split functionality. Once you've told Spring Integration how to split Message<T>, it forwards each result out on the output channel of the splitter component. In a few cases, Spring Integration ships with useful splitters that require no customization. One example is the splitter provided to partition an XML payload along an XPath query, XPathMessageSplitter.

One example of a useful application of a splitter might be a text file with rows of data, each of which must be processed. Your goal is to be able to submit each row to a service that will handle the processing. What's required is a way to extract each row and forward each row as a new Message<T>. The configuration for such a solution looks like this:

```java
@Configuration
@EnableIntegration
public class IntegrationConfiguration {

    @Bean
    public CustomerBatchFileSplitter splitter() {
        return new CustomerBatchFileSplitter();
    }

    @Bean
    public CustomerDeletionServiceActivator customerDeletionServiceActivator() {
        return new CustomerDeletionServiceActivator();
    }

    @Bean
    public IntegrationFlow fileSplitAndDelete(@Value("file:${user.home}/customerstoremove/
    new/") File inputDirectory) throws Exception {

        return IntegrationFlows.from(
            Files.inboundAdapter(inputDirectory).patternFilter("customerstoremove-*.txt"),
            c -> c.poller(Pollers.fixedRate(1, TimeUnit.SECONDS)))
            .split(splitter())
            .handle(customerDeletionServiceActivator())
            .get();
    }
}
```

The configuration for this is not terribly different from the previous solutions. The Java code is just about the same as well, except that the return type of the method annotated by the @Splitter annotation is of type java.util.Collection.

```java
package com.apress.springrecipes.springintegration;

import org.springframework.integration.annotation.Splitter;

import java.io.File;
import java.io.IOException;
import java.nio.file.Files;
import java.util.Collection;

public class CustomerBatchFileSplitter {

    @Splitter
    public Collection<String> splitAFile(File file) throws IOException {
        System.out.printf("Reading %s....%n", file.getAbsolutePath());
        return Files.readAllLines(file.toPath());
    }
}
```

A message payload is passed in as a `java.io.File` component, and the contents are read. The result (a collection or array value; in this case, a `Collection<String>` collection) is returned. Spring Integration executes a kind of `foreach` on the results, sending each value in the collection out on the output channel configured for the splitter. Often, you split messages so that the individual pieces can be forwarded to processing that's more focused. Because the message is more manageable, the processing requirements are dampened. This is true in many different architectures. In map/reduce solutions, tasks are split and then processed in parallel, and the fork/join constructs in a BPM system let control flow proceed in parallel so that the total work product can be achieved quicker.

Use Aggregators

At some point you'll need to do the reverse: combine many messages into one and create a single result that can be returned on the output channel. An `@Aggregator` collects a series of messages (based on some correlation that you help Spring Integration make between the messages) and publishes a single message to the components downstream. Suppose that you know you're expecting 22 different messages from 22 actors in the system, but you don't know when. This is similar to a company that auctions off a contract and collects all the bids from different vendors before choosing the ultimate vendor. The company can't accept a bid until all bids have been received from all companies. Otherwise, there's the risk of prematurely signing a contract that would not be in the best interest of the company. An aggregator is perfect for building this type of logic.

There are many ways for Spring Integration to correlate incoming messages. To determine how many messages to read until it can stop, it uses the class `SequenceSizeCompletionStrategy`, which reads a well-known header value. (Aggregators are often used after a splitter. Thus, the default header value is provided by the splitter, though there's nothing stopping you from creating the header parameters yourself.) The class `SequenceSizeCompletionStrategy` calculates how many it should look for and notes the index of the message relative to the expected total count (e.g., 3/22).

For correlation when you might not have a size but know that you're expecting messages that share a common header value within a known time, Spring Integration provides `HeaderAttributeCorrelationStrategy`. In this way, it knows that all messages with that value are from the same group, in the same way that your last name identifies you as being part of a larger group.

Let's revisit the previous example. Suppose that the file was split (by lines, each belonging to a new customer) and subsequently processed. You now want to reunite the customers and do some cleanup with everyone at the same time. In this example, you use the default completion strategy and correlation strategy, and as such you can use the default `aggregate()` in the integration flow configuration. The result is passed to another service activator, which will print a small summary.

```
package com.apress.springrecipes.springintegration;

import org.springframework.beans.factory.annotation.Value;
import org.springframework.context.annotation.Bean;
import org.springframework.context.annotation.Configuration;
import org.springframework.integration.config.EnableIntegration;
import org.springframework.integration.dsl.IntegrationFlow;
import org.springframework.integration.dsl.IntegrationFlows;
import org.springframework.integration.dsl.Pollers;
import org.springframework.integration.file.dsl.Files;

import java.io.File;
import java.util.concurrent.TimeUnit;
```

```java
@Configuration
@EnableIntegration
public class IntegrationConfiguration {

    @Bean
    public CustomerBatchFileSplitter splitter() {
        return new CustomerBatchFileSplitter();
    }

    @Bean
    public CustomerDeletionServiceActivator customerDeletionServiceActivator() {
        return new CustomerDeletionServiceActivator();
    }

    @Bean
    public SummaryServiceActivator summaryServiceActivator() {
        return new SummaryServiceActivator();
    }

    @Bean
    public IntegrationFlow fileSplitAndDelete(@Value("file:${user.home}/customerstoremove/
new/") File inputDirectory) throws Exception {

        return IntegrationFlows.from(
            Files.inboundAdapter(inputDirectory).patternFilter("customerstoremove-*.txt"),
            c -> c.poller(Pollers.fixedRate(1, TimeUnit.SECONDS)))
            .split(splitter())
            .handle(customerDeletionServiceActivator())
            .aggregate()
            .handle(summaryServiceActivator())
            .get();
    }
}
```

The Java code for SummaryServiceActivator is quite simple.

```java
package com.apress.springrecipes.springintegration;

import org.springframework.integration.annotation.ServiceActivator;

import java.util.Collection;

public class SummaryServiceActivator {

    @ServiceActivator
    public void summary(Collection<Customer> customers) {
        System.out.printf("Removed %s customers.%n", customers.size());
    }
}
```

15-8. Implement Conditional Routing with Routers

Problem

You want to conditionally move a message through different processes based on some criteria. This is the EAI equivalent to an if/else branch.

Solution

You can use a router component to alter the processing flow based on some predicate. You can also use a router to multicast a message to many subscribers (as you did with the splitter).

How It Works

With a router you can specify a known list of channels on which the incoming Message object should be passed. This has some powerful implications. It means you can change the flow of a process conditionally, and it also means you can forward a Message object to as many (or as few) channels as you want. There are some convenient default routers available to fill common needs, such as payload-type–based routing (PayloadTypeRouter) and routing to a group or list of channels (RecipientListRouter).

Imagine, for example, a processing pipeline that routes customers with high credit scores to one service and customers with lower credit scores to another process in which the information is queued up for a human audit and verification cycle. The configuration is, as usual, very straightforward. The following example shows the configuration. One router element, which in turn delegates the routing logic to a class, is CustomerCreditScoreRouter.

```
@Bean
public IntegrationFlow fileSplitAndDelete(@Value("file:${user.home}/customerstoimport/new/")
File inputDirectory) throws Exception {

    return IntegrationFlows.from(
        Files.inboundAdapter(inputDirectory).patternFilter("customers-*.txt"), c ->
        c.poller(Pollers.fixedRate(1, TimeUnit.SECONDS)))
        .split(splitter())
        .transform(transformer())
        .<Customer, Boolean>route(c -> c.getCreditScore() > 770,
            m -> m
                .channelMapping(Boolean.TRUE, "safeCustomerChannel")
                .channelMapping(Boolean.FALSE, "riskyCustomerChannel").applySequence(false)
        ).get();
}
```

You could use a class with a method annotated with @Router instead. It feels a lot like a workflow engine's conditional element, or even a JSF backing-bean method, in that it extricates the routing logic into the XML configuration, away from code, delaying the decision until runtime. In the example, the Strings returned are the names of the channels on which the Message component should pass.

```
package com.apress.springrecipes.springintegration;

import org.springframework.integration.annotation.Router;

public class CustomerCreditScoreRouter {

    @Router
    public String routeByCustomerCreditScore(Customer customer) {
        if (customer.getCreditScore() > 770) {
            return "safeCustomerChannel";
        } else {
            return "riskyCustomerChannel";
        }
    }
}
```

If you decide that you'd rather not let Message<T> pass and want to stop processing, you can return null instead of a String.

15-9. Stage Events Using Spring Batch

Problem

You have a file with a million records in it. This file is too big to handle as one event; it's far more natural to react to each row as an event.

Solution

Spring Batch works very well with these types of solutions. It allows you to take an input file or a payload and reliably and systematically decompose it into events that an ESB can work with.

How It Works

Spring Integration does support reading files into the bus, and Spring Batch does support providing custom, unique endpoints for data. However, just like Mom always says, "just because you can doesn't mean you should." Although it seems as if there's a lot of overlap here, it turns out that there is a distinction (albeit a fine one). While both systems will work with files and message queues, or anything else you could conceivably write code to talk to, Spring Integration doesn't do well with large payloads because it's hard to deal with something as large as a file with a million rows that might require hours of work as an event. That's simply too big a burden for an ESB. At that point, the term *event* has no meaning. A million records in a CSV file isn't an event on a bus; it's a file with a million records, each of which might in turn be events. It's a subtle distinction.

A file with a million rows needs to be decomposed into smaller events. Spring Batch can help here: it allows you to systematically read through, apply validations, and optionally skip and retry invalid records. The processing can begin on an ESB such as Spring Integration. Spring Batch and Spring Integration can be used together to build truly scalable decoupled systems.

Staged event-driven architecture (SEDA) is an architecture style that deals with this sort of processing situation. In SEDA, you dampen the load on components of the architecture by staging it in queues and advance only those the components downstream can handle. Put another way, imagine video processing.

If you ran a site with a million users uploading video that in turn needed to be transcoded and you had only ten servers, your system would fail if your system attempted to process each video as soon as it received the uploaded video. Transcoding can take hours and pegs a CPU (or multiple CPUs!) while the system works. The most sensible thing to do would be to store the file and then, as capacity permits, process each one. In this way, the load on the nodes that handle transcoding is managed. There's always only enough work to keep the machine humming, but not overrun.

Similarly, no processing system (such as an ESB) can deal with a million records at once efficiently. Strive to decompose bigger events and messages into smaller ones. Let's imagine a hypothetical solution designed to accommodate a drop of batch files representing hourly sales destined for fulfillment. The batch files are dropped onto a mount that Spring Integration is monitoring. Spring Integration kicks off processing as soon as it sees a new file. Spring Integration tells Spring Batch about the file and launches a Spring Batch job asynchronously.

Spring Batch reads the file, transforms the records into objects, and writes the output to a JMS topic with a key correlating the original batch to the JMS message. Naturally, this takes half a day to get done, but it does get done. Spring Integration, completely unaware that the job it started half a day ago is now finished, begins popping messages off the topic, one by one. Processing to fulfill the records would begin. Simple processing involving multiple components might begin on the ESB.

If fulfillment is a long-lived process with a long-lived, conversational state involving many actors, perhaps the fulfillment for each record could be farmed to a BPM engine. The BPM engine would thread together the different actors and work lists and allow work to continue over the course of days instead of the small millisecond time frames Spring Integration is more geared to. In this example, we talked about using Spring Batch as a springboard to dampen the load for components downstream. In this case, the component downstream was again a Spring Integration process that took the work and set it up to be funneled into a BPM engine where final processing could begin. Spring Integration could use directory polling as a trigger to start a batch job and supply the name of the file to process. To launch a job from Spring Integration, Spring Batch provides the `JobLaunchingMessageHandler` class. This class takes a `JobLaunchRequest` instance to determine which job with which parameters to start. You have to create a transformer to change the incoming `Message<File>` to a `JobLaunchRequest` instance.

The transformer could look like the following:

```
package com.apress.springrecipes.springintegration;

import org.springframework.batch.core.Job;
import org.springframework.batch.core.JobParametersBuilder;
import org.springframework.batch.integration.launch.JobLaunchRequest;
import org.springframework.integration.annotation.Transformer;

import java.io.File;

public class FileToJobLaunchRequestTransformer {

    private final Job job;
    private final String fileParameterName;

    public FileToJobLaunchRequestTransformer(Job job, String fileParameterName) {
        this.job=job;
        this.fileParameterName=fileParameterName;
    }
```

```
@Transformer
public JobLaunchRequest transform(File file) throws Exception {

    JobParametersBuilder builder = new JobParametersBuilder();
    builder.addString(fileParameterName, file.getAbsolutePath());
    return new JobLaunchRequest(job, builder.toJobParameters());
  }
}
```

The transformer needs a Job object and a filename parameter to be constructed; this parameter is used in the Spring Batch job to determine which file needs to be loaded. The incoming message is transformed in a JobLaunchRequest using the full name of the file as a parameter value. This request can be used to launch a batch job.

To wire everything together, you can use the following configuration (note the Spring Batch setup is missing here; see Chapter 11 for information on setting up Spring Batch):

```
package com.apress.springrecipes.springintegration;

import org.springframework.batch.core.Job;
import org.springframework.batch.core.launch.JobLauncher;
import org.springframework.batch.integration.launch.JobLaunchingMessageHandler;
import org.springframework.beans.factory.annotation.Value;
import org.springframework.context.annotation.Bean;
import org.springframework.integration.dsl.IntegrationFlow;
import org.springframework.integration.dsl.IntegrationFlows;
import org.springframework.integration.dsl.Pollers;
import org.springframework.integration.file.dsl.Files;

import java.io.File;
import java.util.concurrent.TimeUnit;

public class IntegrationConfiguration {

    @Bean
    public FileToJobLaunchRequestTransformer transformer(Job job) {
        return new FileToJobLaunchRequestTransformer(job, "filename");
    }

    @Bean
    public JobLaunchingMessageHandler jobLaunchingMessageHandler(JobLauncher jobLauncher) {
        return new JobLaunchingMessageHandler(jobLauncher);
    }

    @Bean
    public IntegrationFlow fileToBatchFlow(@Value("file:${user.home}/customerstoimport/
new/") File directory, FileToJobLaunchRequestTransformer transformer,
JobLaunchingMessageHandler handler) {
        return IntegrationFlows
            .from(Files.inboundAdapter(directory).patternFilter("customers-*.txt"),
            c -> c.poller(Pollers.fixedRate(10, TimeUnit.SECONDS)))
            .transform(transformer)
```

```
            .handle(handler)
        .get();

    }

}
```

`FileToJobLaunchRequestTransformer` is configured as well as `JobLaunchingMessageHandler`. A file-inbound channel adapter is used to poll for files. When a file is detected, a message is placed on a channel. A chain is configured to listen to that channel. When a message is received, it is first transformed and next passed on to `JobLaunchingMessageHandler`.

Now a batch job will be launched to process the file. A typical job would probably use a `FlatFileItemReader` to actually read the file passed using the `filename` parameter. A `JmsItemWriter` could be used to write messages per read row on a topic. In Spring Integration, a JMS-inbound channel adapter could be used to receive messages and process them.

15-10. Use Gateways

Problem

You want to expose an interface to clients of your service, without betraying the fact that your service is implemented in terms of messaging middleware.

Solution

Use a gateway—a pattern from the classic book *Enterprise Integration Patterns* by Gregor Hohpe and Bobby Woolf—that enjoys rich support in Spring Integration.

How It Works

A gateway is a distinct animal, similar to a lot of other patterns but ultimately different enough to warrant its own consideration. You used adapters in previous examples to enable two systems to speak in terms of foreign, loosely coupled, middleware components. This foreign component can be anything: the file system, JMS queues/topics, Twitter, and so on.

You also know what a façade is, serving to abstract away the functionality of other components in an abbreviated interface to provide courser-grained functionality. You might use a façade to build an interface oriented around vacation planning that in turn abstracts away the minutiae of using a car rental, hotel reservation, and airline reservation system.

You build a gateway, on the other hand, to provide an interface for your system that insulates clients from the middleware or messaging in your system so that they're not dependent on JMS or Spring Integration APIs, for example. A gateway allows you to express compile-time constraints on the inputs and outputs of your system.

You might want to do this for several reasons. First, it's cleaner. Secondly if you have the latitude to insist that clients comply with an interface, this is a good way to provide that interface. Your use of middleware can be an implementation detail. Perhaps your architecture's messaging middleware can be to exploit the performance increases had by leveraging asynchronous messaging, but you didn't intend for those performance gains to come at the cost of a precise, explicit, external-facing interface.

This feature—the capability to hide messaging behind a POJO interface—is interesting and has been the focus of several other projects. Lingo, a project from Codehaus.org that is no longer under active development, had such a feature that was specific to JMS and the Java EE Connector Architecture (JCA)—it was originally used to talk about the Java Cryptography Architecture but is more commonly used for the Java EE Connector Architecture now). Since then, the developers have moved on to work on Apache Camel.

In this recipe, you'll explore Spring Integration's core support for messaging gateways and explore its support for message exchange patterns. Then, you'll see how to completely remove implementation details from the client-facing interface.

SimpleMessagingGateway

The most fundamental support for gateways comes from the Spring Integration class SimpleMessagingGateway. The class provides the ability to specify a channel on which requests should be sent and a channel on which responses are expected. Finally, the channel on which replies are sent can be specified. This gives you the ability to express in-out and in-only patterns on top of your existing messaging systems. This class supports working in terms of payloads, isolating you from the gory details of the messages being sent and received. This is already one level of abstraction. You could, conceivably, use SimpleMessagingGateway and Spring Integration's concept of channels to interface with file systems, JMS, e-mail, or any other system and deal simply with payloads and channels. There are implementations already provided for you to support some of these common endpoints such as web services and JMS.

Let's look at using a generic messaging gateway. In this example, you'll send messages to a service activator and then receive the response. You manually interface with SimpleMessageGateway so that you can see how convenient it is.

```java
package com.apress.springrecipes.springintegration;

import org.springframework.context.ConfigurableApplicationContext;
import org.springframework.context.annotation.AnnotationConfigApplicationContext;
import org.springframework.messaging.MessageChannel;

public class Main {
    public static void main(String[] args) {
        ConfigurableApplicationContext ctx =
            new AnnotationConfigApplicationContext(AdditionConfiguration.class);
        MessageChannel request = ctx.getBean("request", MessageChannel.class);
        MessageChannel response = ctx.getBean("response", MessageChannel.class);

        SimpleMessagingGateway msgGateway = new SimpleMessagingGateway();
        msgGateway.setRequestChannel(request);
        msgGateway.setReplyChannel(response);
        msgGateway.setBeanFactory(ctx);
        msgGateway.afterPropertiesSet();
        msgGateway.start();

        Number result = msgGateway.convertSendAndReceive(new Operands(22, 4));

        System.out.printf("Result: %f%n", result.floatValue());

        ctx.close();

    }
}
```

The interface is straightforward. SimpleMessagingGateway needs a request and a response channel, and it coordinates the rest. In this case, you're doing nothing but forwarding the request to a service activator, which in turn adds the operands and sends them out on the reply channel. The configuration is sparse because most of the work is done in those five lines of Java code.

```java
package com.apress.springrecipes.springintegration;

import org.springframework.context.annotation.Bean;
import org.springframework.context.annotation.Configuration;
import org.springframework.integration.config.EnableIntegration;
import org.springframework.integration.dsl.IntegrationFlow;
import org.springframework.integration.dsl.IntegrationFlows;

@Configuration
@EnableIntegration
public class AdditionConfiguration {

    @Bean
    public AdditionService additionService() {
        return new AdditionService();
    }

    @Bean
    public IntegrationFlow additionFlow() {

        return IntegrationFlows
            .from("request")
            .handle(additionService(), "add")
            .channel("response")
            .get();
    }
}
```

Break the Interface Dependency

The previous example demonstrates what's happening behind the scenes. You're dealing only with Spring Integration interfaces and are isolated from the nuances of the endpoints. However, there are still plenty of inferred constraints that a client might easily fail to comply with. The simplest solution is to hide the messaging behind an interface. Let's look at building a fictional hotel reservation search engine. Searching for a hotel might take a long time, and ideally processing should be offloaded to a separate server. An ideal solution is JMS because you could implement the aggressive consumer pattern and scale simply by adding more consumers. The client would still block waiting for the result, in this example, but the server (or servers) would not be overloaded or in a blocking state.

You'll build two Spring Integration solutions: one for the client (which will in turn contain the gateway) and one for the service itself, which, presumably, is on a separate host connected to the client only by way of well-known message queues.

Let's look at the client configuration first. The first thing that the client configuration does is declare a ConnectionFactory. Then you declare the flow that starts with the gateway for the VacationService interface. The gateway element simply exists to identify the component and the interface, to which the proxy is cast and made available to clients. jms-outbound-gateway is the component that does most of the work. It takes the message you created and sends it to the request JMS destination, setting up the reply headers, and so on. Finally, you declare a generic gateway element, which does most of the magic.

```
package com.apress.springrecipes.springintegration;

import com.apress.springrecipes.springintegration.myholiday.VacationService;
import org.apache.activemq.ActiveMQConnectionFactory;
import org.springframework.context.annotation.Bean;
import org.springframework.context.annotation.Configuration;
import org.springframework.integration.config.EnableIntegration;
import org.springframework.integration.dsl.IntegrationFlow;
import org.springframework.integration.dsl.IntegrationFlows;
import org.springframework.integration.jms.dsl.Jms;
import org.springframework.jms.connection.CachingConnectionFactory;

import java.util.Arrays;

@Configuration
@EnableIntegration
public class ClientIntegrationContext {

    @Bean
    public CachingConnectionFactory connectionFactory() {
        ActiveMQConnectionFactory connectionFactory =
            new ActiveMQConnectionFactory("tcp://localhost:61616");
        connectionFactory.setTrustAllPackages(true);
        return new CachingConnectionFactory(connectionFactory);
    }

    @Bean
    public IntegrationFlow vacationGatewayFlow() {
        return IntegrationFlows
            .from(VacationService.class)
            .handle(
                Jms.outboundGateway(connectionFactory())
                    .requestDestination("inboundHotelReservationSearchDestination")
                    .replyDestination("outboundHotelReservationSearchResultsDestination"))
            .get();
    }

}
```

To be able to use VacationService as a gateway, it needs to be annotated with the @MessagingGateway annotation, and the method that serves as the entry point needs to be annotated with @Gateway.

```
package com.apress.springrecipes.springintegration.myholiday;

import org.springframework.integration.annotation.Gateway;
import org.springframework.integration.annotation.MessagingGateway;

import java.util.List;

@MessagingGateway
public interface VacationService {

    @Gateway
    List<HotelReservation> findHotels(HotelReservationSearch hotelReservationSearch);
}
```

This is the client-facing interface. There is no coupling between the client-facing interface exposed via the gateway component and the interface of the service that ultimately handles the messages. You use the interface for the service and the client to simplify the names needed to understand everything that's going on. This is not like traditional, synchronous remoting in which the service interface and the client interface match.

In this example, you're using two very simple objects for demonstration: HotelReservationSearch and HotelReservation. There is nothing interesting about these objects in the slightest; they are simple POJOs that implement Serializable and contain a few accessor/mutators to flesh out the example domain.

The following client Java code demonstrates how all of this comes together:

```
package com.apress.springrecipes.springintegration;

import com.apress.springrecipes.springintegration.myholiday.HotelReservation;
import com.apress.springrecipes.springintegration.myholiday.HotelReservationSearch;
import com.apress.springrecipes.springintegration.myholiday.VacationService;
import org.springframework.context.ConfigurableApplicationContext;
import org.springframework.context.annotation.AnnotationConfigApplicationContext;

import java.time.LocalDate;
import java.time.ZoneId;
import java.util.Date;
import java.util.List;

public class Main {
    public static void main(String[] args) throws Throwable {
        // Start server
        ConfigurableApplicationContext serverCtx =
            new AnnotationConfigApplicationContext(ServerIntegrationContext.class);

        // Start client and issue search
        ConfigurableApplicationContext clientCtx =
            new AnnotationConfigApplicationContext(ClientIntegrationContext.class);

        VacationService vacationService = clientCtx.getBean(VacationService.class);
```

```
        LocalDate now = LocalDate.now();
        Date start = Date.from(now.plusDays(1).atStartOfDay(ZoneId.systemDefault()).
        toInstant());
        Date stop = Date.from(now.plusDays(8).atStartOfDay(ZoneId.systemDefault()).
        toInstant());
        HotelReservationSearch hotelReservationSearch =
            new HotelReservationSearch(200f, 2, start, stop);
        List<HotelReservation> results = vacationService.findHotels(hotelReservationSearch);

        System.out.printf("Found %s results.%n", results.size());
        results.forEach(r -> System.out.printf("\t%s%n", r));

        serverCtx.close();
        clientCtx.close();
    }
}
```

It just doesn't get any cleaner than that! No Spring Integration interfaces whatsoever. You make a request, searching is done, and you get the result back when the processing is done. The service implementation for this setup is interesting, not because of what you've added but because of what's not there.

```
package com.apress.springrecipes.springintegration;

import com.apress.springrecipes.springintegration.myholiday.VacationServiceImpl;
import org.apache.activemq.ActiveMQConnectionFactory;
import org.springframework.context.annotation.Bean;
import org.springframework.context.annotation.Configuration;
import org.springframework.integration.config.EnableIntegration;
import org.springframework.integration.dsl.IntegrationFlow;
import org.springframework.integration.dsl.IntegrationFlows;
import org.springframework.integration.jms.dsl.Jms;
import org.springframework.jms.connection.CachingConnectionFactory;

import java.util.Arrays;

@Configuration
@EnableIntegration
public class ServerIntegrationContext {

    @Bean
    public CachingConnectionFactory connectionFactory() {
        ActiveMQConnectionFactory connectionFactory =
            new ActiveMQConnectionFactory("tcp://localhost:61616");
        connectionFactory.setTrustAllPackages(true);
        return new CachingConnectionFactory(connectionFactory);
    }

    @Bean
    public VacationServiceImpl vacationService() {
        return new VacationServiceImpl();
    }
```

687

```
    @Bean
    public IntegrationFlow serverIntegrationFlow() {
        return IntegrationFlows.from(
            Jms.inboundGateway(connectionFactory())
                .destination("inboundHotelReservationSearchDestination"))
            .handle(vacationService())
            .get();
    }
}
```

Here, you've defined an inbound JMS gateway. The messages from the inbound JMS gateway are put on a channel, whose messages are forwarded to a service activator, as you would expect. The service activator is what handles actual processing. What's interesting here is that there's no mention of a response channel, either for the service activator or for the inbound JMS gateway. The service activator looks, and fails to find, a reply channel and so uses the reply channel created by the inbound JMS gateway component, which in turn has created the reply channel based on the header metadata in the inbound JMS message. Thus, everything just works without specification.

The implementation is a simple useless implementation of the interface.

```
package com.apress.springrecipes.springintegration.myholiday;

import org.springframework.integration.annotation.ServiceActivator;

import javax.annotation.PostConstruct;
import java.util.Arrays;
import java.util.List;

public class VacationServiceImpl implements VacationService {
    private List<HotelReservation> hotelReservations;

    @PostConstruct
    public void afterPropertiesSet() throws Exception {
        hotelReservations = Arrays.asList(
                new HotelReservation("Bilton", 243.200F),
                new HotelReservation("East Western", 75.0F),
                new HotelReservation("Thairfield Inn", 70F),
                new HotelReservation("Park In The Inn", 200.00F));
    }

    @ServiceActivator
    public List<HotelReservation> findHotels(HotelReservationSearch searchMsg) {
        try {
            Thread.sleep(1000);
        } catch (Throwable th) {
        }

        return this.hotelReservations;
    }
}
```

Summary

This chapter discussed building an integration solution using Spring Integration, an ESB-like framework built on top of the Spring Framework. You were introduced to the core concepts of enterprise application integration. You learned how to handle a few integration scenarios, including JMS and file polling.

In the next chapter, you will explore the capabilities of Spring in the field of testing.

CHAPTER 16

■ ■ ■

Spring Testing

In this chapter, you will learn about basic techniques you can use to test Java applications, as well as the testing support features offered by the Spring Framework. These features can make your testing tasks easier and lead you to better application design. In general, applications developed with the Spring Framework and the dependency injection pattern are easy to test.

Testing is a key activity for ensuring quality in software development. There are many types of testing, including unit testing, integration testing, functional testing, system testing, performance testing, and acceptance testing. Spring's testing support focuses on unit and integration testing, but it can also help with other types of testing. Testing can be performed either manually or automatically. However, since automated tests can be run repeatedly and continuously at different phases of a development process, they are highly recommended, especially in agile development processes. The Spring Framework is an agile framework that fits these kinds of processes.

Many testing frameworks are available on the Java platform. Currently, JUnit and TestNG are the most popular. JUnit has a long history and a large user group in the Java community. TestNG is another popular Java testing framework. Compared to JUnit, TestNG offers additional powerful features such as test grouping, dependent test methods, and data-driven tests.

Spring's testing support features have been offered by the Spring TestContext framework, which abstracts the underlying testing framework with the following concepts:

- *Test context*: This encapsulates the context of a test's execution, including the application context, test class, current test instance, current test method, and current test exception.

- *Test context manager*: This manages a test context for a test and triggers test execution listeners at predefined test execution points, including when preparing a test instance, before executing a test method (before any framework-specific initialization methods), and after executing a test method (after any framework-specific cleanup methods).

- *Test execution listener*: This defines a listener interface; by implementing this, you can listen to test execution events. The TestContext framework provides several test execution listeners for common testing features, but you are free to create your own.

Spring provides convenient TestContext support classes for JUnit and TestNG, with particular test execution listeners preregistered. You can simply extend these support classes to use the TestContext framework without having to know much about the framework details.

After finishing this chapter, you will understand the basic concepts and techniques of testing and the popular Java testing frameworks JUnit and TestNG. You will also be able to create unit tests and integration tests using the Spring TestContext framework.

© Marten Deinum, Daniel Rubio, and Josh Long 2017

M. Deinum et al., *Spring 5 Recipes*, DOI 10.1007/978-1-4842-2790-9_16

16-1. Create Tests with JUnit and TestNG

Problem

You want to create automated tests for your Java application so that they can be run repeatedly to ensure the correctness of your application.

Solution

The most popular testing frameworks on the Java platform are JUnit and TestNG. Both JUnit and TestNG allow you to annotate your test methods with the @Test annotation, so an arbitrary public method can be run as a test case.

How It Works

Suppose you are going to develop a system for a bank. To ensure the system's quality, you have to test every part of it. First, let's consider an interest calculator, whose interface is defined as follows:

```
package com.apress.springrecipes.bank;

public interface InterestCalculator {

    void setRate(double rate);
    double calculate(double amount, double year);
}
```

Each interest calculator requires a fixed interest rate to be set. Now, you can implement this calculator with a simple interest formula, shown here:

```
package com.apress.springrecipes.bank;

public class SimpleInterestCalculator implements InterestCalculator {

    private double rate;

    public void setRate(double rate) {
        this.rate = rate;
    }

    public double calculate(double amount, double year) {
        if (amount < 0 || year < 0) {
            throw new IllegalArgumentException("Amount or year must be positive");
        }
        return amount * year * rate;
    }
}
```

Next, you will test this simple interest calculator with the popular testing frameworks JUnit and TestNG (version 5).

Test with JUnit

A test case is simply a public method with the @Test annotation. To set up data, you can annotate a method with @Before. To clean up resources, you can annotate a method with @After. You can also annotate a public static method with @BeforeClass or @AfterClass to have it run once before or after all test cases in the class.

You have to call the static assert methods declared in the org.junit.Assert class directly. However, you can import all assert methods via a static import statement. You can create the following JUnit test cases to test your simple interest calculator.

■ **Note**   To compile and run test cases created for JUnit, you have to include JUnit on your CLASSPATH. If you are using Maven, add the following dependency to your project:

```
<dependency>
    <groupId>junit</groupId>
    <artifactId>junit</artifactId>
    <version>4.12</version>
</dependency>
```

For Gradle, add the following:

```
testCompile 'junit:junit:4.12'
```

```
package com.apress.springrecipes.bank;

import static org.junit.Assert.*;

import org.junit.Before;
import org.junit.Test;

public class SimpleInterestCalculatorJUnit4Tests {

    private InterestCalculator interestCalculator;

    @Before
    public void init() {
        interestCalculator = new SimpleInterestCalculator();
        interestCalculator.setRate(0.05);
    }

    @Test
    public void calculate() {
        double interest = interestCalculator.calculate(10000, 2);
        assertEquals(interest, 1000.0, 0);
    }
```

```
@Test(expected = IllegalArgumentException.class)
public void illegalCalculate() {
    interestCalculator.calculate(-10000, 2);
}
}
```

JUnit offers a powerful feature that allows you to expect an exception to be thrown in a test case. You can simply specify the exception type in the expected attribute of the @Test annotation.

Test with TestNG

A TestNG test looks similar to a JUnit test, except that you have to use the classes and annotation types defined by the TestNG framework.

■ **Note**   To compile and run test cases created for TestNG, you have to add TestNG to your CLASSPATH. If you are using Maven, add the following dependency to your project:

```
<dependency>
    <groupId>org.testng</groupId>
    <artifactId>testng</artifactId>
    <version>6.11</version>
</dependency>
```

For Gradle, add the following:

```
testCompile 'org.testng:testng:6.11'
```

```
package com.apress.springrecipes.bank;

import static org.testng.Assert.*;

import org.testng.annotations.BeforeMethod;
import org.testng.annotations.Test;

public class SimpleInterestCalculatorTestNGTests {

    private InterestCalculator interestCalculator;

    @BeforeMethod
    public void init() {
        interestCalculator = new SimpleInterestCalculator();
        interestCalculator.setRate(0.05);
    }

    @Test
    public void calculate() {
        double interest = interestCalculator.calculate(10000, 2);
        assertEquals(interest, 1000.0);
    }
```

```java
@Test(expectedExceptions = IllegalArgumentException.class)
public void illegalCalculate() {
    interestCalculator.calculate(-10000, 2);
}
```
}

Tip If you are using Eclipse for development, you can download and install the TestNG Eclipse plug-in from `http://testng.org/doc/eclipse.html` to run TestNG tests in Eclipse. Again, you will see a green bar if all your tests pass and a red bar otherwise.

One of the powerful features of TestNG is its built-in support for data-driven testing. TestNG cleanly separates test data from test logic so that you can run a test method multiple times for different data sets. In TestNG, test data sets are provided by data providers, which are methods with the @DataProvider annotation.

```java
package com.apress.springrecipes.bank;

import org.testng.annotations.BeforeMethod;
import org.testng.annotations.DataProvider;
import org.testng.annotations.Test;

import static org.testng.Assert.assertEquals;

public class SimpleInterestCalculatorTestNGTests {

    private InterestCalculator interestCalculator;

    @BeforeMethod
    public void init() {
        interestCalculator = new SimpleInterestCalculator();
        interestCalculator.setRate(0.05);
    }

    @DataProvider(name = "legal")
    public Object[][] createLegalInterestParameters() {
        return new Object[][]{new Object[]{10000, 2, 1000.0}};
    }

    @DataProvider(name = "illegal")
    public Object[][] createIllegalInterestParameters() {
        return new Object[][]{
            new Object[]{-10000, 2},
            new Object[]{10000, -2},
            new Object[]{-10000, -2}
        };
    }
}
```

```
@Test(dataProvider = "legal")
public void calculate(double amount, double year, double result) {
    double interest = interestCalculator.calculate(amount, year);
    assertEquals(interest, result);
}

@Test(
    dataProvider = "illegal",
    expectedExceptions = IllegalArgumentException.class)
public void illegalCalculate(double amount, double year) {
    interestCalculator.calculate(amount, year);
}
}
```

If you run the preceding test with TestNG, the calculate() method will be executed once, while the illegalCalculate() method will be executed three times, as there are three data sets returned by the illegal data provider.

16-2. Create Unit Tests and Integration Tests

Problem

A common testing technique is to test each module of your application in isolation and then test them in combination. You want to apply this skill in testing your Java applications.

Solution

Unit tests are used to test a single programming unit. In object-oriented languages, a unit is usually a class or a method. The scope of a unit test is a single unit, but in the real world, most units won't work in isolation. They often need to cooperate with others to complete their tasks. When testing a unit that depends on other units, a common technique you can apply is to simulate the unit dependencies with stubs and mock objects, both of which can reduce the complexity of your unit tests caused by dependencies.

A *stub* is an object that simulates a dependent object with the minimum number of methods required for a test. The methods are implemented in a predetermined way, usually with hard-coded data. A stub also exposes methods for a test to verify the stub's internal states. In contrast to a stub, a *mock object* usually knows how its methods are expected to be called in a test. The mock object then verifies the methods actually called against the expected ones. In Java, there are several libraries that can help create mock objects, such as Mockito, EasyMock, and jMock. The main difference between a stub and a mock object is that a stub is usually used for state verification, while a mock object is used for behavior verification.

Integration tests, in contrast, are used to test several units in combination as a whole. They test if the integration and interaction between units are correct. Each of these units should already have been tested with unit tests, so integration testing is usually performed after unit testing.

Finally, note that applications developed using the principle of separating interface from implementation and the dependency injection pattern are easy to test, both for unit testing and for integration testing. This is because that principle and pattern can reduce coupling between different units of your application.

How It Works

First you will explore how to write a unit test for a single class, which will then be extended to testing a class with mocked and/or stubbed colaborates. Finally you will take a look on how to write an integration test.

Create Unit Tests for Isolated Classes

The core functions of your bank system should be designed around customer accounts. First, you create the following domain class, Account, with custom equals() and hashCode() methods:

```
package com.apress.springrecipes.bank;

public class Account {

    private String accountNo;
    private double balance;

    // Constructors, Getters and Setters
    ...

    @Override
    public boolean equals(Object o) {
        if (this == o) return true;
        if (o == null || getClass() != o.getClass()) return false;
        Account account = (Account) o;
        return Objects.equals(this.accountNo, account.accountNo);
    }

    @Override
    public int hashCode() {
        return Objects.hash(this.accountNo);
    }
}
```

Next, you define the following DAO interface for persisting account objects in your bank system's persistence layer:

```
package com.apress.springrecipes.bank;

public interface AccountDao {

    public void createAccount(Account account);
    public void updateAccount(Account account);
    public void removeAccount(Account account);
    public Account findAccount(String accountNo);
}
```

To demonstrate the unit testing concept, let's implement this interface by using a map to store account objects. The AccountNotFoundException and DuplicateAccountException classes are subclasses of RuntimeException that you should be able to create yourself.

```java
package com.apress.springrecipes.bank;

import java.util.Collections;
import java.util.HashMap;
import java.util.Map;

public class InMemoryAccountDao implements AccountDao {

    private Map<String, Account> accounts;

    public InMemoryAccountDao() {
        accounts = Collections.synchronizedMap(new HashMap<String, Account>());
    }

    public boolean accountExists(String accountNo) {
        return accounts.containsKey(accountNo);
    }

    public void createAccount(Account account) {
        if (accountExists(account.getAccountNo())) {
            throw new DuplicateAccountException();
        }
        accounts.put(account.getAccountNo(), account);
    }

    public void updateAccount(Account account) {
        if (!accountExists(account.getAccountNo())) {
            throw new AccountNotFoundException();
        }
        accounts.put(account.getAccountNo(), account);
    }

    public void removeAccount(Account account) {
        if (!accountExists(account.getAccountNo())) {
            throw new AccountNotFoundException();
        }
        accounts.remove(account.getAccountNo());
    }

    public Account findAccount(String accountNo) {
        Account account = accounts.get(accountNo);
        if (account == null) {
            throw new AccountNotFoundException();
        }
        return account;
    }
}
```

Obviously, this simple DAO implementation doesn't support transactions. However, to make it thread-safe, you can wrap the map storing accounts with a synchronized map so that it will be accessed serially.

Now, let's create unit tests for this DAO implementation with JUnit. As this class doesn't depend directly on other classes, it's easy to test. To ensure that this class works properly for exceptional cases as well as normal cases, you should also create exceptional test cases for it. Typically, exceptional test cases expect an exception to be thrown.

```java
package com.apress.springrecipes.bank;

import static org.junit.Assert.*;

import org.junit.Before;
import org.junit.Test;

public class InMemoryAccountDaoTests {

    private static final String EXISTING_ACCOUNT_NO = "1234";
    private static final String NEW_ACCOUNT_NO = "5678";

    private Account existingAccount;
    private Account newAccount;
    private InMemoryAccountDao accountDao;

    @Before
    public void init() {
        existingAccount = new Account(EXISTING_ACCOUNT_NO, 100);
        newAccount = new Account(NEW_ACCOUNT_NO, 200);
        accountDao = new InMemoryAccountDao();
        accountDao.createAccount(existingAccount);
    }

    @Test
    public void accountExists() {
        assertTrue(accountDao.accountExists(EXISTING_ACCOUNT_NO));
        assertFalse(accountDao.accountExists(NEW_ACCOUNT_NO));
    }

    @Test
    public void createNewAccount() {
        accountDao.createAccount(newAccount);
        assertEquals(accountDao.findAccount(NEW_ACCOUNT_NO), newAccount);
    }

    @Test(expected = DuplicateAccountException.class)
    public void createDuplicateAccount() {
        accountDao.createAccount(existingAccount);
    }

    @Test
    public void updateExistedAccount() {
        existingAccount.setBalance(150);
        accountDao.updateAccount(existingAccount);
        assertEquals(accountDao.findAccount(EXISTING_ACCOUNT_NO), existingAccount);
    }
```

```
    @Test(expected = AccountNotFoundException.class)
    public void updateNotExistedAccount() {
        accountDao.updateAccount(newAccount);
    }

    @Test
    public void removeExistedAccount() {
        accountDao.removeAccount(existingAccount);
        assertFalse(accountDao.accountExists(EXISTING_ACCOUNT_NO));
    }

    @Test(expected = AccountNotFoundException.class)
    public void removeNotExistedAccount() {
        accountDao.removeAccount(newAccount);
    }

    @Test
    public void findExistedAccount() {
        Account account = accountDao.findAccount(EXISTING_ACCOUNT_NO);
        assertEquals(account, existingAccount);
    }

    @Test(expected = AccountNotFoundException.class)
    public void findNotExistedAccount() {
        accountDao.findAccount(NEW_ACCOUNT_NO);
    }
}
```

Create Unit Tests for Dependent Classes Using Stubs and Mock Objects

Testing an independent class is easy, because you needn't consider how its dependencies work and how to set them up properly. However, testing a class that depends on results of other classes or services (e.g., database services and network services) would be a little bit difficult. For example, let's consider the following AccountService interface in the service layer:

```
package com.apress.springrecipes.bank;

public interface AccountService {

    void createAccount(String accountNo);
    void removeAccount(String accountNo);
    void deposit(String accountNo, double amount);
    void withdraw(String accountNo, double amount);
    double getBalance(String accountNo);
}
```

The implementation of this service interface has to depend on an AccountDao object in the persistence layer to persist account objects. The InsufficientBalanceException class is also a subclass of RuntimeException that you have to create.

```java
package com.apress.springrecipes.bank;

public class AccountServiceImpl implements AccountService {

    private AccountDao accountDao;

    public AccountServiceImpl(AccountDao accountDao) {
        this.accountDao = accountDao;
    }

    public void createAccount(String accountNo) {
        accountDao.createAccount(new Account(accountNo, 0));
    }

    public void removeAccount(String accountNo) {
        Account account = accountDao.findAccount(accountNo);
        accountDao.removeAccount(account);
    }

    public void deposit(String accountNo, double amount) {
        Account account = accountDao.findAccount(accountNo);
        account.setBalance(account.getBalance() + amount);
        accountDao.updateAccount(account);
    }

    public void withdraw(String accountNo, double amount) {
        Account account = accountDao.findAccount(accountNo);
        if (account.getBalance() < amount) {
            throw new InsufficientBalanceException();
        }
        account.setBalance(account.getBalance() - amount);
        accountDao.updateAccount(account);
    }

    public double getBalance(String accountNo) {
        return accountDao.findAccount(accountNo).getBalance();
    }
}
```

A common technique in unit testing to reduce complexity caused by dependencies is to use stubs. A stub must implement the same interface as the target object so that it can substitute for the target object. For example, you can create a stub for AccountDao that stores a single customer account and implements only the findAccount() and updateAccount() methods, as they are required for deposit() and withdraw().

```java
package com.apress.springrecipes.bank;

import static org.junit.Assert.*;

import org.junit.Before;
import org.junit.Test;
```

```java
public class AccountServiceImplStubTests {

    private static final String TEST_ACCOUNT_NO = "1234";
    private AccountDaoStub accountDaoStub;
    private AccountService accountService;

    private class AccountDaoStub implements AccountDao {

        private String accountNo;
        private double balance;

        public void createAccount(Account account) {}
        public void removeAccount(Account account) {}

        public Account findAccount(String accountNo) {
            return new Account(this.accountNo, this.balance);
        }

        public void updateAccount(Account account) {
            this.accountNo = account.getAccountNo();
            this.balance = account.getBalance();
        }
    }

    @Before
    public void init() {
        accountDaoStub = new AccountDaoStub();
        accountDaoStub.accountNo = TEST_ACCOUNT_NO;
        accountDaoStub.balance = 100;
        accountService = new AccountServiceImpl(accountDaoStub);
    }

    @Test
    public void deposit() {
        accountService.deposit(TEST_ACCOUNT_NO, 50);
        assertEquals(accountDaoStub.accountNo, TEST_ACCOUNT_NO);
        assertEquals(accountDaoStub.balance, 150, 0);
    }

    @Test
    public void withdrawWithSufficientBalance() {
        accountService.withdraw(TEST_ACCOUNT_NO, 50);
        assertEquals(accountDaoStub.accountNo, TEST_ACCOUNT_NO);
        assertEquals(accountDaoStub.balance, 50, 0);
    }

    @Test(expected = InsufficientBalanceException.class)
    public void withdrawWithInsufficientBalance() {
        accountService.withdraw(TEST_ACCOUNT_NO, 150);
    }
}
```

However, writing stubs yourself requires a lot of coding. A more efficient technique is to use mock objects. The Mockito library is able to dynamically create mock objects that work in a record/playback mechanism.

■ **Note**   To use Mockito for testing, you have to add it to your CLASSPATH. If you are using Maven, add the following dependency to your project:

```
<dependency>
    <groupId>org.mockito</groupId>
    <artifactId>mockito-core</artifactId>
    <version>2.7.20</version>
    <scope>test</scope>
</dependency>
```

Or when using Gradle, add the following:

```
testCompile 'org.mockito:mockito-core:2.7.20'
```

```java
package com.apress.springrecipes.bank;

import org.junit.Before;
import org.junit.Test;

import static org.mockito.Mockito.*;

public class AccountServiceImplMockTests {

    private static final String TEST_ACCOUNT_NO = "1234";

    private AccountDao accountDao;
    private AccountService accountService;

    @Before
    public void init() {
        accountDao = mock(AccountDao.class);
        accountService = new AccountServiceImpl(accountDao);
    }

    @Test
    public void deposit() {
        // Setup
        Account account = new Account(TEST_ACCOUNT_NO, 100);
        when(accountDao.findAccount(TEST_ACCOUNT_NO)).thenReturn(account);

        // Execute
        accountService.deposit(TEST_ACCOUNT_NO, 50);

        // Verify
        verify(accountDao, times(1)).findAccount(any(String.class));
        verify(accountDao, times(1)).updateAccount(account);

    }
```

```
    @Test
    public void withdrawWithSufficientBalance() {
        // Setup
        Account account = new Account(TEST_ACCOUNT_NO, 100);
        when(accountDao.findAccount(TEST_ACCOUNT_NO)).thenReturn(account);

        // Execute
        accountService.withdraw(TEST_ACCOUNT_NO, 50);

        // Verify
        verify(accountDao, times(1)).findAccount(any(String.class));
        verify(accountDao, times(1)).updateAccount(account);

    }

    @Test(expected = InsufficientBalanceException.class)
    public void testWithdrawWithInsufficientBalance() {
        // Setup
        Account account = new Account(TEST_ACCOUNT_NO, 100);
        when(accountDao.findAccount(TEST_ACCOUNT_NO)).thenReturn(account);

        // Execute
        accountService.withdraw(TEST_ACCOUNT_NO, 150);
    }
}
```

With Mockito, you can create a mock object dynamically for an arbitrary interface or class. This mock can be instructed to have certain behavior for method calls, and you can use it to selectively verify whether something has happened. In your test you want that in the findAccount method that a certain Account object is returned. You use the Mockito.when method for this, and you can then either return a value, throw an exception, or do more elaborate things with an Answer. The default behavior for the mock is to return null. You use the Mockito.verify method to do selective verification of actions that should have happened. You want to make sure that the findAccount method is called and that the account gets updated.

Create Integration Tests

Integration tests are used to test several units in combination to ensure that the units are properly integrated and can interact correctly. For example, you can create an integration test to test AccountServiceImpl using InMemoryAccountDao as the DAO implementation.

```
package com.apress.springrecipes.bank;

import static org.junit.Assert.*;

import org.junit.After;
import org.junit.Before;
import org.junit.Test;
```

```
public class AccountServiceTests {

    private static final String TEST_ACCOUNT_NO = "1234";
    private AccountService accountService;

    @Before
    public void init() {
        accountService = new AccountServiceImpl(new InMemoryAccountDao());
        accountService.createAccount(TEST_ACCOUNT_NO);
        accountService.deposit(TEST_ACCOUNT_NO, 100);
    }

    @Test
    public void deposit() {
        accountService.deposit(TEST_ACCOUNT_NO, 50);
        assertEquals(accountService.getBalance(TEST_ACCOUNT_NO), 150, 0);
    }

    @Test
    public void withDraw() {
        accountService.withdraw(TEST_ACCOUNT_NO, 50);
        assertEquals(accountService.getBalance(TEST_ACCOUNT_NO), 50, 0);
    }

    @After
    public void cleanup() {
        accountService.removeAccount(TEST_ACCOUNT_NO);
    }
}
```

16-3. Implement Unit Testing for Spring MVC Controllers

Problem

In a web application, you want to test the web controllers developed with the Spring MVC framework.

Solution

A Spring MVC controller is invoked by DispatcherServlet with an HTTP request object and an HTTP response object. After processing a request, the controller returns it to DispatcherServlet for rendering the view. The main challenge of unit testing Spring MVC controllers, as well as web controllers in other web application frameworks, is simulating HTTP request objects and response objects in a unit testing environment. Fortunately, Spring supports web controller testing by providing a set of mock objects for the Servlet API (including MockHttpServletRequest, MockHttpServletResponse, and MockHttpSession).

To test a Spring MVC controller's output, you need to check whether the object returned to DispatcherServlet is correct. Spring also provides a set of assertion utilities for checking the contents of an object.

How It Works

In your bank system, suppose you are going to develop a web interface for bank staff to input the account number and amount of a deposit. You create a controller named DepositController using the techniques you already know from Spring MVC.

```
package com.apress.springrecipes.bank.web;

import org.springframework.beans.factory.annotation.Autowired;
import org.springframework.stereotype.Controller;
import org.springframework.ui.ModelMap;
import org.springframework.web.bind.annotation.RequestMapping;
import org.springframework.web.bind.annotation.RequestParam;

@Controller
public class DepositController {

    private AccountService accountService;

    @Autowired
    public DepositController(AccountService accountService) {
        this.accountService = accountService;
    }

    @RequestMapping("/deposit.do")
    public String deposit(
        @RequestParam("accountNo") String accountNo,
        @RequestParam("amount") double amount,
        ModelMap model) {
        accountService.deposit(accountNo, amount);
        model.addAttribute("accountNo", accountNo);
        model.addAttribute("balance", accountService.getBalance(accountNo));
        return "success";
    }
}
```

Because this controller doesn't deal with the Servlet API, testing it is easy. You can test it just like a simple Java class.

```
package com.apress.springrecipes.bank.web;

import static org.junit.Assert.*;

import com.apress.springrecipes.bank.AccountService;
import org.junit.Before;
import org.junit.Test;
import org.mockito.Mockito;
import org.springframework.ui.ModelMap;
```

```java
public class DepositControllerTests {

    private static final String TEST_ACCOUNT_NO = "1234";
    private static final double TEST_AMOUNT = 50;
    private AccountService accountService;
    private DepositController depositController;

    @Before
    public void init() {
        accountService = Mockito.mock(AccountService.class);
        depositController = new DepositController(accountService);
    }

    @Test
    public void deposit() {
        //Setup
        Mockito.when(accountService.getBalance(TEST_ACCOUNT_NO)).thenReturn(150.0);
        ModelMap model = new ModelMap();

        //Execute
        String viewName =
            depositController.deposit(TEST_ACCOUNT_NO, TEST_AMOUNT, model);

        assertEquals(viewName, "success");
        assertEquals(model.get("accountNo"), TEST_ACCOUNT_NO);
        assertEquals(model.get("balance"), 150.0);
    }
}
```

16-4. Manage Application Contexts in Integration Tests

Problem

When creating integration tests for a Spring application, you have to access beans declared in the application context. Without Spring's testing support, you have to load the application context manually in an initialization method of your tests, a method with @Before or @BeforeClass in JUnit. However, as an initialization method is called before each test method or test class, the same application context may be reloaded many times. In a large application with many beans, loading an application context may require a lot of time, which causes your tests to run slowly.

Solution

Spring's testing support facilities can help you manage the application context for your tests, including loading it from one or more bean configuration files and caching it across multiple test executions. An application context will be cached across all tests within a single JVM, using the configuration file locations as the key. As a result, your tests can run much faster without reloading the same application context many times.

The TestContext framework provides a few test execution listeners that are registered by default, as shown in Table 16-1.

Table 16-1. *Default Test Execution Listeners*

TestExecutionListener	Description
DependencyInjectionTestExecutionListener	This injects dependencies, including the managed application context, into your tests.
DirtiesContextTestExecutionListener, DirtiesContextBeforeModesTestExecutionListener	This handles the @DirtiesContext annotation and reloads the application context when necessary.
TransactionalTestExecutionListener	This handles the @Transactional annotation in test cases and does a rollback at the end of a test.
SqlScriptsTestExecutionListener	This detects @Sql annotations on the test and executes the SQL before the start of the test.
ServletTestExecutionListener	This handles the loading of a web application context when the @WebAppConfiguration annotation is detected.

To have the TestContext framework manage the application context, your test class has to integrate with a test context manager internally. For your convenience, the TestContext framework provides support classes that do this, as shown in Table 16-2. These classes integrate with a test context manager and implement the ApplicationContextAware interface, so they can provide access to the managed application context through the protected field applicationContext.

Table 16-2. *TestContext Support Classes for Context Management*

Testing Framework	TestContext Support Class
JUnit	AbstractJUnit4SpringContextTests
TestNG	AbstractTestNGSpringContextTests

Your test class can simply extend the corresponding TestContext support class for your testing framework.

These TestContext support classes have only DependencyInjectionTestExecutionListener, DirtiesContextTestExecutionListener, and ServletTestExecutionListener enabled.

If you are using JUnit or TestNG, you can integrate your test class with a test context manager by yourself and implement the ApplicationContextAware interface directly, without extending a TestContext support class. In this way, your test class doesn't bind to the TestContext framework class hierarchy, so you can extend your own base class. In JUnit, you can simply run your test with the test runner SpringRunner to have a test context manager integrated. However, in TestNG, you have to integrate with a test context manager manually.

How It Works

First, let's declare an AccountService instance and an AccountDao instance in the configuration class. Later, you will create integration tests for them.

```
package com.apress.springrecipes.bank.config;

import com.apress.springrecipes.bank.AccountServiceImpl;
import com.apress.springrecipes.bank.InMemoryAccountDao;
import org.springframework.context.annotation.Bean;
import org.springframework.context.annotation.Configuration;

@Configuration
public class BankConfiguration {

    @Bean
    public InMemoryAccountDao accountDao() {
        return new InMemoryAccountDao();
    }

    @Bean
    public AccountServiceImpl accountService() {
        return new AccountServiceImpl(accountDao());
    }
}
```

Access the Context with the TestContext Framework in JUnit

If you are using JUnit to create tests with the TestContext framework, you will have two options to access the managed application context. The first option is by implementing the ApplicationContextAware interface or using @Autowired on a field of the ApplicationContext type. For this option, you have to explicitly specify a Spring-specific test runner for running your test SpringRunner. You can specify this in the @RunWith annotation at the class level.

```
package com.apress.springrecipes.bank;

import com.apress.springrecipes.bank.config.BankConfiguration;
import org.junit.After;
import org.junit.Before;
import org.junit.Test;
import org.junit.runner.RunWith;
import org.springframework.beans.factory.annotation.Autowired;
import org.springframework.test.context.ContextConfiguration;
import org.springframework.test.context.junit4.SpringRunner;

import static org.junit.Assert.assertEquals;

@RunWith(SpringRunner.class)
@ContextConfiguration(classes = BankConfiguration.class)
public class AccountServiceJUnit4ContextTests implements ApplicationContextAware {

    private static final String TEST_ACCOUNT_NO = "1234";
    private ApplicationContext applicationContext;
    private AccountService accountService;
```

```
    @Override
    public void setApplicationContext(ApplicationContext applicationContext) throws
    BeansException {
        this.applicationContext=applicationContext;
    }

    @Before
    public void init() {
        accountService = applicationContext.getBean(AccountService.class);
        accountService.createAccount(TEST_ACCOUNT_NO);
        accountService.deposit(TEST_ACCOUNT_NO, 100);
    }

    @Test
    public void deposit() {
        accountService.deposit(TEST_ACCOUNT_NO, 50);
        assertEquals(accountService.getBalance(TEST_ACCOUNT_NO), 150, 0);
    }

    @Test
    public void withDraw() {
        accountService.withdraw(TEST_ACCOUNT_NO, 50);
        assertEquals(accountService.getBalance(TEST_ACCOUNT_NO), 50, 0);
    }

    @After
    public void cleanup() {
        accountService.removeAccount(TEST_ACCOUNT_NO);
    }

}
```

You can specify the configuration classes in the classes attribute of the @ContextConfiguration annotation at the class level. When using XML-based configuration, you can use the locations attribute instead. If you don't specify any test configuration, the TestContext will try to detect one. It will first try to load a file by joining the test class name with -context.xml as the suffix (i.e., AccountServiceJUnit4Tests-context.xml) from the same package as the test class. Next it will scan the test class for any public static inner classes that are annotated with @Configuration. If a file or classes are detected, those will be used to load the test configuration.

By default, the application context will be cached and reused for each test method, but if you want it to be reloaded after a particular test method, you can annotate the test method with the @DirtiesContext annotation so that the application context will be reloaded for the next test method.

The second option to access the managed application context is by extending the TestContext support class specific to JUnit: AbstractJUnit4SpringContextTests. This class implements the ApplicationContextAware interface, so you can extend it to get access to the managed application context via the protected field applicationContext. However, you first have to delete the private field applicationContext and its setter method. Note that if you extend this support class, you don't need to specify SpringRunner in the @RunWith annotation because this annotation is inherited from the parent.

```
package com.apress.springrecipes.bank;
...
import org.springframework.test.context.ContextConfiguration;
import org.springframework.test.context.junit4.AbstractJUnit4SpringContextTests;

@ContextConfiguration(classes = BankConfiguration.class)
public class AccountServiceJUnit4ContextTests extends AbstractJUnit4SpringContextTests {

    private static final String TEST_ACCOUNT_NO = "1234";
    private AccountService accountService;

    @Before
    public void init() {
        accountService = applicationContext.getBean(AccountService.class);
        accountService.createAccount(TEST_ACCOUNT_NO);
        accountService.deposit(TEST_ACCOUNT_NO, 100);
    }
    ...
}
```

Access the Context with the TestContext Framework in TestNG

To access the managed application context with the TestContext framework in TestNG, you can extend the TestContext support class AbstractTestNGSpringContextTests. This class also implements the ApplicationContextAware interface.

```
package com.apress.springrecipes.bank;

import com.apress.springrecipes.bank.config.BankConfiguration;
import org.springframework.test.context.ContextConfiguration;
import org.springframework.test.context.testng.AbstractTestNGSpringContextTests;
import org.testng.annotations.AfterMethod;
import org.testng.annotations.BeforeMethod;
import org.testng.annotations.Test;

import static org.testng.Assert.assertEquals;

@ContextConfiguration(classes = BankConfiguration.class)
public class AccountServiceTestNGContextTests extends AbstractTestNGSpringContextTests {

    private static final String TEST_ACCOUNT_NO = "1234";
    private AccountService accountService;

    @BeforeMethod
    public void init() {
        accountService = applicationContext.getBean(AccountService.class);
        accountService.createAccount(TEST_ACCOUNT_NO);
        accountService.deposit(TEST_ACCOUNT_NO, 100);
    }
```

```java
    @Test
    public void deposit() {
        accountService.deposit(TEST_ACCOUNT_NO, 50);
        assertEquals(accountService.getBalance(TEST_ACCOUNT_NO), 150, 0);
    }

    @Test
    public void withDraw() {
        accountService.withdraw(TEST_ACCOUNT_NO, 50);
        assertEquals(accountService.getBalance(TEST_ACCOUNT_NO), 50, 0);
    }

    @AfterMethod
    public void cleanup() {
        accountService.removeAccount(TEST_ACCOUNT_NO);
    }

}
```

If you don't want your TestNG test class to extend a TestContext support class, you can implement the `ApplicationContextAware` interface just as you did for JUnit. However, you have to integrate with a test context manager by yourself. Please refer to the source code of `AbstractTestNGSpringContextTests` for details.

16-5. Inject Test Fixtures into Integration Tests

Problem

The test fixtures of an integration test for a Spring application are mostly beans declared in the application context. You might want to have the test fixtures automatically injected by Spring via dependency injection, which saves you the trouble of retrieving them from the application context manually.

Solution

Spring's testing support facilities can inject beans automatically from the managed application context into your tests as test fixtures. You can simply annotate a setter method or field of your test with Spring's `@Autowired` annotation or JSR-250's `@Resource` annotation to have a fixture injected automatically. For `@Autowired`, the fixture will be injected by type, and for `@Resource`, it will be injected by name.

How It Works

You will explore how to inject test fixtures with JUnit and TestNG.

Inject Test Fixtures with the TestContext Framework in JUnit

When using the TestContext framework to create tests, you can have their test fixtures injected from the managed application context by annotating a field or setter method with the `@Autowired` or `@Resource` annotation. In JUnit, you can specify `SpringRunner` as your test runner without extending a support class.

```
package com.apress.springrecipes.bank;
...
import org.springframework.beans.factory.annotation.Autowired;
import org.springframework.test.context.ContextConfiguration;
import org.springframework.test.context.junit4.SpringRunner;

@RunWith(SpringRunner.class)
@ContextConfiguration(classes = BankConfiguration.class)
public class AccountServiceJUnit4ContextTests {

    private static final String TEST_ACCOUNT_NO = "1234";

    @Autowired
    private AccountService accountService;

    @Before
    public void init() {
        accountService.createAccount(TEST_ACCOUNT_NO);
        accountService.deposit(TEST_ACCOUNT_NO, 100);
    }
    ...
}
```

If you annotate a field or setter method of a test with @Autowired, it will be injected using autowiring by type. You can further specify a candidate bean for autowiring by providing its name in the @Qualifier annotation. However, if you want a field or setter method to be autowired by name, you can annotate it with @Resource.

By extending the TestContext support class AbstractJUnit4SpringContextTests, you can also have test fixtures injected from the managed application context. In this case, you don't need to specify SpringRunner for your test, as it is inherited from the parent.

```
package com.apress.springrecipes.bank;
...
import org.springframework.beans.factory.annotation.Autowired;
import org.springframework.test.context.ContextConfiguration;
import org.springframework.test.context.junit4.AbstractJUnit4SpringContextTests;

@ContextConfiguration(classes = BankConfiguration.class)
public class AccountServiceJUnit4ContextTests extends AbstractJUnit4SpringContextTests {

    private static final String TEST_ACCOUNT_NO = "1234";

    @Autowired
    private AccountService accountService;
    ...
}
```

Inject Test Fixtures with the TestContext Framework in TestNG

In TestNG, you can extend the TestContext support class `AbstractTestNGSpringContextTests` to have test fixtures injected from the managed application context.

```
package com.apress.springrecipes.bank;
...
import org.springframework.beans.factory.annotation.Autowired;
import org.springframework.test.context.ContextConfiguration;
import org.springframework.test.context.testng.AbstractTestNGSpringContextTests;

@ContextConfiguration(classes = BankConfiguration.class)
public class AccountServiceTestNGContextTests extends AbstractTestNGSpringContextTests {

    private static final String TEST_ACCOUNT_NO = "1234";

    @Autowired
    private AccountService accountService;

    @BeforeMethod
    public void init() {
        accountService.createAccount(TEST_ACCOUNT_NO);
        accountService.deposit(TEST_ACCOUNT_NO, 100);
    }
    ...
}
```

16-6. Manage Transactions in Integration Tests

Problem

When creating integration tests for an application that accesses a database, you usually prepare the test data in the initialization method. After each test method runs, it may have modified the data in the database. So, you have to clean up the database to ensure that the next test method will run from a consistent state. As a result, you have to develop many database cleanup tasks.

Solution

Spring's testing support facilities can create and roll back a transaction for each test method, so the changes you make in a test method won't affect the next one. This can also save you the trouble of developing cleanup tasks to clean up the database.

The TestContext framework provides a test execution listener related to transaction management. It will be registered with a test context manager by default if you don't specify your own explicitly.

`TransactionalTestExecutionListener` handles the `@Transactional` annotation at the class or method level and has the methods run within transactions automatically.

Your test class can extend the corresponding TestContext support class for your testing framework, as shown in Table 16-3, to have its test methods run within transactions. These classes integrate with a test context manager and have `@Transactional` enabled at the class level. Note that a transaction manager is also required in the bean configuration file.

Table 16-3. *TestContext Support Classes for Transaction Management*

Testing Framework	TestContext Support Class*
JUnit	AbstractTransactionalJUnit4SpringContextTests
TestNG	AbstractTransactionalTestNGSpringContextTests

These TestContext support classes have `TransactionalTestExecutionListener` and `SqlScriptsTestExecutionListener` enabled in addition to `DependencyInjectionTestExecutionListener` and `DirtiesContextTestExecutionListener`.

In JUnit and TestNG, you can simply annotate `@Transactional` at the class level or the method level to have the test methods run within transactions, without extending a TestContext support class. However, to integrate with a test context manager, you have to run the JUnit test with the test runner `SpringRunner`, and you have to do it manually for a TestNG test.

How It Works

Let's consider storing your bank system's accounts in a relational database. You can choose any JDBC-compliant database engine that supports transactions and then execute the following SQL statement on it to create the ACCOUNT table. For testing we are going to use an in-memory H2 database.

```
CREATE TABLE ACCOUNT (
    ACCOUNT_NO   VARCHAR(10)    NOT NULL,
    BALANCE      DOUBLE         NOT NULL,
    PRIMARY KEY (ACCOUNT_NO)
);
```

Next, you create a new DAO implementation that uses JDBC to access the database. You can take advantage of JdbcTemplate to simplify your operations.

```
package com.apress.springrecipes.bank;

import org.springframework.jdbc.core.support.JdbcDaoSupport;

public class JdbcAccountDao extends JdbcDaoSupport implements AccountDao {

    public void createAccount(Account account) {
        String sql = "INSERT INTO ACCOUNT (ACCOUNT_NO, BALANCE) VALUES (?, ?)";
        getJdbcTemplate().update(
            sql, account.getAccountNo(), account.getBalance());
    }

    public void updateAccount(Account account) {
        String sql = "UPDATE ACCOUNT SET BALANCE = ? WHERE ACCOUNT_NO = ?";
        getJdbcTemplate().update(
            sql, account.getBalance(), account.getAccountNo());
    }
```

```
    public void removeAccount(Account account) {
        String sql = "DELETE FROM ACCOUNT WHERE ACCOUNT_NO = ?";
        getJdbcTemplate().update(sql, account.getAccountNo());
    }

    public Account findAccount(String accountNo) {
        String sql = "SELECT BALANCE FROM ACCOUNT WHERE ACCOUNT_NO = ?";
        double balance =
            getJdbcTemplate().queryForObject(sql, Double.class, accountNo);
        return new Account(accountNo, balance);
    }
}
```

Before you create integration tests to test the AccountService instance that uses this DAO to persist account objects, you have to replace InMemoryAccountDao with this DAO in the configuration class and configure the target data source as well.

■ **Note**   To use H2, you have to add it as a dependency to your classpath.

```
<dependency>
    <groupId>com.h2database:</groupId>
    <artifactId>h2</artifactId>
    <version>1.4.194</version>
</dependency>
```

Or when using Gradle, add the following:

```
testCompile 'com.h2database:h2:1.4.194'
```

```
@Configuration
public class BankConfiguration {

    @Bean
    public DataSource dataSource() {
        DriverManagerDataSource dataSource = new DriverManagerDataSource();
        dataSource.setUrl("jdbc:h2:mem:bank-testing");
        dataSource.setUsername("sa");
        dataSource.setPassword("");
        return dataSource;
    }

    @Bean
    public AccountDao accountDao() {
        JdbcAccountDao accountDao = new JdbcAccountDao();
        accountDao.setDataSource(dataSource());
        return accountDao;
    }
}
```

```
    @Bean
    public AccountService accountService() {
        return new AccountServiceImpl(accountDao());
    }
}
```

Manage Transactions with the TestContext Framework in JUnit

When using the TestContext framework to create tests, you can have the tests methods run within transactions by annotating @Transactional at the class or method level. In JUnit, you can specify SpringRunner for your test class so that it doesn't need to extend a support class.

```
package com.apress.springrecipes.bank;
...
import org.springframework.beans.factory.annotation.Autowired;
import org.springframework.test.context.ContextConfiguration;
import org.springframework.test.context.junit4.SpringRunner;
import org.springframework.transaction.annotation.Transactional;

@RunWith(SpringRunner.class)
@ContextConfiguration(classes = BankConfiguration.class)
@Transactional
public class AccountServiceJUnit4ContextTests {

    private static final String TEST_ACCOUNT_NO = "1234";

    @Autowired
    private AccountService accountService;

    @Before
    public void init() {
        accountService.createAccount(TEST_ACCOUNT_NO);
        accountService.deposit(TEST_ACCOUNT_NO, 100);
    }

    // Don't need cleanup() anymore
    ...
}
```

If you annotate a test class with @Transactional, all of its test methods will run within transactions. An alternative is to annotate individual methods with @Transactional, not the entire class.

By default, transactions for test methods will be rolled back at the end. You can alter this behavior by disabling the defaultRollback attribute of @TransactionConfiguration, which should be applied to the class level. Also, you can override this class-level rollback behavior at the method level with the @Rollback annotation, which requires a Boolean value.

■ **Note**   Methods with the @Before or @After annotation will be executed within the same transactions as test methods. If you have methods that need to perform initialization or cleanup tasks before or after a transaction, you have to annotate them with @BeforeTransaction or @AfterTransaction.

Finally, you also need a transaction manager configured in the bean configuration file. By default, a bean whose type is PlatformTransactionManager will be used, but you can specify another one in the transactionManager attribute of the @TransactionConfiguration annotation by giving its name.

```
@Bean
public DataSourceTransactionManager transactionManager(DataSource dataSource) {
    return new DataSourceTransactionManager(dataSource);
}
```

In JUnit, an alternative to managing transactions for test methods is to extend the transactional TestContext support class AbstractTransactionalJUnit4SpringContextTests, which has @Transactional enabled at the class level so that you don't need to enable it again. By extending this support class, you don't need to specify SpringRunner for your test, as it is inherited from the parent.

```
package com.apress.springrecipes.bank;
...
import org.springframework.test.context.ContextConfiguration;
import org.springframework.test.context.junit4.
AbstractTransactionalJUnit4SpringContextTests;

@ContextConfiguration(classes = BankConfiguration.class)
public class AccountServiceJUnit4ContextTests extends
AbstractTransactionalJUnit4SpringContextTests {
    ...
}
```

Manage Transactions with the TestContext Framework in TestNG

To create TestNG tests that run within transactions, your test class can extend the TestContext support class AbstractTransactionalTestNGSpringContextTests to have its methods run within transactions.

```
package com.apress.springrecipes.bank;
...
import org.springframework.beans.factory.annotation.Autowired;
import org.springframework.test.context.ContextConfiguration;
import org.springframework.test.context.testng.
AbstractTransactionalTestNGSpringContextTests;

@ContextConfiguration(classes = BankConfiguration.class)
public class AccountServiceTestNGContextTests extends
    AbstractTransactionalTestNGSpringContextTests {

    private static final String TEST_ACCOUNT_NO = "1234";

    @Autowired
    private AccountService accountService;
```

```
@BeforeMethod
public void init() {
    accountService.createAccount(TEST_ACCOUNT_NO);
    accountService.deposit(TEST_ACCOUNT_NO, 100);
}

// Don't need cleanup() anymore
...
}
```

16-7. Access a Database in Integration Tests

Problem

When creating integration tests for an application that accesses a database, especially one developed with an ORM framework, you might want to access the database directly to prepare test data and validate the data after a test method runs.

Solution

Spring's testing support facilities can create and provide a JDBC template for you to perform database-related tasks in your tests. Your test class can extend one of the transactional TestContext support classes to access the precreated JdbcTemplate instance. These classes also require a data source and a transaction manager in the bean configuration file.

How It Works

When using the TestContext framework to create tests, you can extend the corresponding TestContext support class to use a JdbcTemplate instance via a protected field. For JUnit, this class is AbstractTransactionalJUnit4SpringContextTests, which provides similar convenient methods for you to count the number of rows in a table, delete rows from a table, and execute a SQL script.

```
package com.apress.springrecipes.bank;
...
import org.springframework.test.context.ContextConfiguration;
import org.springframework.test.context.junit4.
AbstractTransactionalJUnit4SpringContextTests;

@ContextConfiguration(classes = BankConfiguration.class)
public class AccountServiceJUnit4ContextTests extends AbstractTransactionalJUnit4Spring
ContextTests {
    ...
    @Before
    public void init() {
        executeSqlScript("classpath:/bank.sql",true);
        jdbcTemplate.update(
            "INSERT INTO ACCOUNT (ACCOUNT_NO, BALANCE) VALUES (?, ?)",
            TEST_ACCOUNT_NO, 100);
    }
```

```
    @Test
    public void deposit() {
        accountService.deposit(TEST_ACCOUNT_NO, 50);
        double balance = jdbcTemplate.queryForObject(
            "SELECT BALANCE FROM ACCOUNT WHERE ACCOUNT_NO = ?",
            Double.class, TEST_ACCOUNT_NO);
        assertEquals(balance, 150.0, 0);
    }

    @Test
    public void withDraw() {
        accountService.withdraw(TEST_ACCOUNT_NO, 50);
        double balance = jdbcTemplate.queryForObject(
            "SELECT BALANCE FROM ACCOUNT WHERE ACCOUNT_NO = ?",
            Double.class, TEST_ACCOUNT_NO);
        assertEquals(balance, 50.0, 0);
    }
}
```

Instead of using the executeSqlScript method, you could also put the @Sql annotation on the class or test method to execute some SQL or a script.

```
@ContextConfiguration(classes = BankConfiguration.class)
@Sql(scripts="classpath:/bank.sql")
public class AccountServiceJUnit4ContextTests extends
AbstractTransactionalJUnit4SpringContextTests {

    private static final String TEST_ACCOUNT_NO = "1234";

    @Autowired
    private AccountService accountService;

    @Before
    public void init() {
        jdbcTemplate.update(
            "INSERT INTO ACCOUNT (ACCOUNT_NO, BALANCE) VALUES (?, ?)",
            TEST_ACCOUNT_NO, 100);
    }
}
```

With the @Sql method, you can execute scripts which you can specify in the scripts attribute or put in SQL statements directly in the statements attribute of the annotation. Finally, you can specify when to execute the specified instructions before or after a test method. You can put multiple @Sql annotations on a class/method so you can execute statements before and after the test.

In TestNG, you can extend AbstractTransactionalTestNGSpringContextTests to use a JdbcTemplate instance.

```
package com.apress.springrecipes.bank;
...
import org.springframework.beans.factory.annotation.Autowired;
import org.springframework.test.context.ContextConfiguration;
import org.springframework.test.context.testng.
AbstractTransactionalTestNGSpringContextTests;

@ContextConfiguration(classes = BankConfiguration.class)
public class AccountServiceTestNGContextTests extends
AbstractTransactionalTestNGSpringContextTests {
    ...
    @BeforeMethod
    public void init() {
        executeSqlScript("classpath:/bank.sql",true);
        jdbcTemplate.update(
            "INSERT INTO ACCOUNT (ACCOUNT_NO, BALANCE) VALUES (?, ?)",
            TEST_ACCOUNT_NO, 100);
    }

    @Test
    public void deposit() {
        accountService.deposit(TEST_ACCOUNT_NO, 50);
        double balance = jdbcTemplate.queryForObject(
            "SELECT BALANCE FROM ACCOUNT WHERE ACCOUNT_NO = ?",
            Double.class, TEST_ACCOUNT_NO);
        assertEquals(balance, 150, 0);
    }

    @Test
    public void withDraw() {
        accountService.withdraw(TEST_ACCOUNT_NO, 50);
        double balance = jdbcTemplate.queryForObject(
            "SELECT BALANCE FROM ACCOUNT WHERE ACCOUNT_NO = ?",
            Double.class, TEST_ACCOUNT_NO);
        assertEquals(balance, 50, 0);
    }
}
```

16-8. Use Spring's Common Testing Annotations

Problem

You often have to manually implement common testing tasks, such as expecting an exception to be thrown, repeating a test method multiple times, ensuring that a test method will complete in a particular time period, and so on.

Solution

Spring's testing support provides a common set of testing annotations to simplify your test creation. These annotations are Spring-specific but independent of the underlying testing framework. Of these, the annotations in Table 16-4 are useful for common testing tasks. However, they are supported only for use with JUnit.

Table 16-4. *Spring's Test Annotations*

Annotation	Description
@Repeat	This indicates that a test method has to run multiple times. The number of times it will run is specified as the annotation value.
@Timed	This indicates that a test method must complete in a specified time period (in milliseconds). Otherwise, the test fails. Note that the time period includes the repetitions of the test method and any initialization and cleanup methods.
@IfProfileValue	This indicates that a test method can run only in a specific testing environment. This test method will run only when the actual profile value matches the specified one. You can also specify multiple values so that the test method will run if any of the values is matched. By default, SystemProfileValueSource is used to retrieve system properties as profile values, but you can create your own ProfileValueSource implementation and specify it in the @ProfileValueSourceConfiguration annotation.

You can use Spring's testing annotations by extending one of the TestContext support classes. If you don't extend a support class but run your JUnit test with the test runner SpringRunner, you can also use these annotations.

How It Works

When using the TestContext framework to create tests for JUnit, you can use Spring's testing annotations if you run your test with SpringRunner or extend a JUnit TestContext support class.

```
package com.apress.springrecipes.bank;
...
import org.springframework.test.annotation.Repeat;
import org.springframework.test.annotation.Timed;
import org.springframework.test.context.ContextConfiguration;
import org.springframework.test.context.junit4.
AbstractTransactionalJUnit4SpringContextTests;

@ContextConfiguration(locations = "/beans.xml")
public class AccountServiceJUnit4ContextTests extends
AbstractTransactionalJUnit4SpringContextTests {
    ...
    @Test
    @Timed(millis = 1000)
    public void deposit() {
        ...
    }
```

```
    @Test
    @Repeat(5)
    public void withDraw() {
        ...
    }
}
```

16-9. Implement Integration Tests for Spring MVC Controllers

Problem

In a web application, you want to integration test the web controllers developed with the Spring MVC framework.

Solution

A Spring MVC controller is invoked by `DispatcherServlet` with an HTTP request object and an HTTP response object. After processing a request, the controller returns it to `DispatcherServlet` for rendering the view. The main challenge of integration testing Spring MVC controllers, as well as web controllers in other web application frameworks, is simulating HTTP request objects and response objects in a unit testing environment as well as setting up the mocked environment for a unit test. Fortunately, Spring has the mock MVC part of the Spring Test support. This allows for easy setup of a mocked servlet environment.

Spring Test Mock MVC will set up a `WebApplicationContext` according to your configuration. Next you can use the MockMvc API to simulate HTTP requests and verify the result.

How It Works

In the banking application, you want to integration test your `DepositController`. Before you can start testing, you need to create a configuration class to configure the web-related beans.

```java
package com.apress.springrecipes.bank.web.config;

import org.springframework.context.annotation.Bean;
import org.springframework.context.annotation.ComponentScan;
import org.springframework.context.annotation.Configuration;
import org.springframework.web.servlet.ViewResolver;
import org.springframework.web.servlet.config.annotation.EnableWebMvc;
import org.springframework.web.servlet.view.InternalResourceViewResolver;

@Configuration
@EnableWebMvc
@ComponentScan(basePackages = "com.apress.springrecipes.bank.web")
public class BankWebConfiguration {
```

```
    @Bean
    public ViewResolver viewResolver() {
        InternalResourceViewResolver viewResolver = new InternalResourceViewResolver();
        viewResolver.setPrefix("/WEB-INF/views/");
        viewResolver.setSuffix(".jsp");
        return viewResolver;

    }
}
```

The configuration enables annotation-based controllers by using the @EnableWebMvc annotation; next you want the @Controller annotated beans to be picked up automatically using the @ComponentScan annotation. Finally, there is an InternalResourceViewResolver that turns the name of the view into a URL, which normally would be rendered by the browser, that you will now validate in the controller.

Now that the web-based configuration is in place, you can start to create your integration test. This unit test has to load your BankWebConfiguration class and also has to be annotated with @WebAppConfiguration to inform the TestContext framework you want a WebApplicationContext instead of a regular ApplicationContext.

Integration Test Spring MVC Controllers with JUnit

In JUnit it is the easiest to extend one of the base classes, in this case AbstractTransactionalJUnit4Spring ContextTests because you want to insert some test data and to roll back after the tests complete.

```
package com.apress.springrecipes.bank.web;

import com.apress.springrecipes.bank.config.BankConfiguration;
import com.apress.springrecipes.bank.web.config.BankWebConfiguration;
import org.junit.Before;
import org.junit.Test;
import org.springframework.beans.factory.annotation.Autowired;
import org.springframework.test.context.ContextConfiguration;
import org.springframework.test.context.junit4.AbstractTransactionalJUnit4Spring
ContextTests;
import org.springframework.test.context.web.WebAppConfiguration;
import org.springframework.test.web.servlet.MockMvc;
import org.springframework.test.web.servlet.setup.MockMvcBuilders;
import org.springframework.web.context.WebApplicationContext;

import static org.springframework.test.web.servlet.request.MockMvcRequestBuilders.get;
import static org.springframework.test.web.servlet.result.MockMvcResultHandlers.print;
import static org.springframework.test.web.servlet.result.MockMvcResultMatchers.forwardedUrl;
import static org.springframework.test.web.servlet.result.MockMvcResultMatchers.status;
```

```
@ContextConfiguration(classes= { BankWebConfiguration.class, BankConfiguration.class})
@WebAppConfiguration
public class DepositControllerJUnit4ContextTests extends
AbstractTransactionalJUnit4SpringContextTests {

    private static final String ACCOUNT_PARAM = "accountNo";
    private static final String AMOUNT_PARAM = "amount";

    private static final String TEST_ACCOUNT_NO = "1234";
    private static final String TEST_AMOUNT = "50.0";

    @Autowired
    private WebApplicationContext webApplicationContext;

    private MockMvc mockMvc;

    @Before
    public void init() {
        executeSqlScript("classpath:/bank.sql", true);
        jdbcTemplate.update(
            "INSERT INTO ACCOUNT (ACCOUNT_NO, BALANCE) VALUES (?, ?)",
            TEST_ACCOUNT_NO, 100);
        mockMvc = MockMvcBuilders.webAppContextSetup(webApplicationContext).build();

    }

    @Test
    public void deposit() throws Exception {
        mockMvc.perform(
            get("/deposit.do")
                .param(ACCOUNT_PARAM, TEST_ACCOUNT_NO)
                .param(AMOUNT_PARAM, TEST_AMOUNT))
            .andDo(print())
            .andExpect(forwardedUrl("/WEB-INF/views/success.jsp"))
            .andExpect(status().isOk());
    }
}
```

In the init method, you prepare the MockMvc object by using the convenient MockMvcBuilders. Using the factory method webAppContextSetup, you can use the already loaded WebApplicationContext to initialize the MockMvc object. The MockMvc object basically mimics the behavior of DispatcherServlet, which you would use in a Spring MVC–based application. It will use the passed-in WebApplicationContext to configure the handler mappings and view resolution strategies and will also apply any interceptors that are configured.

There is also some setup of a test account so that you have something to work with.

In the deposit test method, the initialized MockMvc object is used to simulate an incoming request to the /deposit.do URL with two request parameters, accountNo and amount. The MockMvcRequestBuilders. get factory method results in a RequestBuilder instance that is passed to the MockMvc.perform method.

The perform method returns a ResultActions object that can be used to do assertions and certain actions on the return result. The test method prints the information for the created request and returned response using andDo(print()), which can be useful while debugging your test. Finally, there are two assertions to verify that everything works as expected. The DepositController returns success as the viewname, which should lead to a forward to /WEB-INF/views/success.jsp because of the configuration of the ViewResolver. The return code of the request should be 200 (OK), which can be tested with status(). isOk() or status().is(200).

Integration Test Spring MVC Controllers with TestNG

Spring Mock MVC can also be used with TestNG to extend the appropriate base class AbstractTransactionalTestNGSpringContextTests and add the @WebAppConfiguration annotation.

```
@ContextConfiguration(classes= { BankWebConfiguration.class, BankConfiguration.class})
@WebAppConfiguration
public class DepositControllerTestNGContextTests
    extends AbstractTransactionalTestNGSpringContextTests {

    @BeforeMethod
    public void init() {
        executeSqlScript("classpath:/bank.sql", true);
        jdbcTemplate.update(
            "INSERT INTO ACCOUNT (ACCOUNT_NO, BALANCE) VALUES (?, ?)",
            TEST_ACCOUNT_NO, 100);
        mockMvc = MockMvcBuilders.webAppContextSetup(webApplicationContext).build();
    }

}
```

16-10. Write Integration Tests for REST Clients

Problem

You want to write an integration test for a RestTemplate-based client.

Solution

When writing an integration test for a REST-based client, you don't want to rely on the availability of the external service. You can write an integration test using a mock server to return an expected result instead of calling the real endpoint.

How It Works

When working at a bank, you need to validate the account numbers people enter; you could implement your own validation or you could reuse an existing one. You are going to implement an IBAN validation service that will use the API available at http://openiban.com.

First you write an interface defining the contract.

```
package com.apress.springrecipes.bank.web;

public interface IBANValidationClient {

    IBANValidationResult validate(String iban);
}
```

IBANValidationResult contains the results of the call to the validation endpoint.

```
package com.apress.springrecipes.bank.web;

import java.util.ArrayList;
import java.util.HashMap;
import java.util.List;
import java.util.Map;

public class IBANValidationResult {

    private boolean valid;
    private List<String> messages = new ArrayList<>();
    private String iban;

    private Map<String, String> bankData = new HashMap<>();

    public boolean isValid() {
        return valid;
    }

    public void setValid(boolean valid) {
        this.valid = valid;
    }

    public List<String> getMessages() {
        return messages;
    }

    public void setMessages(List<String> messages) {
        this.messages = messages;
    }

    public String getIban() {
        return iban;
    }

    public void setIban(String iban) {
        this.iban = iban;
    }
```

```java
    public Map<String, String> getBankData() {
        return bankData;
    }

    public void setBankData(Map<String, String> bankData) {
        this.bankData = bankData;
    }

    @Override
    public String toString() {
        return "IBANValidationResult [" +
                "valid=" + valid +
                ", messages=" + messages +
                ", iban='" + iban + '\'' +
                ", bankData=" + bankData +
                ']';
    }
}
```

Next write the OpenIBANValidationClient class, which will use a RestTemplate instance to communicate with the API. For easy access to a RestTemplate instance, you can extend RestGatewaySupport.

```java
package com.apress.springrecipes.bank.web;

import org.springframework.stereotype.Service;
import org.springframework.web.client.support.RestGatewaySupport;

@Service
public class OpenIBANValidationClient extends RestGatewaySupport implements
IBANValidationClient {

    private static final String URL_TEMPLATE = "https://openiban.com/validate/{IBAN_NUMBER}?
getBIC=true&validateBankCode=true";

    @Override
    public IBANValidationResult validate(String iban) {

        return getRestTemplate().getForObject(URL_TEMPLATE, IBANValidationResult.class, iban);
    }
}
```

Next you will create a test that will construct a MockRestServiceServer class for the OpenIBANValidationClient class, and you configure it to return a specific result in JSON for an expected request.

```java
package com.apress.springrecipes.bank.web;

import com.apress.springrecipes.bank.config.BankConfiguration;
import org.junit.Before;
import org.junit.Test;
```

```java
import org.junit.runner.RunWith;
import org.springframework.beans.factory.annotation.Autowired;
import org.springframework.core.io.ClassPathResource;
import org.springframework.http.MediaType;
import org.springframework.test.context.ContextConfiguration;
import org.springframework.test.context.junit4.SpringRunner;
import org.springframework.test.web.client.MockRestServiceServer;

import static org.junit.Assert.assertFalse;
import static org.junit.Assert.assertTrue;
import static org.springframework.test.web.client.match.MockRestRequestMatchers.requestTo;
import static org.springframework.test.web.client.response.MockRestResponseCreators.
withSuccess;

@RunWith(SpringRunner.class)
@ContextConfiguration(classes= { BankConfiguration.class})
public class OpenIBANValidationClientTest {

    @Autowired
    private OpenIBANValidationClient client;

    private MockRestServiceServer mockRestServiceServer;

    @Before
    public void init() {
        mockRestServiceServer = MockRestServiceServer.createServer(client);
    }

    @Test
    public void validIban() {

        mockRestServiceServer
            .expect(requestTo("https://openiban.com/validate/NL87TRIO0396451440?getBIC=
            true&validateBankCode=true"))
                .andRespond(withSuccess(new ClassPathResource("NL87TRIO0396451440-result.
                json"), MediaType.APPLICATION_JSON));

        IBANValidationResult result = client.validate("NL87TRIO0396451440");
        assertTrue(result.isValid());
    }

    @Test
    public void invalidIban() {

        mockRestServiceServer
            .expect(requestTo("https://openiban.com/validate/NL28XXXX389242218?getBIC=
            true&validateBankCode=true"))
                .andRespond(withSuccess(new ClassPathResource("NL28XXXX389242218-result.
                json"), MediaType.APPLICATION_JSON));
```

```
        IBANValidationResult result = client.validate("NL28XXXX389242218");
        assertFalse(result.isValid());
    }
}
```

The test class has two test methods, and both are quite similar. In the `init` method, you create a `MockRestServiceService` class using the `OpenIBANValidationClient` class (this is possible because it extends `RestGatewaySupport`; if that wasn't the case, you would have to use the configured `RestTemplate` class to create a mocked server). In the test method, you set up the expectation with a URL, and now when that URL is called, a JSON response, from the classpath, will be returned as the answer.

For testing you probably want to use some well-known responses from the server, and for this you could use some recorded results from a live system or maybe they already provide results for testing.

Summary

In this chapter, you learned about the basic concepts and techniques used in testing Java applications. JUnit and TestNG are the most popular testing frameworks on the Java platform. Unit tests are used for testing a single programming unit, which is typically a class or a method in object-oriented languages. When testing a unit that depends on other units, you can use stubs and mock objects to simulate its dependencies, thus making the tests simpler. In contrast, integration tests are used to test several units as a whole.

In the web layer, controllers are usually hard to test. Spring offers mock objects for the Servlet API so that you can easily simulate web request and response objects to test a web controller. There is also Spring Mock MVC for easy integration testing of your controllers. What applies to controllers also applies to REST-based clients. To help you test these clients, Spring provides the `MockRestServiceServer`, which you can use to mock an external system.

Spring's testing support facilities can manage application contexts for your tests by loading them from bean configuration files and caching them across multiple test executions. You can access the managed application context in your tests, as well as have your test fixtures injected from the application context automatically. In addition, if your tests involve database updates, Spring can manage transactions for them so that changes made in one test method will be rolled back and thus won't affect the next test method. Spring can also create a JDBC template for you to prepare and validate your test data in the database.

Spring provides a common set of testing annotations to simplify your test creation. These annotations are Spring-specific but independent of the underlying testing framework. However, some of these are only supported for use with JUnit.

CHAPTER 17

Grails

When you embark on the creation of a Java web application, you need to put together a series of Java classes, create configuration files, and establish a particular layout, all of which have little to do with the problems an application solves. Such pieces are often called *scaffolding code* or *scaffolding steps* since they are just the means to an end—the end being what an application actually accomplishes.

Grails is a framework designed to limit the amount of scaffolding steps you need to take in Java applications. Based on the Groovy language, which is a Java Virtual Machine–compatible language, Grails automates many steps that need to be undertaken in a Java application on the basis of conventions.

For example, when you create application controllers, they are eventually accompanied by a series of views (e.g., JavaServer Pages [JSP] pages), in addition to requiring some type of configuration file to make them work. If you generate a controller using Grails, Grails automates numerous steps using conventions (e.g., creating views and configuration files). You can later modify whatever Grails generates to more specific scenarios, but Grails undoubtedly shortens your development time since you won't need to write everything from scratch (e.g., write XML configuration files and prepare a project directory structure).

Grails is fully integrated with Spring, so you can use it to kick-start your Spring applications and thus reduce your development efforts.

17-1. Get and Install Grails

Problem

You want to start creating a Grails application but don't know where to get Grails and how to set it up.

Solution

You can download Grails at www.grails.org/. Ensure that you download Grails version 3.2 or higher. Grails is a self-contained framework that comes with various scripts to automate the creation of Java applications. In this sense, you simply need to unpack the distribution and perform a few installation steps to create Java applications on your workstation.

How It Works

After you unpack Grails on your workstation, define two environment variables on your operating system: GRAILS_HOME and PATH. This allows you to invoke Grails operations from anywhere on your workstation. If you use a Linux workstation, you can edit the global bashrc file, located under the /etc/ directory, or a user's .bashrc file, located under a user's home directory. Note that, depending on the Linux distribution, these last file names can vary (e.g., bash.bashrc). Both files use identical syntax to define environment variables, with one file used to define variables for all users and another for a single user. Place the following contents in either one:

```
GRAILS_HOME=/<installation_directory>/grails
export GRAILS_HOME
export PATH=$PATH:$GRAILS_HOME/bin
```

If you use a Windows workstation, go to the Control Panel and click the System icon. In the window that opens, click the Advanced Options tab. Next, click the "Environment variables" box to bring up the environment variable editor. From there, you can add or modify environment variables for either a single user or all users, using the following steps:

1. Click the New box.

2. Create an environment variable with the name GRAILS_HOME and a value corresponding to the Grails installation directory (e.g., /<installation_directory>/grails).

3. Select the PATH environment variable, and click the Modify box.

4. Add the ;%GRAILS_HOME%\bin value to the end of the PATH environment variable.

■ **Caution**   Be sure to add this last value and not modify the PATH environment variable in any other way because this may cause certain applications to stop working.

Once you perform these steps in either a Windows or Linux workstation, you can start creating Grails applications. If you execute the command grails help from any directory on your workstation, you should see Grails' numerous commands.

17-2. Create a Grails Application

Problem

You want to create a Grails application.

Solution

To create a Grails application, invoke the following command wherever you want to create an application: grails create-app <grailsappname>. This creates a Grails application directory, with a project structure in accordance to the framework's design. If this last command fails, consult recipe 17-1. The grails command should be available from any console or terminal if Grails was installed correctly.

How It Works

For example, typing grails create-app court creates a Grails application under a directory named court. Inside this directory, you will find a series of files and directories generated by Grails on the basis of conventions. Figure 17-1 shows the initial project structure for a Grails application.

Figure 17-1. Grails application project structure

■ **Note** In addition to this layout, Grails creates a series of working directories and files (i.e., not intended to be modified directly) for an application. These working directories and files are placed under a user's home directory under the name .grails/<grails_version>/.

As you can note from this last listing, Grails generates a series of files and directories that are common in most Java applications. You'll have a directory called `src\main\groovy` for placing source code files and a `src\main\web-app` directory that includes the common layout for Java web applications (e.g., `/WEB-INF/`, `/META-INF/`, `css`, `images`, and `js`). Right out of the box, Grails saves you time by putting these common Java application constructs together using a single command.

Explore a Grails Application's File and Directory Structure

Since some of these files and directories are Grails specific, we will describe the purpose behind each one:

- `gradle.properties`: Used to define an application's build properties, including the Grails version, the servlet version, and an application's name

- `grails-app`: A directory containing the core of an application, which further contains the following folders:

  - `#.assets`: A directory containing an application's static resources (i.e., `.css` and `.js` files).

  - `conf`: A directory containing an application's configuration sources

  - `controllers`: A directory containing an application's controller files

  - `domain`: A directory containing an application's domain files

  - `i18n`: A directory containing an application's internationalization (i18n) files

  - `services`: A directory containing an application's service files

  - `taglib`: A directory containing an application's tag libraries

  - `utils`: A directory containing an application's utility files

  - `views`: A directory containing an application's view files

- `src\main`: Directory used for an application's source code files; contains a subfolder named `groovy`, for sources written in this language (you could add a `java` subfolder to write Java)

- `src\test`: Directory used for an application's unit test files

- `src\integration-test`: Directory used for an application's integration test files

- `web-app`: Directory used for an application's deployment structure; contains the standard web archive (WAR) files and directory structure (e.g., `/WEB-INF/`, `/META-INF/`, `css`, `images`, and `js`)

Run an Application

Grails comes preconfigured to run applications on an Apache Tomcat web container. Similar to the creation of creating a Grails application, the process of running Grails applications is highly automated.

Placed under the root directory of a Grails application, invoke `grails run-app`. This command will trigger the build process for an application if it's needed, as well as start the Apache Tomcat web container and deploy the application.

Since Grails operates on conventions, an application is deployed under a context named after the project name. So, for example, the application named `court` is deployed to the URL `http://localhost:8080/`. Figure 17-2 illustrates the default main screen for Grails applications.

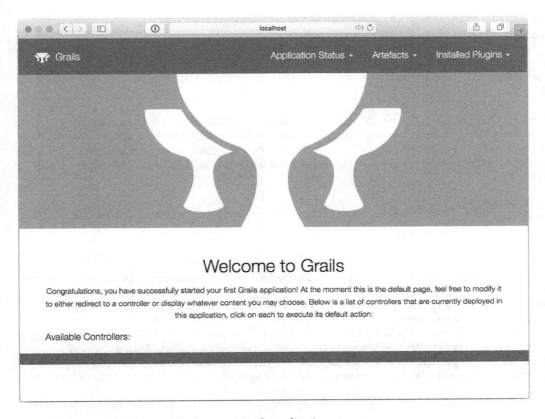

Figure 17-2. *Default main screen for court Grails application*

The application is still in its out-of-the-box state. Next, we will illustrate how to create your first Grails construct in order to realize more time-saving procedures.

Create Your First Grails Application Construct

Now that you have seen how easy it is to create a Grails application, let's incorporate an application construct in the form of a controller. This will further illustrate how Grails automates a series of steps in the development process of Java applications.

Placed under the root directory of a Grails application, invoke `grails create-controller welcome`. Executing this command will perform the following steps:

1. Create a controller named `WelcomeController.groovy` under the application directory `grails-app/controllers`.

2. Create a directory named `welcome` under the application directory `grails-app/views`.

3. Create a test class named `WelcomeControllerSpec.groovy` under the application directory `src/u`.

As a first step, let's analyze the contents of the controller generated by Grails. The contents of the `WelcomeController.groovy` controller are as follows:

```
class WelcomeController {
    def index {}
}
```

If you're unfamiliar with Groovy, the syntax will seem awkward. But it's simply a class named `WelcomeController` with a method named `index`. The purpose is the same as the Spring MVC controllers you created in Chapter 3. `WelcomeController` represents a controller class, whereas the method `index` represents a handler method. However, in this state the controller isn't doing anything. Modify it to reflect the following:

```
class WelcomeController {
    Date now = new Date()
    def index = {[today:now]}
}
```

The first addition is a `Date` object assigned to the `now` class field, to represent the system date. Since `def index {}` represents a handler method, the addition of `[today:now]` is used as a return value. In this case, the return value represents a variable named `today` with the `now` class field, and that variable's value will be passed onto the view associated with the handler method.

Having a controller and a handler method that returns the current date, you can create a corresponding view. If you place yourself under the directory `grails-app/views/welcome`, you will not find any views. However, Grails attempts to locate a view for the `WelcomeController` controller inside this directory, in accordance with the name of the handler method; this, once again, is one of the many conventions used by Grails.

Therefore, create a GSP page named `index.gsp` inside this directory with the following contents:

```
<!DOCTYPE html>
<html>
<head>
    <title>Welcome</title>
</head>

<body>
<h2>Welcome to Court Reservation System</h2>
Today is <g:formatDate format="yyyy-MM-dd" date="${today}"/>
</body>
</html>
```

This is a standard GSP page, which makes use of the expressions and a tag library. When writing GSP pages, the default tag library is available using the g tag. The `formatDate` tag renders a variable named `${today}`, which is precisely the name of the variable returned by the controller handler method named `index`.

Next, from the root directory of the Grails application, invoke the command `grails run-app`. This automatically builds the application, compiling the controller class and copying files where they are needed as well as starting the Apache Tomcat web container and deploying the application.

Following the same Grails convention process, the `WelcomeController` along with its handler methods and views will be accessible from the context path `http://localhost:8080/welcome/`. Since `index` is the default page used for context paths, if you open a browser and visit `http://localhost:8080/welcome/` or the explicit URL `http://localhost:8080/welcome/` index, you will see the previous JSP page that renders the current date as returned by the controller. Note the lack of view extensions in the URLs (i.e., `.html`). Grails hides the view technology by default; the reasons for this will become more evident in more advanced Grails scenarios.

As you repeat the simple steps needed to create an application controller and view, bear in mind you didn't have to create or modify any configuration files, manually copy files to different locations, or set up a web container to run the application. As an application moves forward, avoiding these scaffolding steps that are common in Java web applications can be a great way to reduce development time.

Export a Grails Application to a WAR

The previous steps were all performed in the confines of a Grails environment. That is to say, you relied on Grails to bootstrap a web container and run applications. However, when you want to run a Grails application in a production environment, you will undoubtedly need to generate a format in which to deploy the application to an external web container, which is a WAR file in the case of Java applications.

Placed under the root directory of a Grails application, invoke `grails war`. Executing this command generates a WAR file under the root directory in the form `<application-name>-<application-version>.war`. This WAR is a self-contained file with all the necessary elements needed to run a Grails application on any Java standard web container. In the case of the court application, a file named `court-0.1.war` is generated in the root directory of the Grails application, and the application version is taken from the parameter `app.version` defined in the `application.properties` file.

In accordance with Apache Tomcat deployment conventions, a WAR named `court-0.1.war` would be accessible at a URL in the form `http://localhost:8080/court-0.1/`. WAR deployment to URL conventions may vary depending on the Java web container (e.g., Jetty or Oracle WebLogic).

17-3. Get Grails Plug-Ins

Problem

You want to use functionality from a Java framework or Java API inside Grails applications, while taking advantage of the same Grails techniques to save scaffolding. The problem isn't simply using a Java framework or Java API in an application; this can be achieved by simply dropping the corresponding JARs into an application's `lib` directory. But rather having a Java framework or Java API tightly integrated with Grails, something that is provided in the form of Grails plug-ins.

By tightly integrated with Grails, we mean having the capacity to use shortcut instructions (e.g., `grails <plug-in-task>`) for performing a particular Java framework or Java API task or the ability to use functionality inside an application's classes or configuration files without resorting to scaffolding steps.

Solution

Grails actually comes with a few preinstalled plug-ins, even though this is not evident if you stick to using Grails' out-of-the-box functionality. However, there are many Grails plug-ins that can make working with a particular Java framework or Java API as productive a process as using Grails core functionality. Some of the more popular Grails plug-ins follow:

- *App Engine*: Integrates Google's App Engine SDK and tools with Grails

- *Quartz*: Integrates the Quartz Enterprise Job Scheduler to schedule jobs and have them executed using a specified interval or cron expression

737

- *Spring WS*: Integrates and supports the provisioning of web services, based on the Spring Web Services project

- *Clojure*: Integrates Clojure and allows Clojure code to be executed in Grails artifacts

To obtain a complete list of Grails plug-ins, you can execute the command `grails list-plugins`. This last command connects to the Grails plug-in repository and displays all the available Grails plug-ins. In addition, the command `grails plugin-info <plugin_name>` can be used to obtain detailed information about a particular plug-in. As an alternative, you can visit the Grails plug-in page located at `http://grails.org/plugin/home`.

Installing a Grails plug-in is as easy as adding a dependency to your `build.gradle` file; uninstalling is the reverse, removing it from the `build.gradle` file.

How It Works

A Grails plug-in follows a series of conventions that allow it to tightly integrate a particular Java framework or Java API with Grails. By default, Grails comes with the Apache Tomcat and Hibernate plug-ins preinstalled.

Besides these default plug-ins, additional plug-ins can be installed on a per-application basis. For example, to install the Clojure plug-in, you would add the following dependency to your `build.gradle` file:

```
dependencies {
    compile "org.grails.plugins:clojure:2.0.0.RC4"
}
```

17-4. Develop, Produce, and Test in Grails Environments

Problem

You want to use different parameters for the same application on the basis of the environment (e.g., development, production, and testing) it's being run in.

Solution

Grails anticipates that a Java application can undergo various phases that require different parameters. These phases, or *environments* as they are called by Grails, can be, for instance, development, production, and testing.

The most obvious scenario involves data sources, where you are likely to use a different permanent storage system for development, production, and testing environments. Since each of these storage systems will use different connection parameters, it's easier to configure parameters for multiple environments and let Grails connect to each one depending on an application's operations.

In addition to data sources, Grails provides the same feature for other parameters that can change in between application environments, such as server URLs for creating an application's absolute links.

Configuration parameters for a Grails application environment are specified in the files located under an application's `/grails-app/conf/` directory.

How It Works

Depending on the operation you're performing, Grails automatically selects the most suitable environment: development, production, or testing. For example, when you invoke the command `grails run-app`, this implies that you are still developing an application locally, so a development environment is assumed. In fact, when you execute this command, among the output you can see a line that reads as follows:

```
Environment set to development
```

This means that whatever parameters are set for a development environment are used to build, configure, and run the application. Another example is the `grails war` command. Since exporting a Grails application to a stand-alone WAR implies you will be running it on an external web container, Grails assumes a production environment. In the output generated for this command, you will find a line that reads as follows:

```
Environment set to production
```

This means that whatever parameters are set for a production environment are used to build, configure, and export the application. Finally, if you run a command like `grails test-app`, Grails assumes a testing environment. This means that whatever parameters are set for a testing environment are used to build, configure, and run tests. In the output generated for this command, you will find a line that reads as follows:

```
Environment set to test
```

Inside the `application.yml` file located in an application's directory `/grails-app/conf/`, you can find sections in the following form:

```
environments:
    development:
        dataSource:
            dbCreate: create-drop
            url: jdbc:h2:mem:devDb;MVCC=TRUE;LOCK_TIMEOUT=10000;DB_CLOSE_ON_EXIT=FALSE
    test:
        dataSource:
            dbCreate: update
            url: jdbc:h2:mem:testDb;MVCC=TRUE;LOCK_TIMEOUT=10000;DB_CLOSE_ON_EXIT=FALSE
    production:
        dataSource:
            dbCreate: none
            url: jdbc:h2:./prodDb;MVCC=TRUE;LOCK_TIMEOUT=10000;DB_CLOSE_ON_EXIT=FALSE
```

In this last listing, different connection parameters are specified for permanent storage systems on the basis of an application's environment. This allows an application to operate on different data sets, as you will surely not want development modifications to take place on the same data set used in a production environment. It should be noted that this doesn't mean these last examples are the only parameters that are allowed to be configured on the basis of an application's environment. You can equally place any parameter inside the corresponding environments section. These last examples simply represent the most likely parameters to change in between an application's environments.

It's also possible to perform programming logic (e.g., within a class or script) on the basis of a given application's environment. This is achieved through the `grails.util.Environment` class. The following listing illustrates this process:

```
import grails.util.Environment
...
...
switch(Environment.current) {
    case Environment.DEVELOPMENT:
        // Execute development logic
    break
    case Environment.PRODUCTION:
        // Execute production logic
    break
}
```

This last code snippet illustrates how a class first imports the `grails.util.Environment` class. Then, on the basis of the `Environment.current` value, which contains the environment an application is being run on, the code uses a switch conditional to execute logic depending on this value.

Such a scenario can be common in areas such as sending out e-mails or performing geolocation. It would not make sense to send out e-mails or determine where a user is located on a development environment, given that a development team's location is irrelevant in addition to not requiring an application's e-mail notifications.

Finally, it's worth mentioning that you can override the default environment used for any Grails command.

For example, by default, the `grails run-app` command uses the parameters specified for a development environment. If for some reason you want to run this command with the parameters specified for a production environment, you can do so using the following instruction: `grails prod run-app`. If you want to use the parameters specified for a test environment, you can also do so by using the following instruction: `grails test run-app`.

By the same token, for a command such as `grails test-app`, which uses the parameters specified for a test environment, you can use the parameters belonging to a development environment by using the command `grails dev test-app`. The same case applies for all other commands, by simply inserting the prod, test, or dev keyword after the `grails` command.

17-5. Create an Application's Domain Classes

Problem

You need to define an application's domain classes.

Solution

Domain classes are used to describe an application's primary elements and characteristics. If an application is designed to attend reservations, it's likely to have a domain class for holding reservations. Equally, if reservations are associated with a person, an application will have a domain class for holding people.

In web applications, domain classes are generally the first things to be defined, because these classes represent data that is saved for posterity—in a permanent storage system—so it interacts with controllers, as well as representing data displayed in views.

In Grails, domain classes are placed under the /grails-app/domain/ directory. The creation of domain classes, like most other things in Grails, can be carried out by executing a simple command in the following form:

```
grails create-domain-class <domain_class_name>
```

This last command generates a skeleton domain class file named <domain_class_name>.groovy inside the /grails-app/domain/ directory.

How It Works

Grails creates skeleton domain classes, but you still need to modify each domain class to reflect the purpose of an application.

Let's create a reservation system, similar to the one you created in Chapter 4 to experiment with Spring MVC. Create two domain classes, one named Reservation and another named Player. To do so, execute the following commands:

```
grails create-domain-class Player
grails create-domain-class Reservation
```

By executing these commands, a class file named Player.groovy and another one named Reservation.groovy are placed under an application's /grails-app/domain/ directory. In addition, corresponding unit test files are generated for each domain class under an application's src/test/groovy directory, though testing will be addressed in recipe 17-10. Next, open the Player.groovy class to edit its contents to the following:

```
class Player {
    static hasMany = [ reservations : Reservation ]
    String name
    String phone
    static constraints = {
        name(blank:false)
        phone(blank:false)
    }
}
```

The first addition, static hasMany = [reservations : Reservation], represents a relationship among domain classes. This statement indicates that the Player domain class has a reservations field that has many Reservation objects associated with it. The following statements indicate that the Player domain class also has two String fields, one called name and another called phone.

The remaining element, static constraints = { }, defines constraints on the domain class. In this case, the declaration name(blank:false) indicates that a Player object's name field cannot be left blank. The declaration phone(blank:false) indicates that a Player object cannot be created unless the phone field is provided with a value. Once you modify the Player domain class, open the Reservation.groovy class to edit its contents.

```
package court

import java.time.DayOfWeek
import java.time.LocalDateTime
```

```
class Reservation {

    static belongsTo = Player
    String courtName;
    LocalDateTime date;
    Player player;
    String sportType;
    static constraints = {
        sportType(inList: ["Tennis", "Soccer"])
        date(validator: { val, obj ->
            if (val.getDayOfWeek() == DayOfWeek.SUNDAY && (val.getHour() < 8 || val.
            getHour() > 22)) {
                return ['invalid.holidayHour']
            } else if (val.getHour() < 9 || val.getHour() > 21) {
                return ['invalid.weekdayHour']
            }
        })
    }
}
```

The first statement added to the Reservation domain class, static belongsTo = Player, indicates that a Reservation object always belongs to a Player object. The following statements indicate the Reservation domain class has a field named courtName of the type String, a field named date of the type LocalDateTime, a field named player of the type Player, and another field named sportType of the type String.

The constraints for the Reservation domain class are a little more elaborate than the Player domain class. The first constraint, sportType(inList:["Tennis", "Soccer"]), restricts the sportType field of a Reservation object to a string value of either Tennis or Soccer. The second constraint is a custom-made validator to ensure the date field of a Reservation object is within a certain hour range depending on the day of the week.

Now that you have an application's domain classes, you can create the corresponding views and controllers for an application.

Before proceeding, though, a word on Grails domain classes is in order. While the domain classes you created in this recipe provide you with a basic understanding of the syntax used to define Grails domain classes, they illustrate only a fraction of the features available in Grails domain classes.

As the relationship between domain classes grows more elaborate, more sophisticated constructs are likely to be required for defining Grails domain classes. This comes as a consequence of Grails relying on domain classes for various application functionalities.

For example, if a domain object is updated or deleted from an application's permanent storage system, the relationships between domain classes need to be well established. If relationships are not well established, there is a possibility for inconsistent data to arise in an application (e.g., if a person object is deleted, its corresponding reservations also need to be deleted to avoid an inconsistent state in an application's reservations).

Equally, a variety of constraints can be used to enforce a domain class's structure. Under certain circumstances, if a constraint is too elaborate, it's often incorporated within an application's controller prior to creating an object of a certain domain class. Though for this recipe, model constraints were used to illustrate the design of Grails domain classes.

17-6. Generate CRUD Controllers and Views for an Application's Domain Classes

Problem

You need to generate create, read, update, and delete (CRUD) controllers and views for an application's domain classes.

Solution

An application's domain classes by themselves are of little use. The data mapped to domain classes still needs to be created, presented to end users, and potentially saved for future use in a permanent storage system.

In web applications backed by permanent storage systems, these operations on domain classes are often referred to as CRUD operations. In the majority of web frameworks, generating CRUD controllers and views entails a substantial amount of work. This is on account of needing controllers capable of creating, reading, updating, and deleting domain objects to a permanent storage system, as well as creating the corresponding views (e.g., JSP pages) for an end user to create, read, update, and delete these same objects.

However, since Grails operates on the basis of conventions, the mechanism for generating CRUD controllers and views for an application's domain classes is easy. You can execute the following command to generate the corresponding CRUD controller and views for an application's domain class:

```
grails generate-all <domain_class_name>
```

How It Works

Grails is capable of inspecting an application's domain classes and generating the corresponding controllers and views necessary to create, read, update, and delete instances belonging to an application's domain classes.

For example, take the case of the Player domain class you created earlier. To generate its CRUD controller and views, you only need to execute the following command from an application's root directory:

```
grails generate-all court.Player
```

A similar command would apply to the Reservation domain class. Simply execute the following command to generate its CRUD controller and views:

```
grails generate-all court.Reservation
```

So, what is actually generated by executing these steps? If you saw the output for these commands, you will have a pretty good idea, but I will recap the process here nonetheless.

1. Compile an application's classes.

2. Generate 12 properties files under the directory grails-app/i18n to support an application's internationalization (e.g., messages_<language>.properties).

3. Create a controller named <domain_class>Controller.groovy with CRUD operations designed for an RDBMS, placed under an application's grails-app/controllers directory.

4. Create four views corresponding to a controller class's CRUD operations named `create.gsp`, `edit.gsp`, `index.gsp`, and `show.gsp`. Note that the `.gsp` extension stands for "Groovy Server Pages," which is equivalent to JavaServer Pages except it uses Groovy to declare programmatic statements instead of Java. These views are placed under an application's `grails-app/views/<domain_class>` directory.

Once you finish these steps, you can start the Grails application using `grails run-app` and work as an end user with the application. Yes, you read correctly; after performing these simple commands, the application is now ready for end users. This is the mantra of Grails operating on conventions, to simplify the creation of scaffolding code through one-word commands. After the application is started, you can perform CRUD operations on the `Player` domain class at the following URLs:

- *Create*: `http://localhost:8080/player/create`

- *Read*: `http://localhost:8080/player/list` (for all players) or `http://localhost:8080/court/player/show/<player_id>;`

- *Update*: `http://localhost:8080/player/edit/<player_id>`

- *Delete*: `http://localhost:8080/player/delete/<player_id>`

The page navigation between each view is more intuitive than these URLs have it to be, but we will illustrate with a few screenshots shortly. An important thing to be aware about these URLs is their conventions. Notice the pattern `<domain>/<app_name>/<domain_class>/<crud_action>/<object_id>`, where `<object_id>` is optional depending on the operation.

In addition to being used to define URL patterns, these conventions are used throughout an application's artifacts. For example, if you inspect the `PlayerController.groovy` controller, you can observe there are handler methods named like the various `<crud_action>` values. Similarly, if you inspect an application's backing RDBMS, you can note that the domain class objects are saved using the same `<player_id>` used in a URL.

Now that you're aware of how CRUD operations are structured in Grails applications, create a `Player` object by visiting the address `http://localhost:8080/player/create`. Once you visit this page, you can see an HTML form with the same field values you defined for the `Player` domain class.

Introduce any two values for the name and phone fields and submit the form. You've just persisted a `Player` object to an RDBMS. By default, Grails comes preconfigured to use HSQLDB, an in-memory RDBMS. A future recipe will illustrate how to change this to another RDBMS; for now, HSQLDB will suffice.

Next, try submitting the same form but, this time, without any values. Grails will not persist the `Player` object; it will instead show two warning messages indicating that the name and phone fields cannot be blank, as shown in Figure 17-3.

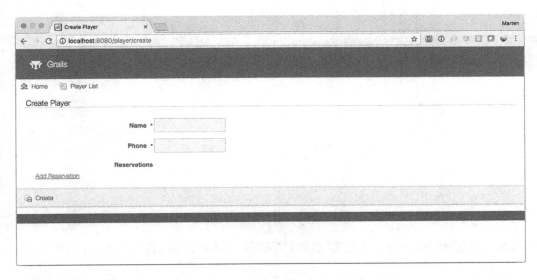

***Figure 17-3.** Grails domain class validation taking place in a view (in this case, an HTML form)*

This validation process is being enforced on account of the statements, name(blank:false) and phone(blank:false), which you placed in the Player domain class. You didn't need to modify an application's controllers or views or even create properties files for these error messages; everything was taken care of by the Grails convention-based approach.

■ **Note** When using an HTML5-capable browser, you won't be allowed to submit the form. Both input elements are marked required, which prevents the form submission in these browsers. These rules are also added based on the statements mentioned earlier.

Experiment with the remaining views available for the Player domain class, creating, reading, updating, and deleting objects directly from a web browser to get a feel for how Grails handles these tasks.

Moving along the application, you can also perform CRUD operations on the Reservation domain class at the following URLs:

- *Create*: http://localhost:8080/reservation/create

- *Read*: http://localhost:8080/reservation/list (for all reservations) or http://localhost:8080/court/reservation/show/<reservation_id>

- *Update*: http://localhost:8080/reservation/edit/<reservation_id>

- *Delete*: http://localhost:8080/reservation/delete/<reservation_id>

These last URLs serve the same purpose as those for the Player domain class: the ability to create, read, update, and delete objects belonging to the Reservation domain class from a web interface.

Next, let's analyze the HTML form used for creating Reservation objects, available at the URL http://localhost:8080/reservation/create. Figure 17-4 illustrates this form.

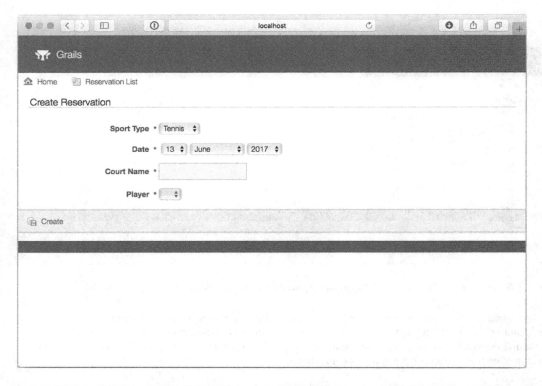

Figure 17-4. *Grails domain class HTML form, populated with domain objects from separate class*

Figure 17-4 is interesting in various ways. Though the HTML form is still created on the basis of the fields of the Reservation domain class, just like the HTML form for the Player domain class, notice that it has various prepopulated HTML select menus.

The first select menu belongs to the sportType field. Since this particular field has a definition constraint to have a string value of either Soccer or Tennis, Grails automatically provides a user with these options instead of allowing open-ended strings and validating them afterward.

The second select menu belongs to the date field. In this case, Grails generates various HTML select menus representing a date to make the date-selection process easier, instead of allowing open-ended dates and validating them afterward.

The third select menu belongs to the player field. This select menu's options are different in the sense they are taken from the Player objects you've created for the application. The values are being extracted from querying the application's RDBMS; if you add another Player object, it will automatically become available in this select menu.

In addition, a validation process is performed on the date field. If the selected date does not conform to a certain range, the Reservation object cannot be persisted, and a warning message appears on the form.

Currently you cannot submit a valid Reservation because the date field only accepts a date and not a time. To fix this, open the create.gsp (and also the edit.gsp) file under the views/reservation directory. This contains an <f:all bean="reservation" /> tag. This tag is responsible for creating the HTML form, and based on the type of field, it will render an HTML input element. To be able to input time as well, add a <g:datePicker /> tag and exclude the date field from the default form.

```
<fieldset class="form">
    <f:all bean="reservation" except="date" />
    <div class="fieldcontain required">
        <label for="date">Date</label>
        <g:datePicker name="date" value="${reservation?.date}" precision="minute"/>
    </div>
</fieldset>
```

The `<g:datePicker />` tag allows you to specify a `precision` value. When set to `minute`, it allows for setting the hour and minutes next to the date. Now when selecting a proper range, a `Reservation` can be stored.

Try experimenting with the remaining views available for the `Reservation` domain class, creating, reading, updating, and deleting objects directly from a web browser.

Finally, just to keep things in perspective, realize what your application is already doing in a few steps: validating input; creating, reading, updating, and deleting objects from an RDBMS; completing HTML forms from data in an RDBMS; and supporting internationalization. And you haven't even modified a configuration file, been required to use HTML, or needed to deal with SQL or object-relational mappers (ORMs).

17-7. Implement Internationalization (I18n) for Message Properties

Problem

You need to internationalize values used throughout a Grails application.

Solution

By default, all Grails applications are equipped to support internationalization. Inside an application's `/grails-app/i18n/` folder, you can find a series of `*.properties` files used to define messages in 12 languages. The values declared in these `*.properties` files allow Grails applications to display messages based on a user's languages preferences or an application's default language. Within a Grails application, the values declared in `*.properties` files can be accessed from places that include views (JSP or GSP pages) or an application's context.

How It Works

Grails determines which locale (i.e., from an internationalization properties file) to use for a user based on two criteria:

- The explicit configuration inside an application's `/grails-app/conf/spring/resource.groovy` file
- A user's browser language preferences

Since the explicit configuration of an application's locale takes precedence over a user's browser language preferences, there is no default configuration present in an application's `resource.groovy` file. This ensures that if a user's browser language preferences are set to Spanish (`es`) or German (`de`), a user is served messages from the Spanish or German properties files (e.g., `messages_es.properties` or `messages_de.properties`). On the other hand, if an application's `resource.groovy` file is configured to use Italian (`it`),

747

it won't matter what a user's browser language preferences are; a user will always be served messages from the Italian properties file (e.g., messages_it.properties).

Therefore, you should define an explicit configuration inside an application's /grails-app/conf/ spring/resource.groovy file, only if you want to coerce users into using a specific language locale. For example, maybe you don't want to update several internationalization properties files or maybe you simply value uniformity.

Since Grails internationalization is based on Spring's Locale Resolver, you need to place the following contents inside an application's /grails-app/conf/spring/resource.groovy file to force a specific language on users:

```
import org.springframework.web.servlet.i18n.SessionLocaleResolver

beans = {
    localeResolver(SessionLocaleResolver) {
        defaultLocale= Locale.ENGLISH
        Locale.setDefault (Locale.ENGLISH)
    }
}
```

By using this last declaration, any visitor is served messages from the English properties files (e.g., messages_en.properties) irrespective of his or her browser's language preferences. It's also worth mentioning that if you specify a locale for which there are no available properties files, Grails reverts to using the default messages.properties file, which by default is written in English though you can easily modify its values to reflect another language if you prefer. This same scenario applies when a user's browser language preferences are the defining selection criteria (e.g., if a user browser's language preferences are set for Chinese and there is no Chinese properties file, Grails falls back to using the default messages.properties file).

Now that you know how Grails determines which properties file to choose from in order to serve localized content, let's take a look at the syntax of a Grails *.properties file:

```
default.paginate.next=Next
typeMismatch.java.net.URL=Property {0} must be a valid URL
default.blank.message=Property [{0}] of class [{1}] cannot be blank
default.invalid.email.message=Property [{0}] of class [{1}] with value [{2}] is not a valid
e-mail address
default.invalid.range.message=Property [{0}] of class [{1}] with value [{2}] does not fall
within the valid range from [{3}] to [{4}]
```

The first line is the simplest declaration possible in a *.properties file. If Grails encounters the property named default.paginate.next in an application, it will substitute it for the value Next, or whatever other value is specified for this same property based on a user's determining locale.

On certain occasions, it can be necessary to provide more explicit messages that are best determined from wherever a localized message is being called. This is the purpose of the keys {0}, {1}, {2}, {3}, and {4}. They are parameters used in conjunction with a localized property. In this manner, the localized message displayed to a user can convey more detailed information. Figure 17-5 illustrates localized and parameterized messages for the court application determined on a user browser's language preferences.

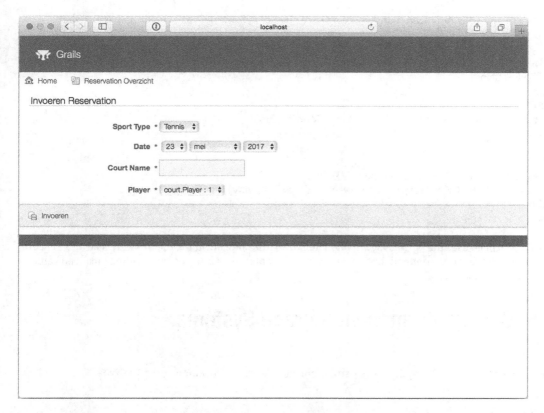

Figure 17-5. *Grails localized and parameterized messages, determined on a user browser's language preferences (left-right, top-down: Spanish, German, Italian, and French)*

Armed with this knowledge, define the following four properties inside Grails `message.properties` files:

```
invalid.holidayHour=Invalid holiday hour
invalid.weekdayHour=Invalid weekday hour
welcome.title=Welcome to Grails
welcome.message=Welcome to Court Reservation System
```

Next, it's time to explore how property placeholders are defined in Grails applications.

In recipe 17-5, you might not have realized it, but you declared a localized property for the `Reservation` domain class. In the validation section (`static constraints = { }`), you created this statement in the following form:

```
return ['invalid.weekdayHour']
```

If this statement is reached, Grails attempts to locate a property named `invalid.weekdayHour` inside a properties file and substitute its value on the basis of a user's determining locale. It's also possible to introduce localized properties into an application's views. For example, you can modify the GSP page

749

created in recipe 17-2 and located under /court/grails-app/views/welcome/index.gsp to use the following:

```
<html>
<!DOCTYPE html>
<html>
<head>
    <title><g:message code="welcome.title"/></title>
</head>

<body>
<h2><g:message code="welcome.message"/></h2>
Today is <g:formatDate format="yyyy-MM-dd" date="${today}"/>
</body>
</html>
```

This GSP page uses the <g:message/> tag. Then using the code attribute, the properties welcome.title and welcome.messsage are defined, both of which will be replaced with the corresponding localized values once the JSP is rendered.

17-8. Change Permanent Storage Systems

Problem

You want to change a Grails application's permanent storage system to your favorite RDBMS.

Solution

Grails is designed to use an RDBMS as a permanent storage system. By default, Grails comes preconfigured to use HSQLDB. HSQLDB is a database that is automatically started by Grails upon deploying an application (i.e., executing grails run-app).

However, the simplicity of HSQLDB can also be its primary drawback. Every time an application is restarted in development and testing environments, HSQLDB loses all its data since it's configured to operate in memory. And even though Grails applications in a production environment are configured with HSQLDB to store data permanently on a file, the HSQLDB feature set may be seen as limited for certain application demands.

You can configure Grails to use another RDBMS by modifying an application's application.yml file, located under the grails-app/conf directory. Inside this file, you can configure up to three RDBMSs, one for each environment—development, production, and testing—undertaken by an application. See recipe 17-4 for more on development, production, and testing environments in Grails applications.

How It Works

Grails relies on the standard Java JDBC notation to specify RDBMS connection parameters, as well as on the corresponding JDBC drivers provided by each RDBMS vendor, to create, read, update, and delete information.

One important aspect you need to be aware of if you change RDBMSs is that Grails uses an ORM called Groovy Object Relational Mapper (GROM) to interact with an RDBMS. The purpose behind GROM is the same as all other ORM solutions—to allow you to concentrate on an application's business logic, without worrying about the particularities of an RDBMS implementation, which can range from discrepancies in data types to working with SQL directly. GROM allows you to design an application's domain classes and maps your design to the RDBMS of your choice.

Set Up an RDBMS Driver

The first step you need to take in changing the Grails default RDBMS is to add the JDBC driver for the RDBMS of your choice to the gradle.build file. This allows the application access to the JDBC classes needed to persist objects to a particular RDBMS.

Configure an RDBMS Instance

The second step consists of modifying the application.yml file located under an application's grails-app/conf directory. Inside this file, there are three sections for defining an RDBMS instance.

Each RDBMS instance corresponds to a different possible application environment: development, production, and testing. Depending on the actions you take, Grails chooses one of these instances to perform any permanent storage operations an application is designed to do. See recipe 17-4 for more on development, production, and testing environments in Grails applications.

However, the syntax used for declaring an RDBMS in each of these sections is the same. Table 17-1 contains the various properties that can be used in a dataSource definition for the purpose of configuring an RDBMS.

Table 17-1. dataSource Properties for Configuring an RDBMS

Property	Definition
driverClassName	Class name for the JDBC driver
username	Username to establish a connection to an RDBMS
password	Password to establish a connection to an RDBMS
url	URL connection parameters for an RDBMS
pooled	Indicates whether to use connection pooling for an RDMBS; defaults to true
jndiName	Indicates a JNDI connection string for a data source (this is an alternative to configuring driverClassName, username, password, and url directly in Grails and instead relying on a data source being configured in a web container)
logSql	Indicates whether to enable SQL logging
dialect	Indicates the RDBMS dialect to perform operations
properties	Used to indicate extra parameters for RDBMS operation
dbCreate	Indicates autogeneration of RDBMS data definition language (DDL)

	dbCreate Value	Definition
	create-drop	Drops and re-creates the RDBMS DDL when Grails is run (warning: deletes all existing data in the RDBMS)
	create	Creates the RDBMS DDL if it doesn't exist but doesn't modify if it does (warning: deletes all existing data in the RDBMS)
	update	Creates the RDBMS DDL if it doesn't exist or updates if it does

If you've used a Java ORM, such as Hibernate or EclipseLink, the parameters in Table 17-1 should be fairly familiar. The following code illustrates the dataSource definition for a MySQL RDBMS:

```
dataSource:
    dbCreate: update
    pooled: true
    jmxExport: true
    driverClassName: com.mysql.jdbc.Driver
    username: grails
    password: groovy
```

Of the properties in the previous definition, the one you should be most careful with is dbCreate since it can destroy data in an RDBMS. In this case, the update value is the most conservative of all three available values, as explained in Table 17-1.

If you're using a production RDBMS, then dbCreate="update" is surely to be your preferred strategy, since it doesn't destroy any data in the RDBMS. If, on the other hand, a Grails application is undergoing testing, you are likely to want data in an RDBMS being cleaned out on every test run; thus, a value like dbCreate="create" or dbCreate="create-drop" would be more common. For a development RDBMS, which of these options you select as the better strategy depends on how advanced a Grails application is in terms of development.

Grails also allows you to use an RDBMS configured on a web container. In such cases, a web container, such as Apache Tomcat, is set up with the corresponding RDBMS connection parameters, and access to the RDBMS is made available through JNDI. The following code illustrates the dataSource definition to access the RDBMS via JNDI:

```
dataSource:
    jndiName: java:comp/env/grailsDataSource
```

Finally, it's worth mentioning that you can configure a dataSource definition to take effect on an application's various environments, while further specifying properties for each specific environment. This configuration is illustrated in the following code:

```
dataSource:
    driverClassName: com.mysql.jdbc.Driver
    username: grails

environments:
    production:
        dataSource:
            url: jdbc:mysql://localhost/grailsDBPro
            password: production
    development:
        dataSource:
            url: jdbc:mysql://localhost/grailsDBDev
            password: development
```

As the previous code illustrates, a dataSource's driverClassName and username properties are defined globally, taking effect on all environments, while other dataSource properties are declared specifically for each individual environment.

17-9. Customize Log Output

Problem

You want to customize the logging output generated by a Grails application.

Solution

Grails relies on Logback to perform its logging operations. In doing so, all configuration parameters are specified inside the `logback.groovy` file located under an application's `/grails-app/conf` directory. Note you could replace this with a `logback.xml` file if you are more familiar with the XML configuration of Logback.

Given Logback's logging versatility, a Grails application logging can be configured in various ways. This includes creating custom appenders, logging levels, console output, logging by artifacts, and custom logging layouts.

How It Works

Grails comes preconfigured with a basic set of parameters. Defined inside the `logback.groovy` file located under an application's `/grails-app/conf` directory, these parameters are as follows:

```
import grails.util.BuildSettings
import grails.util.Environment
import org.springframework.boot.logging.logback.ColorConverter
import org.springframework.boot.logging.logback.WhitespaceThrowableProxyConverter

import java.nio.charset.Charset

conversionRule 'clr', ColorConverter
conversionRule 'wex', WhitespaceThrowableProxyConverter

// See http://logback.qos.ch/manual/groovy.html for details on configuration
appender('STDOUT', ConsoleAppender) {
    encoder(PatternLayoutEncoder) {
        charset = Charset.forName('UTF-8')

        pattern =
            '%clr(%d{yyyy-MM-dd HH:mm:ss.SSS}){faint} ' + // Date
                '%clr(%5p) ' + // Log level
                '%clr(---){faint} %clr([%15.15t]){faint} ' + // Thread
                '%clr(%-40.40logger{39}){cyan} %clr(:){faint} ' + // Logger
                '%m%n%wex' // Message
    }
}

def targetDir = BuildSettings.TARGET_DIR
if (Environment.isDevelopmentMode() && targetDir != null) {
    appender("FULL_STACKTRACE", FileAppender) {
        file = "${targetDir}/stacktrace.log"
        append = true
```

```
        encoder(PatternLayoutEncoder) {
            pattern = "%level %logger - %msg%n"
        }
    }
    logger("StackTrace", ERROR, ['FULL_STACKTRACE'], false)
}
root(ERROR, ['STDOUT'])
```

In logging parlance, each package is known as a *logger*. Logback supports the following logging levels: error, warn, info, debug, and trace. error is the most severe. Grails thus follows a conservative default logging policy by using the error level on most of its packages. Specifying a less severe level (e.g., debug) would result in greater volumes of logging information, which may not be practical for most cases.

By default, all logging messages are sent to the stacktrace.log file located under an application's root directory and, if applicable, to the standard output (i.e., console) of a running application. When you execute a Grails command, you will observe logging messages sent to standard output.

Configuring Custom Appenders and Loggers

Logback relies on appenders and loggers to offer versatile logging functionality. An appender is a location where logging information is sent (e.g., a file or standard output), whereas a logger is a location where logging information is generated (e.g., a class or package).

Grails is configured with a root logger, from which all other loggers inherit their behavior. The default logger can be customized in a Grails application using the following statement within an application's Logback.groovy file:

```
root(ERROR, ['STDOUT'])
```

This last statement defines a logger so that messages of an error level, or a more severe one, are logged to standard output. This is the reason you can see logging messages from other loggers (e.g., a class or package) being sent to standard output; they all inherit the root logger's behavior, in addition to specifying their own log level. On the other hand, Logback appenders provide a means to send logging messages to various locations. There are four types of appenders available by default.

- jdbc : An appender that logs to a JDBC connection
- console: An appender that logs to standard output
- file: An appender that logs to a file
- rollingFile: An appender that logs to a rolling set of files

To define appenders in a Grails application, you need to declare them within the application's Logback.groovy file, as follows:

```
def USER_HOME = System.getProperty("user.home")

appender('customlogfile', FileAppender) {
    encoder(PatternLayoutEncoder) {
        Pattern = "%d %level %thread %mdc %logger - %m%n"
    }
    file = '${USER_HOME}/logs/grails.log'
}
```

```
appender('rollinglogfile', RollingFileAppender) {
    encoder(PatternLayoutEncoder) {
        Pattern = "%d %level %thread %mdc %logger - %m%n"
    }

    rollingPolicy(TimeBasedRollingPolicy) {
        FileNamePattern = "${USER_HOME}/logs/rolling-grails-%d{yyyy-MM}.log"
    }
}
```

To use appenders, you simply need to add them to a corresponding logger where they can receive input.

The following declaration illustrates how to put together the use of appenders, loggers, and logging levels:

```
root(DEBUG, ['STDOUT','customlogfile'])
```

This last listing overrides the default root logger. It indicates to use a debug level for outputting logging messages to both the stdout appender (i.e., standard output or console) as well as the customlogfile appender, the last of which represents a file defined in the appender section. Be aware that a debug level generates a lot of logging information.

17-10. Run Unit and Integration Tests

Problem

To make sure that your application's classes are working as specified, you need to perform unit and integration tests on them.

Solution

Grails has built-in support for running both unit and integration tests on an application. Earlier when you generated Grails artifacts, such as an application's domain classes, you might recall a series of test classes were automatically generated.

In a Grails application, tests are placed under an application's src/test or src/integration-test directory. Similar to other functionality offered by Grails, much of the drudgery involved in setting up and configuring application tests is handled by Grails. You simply need to concentrate on designing tests.

Once you've designed an application's tests, running tests in Grails is as simple as executing the grails test-app command from an application's root directory.

How It Works

Grails bootstraps an environment necessary to perform application tests. This environment includes the libraries (i.e., JARs) and permanent storage system (i.e., RDBMS), as well as any other artifact necessary to carry out unit and integration tests.

Let's start by analyzing the output of executing the grails test-app command, illustrated in Figure 17-6.

```
court — marten@iMac-van-Marten — ..th/ch17/court — -zsh — 160×68
→  court git:(master) ✗ grails test-app
:compileJava UP-TO-DATE
:compileGroovy
:buildProperties UP-TO-DATE
:processResources
:classes
:compileTestJava UP-TO-DATE
:compileTestGroovy
:processTestResources UP-TO-DATE
:testClasses
:test

court.PlayerControllerSpec > Test the save action correctly persists an instance FAILED
    org.spockframework.runtime.ConditionNotSatisfiedError at PlayerControllerSpec.groovy:15

court.PlayerControllerSpec > Test that the show action returns the correct model FAILED
    org.spockframework.runtime.ConditionNotSatisfiedError at PlayerControllerSpec.groovy:15

court.PlayerControllerSpec > Test that the edit action returns the correct model FAILED
    org.spockframework.runtime.ConditionNotSatisfiedError at PlayerControllerSpec.groovy:15

court.PlayerControllerSpec > Test the update action performs an update on a valid domain instance FAILED
    org.spockframework.runtime.ConditionNotSatisfiedError at PlayerControllerSpec.groovy:15

court.PlayerControllerSpec > Test that the delete action deletes an instance if it exists FAILED
    org.spockframework.runtime.ConditionNotSatisfiedError at PlayerControllerSpec.groovy:15

court.PlayerSpec > test something FAILED
    org.spockframework.runtime.SpockComparisonFailure at PlayerSpec.groovy:20

court.ReservationControllerSpec > Test the save action correctly persists an instance FAILED
    org.spockframework.runtime.ConditionNotSatisfiedError at ReservationControllerSpec.groovy:15

court.ReservationControllerSpec > Test that the show action returns the correct model FAILED
    org.spockframework.runtime.ConditionNotSatisfiedError at ReservationControllerSpec.groovy:15

court.ReservationControllerSpec > Test that the edit action returns the correct model FAILED
    org.spockframework.runtime.ConditionNotSatisfiedError at ReservationControllerSpec.groovy:15

court.ReservationControllerSpec > Test the update action performs an update on a valid domain instance FAILED
    org.spockframework.runtime.ConditionNotSatisfiedError at ReservationControllerSpec.groovy:15

court.ReservationControllerSpec > Test that the delete action deletes an instance if it exists FAILED
    org.spockframework.runtime.ConditionNotSatisfiedError at ReservationControllerSpec.groovy:15

court.ReservationSpec > test something FAILED
    org.spockframework.runtime.SpockComparisonFailure at ReservationSpec.groovy:20

court.WelcomeControllerSpec > test something FAILED
    org.spockframework.runtime.SpockComparisonFailure at WelcomeControllerSpec.groovy:20

17 tests completed, 13 failed
:test FAILED

FAILURE: Build failed with an exception.

* What went wrong:
Execution failed for task ':test'.
> There were failing tests. See the report at: file:///Users/marten/Repositories/spring-recipes-4th/ch17/court/build/reports/tests/test/index.html

* Try:
Run with --stacktrace option to get the stack trace. Run with --info or --debug option to get more log output.

BUILD FAILED

Total time: 18.166 secs
| Tests FAILED Test execution failed
→  court git:(master) ✗
```

Figure 17-6. *Test output*

The first section indicates the execution of the tests, which are taken from the `src/test/groovy` directory under an application's root directory. In this case, 13 failed and 4 successful unit tests are performed, which correspond to the skeleton test classes generated upon creation of an application's domain classes. Since these test classes contain a test skeleton, most of them fail.

The second section indicates if it was a success or failure; in this case, it was a failure. The results are available as HTML reports for which the link is shown; they can be found in the `build/reports/tests/test` directory of the project.

Now that you know how Grails executes tests, let's modify the preexisting unit test classes to incorporate unit tests based on a domain class's logic. Given that Grails testing is based on the foundations of the JUnit testing framework (`www.junit.org/`). If you're unfamiliar with this framework, we advise you to look over its documentation to grasp its syntax and approach. The following sections assume a basic understanding of JUnit (see also chapter 16).

Add the following methods (i.e., unit tests) to the PlayerSpec.groovy class located under an application's src/test/groovy directory and remove the "test something" method:

```
void "A valid player is constructed"() {
    given:
        def player = new Player(name: 'James', phone: '120-1111')
    when: "validate is called"
        def result = player.validate();
    then: "it should be valid"
        result
}

void "A player without a name is constructed"() {
    given:
        def player = new Player(name: '', phone: '120-1111')
    when: "validate is called"
        def result = player.validate();
    then: "The name should be rejected"
        !result
        player.errors['name'].codes.contains('nullable')
}

void "A player without a phone is constructed"() {
    given:
        def player = new Player(name: 'James', phone: '')
    when: "validate is called"
        def result = player.validate()
    then: "The phone number should be rejected."
        !result
        player.errors['phone'].codes.contains('nullable')
}
```

The first unit test creates a Player object and instantiates it with both a name field and a phone field. In accordance with the constraints declared in the Player domain class, this type of an instance should always be valid. Therefore, the statement assertTrue player.validate() confirms the validation of this object is always true.

The second and third unit tests also create a Player object. However, notice in one test the Player object is instantiated with a blank name field, and in another, the Player object is instantiated with a blank phone field. In accordance with the constraints declared in the Player domain class, both instances should always be invalid. Therefore, the !result statements in the then: block to confirm the validation of such objects are always false. The player.errors['phone'].codes.contains('nullable') part checks whether the validation contains the excepted code for the validation exception.

Next, add the following methods (i.e., unit tests) to the ReservationSpec.groovy class located under an application's src/test/groovy directory:

```
void testReservation() {
    given:
    def calendar = LocalDateTime.of(2017, 10, 13, 15, 00)
        .toInstant(ZoneOffset.UTC)
    def validDateReservation = Date.from(calendar)
```

```
    def reservation = new Reservation(
        sportType:'Tennis', courtName:'Main',
        date:validDateReservation,player:new Player(name:'James',phone:'120-1111'))

    expect:
        reservation.validate()
}

void testOutOfRangeDateReservation() {
    given:
    def calendar = LocalDateTime.of(2017, 10, 13, 23, 00)
        .toInstant(ZoneOffset.UTC)

    def invalidDateReservation = Date.from(calendar)
    def reservation = new Reservation(
        sportType:'Tennis',courtName:'Main',
        date:invalidDateReservation,player:new Player(name:'James',phone:'120-1111'))

    expect:
        !reservation.validate()
        reservation.errors['date'].code == 'invalid.weekdayHour'
}

void testOutOfRangeSportTypeReservation() {
    given:
    def calendar = LocalDateTime.of(2017, 10, 13, 15, 00)
        .toInstant(ZoneOffset.UTC)
    def validDateReservation = Date.from(calendar)
    def reservation = new Reservation(
        sportType:'Baseball',courtName:'Main',
        date:validDateReservation,player:new Player(name:'James',phone:'120-1111'))

    expect:
        !reservation.validate()
        reservation.errors['sportType'].codes.contains('not.inList')
}
```

This last listing contains three unit tests designed to validate the integrity of Reservation objects. The first test creates a Reservation object instance and confirms that its corresponding values pass through the Reservation domain class's constraints. The second test creates a Reservation object that violates the domain class's date constraint and confirms such an instance is invalid. The third test creates a Reservation object that violates the domain class's sportType constraint and confirms such an instance is invalid.

If you execute the grails test-app command, Grails automatically executes all the previous tests and outputs the test results to the application's build directory.

There are still failing tests, specifically PlayerControllerSpec and ReservationControllerSpec. When open, there is a method called populateValidParams that contains an @TODO.

```
def populateValidParams(params) {
    assert params != null

    // TODO: Populate valid properties like...
    //params["name"] = 'someValidName'
    assert false, "TODO: Provide a populateValidParams() implementation for this generated
    test suite"
}
```

To fix the tests, it needs to be modified to submit proper values to the controller. For
PlayerControllerSpec, modify populateValidParams to include params["name"] and params["phone"].

```
def populateValidParams(params) {
    assert params != null

    params["name"] = 'J. Doe'
    params["phone"] = '555-123-4567'
}
```

And the following for ReservationControllerSpec:

```
def populateValidParams(params) {
    assert params != null

    def calendar = LocalDateTime.of(2017, 10, 13, 12, 00)
        .toInstant(ZoneOffset.UTC)

    params["courtName"] = 'Tennis Court #1'
    params["sportType"] = "Tennis"
    params["date"] = Date.from(calendar)
    params["player"] = new Player(name: "J. Doe", phone: "555-432-1234")
}
```

Now the only remaining failing test is WelcomeControllerSpec, which you can remove to have a
successful build.

Now that you've created unit tests for a Grails application, let's explore the creation of integration tests.

Unlike unit tests, integration tests validate more elaborate logic undertaken by an application.
Interactions between various domain classes or operations performed against an RDBMS are the realm of
integration testing. In this sense, Grails aids the integration testing process by automatically bootstrapping
an RDBMS and other application properties to perform integration tests. The "Grails Differences for
Running Unit and Integration Tests" sidebar contains more details on the different aspects provided by
Grails for running both unit and integration tests.

Unit tests are designed to validate the logic contained in a single domain class. Because of this fact,
besides automating the execution of such tests, Grails provides no type of bootstrapping properties for
performing these types of tests.

Integration tests are designed to validate more elaborate logic that can span a series of application
classes. Therefore, Grails bootstraps not only an RDBMS for the purpose of running tests against this type of
permanent storage system but also bootstraps a domain class's dynamic methods to simplify the creation of
such tests. This of course entails additional overhead for performing such tests, compared to unit tests.

It's also worth mentioning that if you look closely at the skeleton test classes generated by Grails for both
unit and integration tests, there isn't any difference among them. The only difference is that tests placed

inside the integration directory have access to the series of provisions mentioned earlier, whereas those inside the unit directory do not. You could go down the route of placing unit tests inside the integration directory, but this is a matter for you to decide by considering convenience versus overhead.

Next, create an integration class for the application by executing the following command: `grails create-integration-test CourtIntegrationTest`. This generates an integration test class inside the application's `src/integration-test/groovy` directory.

Incorporate the following method (i.e., the integration test) into this last class to validate the RDBMS operations performed by the application:

```
void testQueries() {
    given: "2 Existing Players"
        // Define and save players
        def players = [ new Player(name:'James',phone:'120-1111'),
                        new Player(name:'Martha',phone:'999-9999')]
        players*.save()

        // Confirm two players are saved in the database
        Player.list().size() == 2
    when: "Player James is retrieved"
        // Get player from the database by name
        def testPlayer = Player.findByName('James')
    then:   "The phone number should match"
        // Confirm phone
        testPlayer.phone == '120-1111'
    when: "Player James is Updated"
        // Update player name
        testPlayer.name = 'Marcus'
        testPlayer.save()

    then: "The name should be updated in the DB"
        // Get updated player from the database, but now by phone
        def updatedPlayer = Player.findByPhone('120-1111')

        // Confirm name
        updatedPlayer.name == 'Marcus'

    when: "The updated player is deleted"
        // Delete player
        updatedPlayer.delete()

    then: "The player should be removed from the DB."
        // Confirm one player is left in the database
        Player.list().size() == 1

        // Confirm updatedPlayer is deleted
        def nonexistantPlayer = Player.findByPhone('120-1111')
        nonexistantPlayer == null
}
```

This last listing performs a series of operations against an application's RDBMS, starting from saving two Player objects and then querying, updating, and deleting those objects from the RDBMS. After each operation, a validation step is performed to ensure the logic—in this case contained in the PlayerController controller class—operates as expected (i.e., the controller list() method returns the correct number of objects in the RDBMS).

By default, Grails performs RDBMS test operations against HSQLDB. However, you can use any RDBMS you like. See recipe 17-8 for details on changing the Grails RDBMS.

Finally, it's worth mentioning that if you want to execute a single type of test (i.e., unit or integration), you can rely on the command flag -unit or -integration. Executing the grails test-app -unit command performs only an application's unit tests, whereas executing the grails test-app -integration command performs only an application's integration tests. This can be helpful if you have a large amount of both tests since it can cut down on the overall time needed to perform tests.

17-11. Use Custom Layouts and Templates

Problem

You need to customize layouts and templates to display an application's content.

Solution

By default, Grails applies a global layout to display an application's content. This allows views to have a minimal set of display elements (e.g., HTML, CSS, and JavaScript) and inherit their layout behavior from a separate location.

This inheritance process allows application designers and graphic designers to perform their work separately, with application designers concentrating on creating views with the necessary data and graphic designers concentrating on the layout (i.e., aesthetics) of such data.

You can create custom layouts to include elaborate HTML displays, as well as custom CSS or JavaScript libraries. Grails also supports the concept of templates, which serve the same purpose as layouts except applied at a more granular level. In addition, it's also possible to use templates for rendering a controller's output, instead of a view as in most controllers.

How It Works

Inside the /grails-app/view/ directory of an application, you can find a subdirectory called layouts, containing the layouts available to an application. By default, there is a file named main.gsp whose contents is the following:

```
<!doctype html>
<html lang="en" class="no-js">
<head>
    <meta http-equiv="Content-Type" content="text/html; charset=UTF-8"/>
    <meta http-equiv="X-UA-Compatible" content="IE=edge"/>
    <title>
        <g:layoutTitle default="Grails"/>
    </title>
```

```
    <meta name="viewport" content="width=device-width, initial-scale=1"/>

    <asset:stylesheet src="application.css"/>

    <g:layoutHead/>
</head>
<body>

    <div class="navbar navbar-default navbar-static-top" role="navigation">
        <div class="container">
            <div class="navbar-header">
                <button type="button" class="navbar-toggle" data-toggle="collapse"
                data-target=".navbar-collapse">
                    <span class="sr-only">Toggle navigation</span>
                    <span class="icon-bar"></span>
                    <span class="icon-bar"></span>
                    <span class="icon-bar"></span>
                </button>
                <a class="navbar-brand" href="/#">
                    <i class="fa grails-icon">
                        <asset:image src="grails-cupsonly-logo-white.svg"/>
                    </i> Grails
                </a>
            </div>
            <div class="navbar-collapse collapse" aria-expanded="false" style="height: 0.8px;">
                <ul class="nav navbar-nav navbar-right">
                    <g:pageProperty name="page.nav" />
                </ul>
            </div>
        </div>
    </div>

    <g:layoutBody/>

    <div class="footer" role="contentinfo"></div>

    <div id="spinner" class="spinner" style="display:none;">
        <g:message code="spinner.alt" default="Loading&hellip;"/>
    </div>

    <asset:javascript src="application.js"/>

</body>
</html>
```

Though apparently a simple HTML file, this last listing contains several elements that are used as placeholders in order for application views (i.e., JSP and GSP pages) to inherit the same layout.

The first of such elements are Groovy tags appended to the <g:*> namespace. The <g:layoutTitle> tag is used to define the contents of a layout's title section. If a view inherits the behavior from this layout and lacks such a value, Grails automatically assigns the Grails value, as indicated by the default attribute. On the other hand, if an inheriting view has such a value, it's displayed in its place.

The `<g:layoutHead>` tag is used to define the contents of a layout's head section. Any values declared in the head of a view head inheriting this layout are placed in this location upon rendering.

The `<asset:javascript src="application">` tag allows any view inheriting this layout automatic access to JavaScript libraries. Upon rendering, this element is transformed into the following: `<script type="text/javascript" src="/court/assets/application.js"></script>`. Bear in mind JavaScript libraries have to be placed inside the Grails `/<app-name>/web-app/assets/javascripts` subdirectory; `<app-name>` in this case corresponds to court.

Moving along, you will also find several declarations in the form `${assetPath*}` with a src attribute. Such statements are translated by Grails to reflect a resource contained in an application. So, for example, the statement `${assetPath(src: 'favicon.ico')}` is transformed into `/court/assets/images/favicon.ico`. Notice the addition of the application's name (i.e., context path) to the transformed values. This allows the layout to be reused in several applications while referencing the same image, the last of which should be placed under the Grails `/court/web-app/assets/images` subdirectory.

Now that you know how a Grails layout is structured, let's take a look at how a view inherits its behavior. If you open any of the views generated by the application controllers created earlier—player, reservation, or welcome (also located under the views directory)—you will find the following statement used to inherit behavior from a Grails layout:

```
<meta name="layout" content="main"/>
```

The `<meta>` tag is a standard HTML tag that has no effect on a page's display but is used by Grails to detect the layout from which a view should inherit its behavior. By using this last statement, a view is automatically rendered with the layout named main, which is precisely the template described earlier.

Looking further into a view's structure, you will notice that all generated views are structured as stand-alone HTML pages; they contain `<html>`, `<body>`, and other such HTML tags, similar to the layout template. This doesn't mean, however, that a page will contain duplicate HTML tags upon rendering. Grails automatically sorts out the substitution process by placing a view's `<title>` content inside the `<g:layoutTitle>` tag, a view's `<body>` content inside the `<g:layoutBody />` tag, and so on.

What happens if you remove the `<meta>` tag from a Grails view? On the face of it, the answer to this question is obvious: no layout is applied upon rendering a view, which also implies no visual elements are rendered (e.g., images, menus, and CSS borders). However, since Grails operates on the basis of conventions, Grails always attempts to apply a layout on the basis of a controller's name.

For example, even if the views corresponding to the reservation controller have no `<meta name="layout">` tag declaration's associated with them, if a layout named reservation.gsp is present inside an application's layout directory, it will be applied to all views corresponding to the controller.

Though layouts provide an excellent foundation on which to modularize an application's views, they are applicable only to a view's entire page. Providing a more granular approach, templates allow certain chunks of a view's page be made reusable.

Take the case of an HTML section used to display a player's reservations. You'd like to display this information on all views corresponding to this controller as a reminder. Placing this HTML section explicitly on all views not only results in more initial work but can also result in more ongoing work in case such an HTML section changes. To facilitate this inclusion process, a template can be used. The following code illustrates the contents of a template named _reservationList.gsp:

```
<table>
    <g:each in="${reservationInstanceList}" status="i" var="reservationInstance">
        <tr class="${(i % 2) == 0 ? 'odd' : 'even'}">
            <td><g:link action="show" id="${reservationInstance.id}">
                ${fieldValue(bean:reservationInstance, field:'id')}</g:link></td>
            <td>${fieldValue(bean:reservationInstance, field:'sportType')}</td>
            <td>${fieldValue(bean:reservationInstance, field:'date')}</td>
```

```
            <td>${fieldValue(bean:reservationInstance, field:'courtName')}</td>
            <td>${fieldValue(bean:reservationInstance, field:'player')}</td>
        </tr>
    </g:each>
</table>
```

This last template generates an HTML table relying on the Groovy tag <g:each> with a list of reservations. The underscore (_) prefix used to name the file is a notation by Grails to differentiate between templates and stand-alone views; templates are always prefixed with an underscore.

To use this template inside a view, you need to use the <g:render> tag illustrated here:

```
<g:render template="reservationList" model="[reservationList:reservationInstanceList]" />
```

In this case, the <g:render> tag takes two attributes: the template attribute to indicate the name of a template and the model attribute to pass reference data needed by a template. Another variation of the <g:render> tag includes a template's relative and absolute locations. By declaring template="reservationList", Grails attempts to locate a template in the same directory as the view in which it's declared. To facilitate reuse, templates can be loaded from a common directory for which absolute directories are used. For example, a view with a statement in the form template="/common/reservationList" would attempt to locate a template named _reservationList.gsp under an application's grails-app/views/common directory.

Finally, it's worth mentioning that a template can also be used by a controller to render its output. For example, most controllers return control to a view using the following syntax:

```
render view:'reservations', model:[reservationList:reservationList]
```

However, it's also possible to return control to a template using the following syntax:

```
render template:'reservationList', model:[reservationList:reservationList]
```

By using this last render statement, Grails attempts to locate a template by the name _reservationList.gsp.

17-12. Use GORM Queries

Problem

You want to perform queries against an application's RDBMS.

Solution

Grails performs RDBMS operations using GORM (http://gorm.grails.org/latest/). GORM is based on the popular Java ORM Hibernate, allowing Grails applications to perform queries using Hibernate Query Language (HQL). However, in addition to supporting the use of HQL, GORM also has a series of built-in functionalities that make querying an RDBMS very simple.

How It Works

In Grails, queries against an RDBMS are generally performed from within controllers. If you inspect any of the court application controllers, one of the simplest queries is the following:

```
Player.get(id)
```

This query is used to obtain a `Player` object with a particular ID. Under certain circumstances, though, an application can be required to perform queries on another set of criteria. For example, `Player` objects in the court application have the name and phone fields, as defined in the `Player` domain class. GORM supports the querying of domain objects on the basis of its field names. It does so by offering methods in the form `findBy<field_name>`, as illustrated here:

```
Player.findByName('Henry')
Player.findByPhone('120-1111')
```

These two statements are used to query an RDBMS and obtain a `Player` object on the basis of a name and phone. These methods are called *dynamic finders* since they are made available by GORM on the basis of a domain class's fields.

In a similar fashion, the `Reservation` domain class having its own field names will have dynamic finders like `findByPlayer()`, `findByCourtName()`, and `findByDate()`. As you can see, this process simplifies the creation of queries against an RDBMS in Java applications.

In addition, dynamic finder methods can also use comparators to further refine a query's results. The following snippet illustrates how to use a comparator to extract `Reservation` objects in a particular date range:

```
def now = new Date()
def tomorrow = now + 1
def reservations = Reservation.findByDateBetween( now, tomorrow )
```

Besides the Between comparator, another comparator that can be of use in the court application is the Like comparator. The following snippet illustrates the use of the Like comparator to extract `Player` objects with names starting with the letter *A*:

```
def letterAPlayers = Player.findByNameLike('A%')
```

Table 17-2 describes the various comparators available for dynamic finder methods.

Table 17-2. GORM Dynamic Finder Comparators

GORM Comparator	Query
InList	If value is present in a given list of values
LessThan	For lesser object(s) than the given value
LessThanEquals	For lesser or equal object(s) than the given value
GreaterThan	For greater object(s) than the given value
GreaterThanEquals	For greater or equal object(s) than the given value
Like	For object(s) like the given value
Ilike	For object(s) like the given value in a case insensitive manner
NotEqual	For object(s) not equal to the given value
Between	For object(s) between to the two given values
IsNotNull	For not null object(s); uses no arguments
IsNull	For null object(s); uses no arguments

GORM also supports the use of Boolean logic (and /or) in the construction of dynamic finder methods. The following snippet demonstrates how to perform a query for Reservation objects that satisfy both a certain court name and a date in the future:

```
def reservations = Reservation.findAllByCourtNameLikeAndDateGreaterThan("%main%",
new Date()+7)
```

In a similar fashion, the Or statement (instead of And) could have been used in this last dynamic finder method to extract Reservation objects that satisfy at least one of the criteria.

Finally, dynamic finder methods also support the use of pagination and sorting to further refine queries. This is achieved by appending a map to the dynamic finder method. The following snippet illustrates how to limit the number of results in a query, as well as define its sorting and order properties:

```
def reservations = Reservation.findAllByCourtName("%main%", [ max: 3, sort: "date",
order: "desc"] )
```

As outlined at the start of this recipe, GORM also supports the use HQL to execute queries against an RDBMS. Though more verbose and error prone than the preceding listing, the following one illustrates several equivalent queries using HQL:

```
def letterAPlayers = Player.findAll("from Player as p where p.name like 'A%'")
def reservations = Reservation.findAll("from Reservation as r
    where r.courtName like '%main%' order by r.date desc", [ max: 3] )
```

17-13. Create Custom Tags

Problem

You want to execute logic inside a Grails view that is not available through a prebuilt GSP or JSTL tag and yet not resort to the inclusion of code in a view.

Solution

A Grails view can contain display elements (e.g., HTML tags), business logic elements (e.g., GSP or JSTL tags), or straightforward Groovy or Java code to achieve its display objectives. On certain occasions, a view can require a unique combination of display elements and business logic. For example, displaying the reservations of a particular player on a monthly basis requires the use of custom code. To simplify the inclusion of such a combination and facilitate its reuse in multiple views, you can use a custom tag.

How It Works

To create custom tags, you can use the grails create-taglib <tag-lib-name> command. This command creates a skeleton class for a custom tag library under an application's /grails-app/tag-lib/ directory.

Knowing this, let's create a custom tag library for the court application designed to display special reservation offers. The first custom tag will detect the current date and based on this information display special reservation offers. The end result is the ability to use a tag like <g:promoDailyAd/> inside an application's view, instead of placing inline code in a view or performing this logic in a controller.

Execute the grails create-taglib DailyNotice command to create the custom tag library class. Next, open the generated DailyNoticeTagLib.groovy class located under an application's /grails-app/taglib/ directory, and add the following method (i.e., custom tag):

```
def promoDailyAd = { attrs, body ->
    def dayoftheweek = Calendar.getInstance().get(Calendar.DAY_OF_WEEK)
    out << body() << (dayoftheweek == 7 ?
        "We have special reservation offers for Sunday!": "No special offers")
}
```

The name of this method defines the name of the custom tag. The first declarations of the method (attrs, body) represent the input values of a custom tag—its attributes and body. Next, the day of the week is determined using a Calendar object.

After that, you can find a conditional statement based on the day of the week. If the day of the week is 7 (Saturday), the conditional statement resolves to the string "We have special reservation offers for Saturday!". Otherwise, it resolves to "No special offers".

The string is outputted through << and is first assigned through the body() method, which represents the custom tag's body, then throughout, which represents the custom tag's output. In this manner, you declare the custom tag in an application's view using the following syntax:

```
<h3><g:promoDailyAd /></h3>
```

When the view containing this custom tag is rendered, Grails executes the logic in the backing class method and supplants it with the results. This allows a view to display results based on more elaborate logic by means of a simple declaration.

■ **Caution** This type of tag is automatically available in GSP pages but not JSP pages. For this custom tag to function properly in JSP, it's necessary to add it to the corresponding tag library definition (TLD) called grails. tld. TLDs are located in an application's /web-app/WEB-INF/tld/ directory.

Custom tags can also rely on input parameters passed in as tag attributes to perform a backing class's logic. The following code illustrates another custom tag that expects an attribute named offerdate to determine its results:

```
def upcomingPromos  = { attrs, body ->
    def dayoftheweek = attrs['offerdate']
    out << body() << (dayoftheweek == 7 ?
        "We have special reservation offers for Saturday!": "No special offers")
}
```

Though similar to the earlier custom tag, this last listing uses the statement attrs['offerdate'] to determine the day of the week. In this case, attrs represents the attributes passed as input parameters to the class method (i.e., those declared in the view). Therefore, to use this last custom tag, a declaration like the following is used:

```
<h3><g:upcomingPromos offerdate='saturday'/></h3>
```

This type of custom tag allows more flexibility since its logic is executed on the basis of data provided in a view. Inclusively, it's also possible to use a variable representing data passed by a controller into a view, as illustrated here:

```
<h3><g:upcomingPromos offerdate='${promoDay}'/></h3>
```

Finally, a word about the namespace used in Grails custom tags—by default, Grails assigns custom tags to the `<g:>` namespace. To use a custom namespace, it's necessary to declare the namespace field at the top of the custom tag library class.

```
class DailyNoticeTagLib {
    static namespace = 'court'
    def promoDailyAd = { attrs, body ->
    ...
    }
    def upcomingPromos  = { attrs, body ->
    ...
    }
}
```

By using this last statement, a class's custom tags are assigned their own custom namespace named court. With the custom tag, the declarations made in a view need to be changed to the following:

```
<h3><court:promoDailyAd/></h3>
<h3><court:upcomingPromos offerdate='${promoDay}'/></h3>
```

17-14. Add Security

Problem

You want to secure your application using Spring Security.

Solution

Use the Grails Spring Security plug-in (see recipe 17-3 about plug-ins in general) to have security applied to your application.

How It Works

To secure an application, you need to add the Grails plug-in `spring-security-core` to the application. To do this, open the `build.gradle` file and add the plug-in to it.

```
dependencies {
    compile "org.grails.plugins:spring-security-core:3.1.2"
}
```

Now that the plug-in is added, running `grails compile` will download and install the plug-in.

After installing the plug-in, security can be set up using the s2-quickstart command. This command takes a package name and names of the classes to use for representing the user and its authorities.

```
grails s2-quickstart court SecUser SecRole
```

Running this will create a SecUser and SecRole domain object. It will also modify (or create) the grails-app/conf/application.groovy file. This will have a security section added.

```
// Added by the Spring Security Core plugin:
grails.plugin.springsecurity.userLookup.userDomainClassName = 'court.SecUser'
grails.plugin.springsecurity.userLookup.authorityJoinClassName = 'court.SecUserSecRole'
grails.plugin.springsecurity.authority.className = 'court.SecRole'
grails.plugin.springsecurity.controllerAnnotations.staticRules = [
    [pattern: '/',              access: ['permitAll']],
    [pattern: '/error',         access: ['permitAll']],
    [pattern: '/index',         access: ['permitAll']],
    [pattern: '/index.gsp',     access: ['permitAll']],
    [pattern: '/shutdown',      access: ['permitAll']],
    [pattern: '/assets/**',     access: ['permitAll']],
    [pattern: '/**/js/**',      access: ['permitAll']],
    [pattern: '/**/css/**',     access: ['permitAll']],
    [pattern: '/**/images/**',  access: ['permitAll']],
    [pattern: '/**/favicon.ico', access: ['permitAll']]
]
grails.plugin.springsecurity.filterChain.chainMap = [
    [pattern: '/assets/**',     filters: 'none'],
    [pattern: '/**/js/**',      filters: 'none'],
    [pattern: '/**/css/**',     filters: 'none'],
    [pattern: '/**/images/**',  filters: 'none'],
    [pattern: '/**/favicon.ico', filters: 'none'],
    [pattern: '/**',            filters: 'JOINED_FILTERS']
]
```

When running the application with grails run-app, the application will start and have security applied. If you try to access the application, you will be prompted with a login screen asking for a username and password (see Figure 17-7).

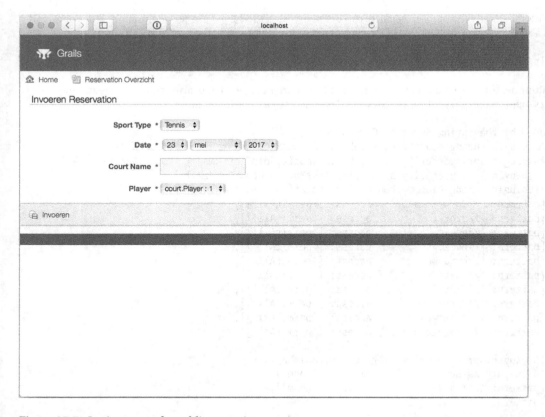

Figure 17-7. *Login screen after adding security*

Currently there are no users and roles in the system, so logging on to the system isn't possible at the moment.

Bootstrap Security

To use the system, you need users who have passwords and roles in a live application. These would come from a database, LDAP directory, or maybe some files on the file system. You will add some users in the bootstrap script of the application. Open the BootStrap.groovy file in the grails-app/init directory and add two users and two roles to the system.

```
class BootStrap {
def init = { servletContext ->
def adminRole = new court.SecRole(authority: 'ROLE_ADMIN').save(flush: true)
def userRole = new court.SecRole(authority: 'ROLE_USER').save(flush: true)
def testUser = new  court.SecUser(username: 'user', password: 'password')
testUser.save(flush: true)
def testAdmin = new  court.SecUser(username: 'admin', password: 'secret')
testAdmin.save(flush: true)
court.SecUserSecRole.create testUser, userRole, true
court.SecUserSecRole.create testAdmin, adminRole, true
    }
    ...
}
```

The first two roles, ROLE_ADMIN and ROLE_USER, are added to the system. The next two users are added both with a username and password. Finally, the link between the user and the role is made.

Now that everything is in place, restart the application and log on to the system (see Figure 17-8).

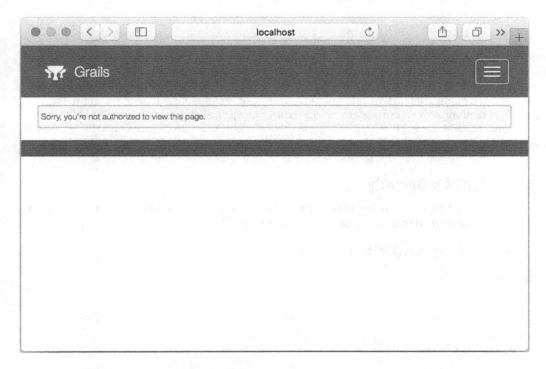

Figure 17-8. *The system after logging in with a user*

Although you are able to log in, you will be greeted with a page telling you that you aren't allowed to access the page you requested. Although there are now users in the system, the system doesn't know that those are allowed to access the page requests. For this, you need to add the configuration to make clear which URLs are allowed to be accessed.

Secure URLs

After creating the security configuration, only some default URLs are added to it, and this doesn't include the specific URLs for your application. For this, open the application.groovy file in the grails-app/conf directory.

```
grails.plugin.springsecurity.controllerAnnotations.staticRules = [
    [pattern: '/',              access: ['permitAll']],
    [pattern: '/error',         access: ['permitAll']],
    [pattern: '/index',         access: ['permitAll']],
    [pattern: '/index.gsp',     access: ['permitAll']],
    [pattern: '/shutdown',      access: ['permitAll']],
    [pattern: '/assets/**',     access: ['permitAll']],
    [pattern: '/**/js/**',      access: ['permitAll']],
```

```
    [pattern: '/**/css/**',       access: ['permitAll']],
    [pattern: '/**/images/**',    access: ['permitAll']],
    [pattern: '/**/favicon.ico',  access: ['permitAll']],
    [pattern: '/player/**',       access: ['isAuthenticated()']],
    [pattern: '/reservation/**',  access: ['isAuthenticated()']]
]
```

Notice the two new additions, one for the players section of the site and one for the reservation section of the site. The expression /player/** is a so-called Ant-style pattern that matches everything that starts with /player. permitAll means everyone even no users can access those parts of the web site (mostly useful for static and public content). With isAuthenticated(), only authenticated users are allowed to access the site. For more allowed expressions, see the recipes on Spring Security in Chapter 7.

After rebuilding and starting the application, you should be able to access the player and reservations screens again.

Use Annotations for Security

In addition to securing URLs, it is possible to secure methods; for this you can use the @Secured annotation. Let's secure the create method so that only admins can create new players.

```
import grails.plugin.springsecurity.annotation.Secured

class PlayerController {
...

    @Secured(['ROLE_ADMIN'])
    def create() {
        respond new Player(params)
    }
}
```

Notice the addition of the @Secured annotation to the create method. The annotation takes an array of roles that are allowed access. Here ROLE_ADMIN is specified, as access is limited to administrators only. The @Secured annotation can also be placed on the class level instead of the method level, and this will add security to all methods in the class. Logging in as a normal user (using user/password) and trying to create a new player will result in an access denied page (the same as shown in Figure 17-8). When doing the same with an administrator (using *admin/secret*), you will be allowed to enter a new player.

Summary

In this chapter, you learned how to develop Java web applications using the Grails framework. You started by learning the structure of a Grails application and quickly followed that by working with a sample application that demonstrated the automation of several steps undertaken in a web application.

Throughout the various recipes, you learned how Grails uses conventions in its automation process to create an application's views, controllers, models, and configuration files. In addition, you learned about the existence of Grails plug-ins to automate tasks for related Java APIs or frameworks in the context of Grails. You then explored how Grails separates configuration parameters and executes tasks on the basis of an application's working environment, which can be development, testing, or production.

You then learned how, from an application's domain classes, Grails generates the corresponding controller and views used to perform CRUD operations against an RDBMS. Next, you explored Grails internationalization, logging, and testing facilities.

Next, you explored Grails layouts and templates used to modularize an application's display and followed that with a look at the Grails Object Relational Mapping facilities, as well as the creation of custom tags.

Finally, you explored how to apply Spring Security to a Grails project and how to configure and use it to secure URLs and methods.

Deploying to the Cloud

Over the last couple of years, the cloud has grown considerably, and a lot of companies now offer these types of cloud solutions:

- Platform as a service

- Infrastructure as a service

- Software as a service

A *platform as a service* is, as the name implies, a full platform to run your applications on. Often you can choose some of the services (database, messaging, logging, etc.) you want to use for your applications. These services are provided by companies such as Google (Google Cloud Platform), Pivotal (CloudFoundry), and Amazon (Amazon Web Services).

Infrastructure as a service provides infrastructure such as virtual machines and other resources to build your own platform for deployment. Some examples are VMware ESX and Oracle VirtualBox.

Software as service is a piece of software or pieces of software delivered through the cloud, such as Office 365 and Google Apps for Work.

This chapter will focus on the platform as a service cloud solution, specifically the cloud solution offered by Pivotal named CloudFoundry.

A-1. Sign Up for CloudFoundry

Problem

You want to use CloudFoundry to deploy your applications.

Solution

Sign up with CloudFoundry at `http://run.pivotal.io`.

© Marten Deinum, Daniel Rubio, and Josh Long 2017
M. Deinum et al., *Spring 5 Recipes*, DOI 10.1007/978-1-4842-2790-9

How It Works

To be able to deploy to CloudFoundry, you need an account. Navigate to `http://run.pivotal.io` and click the Sign Up For Free button (see Figure A-1).

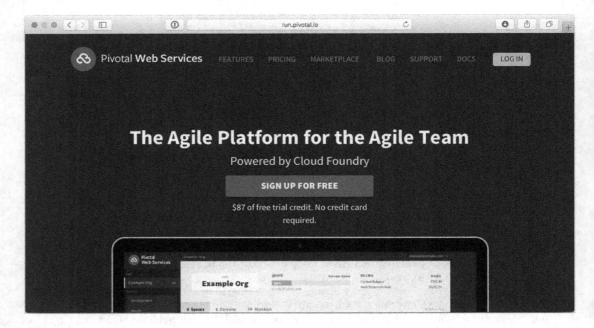

Figure A-1. *Sign-up screen for CloudFoundry*

Signing up for CloudFoundry is as easy as entering your name, your e-mail address, and a password followed by clicking the Sign Up button (see Figure A-2).

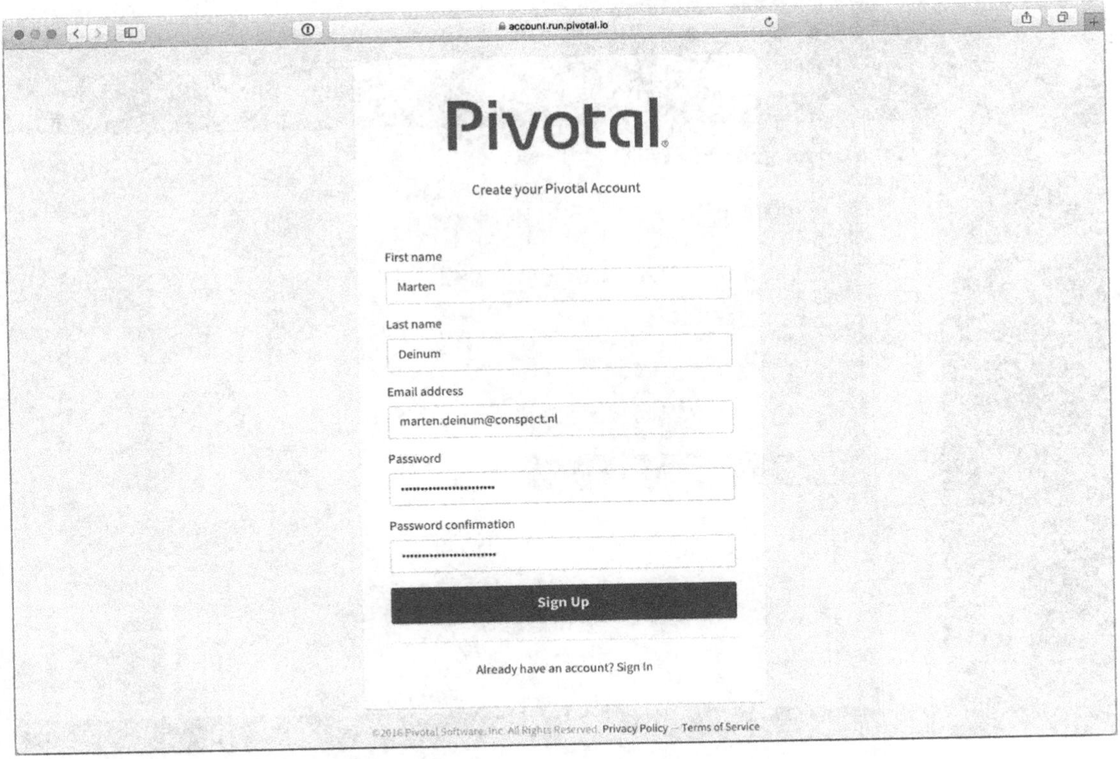

Figure A-2. *Sign-up form for CloudFoundry*

After clicking the button, you will receive a confirmation e-mail with a link. After clicking this link, you will be transferred to the confirmation page (see Figure A-3).

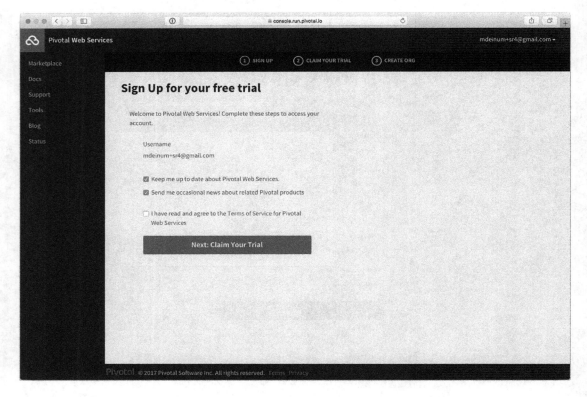

Figure A-3. *CloudFoundry confirmation page*

After accepting the terms of service and clicking the Next: Claim Your Trial button, you will be transferred to the account verification page (see Figure A-4) where you are asked to enter your mobile number.

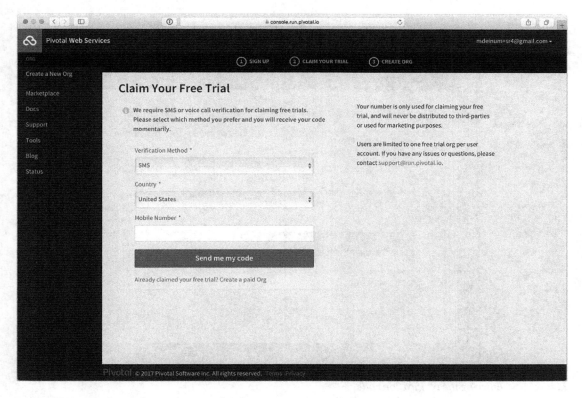

Figure A-4. *CloudFoundry account verification page*

After clicking the "Send me my code" button, you will receive a text message on your mobile phone with a verification code. You can enter this code on the next verification page (see Figure A-5).

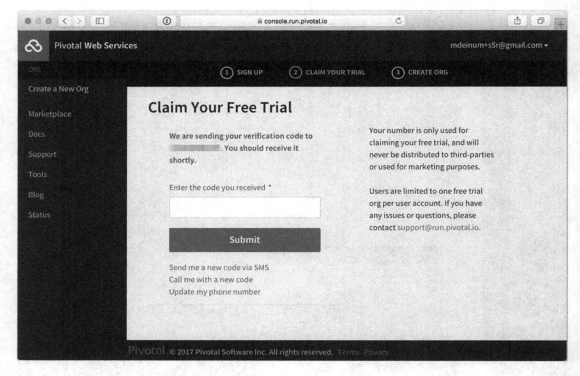

Figure A-5. *Entering the verification code*

After you enter the verification code, you are asked to create an organization (see Figure A-6). This can be the name of the project or your organization name. The organization name has to be unique, and you will receive an error if you try to reuse an existing organization name.

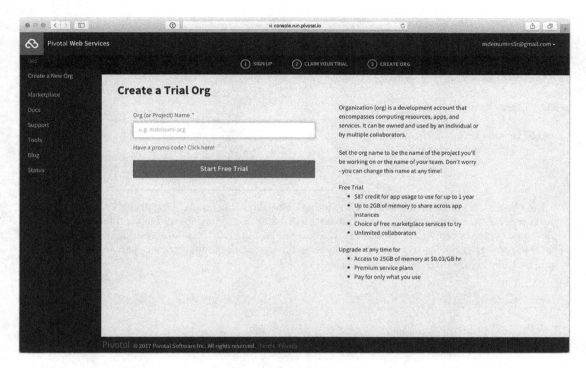

Figure A-6. *Entering an organization name*

A-2. Install and Use the CloudFoundry CLI

Problem

You want to use the CloudFoundry CLI tooling to push your application.

Solution

Download and install the CloudFoundry CLI tools.

How It Works

To be able to manipulate your CloudFoundry instance, you need some tools. You can find tools in different IDEs such as Spring Source's Spring Tool Suite and Intellij's IDEA. However, the most powerful are the command-line tools. To install the command-line tools, first download the version for your system from `https://github.com/cloudfoundry/cli/releases`, or you can use a package manager to install them. Select and download the installer for your system. After installation, the tools are available on the command line.

Now you need to set up the command-line tools, so open a terminal and type `cf login`. This will prompt you for the API, e-mail, and password. The URL for the API is the URL to your CloudFoundry instance. For this recipe, you are using the public API, so the URL is `https://api.run.pivotal.io`. The e-mail address and password are the ones you used for registration.

Next it will ask for the org and space to use. You can skip these because you have only a single org and single space at the moment.

After filling out the questions, the configuration is written to a `config.json` file in the `.cf` directory in the user's home directory.

Let's create a simple Hello World application and deploy that to CloudFoundry.

```
package com.apress.springrecipes.cloud;

public class Main {

    public static void main(String[] args) {
        System.out.println("Hello World from CloudFoundry.");
    }
}
```

The class is a basic Java class with a `main` method. The only thing that is being printed is a message to the console. After compiling the file and creating a JAR for it, it can be deployed to CloudFoundry. To deploy, type `cf push <application-name> -p Recipe_a_2_i-4.0.0.jar` on the command line, where `<application-name>` is a nice name you can make up for your application. During deployment, the output should look like Figure A-7.

Figure A-7. Output for application deployment

The first thing to notice is that, apparently, starting the application failed. Actually, it did start, but it only printed a message in the console and quit right after that. For the CloudFoundry tooling, it looks like it failed to start because it already shut down before it was able to detect that it was up.

The first thing in the output is the creation of the application on CloudFoundry. It reserves some space and assigns memory to it (the default is 1GB). Next it creates the route `<application-name>.cfapps.io` for public applications. This route is the entry point for an application with a web interface. For the current application, it has little use (adding the `--no-route` option to the `cf push` command prevents a route from being created).

After creation, the JAR file is uploaded. After uploading, CloudFoundry does detection on what kind of application it has to deal with. When it has determined the type, the corresponding buildpack is downloaded and added. In this case, that means the Java buildpack is installed. After that, the application is started, and the tooling will try to detect the successful start of the application. In this case, it appears to have failed.

Type `cf logs <application-name> --recent`, which will give you the last logging of the application (see Figure A-8).

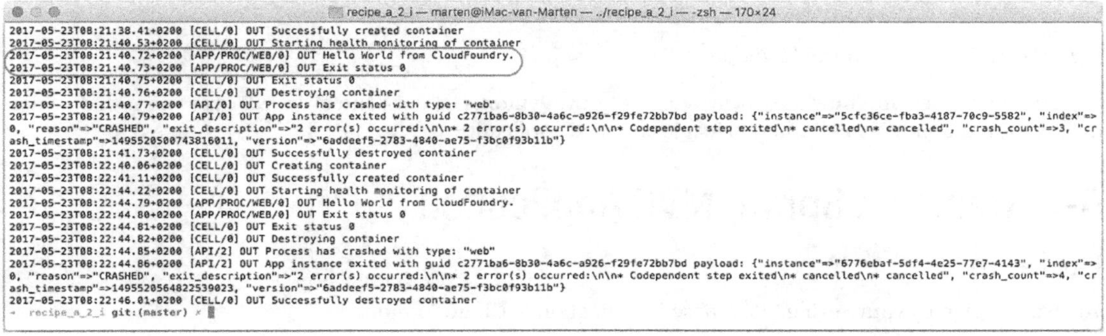

```
2017-05-23T08:21:38.41+0200 [CELL/0] OUT Successfully created container
2017-05-23T08:21:40.53+0200 [CELL/0] OUT Starting health monitoring of container
2017-05-23T08:21:40.72+0200 [APP/PROC/WEB/0] OUT Hello World from CloudFoundry.
2017-05-23T08:21:40.73+0200 [APP/PROC/WEB/0] OUT Exit status 0
2017-05-23T08:21:40.75+0200 [CELL/0] OUT Exit status 0
2017-05-23T08:21:40.76+0200 [CELL/0] OUT Destroying container
2017-05-23T08:21:40.77+0200 [API/0] OUT Process has crashed with type: "web"
2017-05-23T08:21:40.79+0200 [API/0] OUT App instance exited with guid c2771ba6-8b30-4a6c-a926-f29fe72bb7bd payload: {"instance"=>"5cfc36ce-fba3-4187-70c9-5582", "index"=>
0, "reason"=>"CRASHED", "exit_description"=>"2 error(s) occurred:\n\n* 2 error(s) occurred:\n\n* Codependent step exited\n* cancelled\n* cancelled", "crash_count"=>3, "cr
ash_timestamp"=>1495520500743816011, "version"=>"6addeef5-2783-4840-ae75-f3bc0f93b11b"}
2017-05-23T08:21:41.73+0200 [CELL/0] OUT Successfully destroyed container
2017-05-23T08:22:40.06+0200 [CELL/0] OUT Creating container
2017-05-23T08:22:41.11+0200 [CELL/0] OUT Successfully created container
2017-05-23T08:22:44.22+0200 [CELL/0] OUT Starting health monitoring of container
2017-05-23T08:22:44.79+0200 [APP/PROC/WEB/0] OUT Hello World from CloudFoundry.
2017-05-23T08:22:44.80+0200 [APP/PROC/WEB/0] OUT Exit status 0
2017-05-23T08:22:44.81+0200 [CELL/0] OUT Exit status 0
2017-05-23T08:22:44.82+0200 [CELL/0] OUT Destroying container
2017-05-23T08:22:44.85+0200 [API/2] OUT Process has crashed with type: "web"
2017-05-23T08:22:44.86+0200 [API/2] OUT App instance exited with guid c2771ba6-8b30-4a6c-a926-f29fe72bb7bd payload: {"instance"=>"6776ebaf-5df4-4e25-77e7-4143", "index"=>
0, "reason"=>"CRASHED", "exit_description"=>"2 error(s) occurred:\n\n* 2 error(s) occurred:\n\n* Codependent step exited\n* cancelled\n* cancelled", "crash_count"=>4, "cr
ash_timestamp"=>1495520564822539023, "version"=>"6addeef5-2783-4840-ae75-f3bc0f93b11b"}
2017-05-23T08:22:46.01+0200 [CELL/0] OUT Successfully destroyed container
→  recipe_a_2_i git:(master) ✗
```

Figure A-8. *Logging output for application*

The logging contains the line you have put in `System.out`. So, it actually did start but ended right after that, which made it unavailable to the health check, which signaled that it crashed.

As mentioned, CloudFoundry uses so-called buildpacks to (optionally) build and run applications. CloudFoundry supports a variety of different buildpacks. Typing `cf buildpacks` on the command line will give a list of default supported buildpacks (see Figure A-9).

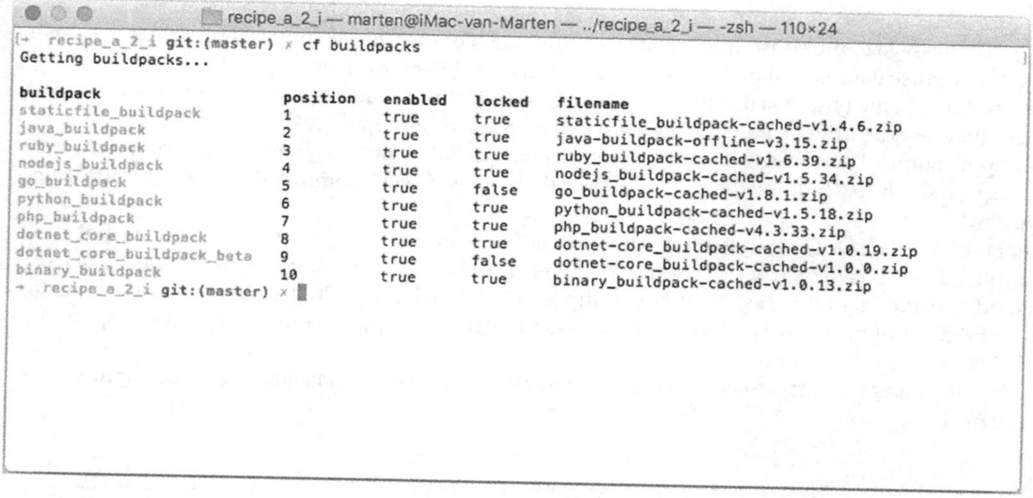

Figure A-9. *Default supported buildpacks*

As you can see, multiple languages such as Ruby, Python, Go, Java, and even .NET are supported, which means CloudFoundry isn't limited to just Java-based applications.

A-3. Deploy a Spring MVC Application

Problem

You want to deploy your Spring MVC–based application to CloudFoundry.

Solution

Use `cf push` to push the WAR to CloudFoundry.

How It Works

First you will create a web application to deploy to CloudFoundry. Before deploying the created application to CloudFoundry you will learn how to add configuration specific for the cloud and how to bind to services. When all that is done you will use cf push to publish the application to CloudFoundry.

Create the Application

Let's start by creating a simple Spring MVC–based web application. First create a `ContactRepository` interface.

```
package com.apress.springrecipes.cloud;

import java.util.List;

public interface ContactRepository {

    List<Contact> findAll();
    void save(Contact c);
}
```

Now create a Map-based implementation for this interface.

```java
package com.apress.springrecipes.cloud;

import org.springframework.stereotype.Repository;

import java.util.ArrayList;
import java.util.HashMap;
import java.util.List;
import java.util.Map;
import java.util.concurrent.atomic.AtomicLong;

@Repository
public class MapBasedContactRepository implements ContactRepository {

    private final AtomicLong SEQUENCE = new AtomicLong();
    private Map<Long, Contact> contacts = new HashMap<>();

    @Override
    public List<Contact> findAll() {
        return new ArrayList<>(contacts.values());
    }

    @Override
    public void save(Contact c) {
        if (c.getId() <= 0) {
            c.setId(SEQUENCE.incrementAndGet());
        }
        contacts.put(c.getId(), c);
    }
}
```

Of course, there needs to be a Contact entity; this is just a simple class with three properties.

```java
package com.apress.springrecipes.cloud;

public class Contact {

    private long id;
    private String name;
    private String email;

    public long getId() {
        return id;
    }

    public void setId(long id) {
        this.id = id;
    }
```

```java
    public String getName() {
        return name;
    }

    public void setName(String name) {
        this.name = name;
    }

    public String getEmail() {
        return email;
    }

    public void setEmail(String email) {
        this.email = email;
    }
}
```

As this is a web application, let's create a controller.

```java
package com.apress.springrecipes.cloud.web;

import com.apress.springrecipes.cloud.Contact;
import com.apress.springrecipes.cloud.ContactRepository;
import org.springframework.beans.factory.annotation.Autowired;
import org.springframework.stereotype.Controller;
import org.springframework.ui.Model;
import org.springframework.web.bind.annotation.GetMapping;
import org.springframework.web.bind.annotation.ModelAttribute;
import org.springframework.web.bind.annotation.PostMapping;
import org.springframework.web.bind.annotation.RequestMapping;

@Controller
@RequestMapping("/contact")
public class ContactController {

    private final ContactRepository contactRepository;

    @Autowired
    public ContactController(ContactRepository contactRepository) {
        this.contactRepository = contactRepository;
    }

    @GetMapping
    public String list(Model model) {
        model.addAttribute("contacts", contactRepository.findAll());
        return "list";
    }
```

```java
@GetMapping("/new")
public String newContact(Model model) {
    model.addAttribute(new Contact());
    return "contact";
}

@PostMapping("/new")
public String newContact(@ModelAttribute Contact contact) {
    contactRepository.save(contact);
    return "redirect:/contact";
}
}
```

The controller is simple. It has a method for showing a list of currently available contacts, and it has a method to add a new contact. The next two views need to be created in the /WEB-INF/views directory. First, here's the list.jsp file:

```jsp
<%@ taglib prefix="c" uri="http://java.sun.com/jsp/jstl/core" %>
<!doctype HTML>
<html>
<head>
    <title>Spring Recipes - Contact Sample</title>
</head>
<body>
<h1>Contacts</h1>
<table>
    <tr><th>Name</th><th>Email</th></tr>
    <c:forEach items="${contacts}" var="contact">
        <tr><td>${contact.name}</td><td>${contact.email}</td></tr>
    </c:forEach>
</table>
<a href="<c:url value="/contact/new"/>">New Contact</a>
</body>
</html>
```

Next, here's the contact.jsp file for adding new contacts:

```jsp
<%@ taglib prefix="c" uri="http://java.sun.com/jsp/jstl/core" %>
<%@ taglib prefix="form" uri="http://www.springframework.org/tags/form" %>
<!doctype HTML>
<html>
<head>
    <title>Spring Recipes - Contact Sample</title>
</head>
<body>
<h1>Contact</h1>
<form:form method="post" modelAttribute="contact">
    <fieldset>
        <legend>Contact Information</legend>
        <div>
```

```
            <div><form:label path="name">Name</form:label></div>
            <div><form:input path="name"/></div>
        </div>
        <div>
            <div><form:label path="email">Email Address</form:label></div>
            <div><form:input path="email" type="email"/></div>
        </div>
        <div><button>Save</button></div>
    </fieldset>
    <form>
</form:form>
</html>
```

That is all the application code. What remains is the application configuration and a class to start the application. First, here's the application configuration:

```
package com.apress.springrecipes.cloud.config;

import org.springframework.context.annotation.ComponentScan;
import org.springframework.context.annotation.Configuration;

@ComponentScan(basePackages = {"com.apress.springrecipes.cloud"})
@Configuration
public class ContactConfiguration {}
```

The application configuration is quite empty. It only defines a component scan annotation to detect the service and controller. Next, a configuration for the web-related part is needed.

```
package com.apress.springrecipes.cloud.web;

import org.springframework.context.annotation.Bean;
import org.springframework.context.annotation.Configuration;
import org.springframework.web.servlet.config.annotation.DefaultServletHandlerConfigurer;
import org.springframework.web.servlet.config.annotation.EnableWebMvc;
import org.springframework.web.servlet.config.annotation.ViewControllerRegistry;
import org.springframework.web.servlet.config.annotation.WebMvcConfigurer;
import org.springframework.web.servlet.view.InternalResourceViewResolver;

@Configuration
@EnableWebMvc
public class ContactWebConfiguration implements WebMvcConfigurer {

    @Override
    public void configureDefaultServletHandling(DefaultServletHandlerConfigurer configurer) {
        configurer.enable();
    }
```

```java
    @Override
    public void addViewControllers(ViewControllerRegistry registry) {
        registry.addViewController("/").setViewName("redirect:/contact");
    }

    @Bean
    public InternalResourceViewResolver internalResourceViewResolver() {
        InternalResourceViewResolver viewResolver = new InternalResourceViewResolver();
        viewResolver.setPrefix("/WEB-INF/views/");
        viewResolver.setSuffix(".jsp");
        return viewResolver;
    }
}
```

The final missing part is the application initializer.

```java
package com.apress.springrecipes.cloud.web;

import com.apress.springrecipes.cloud.config.ContactConfiguration;
import org.springframework.web.servlet.support.
AbstractAnnotationConfigDispatcherServletInitializer;

public class ContactWebApplicationInitializer extends
AbstractAnnotationConfigDispatcherServletInitializer {
    @Override
    protected Class<?>[] getRootConfigClasses() {
        return null;
    }

    @Override
    protected Class<?>[] getServletConfigClasses() {
        return new Class[] {ContactConfiguration.class, ContactWebConfiguration.class};
    }

    @Override
    protected String[] getServletMappings() {
        return new String[] {"/"} ;
    }
}
```

Now everything is in place. After building the WAR file, push it to CloudFoundry by entering cf push <application-name> -p contact.war on the command line. This will show the progress of uploading, installing the buildpack, and installing Tomcat. After a successful deployment, the application is available at <application-name>.cfapps.io (see Figure A-10).

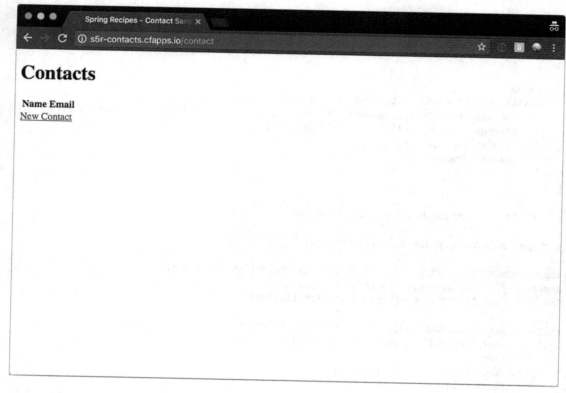

Figure A-10. *Contact application on CloudFoundry*

Use a Data Source

At the moment, the application stores the contact information in a HashMap. This is nice for testing purposes, but for a real application the data needs to be stored in a database. First, create a JDBC-driven ContactRepository implementation.

```
package com.apress.springrecipes.cloud;

import org.springframework.beans.factory.annotation.Autowired;
import org.springframework.jdbc.core.support.JdbcDaoSupport;
import org.springframework.stereotype.Service;

import javax.sql.DataSource;
import java.util.List;

@Service
public class JdbcContactRepository extends JdbcDaoSupport implements ContactRepository {

    @Autowired
    public JdbcContactRepository(DataSource dataSource) {
        super.setDataSource(dataSource);
    }
```

```java
    @Override
    public List<Contact> findAll() {
        return getJdbcTemplate().query("select id, name, email from contact", (rs, rowNum) -> {
            Contact contact = new Contact();
            contact.setId(rs.getLong(1));
            contact.setName(rs.getString(2));
            contact.setEmail(rs.getString(3));
            return contact;
        });
    }

    @Override
    public void save(Contact c) {
        getJdbcTemplate().update("insert into contact (name, email) values (?, ?)",
        c.getName(), c.getEmail());
    }
}
```

Next, update the configuration and add DataSource and DataSourceInitializer classes.

```java
package com.apress.springrecipes.cloud.config;

import com.apress.springrecipes.cloud.ContactRepository;
import com.apress.springrecipes.cloud.JdbcContactRepository;
import org.springframework.context.annotation.Bean;
import org.springframework.context.annotation.ComponentScan;
import org.springframework.context.annotation.Configuration;
import org.springframework.core.io.ClassPathResource;
import org.springframework.jdbc.core.JdbcTemplate;
import org.springframework.jdbc.datasource.embedded.EmbeddedDatabaseBuilder;
import org.springframework.jdbc.datasource.embedded.EmbeddedDatabaseType;
import org.springframework.jdbc.datasource.init.DataSourceInitializer;
import org.springframework.jdbc.datasource.init.ResourceDatabasePopulator;

import javax.sql.DataSource;

@ComponentScan(basePackages = {"com.apress.springrecipes.cloud"})
@Configuration
public class ContactConfiguration {

    @Bean
    public DataSource dataSource() {
        return new EmbeddedDatabaseBuilder().setType(EmbeddedDatabaseType.H2).build();
    }

    @Bean
    public DataSourceInitializer dataSourceInitializer(DataSource dataSource) {
        ResourceDatabasePopulator populator = new ResourceDatabasePopulator();
        populator.addScript(new ClassPathResource("/sql/schema.sql"));
        populator.setContinueOnError(true);
```

791

```
DataSourceInitializer initializer = new DataSourceInitializer();
initializer.setDataSource(dataSource);
initializer.setDatabasePopulator(populator);
return initializer;
    }
}
```

For testing and local deployment, the in-memory H2 database is used to configure this instance. The `EmbeddedDatabaseBuilder` class is used to create the DataSource, and the `DataSourceInitializer` class takes care of executing the create script.

After building the WAR file again and deploying to CloudFoundry, the application should still be running and using the in-memory database. However, instead of the in-memory database, you want to use a real database so that content survives redeployments, outages, and so on.

CloudFoundry provides several services that are available in the marketplace. To get an overview, type `cf marketplace` (or `cf m`) on the command line (see Figure A-11).

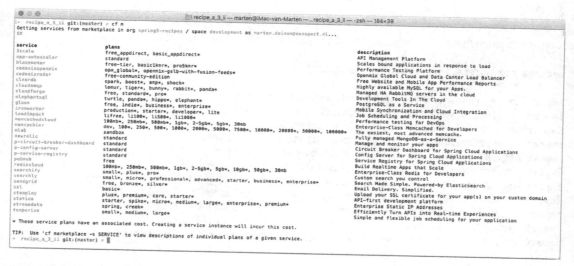

Figure A-11. *Overview of CloudFoundry services*

As you can see, there are different services such as database implementations, messaging, and e-mail. For this recipe, a database instance is needed. There are two database options: MySQL and PostgreSQL. Choose which one you like and create an instance. To construct a basic MySQL instance, type `cf create-service cleardb spark contacts-db`. After the database has been created, you need to bind it (make it available for access) to your application. Type `cf bind-service <application-name> contacts-db`.

Now the database is ready to be used. To use it, simply restart or redeploy the application.

CloudFoundry has a feature called *autoreconfiguration*, which is enabled by default. It finds a bean of a certain type, in this case, a `DataSource`. It will try to replace it with one provided by your configured services. This will, however, work only when there is a single service and a single bean of that type. If you have multiple data sources, autoreconfiguration won't work. It will work for all the provided services, such as AMQP connection factories and MongoDB instances.

Access the Cloud Service

Although autoreconfiguration is a nice feature, as already mentioned, it doesn't always work. However, there is an easy way to explicitly tell which service to use when deployed to CloudFoundry. Another nice thing that CloudFoundry does is that it activates a profile called cloud. This profile can be used to determine whether the application is deployed on CloudFoundry or not, and as such certain beans can be accessed specifically when deployed here.

Two additional dependencies are needed.

```
<dependency>
    <groupId>org.springframework.cloud</groupId>
    <artifactId>spring-cloud-cloudfoundry-connector</artifactId>
    <version>1.2.4.RELEASE</version>
</dependency>
<dependency>
    <groupId>org.springframework.cloud</groupId>
    <artifactId>spring-cloud-spring-service-connector</artifactId>
    <version>1.2.4.RELEASE</version>
</dependency>
```

These two dependencies make it easy to interact with the CloudFoundry instance and the provided services. Now that these are available, it is just a matter of a reconfiguration.

```
package com.apress.springrecipes.cloud.config;

import org.springframework.cloud.config.java.AbstractCloudConfig;
import org.springframework.context.annotation.Profile;
...
@Configuration
@ComponentScan(basePackages = {"com.apress.springrecipes.cloud"})
public class ContactConfiguration {

    @Configuration
    @Profile("default")
    public static class LocalDatasourceConfiguration {
        @Bean
        public DataSource dataSource() {
            return new EmbeddedDatabaseBuilder().setType(EmbeddedDatabaseType.H2).build();
        }
    }

    @Configuration
    @Profile("cloud")
    public static class CloudDatasourceConfiguration extends AbstractCloudConfig {

        @Bean
        public DataSource dataSource() {
            return connectionFactory().dataSource("contacts-db");
        }
    }
}
```

Notice the two inner configuration classes. Both have the @Profile annotation. LocalDataSource Configuration is available when there is no cloud profile active. CloudDataSourceConfiguration is available only when deployed to the cloud. The latter extends the AbstractCloudConfig class, which has convenient methods to access the provided services. To get a reference to the data source, use the dataSource() lookup method on the connectionFactory() method. For default services (data sources, MongoDB, Redis, etc.), it provides convenient access methods. If you have developed and deployed custom services, they can be accessed using the general service() method.

After rebuilding the WAR and pushing it to CloudFoundry, it will still be working.

A-4. Remove an Application

Problem

You want to remove an application from CloudFoundry.

Solution

Use the CloudFoundry tools to delete the application from your space.

How It Works

To remove an application, you issue a delete command, instead of push, to let CloudFoundry remove the application. To remove the application, type cf delete <application-name> on the command line. After confirming that you really want to delete the application, CloudFoundry will start to remove the application.

The output should look like that in Figure A-12.

```
recipe_a_3_iii — marten@iMac-van-Marten — ..ecipe_a_3_iii — -zsh — 125×19
[→  recipe_a_3_iii git:(master) ✗ cf delete s5r-contacts

Really delete the app s5r-contacts?> y
Deleting app s5r-contacts in org spring5-recipes / space development as marten.deinum@conspect.nl...
OK
→  recipe_a_3_iii git:(master) ✗ ▮
```

Figure A-12. *Output of removing an application from CloudFoundry*

Summary

In this chapter, you explored how to deploy to and remove an application from the cloud platform provided by Pivotal's CloudFoundry. First you deployed a basic web application without any external connections. After that, you added a data source, and you learned how to create and bind a service to your application. As soon as the service was available, you experienced the autoreconfiguration feature provided by CloudFoundry.

Finally, you explored how to interact with the cloud from within your application configuration and not to rely on autoreconfiguration.

Caching

When a heavy computation is done in a program, when retrieval of data is slow, or when the retrieved data hardly ever changes, it can be useful to apply caching. *Caching* is the ability to store and retrieve data transparently so that data can be served quicker to the client.

In the Java ecosystem, there are multiple cache implementations, ranging from the use of a simple Map implementation to a fully distributed cache solution (Oracle Coherence, for instance). However, there is also the proven and trusted Ehcache.

As of Java Enterprise Edition 7, there is also a general caching API (JSR-107) named JCache. For this specification, several implementations exist (such as Apache JCS, Hazelcast, and Oracle Coherence, which is JCache compliant).

Spring provides a cache abstract to make it easier to work with any of these implementations, which makes it quite easy to add caching to your application. For testing, you could use a simple Map-based implementation, whereas your real system would use an Oracle Coherence cluster for caching.

In this appendix, you will explore Spring's caching abstraction and will take a look at different strategies of applying caching to your application.

B-1. Implement Caching with Ehcache

Problem

You have an application with some heavy computation tasks, and you want to cache the result and reuse it.

Solution

Use Ehcache to store the result of your computation. For each computation, check whether a result is already present. If it is, return the cached value, and if it is not, calculate and put it in the cache.

How It Works

Let's create `CalculationService`, which simulates a heavy computation by using a `Thread.sleep()` method.

```java
package com.apress.springrecipes.caching;

import java.math.BigDecimal;

public class PlainCalculationService implements CalculationService {

    @Override
    public BigDecimal heavyCalculation(BigDecimal base, int power) {
        try {
```

© Marten Deinum, Daniel Rubio, and Josh Long 2017
M. Deinum et al., *Spring 5 Recipes*, DOI 10.1007/978-1-4842-2790-9

```
        Thread.sleep(500);
    } catch (InterruptedException e) {}
    return base.pow(power);
    }
}
```

As you can see, calculating the power of something is a heavy computation to do. Create a Main class to run this program in a couple of iterations.

```
package com.apress.springrecipes.caching;

import java.math.BigDecimal;

public class Main {

    public static final void main(String[] args) throws Exception {

        CalculationService calculationService = new PlainCalculationService();
        for (int i = 0; i < 10 ;i++) {
            long start = System.currentTimeMillis();
            System.out.println(calculationService.heavyCalculation(BigDecimal.valueOf(2L), 16));
            long duration = System.currentTimeMillis() - start;
            System.out.println("Took: " + duration);
        }
    }
}
```

The Main class will run the computation ten times and output the result as well as the time it took to calculate the result. When it's running, you will see that the time for each computation is about 500 milliseconds, mainly because of Thread.sleep().

Use Ehcache Without Spring

Let's improve the system by introducing caching. For this you are going to use plain Ehcache. The modified service looks like this:

```
package com.apress.springrecipes.caching;

import net.sf.ehcache.Ehcache;
import net.sf.ehcache.Element;

import java.math.BigDecimal;

public class PlainCachingCalculationService implements CalculationService {

    private final Ehcache cache;

    public PlainCachingCalculationService(Ehcache cache) {
        this.cache = cache;
    }
```

```java
@Override
public BigDecimal heavyCalculation(BigDecimal base, int power) {
    String key = base +"^"+power;
    Element result = cache.get(key);
    if (result != null) {
        return (BigDecimal) result.getObjectValue();
    }
    try {
        Thread.sleep(500);
    } catch (InterruptedException e) {}
    BigDecimal calculatedResult = base.pow(power);
    cache.putIfAbsent(new Element(key, calculatedResult));
    return calculatedResult;
    }
}
```

First notice the addition of a cache variable in the service. This cache is injected through the constructor. Let's take a look at the updated heavyCalculation method. First it generates a unique key based on the method arguments; this key is used to look up a result from the cache. If found, it is returned. If there is no cached result, the calculation proceeds as normal, and after the calculation, it is added to the cache; finally, the value is returned.

Because of the need for an Ehcache cache, the Main class needs to be modified to bootstrap Ehcache and look up a cache before constructing the service. The updated Main class looks like this:

```java
package com.apress.springrecipes.caching;

import net.sf.ehcache.CacheManager;
import net.sf.ehcache.Ehcache;
...
public class Main {

    public static final void main(String[] args) throws Exception {
        CacheManager cacheManager = CacheManager.getInstance();
        Ehcache cache = cacheManager.getEhcache("calculations");
        CalculationService calculationService = new PlainCachingCalculationService(cache);
        ...
        cacheManager.shutdown();
    }
}
```

First there needs to be a CacheManager instance constructed. For this, use the getInstance method on the CacheManager class. This class will try to read a file called ehcache.xml from the root of the classpath to configure the cache. Next a cache instance is requested with the name calculations; the resulting cache is injected into the PlainCachingCalculationService instance.

The ehcache.xml file is the configuration file for Ehcache, and it contains the following:

```xml
<ehcache>
    <diskStore path="java.io.tmpdir"/>

    <defaultCache
        maxElementsInMemory="1000"
```

```
            eternal="false"
            timeToIdleSeconds="120"
            timeToLiveSeconds="120"
            overflowToDisk="true"
        />

    <cache name="calculations"
            maxElementsInMemory="100"
            eternal="false"
            timeToIdleSeconds="600"
            timeToLiveSeconds="3600"
            overflowToDisk="true"
        />
</ehcache>
```

This configures Ehcache and the specific cache you want to use. It keeps 100 results in memory (maxElementsInMemory) for 1 hour (timeToLiveSeconds). When there are more elements, it will store those on disk (overflowToDisk).

When running the Main class, the first computation takes about 500 milliseconds, whereas the next computations take a lot less time, around 0 to 1 milliseconds.

Use Ehcache with Spring for Configuration

The application is integrated with Spring, and Spring will be leveraged for configuring CacheManager and constructing the service. To make this work, you need to do some Spring configuration and use an ApplicationContext object to load everything. The configuration is as follows:

```
package com.apress.springrecipes.caching.config;

import com.apress.springrecipes.caching.CalculationService;
import com.apress.springrecipes.caching.PlainCachingCalculationService;
import net.sf.ehcache.CacheManager;
import net.sf.ehcache.Ehcache;
import org.springframework.context.annotation.Bean;
import org.springframework.context.annotation.Configuration;

@Configuration
public class CalculationConfiguration {

    @Bean
    public CacheManager cacheManager() {
        return CacheManager.getInstance();
    }

    @Bean
    public CalculationService calculationService() {
        Ehcache cache = cacheManager().getCache("calculations");
        return new PlainCachingCalculationService(cache);
    }
}
```

You also need a modified Main class that loads the configuration and obtains the CalculationService class from the context.

```
package com.apress.springrecipes.caching;

import com.apress.springrecipes.caching.config.CalculationConfiguration;
import org.springframework.context.ApplicationContext;
import org.springframework.context.annotation.AnnotationConfigApplicationContext;

import java.math.BigDecimal;

public class Main {

    public static final void main(String[] args) throws Exception {

        ApplicationContext context =
            new AnnotationConfigApplicationContext(CalculationConfiguration.class);
        CalculationService calculationService = context.getBean(CalculationService.class);

        for (int i = 0; i < 10 ;i++) {
            long start = System.currentTimeMillis();
            System.out.println(
                calculationService.heavyCalculation(BigDecimal.valueOf(2L), 16));
            long duration = System.currentTimeMillis() - start;
            System.out.println("Took: " + duration);
        }
        ((AbstractApplicationContext) context).close();
    }
}
```

Although this reduces the direct references to Ehcache from the bootstrapping code, the implementation of the CalculationService class is still riddled with references to Ehcache. Not to mention, manual caching is quite cumbersome and an erroneous task that pollutes the code. It would be nice if caching could just be applied, just like transactions, with AOP.

Use Spring to Configure Ehcache

Spring contains some Ehcache support classes to make it easier to configure Ehcache and easier to obtain a cache instance. To configure the Ehcache CacheManager, you can use Spring's EhCacheManagerFactoryBean. To obtain a Cache instance, there is EhCacheFactoryBean.

The advantage of using EhCacheManagerFactoryBean is that it can leverage Spring's resource-loading mechanism to load the configuration file for Ehcache. It also allows for easy reuse of an already existing CacheManager and allows you to register it with a certain name.

EhCacheFactoryBean will create a cache automatically if one doesn't exist yet. In the code so far, the cache that was used was explicitly defined. EhCacheFactoryBean will first try to locate an existing explicitly configured cache; if one doesn't exist, one is created using the defaultCache element from ehcache.xml.

The modified configuration looks like this:

```
package com.apress.springrecipes.caching.config;

import com.apress.springrecipes.caching.CalculationService;
import com.apress.springrecipes.caching.PlainCachingCalculationService;
import org.springframework.cache.ehcache.EhCacheFactoryBean;
import org.springframework.cache.ehcache.EhCacheManagerFactoryBean;
import org.springframework.context.annotation.Bean;
import org.springframework.context.annotation.Configuration;
import org.springframework.core.io.ClassPathResource;

@Configuration
public class CalculationConfiguration {

    @Bean
    public EhCacheManagerFactoryBean cacheManager() {
        EhCacheManagerFactoryBean factory = new EhCacheManagerFactoryBean();
        factory.setConfigLocation(new ClassPathResource("ehcache.xml"));
        return factory;
    }

    @Bean
    public EhCacheFactoryBean calculationsCache() {
        EhCacheFactoryBean factory = new EhCacheFactoryBean();
        factory.setCacheManager(cacheManager().getObject());
        factory.setCacheName("calculations");
        return factory;
    }

    @Bean
    public CalculationService calculationService() {
        return new PlainCachingCalculationService(calculationsCache().getObject());
    }
}
```

B-2. Cache with Spring's Cache Abstraction

Problem

You have an application with some heavy computation tasks. You want to cache the result and reuse it, but at the same time you don't want to be bound to a single cache implementation.

Solution

Use Ehcache to store the result of your computation through Spring's cache abstraction. For each computation, check whether a result is already present. If it is, return the cached value; if it is not, calculate and put it in the cache.

How It Works

First, add caching to your application using Spring's Cache class. Second, check whether a result is already present using the get() method. If it is, present return; if it is not, continue with the program. After the calculation, the value is added to the cache.

```
package com.apress.springrecipes.caching;

import org.springframework.cache.Cache;

import java.math.BigDecimal;

public class PlainCachingCalculationService implements CalculationService {

    private final Cache cache;

    public PlainCachingCalculationService(Cache cache) {
        this.cache = cache;
    }

    @Override
    public BigDecimal heavyCalculation(BigDecimal base, int power) {
        String key = base +"^"+power;
        BigDecimal result = cache.get(key, BigDecimal.class);
        if (result != null) {
            return result;
        }
        try {
            Thread.sleep(500);
        } catch (InterruptedException e) {}

        BigDecimal calculatedResult = base.pow(power);
        cache.put(key, calculatedResult);
        return calculatedResult;
    }
}
```

Next, the CacheManager class needs to be configured. First configure a simple Map-based cache by using ConcurrentMapCacheManager, which, as the name implies, uses ConcurrentMap underneath for caching.

```
package com.apress.springrecipes.caching.config;
...
import org.springframework.cache.CacheManager;
import org.springframework.cache.concurrent.ConcurrentMapCacheManager;

@Configuration
public class CalculationConfiguration {

    @Bean
    public CacheManager cacheManager() {
        return new ConcurrentMapCacheManager();
    }
}
```

```
    @Bean
    public CalculationService calculationService() {
        return new PlainCachingCalculationService(cacheManager().getCache("calculations"));
    }
}
```

You can leave the Main class unchanged.

Use Ehcache with Spring's Cache Abstraction

Although ConcurrentMapCacheManager appears to do its job, it is not a full cache implementation. It will only add things to the cache; there is no cache eviction or cache overflowing. Ehcache, on the other hand, has all of this. Using Ehcache (or another cache implementation like JCS or Hazelcast) is just a matter of configuration.

To use Ehcache, first configure Ehcache using EhCacheManagerFactoryBean and next use EhCacheCacheManager to hook it up with Spring's cache abstraction. PlainCachingCalculationService can remain untouched because that already uses Spring's cache abstraction to use a cache.

```
package com.apress.springrecipes.caching.config;
...
import org.springframework.cache.CacheManager;
import org.springframework.cache.ehcache.EhCacheCacheManager;
import org.springframework.cache.ehcache.EhCacheManagerFactoryBean;

@Configuration
public class CalculationConfiguration {

    @Bean
    public CacheManager cacheManager() {
        EhCacheCacheManager cacheManager = new EhCacheCacheManager();
        cacheManager.setCacheManager(ehCacheManagerFactoryBean().getObject());
        return cacheManager;
    }

    @Bean
    public EhCacheManagerFactoryBean ehCacheManagerFactoryBean() {
        EhCacheManagerFactoryBean factory = new EhCacheManagerFactoryBean();
        factory.setConfigLocation(new ClassPathResource("ehcache.xml"));
        return factory;
    }

    @Bean
    public CalculationService calculationService() {
        return new PlainCachingCalculationService(cacheManager().getCache("calculations"));
    }
}
```

B-3. Implement Declarative Caching with AOP

Problem

Caching is a kind of crosscutting concern. Applying caching manually can be tedious and error prone. It is simpler to specify declaratively what behavior you are expecting and to not prescribe how that behavior is to be achieved.

Solution

Spring (since version 3.1) offers a cache advice that can be enabled with @EnableCaching.

How It Works

To enable declarative caching, you have to add @EnableCaching to the configuration class. This will register a CacheInterceptor or AnnotationCacheAspect class (depending on the mode), which will detect, among others, the @Cacheable annotation.

```
public BigDecimal heavyCalculation(BigDecimal base, int power) {
    String key = base +"^"+power;
    Element result = cache.get(key);
    if (result != null) {
        return (BigDecimal) result.getObjectValue();
    }
    try {
        Thread.sleep(500);
    } catch (InterruptedException e) {}
    BigDecimal calculatedResult = base.pow(power);
    cache.putIfAbsent(new Element(key, calculatedResult));
    return calculatedResult;
}
```

The registered advice replaces the code in bold because that is mainly boilerplate and would need to be duplicated in each method in which you want to introduce caching. When the boilerplate code is removed, the following code is what would remain:

```
@Override
public BigDecimal heavyCalculation(BigDecimal base, int power) {
    try {
        Thread.sleep(500);
    } catch (InterruptedException e) {}
    return base.pow(power);
}
```

To enable caching for this method, you need to place a @Cacheable annotation on the method. This annotation requires the name of the cache to use to be specified (by using the value attribute of the annotation).

```
@Override
@Cacheable("calculations")
public BigDecimal heavyCalculation(BigDecimal base, int power) { ... }
```

803

This annotation has three other attributes: key, condition, and unless. Each of these attributes takes a SpEL expression that is evaluated at runtime. The key attribute specifies which method arguments to use to calculate the key used for caching. The default is to use all method arguments. The condition attribute can be used to define the condition for which the cache is applied. The default is to always cache and is invoked before the actual method is invoked. The unless attribute works like the condition attribute; however, this is invoked after the actual method invocation.

Use Spring AOP

The default operation mode for the @EnableCachin annotation is to use plain Spring AOP. This means a proxy will be created for CalculationService. The configuration looks like this:

```
package com.apress.springrecipes.caching.config;

import com.apress.springrecipes.caching.CalculationService;
import com.apress.springrecipes.caching.PlainCalculationService;
import org.springframework.cache.CacheManager;
import org.springframework.cache.annotation.EnableCaching;
import org.springframework.cache.ehcache.EhCacheCacheManager;
import org.springframework.cache.ehcache.EhCacheManagerFactoryBean;
import org.springframework.context.annotation.Bean;
import org.springframework.context.annotation.Configuration;
import org.springframework.core.io.ClassPathResource;

@Configuration
@EnableCaching
public class CalculationConfiguration {

    @Bean
    public CacheManager cacheManager() {
        EhCacheCacheManager cacheManager = new EhCacheCacheManager();
        cacheManager.setCacheManager(ehCacheManagerFactoryBean().getObject());
        return cacheManager;
    }

    @Bean
    public EhCacheManagerFactoryBean ehCacheManagerFactoryBean() {
        EhCacheManagerFactoryBean factory = new EhCacheManagerFactoryBean();
        factory.setConfigLocation(new ClassPathResource("ehcache.xml"));
        return factory;
    }

    @Bean
    public CalculationService calculationService() {
        return new PlainCalculationService();
    }
}
```

The configuration now has a @EnableCaching annotation, and CalculationService has only the @Cacheable annotation; there's no dependency on the caching framework.

Use AspectJ

Using the AspectJ mode for caching is as easy as setting the mode attribute of the @EnableCaching annotation to ASPECTJ. Depending on whether you use compile-time or load-time weaving, it might be necessary to add @EnableLoadTimeWeaving. For the sample, it is assumed that the code uses load-time weaving. For this, add the aforementioned annotation to the configuration class.

```
package com.apress.springrecipes.caching.config;
...
import org.springframework.cache.annotation.EnableCaching;
import org.springframework.context.annotation.EnableLoadTimeWeaving;

@Configuration
@EnableLoadTimeWeaving
@EnableCaching(mode = AdviceMode.ASPECTJ)
public class CalculationConfiguration { ... }
```

You can find more information on load-time weaving in recipe 3-19. To run the main application, you have to start it with a so-called Java agent. To run the program with load-time weaving, use java -javaagent:./lib/spring-instrument-5.0.0.RELEASE.jar -jar Recipe_19_3_ii-4.0.0.jar (from the build/libs directory of this recipe).

B-4. Configure a Custom KeyGenerator

Problem

The default KeyGenerator generates a key based on the method parameters. You want to modify this behavior.

Solution

Implement a custom KeyGenerator with the desired strategy and configure the caching support to use this custom KeyGenerator.

How It Works

The caching abstraction uses a KeyGenerator interface as a callback mechanism for the key generation. By default it uses the SimpleKeyGenerator class for key generation. This class takes all method arguments and calculates a hash code. This hash is used as a key.

It is possible to implement your own generation strategy and use that to generate the keys. To do this, create a class that implements the KeyGenerator interface and implements the generate method.

```
package com.apress.springrecipes.caching;

import org.springframework.cache.interceptor.KeyGenerator;

import java.lang.reflect.Method;

public class CustomKeyGenerator implements KeyGenerator {
```

```
    @Override
    public Object generate(Object target, Method method, Object... params) {
        return params[0] + "^" + params[1];
    }
}
```

CustomKeyGenerator takes the first and second parameters and appends them with a ^ in between (the same as was done in the samples when you generated your own key for the cache).

Next wire up the custom implementation with the caching support in Spring. For this, use the CachingConfigurer interface, which further configures the caching support in Spring. To implement it, you can use the CachingConfigurerSupport class to override only those parts of the configuration you want to override. Here you will override keyGenerator and cacheMananger.

■ **Note** Don't forget to put @Bean on the overridden methods or the created instances won't be managed by the Spring container.

```
package com.apress.springrecipes.caching.config;

import org.springframework.cache.CacheManager;
import org.springframework.cache.annotation.CachingConfigurerSupport;
import org.springframework.cache.annotation.EnableCaching;
import org.springframework.cache.ehcache.EhCacheCacheManager;
import org.springframework.cache.ehcache.EhCacheManagerFactoryBean;
import org.springframework.cache.interceptor.KeyGenerator;
import org.springframework.context.annotation.Bean;
import org.springframework.context.annotation.Configuration;
import org.springframework.core.io.ClassPathResource;

import com.apress.springrecipes.caching.CalculationService;
import com.apress.springrecipes.caching.CustomKeyGenerator;
import com.apress.springrecipes.caching.PlainCalculationService;

@Configuration
@EnableCaching
public class CalculationConfiguration extends CachingConfigurerSupport {

    @Bean
    @Override
    public CacheManager cacheManager() {
        EhCacheCacheManager cacheManager = new EhCacheCacheManager();
        cacheManager.setCacheManager(ehCacheManagerFactoryBean().getObject());
        return cacheManager;
    }

    @Bean
    @Override
    public KeyGenerator keyGenerator() {
        return new CustomKeyGenerator();
    }
```

```
@Bean
public EhCacheManagerFactoryBean ehCacheManagerFactoryBean() {
    EhCacheManagerFactoryBean factory = new EhCacheManagerFactoryBean();
    factory.setConfigLocation(new ClassPathResource("ehcache.xml"));
    return factory;
}

@Bean
public CalculationService calculationService() {
    return new PlainCalculationService();
}

}
```

First notice the addition of CustomKeyGenerator as a bean so that it is available for use. Next you'll see the inner class for CachingConfigurer (you can also create a normal class as long as it implements the CachingConfigurer interface). The implementation for CachingConfigurer returns the already configured CacheManager as well as the KeyGenerator. When using CachingConfigurer, CacheManager is no longer autodetected and must be configured through CachingConfigurer.

B-5. Add and Remove Objects from the Cache

Problem

You want to use cache eviction and cache puts when objects get created, updated, or removed.

Solution

Use the @CachePut and @CacheEvict annotations on methods that you want to update or when you want to invalidate objects in the cache.

How It Works

In addition to @Cacheable, Spring has the @CachePut and @CacheEvict annotations, which, respectively, add or remove objects (or invalidate the whole cache) to/from a cache.

When using caches, you don't only want your cache to fill up; you also want it to keep in sync with what is happening inside your application, including object updates and removal. For methods whose results update the cache, add the @CachePut annotation; for methods that invalidate objects inside the cache, use the @CacheEvict annotation.

When using CustomerRepository, obtaining the customers from the underlying data source is time-consuming. You decide to add caching to the repository. First create the CustomerRepository interface.

```
package com.apress.springrecipes.caching;

public interface CustomerRepository {

    Customer find(long customerId);
    Customer create(String name);
    void update(Customer customer);
    void remove(long customerId);
}
```

You also need a Customer class.

```
package com.apress.springrecipes.caching;

import java.io.Serializable;

public class Customer implements Serializable {

    private final long id;
    private String name;

    public Customer(long id) {
        this.id = id;
    }

    public long getId() {
        return id;
    }

    public String getName() {
        return name;
    }

    public void setName(String name) {
        this.name = name;
    }

    @Override
    public String toString() {
        return String.format("Customer [id=%d, name=%s]", this.id, this.name);
    }
}
```

Finally, the implementation of the CustomerRepository interface is based on a HashMap because it is just for testing purposes. The slow retrieval is faked with a call to Thread.sleep().

```
package com.apress.springrecipes.caching;

import org.springframework.cache.annotation.Cacheable;

import java.util.HashMap;
import java.util.Map;
import java.util.UUID;

public class MapBasedCustomerRepository implements CustomerRepository {

    private final Map<Long, Customer> repository = new HashMap<>();

    @Override
    @Cacheable(value = "customers")
    public Customer find(long customerId) {
```

```
        try {
            Thread.sleep(500);
        } catch (InterruptedException e) {}
        return repository.get(customerId);
    }

    @Override
    public Customer create(String name) {
        long id = UUID.randomUUID().getMostSignificantBits();
        Customer customer = new Customer(id);
        customer.setName(name);
        repository.put(id, customer);
        return customer;
    }

    @Override
    public void update(Customer customer) {
        repository.put(customer.getId(), customer);
    }

    @Override
    public void remove(long customerId) {
        repository.remove(customerId);
    }
}
```

Next everything needs to be configured with a configuration class.

```
package com.apress.springrecipes.caching.config;

import com.apress.springrecipes.caching.CustomerRepository;
import com.apress.springrecipes.caching.MapBasedCustomerRepository;
import org.springframework.cache.CacheManager;
import org.springframework.cache.annotation.EnableCaching;
import org.springframework.cache.ehcache.EhCacheCacheManager;
import org.springframework.cache.ehcache.EhCacheManagerFactoryBean;
import org.springframework.context.annotation.Bean;
import org.springframework.context.annotation.Configuration;
import org.springframework.core.io.ClassPathResource;

@Configuration
@EnableCaching
public class CustomerConfiguration {

    @Bean
    public CacheManager cacheManager() {
        EhCacheCacheManager cacheManager = new EhCacheCacheManager();
        cacheManager.setCacheManager(ehCacheManagerFactoryBean().getObject());
        return cacheManager;
    }
```

```
    @Bean
    public EhCacheManagerFactoryBean ehCacheManagerFactoryBean() {
        EhCacheManagerFactoryBean factory = new EhCacheManagerFactoryBean();
        factory.setConfigLocation(new ClassPathResource("ehcache.xml"));
        return factory;
    }

    @Bean
    public CustomerRepository customerRepository() {
        return new MapBasedCustomerRepository();
    }
}
```

Last but not least, to be able to run this program, you need a Main class.

```
package com.apress.springrecipes.caching;

import org.springframework.context.ApplicationContext;
import org.springframework.context.annotation.AnnotationConfigApplicationContext;
import org.springframework.context.support.AbstractApplicationContext;
import org.springframework.util.StopWatch;

import com.apress.springrecipes.caching.config.CustomerConfiguration;

public class Main {

    public static final void main(String[] args) throws Exception {

        ApplicationContext context =
            new AnnotationConfigApplicationContext(CustomerConfiguration.class);
        CustomerRepository customerRepository = context.getBean(CustomerRepository.class);
        StopWatch sw = new StopWatch("Cache Evict and Put");

        sw.start("Get 'Unknown Customer'");
        Customer customer = customerRepository.find(1L);
        System.out.println("Get 'Unknown Customer' (result) : " + customer);
        sw.stop();

        sw.start("Create New Customer");
        customer = customerRepository.create("Marten Deinum");
        System.out.println("Create new Customer (result) : " + customer);
        sw.stop();

        long customerId = customer.getId();

        sw.start("Get 'New Customer 1'");
        customer = customerRepository.find(customerId);
        System.out.println("Get 'New Customer 1' (result) : " + customer);
        sw.stop();
```

```
sw.start("Get 'New Customer 2'");
customer = customerRepository.find(customerId);
System.out.println("Get 'New Customer 2' (result) : " + customer);
sw.stop();

sw.start("Update Customer");
customer.setName("Josh Long");
customerRepository.update(customer);
sw.stop();

sw.start("Get 'Updated Customer 1'");
customer = customerRepository.find(customerId);
System.out.println("Get 'Updated Customer 1' (result) : " + customer);
sw.stop();

sw.start("Get 'Updated Customer 2'");
customer = customerRepository.find(customerId);
System.out.println("Get 'Updated Customer 2' (result) : " + customer);
sw.stop();

sw.start("Remove Customer");
customerRepository.remove(customer.getId());
sw.stop();

sw.start("Get 'Deleted Customer 1'");
customer = customerRepository.find(customerId);
System.out.println("Get 'Deleted Customer 1' (result) : " + customer);
sw.stop();

sw.start("Get 'Deleted Customer 2'");
customer = customerRepository.find(customerId);
System.out.println("Get 'Deleted Customer 2' (result) : " + customer);
sw.stop();

System.out.println();
System.out.println(sw.prettyPrint());

((AbstractApplicationContext) context).close();
    }
}
```

The first thing to notice is the number of System.out calls that use StopWatch. These are there to show the behavior of what is happening to the program. After running this class, there should be output similar to that in Figure B-1.

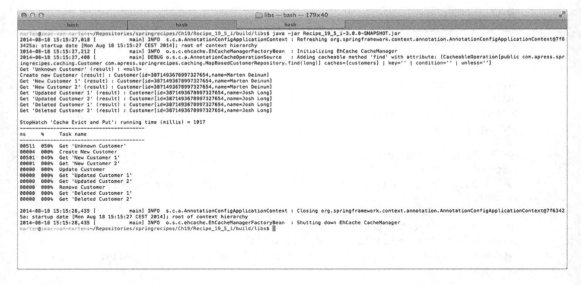

Figure B-1. *Initial output of running Main*

There are a couple of things to notice in the output after running the program. First, after removing the customer, you still get a result when trying to find the deleted customer. This is because the object is removed from the repository only if it still is in the cache that is being used. Second, the first get after creating the customer is taking a long time; it would be more efficient to have the created customer cached immediately. Third, although not directly apparent from the output, the first get after the update of the object is really fast. After updating the object, the cached instance should be removed.

■ **Note**   The update only appears to be working because we are updating the same `Customer` instance as is in the cache. If the update were a real JDBC update, the cache wouldn't reflect the update!

Use @CacheEvict to Remove Invalid Objects

When an object is removed from the underlying repository, it has to be removed from the cache (or maybe the whole cache needs to be invalidated). To do this, add the @CacheEvict annotation to the remove method. Now when this method is called, the object with the same key will be removed from the cache.

```
package com.apress.springrecipes.caching;

import org.springframework.cache.annotation.CacheEvict;
...

public class MapBasedCustomerRepository implements CustomerRepository {
...
    @Override
    @CacheEvict(value="customers")
    public void remove(long customerId) {
        repository.remove(customerId);
    }
}
```

Notice the @CacheEvict annotation on the remove method needs the name of the cache from which to remove the item. In this case, the cache name is customers. It has a few other attributes that can be used (see Table B-1).

Table B-1. *@CacheEvict Attributes*

Attribute	Description
key	SpEL expression for computing the key. The default is to use all method arguments.
condition	The condition on which the cache will or will not be invalidated.
allEntries	Sets whether the whole cache should be evicted; the default is false.
beforeInvocation	Sets whether the cache should be invalidated before or after (the default) method invocation. When invoked before the method, the cache will invalidate regardless of the method outcome.

When running the Main program again, the output has changed a little (see Figure B-2).

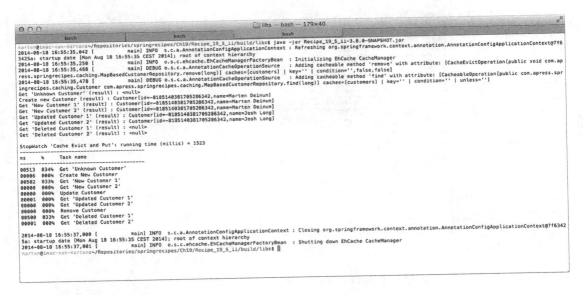

Figure B-2. *Output after adding @CacheEvict to remove method*

Looking at the output, it is apparent that when a customer is removed, there is no more result. When retrieving the deleted customer, null is returned instead of a cached instance. Next let's add the @CacheEvict annotation to the update method; after an update, the object should be retrieved from the underlying data source again. Adding it to the update method, however, yields a problem. The method argument is a Customer value, whereas the cache uses the ID of the customer as a key. (Remember that the default key generation strategy uses all method arguments to generate the key; the find and remove methods both have a long as method argument.)

To overcome this, you can write a little SpEL expression in the key attribute. You want it to use the id property of the first argument as the key. The #customer.id expression will take care of that. It will reference the method argument named customer.

813

The modified update method looks like the following:

```
package com.apress.springrecipes.caching;
...
import org.springframework.cache.annotation.CacheEvict;

public class MapBasedCustomerRepository implements CustomerRepository {
...
    @Override
    @CacheEvict(value="customers", key="#customer.id")
    public void update(Customer customer) {
        repository.put(customer.getId(), customer);
    }
}
```

After running the Main class, the timing information shows that the first lookup for the updated customer takes a little longer (see Figure B-3).

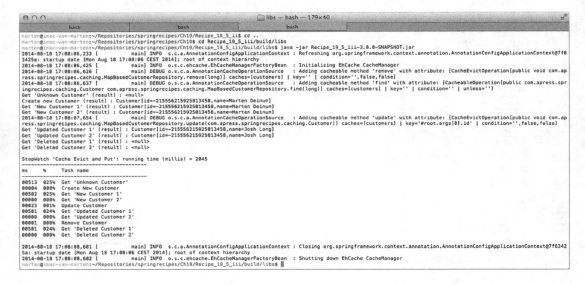

Figure B-3. *Output after adding @CacheEvict to update method*

Use @CachePut to Place Objects in the Cache

The create method creates a Customer object based on the input at the moment. The first find operation for this object after the creation takes some time to finish. Although it works, it can be made faster by having the create method place the object into the cache.

To make a method put a value in the cache, you can use the @CachePut annotation. The annotation requires the name of the cache to add the object to. This is done through the value attribute. Just like the other annotations, there are also the key, condition, and unless attributes.

```
package com.apress.springrecipes.caching;

import org.springframework.cache.annotation.CachePut;
...
```

```
public class MapBasedCustomerRepository implements CustomerRepository {

    @Override
    @CachePut(value="customers", key = "#result.id")
    public Customer create(String name) { ... }
}
```

First notice the @CachePut annotation on the update method. It is given the name of the cache, customers, through the value attribute. The key attribute is needed because in general a method that creates an object returns the actual object to be cached. The key, however, is generally not the object itself, which is why you need to specify an SpEL expression for the key attribute. The #result placeholder gives access to the returned object. As the id of the Customer object is the key, the expression #result.id yields the desired result.

The result of running the main program should look like Figure B-4.

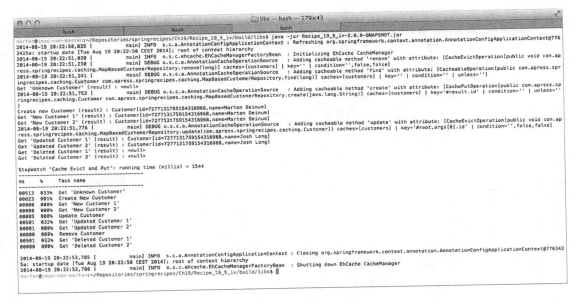

Figure B-4. *The result after adding @CachePut to the update method*

The first retrieval of the newly created customer is now a lot faster as the object is returned from the cache instead of being looked up from the repository.

Veto Results for the @Cacheable Annotation

At the moment, the find method caches all the results even when the method returns null. It can be undesirable to disable caching. For certain results, you can use the unless attribute on the @Cacheable annotation. When the criteria (an SpEL expression) are met, the returned object is not cached.

```
package com.apress.springrecipes.caching;

import org.springframework.cache.annotation.Cacheable;
...
```

```
public class MapBasedCustomerRepository implements CustomerRepository {

    @Override
    @Cacheable(value = "customers", unless="#result == null")
    public Customer find(long customerId) { ... }
...
}
```

Notice the expression in the `unless` attribute. If the result is `null`, the caching will be vetoed. The `#result` placeholder gives you access to the object returned from the called method. This can be used to write an expression. The expression here is a simple `null` check.

Figure B-5 shows the results after excluding `null` from being cached. Both lookups for the deleted customer take approximately the same amount of time.

Figure B-5. *Results after excluding null from being cached*

B-6. Synchronize Caching with a Transactional Resource

Problem

You want your cache to be transaction aware.

Solution

Some of the Spring-provided CacheManager implementations can be made aware of the fact that they are running in a transactional context. EhCacheCacheManager is one of them. To switch on the transaction awareness, set the transactionAware property to true.

How It Works

First create a transactional implementation of CustomerRepository, for instance, using JDBC.

```java
package com.apress.springrecipes.caching;

import java.sql.Connection;
import java.sql.PreparedStatement;
import java.sql.ResultSet;
import java.sql.SQLException;

import javax.sql.DataSource;

import org.springframework.cache.annotation.CacheEvict;
import org.springframework.cache.annotation.CachePut;
import org.springframework.cache.annotation.Cacheable;
import org.springframework.jdbc.core.JdbcTemplate;
import org.springframework.jdbc.core.PreparedStatementCreator;
import org.springframework.jdbc.core.RowMapper;
import org.springframework.jdbc.support.GeneratedKeyHolder;
import org.springframework.jdbc.support.KeyHolder;
import org.springframework.stereotype.Repository;
import org.springframework.transaction.annotation.Transactional;

@Repository
@Transactional
public class JdbcCustomerRepository implements CustomerRepository {

    private final JdbcTemplate jdbc;

    public JdbcCustomerRepository(DataSource dataSource) {
        this.jdbc = new JdbcTemplate(dataSource);
    }

    @Override
    @Cacheable(value = "customers")
    public Customer find(long customerId) {
        final String sql = "SELECT id, name FROM customer WHERE id=?";
        return jdbc.query(sql, (rs, rowNum) -> {
            Customer customer = new Customer(rs.getLong(1));
            customer.setName(rs.getString(2));
            return customer;
        }, customerId).stream().findFirst().orElse(null);
    }
    @Override
    @CachePut(value="customers", key = "#result.id")
    public Customer create(String name) {

        final String sql = "INSERT INTO customer (name) VALUES (?);";
        KeyHolder keyHolder = new GeneratedKeyHolder();
        jdbc.update(con -> {
            PreparedStatement ps = con.prepareStatement(sql);
```

817

```
                ps.setString(1, name);
                return ps;
        }, keyHolder);

        Customer customer = new Customer(keyHolder.getKey().longValue());
        customer.setName(name);

        return customer;
    }

    @Override
    @CacheEvict(value="customers", key="#customer.id")
    public void update(Customer customer) {
        final String sql = "UPDATE customer SET name=? WHERE id=?";
        jdbc.update(sql, customer.getName(), customer.getId());
    }

    @Override
    @CacheEvict(value="customers")
    public void remove(long customerId) {
        final String sql = "DELETE FROM customer WHERE id=?";
        jdbc.update(sql, customerId);
    }
}
```

Now you need to add DataSource and DataSourceTransactionManager to your configuration and of course JdbcCustomerRepository.

```
@Bean
public CustomerRepository customerRepository(DataSource dataSource) {
    return new JdbcCustomerRepository(dataSource);
}
@Bean
public DataSourceTransactionManager transactionManager(DataSource dataSource) {
    return new DataSourceTransactionManager(dataSource);
}

@Bean
public DataSource dataSource() {
    return new EmbeddedDatabaseBuilder()
        .setType(EmbeddedDatabaseType.H2)
        .setName("customers")
        .addScript("classpath:/schema.sql").build();
}
```

The CUSTOMER table is defined in the following schema.sql:

```
CREATE TABLE customer (
    id bigint AUTO_INCREMENT PRIMARY KEY,
    name VARCHAR(255) NOT NULL,
);
```

818

Finally, set the transactionAware property of EhCacheCacheManager to true. Setting this to true will wrap the actual Cache instances with TransactionAwareCacheDecorator, which will register the operations on the cache with the current ongoing transaction (or execute directly if no transaction is available).

```
@Bean
public CacheManager cacheManager() {

    EhCacheCacheManager cacheManager = new EhCacheCacheManager();
    cacheManager.setCacheManager(ehCacheManagerFactoryBean().getObject());
    cacheManager.setTransactionAware(true);
    return cacheManager;
}
```

Now when you run the application, everything should still look normal, but all caching operations are bound to the successful execution of a transaction. So, if the delete operation fails with an exception, the Customer would still be in the cache.

B-7. Use Redis as a Cache Provider

Problem

You want to use Redis as a caching provider.

Solution

Use Spring Data Redis and configure a RedisCacheManager object to connect to a Redis instance. See also Chapter 12 for more information on Redis and Spring Data Redis.

How It Works

First make sure you have Redis up and running.

■ **Note**   There is a redis.sh file in the bin directory that starts a Dockerized version of Redis.

Configure RedisCacheManager

To be able to use Redis for caching, you need to set up RedisCacheManager, which will delegate caching to Redis. RedisCacheManager in turn requires a RedisTemplate class to use for its operations.

```
@Configuration
@EnableCaching
public class CustomerConfiguration {

    @Bean
    public RedisCacheManager cacheManager(RedisConnectionFactory connectionFactory) {
        return RedisCacheManager.create(connectionFactory);
    }
}
```

```
@Bean
public RedisConnectionFactory redisConnectionFactory() {
    return new JedisConnectionFactory();
}

@Bean
public CustomerRepository customerRepository() {
    return new MapBasedCustomerRepository();
}
}
```

To connect to Redis, you set up `JedisConnectionFactory`, which itself is used to configure `RedisCacheManager`. To create a `RedisCacheManager` object, you can pass the connection factory to the create method, or if you want to customize the cache, you can use the `builder` method instead. When using builder, you can customize things such as cache names, transaction awareness, and so on.

You can leave the remaining code untouched. When running the main program, it will show, among others things, the adding and removing of objects to the cache.

Summary

In this chapter, you discovered how to add caching to your application and that it is quite cumbersome to do so, especially if you want to introduce this in multiple parts of your code. You explored both the plain Ehcache API and Spring's cache abstraction. After doing manual caching, you explored applying caching with AOP, both with plain Spring AOP using proxies and with AspectJ using load-time weaving.

Next you learned about the different annotations, @Cacheable, @CacheEvict, and @CachePut, and how those influence the caching behavior of your application. You also learned how to use a SpEL expression to retrieve the correct key for caching or cache invalidation and how to influence the caching behavior of the @Cacheable annotation.

The final recipe introduced Spring Gemfire as a caching solution and explored how it can be used as a local or remote caching solution.

Index

© Marten Deinum, Daniel Rubio, and Josh Long 2017
M. Deinum et al., *Spring 5 Recipes*, DOI 10.1007/978-1-4842-2790-9

■ X, Y, Z

Get the eBook for only $5!

Why limit yourself?

With most of our titles available in both PDF and ePUB format, you can access your content wherever and however you wish—on your PC, phone, tablet, or reader.

Since you've purchased this print book, we are happy to offer you the eBook for just $5.

To learn more, go to http://www.apress.com/companion or contact support@apress.com.

Apress®

CPSIA information can be obtained
at www.ICGtesting.com
Printed in the USA
LVHW101244270820
664174LV00015B/26